RESEARCH IN INTERNATIONAL BUSINESS AND FINANCE

Supplement 1 • 1996

To our family and friends
with love and gratitude

RESEARCH IN INTERNATIONAL BUSINESS AND FINANCE

Editors: JOHN DOUKAS
Department of Finance
Graduate School of Business
Old Dominion University

LARRY LANG
Department of Finance
Faculty of Business Administration
Chinese University of Hong Kong

SUPPLEMENT 1 • 1996

JAI PRESS INC.

Greenwich, Connecticut *London, England*

55 Old Post Road No. 2
Greenwich, Connecticut 06836

JAI PRESS LTD.
38 Tavistock Street
Covent Garden
London WC2E 7PB
England

ISBN: 0-7623-0110-4

Manufactured in the United States of America

CONTENTS

LIST OF CONTRIBUTORS

Reena Aggarwal	School of Business Georgetown University
Alan Alford	Finance Department IESA
Nabeel E. Al-Loughani	Department of Business Administration Kuwait University
Bala Arshanapalli	Division of Business & Economics Indiana University Northwest
Jacqueline Chavez	Department of Finance and Insurance Laval University
C. Sherman Cheung	School of Business McMaster University
Thomas C. Chiang	Department of Finance Drexel University
Young-Kwon Cho	Department of Economics University of Connecticut
Jongmoo Jay Choi	Department of Finance Temple University
Steven R. Cunningham	Department of Economics University of Connecticut
John Doukas	Finance Department Graduate School of Business Old Dominion University
Babak Eftekhari	Fitzwilliam College Cambridge University

Venkat R. Eleswarapu	Department of Accounting and Finance University of Auckland
Klaus P. Fischer	Department of Finance and Insurance Laval University
Dan W. French	Department of Finance New Mexico State University
Joseph Friedman	Department of Economics and Department of Finance Temple University
Hung-Gay Fung	Department of Economics & Finance University of Baltimore
Martin J. Herrera	ITESM, Guadalajara
Qaizar Hussain	Department of Economics Gothenberg University
Bang Nam Jeon	Department of Economics Drexel University
Dimitris G. Kirikos	Department of Economics University of Crete
Chandrasekhar Krishnamurthi	Department of Management Studies Indian Institute of Science
Mukund S. Kulkarni	School of Business Administration The Pennsylvania State University, Harrisburg
Clarence C.Y. Kwan	Finance and Business Economics Area McMaster University
Ricardo Leal	Finance Department University of Nevada, Reno
Moon Hoe Lee	Department of Finance and Management Science University of Saskatchewan
Wai Lee	Graduate School of Business Harvard University

Che-Peng Lin	Department of Finance Feng Chic University Taiwan
Wai-Chung Lo	City University of Hong Kong
Jacques Lussier	GUDL and Haute Etudes Commerciales Montreal
A.G. Malliaris	Department of Economics Loyola University, Chicago
Imad A. Moosa	School of Economics LaTrobe University
Kap-Soo Oh	Department of Finance Drexel University
Edgar Ortiz	Universidad Nacional Autonoma de Mexico
Michael G. Papaioannou	Bank of Greece
Osman Luis C. Ranit	Graduate School of Business and Economics DeLaSalle University
Stephen E. Satchell	Trinity Collage Cambridge University
Yochanan Shachmurove	Department of Economics University of Pennsylvania
Janet M. Tanski	Department of Economics & International Business New Mexico State University
Hugh A. Thomas	Finance and Business Economics Area McMaster University
Jorge L. Urrutia	Department of Finance Loyola University, Chicago
M. Mark Walker	Department of Economics and Finance University of Mississippi

ABOUT THE EDITORS

John Doukas, Ph.D., is Professor of Finance and International Finance at Old Dominion University. His current research interests are in the areas of international financial management, foreign exchange markets, and international asset pricing. Dr. Doukas has published in many journals including the *Journal of Finance, Journal of Financial and Quantitative Analysis, Journal of Banking and Finance, Journal of International Business Studies, Financial Review,* and *Journal of Futures Markets.* He is the founding editor of the *European Financial Management Journal* and founder of the European Financial Management Association.

Dr. Larry H.P. Lang earned his Ph.D. in Finance at the Wharton School, University of Pennsylvania in 1986. He has taught at several prestigious U.S. business schools including the Wharton School, Michigan State University, Ohio State University, and New York University. Dr. Lang is currently a Professor in Finance at the Chinese University of Hong Kong, Dr. Lang's main research interests are in the areas of corporate finance and investments. More specifically, he has extensively researched issues in the fields of corporate restructuring, merger and acquisition, bankruptcy, managerial incentive schemes, direct investments, and asset pricing. He has published numerous academic papers in the world's leading journals, such as *Journal of Political Economy, Journal of Financial Economics, Journal of Finance*, and *Journal of Accounting Research*. Dr. Lang has also served as editor and associate editor for several international academic journals and research manuals including *European Financial Management Journal*, *Pacific*

Basin Finance Journal, *Research in International Business and Finance*, *Hong Kong Journal of Business Management*, *Journal of Financial Studies*, and *Asian Journal of Financial Management*. Dr. Lang's research is widely recognized in the academic world (as evidenced by the high number of citations his work has received), and has also been widely publicized by the popular media including *The New York Times*, *Business Week*, *Investor Dealers' Digest*, *Cincinnati Enquirer*, *Philadelphia Inquirer*, *Investor's Business Daily*, CNBC TV station, and *The Journal of High Yield Bond Research by Merrill Lynch*, and so forth.

ACKNOWLEDGMENTS

The editors of this volume are grateful to Angelos Doukas for excellent editorial assistance in preparation of this research volume. Support from Old Dominion University and Chinese University of Hong Kong is also acknowledged.

INTRODUCTION

In the last two decades international investment flows have been growing at a very rapid pace. This is often attributed to the deregulation of capital markets, removal of barriers to international investments, and improvements in computer and communication technology that have substantially reduced the cost of cross-border information flows and financial transactions. Investors' increasing awareness of the importance of global investment opportunities and the growing role of the privatization process in many countries are expected to enhance the interaction among national capital markets leading eventually to a more integrated global economy. This volume presents a set of research papers that do examine the degree of capital markets' interaction and major financial issues in emerging capital markets. Further, it provides a setting for understanding the nature of the integration process as well as the behavior of national stock-price movements.

The first study by Shachmurove investigates the linkages among Latin American and other major world stock markets over the 1987–1994 period. The Latin American countries involved in this study are: Mexico, Brazil, Chile, and Argentina. The methodology used in this paper is based on the Vector Auto Regressive (VAR) model. The evidence reported suggests that there are dynamic linkages among these capital markets that can be exploited by the international investor. Further, it is argued that these markets respond differently to shocks of information and hence investors may enjoy the benefits of diversification by investing in these capital markets.

The next paper by Friedman and Shachmurove investigates whether European Community stock markets behave as a single market. They use a Vector Auto-Regressive (VAR) model to identify the degree of integration and the daily dynamic linkages among eight major EC stock exchanges over the 1988–1992 period. While the impulse evidence reported in this paper suggests that innovations in one stock market are transmitted to other EC markets, most of this information is absorbed within one to two trading days. The decomposition of the forecast variance shows varying degrees of interdependence among EC stock markets. No market, however, was found to act independently from the other stock markets. The U.K. stock exchange was found to play a leading role in explaining most of the EC stock market innovations. While smaller markets such as Belgium, Denmark, and Italy appear to have no impact on other EC stock markets, larger stock markets such as France and Germany were found to exert substantial influence on neighboring countries.

Kulkarni's study analyzes the extent of interaction between capital markets of the southern European countries of Greece, Italy, Spain, and Turkey with the United States. The paper uses weekly stock index data for the period of January 1987 to March 1994. The empirical evidence supports the existing empirical literature which shows growing interdependence among major world financial markets. Specifically, his results show that all four southern European capital markets are cointegrated with one cointegrating vector throughout the 1987–1994 period. The degree of cointegration, however, appears to be stronger among the four southern European stock exchanges. In this set of four capital markets he finds the number of cointegrating vectors to be four implying a strong underlying equilibrium relationship among the stock markets of these southern European capital markets. Finally, the error correction regression results do confirm the findings of growing stock market interactions between the United States and the four southern European capital markets.

The next paper by Aggarwal and Leal examines the integration and the behavior of daily stock market indexes in the ten largest emerging markets of Asia and Latin America over the 1982 to 1991 period. The evidence of this study points out that Latin American markets are subject to greater volatility than Asian markets. The daily linkages between Asian emerging markets and the U.S. market, as well as between Japan and the United States, appear to have increased overtime. Latin American stock markets, however, appear to be less integrated than the emerging Asian markets. As expected, during the crash period, the linkages between the various markets were found to be distinctly profound. Multivariate analysis was also conducted to investigate a series of anomalies in the stock market return series of the emerging markets. The evidence suggests that Asian markets have a weekend effect of their own as well as a "Tuesday effect" which is argued to be driven by New York's performance the day before. The Monday effect appears to be present in all four Latin American markets of this study (i.e., Argentina, Brazil, Chile, and

Mexico). No month-of-the-year, turn-of-the-month, or January effect was detected in most markets. However, the "twist" of the Monday effect was found to be present in many countries.

Arshanapalli and Doukas examine the relations among security prices across three major Asian stock markets: Japan, Hong Kong, and Singapore. The focus of this study is on the extent to which security price innovations in one market influence the opening prices in the next market to trade using daily open and close daily prices for the 1991–1992 period. Their study uses Johansen's (1991) multivariate cointegration methodology which is designed to identify linkages across time series characterized by unit roots. Evidence of cointegration would imply that the three Asian stock markets have an underlying cointegrating equilibrium relationship that prohibits any one market to drift far apart from this common equilibrium path. Absence of cointegration, however, from this three-stock-markets system would imply lack of interaction among them. The results of this paper do not favor cointegration implying that there is no underlying equilibrium relationship in this system of the three Asian stock markets. The cointegration analysis is conducted using open as well as closed stock exchange indexes. The results appear to be basically similar whether open or closed stock indexes are used. It is also reported that Japan's stock market innovations a day before or an hour prior to the opening of the Hong Kong and Singapore markets do not have any impact on the performance of the other two stock exchanges. These results reinforce previous findings in the literature which show that Japan's stock market has very little, if any, influence on other world stock exchanges.

The next paper by Jeon, Oh, and Chiang analyzes the time-series properties of stock prices in two emerging markets (i.e., Taiwan and Korea) for the period January 1975 through December 1990. Despite the lack of significant linear dependence, stock price changes in both Asian markets show stochastic nonlinear time dependence properties and substantial ARCH effects. While various classes of autoregressive models with conditional variance processes were fit to the data, the AR (12)-ARCH (3) model appeared to fit best the stock price data for both Asian stock markets. This model was shown to account for most of the second-movement nonlinearity and time-varying conditional heteroskedasticity in the data. Furthermore, the evidence shows that nonlinearity enters through variances rather than through means in the stock price behavior of Taiwanese and Korean stock markets. The AR (12)-ARCH (3) model was also used to examine the linkages between these two Asian stock markets and the major stock market exchanges. The results show that their linkages with major world stock markets have increased considerably in recent years.

The seventh paper in this research volume by Malliaris and Urrutia empirically investigates the economic significance of the Gulf Crisis on the oil and world equity markets, using event type and Granger causality methodologies. The major event days are August 2, 1990, the day the Iraqi army invaded Kuwait, January 16, 1991, the day the war started, and January 24, 1991, the day the Allied Forces initiated the ground attack. Cumulative abnormal returns for 13 national stock markets around these event dates suggest that the invasion of Kuwait had a bigger negative impact on world stock prices than the initiation of the war and the ground attack. The evidence with respect to oil exporting and oil importing countries suggests that the negative abnormal returns around the day the Iraqi army invaded Kuwait were much larger for the oil importing than for the oil exporting countries. The abnormal returns appear to be positive and significant, but larger for the oil importing countries, two days after the day the war started on January 16, 1991. This result is consistent with the reactions of the individual stock markets. This study also examines the changes caused by the Persian Gulf Crisis in the lead-lag relationships between the oil and national equity markets. No causality was found for the preinvasion of Kuwait period. For the post-invasion period, however, the evidence supports strong contemporaneous causality, an increase in lead-lag relationships, and a strong feedback between oil and equity markets. Hence, this study concludes that oil and national stock markets reacted simultaneously to the Gulf Crisis while they affected each other during the Gulf War.

Choi and Papaioannou examine the determinants of relative stock market valuation ratios of Canada, France, Germany, Japan, and the U.K. relative to the United States. This study uses monthly data for the period of January 1974–1988. The authors of this study begin their analysis by pointing out the disparities across stock valuation ratios (i.e., price-earnings, price-cash flow, price-book value, capital gains, and dividend yield) among the six major industrialized countries throughout the 1974–1988 period. Thus, the paper proceeds with the development of a simple comparative valuation model to examine the United States as the reference country. This model identifies a set of determinants such as the relative cost of capital, earnings growth rates, exchange rates, and the dividend payout ratios as potential explanatory variables. The reported results show exchange rate changes as the most significant and consistent determinant of the relative stock market valuations for all countries and for different specifications of the model. The cost of capital appears to be less influential but still an important determinant of relative stock valuation ratios for most countries. Specifically, the cost of capital has a significant negative effect on both the relative P/B and P/C ratios for all countries in 18 out of 20 times. The dividend payout ratio has a divergent impact depending on the ratios and countries. The P/E ratios are found to be affected by dividend payout ratios. The effects of dividend payout ratios are significantly positive for all countries but Japan. This implies that high dividend payout is viewed positively by investors with Japan being the exception. Japan also appears to be the exception with respect to exchange rate movements. An appreciation of the yen is found to exert a strong increase in the Japanese valuation ratios (i.e., P/E, P/B, and PC ratios). In all other countries the exchange rate seems to have the opposite influence on the relative valuation ratios compared to Japan.

The second part of this volume deals with major financial issues in the emerging capital markets that are expected to enhance our understanding with respect to their functioning in the presence of regulatory and nonregulatory changes taking place nationally and internationally.

Chavez, Fisher, and Ortiz address the issue of financial liberalization and bank solvency for Brazil, Greece, Mexico, and Thailand. Specifically, the authors are evaluating and measuring the effect of financial liberalization processes on bank risk exposure and provide policy tools for bank regulators that must use to oversee the financial liberalization process. They use an option pricing theory model to obtain first and second moments of bank-asset values and measures of bank risk. The results of this paper suggest that banks' risk exposure increases following a financial liberalization program. This is the case even for banks operating in countries that have adopted very cautious financial liberalization programs such as Thailand. The authors suggest that supervisory authorities need to perform a very intense scrutiny of all critical variables linked to bank performance during periods of financial liberalization.

The next paper by Moosa and Al-Loughani examines the effect of deposit variability on the portfolio behavior of commercial banks in the emerging market of Kuwait over the 1980–1992 period. The empirical evidence based on cointegration tests shows that domestic credit is inversely related while the acquisition of foreign assets is positively related to deposit variability in the long run. Causality tests show that the variability of certain deposit categories has a short-run effect on domestic credit and on commercial banks' tendency to borrow from the offshore market.

Cho and Cunningham provide a historical account of the institutional and regulatory developments of the Korean stock market from 1953 through the more recent period. They address a set of issues such as market liberalization processes, microstructure characteristics, policy tools used to reduce market volatility, the role of investment trusts, the status of the securities industry, stock ownership, and the real-name reforms. The authors conclude with a set of policy recommendations as the Korean stock market is expected to undergo complete liberalization.

For the market to become more efficient, it is suggested that the government may have to keep a "hands-off" policy toward the market. The government has often taken measures to boost the stock market. It is argued that such discretionary policy measure should be avoided. It is also recommended that the range of daily price fluctuations limit (DPFL), applied to stocks, beneficiary certificates, equity related debt securities such as convertible bonds and bonds with stock purchase warrants, must be increased to allow the market to adjust faster to the arrival of new information. Furthermore, it is suggested that the adoption of one agency supervision (i.e., Securities Supervisory Board) is more desirable in terms of reducing market volatility as opposed to multiple supervision authorities in place. Finally, it is argued that a study needs to be undertaken and address the relevance of margin requirements.

The next paper by Alford and Lussier examines how the price of risk has changed in the emerging markets from 1989 through 1992. The evidence reported in this study shows that emerging markets are not collapsing toward a common core grouping. Instead, the results indicate that the price of risk is different among emerging markets. That is, the evidence shows that the emerging markets do not have the same price of risk as do the developed markets. It is argued that emerging markets have a larger sensitivity to international events, but that their responsiveness is "dwarfed" by their reaction to local news. Hence, the authors' empirical evidence seems to be consistent with the view that there is no common factor that determines the price of risk across emerging markets.

Cheung, Kwan, and Thomas investigate the design of restrictions to foreign portfolio equity investment in an international asset pricing framework and offer a theoretical explanation for the empirical discount puzzle for the B shares of China. In addition, they draw policy implications concerning the design of restrictions for other Asia Pacific countries. The authors also address the question why closed-end, single-country, equity funds, which invest in countries restricting foreign shareholding, do not always trade at a premium. Specifically, it is shown that the irrationally rigid design of China's A-share and B-share segmentation and the exchange rate controls in place lead to a discount on the price of B shares. As a result domestic firms considering going public prefer issuing domestic A shares in order to obtain better pricing and hence achieve a lower cost of capital. Finally, they show that a binding restriction imposed on foreign investors does not always lead to a premium on the net asset value (NAV) of the fund investing in a foreign country. The existence of the premium is shown to be a function of the design of the restriction.

Eftekhari and Satchell estimate and compare mean-variance (MV) and mean-lower partial (MLP) betas for emerging markets over the 1985–1994 period. Estimating Beta-Jarque statistics, the authors of this study conclude that none of these markets have normal returns. Comparison between MV and LPM betas shows that in only four cases non-normality of returns is responsible for statistical differences in betas. This result suggests that traditional betas are not different from alternative beta estimates robust to non-normality. Hence, it is argued that investors can rely on the standard risk analysis packages such as APT, BARRA, and QUANTC of all which use mean-variance analysis and are based on the decomposition of risk into sub-factors.

The next paper by Kirikos examines the validity of the efficient market model in the context of the Greek capital market using monthly observations from the Athens stock exchange over the 1981–1993 period. With the exception of the 1989–1990 period, which is generally characterized as politically unstable, the efficient market model is found to be economically significant for this emerging market. This evidence is in sharp contrast with the findings reported in previous studies of developed capital markets. Specifically, it is documented that investors are risk averse and that the market efficiency model, with varying discount factors, seems to explain fairly well the stock-price movements of the Athens stock exchange. Hence, the evidence appears to be consistent with the view that risk is a major concern for investment decisions in less organized (emerging) capital markets. According to Kirikos, this is mainly due to the presence of a deficient institutional setting and absence of financial instruments (i.e., derivatives and others) for hedging financial risk.

The study by Eleswarapu and Krishnamurthi concentrates on the problem of illiquidity that characterizes the Bombay stock exchange. This study is based on a random sample of 250 firms traded in the BSE over the 1989–1993 period. Specifically, the authors of this study focus on the factors causing differential levels of trading frequency on the BSE and particularly on the ownership structure factor. The evidence presented in this paper indicates that there is a liquidity premium for stocks traded in the Bombay stock exchange with expected returns being inversely related to the trading frequency. It is also documented that trading frequency increases with the number of shareholders and number of outstanding shares. Finally, it is shown that ownership structure does matter with insiders and government playing nonconstructive role in the companies in which they have big stock stakes.

Lee, Fung, and Lo investigate the time-varying behavior of expected returns of a sample of Hong Kong common stocks and industry groups for the period of 1986–1995. Using Ferson, Forester, and Keim's (1993) latent variable method that allows for conditional heteroskedasticity, a smaller number of latent variables is found for Hong Kong than for U.S. stock returns. Specifically, weak evidence against the joint hypothesis of linear expectations and one latent variable is reported. Furthermore, when the linear expectations restrictions is related, the evidence continues to support the hypothesis of one latent variable in the mean-variance pricing framework of the Hong Kong stock returns. This result is consistent and robust across time intervals and different sets of assets, implying co-movement in asset returns. Therefore, it is argued that this unique behavior of assets traded in the stock market of Hong Kong is driven by a few common factors. It is conjectured that political and economic influences together seem to dominate other seemingly relevant asset pricing determination forces.

Lee and Ranit examine the volatility structure of the Philippines interest rate futures contract introduced in October 1992. Specifically, this study addresses whether the Philippines interest rate futures contracts are characterized by mean reversion. The empirical findings listed in this paper show strong evidence in favor of mean reversion. In addition, nearby interest rate futures contracts are found to have higher price volatility than more distant contracts. This result is interpreted by the authors to be consistent with Samuelson's hypothesis which postulates that near maturity, forward contracts are more volatile than contracts with distant maturity. Finally, the empirical results of this study do not favor monotonicity in the volatility structure of interest rate futures contracts traded in the Manila international futures exchange.

French, Herrera, and Tanski study the valuation effects of environmental regulation on stock prices traded on the Mexican stock exchange from 1987 to 1991. They show that the market's reaction is negative to new environmental regulations. The negative returns associated with the environmental announcements appear to have a lasting effect for several days after the announcement day indicating that the market does not absorb the environmental news immediately. Overall, the evidence seems to suggest that the stock market is sensitive to environmental regulatory changes.

The next paper by Lin and Walker examines the day-of-the-week effect in the emerging market of Taiwan during the 1986–1994 period. Unlike previous studies, the results of this paper indicate lack of a significant Monday or Tuesday effect. Average returns for Saturdays are found, however, to be significantly positive and the largest across the days of the week. Additional tests, after controlling for problems associated with the sample size and the assumptions of OLS error terms, revealed lack of abnormal Saturday returns. Hence, the authors of this study conclude that the evidence from the Taiwan stock market appears to be consistent with the efficient market hypothesis and in line with those reported by Connolly (1989, 1991) for U.S. stocks.

The last paper of this volume deals with the interesting topics of cost of capital and debt-equity ratios in emerging markets. Specifically, Hussain's study concentrates on the determinants of average cost of capital and debt equity ratios in Indonesia and Malaysia following banking deregulation in the early 1980s. In contrast to other empirical studies, it is reported that shareholder concentration is an important source of financial distortions and is a determinant of the cost of capital and debt-equity ratios. However, shareholder concentration appears to have a differential impact on the cost of capital and the debt equity ratios for Indonesia and Malaysia. It raises the debt-equity ratios and the cost of capital in Indonesia but has an insignificant influence on the same variables in Malaysia. It is argued that the highly concentrated shareholder sector in Indonesia exerts a supply constraint in the sense that it discourages firms from issuing new equity to finance their projects, thus strengthening their reliance on bank funding. It is also found that profitable firms in both countries tend to rely more on equity than debt. However, long-term debt is strongly preferred to short-term debt. This study concludes with a set of reforms required to speed up the development of financial sectors in both countries. Reform should include: (1) tax incentives to issuing companies especially those with large public ownership, (2) requirements for greater information disclosure by shareholders and firms, (3) restriction of bank loans to undercapitalized firms, (4) imposition of taxes on bank deposits in order to reduce the return differential between equity and bank deposits, and (5) elimination of restrictions on international capital flows.

John Doukas
Larry Lang

PART I

INTERNATIONAL CAPITAL MARKET INTERACTIONS

DYNAMIC LINKAGES AMONG LATIN AMERICAN AND OTHER MAJOR WORLD STOCK MARKETS

Yochanan Shachmurove

ABSTRACT

Vector Auto Regression (VAR) models are used to trace the dynamic linkages across daily returns of national stock market indexes of Latin America, and among the Latin American and major world stock market indexes. The Latin American indexes include Argentina, Brazil, Chile, and Mexico. The major world stock market indexes include the United States; the world excluding the United States, United Kingdom, Japan, Germany, France, and Canada. Although most of the impulse responses die out very quickly, it is still possible to trace the dynamic linkages among markets. The dynamic linkages among the Latin American markets and among the Latin American markets and major world stock markets are found to be relatively small. The conclusion is that although markets are efficient and cleared out in a few trading days, there are dynamic linkages that can be explored and exploited to the benefit of the diversified international investor.

Research in International Business and Finance, Supplement 1, pages 3–33.

ISBN: 0-7623-0110-4

INTRODUCTION

This paper studies the dynamic linkages across national stock indexes of the newly emerging markets of South America. The late 1980s saw a gradual increase in international investment in the emerging markets of the newly industrialized Latin American countries like Mexico, Brazil, Argentina, and Chile.[1] These newly emerging infant stock markets have been profitable for some daring investors. Yet, many market analysts have pointed out that such markets are somewhat of an anomaly, in that they tend to be characterized by thin and narrow markets driven by poorly informed individuals rather than by fundamentals.[2]

One of the prominent examples that typify this new type of market is the Mexican stock market. In December of 1994, after six years of hard-won stability, the Mexican market lost about 36% of its stock index value in U.S. dollars (and 50.6% in the peso dollar exchange rate in the year 1994). This in turn has caused the Brazilian stock index to plunge by 16.4% since the start of the Mexican currency crisis. Despite this example, we cannot conclude that investment in the emerging stock markets is, as a whole, riskier than in developed countries, given their expected returns. What it does suggest is that the international investor would do better to diversify rather than concentrate his investments in a particular emerging market that is currently yielding high returns. The purpose behind global diversification is that stock markets are not highly correlated and consequently do not move in lock step with one another. Thus, a portfolio with a broad global mix can pay a higher return, than, say, the U.S. stock market alone while at the same time such diversification reduces overall risk.

Moreover, U.S. investors are increasingly aware of the opportunities for investing in foreign exchanges.[3] Global diversification has generally paid off well: in a ten-year period ending in October 1994, the U.S. portion of Morgan Stanley Capital International's world index was up by 296%, (with dividends reinvested but before subtracting withholding taxes), while Morgan Stanley's 20-stock-market Europe-Australia-Far-East (EAFE) Index was up 455%! Its world stock index climbed 345%.

There are some that claim that the logic behind international diversification may not hold in the future.[4] Expanding links between national economies and increasing intra-regional trade, combined with the explosive growth in cross-border portfolio investment, could create a world in which stock markets are synchronized. Moreover, the experts directing those funds are all increasingly using the same information or have access to those same sources of information. Given the proliferation of similar databases or similar sources of information in the investment world, the argument says that there will undoubtedly be a convergence in the decision-making process. Another argument for the convergence of national stock markets is that many stock markets are becoming more accessible through deregulation, including an easing of rules on foreign investment. Additionally, the trend for increased privatization of government-owned industries extends the list of blue-chip opportunities for investors interested in markets like Mexico, Chile, Brazil, and Argentina. These developments mean that the prices of foreign stocks are being influenced more and more by U.S. investor sentiment.[5] Furthermore, the emergence of regional economic blocs like the European Community, the North American Free Trade Agreement, and nascent groupings in Asia and Latin America means that national economies—including stock markets—inevitably will move more in tandem. Regional integration is on the political agenda in Latin America in the 1990s. This stands in contrast to the 1960s, when regional economic integration was linked to state planning and managed trade rather than free trade and less government intervention.[6]

One crucial question is the role of the United States as the one major developed country in the region (this assumption is made because Latin American trade with Canada is generally small). Countries like Mexico, Chile, and Costa Rica have strongly supported closer economic ties with the United States through regional free-trade agreements. However, countries like Brazil, Venezuela, and Argentina, while recognizing the need for good economic relationships with the United States, also like to maintain a certain distance, both economically and politically, from the regional hegemonic power. At the same time, closer integration in the whole of the Americas also depends strongly on the attitude of the United States.[7]

Still, even while some stock markets are more likely to become mirror images of each other, it is unlikely that different regions will be marching to the same tune at the same time. Perceptive investors will spot interregional differences, and be able to capitalize on these differences.[8]

However, Solonik has found that in the mid-1970s, the U.S. stock market's correlation with Morgan Stanley's EAFE (Europe Australia Far East) Index was 0.7, just about where it is now. Moreover, Solonik's analysis of the performance of the U.S. and seven other major stock markets over the past 34 years shows that there has been only a slight increase in correlations, although correlations increased during periods of high volatility, such as the oil shocks of the 1970s and the 1987 crash.[9] Another reason why an increase in correlation among stock markets is not likely to materialize is that countries are different in their industrial compositions and endowments. This indicates that when an investor invests in different stock markets he is buying different sets of cash flows.[10]

Table 1. Overview of Emerging Latin American Stock Markets, Third Quarter 1990

Country	*Market Capitalization (USD Millions)*	*Number of Listed Companies*	*Average Daily Value Traded for Quarter (USD Millions)*	*Price/Earnings Ratio*
Argentina	3,438	174	3.16	–4.35
Brazil	24,907	584	17.56	7.18
Chile	11,216	216	2.82	6.17
Mexico	27,998	205	52.65	10.27

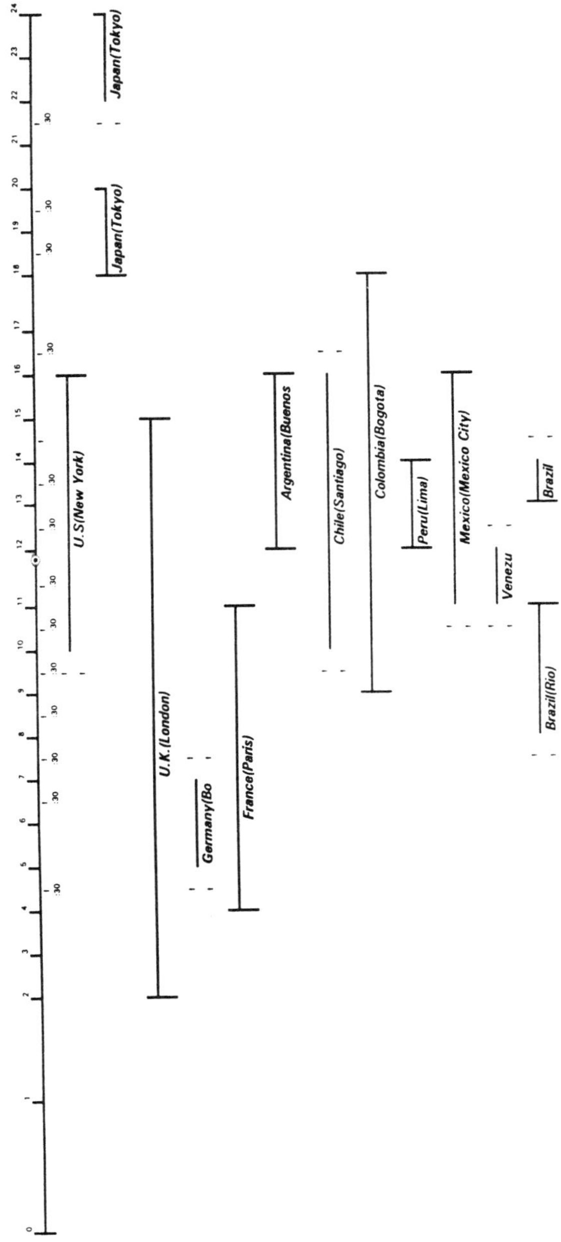
Japan(Tokyo)
Japan(Tokyo)
U.S(New York)
U.K.(London)
Germany(Bo
France(Paris)
Argentina(Buenos
Chile(Santiago)
Colombia(Bogota)
Peru(Lima)
Mexico(Mexico City)
Venezu
Brazil
Brazil(Rio)

Figure 1.

The dynamic linkages among the world's major markets have been studied since the late 1960s (Grubel 1968; Granger and Morgenstern 1970; Levy and Sarnat 1970; Grubel and Fadner 1971; Agmon 1972; Bertoneche 1979; Hilliard 1979) and more recently (Schollhammer and Sands 1985; Grauer and Hackansson 1987; Eun and Shim 1989; Meric and Meric 1989; Von Furstenberg and Jeon 1989; Jeon and Von Furstenberg 1990; Hamao, Masulis, and Ng 1990; Koch and Koch 1991; Birati and Shachmurove 1992; Chan, Gup, and Pan 1992; Malliaris and Urrutia 1992; Roll 1992; Friedman and Shachmurove 1995). However, this study is the first to investigate the dynamic linkages across national indexes of the newly emerging markets of South America.

Table 1 presents an overview of emerging Latin American stock markets as of the third quarter of 1990. Determining which country takes the leading position in market size depends on how well each country's stock market and currency happens to be doing at the time, so it is not of great significance. Yet, the ordering presented is true for the period studied in this paper. The Mexican stock market is the biggest market followed by the Brazilian, Chilean, and the Argentinean.

Since stock markets in different countries operate in different time zones with different closing and opening times, their returns on a given calendar day represent returns that are realized over different real-time periods. Figure 1 presents the operating times of each market relative to other markets in a real-time scale using New York time. As can be seen from the figure, the Brazilian stock exchange closes at 2:30 p.m., Mexico and Argentina at 4:00 p.m., and Chile at 4:30 p.m., New York time.

The remainder of this paper is organized in the following sections. The second section summarizes the Vector Auto Regressions (VAR) model. The third section describes the data used in this study. The fourth section presents the empirical results for the South American markets. The fifth section investigates the influences of major world stock markets on the South American markets. The sixth section presents a mean-variance optimum portfolio for the four South American markets from the point of view of an international investor. The last section summarizes.

THE VAR MODEL—ECONOMETRIC SPECIFICATION

The methodology employed in this paper is the Vector Auto Regressive (VAR) model. This methodology provides identification of the responses to shocks originating in different stock markets. If markets do not behave as a single regional market, the benefits from diversification may be exploited.

A vector autoregression may be written as:

$$Y(t) = C + \sum_{s=1}^{L} A(s) \cdot Y(t-s) + e(t), \tag{1}$$

where L denotes the number of lags, $Y(t)$ is an $n \cdot 1$ vector of daily rates of return of the stock markets, C is an $n \cdot 1$ vector of constants, $A(s)$ is $n \cdot n$ matrixes of coefficients, and $e(t)$ is $n \cdot 1$ column-vector of forecast errors of the best linear predictor of $Y(t)$ using all past $Y(s)$ up to $Y(t-L)$. By design, $e(t)$ is uncorrelated with all the past $Y(s)$. If this is combined with the assumption that $e(t)$ is also a linear combination of current and past $Y(t)$, then $e(t)$ is serially uncorrelated. The *i,j-th* component of $A(s)$ measures the direct effect that a change in the return to the *j-th* market would have on the *i-th* market in time period s.[11] It is more insightful (Sims 1980) to analyze the reaction or the response of the system of equations to typical random shocks by tracing out the following moving average representation (MAR) of the VAR:

$$Y(t) = \sum_{s=0}^{\infty} B(s) \cdot e(t-s), \tag{2}$$

where the $n \cdot n$ matrix of coefficients $B(s)$ is derived from equation (1). Equation (2) expresses $Y(t)$ as a linear combination of current and past one-step ahead forecast errors or innovations.[12]

The vector $e(t)$ is, by assumption, serially uncorrelated. However, each element of the vector $e(t)$ may be contemporaneously correlated. Thus, the error term may be transformed in different ways. Following Sims (1980) and Litterman (1984) we choose a lower triangular matrix V, utilizing the Cholesky factorization, and derive the orthogonalized innovations u from $e = V \cdot u$.[13] The orthogonalized transformation of $e(t)$ implies that equation (2) may be expressed as the following equation:

$$Y(t) = \sum_{s=0}^{\infty} C(s) \cdot u(t-s), \tag{3}$$

where $C(s) = B(s) \cdot V$. The *i,j-th* element of $C(s)$ represents the impulse response of the *i-th* market in s periods to a shock of one standard error in the *j-th* stock market. The orthogonalized innovation enables one to allocate the variance of each element in Y to sources in elements of u, since u is both serially and contemporaneously uncorrelated. This enables decomposition of forecast error variance into the different markets. Such a decomposition measures the overall relative importance of the markets in generating fluctuations in stock returns in all markets, including their own market. A leading market is a market that helps explain the variance of its forecast errors and can explain a high proportion of the variance of forecast errors (VFE) of other markets. A follower stock market is a market that is explained largely by other markets and is not able to explain the VFE of other stock markets.

DESCRIPTION OF THE DATA

The database for this study consists of daily stock market indexes of the four major Latin American stock markets at closing time. The countries are Mexico, Brazil, Chile, and Argentina. In addition, major stock indexes are used in order to investigate external shocks to the South American markets. These stock market indexes are: the United States, the world excluding United States (EXUS), United Kingdom (UK), Japan, Germany, France, and Canada. The indexes were calculated by Morgan Stanley Capital International Perspective, Geneva (MSCIP). The database covers the period December 31, 1987 through June 14, 1994, with a total of 1,684 observations per stock market. These stock market indexes are transformed to daily rates of return, which are then used in the VAR analysis. One of the main advantages of the stock market indexes compiled by the MSCIP is that these indexes do not double-count those stocks that are multiple-listed on other foreign stock exchanges. Thus, any observed interdependence among stock markets cannot be attributed to the multiple listings (Eun and Shim 1989).

EMPIRICAL RESULTS

Correlation Matrix of Daily Returns

Table 2 presents the correlation matrix of daily returns for the transformed data, that is, in rates of return for the four major Latin American and the world stock markets. In this section we concentrate on the Latin American markets. Two interesting points should be noted from the table. First, all correlation coefficients are below 10%, the highest correlation coefficient is between Mexico and Brazil (0.088) and a close second is between Mexico and Chile (0.080). Second, the

Table 2. Correlation Matrix of Daily Returns for Major Stock Market Indexes 1987–1994

	ARG	*MEX*	*BRAZ*	*CHIL*	*CAN*	*FRN*	*GER*	*JAP*	*UK*	*EXUS*	*US*
ARG	1.000	0.031	–0.028	0.054	0.023	–0.036	–0.001	–0.005	–0.005	–0.007	0.016
MEX	0.031	1.000	0.088	0.080	0.026	0.001	–0.011	–0.022	0.054	0.033	–0.013
BRAZ	–0.028	0.088	1.000	0.067	0.026	0.022	–0.020	0.029	0.041	0.023	0.043
CHIL	0.054	0.080	0.067	1.000	–0.011	–0.032	0.027	0.018	0.004	–0.009	0.003
CAN	0.023	0.026	0.026	–0.011	1.000	0.041	0.016	–0.067	0.038	0.410	0.645
FRN	–0.036	0.001	0.022	–0.032	0.041	1.000	0.628	0.288	0.554	0.168	–0.048
GER	–0.000	–0.011	–0.020	0.027	0.016	0.628	1.000	0.336	0.463	0.088	–0.046
JAP	–0.005	–0.022	0.029	0.018	–0.067	0.288	0.336	1.000	0.359	0.031	–0.052
UK	–0.005	0.054	0.041	0.004	0.038	0.554	0.463	0.359	1.000	0.140	–0.057
EXUS	–0.007	0.033	0.023	–0.009	0.410	0.168	0.088	0.031	0.140	1.000	0.246
US	0.016	–0.013	0.043	0.003	0.645	–0.048	–0.046	– 0.052	–0.057	0.246	1.000

correlation coefficient of daily stock market returns between Argentina and Brazil is negative. This is interesting because international diversification of stock market portfolios will be able to exploit such a negative correlation, that is, the aggregate variance may be reduced in expectations. In addition, based on Table 2, it seems that Mexico has higher correlation with Brazil and Chile. The Argentine stock market is more independent of the other markets.

Unit-roots Tests

Appendix A presents a series of unit-roots tests that are calculated. When the data are transformed to rates of return, that is, the natural log of the stock index in market j at time t, minus the natural log of the stock index in market j at time $(t-1)$ (and multiplied by 100), the hypotheses for unit roots are rejected for each and every stock market j.

Choosing the Lag Length of the VAR Model

Appendix B details different tests for choosing the lag length of the VAR system. Based on the Likelihood Ratio Test (Sims 1980) it seems that a lag length of 15 lags captures most of the dynamics in the data.

Contemporaneous Residual Correlation Coefficients

As with the correlation of daily returns it is apparent that the contemporaneous residual correlation coefficients are not high. The highest correlation coefficient, between Mexico and Chile, is less than 10%. The residuals, or innovations, represent abnormal stock market returns that were not predicted on the basis of all the information reflected in past returns. The contemporaneous correlations of daily residual returns measure the degree of correlation between abnormal returns in two markets on the same calendar day. The more integrated any two of the economies are, the more strongly movements in one stock market will be correlated with those in another market. It is interesting to note (see Table 3) that the Chilean stock market is relatively highly correlated with the relatively geographically far away market of Mexico. The two geographically close markets of Chile and Argentina, who share a long, but not always easy to cross, border, have a contemporaneous correlation

Table 3. Covariance\Correlation Matrixes of Residuals Daily Returns for a VAR with 15 Lags

	R_ARG	*R_MEX*	*R_BRAZ*	*R_CHIL*
R_ARG	27.133	0.031	–0.021	0.062
R_MEX	0.247	2.298	0.073	0.099
R_BRAZ	–0.353	0.359	10.278	0.058
R_CHIL	0.419	0.194	0.244	1.677

Table 4. F-Tests for Granger Causality VAR with 15 Lags of Daily Returns for Four Major Latin American Stock Markets

Countries Affecting	*Affected Market F–Statistic*			
	Argentina	*Mexico*	*Brazil*	*Chile*
Argentina	6.753**	0.605	2.715**	0.737
Mexico	1.042	10.035**	1.304	0.759
Brazil	0.819	0.713	6.083**	0.702
Chile	1.031	0.353	1.161	4.721**

Note: ** Statistically significant at one percent.

of only 0.06. These results are in contrast with both Eun and Shim (1989) and Friedman and Shachmurove (1995) who found that geographical proximity matters.

Granger Causality Tests

Having decided on the lag length of 15 trading days, Table 4 presents the block-F test, or Granger Causality tests. The tests indicate whether a variable, say the return in the Mexican stock exchange helps to forecast the stock market return of the Argentinean stock exchange one-step ahead. It is worth noting that the Mexican return can still affect, for example, the Argentinean return through other equations in the system.

The rows in Table 4 are the affecting or influencing markets whereas the columns are the affected markets. In other words, each column represents an equation where the dependent variable is written at the column's heading and the rows are the regressors or the independent variables. The VAR system includes 15 lagged daily returns for each stock market, a constant and a trend. The Argentinean, the Mexican, and the Chilean stock markets are affected only by their own lags. The Brazilian stock market is affected both by its own lagged values as well as by the Argentinean market. Based on the block-F tests it seems that the most influential market in the South American major markets is the Argentinean market which Granger-cause the Brazilian stock market, and the only affected market is the Brazilian stock exchange.

Decomposition of Forecast Variance

Tables 5A–5B present the results of the decomposition of variances. Table 5A shows a system that responds to a shock according to the closing time of the exchanges; first, the Brazilian market and then the two markets of Mexico and Argentina and finally the Chilean market (see Figure 1). About 4% of the variance of Brazil is explained by its neighbors, especially by Argentina. Mexico seems more

Table 5A. Decomposition of Variances for (DCOVF) Major Latin American Stock Markets According to Market Closing Time. The Order is Brazil, Mexico, Argentina, Chile—15 Lags

DCOVF	*Step*	*Standard Error*	*Brazil*	*Mexico*	*Argentina*	*Chile*
Brazil	5	3.289	99.147	0.153	0.617	0.080
	10	3.335	97.193	0.412	1.966	0.427
	15	3.359	96.053	0.783	2.149	1.013
	20	3.362	95.996	0.821	2.163	1.017
	24	3.363	95.983	0.829	2.167	1.019
Mexico	5	1.569	0.570	99.134	0.153	0.141
	10	1.585	0.816	98.718	0.289	0.175
	15	1.593	1.039	98.211	0.514	0.235
	20	1.595	1.052	98.145	0.533	0.268
	24	1.595	1.053	98.135	0.536	0.274
Argentina	5	5.336	0.409	0.501	98.969	0.120
	10	5.399	0.663	0.759	98.189	0.386
	15	5.421	0.750	0.930	97.807	0.510
	20	5.439	0.752	0.958	97.432	0.856
	24	5.440	0.758	0.967	97.417	0.856
Chile	5	1.323	0.468	1.074	0.585	97.871
	10	1.329	0.519	1.495	0.921	97.063
	15	1.337	1.036	1.617	1.045	96.300
	20	1.339	1.112	1.758	1.068	96.061
	24	1.339	1.114	1.765	1.081	96.039

Note: DCOVF denotes Decomposition of Variance for.

independent; only about 2% of its variance of forecasted error is explained by the other South American markets. The same is true for Argentina. The market of Chile is influenced by all three of the other markets. The markets of Brazil and Chile are more affected by Argentina and Mexico. These patterns seem to carry over in the other ordering of the stock markets (Table 5B and other tables that are available from the author).

The Moving Average Representations For the Four South American Stock Markets

Further insights into the dynamic correlations can be obtained by plotting the impulse responses against forecast horizons in trading days that result from different simulations. A shock of one standard deviation is introduced to one of the markets and its dynamic effects in the following 24 trading days are plotted. In this way it is possible to study the dynamic responses of each of the markets to

Table 5B. Decomposition of Variances for Major Latin American Stock Markets According to Market Capitalization. Mexico, Brazil, Chile, Argentina—15 Lags

DCOVF	*Step*	*Standard Error*	*Mexico*	*Brazil*	*Chile*	*Argentina*
Mexico	5	1.569	99.648	0.056	0.129	0.166
	10	1.585	99.292	0.242	0.163	0.302
	15	1.593	98.791	0.458	0.235	0.513
	20	1.595	98.722	0.475	0.269	0.532
	24	1.595	98.712	0.476	0.274	0.536
Brazil	5	3.289	0.731	98.570	0.084	0.613
	10	3.335	0.992	96.613	0.470	1.923
	15	3.359	1.320	95.516	1.035	2.127
	20	3.362	1.353	95.465	1.039	2.141
	24	3.363	1.359	95.452	1.041	2.146
Chile	5	1.323	1.169	0.373	98.310	0.146
	10	1.329	1.581	0.432	97.496	0.488
	15	1.337	1.729	0.924	96.730	0.615
	20	1.339	1.884	0.985	96.493	0.636
	24	1.339	1.892	0.986	96.471	0.648
Argentina	5	5.336	0.524	0.385	0.543	98.546
	10	5.399	0.774	0.648	0.862	97.713
	15	5.421	0.940	0.740	0.975	97.342
	20	5.439	0.968	0.742	1.296	96.992
	24	5.440	0.977	0.748	1.297	96.977

innovations in a particular market using the simulated responses of the estimated VAR model. Figures 2–5 plot the simulated responses in each market to a shock in each of the four stock markets. The vertical axis represents the deviation from the benchmark case, while the horizontal axis represents the horizon days from the day of the shock up to 24 trading days. Figure 2 plots the responses to the Brazilian market. Figure 3 plots the responses to the Mexican, Figure 4 to the Argentinean, and Figure 5 to the Chilean markets. Figures 6–9 present simulated responses of each market to a one standard deviation shock in each market, including its own market. By and large, there are dynamic linkages among the markets, although the responses are small. The main effects take place in the first two to three days. Brazil is affected by Argentina and by Chile. Mexico affects Argentina, and Mexico is affected by Brazil, Argentina affects Chile even after nine trading days.

Friedman and Shachmurove (1995) advance the idea of an event in one market that is directly transmitted to another market, rather than the heat-waves and meteor showers hypotheses, first introduced in the foreign exchange markets (Engle, Ito, and Lin 1990; Ito, Engle and Lin 1992). The heat-wave hypothesis assumes that volatility has only country-specific autocorrelations. The meteor shower hypothesis

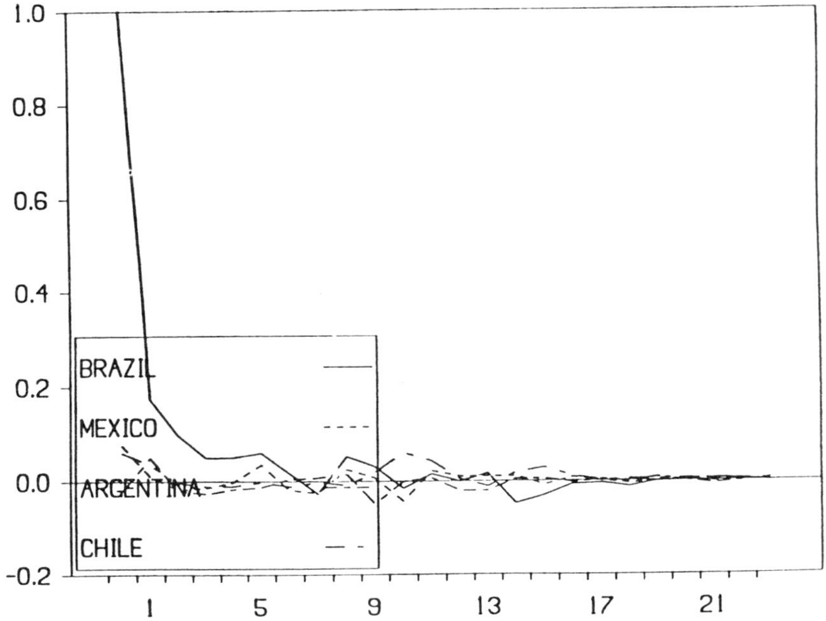

Figure 2. Plot of Responses to Brazil

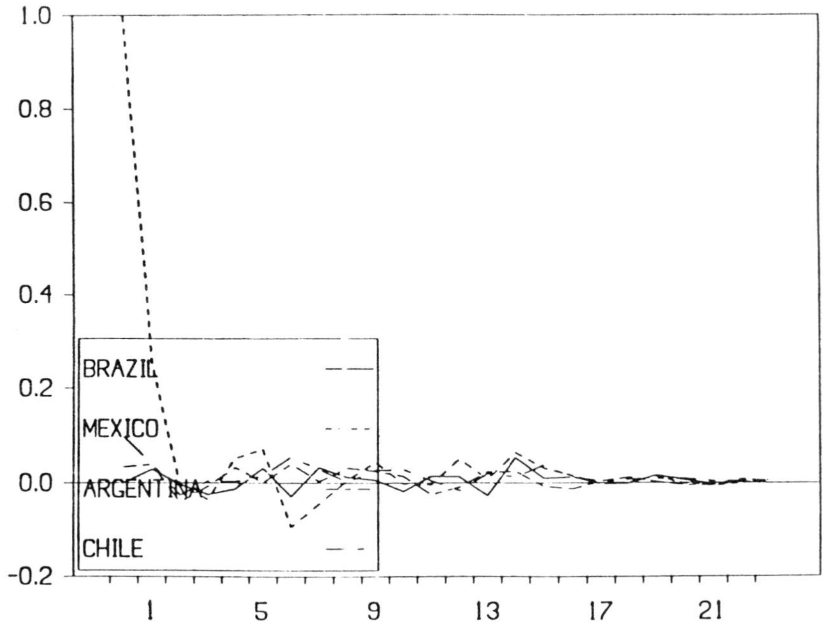

Figure 3. Plot of Responses to Mexico

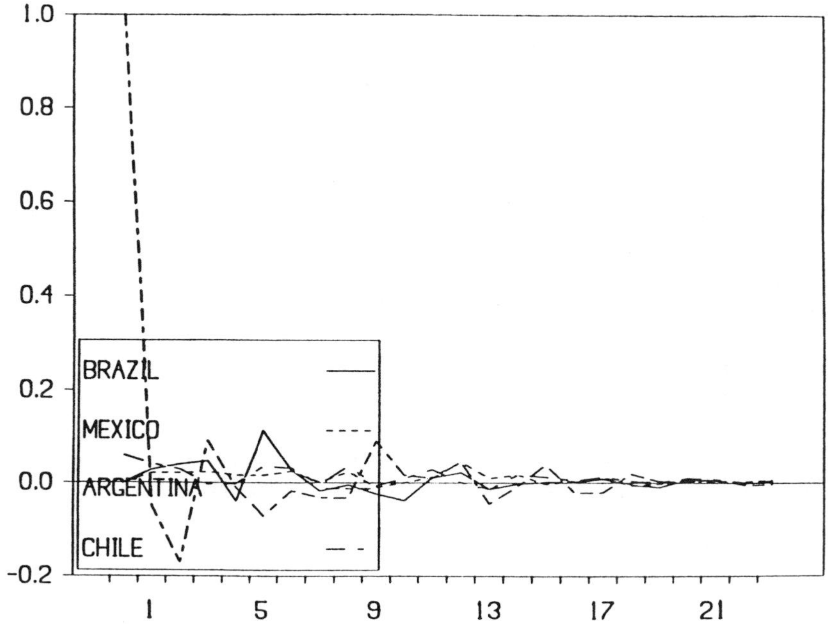

Figure 4. Plot of Responses to Argentina

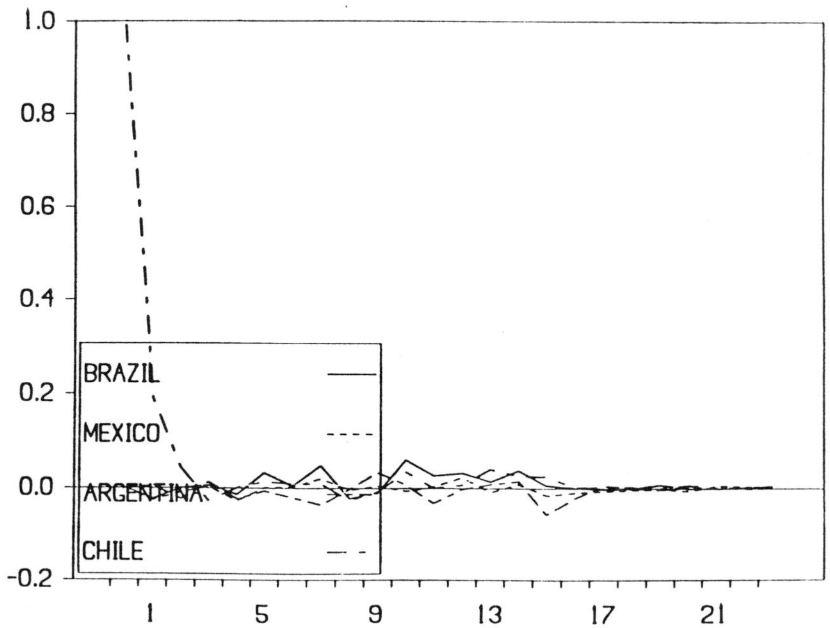

Figure 5. Plot of Responses to Chile

allows volatility spillovers across markets, from one to the other in some order of the stock exchanges. The following simulations can be visualized as a hand grenade that explodes in one market and ricochets to other markets, ignoring its effects, or the ordering on other markets. Figures 6–9 present such simulations. The figures are presented in columns and then the rows from left to right. Figure 6 presents the effects of the Brazilian market on itself, on Mexico, on Argentina, and on Chile. The Brazilian market, shocked positively by one standard deviation is affected for more than five trading days after the shock. The effects on the Mexican and the Chilean markets die after one trading day. The effect on the Argentinean market is felt mostly on the second day (about 25% of the size of the standard deviation) followed by negative adjustments. Figure 7 presents the effect of Mexico on Mexico and the other South American stock markets. The Mexican shock dies out in two days in its own market. The Mexican market affects the markets of Argentina and Brazil with a size of about 20% of the standard error, and the market of Chile by about 10% of the standard error. The effect of the Argentinean market (Figure 8) is interesting as well. There are almost erratic, although dampening, jumps of over and under shooting from the long-run position. We see a strong effect on Brazil, particularly six days after the event and almost no effects on the Mexican and Chilean markets. The Chilean shock dies out after three days in its own market. The

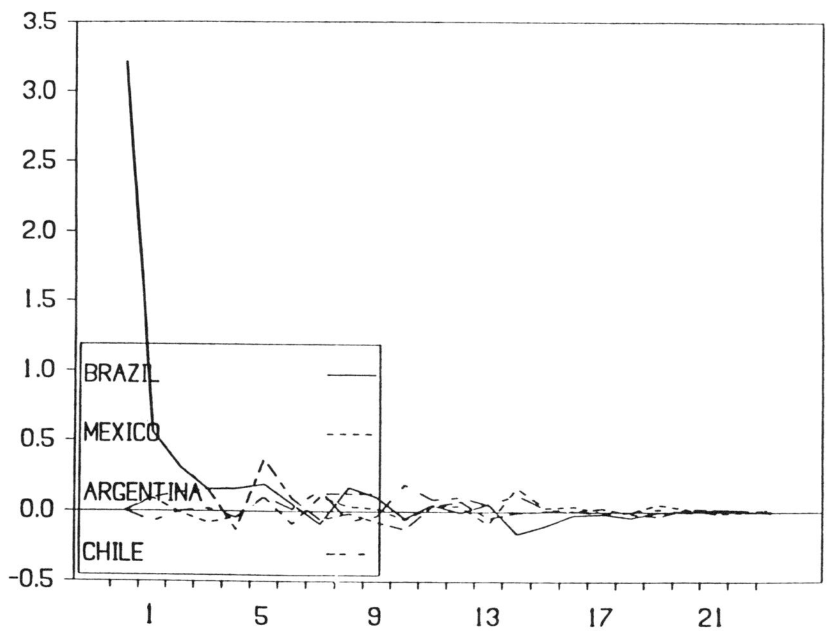

Figure 6. Plot of Responses of Brazil

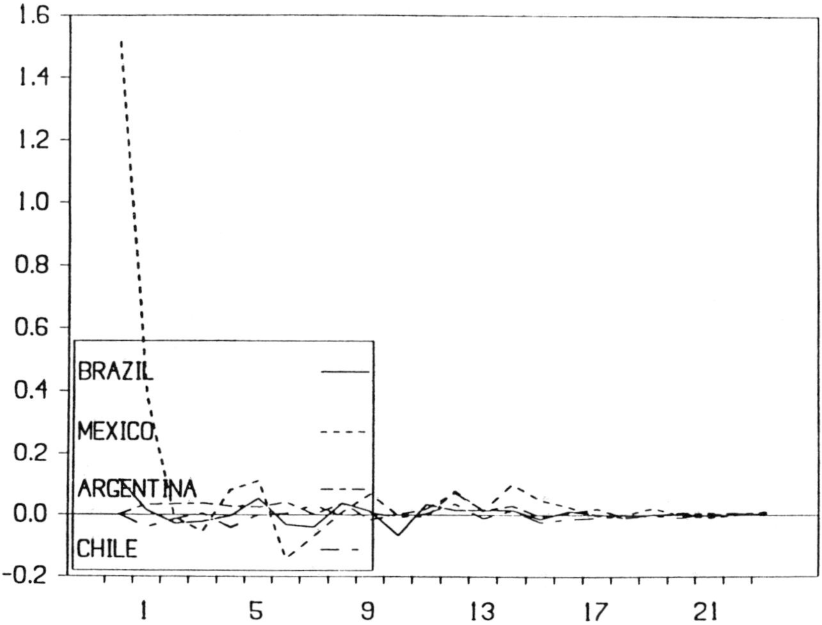

Figure 7. Plot of Responses of Mexico

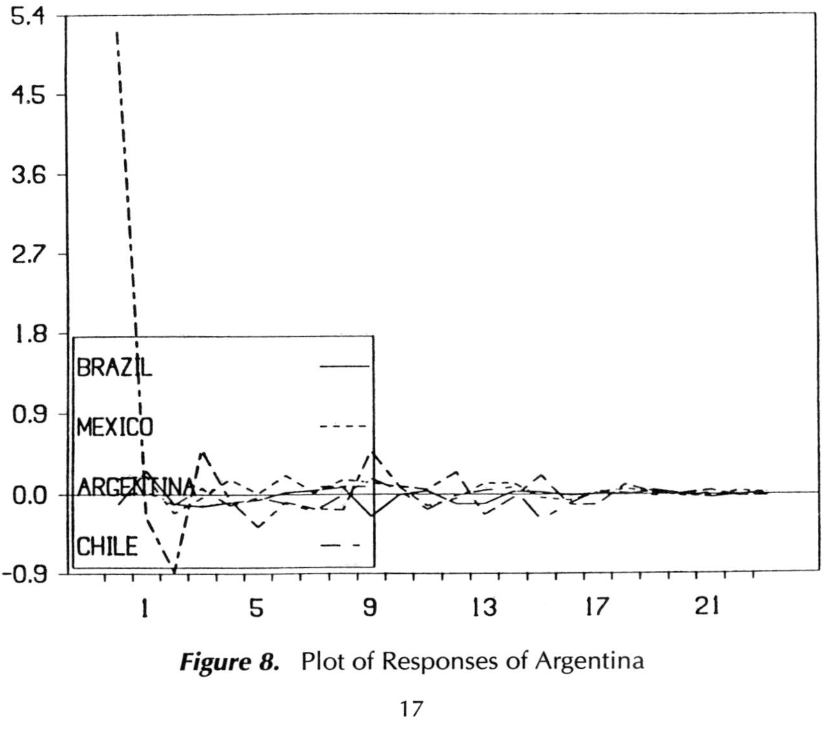

Figure 8. Plot of Responses of Argentina

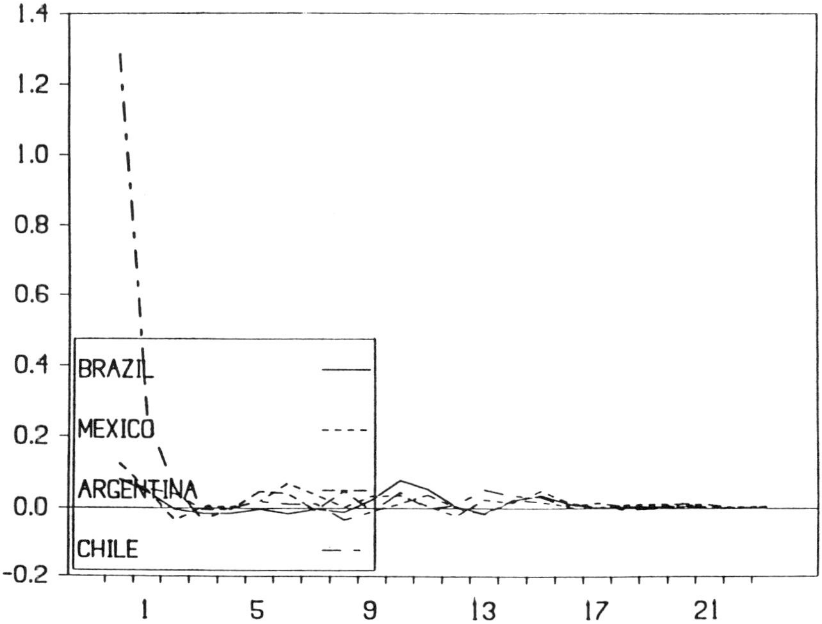

Figure 9. Plot of Responses of Chile

effect on the Argentinean market is interesting with both positive and negative adjustments. Figure 9 plots the effects of the Chilean market. Of a particular interest is the Chilean effect on the Argentinean market (above 0.3 in the first day after the shock to the Chilean market).

EXTERNAL SHOCKS TO SOUTH AMERICAN MARKETS

In this section we investigate the interrelationships among the major South American markets that we have been studying thus far and major world markets. These indexes are: Mexico, Brazil, Chile, Argentina, the United States, world excluding the United States, UK, Japan, Germany, France, and Canada.

Correlation Matrix of Daily Returns

Table 2 presents the correlation matrix of daily returns for major South American and major world markets in the period studied in this paper. Argentinean stock market daily returns are negatively correlated with those of France (–0.04), and have negative or almost zero correlation with those of Germany, Japan, UK, and the world excluding the United States (EXUS). It is positively correlated with the

United States (0.02). Mexico is positively correlated with the Canadian (0.03), the UK (0.05), and EXUS (0.04). Mexico is also negatively correlated with the Japanese and the German markets. Brazil is positively correlated with the UK and the United States (about 4% each) and with EXUS, Japan, and France (about 2% each) and negatively correlated with Germany (–0.02). Chile is correlated mainly with Germany and Japan.

Granger Causality Tests

The F-tests for the affects of major non-South American markets and the South American markets are presented next in Tables 6A–6B. Each VAR system consists of the four South American markets and an additional non-South American market. In all the five-equation VARs, as above in the VARs for the four South American markets, the Brazilian market is affected by Argentina in addition to its own lags. The U.S., Canadian, French, German, UK, and the world excluding U.S. stock indexes are influenced by the Chilean market. The French stock market is affected by the Chilean market as well. The Japanese stock market is affected to a lesser extent, relative to the French, by the Chilean market, and the Chilean market is affected by the Japanese stock market, in addition to its past lags. Finally, Table 6B presents the VAR system with all the available 11 daily stock returns. All countries are affected by their own lags. In addition, Argentina is affected by France, Mexico by the world excluding the U.S. index, Brazil is affected by Argentina, and Chile is affected by Japan, the UK, and the EXUS. The conclusion is that dynamic interrelationships exist among the South American emerging markets and the other major developing countries' stock indexes.

Decomposition of Forecast Variance for South America and World Stock Indexes

The decompositions of variances are presented for the four South American markets and the external stock index of the United States appears in Table 7. It is interesting to note that the Chilean stock index explains about 3.5% of the forecast error variance for the United States. Furthermore, about 7.2% of the forecast variance of the U.S. stock market is explained by the four South American markets. Moreover, the U.S. market has less affect on the South American markets. Similar results, to varying degrees are true for all the external markets investigated and are available from the author. The conclusion is that although we have seen opportunities for diversifications, dynamic linkages exist and should not be played down. The fact that these correlations are small enables an investor to diversify, and thus decrease his risk for a given return on his portfolio. Similar conclusions can be reached using the other external markets.

Table 6A. F-Tests for Granger Causality VAR with 15 Lags of Daily Returns for Four Major South American and an External Stock Market

	Affected Market				
Countries Affecting	*External Market*	*Argentina*	*Mexico*	*Brazil*	*Chile*
US	2.2333**	0.5897	0.6798	0.7179	0.7050
Argentina	0.6125	6.7336**	0.6231	2.6478**	0.7335
Mexico	0.9171	1.0359	10.0575**	1.3136	0.7782
Brazil	1.1473	0.8213	0.7384	5.7797**	0.7253
Chile	3.9559**	1.1502	0.3666	1.1079	4.6129**
Canada	5.2026**	0.8895	0.9509	0.7651	0.6799
Argentina	0.7803	6.7582**	0.6037	2.6978**	0.7533
Mexico	0.7000	1.0458	9.8176**	1.2712	0.7663
Brazil	0.8558	0.8421	0.6496	5.9696**	0.7243
Chile	7.0376**	1.1637	0.3885	1.1909	4.7737**
France	1.8237*	1.4432	1.3452	0.9291	0.7721
Argentina	0.9382	6.3951**	0.6243	2.6687**	0.7028
Mexico	0.6113	1.0599	10.0265**	1.2358	0.7918
Brazil	1.0900	0.9067	0.7176	5.9567**	0.7787
Chile	1.8725*	1.1451	0.3750	1.1083	4.6938**
Germany	1.0380	1.0503	1.4809	1.2661	0.7353
Argentina	0.8763	6.6256**	0.6713	2.6071**	0.7688
Mexico	0.6568	1.0885	9.8085**	1.1989	0.7576
Brazil	1.4000	0.8252	0.6947	6.1441**	0.7606
Chile	1.7521*	1.1688	0.3653	1.0592	4.7289**
Japan	2.6511**	0.6582	1.1549	1.0846	2.6809**
Argentina	0.6433	6.5490**	0.5885	2.8700**	0.7849
Mexico	0.7383	1.0418	9.8905**	1.3005	0.9046
Brazil	0.7497	0.7614	0.7019	6.1428**	0.7248
Chile	1.5721#	0.9912	0.4364	1.2368	5.0996**
UK	1.7748*	0.6580	0.9352	1.1484	0.6016
Argentina	0.7416	6.6730**	0.6134	2.7606**	0.7774
Mexico	1.2001	1.0404	10.1271**	1.2792	0.7068
Brazil	1.2632	0.8389	0.7364	6.0206**	0.7865
Chile	3.1835**	1.0478	0.3950	1.1966	4.6659**
Exus	2.7848**	0.7929	1.7633*	1.2403	0.7271
Argentina	0.9208	6.7586**	0.6088	2.8361**	0.7771
Mexico	0.7530	1.0695	10.0685**	1.2603	0.7458
Brazil	1.2467	0.8108	0.7429	6.0927**	0.7883
Chile	4.0657**	1.0788	0.5300	1.1253	4.6548**

Notes: ** Statistically significant at one percent.
*Statistically significant at three percent.
Statistically significant at ten percent.

Table 6B. F-Tests for Granger Causality VAR with 15 Lags of Daily Returns for Four Major South American and the World Stock Markets

Countries Affecting	*Affected Market F-Statistic*										
	ARG	*Mexico*	*Brazil*	*Chile*	*Canada*	*France*	*Ger*	*Japan*	*UK*	*Exus*	*US*
ARG	5.9558**	0.7453	2.9373**	0.8137	0.7276	1.4330	0.8425	0.6227	0.7518	1.0889	0.3750
MEX	1.0721	9.1855**	1.2298	1.0038	0.6393	0.6998	1.2231	0.6216	1.9854**	0.8404	0.8810
BRAZ	0.8957	0.6835	5.8353**	0.9441	0.9656	0.5878	1.3732	0.8179	0.7980	1.2253	1.3053
CHIL	1.3391	0.6205	1.3519	5.1998**	3.4209**	1.2441	1.3991	0.5515	1.2158	2.0772**	2.0341**
CAN	0.6615	0.6984	1.3142	0.7500	3.9787**	1.2498	0.9797	2.8186**	2.5605**	0.9692	2.8744**
FRN	1.8515*	1.2120	1.1207	1.1411	2.3066**	0.7857	1.4690#	0.8990	1.8189*	1.0732	2.0088**
GER	1.3800	1.2683	1.0245	0.9582	0.9067	1.5562#	1.1576	1.5042	1.0841	1.3185	1.1301
JAP	1.0597	1.0345	0.5760	5.2983**	6.0972**	1.1596	1.1539	6.1265**	1.3566	3.3048**	11.7432**
UK	0.6050	0.9085	1.0001	1.4961*	1.7485	2.0271**	1.3643	2.4657**	2.1443**	0.5755	1.8577*
EXUS	1.1301	1.8361*	0.6313	3.0322**	5.5301**	35.0110**	34.6524**	179.9861**	45.5545**	2.4443**	10.1818**
US	0.3883	0.5360	1.4301	1.1018	7.0803**	5.6353**	4.1006**	1.3853	3.0376**	10.4025**	3.6497**

Notes: ** Statistically significant at one percent.
*Statistically significant at three percent.
Statistically significant at ten percent.

Table 7. Decomposition of Variance for (DCOVF): South America and the United States

DCOVF	*Step*	*Standard Error*	*US*	*Argentina*	*Mexico*	*Brazil*	*Chile*
US	10	1.101	95.773	0.250	0.532	0.626	2.816
	20	1.114	93.924	0.692	0.813	1.052	3.517
	24	1.114	93.881	0.695	0.829	1.060	3.533
ARG	10	5.394	0.517	97.864	0.654	0.579	0.384
	20	5.438	0.656	96.982	0.861	0.672	0.826
	24	5.439	0.658	96.950	0.877	0.681	0.832
MEX	10	1.583	0.325	0.415	98.821	0.236	0.201
	20	1.595	0.517	0.674	98.055	0.463	0.288
	24	1.595	0.523	0.677	98.034	0.465	0.298
BRA	10	3.329	0.733	1.883	1.004	95.945	0.433
	20	3.362	1.074	2.095	1.346	94.452	1.031
	24	3.362	1.074	2.099	1.352	94.440	1.032
CHIL	10	1.327	0.282	0.942	1.533	0.455	96.786
	20	1.338	0.590	1.083	1.841	1.035	95.447
	24	1.339	0.594	1.096	1.848	1.038	95.422

Note: DCOVF denotes Decomposition of Variance for

The Moving Average Representations with External Markets

Because of space limitations, the figures for a VAR system that includes the four South American and one external market are presented only for the U.S. market. The order is according to closing time of the exchanges (Figure 1). Figures 10–14 present the simulation results for the United States. Figure 10 presents the simulation of the U.S. effects on itself and on the other four South American markets. This figure can be compared to the results reported in Eun and Shim (1989). Eun and Shim (1989) report the effects of the United States in a VAR model on eight developed countries for the period January 1980 to December 1985. The countries they studied include, in addition to the United States, the stock markets of Australia, Canada, France, Germany, Hong Kong, Japan, Switzerland, and the UK. They found that innovations in the U.S. stock market are rapidly transmitted to all the other markets in responses of sizes of between 0.2 to 0.4 (except, the Canadian with a high response of 0.6). In our sample, and for the South American emerging stock exchanges, the U.S. market affects mainly Argentina and Brazil. The response of Argentina is about 0.18 and the response of Brazil is about 0.15 in the first two days after the shock. The responses of Mexico and Chile are almost zero. Chile affects the United States on the ninth business day. The simulations of the impulse responses for other external markets and the South American markets are available from the author.

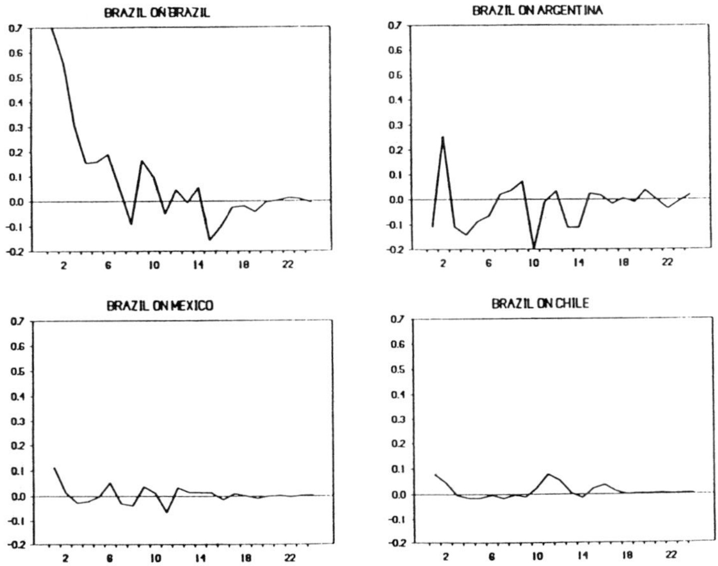

Figure 10.

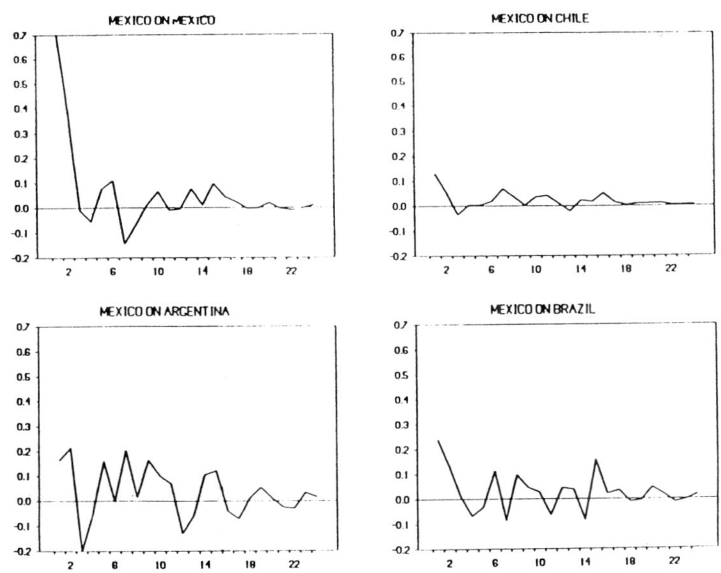

Figure 11.

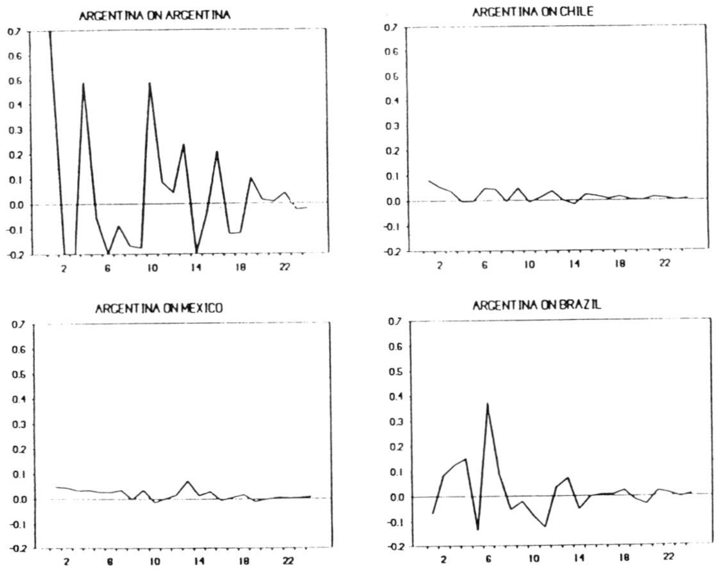

Figure 12.

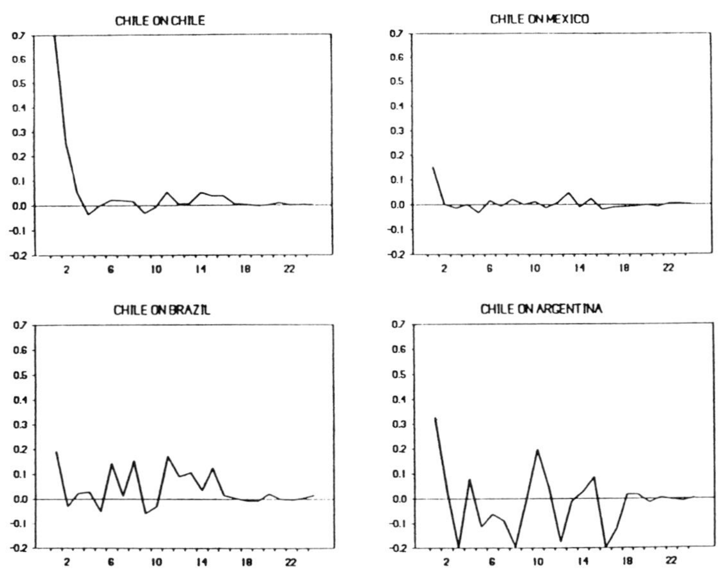

Figure 13.

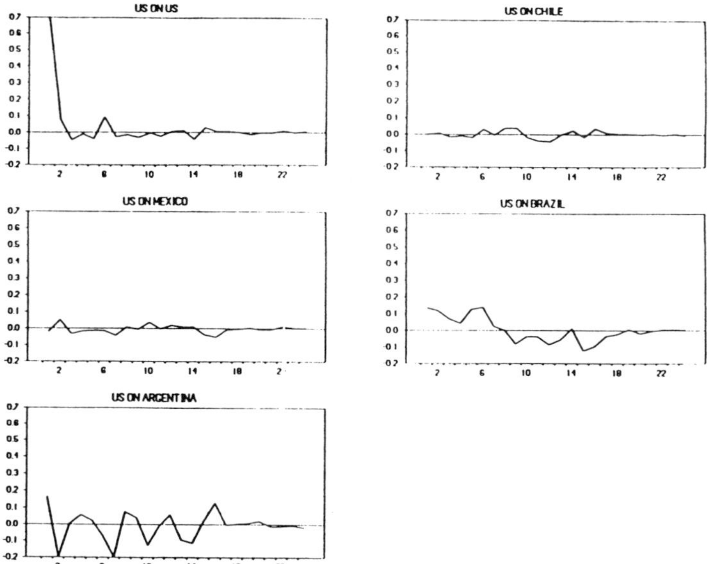

Figure 14.

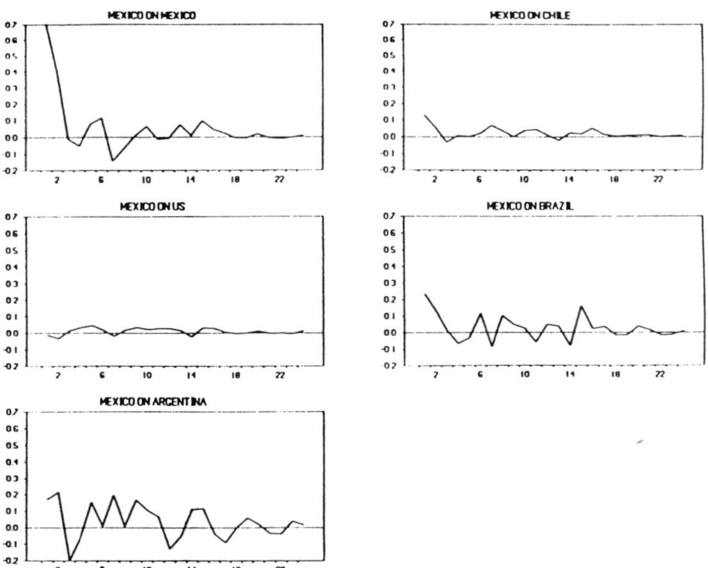

Figure 15.

Table 8. A Mean-Variance Optimum Portfolio

Country	*Expected Annual Return*	*S.D.*	*Weight*
Argentina	1.101	1.009	7.85%
Mexico	0.627	0.312	40.17%
Brazil	0.562	0.636	7.92%
Chile	0.492	0.254	44.06%
PORTFOLIO	0.599	0.218	0.218

A Mean-variance Optimum Portfolio

In this section we present the optimum portfolio (Grauer and Hakansson 1987). Figure 15 and Table 8 present the optimum portfolio of the four stock markets where the U.S. T-bill represents the return on the safe asset. The optimal weights are 7.85% for Argentina, 40.1% for Mexico, about 8% for Brazil and 44% for Chile. The expected annual return on such a portfolio is about 60% with a standard deviation of 21%.

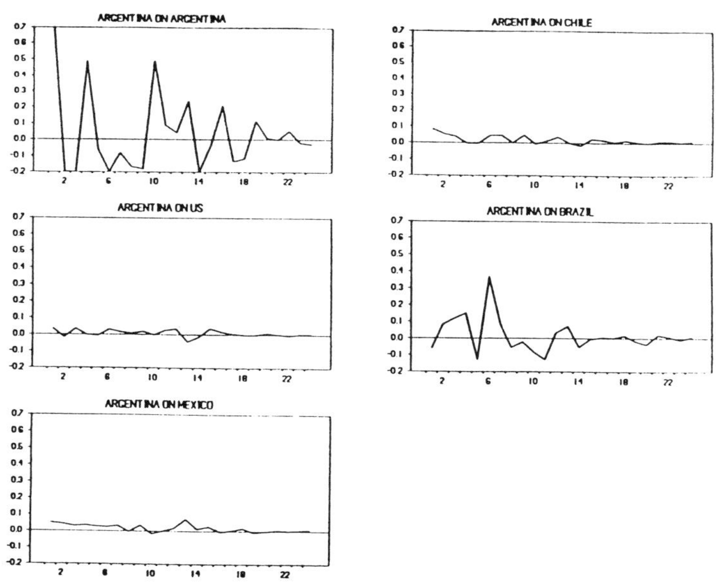

Figure 16.

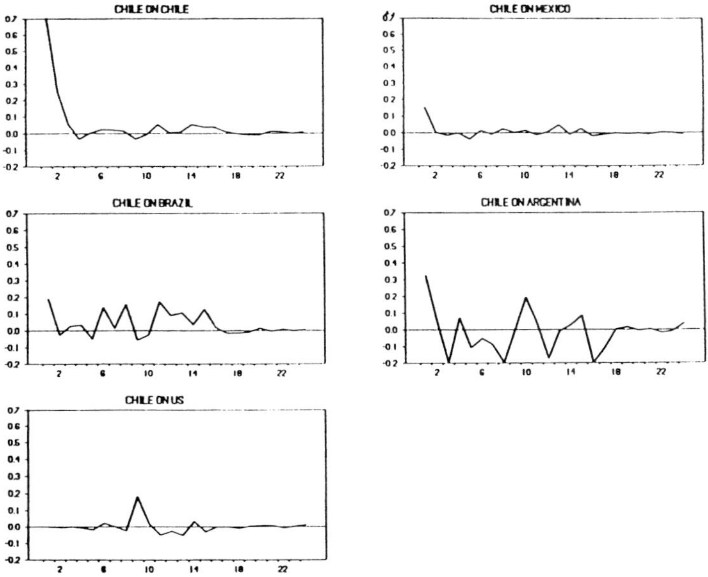

Figure 17.

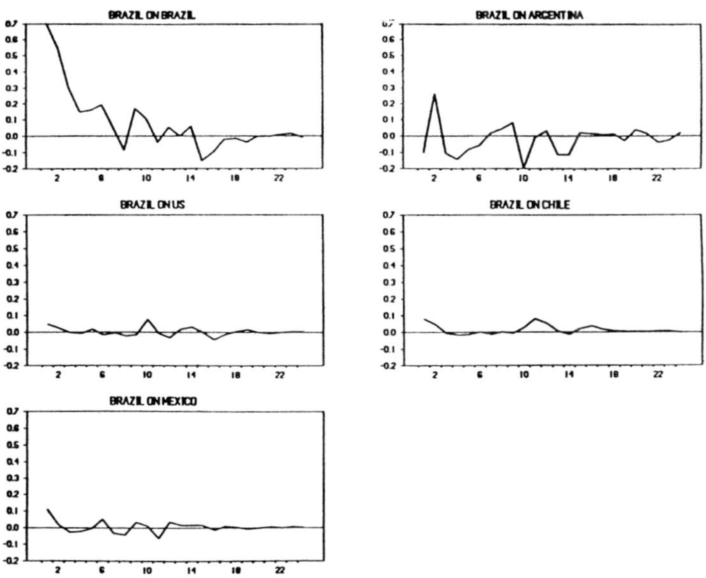

Figure 18.

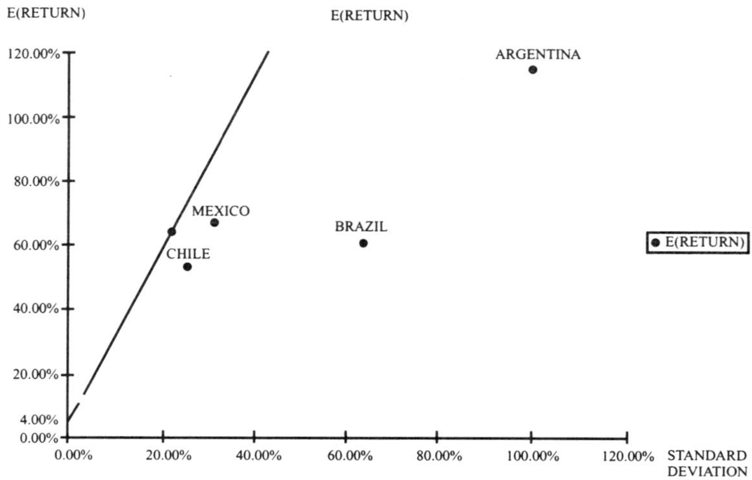

Figure 19.

CONCLUSIONS

This paper formulates and estimates a series of VAR econometric models. The models are used to study the dynamic interrelationships among the four major stock markets of South America and among the South American markets and the major world stock markets. Through a series of simulations the dynamic responses are studied and analyzed. Although most of the impulse responses die out very quickly, it is still possible to trace the dynamic linkages among markets. These linkages are nonlinear functions involving 15 lags and tens (in the four-variable VARs) or hundreds of coefficients (in the 11-variable VARS). Within the South American markets, no market is found to be completely independent. Moreover, different simulations yield different results indicating that different shocks that are transmitted differently from one market to the other are going to affect the stock markets differently. The conclusion is thus, that although markets are efficient and cleared out in few trading days, there are dynamic linkages that can be explored and exploited to the benefits of the international investor. Stock markets do not march to the beat of the same drummer. Thus, diversification makes sense even when global markets become more accessible.

APPENDIX A

This appendix details the unit roots tests performed in this paper. Four tests are displayed. The first test, DFT, presented in column one of Table A1, is the Dickey-Fuller test. The methodology allows for testing a unit root in AR(1 + LAGS)

Table A1.1. Unit Roots Tests on the Levels of the Stock Markets Indexes 1987–1994

Country	*DFT*	*ADF*	*PPT*	*BURT*
Argentina	–1.938	–2.136	–1.932	0.991
Mexico	–0.282	–0.494	–0.442	0.997
Brazil	–3.794	–5.925	–5.480	0.981
Chile	1.387	1.146	1.165	0.992

Notes: DFT is the Dickey-Fuller Test with 0 Lag.
ADF is the Augmented Dickey-Fuller Test with 1 lag.
PPT is the Phillips-Perron Test with 4 Lags.
BURT is the Bayesian Unit Root Test suggested by Sims.

representation (Fuller 1976; Dickey and Fuller 1979). With a positive value for LAGS the test is the Augmented Dikey-Fuller test, ADF. The results of the Augmented Dickey-Fuller test, ADF, is presented in column 2 of Table A1. The third test, PPT, is the Phillips-Perron unit root test (Phillips 1987; Phillips and Perron 1988) presented in column number 3 of the table. The fourth test, BURT implements the Bayesian Unit Root Test suggested by Sims (Sims 1988) and corrected by Doan (Doan 1994). A small value of Marginal Alpha indicates that the data evidence is strongly against the unit-root hypothesis. The BURT is presented in column 4 of Table A1. The results presented in Table A1 are first for the raw data in levels, Table A1.1, then in natural logs, Table A1.2, and finally in rate of return, Table A1.3. The existence of unit roots cannot be rejected for all markets when the

Table A1.2. Unit Roots Tests on the Log of the Levels of the Stock Markets Indexes 1987–1994

Country	*DFT*	*ADF*	*PPT*	*BURT*
Argentina	–4.013	–3.710	–3.362	0.973
Mexico	–1.448	–1.679	–1.595	0.988
Brazil	–4.726	–6.784	–7.005	0.970
Chile	–0.287	–0.458	–0.404	0.997

Table A1.3. Unit Roots Tests on the Daily Returns of the Stock Markets Indexes 1987–1994

Country	*DFT*	*ADF*	*PPT*	*BURT*
Argentina	–1773.085	–2523.299	–1647.713	0.000
Mexico	–1241.076	–1402.610	–1213.767	0.000
Brazil	–1377.423	–1188.892	–1463.661	0.000
Chile	1399.133	–1367.877	–1317.661	0.000

indexes are measured in their levels or in their natural logarithms. However, it is clear that when the data are transformed to rates of return, that is, the natural log of the stock index in market j at time t, minus the natural log of the stock index in market j at time $(t-1)$ (and multiplied by 100),—the hypotheses for unit roots are rejected for each and every stock market j.

APPENDIX B

This appendix presents the tests for choosing the lag length of the VAR system. In general three tests are proposed for choosing the lag length. The first is the Akaike Information Criterion, AIC, (Akaike 1973), the second is the Schwarz Criterion (Schwarz 1978), and the third is the Likelihood ratio test as modified by Sims (Sims 1980). The first two tests are really single-equation tests that use a function of the residual sum of squares together with a penalty for large numbers of parameters. The selection of the lag length is based on minimizing the criterion function over different alternatives for the lag length. Since the Schwarz Criterion places a heavier penalty on additional parameters, the Criterion never chooses a lag length which is larger than the one chosen by the Akaike Criterion. Specifically, the Akaike Criterion minimizes the expression:

$$T \cdot \log(RSS) + 2 \cdot K,$$

where T is the number of observations, RSS is the sum of squared residuals, and K is the number of regressors. The Schwarz Criterion minimizes the expression:

$$T \cdot \log(RSS) + K \cdot (\log T).$$

I have tested for lag length ranging from 1 to 30 lags. For Argentina, the lag length is three and two for Akaike and Schwarz, respectively. For Mexico, the lag length is two and one lag. For Brazil, five lags for the first criterion and only one lag for the second criteria. For Chile, the lag length is one lag based on the two criteria.

However, in a VAR system, the hypotheses to be tested include more than one equation. The test recommended in this case is based on the Likelihood Ratio Test as follows:

$$(T - C) \cdot (\log | \Sigma_r - \Sigma_u |)$$

where T is the number of observations, C is the correction suggested by Sims to improve small sample properties (Sims 1980, p. 17), Σ_r and Σ_u are the restricted and the unrestricted covariance matrixes. The correction, C is equal to the number of variables in each unrestricted equation in the system. The above expression is asymptotically distributed as a χ^2 with degrees of freedom equal to the number of restrictions. I have experimented with length lags of up to 30 lags. It seems that a lag length of 15 lags captures most of the dynamics in the data (detailed results are available upon a request). Similar results were found in Eun and Shim (1989) for daily stock markets of nine major world markets and Friedman and Shachmurove (1995) study of the European stock markets. The lesson that should be inferred from the above exercises is that researchers need to take into account that the estimation is of a system of equations rather than single-equation. Applying such a measure will lead to inclusion of 15 lags in the VAR system.

ACKNOWLEDGMENTS

For many useful discussions and comments, I would like to thank Gerard Adams, Jere Behrman, Martin Cherkes, Betty Daniel, Francis Diebold, Elyas Elyasiani, Joseph Friedman, Alan Heston, Lawrence Klein, Robert Mariano, and seminar participants of the North American Economics and Finance Association Annual Meeting Washington DC, January 1995 and the Graduate School and University Center, The City University of New York, May 1995. Financial support from the University of Pennsylvania Institute for Economic Research and University of Pennsylvania Center for Economic Research in Economics and the Social Sciences are gratefully acknowledged.

NOTES

1. This trend for increased international investment is also occurring in the newly developing markets of East and South Asia (Korea, Philippines, Taiwan and India, Indonesia, Thailand), in Europe (Greece, Portugal, Turkey), and in Africa (Nigeria and Zimbabwe).

2. In fact, the International Finance Corporation (IFC), which helps countries to develop their stock markets, has attempted to establish regulatory criteria for these stock markets. Of the emerging markets, only the countries of Brazil, Chile, Mexico, India, South Korea, and the Philippines have accounting standards, according to the IFC, that are acceptable internationally.

3. In 1993 the United States invested a net of $67.8 billion in foreign exchanges. This figure was more than double what U.S. investors bought in each of the two preceding years and more than seven times the 1990 level.

4. See, *WSJ* "Going Global" December 9, 1994 p. R8.

5. An example of this development is Telefonos de Mexico SA, Mexico's national telephone company and that country's largest stock in terms of market capitalization, whose price is said to be set in New York, where the company's American Depository Receipts (ADRs) are listed, and not in Mexico City.

6. A Pan-American summit ended in December 1994 with plans to establish a free-trade zone. Thirty-four Western Hemisphere leaders agreed to establish a Free Trade Area of the Americas by 2005. The proposed free-trade zone would be the largest in the world, encompassing 850 million people with $13 trillion in purchasing power. Meanwhile, the United States invited Chile to begin negotiations to join NAFTA, which currently comprises the United States, Canada, and Mexico. Along with NAFTA, the major free-trade pacts in Central and Latin America are: Mercosur, which includes Brazil, Argentina, Paraguay, and Uruguay; the Andean group, which includes Venezuela, Colombia, Bolivia, Ecuador, and Peru; the Central American Common Market; and the Caribbean Community (Gwynne 1994; Alonso 1994). It is both economically and politically interesting to note that the previous summit before last December took place 27 years ago, and was held in Punta del Este, Uruguay. Latin America has changed enormously since that summit. The cold war is over and, with the single exception of Cuba, all the region's countries are democracies and believers in open markets.

7. In this context, Bhagwati has claimed that if the United States pushes Free Trade Areas only southward, it will certainly invite a defensive, if not retaliatory, bloc in Asia (Bhagwati 1993, p. 161).

8. To borrow an example from Asia, Singapore will probably be more developed—even in the year 2000—than China. Thus, the emerging growth stocks listed on China's stock market, will not be as correlated as the big name companies who are cross-listed in Singapore's stock market, as well as the major stock markets all over the world.

9. Such correlations reduce the benefits from international risk diversifications, because it is precisely when markets are volatile that investors would like to bear the benefits of risk diversifications. However, Solonik suggests that U.S. investors should have about 40% of their assets abroad, a figure that is higher than the 10 to 15% advocated by many market analysts.

10. For example, energy stocks represent merely 8% of the U.S. stock market's total capitalization. In Germany and Switzerland they account for none of the stock market capitalization. However, in the Netherlands and in Norway, energy stocks make up 43 and 41%, respectively of the total stock market capitalization. This indicates that when an investor invests in different stock markets he is buying different sets of cash flows. Coffee and banana plantations are going to stay in South America; they are not going to sprout up in Germany or the United Kingdom.

11. There are a total of $n^2 \cdot L$ free coefficients in this model. Since the right-hand side (RHS) of each equation in the system of equation (1), includes the same regressors, a constant, lagged values of each variable, and the error term, estimation is relatively straight forward. However, such a system of equations contains complicated cross-equation feedback restrictions.

12. Each element in $B(s)$, say the i,j-th element gives the response of the *i-th* market in s periods after a unit random shock in the *j-th* market and none in other markets, conditional on the information available at time t.

13. The transformed innovation $u(t)$ has an identity covariance matrix, such that $E(e \cdot e') = S$ and $V \cdot V' = S$.

REFERENCES

Agmon, T. 1972. "The Relations Among Equity Markets: A Study of Share Price Co-Movements in the United States, United Kingdom, Germany, and Japan." *Journal of Finance* (September): 839–855.

Akaike, H. 1973. "Information Theory and the Extension of the Maximum Likelihood Principle." In *2nd International Symposium on Information Theory*, edited by B.N. Petrov and F. Csaki. Budapest.

Alonso, I.T. de. (ed.). 1994. *Trade, Industrialization, and Integration in Twentieth-Century Central America*. Publishers. Westport, CT: Praeger Publishers.

Bertoneche, M.L. 1979. "Spectral Analysis of Stock Market Prices." *Journal of Banking and Finance* 3: 201–208.

Bhagwati, J.N. 1993. "Beyond NAFTA: Clinton's Trading Choices." *Foreign Policy* 91: 155–162.

Birati A., and Y. Shachmurove. 1992. "International Stock Price Movements Before and During the Gulf Crisis." *Atlantic Economic Society: Best Papers Proceedings* 2(2): 42–47.

Chan C.K., B.E. Gup, and M.-S. Pan. 1992. "An Empirical Analysis of Stock Prices in Major Asian Markets and the United States." *The Financial Review* 27(2): 289–307.

Dickey, D., and W.A. Fuller. 1979. "Distribution of the Estimators for Time Series Regressions with a Unit Root." *Journal of the American Statistical Association* 74: 427–431.

Engle, R., T. Ito, and W. Lin. 1990. "Meteor Showers or Heat Waves? Heteroskedastic Intra-daily Volatility in the Foreign Exchange Market." *Econometrica* 58(3): 525–542.

Eun C.S., and S. Shim. 1989. "International Transmission of Stock Market Movements." *Journal of Financial and Quantitative Analysis* 24(2): 241–256.

Friedman J., and Y. Shachmurove. 1995. "Dynamic Linkages Among European Stock Markets." In *Advances in International Stock Market Relationships and Interactions*, edited by J. Doukas. Westport, CT: Greenwood Publishing.

Fuller, W.A. 1976. *Introduction to Statistical Time Series*. New York: Wiley.

Granger C.W., and O. Morgenstern. 1970. *Predictability of Stock Market Prices.* Lexington, KY: Heath-Lexington Books.

Grauer R.R., and N. Hakansson. 1987. "Gains from International Diversifications: 1968–85 Returns on Portfolios of Stocks and Bonds." *Journal of Finance* 42(3): 721–739.

Grubel, H.G. 1968. "Internationally Diversified Portfolios." *The American Economic Review* 58: 1299–1314.

Grubel, H., and K. Fadner. 1971. "The Interdependence of International Equity Markets." *Journal of Finance* 26: 89–94.

Gwynne, R. 1994. "Regional Integration in Latin America: The Revival of a Concept?" In *Continental Trading Blocs—The Growth of Regionalism in the World Economy*, edited by R. Gibb and W. Michalak. New York: John Wiley and Sons.

Hamao, Y., R.W. Masulis, and V. Ng. 1990. "Correlations in Price Changes and Volatility Across International Stock Markets." *Review of Financial Studies* 3: 281–307.

Hilliard, J.E. 1979. "The Relationship Between Equity Indices on World Exchanges." *Journal of Finance* 34: 103–114.

Ito, T., R. Engle, and W. Lin. 1992. "Where Does the Meteor Shower Come From? The Role of Stochastic Policy Coordination." *Journal of International Economics* 32(3–4): 221–240.

Jeon, B.N., and G.M. Von Furstenberg. 1990. "Growing International Co-Movement in Stock Price Indexes." *The Quarterly Review of Economics and Business* 30(3): 15–30.

Koch, P.D., and T. Koch. 1991. "Evolution in Dynamic Linkages Across Daily National Stock Indexes." *Journal of International Money and Finance* 10(2): 231–251.

Levy, H., and M. Sarnat. 1970. "International Diversification of Investment Portfolios." *The American Economic Review* 60: 668–675.

Litterman, R. 1984. "A Bayesian Procedure for Forecasting with Vector Autoregressions." Working Paper, Federal Reserve Bank of Minneapolis.

Malliaris A.G., and J. Urrutia. 1992. "The International Crash of October 1987: Causality Tests." *Journal of Financial and Quantitative Analysis* 27(3): 353–364.

Meric, I., and G. Meric. 1989. "Gains from International Portfolio Diversification and Inter-Temporal Stability and Seasonality in International Stock Market Relationships." *Journal of Banking and Finance* 13(4–5): 627–640.

Phillips, P.C.B. 1987. "Time Series Regression With A Unit Root." *Econometrica* 55(2): 277–301.

Phillips, P.C.B., and P. Perron. 1988. "Testing for a Unit Root in Time Series Regressions." *Biometrica* 65: 335–346.

Roll, R. 1992. "Industrial Structure and the Comparative Behavior of International Stock Market Indices." *Journal of Finance* 1(4): 3–41.

Schwarz, G. 1978. "Estimating the Dimension of a Model." *Annals of Statistics* 6: 461–464.

Schollhammer, H., and O. Sands. 1985. "The Interdependence Among the Stock Markets of Major European Countries and the United States: An Empirical Investigation of Interrelationships Among National Stock Prices Movements." *Management International Review* 25(1): 17–26.

———. 1987. "Lead-Lag Relationships Among National Equity Markets: An Empirical Investigation." In *Recent Developments in International Banking and Finance* volume 1, edited by S.J. Khoury and A. Ghosh. Lexington, MA: Lexington.

Sims, C.A. 1972. "Money, Income and Causality." *American Economic Review* 62: 540–552.

———. 1980. "Macroeconomics and Reality." *Econometrica* 48: 1–49.

———. 1988. "Bayesian Skepticism on Unit Root Econometrics," *Journal of Economic Dynamics and Control* 12: 463–474.

Von Furstenberg, G.M., and B.N. Jeon. 1989. "International Stock Price Movements: Links and Messages." *Brookings Papers on Economic Activity* 1: 125–179.

INTERNATIONAL TRANSMISSION OF INNOVATIONS AMONG EC STOCK MARKETS

Joseph Friedman and Yochanan Shachmurove

ABSTRACT

This paper examines the dynamic linkages among the eight major stock markets of the European Communities countries. A Vector Autoregression (VAR) model was calibrated using daily stock market returns. The returns are expressed in terms of the U.S. dollar, reflecting the outlook of American investors. The model is used to investigate through simulations how a shock in one market is transmitted to other EC markets. The four larger stock markets of Britain, France, Germany, and the Netherlands were found to be highly related, while the smaller stock markets (Belgium, Denmark, Italy, and Spain) were found to be more independent.

INTRODUCTION

In the past two decades investors in many countries have adopted a global view. Most advanced economies deregulated their capital markets, removed barriers to international investments, and improved the accessibility to information. These

Research in International Business and Finance, Supplement 1, pages 35–64.

ISBN: 0-7623-0110-4

global trends are especially pronounced in Europe where European Community (EC) countries have embarked on a process of unifying their economies and their financial markets. The Maastricht Treaty, which was agreed to by EC leaders in December 1991, established the steps toward a currency union and closer political integration. Moreover, by 1996 the EC Investment Services Directive will permit stockbrokers to operate across national borders without the need to establish local subsidiaries.

Global trends notwithstanding, European financial intermediaries, investors, and corporations are national rather than pan-European in character. There are substantial differences among EC countries in the regulation of national securities markets, taxes, corporate laws, and accounting practices. Barriers to cross-border investments, for example, pension funds, still exist. The purpose of this study is to examine the dynamic linkages among the eight major EC stock markets and the extent and speed of transmission of innovations (shocks) from one market to another.

The interdependence among national stock markets has been the subject of several recent papers (Schollhammer and Sands 1985, 1987; Eun and Shim 1989; Meric and Meric 1989; Von Furstenberg and Jeon 1989, 1991; Koch and Koch 1991). These studies were motivated by growing recognition of the benefits of international portfolio diversification (e.g., Grubel 1968; Grubel and Fadner 1971; Levy and Sarnat 1970; Agmon 1972) and the international propagation of the October 1987 crash (e.g., Malliaris and Urrutia 1992). None of these studies solely focused on Europe.

The paper uses a Vector Auto Regressive (VAR) model to study whether EC stock markets behave like a single, integrated multiregional market. The VAR model is suitable for the analysis of dynamic linkages among the various markets since it can identify the main channels of interactions and simulates the responses of a given market to innovations in other markets. The EC stock markets operate within a single time zone and should all respond to a global news event simultaneously. Engle, Ito, and Lin (1990) and Ito, Engle, and Lin (1991) argued that shocks are transmitted as meteor showers rather than heat waves. The heat-waves hypothesis assumes that volatility has only country-specific autocorrelation. An innovation in a particular market will persist only in that market and will not have a spillover effect to other markets. The meteor-shower hypothesis asserts that innovations are transmitted from one market to others. A shock in one market tends to continue after that market closes, producing volatility in geographical distant markets opening several hours later. This is similar to the effect of meteor showers on earth as the globe turns. Since the hours of operations of EC securities markets overlap substantially, the meteor-showers paradigm does not apply. Instead, an alternative paradigm is postulated: we simulated shocks that resemble a hand-grenade explosion, where an innovation in one market is directly, rather than serially, transmitted to all other markets.

The rest of the paper is organized as follows: The second section presents the VAR econometric model. The third section discusses the data used in this study and their statistical properties. The fourth section details empirical results. Finally, the last section offers summary and conclusions.

THE VAR MODEL

The VAR model assumes that each variable depends on its own past values and on the past values of all other variables in the system of equations. The model can be expressed as:

$$Y_t = X_t \cdot \beta + \sum_{s=1}^{L} A_s \cdot Y_{t-s} + U_t \tag{1}$$

$$E\,[U_t \cdot U_t'] = \Psi \tag{2}$$

where Y_t is an $n\times 1$ vector of daily returns, $X_t\cdot\beta$ is the deterministic component of Y_t, U_t is an $n\times 1$ vector of serially uncorrelated errors, A_s is an $n\times$n matrix of coefficients, and L is the number of lags. The moving average representation (MAR) of the VAR model can be written as:

$$Y_t = X_t\cdot\beta + \sum_{s=0}^{\infty} B_s\cdot E_{t-s} \tag{3}$$

where, E_{t-s} for $s = 0, \ldots, \infty$ is an n-variate white noise process, and E_t and E_s are uncorrelated for $t \neq s$ (Sims 1980).

There are many equivalent representations for this model. For any nonsingular matrix G, the matrix of coefficients B_s can be replaced by $B_s\cdot G$ and E by $G^{-1}\cdot E$. A particular version is obtained by choosing some normalization.

If B_0 is normalized to be the identity matrix, each component of E_t is the error that results from the one-step-ahead forecast of the corresponding components of Y_t. These are the non-orthogonal innovations in the components of Y because, in general, the covariance matrix $\Phi = E[E_t \cdot E_t']$ is not diagonal.

It is more useful to look at the moving average representation of the system with orthogonalized innovations. If any matrix G is constructed to satisfy

$$G^{-1}\cdot\Phi\cdot G^{-1} = I \tag{4}$$

then the new innovations $v_t = E_t \cdot G^{-1}$ satisfy:

$$E[v(t)\cdot v(t)'] = I \tag{5}$$

These orthogonalized innovations have the important property that they are uncorrelated across time and across equations. Such a matrix G can be any solution that satisfies the condition that $GG' = \Phi$. The problem is that there are many such factorizations of a positive definite matrix Φ.

The literature on time series suggests a number of ways to accomplish the factorization of Φ. Some techniques are based on the Choleski factorization, where G is restricted to be a lower triangular matrix. Other techniques are based on orthogonalization using the eigenvalues. Sims (1980) suggested imposing restrictions on the Φ matrix by constraining it to be a lower triangular matrix.

In general, the moving average model (4) is diagonalized as follows:

$$BU(t) = V(t) \tag{6}$$

and

$$E[V(t) \cdot V(t)'] = D \tag{7}$$

where D is a diagonal matrix. The model can be estimated by minimizing the log likelihood function with respect to the free parameters in the matrixes, A and D, that is, minimize:

$$-2\log|A| + \log|D| + \mathrm{trace}(D^{-1} \cdot A \cdot S \cdot A') \tag{8}$$

where S is the sample covariance matrix of residuals and A is the coefficients matrix of (1).

DESCRIPTION OF THE DATA

The data for this study comprises time series of daily stock market indexes for the eight major EC stock exchanges: Belgium, Britain, Denmark, France, Germany, Italy, the Netherlands, and Spain. The indexes were computed by Morgan Stanley Capital International Perspective (MSCIP) for January 1, 1988 to December 31, 1992. The MSCIP indexes do not double count those stocks that are listed in more than one exchange. Thus, any observed interdependence among markets cannot be attributed to multiple listing (Eun and Shim 1989). For each country, daily returns, r_t, are computed as the first differences of the natural logarithms of the daily close values of the indexes, P_t, multiplied by 100: $r_t = 100(\ln P_t - \ln P_{t-1})$. For the analysis reported here all daily returns are expressed in terms of US$ returns (results for local currency returns are similar and are available from the authors upon request).

The correlations among the daily returns for the eight major EC stock markets are shown in Table 1. It is interesting to note that the EC stock markets are quite independent. Most correlation coefficients are below 0.5 with the exception of the correlation between Britain and the Netherlands, which equals 0.551. In addition, it seems that geographical proximity matters: the correlations among the stock markets of Germany, France, the Netherlands, and Belgium are higher than the correlations among the other markets. The least integrated stock market within the EC is Italy with very low correlations with all other markets.

Table 1. Correlation Matrix of Daily Returns for EC Stock Market Indexes: 1982–1992

	BRT	*FRN*	*GRM*	*NDR*	*BLG*	*DNM*	*ITL*	*SPN*
BRT	1.000	0.459	0.289	0.551	0.205	0.198	0.189	0.308
FRN		1.000	0.463	0.459	0.324	0.254	0.217	0.347
GRM			1.000	0.420	0.342	0.271	0.250	0.296
NDR				1.000	0.270	0.253	0.196	0.307
BLG					1.000	0.326	0.261	0.311
DNM						1.000	0.295	0.263
ITL							1.000	0.320
SPN								1.000

Notes: Key: BRT Britain
FRN France
GRM Germany
NDR Netherlands
BLG Belgium
DNM Denmark
ITL Italy
SPN Spain

Each country's series of daily returns was tested for the presence of a unit root using three alternative tests suggested by Dickey and Fuller (1979), Phillips and Perron (1988), and Sims (1988). All three tests, presented in Table 2, rejected the assumption of a unit root for all time series considered, implying that the relationships among the various variables analyzed below are not spurious.

Table 2. Unit-Root Tests

	DF	*PP*	*SMA*
Britain	–24.88**	–30.23**	0.00
France	–24.01**	–28.70**	0.00
Germany	–23.36**	–28.31**	0.00
Netherlands	–24.86**	–33.14**	0.00
Belgium	–21.86**	–26.87**	0.00
Denmark	–22.15**	–25.43**	0.00
Italy	–22.81**	–25.68**	0.00
Spain	–20.68**	–26.51**	0.00

Notes: DF - Dickey-Fuller Test with one lag.
PP - Phillips-Perron Test with one lag.
SMA - Sims' Marginal Alpha (Bayesian Unit Root Test).
** Statistically significant at the 1% level.
The SMA is the value for alpha at which the posterior odds for and against the unit root are even. A small value indicates that the data evidence is strongly against the unit-root hypothesis.

EMPIRICAL RESULTS

A VAR model of the daily returns was estimated with 15 lags for each variable in each equation. Thus, each equation has 8 × 15 unrestricted coefficients plus two coefficients for a constant and a trend. The number of lags was chosen using Likelihood Ratio tests (Sims 1972) and the Information Criteria suggested by Akaike (1973) and Schwarz (1978). While the Akaike and Schwarz tests indicated that as few as two lagged daily returns may be sufficient, the Sims test suggested that 15 lags are needed. We used 15 lags to ensure that we capture all the dynamics in the data (Eun and Shin 1989 also used 15 lags).

Granger Causality Tests

A relatively simple way to ascertain which markets are affected by innovations in other markets is the Granger Causality test. The test indicates whether innovations in one market help forecast a one-step-ahead returns in another market. An important advantage of the test is its insensitivity to the order of the equations in the VAR system. The test statistics are summarized in Table 3. Each column contains the values of F-statistics testing the marginal effect of inclusion of lagged returns of the market in the row on the market in the column's heading. Each market,

Table 3. F-Tests for Granger Causality

	Affected Markets							
Affecting Market	*BRT (1)*	*FRN (2)*	*GRM (3)*	*NDR (4)*	*BLG (5)*	*DNM (6)*	*ITL (7)*	*SPN (8)*
BRT	5.43**	1.06	3.13**	1.93*	1.89*	2.28**	1.26	1.30
FRN	0.87	8.63**	5.16**	1.25	5.77**	2.22**	0.60	3.73**
GRM	0.76	1.50	4.22**	2.11*	1.93*	0.75	0.95	1.56
NDR	1.31	1.59	0.88	1.44	0.88	1.36	0.65	2.46**
BLG	1.06	1.20	1.56	2.19*	3.24**	1.19	0.52	1.26
DNM	0.92	0.39	1.31	1.08	0.86	11.11**	1.35	0.87
ITL	1.26	1.59	0.26	1.02	1.04	1.12	9.54**	1.41
SPN	0.62	1.96*	1.85*	1.23	0.91	0.24	1.86*	6.58**

Notes: *Statistically significant at a 0.05 critical value.
** Statistically significant at a 0.01 critical value.
Key: BRT Britain
FRN France
GRM Germany
NDR the Netherlands
BLM Belgium
DNM Denmark
ITL Italy
SPN Spain

except the Dutch market, is affected by its own lagged returns. Column 1 shows that the British market is not influenced by other EC returns in the Granger-Causality sense; the French market (column 2) is influenced by the Spanish market. The German market (column 3) is influenced by Britain, France, and Spain. The Dutch market (column 4) is influenced by Britain, Germany, and Spain. The Belgian market (column 5) is influenced by Britain, Germany, and France; the Danish market (column 6) is influenced by Britain and France; the Italian market (column 7) is influenced by Spain and, finally; the Spanish market (column 8) is influenced by France and the Netherlands. Since many EC markets are influenced by lagged returns of other markets, the heat-wave hypothesis is refuted. Further insight is gained by looking at the rows of Table 3, rather than the columns. Each row of the table reveals the effects of a particular market on all markets. It is evident that the British and French markets are the most influential in the EC. The British market affects the German, Dutch, Belgian, and Danish markets. The French market affects the German, Belgian, Danish, and Spanish markets. The German market affects only the Dutch and Belgian markets. It is interesting to note that the Belgian market affects only its neighbor, the Netherlands, while Spain affects the German, French, and Italian markets.

An important caveat about the above *F*-Tests must be noted. Although they indicate whether other markets Granger-cause a given market, it is still possible that other markets can influence that market through other equations in the system. For example, the analysis that follows shows that the German market is as influential as the French market. For this reason we turn to the decompositions of the variances of forecast errors.

Decomposition of Variance and Residual Correlation

The transmission of innovations among markets may occur via many channels. When decomposition matrixes are analyzed, the order of transition must be determined. Eun and Shim (1989) and Von Furstenberg and Jeon (1990) assume that shocks are transmitted according to the meteor-shower hypothesis. In a given calendar day, a shock that originates in the United States moves to Japan and then to Europe. However, within the EC, trading hours largely overlap and there is no a priori to specify how shocks move from one market to another.

The decomposition of the variance of the forecast errors of the returns of a given market indicates the relative importance of the various markets in causing the fluctuations in returns of that market. The decomposition allocates the variance of the forecast error into percentages that are accounted for by innovations in all markets including the market's own innovations. The decomposition of variances is sensitive to the assumed origin of the shock and to the order it is transmitted to other markets. This may be a problem when the contemporaneous correlations of the residuals of the VAR model are high. These residuals are that component of returns not explained by lagged returns of all eight EC markets. The correlations

Table 4. Correlation Matrix of Residual Returns

	FRN	*GRM*	*NDR*	*BLG*	*DNM*	*ITL*	*SPN*
BRT	0.445	0.247	0.542	0.166	0.176	0.156	0.297
FRN		0.421	0.454	0.287	0.223	0.195	0.329
GRM			0.396	0.227	0.209	0.216	0.262
NDR				0.251	0.251	0.177	0.301
BLG					0.274	0.180	0.244
DNM						0.200	0.233
ITL							0.267

Notes: Each entry represents the correlation of the residuals between pairs of markets. The residuals are the part of return not explained by lagged returns of all eight EC markets.

Key: BRT Britain
FRN France
GRM Germany
NDR the Netherlands
BLG Belgium
DNM Denmark
ITL Italy
SPN Spain

indicate the extent of shared responses of all markets to new information in one market. Table 4 indicates that an innovation of an unknown source affects the larger EC markets in a similar manner. The high correlations among the large markets are likely to affect inferences from the variance decompositions tables discussed below. The pairwise correlations between the Netherlands and the large markets of Britain, France, and Germany are quite high (0.542, 0.454, and 0.396, respectively). This indicates that the Dutch stock market is responsive to news from the other markets. In general, the larger EC markets appear to be integrated, that is, the correlation between the residuals of Britain and France is 0.445 and the corresponding correlation between Germany and France is 0.421. On the other hand, correlations with the smaller countries are relatively low.

Given the pattern of correlations of residuals, we begin by considering the effect of a shock that originates in Britain and then moves to France, Germany, the Netherlands, Belgium, Denmark, Italy, and Spain. A leading market is one which explains a large percentage of the forecast error's variance of other markets while its own forecast error is not explained by innovations in other markets. Table 5 presents the decomposition of the forecast error variance for 5-day, 10-day, and 15-day horizons. Each row displays the percentage of forecast error variance explained by the market in the column heading. The table shows that none of the EC stock markets are isolated from the rest, since no variance is completely accounted for by its own innovations. At the 15-day horizon the percentage of forecast error for the British market explained by its own innovations is 91; for Denmark and Italy this percentage is about 80; the corresponding values for

Table 5. Decomposition of Forecast Variance

Market	*HZ*	*BRT*	*FRN*	*GRM*	*NDR*	*BLG*	*DNM*	*ITL*	*SPN*	*AOM*
BRT	5	96.98	0.34	0.13	0.72	0.40	0.33	0.66	0.44	3.02
	10	94.18	1.23	0.43	1.22	0.85	0.64	0.80	0.65	5.82
	15	91.24	1.81	0.76	1.28	1.30	0.64	1.52	1.44	8.76
FRN	5	18.68	78.37	0.29	0.63	0.69	0.28	0.21	0.84	21.63
	10	18.35	76.11	0.97	1.02	0.78	0.55	0.91	1.31	23.89
	15	17.93	73.33	1.16	2.32	1.13	0.82	1.65	1.68	26.67
GRM	5	11.04	13.75	72.09	0.15	1.00	0.37	0.27	1.33	27.91
	10	11.30	14.51	69.88	0.48	1.13	0.67	0.57	1.46	30.12
	15	11.21	14.14	67.51	1.16	1.98	0.90	1.10	2.00	32.49
NDR	5	28.96	5.82	4.07	58.50	0.88	0.33	0.58	0.86	41.50
	10	27.69	7.07	4.69	56.01	1.52	0.84	0.78	1.41	43.99
	15	27.17	6.97	4.77	54.02	2.10	1.33	1.74	1.89	45.98
BLG	5	8.37	11.64	3.57	1.06	74.71	0.20	0.08	0.37	25.29
	10	9.10	13.15	4.28	1.24	69.79	0.98	0.87	0.60	30.21
	15	9.89	12.79	4.38	1.41	67.42	1.52	1.10	1.50	32.58
DNM	5	6.48	4.32	1.41	1.48	3.30	82.30	0.52	0.17	17.70
	10	6.73	4.58	1.65	2.56	3.32	79.69	0.74	0.74	20.31
	15	6.79	4.73	1.10	3.06	3.56	78.06	0.99	1.02	21.94
ITL	5	5.61	2.36	2.48	0.20	1.17	2.08	85.45	0.66	14.55
	10	5.53	2.91	2.78	0.44	1.31	2.92	82.48	1.62	17.52
	15	6.44	3.19	2.80	0.82	1.51	3.03	80.18	2.03	19.82
SPN	5	10.34	6.07	1.57	0.94	1.68	1.05	2.80	75.55	24.45
	10	9.88	8.73	2.16	1.37	2.17	2.08	3.68	69.90	30.10
	15	9.85	8.74	2.35	2.98	2.17	2.64	4.03	67.23	32.77

Note: The order of the decomposition is Britain, France, Germany, The Netherlands, Belgium, Denmark, Italy, Spain. The last column of the table, AOM, shows the percentage of forecast error variance of the market of the first column explained by all other markets except the market's own innovations.

Belgium, France, Germany, and Spain are about 70. The lowest percentage is for the Netherlands—about 54. Britain's market is the most influential among the EC markets. In addition to explaining 91% of its own innovations, it explains 27% of the Netherlands' variance, 18% of the French variance, 11% of German variance, about 10% of the variances of Belgium and Spain, and about 7% of the variance of Denmark and Italy. The French market influences mainly its neighbors: it accounts for 14% of the German variance, about 13% of Belgium's variance, and about 9% of Spain's variance, confirming the hypothesis that geographical proximity matters. The German market explains about 5% of the variance of the Netherlands, 4% the Belgian variance, and smaller percentages for the other EC markets. The other EC countries play a much smaller role, each explaining at most 4% of other countries' variances.[1]

Since the correlation of residuals between France and Germany is high (0.421), we examine the effect of changing the order of the two countries. Table 6 presents the decomposition of variance for a shock that originates in Britain and then moves to Germany, France, the Netherlands, Belgium, Denmark, Italy, and Spain. This reordering affects only results for France and Germany, without affecting explanatory power of the other markets. After the reordering, Germany explains more of its own variance (78% vs. 67%) and 11% of the French variance (vs. 1% before). The effects of Germany on the other EC markets almost double. On the other hand, France explains a smaller fraction of its own variance (64% vs. 73%). France now explains 3% of the German variance, compared to 14% before. The effect of France on the other EC markets is approximately halved. These two experiments show that Britain, France, and Germany are the most integrated markets in the EC.

The above discussion demonstrates the difficulty resulting from the inability to determine a correct order. One way to overcome this indeterminacy is by conduct-

Table 6. Decomposition of Forecast Variance

Market	*HZ*	*BRT*	*GRM*	*FRN*	*NDR*	*BLG*	*DNM*	*ITL*	*SPN*	*AOM*
BRT	5	96.98	0.29	0.19	0.72	0.40	0.33	0.66	0.44	3.02
	10	94.18	0.78	0.88	1.22	0.85	0.64	0.80	0.65	5.82
	15	91.24	1.00	1.58	1.28	1.30	0.64	1.52	1.44	8.76
GRM	5	18.68	83.98	1.85	0.15	1.00	0.37	0.27	1.33	16.02
	10	18.35	81.03	3.35	0.48	1.13	0.67	0.57	1.46	18.97
	15	17.93	78.25	3.40	1.16	1.98	0.90	1.00	2.00	21.75
FRN	5	11.04	10.58	68.08	0.63	0.69	0.28	0.21	0.84	31.92
	10	11.30	10.75	66.33	1.02	0.78	0.55	0.91	1.31	33.67
	15	11.21	10.56	63.93	2.32	1.13	0.82	1.65	1.68	36.07
NDR	5	28.96	7.49	2.40	58.50	0.88	0.33	0.58	0.86	41.50
	10	27.69	8.39	3.37	56.01	1.52	0.84	0.78	1.41	43.99
	15	27.17	8.31	3.43	54.02	2.10	1.33	1.74	1.89	45.98
BLG	5	8.37	8.57	6.65	1.06	74.71	0.20	0.08	0.37	25.29
	10	9.10	8.79	8.64	1.24	69.79	0.98	0.87	0.60	30.21
	15	9.89	8.74	8.44	1.41	67.42	1.52	1.10	1.50	32.58
DNM	5	6.48	3.04	2.69	1.48	3.30	82.30	0.52	0.17	17.70
	10	6.73	3.12	3.11	2.56	3.32	79.69	0.74	0.74	20.31
	15	6.79	3.21	3.32	3.06	3.56	78.06	0.99	1.02	21.94
ITL	5	5.61	3.95	0.89	0.20	1.17	2.08	85.45	0.66	14.55
	10	5.53	4.48	1.22	0.44	1.31	2.92	82.48	1.62	17.52
	15	6.44	4.46	1.53	0.82	1.51	3.03	80.18	2.03	19.82
SPN	5	10.34	4.12	3.52	0.94	1.68	1.05	2.80	75.55	24.45
	10	9.88	4.68	6.22	1.37	2.17	2.08	3.68	69.90	30.10
	15	9.85	4.65	6.45	2.98	2.17	2.64	4.03	67.23	32.77

Note: The decomposition order is Britain, Germany, France, The Netherlands, Belgium, Denmark, Italy, Spain. The last column of the table, AOM, shows the percentage of forecast error variance of the market of the first column explained by all other markets except the market's own innovations.

ing different simulations. One interesting simulation is to examine what is, for example, the immediate effect on the German market of a news event (an innovation) that occurs in Spain. In contrast to the heat-waves and meteor-showers paradigms discussed in the introduction, an innovation in this experiment is viewed as similar to a hand grenade that explodes in one market and ricochets to other markets. This is done by tracing the effects of a shock that bursts in one market, j, and ricochets directly to another market, i, ignoring effects on other markets. Table 7 summarizes the results: each entry a_{ij} shows the effect of a one-standard deviation shock originated in market j and directly transmitted to market i. The larger markets of Britain, France, Germany, and the Netherlands are affecting one another substantially, with Britain and the Netherlands being the most interrelated. In addition, France exhibits considerable dominance of its neighbors, Belgium and Spain. The smaller EC markets, Belgium, Denmark, and Italy are less influential than the larger markets. Note that a shock that begins in Spain, though a small market, directly explains about 10% of the variance of Britain, France, the Netherlands, and Italy. It appears that Spain is more influential in the EC than the other smaller markets, for example, Italy.

Moving Average Representations

Further insight into the dynamic interrelations among the EC stock markets is obtained by simulating the VAR system of equations and observing its dynamic response to shocks through Moving Average Representations (MAR) (Sims 1980; Litterman 1984). A shock of one standard deviation is introduced in a given market and its dynamic effects are traced throughout the system for the next 15 trading days. These impulse responses are highly nonlinear functions of the estimated parameters with numerous coefficients. The confidence bands presented below were computed using Monte Carlo integration. Figures 1 to 8 depict the dynamic

Table 7. Decomposition of Forecast Variance: The Effect of Directly Transmitted Innovation After 15-Day Forecast Horizon

Market	*BRT*	*FRN*	*GRM*	*NDR*	*BLG*	*DNM*	*ITL*	*SPN*
BRT	91.24	19.70	6.56	26.58	3.78	3.87	3.96	9.55
FRN	17.93	90.04	17.00	19.26	7.73	5.41	5.00	10.67
GRM	11.21	21.29	84.72	16.90	7.47	4.84	5.05	6.89
NDR	27.17	19.89	15.81	88.17	6.89	6.68	4.66	9.57
BLG	9.89	20.14	12.45	11.67	80.46	7.80	4.78	8.73
DNM	6.79	8.53	5.01	8.42	6.78	89.56	5.76	6.43
ITL	6.44	6.52	6.56	5.55	3.73	6.40	89.87	10.20
SPN	9.85	13.43	7.31	9.60	5.69	6.45	8.35	85.87

Note: Each entry a_{ij} represents the effect of a one standard deviation innovation originating in country j and is transmitted first to country i.

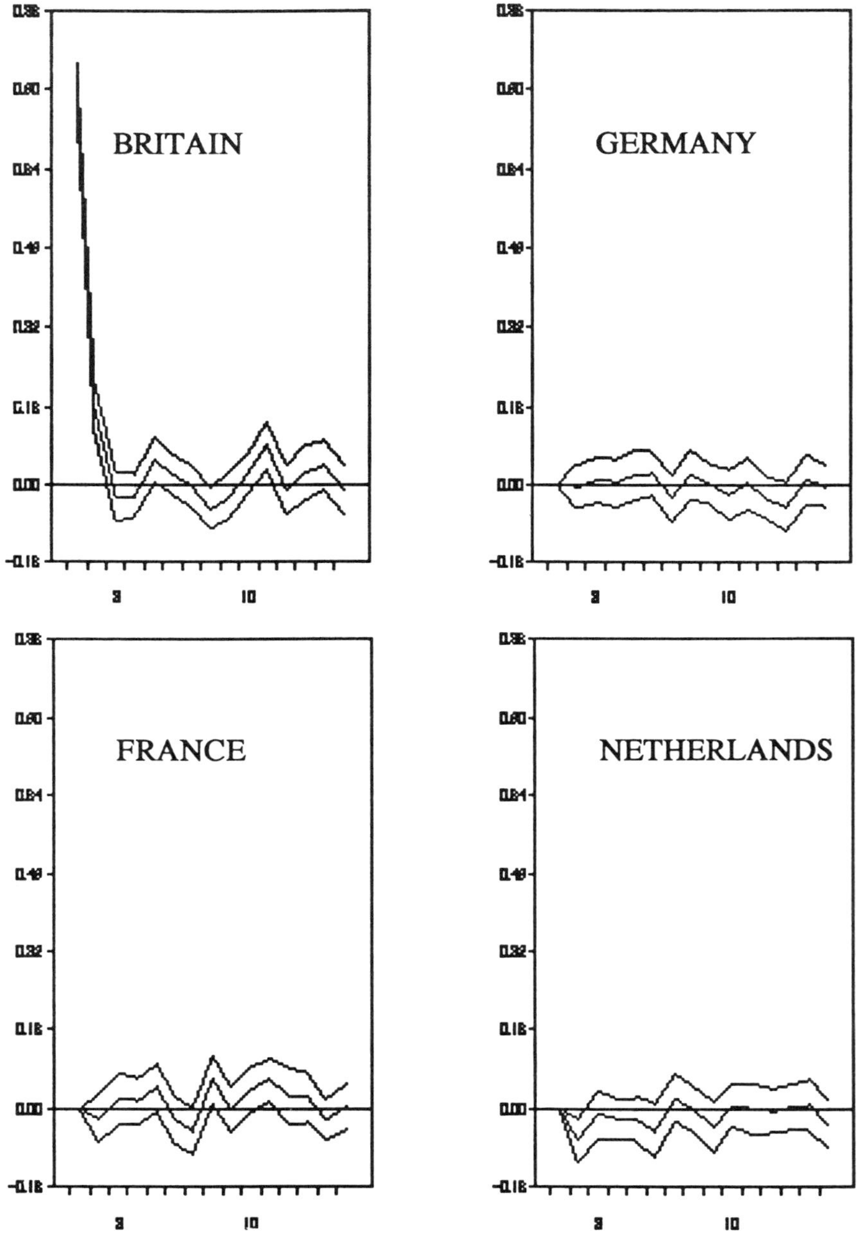

Figure 1. The Effect of a Shock in Britain on EC Stock Markets

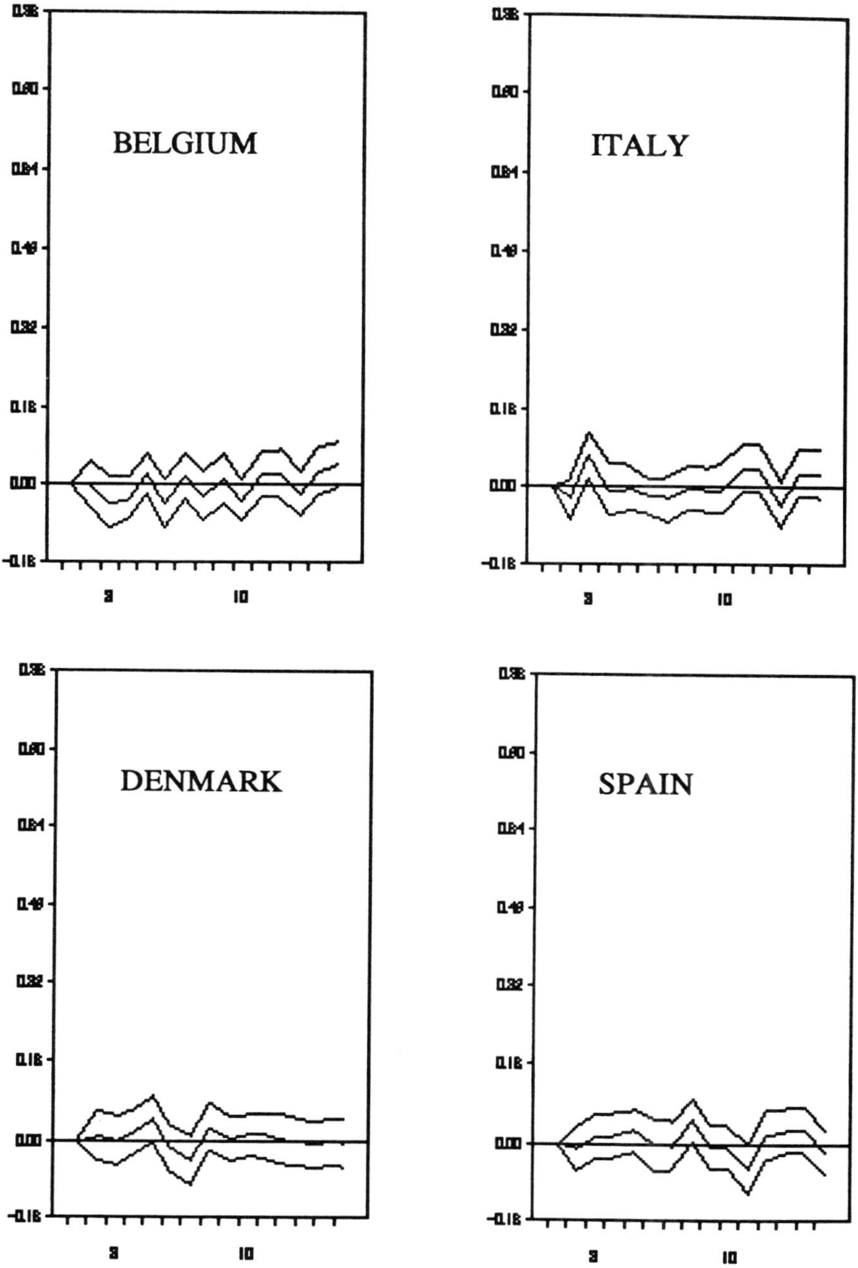

Figure 1. (Continued)

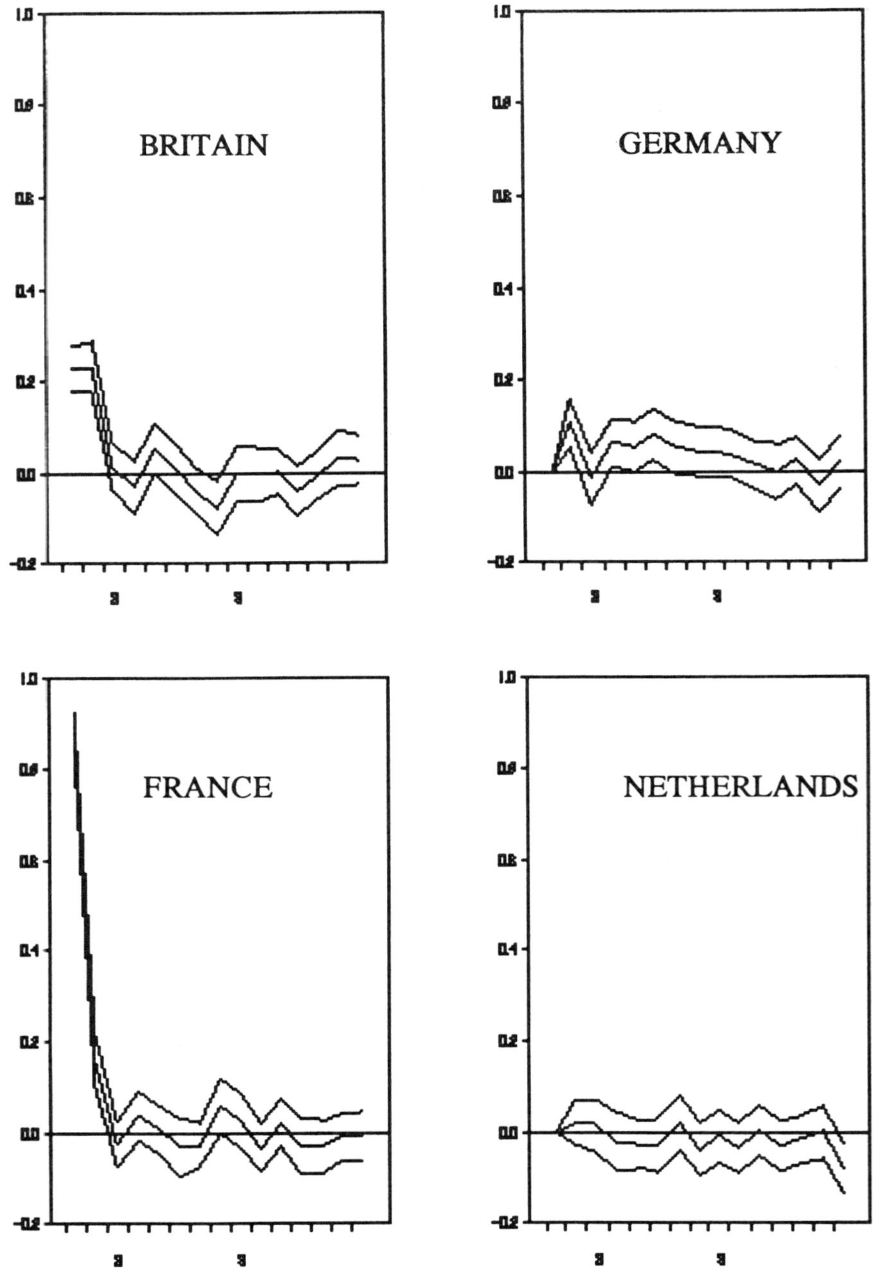

Figure 2. The Effect of a Shock in France on EC Stock Markets

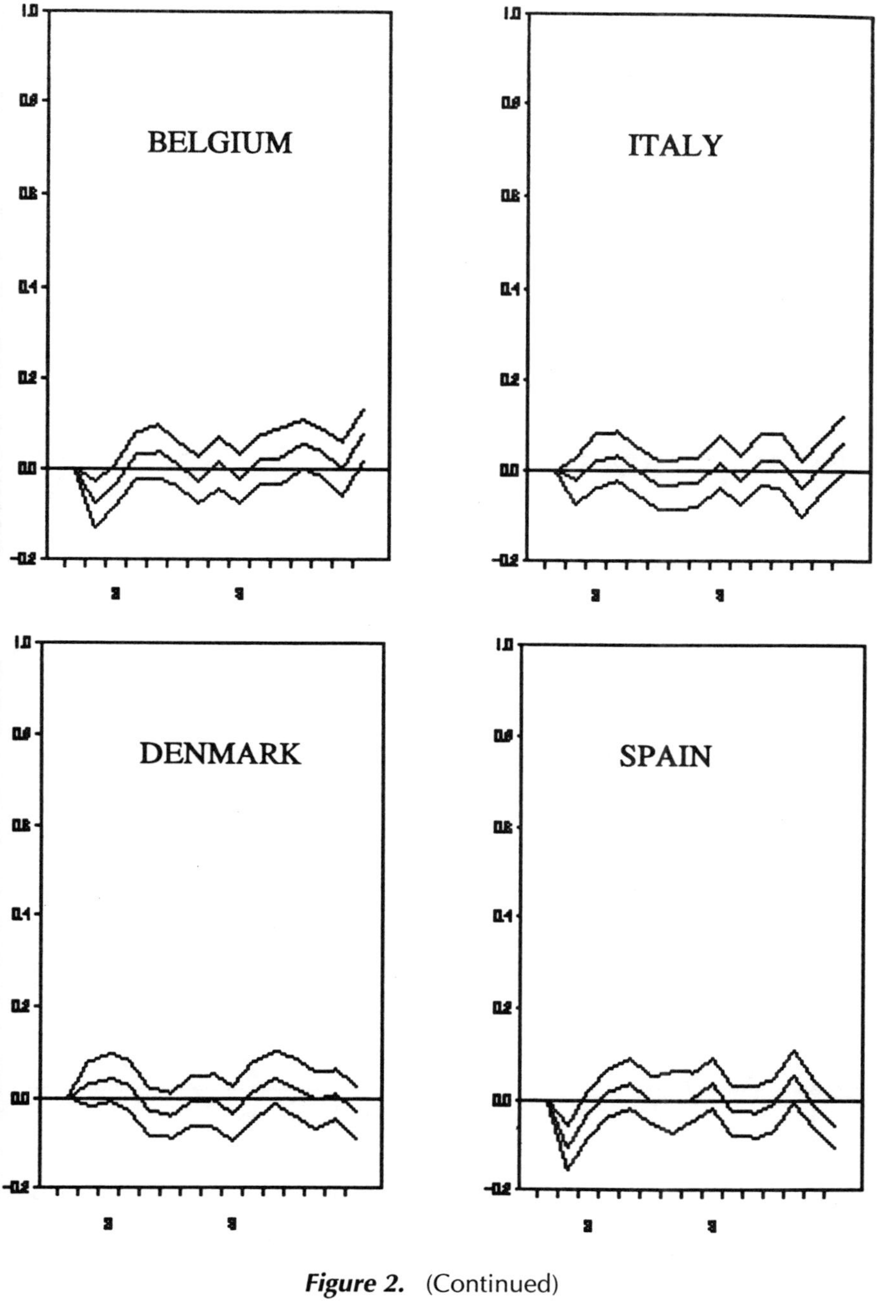

Figure 2. (Continued)

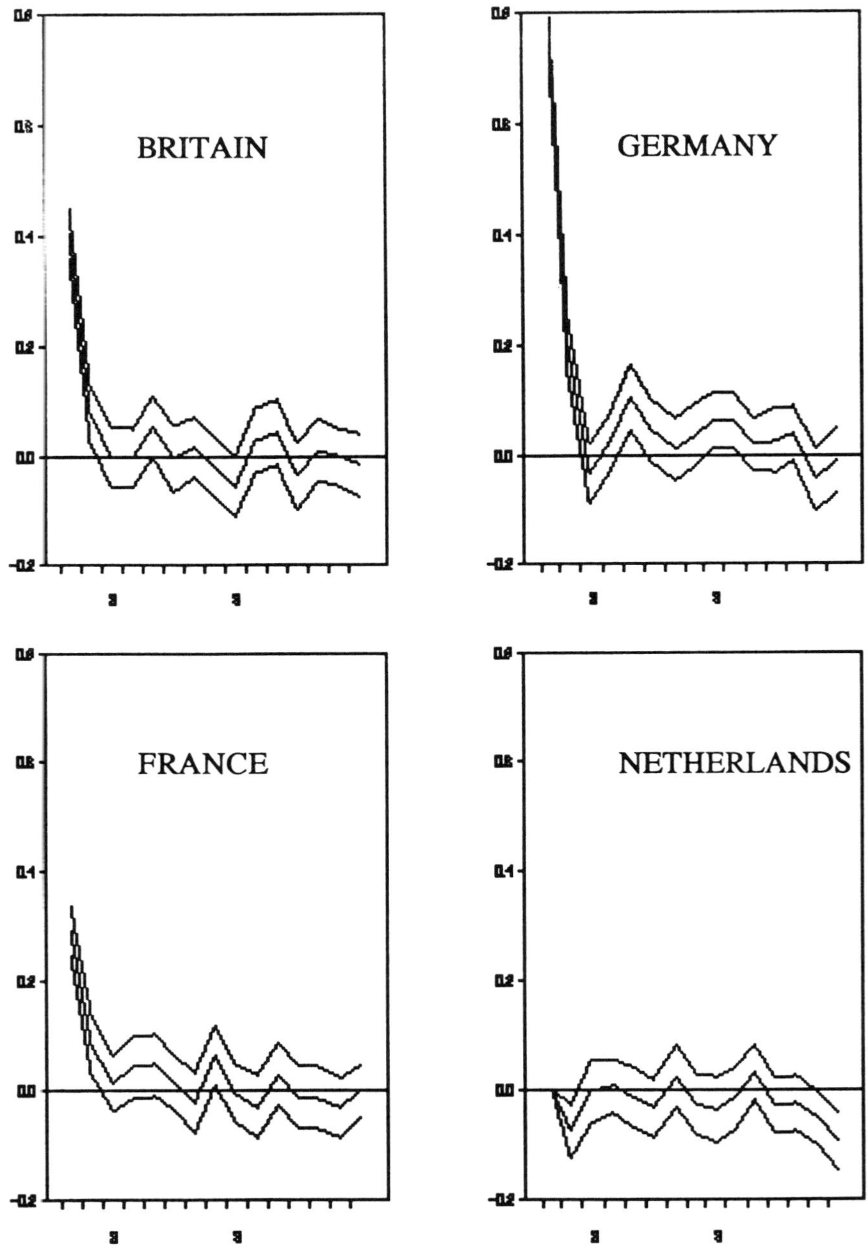

Figure 3. The Effect of a Shock in Germany on EC Stock Markets

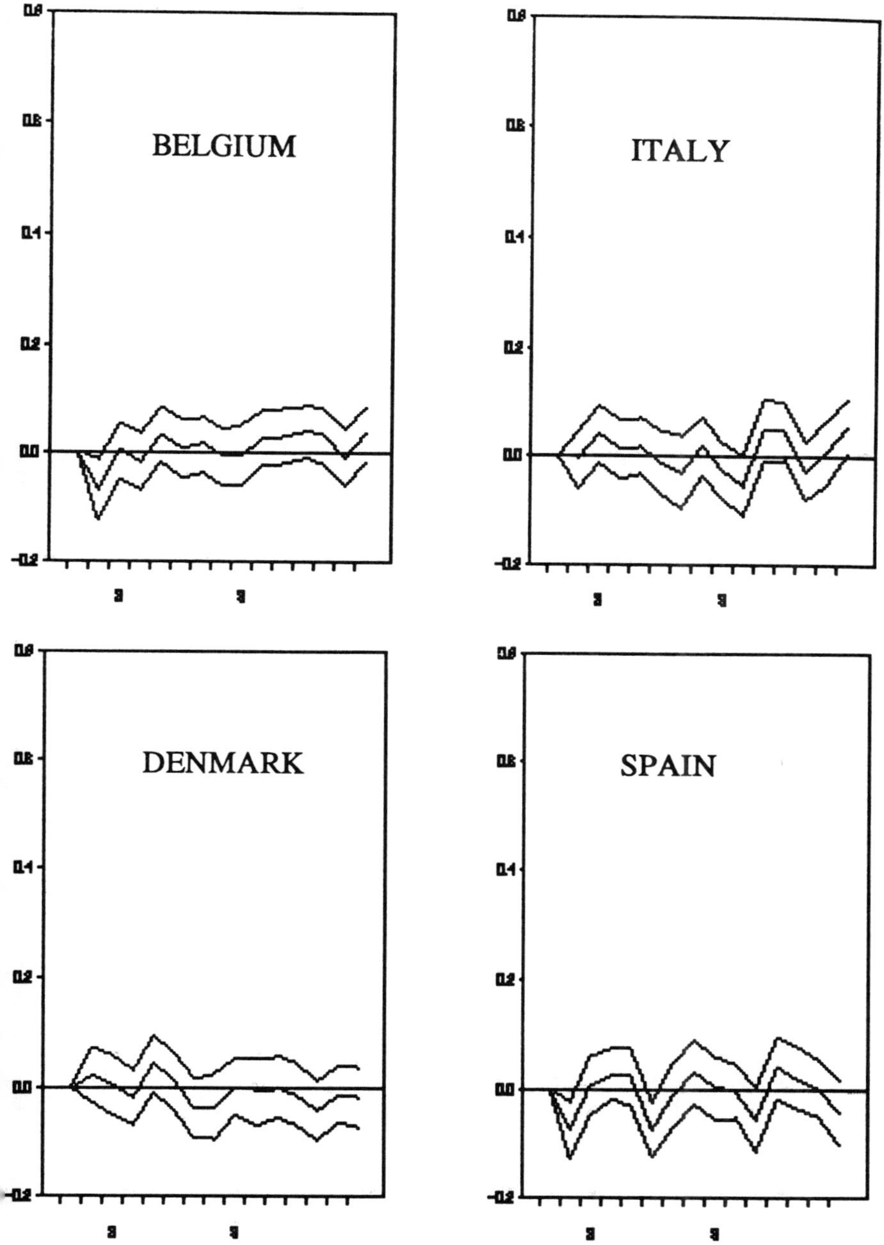

Figure 3. (Continued)

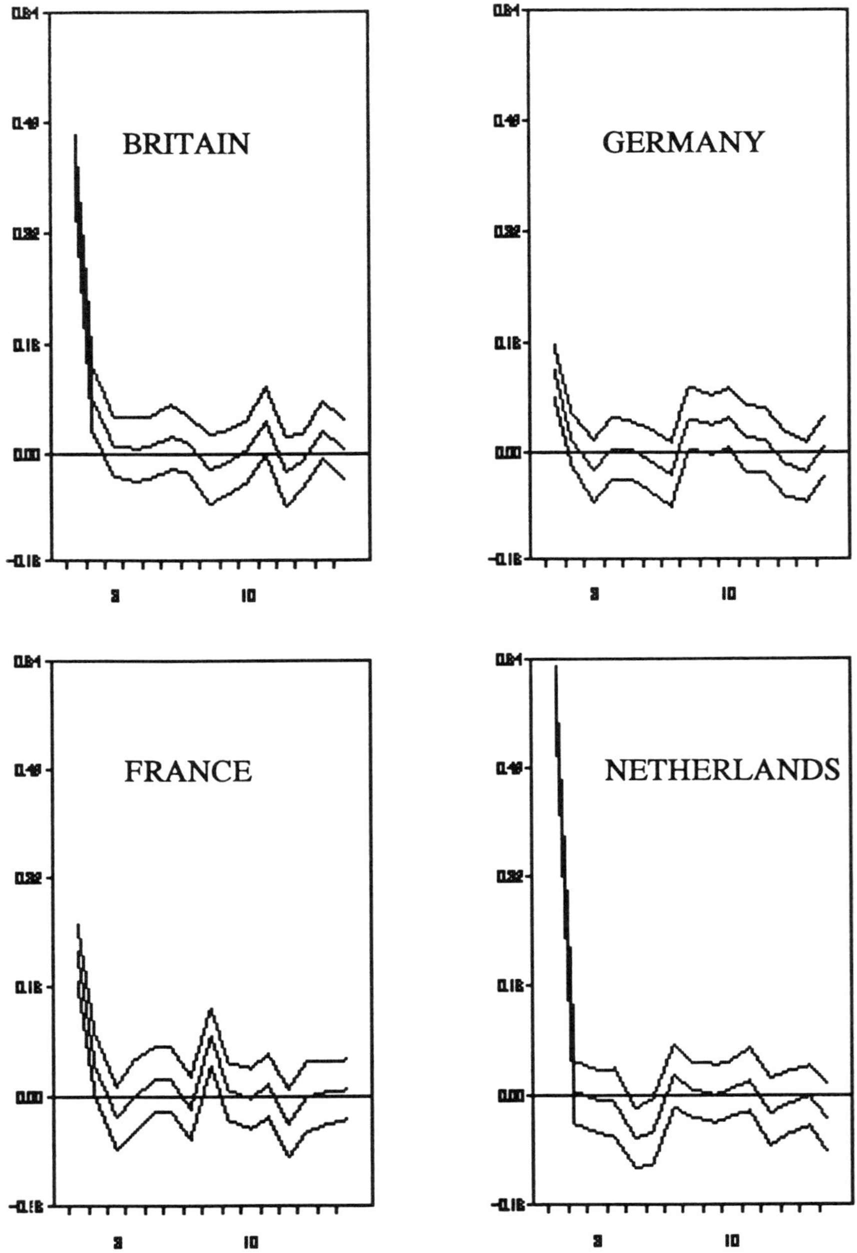

Figure 4. The Effect of a Shock in Netherlands on EC Stock Markets

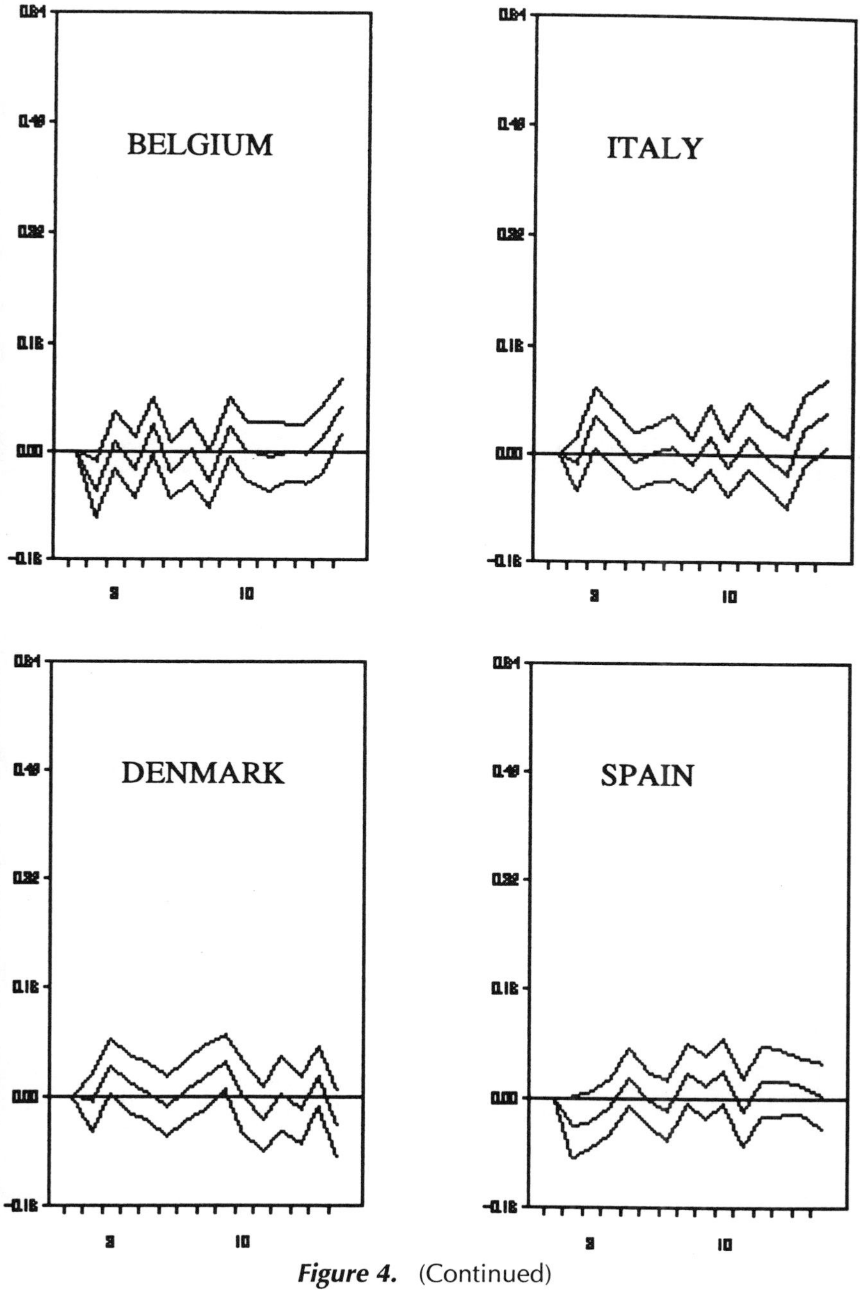

Figure 4. (Continued)

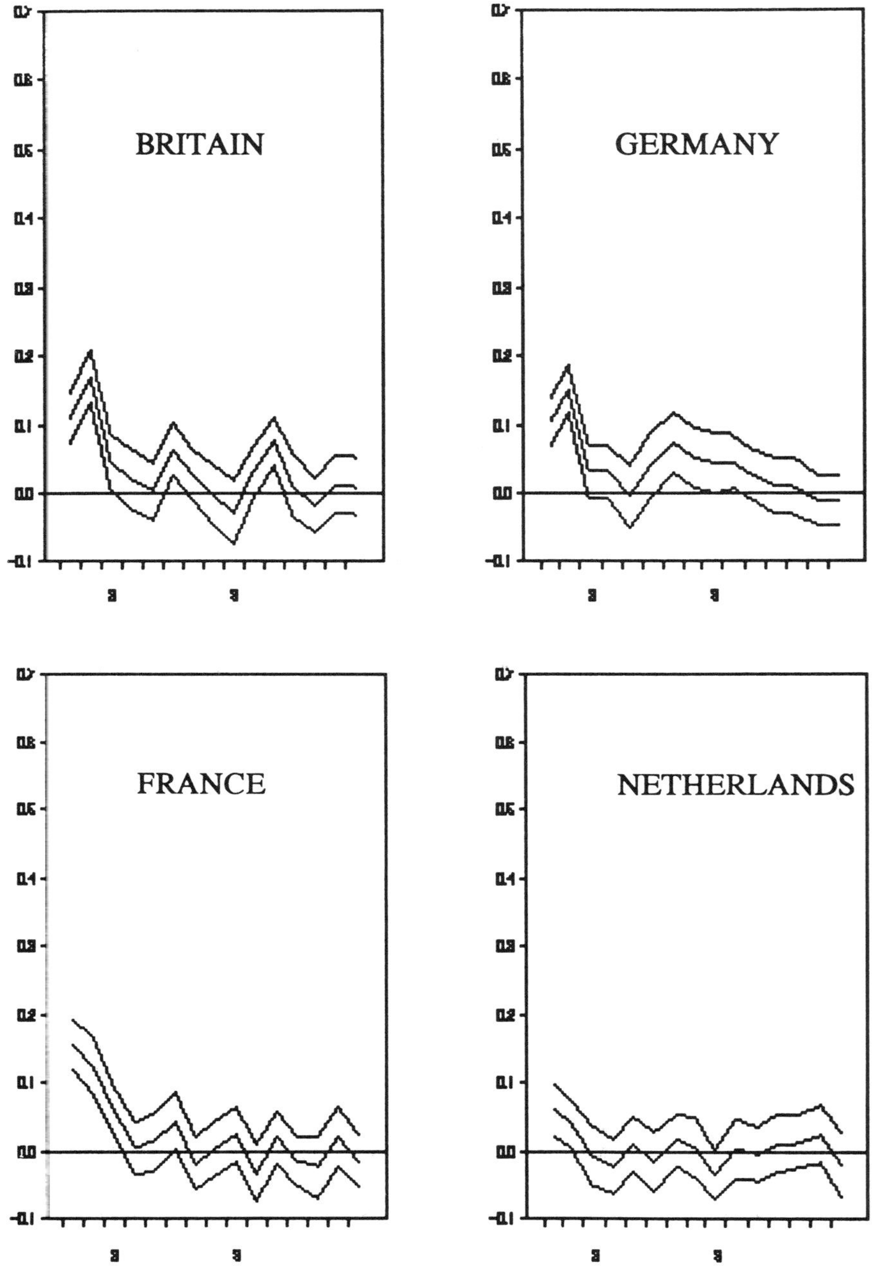

Figure 5. The Effect of a Shock in Belgium on EC Stock Markets

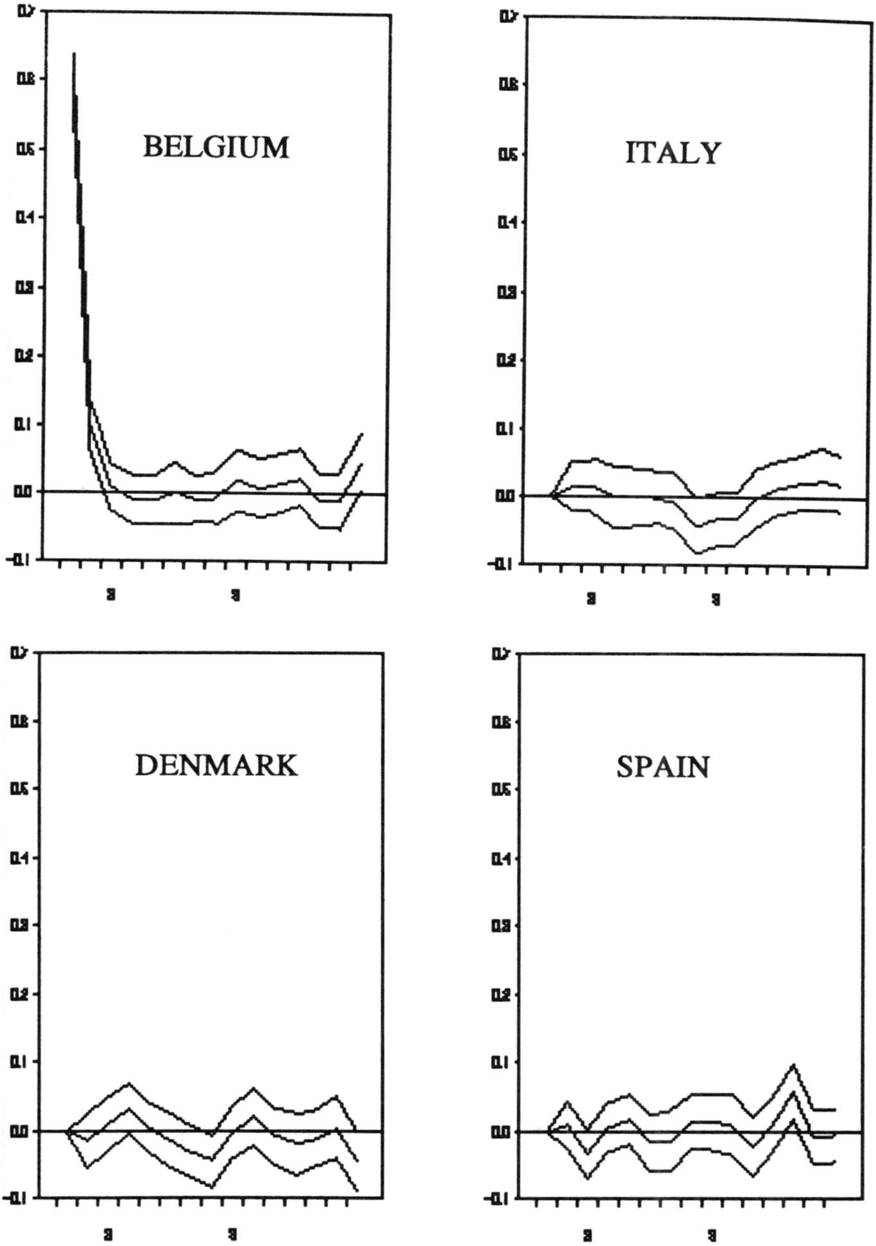

Figure 5. (Continued)

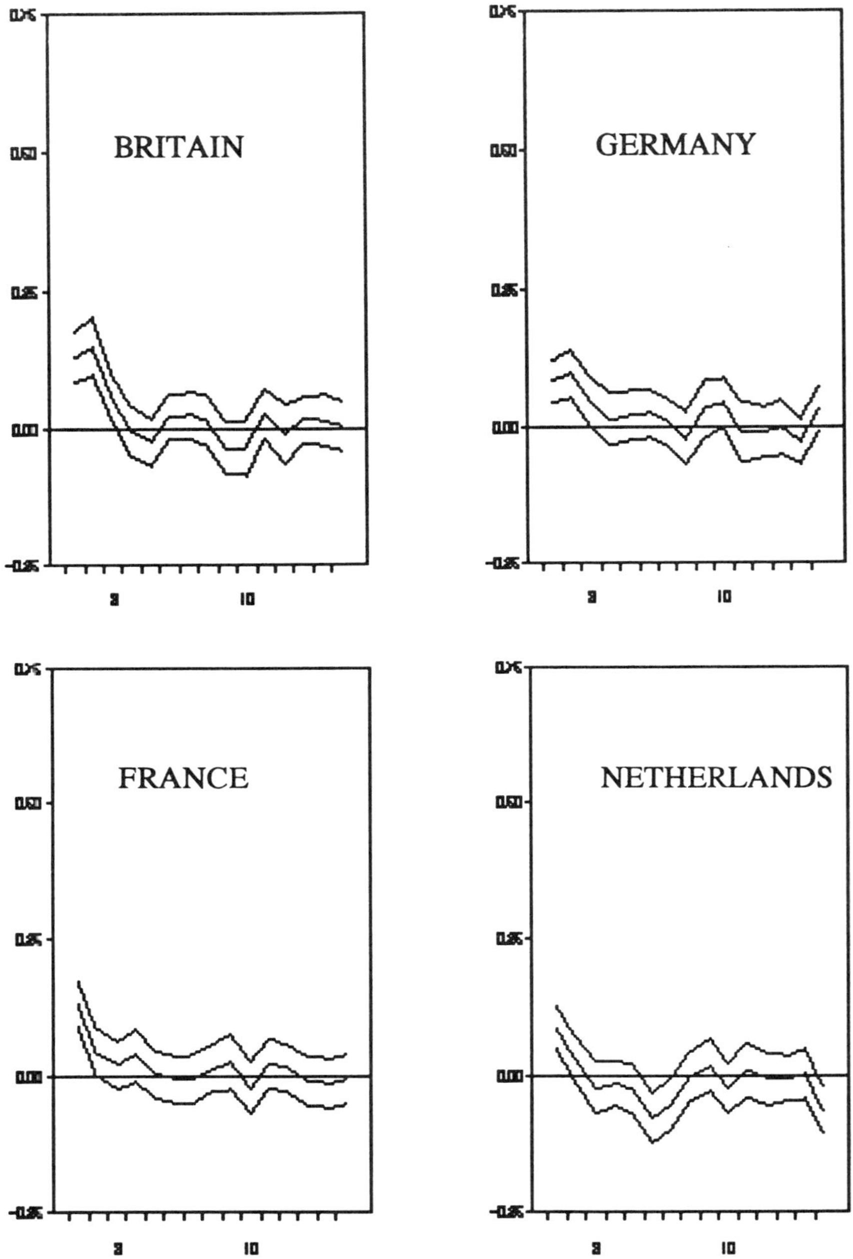

Figure 6. The Effect of a Shock in Denmark on EC Stock Markets

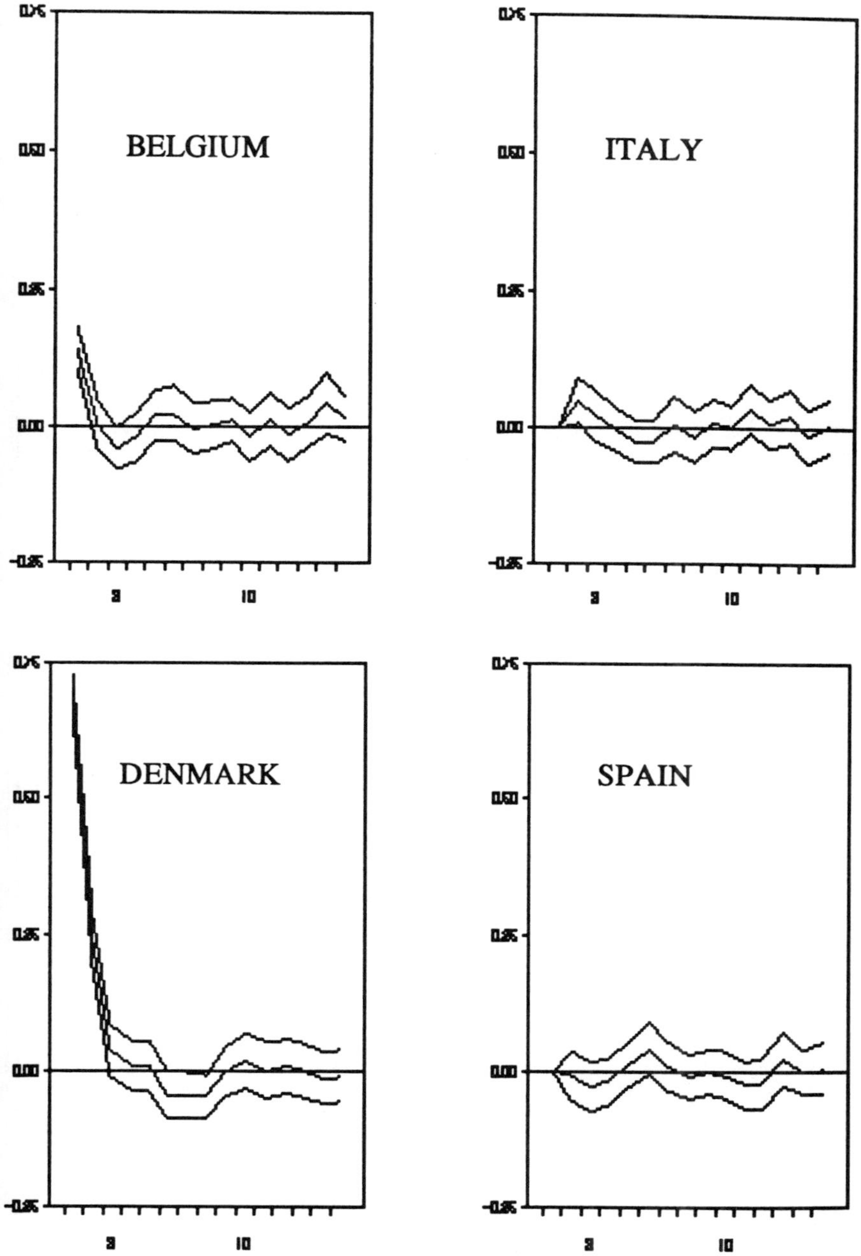

Figure 6. (Continued)

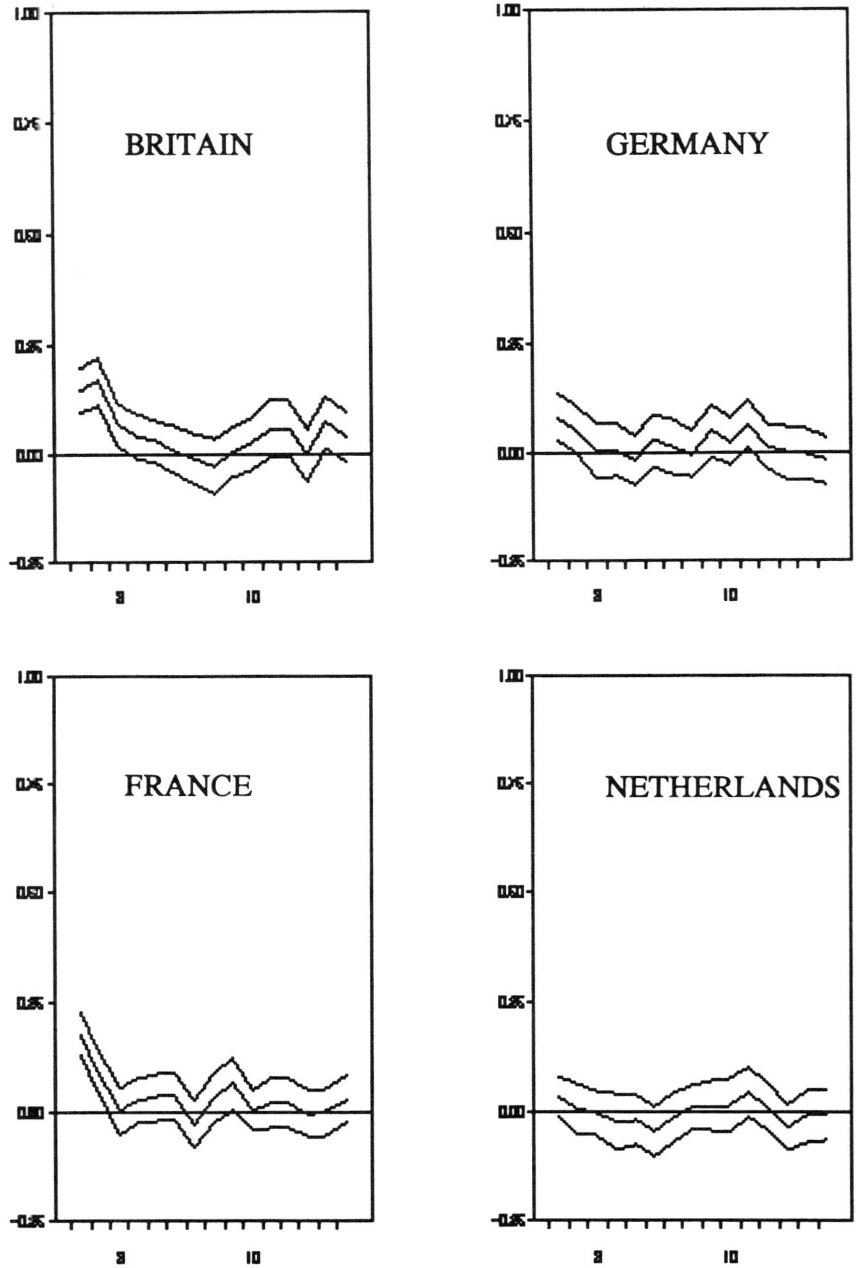

Figure 7. The Effect of a Shock in Italy on EC Stock Markets

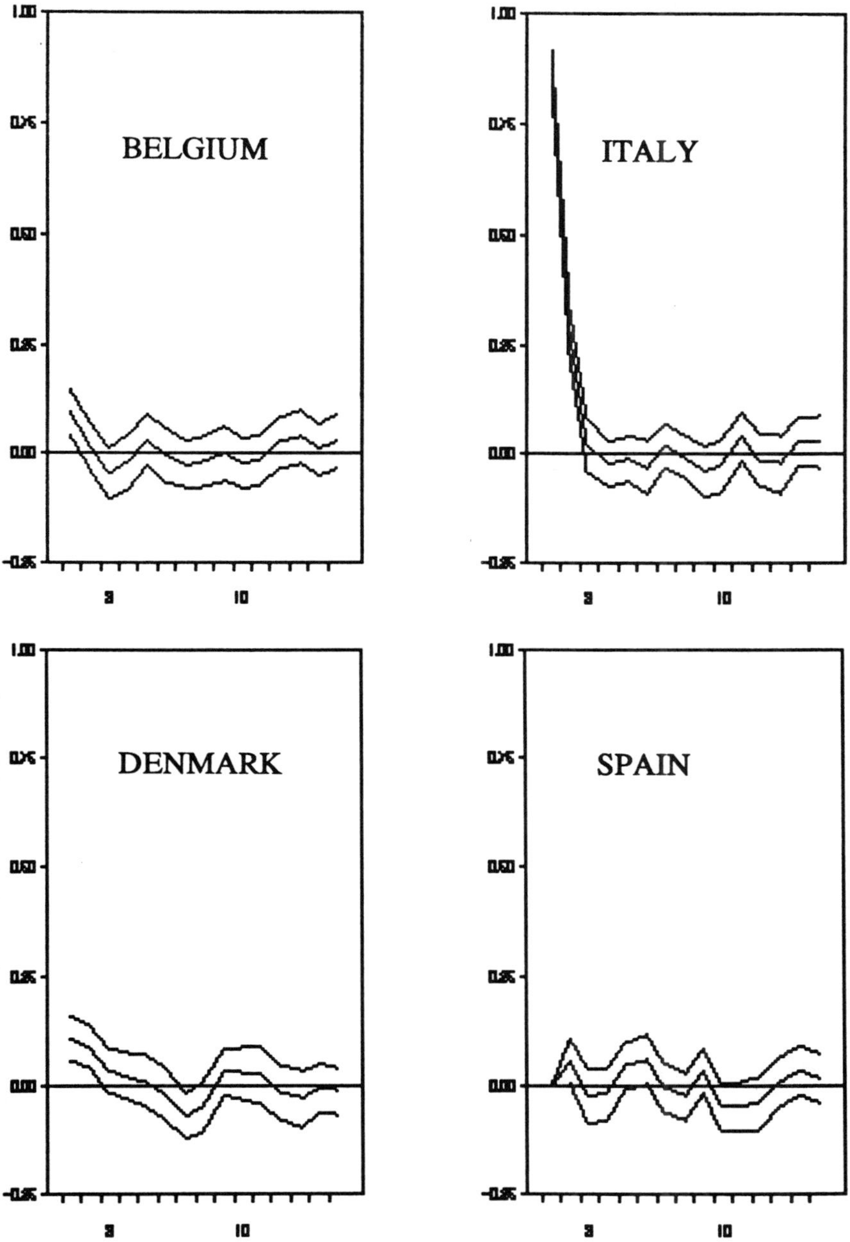

Figure 7. (Continued)

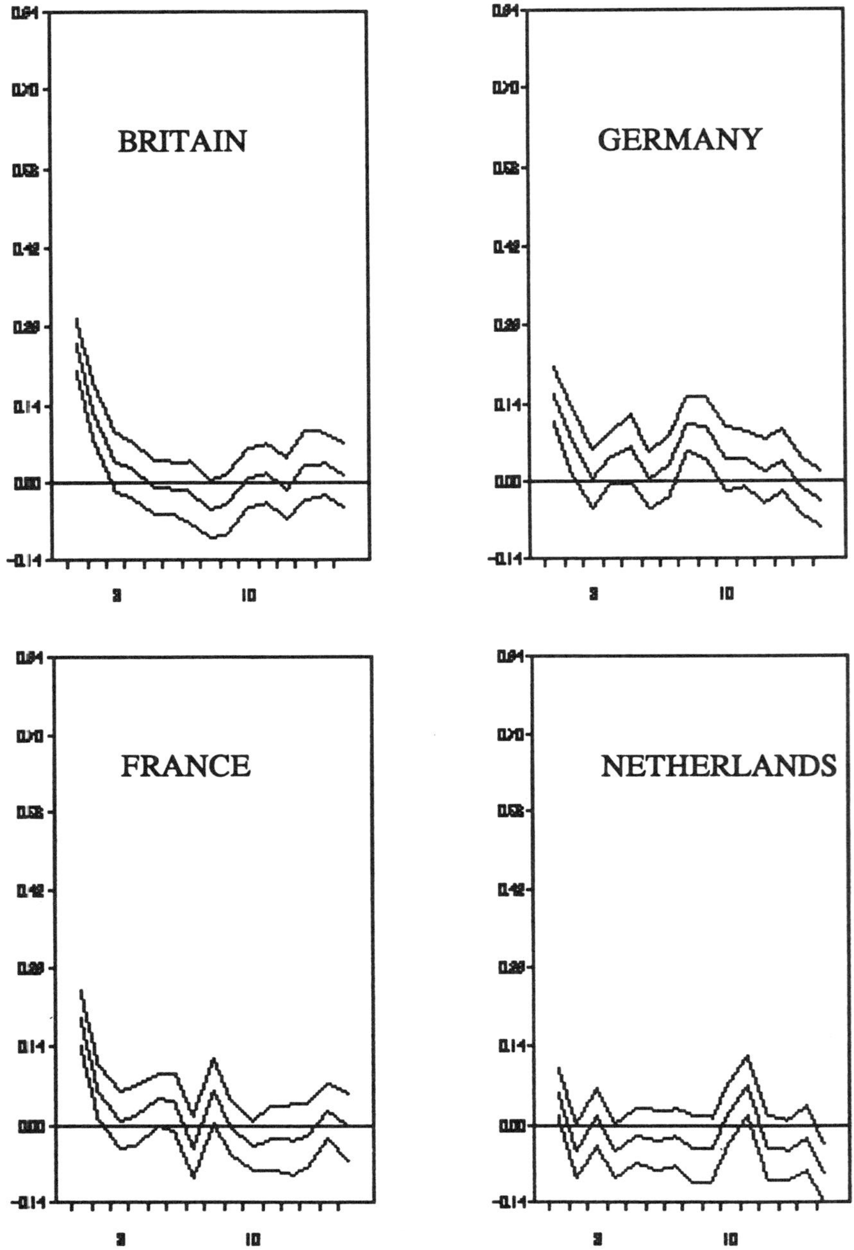

Figure 8. The Effect of a Shock in Spain on EC Stock Markets

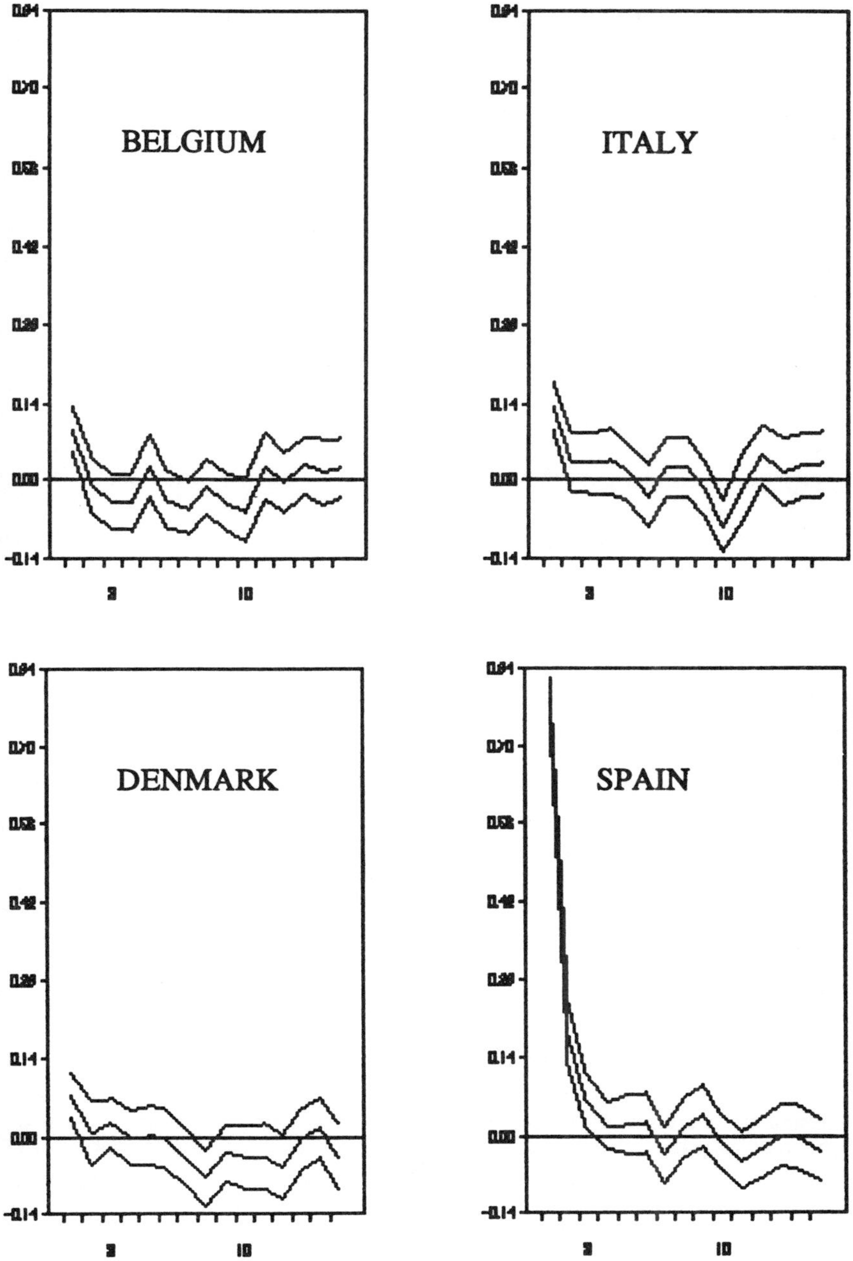

Figure 8. (Continued)

behavior of the system of eight countries ordered as follows: Britain, France, Germany, the Netherlands, Belgium, Denmark, Italy, and Spain. In each graph, the center line represents the impulse responses and the two outer lines represent the two-standard-deviations band. All innovations taper off in at most three trading days, often within one or two days. Furthermore, only a few markets influence other markets considerably. Figure 1 shows the influence of a shock in Britain on other EC markets. No significant response is evident, since the confidence bands all markets other than Britain include the zero line. Figure 2 shows that a shock in the French market affects only Britain, causing a half standard deviation jump. Figure 3 shows that the German market affects only the British and the French markets, causing a one-third standard deviation jump. Figure 4 shows that the Dutch market affects Britain—inducing a half standard deviation jump. France and Germany are also affected, but only to a smaller extent. Figures 5, 6, and 7 show that shocks in Belgium, Denmark, and Italy hardly influence the other markets. Innovations in these markets have only small effects on other markets (less than 20% of the corresponding standard deviations). Figure 8 shows that the Spanish market affects the French and UK markets, reaffirming the finding that Spain seems to be more influential than other small EC markets. Evidently, innovations in the larger markets are transmitted to other markets, especially if they are neighboring markets.[2]

CONCLUSIONS

This paper formulates and estimates a VAR model of the daily stock market returns for eight major EC countries. The model is used to investigate the dynamic linkages among the various markets, and to simulate the responses of a given market to innovations in other markets. If EC markets are integrated, there will be little benefit from diversifying an investment portfolio among them. In contrast, if substantial segmentation exists, there may be rationale for intra EC diversification.

The Granger Causality tests may lead one to suspect that EC markets are inefficient, since current returns are predicted by their own and by other markets' lagged values. However, the impulse response analyses indicate that although innovations are transmitted from some markets to others, most of the responses vanish within one or two days. These patterns are consistent with international market efficiency.

The decomposition of forecast variance indicates varying degrees of interdependence among EC markets. Regardless of the order of the decomposition, no market is found to be completely isolated from the others, since no forecast variance is fully explained by its own innovations. Britain is a leading market within the EC because it explains most of its own innovations (91%) and significant parts of the innovations in other markets. In general, larger markets such as France and Germany, influence their neighbors. In contrast, smaller markets, such as Belgium, Denmark, and Italy have no impact on other markets. Simulations of shocks resembling a hand-grenade explosion, where an innovation in one market is directly transmitted to all other markets, rather than serially, show that the larger markets (Britain, France, Germany, and the Netherlands) are substantially affecting one another.

Further insight is gained by impulse-response analysis which dynamically simulates the model. The responses, as depicted by the graphs, confirm that Britain is a leading market that affects France, the Netherlands, and Germany. In addition, the graphs show that Britain, France, Germany, and the Netherlands form a cluster of highly interdependent markets. The graphs reinforce the finding that smaller markets do not influence larger markets.

One implication of these findings is that investors will achieve larger benefits from international portfolio diversification by including the smaller markets in their opportunity set.

ACKNOWLEDGMENTS

A previous version of this paper was presented at the Second Annual Conference on European Financial Management Issues, May 28–29, 1993, Virginia Beach, VA. The authors wish to thank the conference participants, Kent Becker, John Doukas, Hebert Phillips, and Jorge Urrutia for helpful discussions and comments. The usual disclaimer applies. Please address correspondence to Joseph Friedman.

NOTES

1. The orthogonalization as reported in Table 5 is ordered as the order of the columns in the table suggests, namely, Britain, France, Germany, the Netherlands, Belgium, Denmark, Italy, and Spain. However, since the decomposition of variance is sensitive to the ordering of the markets' returns when the innovations in different markets are correlated, we experimented with changing the order among markets with high correlations.
2. Different orderings produce somewhat different figures and they are available from the authors upon request.

REFERENCES

Agmon, T. 1972. "The Relations Among Equity Markets: A Study of Share Price Co-Movements in the United States, United Kingdom, Germany, and Japan." *Journal of Finance* (September) 839–855.

Akaike, H. 1973. "Information Theory and the Extension of the Maximum Likelihood Principle." In *2nd International Symposium on Information Theory*, edited by B.N. Petrov and F. Csaki. Budapest.

Dickey, D., and W.A. Fuller. 1979. "Distribution of the Estimators for Time Series Regressions with a Unit Root." *Journal of the American Statistical Association* 74: 427–431.

Engle, R., T. Ito, and W. Lin. 1990. "Meteor Showers or Heat Waves? Heteroskedastic Intra-daily Volatility in the Foreign Exchange Market." *Econometrica* 58(3): 525–542.

Eun C.S., and S. Shim. 1989. "International Transmission of Stock Market Movements." *Journal of Financial and Quantitative Analysis* 24(2): 241–256.

Grubel, H.G. 1968. "Internationally Diversified Portfolios." *The American Economic Review* 58: 1299–1314.

Grubel, H., and K. Fadner. 1971. "The Interdependence of International Equity Markets." *Journal of Finance* 26: 89–94.

Ito, T., R. F. Engle, and W. Lin. 1992. "Where Does the Meteor Shower Come From? The Role of Stochastic Policy Coordination." *Journal of International Economics* 32(3–4): 221–240.

Jeon, B.N., and G.M. Von Furstenberg. 1990. "Growing International Co-Movement in Stock Price Indexes." *The Quarterly Review of Economics and Business* 30(3): 15–30.

Koch, P.D., and T. Koch. 1991. "Evolution in Dynamic Linkages Across Daily National Stock Indexes." *Journal of International Money and Finance* 10(2): 231–251.

Levy, H., and M. Sarnat. 1970. "International Diversification of Investment Portfolios." *The American Economic Review* 60: 668–675.

Litterman, R. 1984. "A Bayesian Procedure for Forecasting with Vector Autoregressions." Working Paper, Federal Reserve Bank of Minneapolis.

Malliaris, A.G., and J. Urrutia. 1992. "The International Crash of October 1987: Causality Tests." *Journal of Financial and Quantitative Analysis* 27(3): 353–364.

Meric, I., and G. Meric. 1989. "Gains from International Portfolio Diversification and Inter-Temporal Stability and Seasonality in International Stock Market Relationships." *Journal of Banking and Finance* 13(4–5): 627–640.

Phillips, P.C.B., and P. Perron. 1988. "Testing for a Unit Root." *Econometrica* 55: 277–301.

Schwarz, G. 1978. "Estimating the Dimension of a Model." *Annals of Statistics* 6: 461–464.

Schollhammer, H., and O. Sand. 1985. "The Interdependence Among the Stock Markets of Major European Countries and the United States: An Empirical Investigation of Interrelationships Among National Stock Prices Movements." *Management International Review* 25(1): 17–26.

———. 1987. "Lead-Lag Relationships Among National Equity Markets: An Empirical Investigation." In *Recent Developments in International Banking and Finance* volume 1, edited by S.J. Khoury and A. Ghosh. Lexington, MA: Lexington.

Sims, C.A. 1972. "Money, Income and Causality." *American Economic Review* 62: 540–552.

———. 1980. "Macroeconomics and Reality." *Econometrica* 48: 1–49.

———. 1988. "Bayesian Skepticism on Unit Root Econometrics." *Journal of Economic Dynamics and Control* 12: 463–474.

Von Furstenberg, G.M., and B.N. Jeon. 1989. "International Stock Price Movements: Links and Messages." *Brookings Papers on Economic Activity* 1: 125–179.

STOCK MARKET LINKAGES BETWEEN THE UNITED STATES AND SOUTHERN EUROPEAN COUNTRIES

Mukund S. Kulkarni

ABSTRACT

This paper, using the statistical methods of cointegration, examines long-run linkages among the stock markets of Greece, Italy, Spain, Turkey, and the United States for the period of December 1987–April 1994. The empirical evidence indicates that there is significant interdependence between the United States and the southern European stock markets, but the degree of interdependence is even greater among the four southern European stock markets themselves. The results, while supporting the notion of international financial market interdependence, are different as they show weaker linkage between the southern European countries and the U.S. stock market.

This paper examines the extent of interaction between the capital markets of the southern European countries of Greece, Italy, Spain, and Turkey with the United States and also among themselves, for the period January 1987 through April 1994. The empirical results indicate that there is significant interdependence between the New York Stock Exchange (NYSE) and the southern European stock markets, but

Research in International Business and Finance, Supplement 1, pages 65–74.

ISBN: 0-7623-0110-4

interestingly enough, the results also suggest that there exist even stronger long-run relationships among the four southern European stock markets themselves. While the results provide additional support to the growing body of literature that has hypothesized interdependence among world financial markets, they also indicate that the NYSE, the most dominant stock market in the world, does not play as an important role as it does in cases of many other countries. This study, therefore, provides results that are different than some findings of other recent studies (Arshanapalli and Doukas 1993). This study is useful for two additional reasons. In contrast to most studies on this topic, which are based on the major industrial countries such as the United States, the United Kingdom, Germany, and Japan, this study examines interdependence among the stock markets of countries which are generally not studied as extensively. Second, the empirical analysis of this paper relies on the recent methods based on the theory of cointegration for testing linkages between several economic time series.

PERSPECTIVE

Some recent changes indicate that world capital markets may be coming closer and becoming interdependent faster. The controls on flow of capital across international borders are being relaxed along with other economic deregulation. Multinational corporations are expanding their operations worldwide. Stocks of major corporations are listed and traded on stock exchanges around the world. Dissemination of information is fast and inexpensive providing easy access to international financial and stock markets.

These and many other changes have contributed greatly to increase the world commerce and economic interdependence. One of the consequences of international economic interdependence is to expose domestic economies to the international economic disturbances. The near simultaneous collapse of stock markets around the world in October 1987 is attributed to economic integration of several national economies (Furstenberg and Jeon 1989).

Several studies have tried to examine the extent of capital market interdependence and integration. The evidence from these studies is rather mixed. Studies done in the late 1960s and 1970s generally report lack of interdependence among national stock markets (Grubel 1968; Levy and Sarnat 1970; Aqmon 1972). However, their evidence does not negate the possibilities that stock markets may be more interdependent now than ever, particularly since the early 1980s when the wave of domestic economic deregulation began. The British government, under the Thatcher regime, began selling state-owned companies including the largest sale ever of stock to the public of over $7 billion of British Telecom. Even the French socialist government of Mitterand reversed its economic policies and began a major privatization program. In the United States, economic deregulation began under the Reagan administration with the Depository Institutions Deregulation and Monetary Control Act of 1980. Many other countries, particularly after the collapse of the former Soviet Union, began deregulation of their economies. Along with domestic economic liberalization, barriers to foreign trade and controls on flow of capital movements began to disappear. It is, therefore, hypothesized that these changes might have brought about more economic interdependence among many countries in the 1980s and 1990s.

Recent studies of Bennett and Kelleher (1988) and Friedman and Waller (1987) indicate that stock prices in different countries show co-movements particularly in the 1980s than during earlier periods. Somewhat similar results are reported by Jaffe and Westerfield (1985) and Eun and Shim (1989). Arshanapalli and Doukas (1993), using methods of cointegration, found evidence in sharp contrast to the hypothesis of major world stock market interdependence for the pre-1987 period. However, they report substantial increase in stock price co-movements in the post-1987 period and furthermore they found the NYSE as exercising considerable impact on the French, German, and the United Kingdom markets. Dwyer and Hafer (1988) report similar results. This issue, therefore, is far from settled.

Most of the research in this area is done with data from major world stock markets in developed countries including the United States, the United Kingdom, Germany, France, and Japan. This paper examines stock market interdependence of the southern European countries of Italy, Spain, Greece, and Turkey with the United States. Even though the economies of these countries do not get the kind of attention that their dominant northern countries do, it will be useful to examine the extent of their interdependence with the United States particularly as these countries have embarked upon policies aimed at improving the domestic economy by way of market forces and international trade. Spain and Italy have initiated economic policies to rein in inflation and reduce the domestic budget deficit. Spain virtually eliminated exchange controls in February 1992, and significantly liberalized investment regulations. The Greek economy is responding to the market-oriented economic policies of the recent past. The deregulation and privatization policies are being pursued along with liberalization of the financial markets. Restrictions on capital movements have been lifted. Turkey has taken similar steps; along with domestic economic liberalization, its currency is fully convertible since 1990. In recent times both imports and exports have been rising considerably. Thus, all of these economies have undertaken economic policies of deregulation and liberalization of international trade and capital movements. It is, therefore, hypothesized that these countries' capital markets also may have developed strong economic linkages with outside economies, particularly with the world's largest stock market, the New York Stock Exchange.

DATA AND METHODOLOGY

Weekly stock market index prices on the national stock markets of Italy (Milan), Spain (Madrid), Greece (Athens), and Turkey were used for the period of January 6, 1987 to March 22, 1994, a total of 377 observations. In the case of the United

States, the New York Stock Exchange index values from January 6, 1987 to April 19, 1994 were used. The stock index prices were converted from local currencies to the U.S. dollar values. The study period is important as it includes the time period during which most economic liberalization policies were put in place by these countries. Portugal, also a southern European country, was not included in the sample because its economy is relatively small in comparison with other sample countries.

Several past studies have examined the stock market linkages using long established statistical methods such as variance-covariance and correlation statistics or some other similar methods (Gruber 1968; Levy and Sarnat 1970; Aqmon 1972). Engle and Granger's (1987) theory of cointegration provides a new method for testing linkages across national borders. Cointegration among various stock indexes implies that even if the indexes themselves are nonstationary, they rarely drift apart in the long run. Lack of cointegration on the other hand provides evidence that the stock market indexes have no linkages in the long run. Schollhammer and Sand (1985) and Eun and Shim (1989) report that stock price indexes for several countries are nonstationary. It becomes, therefore, necessary to convert the nonstationary time series to a stationary one, by taking the first differences of the series, for certain statistical procedures. The first differencing, as Arshanapalli and Doukas (1993) point out, filters out potentially important information regarding long-run common trends among nonstationary stock indexes. The statistical techniques based on the theory of cointegration avoids this problem.

Following Engle and Granger (1987), if x_t and y_t are both integrated of order one, $I(1)$, there exists a linear combination

$$Z_t = X_t - Ay_t \tag{1}$$

that is covariance stationary, $I(0)$. Then x_t and y_t are defined to be cointegrated of order 1,1 and z_t is construed as being the equilibrium error. Cointegration implies that at least one linear combination of the economic time series is stationary. If the time series are cointegrated, then it implies that they have a long-run relationship. Also, if x_t and y_t are cointegrated they may be considered to be generated by an error-correcting model of the form

$$\Delta x_t = \rho_1 z_{t-1} + \text{lagged}(\Delta x_t, \Delta y_t) + \varepsilon_x t \tag{2}$$

$$\Delta y_t = \rho_2 z_{t-1} + \text{lagged}(\Delta x_t, \Delta y_t) + \varepsilon_{yt} \tag{3}$$

where at least one of ρ1, ρ2 is nonzero, z_t is from equation (1), and ε_{xt}, ε_{yt} are jointly white noise error terms.

The error-correction model has simple interpretation: the change in x_t is due to the immediate, short-run effect from the change in y_t and to the last period's error, z_{t-1}, which represents the long-run adjustment to past disequilibrium. Therefore, estimation of the error-correction equations is also expected to provide evidence about the long-run relationship and the nature of the adjustment process within the stock markets.

EMPIRICAL ANALYSIS

The empirical analysis is done in three steps. Initially, the individual stock index price series are tested for the presence of unit roots. This is done using the Augmented Dickey Fuller (ADF) analysis (Dickey and Fuller 1979, 1981). The next step involves identification of a long-run equilibrium relationship between the time series using Johansen's (1988) method. In the Johansen method, the null hypothesis is that cointegrating vector (k) is equal to zero; the alternative hypothesis being $k = 1,2,3,4$. Rejection of null hypothesis implies that there is a stable long-run relationship between the economic time series under review. Should there exist a stable long-run relationship between the time series, then it is assumed that changes in a variable are influenced, among others, by previous period's error. Thus, the error term, (z_{t-1}), is expected to "correct" the time series. The last step, therefore, involves estimation of an error correction model.

The order of integration of the national stock indexes is tested by performing the Augmented Dickey Fuller (ADF) tests. The null hypothesis is that the stock indexes have a unit root, against the hypothesis that they do not. The results are presented in Table 1. The test statistics indicate that the null hypothesis can not be rejected in the level but when first differences are taken we can reject the null hypothesis at

Table 1. Tests for Unit Roots
December 23, 1986–March 22, 1994 ($N = 377$)

Country	*ADF*[a]	*ADF (differences)*[b]
U.S.	−1.425991	−9.222330 (1)*
Greece	−2.143727	−8.078304 (1)*
Italy	−1.847839	−6.954144 (1)*
Spain	−2.716745	−9.292662 (1)*
Turkey	−1.994215	−7.581856 (1)*

Notes: [a]ADF denotes the Augmented Dickey-Fuller test. The ADF test is based on the following regression:

$$\Delta x_t = a_0 + a_1\, x_{t-1} + \sum_{j=1}^{m} b_j \Delta x_{t-j} + v_t$$

where x_t represents the weekly stock index prices and v_t the error term.

[b]The number in parentheses denotes the minimum value of m required to achieve white noise errors, v_t.

The * indicates statistical significance at the one percent level or rejection of a unit root occurs at the one percent level. The critical value is −3.4495 as reported in Engle and Yoo (1987).

5% level. The results confirm that individual stock indexes are nonstationary in the level but stationary in the first differences of order one.

Having confirmed that all the stock market price series are integrated, $I(1)$, it is necessary to examine if they are also cointegrated. In Table 2, results of the test for cointegration for the national stock indexes series using Johansen's (1988) method are reported in two separate panels. Test results of cointegration among the four southern European stock markets and the NYSE are reported in Panel A, whereas Panel B shows test statistics on cointegration among the four southern European stock markets only.

The likelihood ratio test statistics reported in Panel A reject the hypothesis that there are no cointegrating vectors in favor of the alternative hypothesis that there is only one cointegrating vector. In other words it implies that there exists a long-run equilibrium relationship between the NYSE and the stock markets of four southern European countries. These results provide additional support to similar findings reported by Jaffe and Westerfield (1985), Schollhammer and Sand (1985), and Eun and Shim (1989). It should be noted that these studies cover the time period prior to the international stock market collapse of October 1987 whereas the present study covers the time period of January 1987 to April 1994. Arshanapalli and Doukas (1993) report results for both the pre- and post-October 1987 period. They found weaker linkage among the stock markets of the United States, the U.K., Germany, and France for the pre-October 1987 period.

These contradictory findings should be kept in perspective when interpreting the results presented in Panel B which shows results for the four southern European countries without the presence of the United States. The test statistics reject the null hypothesis of zero cointegrating vectors and reveals that there are four cointegrating vectors. In the theory of cointegration, it is assumed that an economic system is more stable if it has more number of cointegrating vectors. Each cointegrating vector is viewed as a constraint on the time series and these constraints are expected to bring in more long-run stability to the economic system (Dickey, Jansen, and Thornton 1991). From the results reported in Panel B, it is clear that the long-run relationship among the four countries of southern Europe is much more stable than their relationship with the United States. (Panel A). These results are different than those reported by Arshanapalli and Doukas (1993). For the post-October 1987 period, Arshanapalli and Doukas report greater interdependence between the stock markets of the United States, the United Kingdom, Germany, and France, with the United States having substantial impact on the three European stock markets. In comparison, findings reported in Table 2 show a much weaker linkage between the NYSE and the four southern European countries. Overall the results support the notion of interdependence among the international financial markets.

Next, the extent of interaction between these stock markets is examined by estimating the error correction equation as per Granger (1969) and Engle and Granger (1987). The results are reported in Table 3. The error correction model in general implies that a change x_t is due to the immediate and short-run effect from

Table 2. Johansen Cointegration Test Among the Stock Indexes:

Panel A:
NYSE, Greece, Italy, Spain, Turkey
December 2, 1986–April 19, 1994 (*N* = 377)

Hypothesized No. of Ks	*Eigenvalue*	*Likelihood Ratio*	*5 Percent Critical Value*
$K = 0$	0.084876	70.59100	68.52*
$K \leq 1$	0.040978	37.15282	47.21
$K \leq 2$	0.029613	21.37877	29.68
$K \leq 3$	0.021612	10.04596	15.41
$K \leq 4$	0.004787	1.808952	3.76

Notes: *Likelihood ratio test indicates at least 1 cointegrating equation at 5% significance level.
K represents number of cointegrating equations.

Panel B:
Greece, Italy, Spain, Turkey
December 2, 1986–April 21, 1994 (*N* = 379)

Hypothesized No. of Ks	*Eigenvalue*	*Likelihood Ratio*	*5 Percent Critical Value*
$K = 0$	0.065131	57.81879	47.21*
$K \leq 1$	0.038015	32.29374	29.68*
$K \leq 2$	0.030778	17.60500	15.41*
$K \leq 3$	0.015074	5.756713	3.76*

Notes: *Likelihood ratio test indicates 4 cointegrating equations at 5% significance level.
K represents number of cointegrating equations.

the change in y_t and to last period's error, z_{t-1}. The error (z_{t-1}) represents the long-run adjustment to the past disequilibrium. The underlying assumption here is that the economic time series have tendencies to drift away from each other though they are expected to return back to equilibrium. The "drifting away" is estimated by the error term (z_t) which also provides the correction to the series for the next period. It is, therefore, necessary to take cognizance of the error term (z_{t-1}) as it becomes important in bringing about equilibrium to the time series. In other words, the estimation of the error correction equation is expected to provide support about the existence of long-run relationship and also about the nature of the adjustment process among the national stock markets.

The results presented in Table 3 show that error term is significant, except in the case of Italy. The test statistics, though not large, confirm the earlier findings presented in Table 2. These results imply that previous period's error correcting term is a factor in predicting next period's stock market index price changes particularly in the case of the stock markets of Greece, Spain, and Turkey.

Table 3. Vector Error Correction Regression Estimates in Stock Market Indexes

Dependent Variable	*D(NYSE)*	*D(GREECE)*	*D(SPAIN)*	*D(ITALY)*	*D(TURKEY)*
Z_{t-1}	–0.002097	0.044661*	0.013909*	–0.000482	0.037606*
	(–0.56769)	(4.66749)	(2.80436)	(–0.10344)	(2.35209)
D(NYSE(–1))	0.006377	0.229668	0.041447	–0.169814*	0.117168
	(0.12380)	(1.72095)	(0.59914)	(–2.61095)	(0.52543)
D(NYSE(–2))	–0.003323	0.091258	0.114916	0.143770*	–0.167018
	(–0.06416)	(0.68011)	(1.65215)	(2.19853)	(–0.74491)
D(GREECE(–1))	0.034634	0.024505	–0.008409	0.020993	0.035907
	(1.77028)	(0.48346)	(–0.32004)	(0.84983)	(0.42396)
D(GREECE(–2))	0.034268	0.048151	–0.052289	–0.019599	0.096182
	(1.75254)	(0.95050)	(–1.99119)	(–0.79384)	(1.13625)
D(SPAIN(–1))	0.027961	0.092684	0.134715*	0.270098*	–0.057953
	(0.71163)	(0.91047)	(2.55292)	(5.44427)	(–0.34070)
D(SPAIN(–2))	0.029428	0.394564*	0.071605	0.047708	0.541022
	(0.72074)	(3.72990)	(1.30583)	(0.92541)	(3.06078)
D(ITALY–1))	0.007426	–0.017760	–0.004475	0.074158	0.074063
	(0.17681)	(–0.16322)	(–0.07934)	(1.39842)	(0.40734)
D(ITALY(–2))	0.106425*	–0.026238	0.005557	0.056076	–0.342462
	(2.65245)	(–0.25240)	(0.10312)	(1.10687)	(–1.97157)
D(TURKEY(–1))	–0.001132	–0.037764	0.004116	–0.009533	0.009748
	(–0.09153)	(–1.17842)	(0.24779)	(–0.61041)	(–0.18203)
D(TURKEY(–2))	–0.007531	–0.026910	0.003784	–0.000159	0.097361
	(–0.60748)	(–0.83785)	(0.22731)	(–0.01017)	(1.81420)
CONSTANT	0.001592	–0.003206	–0.000968	–4.27E–06	–0.003004
	(0.00115)	(0.00299)	(0.00155)	(0.00146)	(0.00499)

Notes: *t*-statistics in parenthesis.
*Indicates significance at 5% or better level of significance.

CONCLUDING REMARKS

This study examined the nature of the relationship between the NYSE and the stock markets of four southern European countries of Greece, Italy, Spain, and Turkey during the period of January 1987 to April 1994, using weekly data. In addition to using the recent data, the study is useful as it includes the southern European countries that generally remain neglected in such analysis. However all of these four countries have begun serious efforts of economic liberalization both domestically and also with respect to international trade, investments, and capital movements. It was, therefore, expected that these economic policies might have brought the financial markets of these countries closer to the world economy. Thus the extent of interdependence of the stock markets of these countries with the world's most dominant stock market, the NYSE, was examined.

The study used the analytical techniques based on the theory of cointegration. Overall the results support the hypothesis of interdependence among the stock markets of these countries. However, the strength of interdependence of the stock markets of Greece, Italy, Spain, and Turkey with the United States is weaker in comparison with the interdependence among the four southern European countries themselves. These results, though not unexpected, are different particularly with respect to the lack of predominance of the U.S. stock market. Their northern partners, the U.K., Germany, and France, seem to have a much stronger relationship with the United States as reported by Arshanapalli and Doukas (1993). Thus, the study reports interesting findings while providing additional evidence in support of the notion of interdependence of world stock markets.

REFERENCES

Aqmon, T. 1972. "The Relations Among Equity Markets: A Study of Share Price Co-movements in the United States, United Kingdom, Germany and Japan." *Journal of Finance* 27: 839–855.

Arshanapalli, B., and J. Doukas. 1993a. "International Stock Market Linkages: Evidence from Pre- and Post-October 1987 Period." *Journal of Banking and Finance* 17: 193–208.

———. 1993b. "Integration of Euro-Money Markets." *The Journal of Multinational Financial Management* 107: 126.

Bennett, P., and J. Kelleher. 1988. "The International Transmission of Stock Price Disruption in October 1987." Federal Reserve Bank of New York *Quarterly Review* 13: 17–33.

Dickey, D.A., and W.A. Fuller. 1979. "Distribution of the Estimates for Autoregressive Time Series with a Unit Root." *Journal of the American Statistical Association* 24: 427–31.

———. 1981. "Likelihood Ratio Statistics for Autoregressive Time Series with a Unit Root." *Econometrica* 49: 1057–1072.

Dickey, D.A., D.W. Jensen, and D.L. Thronton. 1991. "A Primer on Cointegration with an Application to Money and Income." *Review*, Federal Reserve Bank of St. Louis (March/April): 58–78.

Dwyer, G.P., and R.W. Hafer. 1988. "Are National Stock Markets Linked?" Federal Reserve Bank of St. Louis, *Review* 39: 314.

Engle, R.F., and E.W.J. Granger. 1987. "Cointegration and Error-Correction: Representation, Estimation and Testing." *Econometrica* 35: 251–76.

Engle, R.F., and G.S. Yoo. 1987. "Forecasting and Testing in Cointegrated Systems." *Journal of Econometrics* (May) 143–59.

Eun, C.S., and S. Shim. 1989. "International Transmission of Stock Market Movements." *Journal of Financial and Quantitative Analysis* 24: 241–256.

Friedman, B.M., and K.J. Waller. 1987. "The Substitutability of United States and Foreign Assets." Pp. 159–193 in *Research Papers on International Integration of Financial Markets and U.S. Monetary Policy.* New York: Federal Reserve Bank of New York.

Grubel, H.G. 1970. "Internationally Diversified of Investment Portfolio's." *American Economic Review* 60: 668–675.

Harvey, C.R. 1991. "The World Price of Covariance Risk." *Journal of Finance* 46: 111–157.

Hilliard, J.E. 1991. "The Relationship Between Equity Indices on World Exchanges." *Journal of Finance* 34: 103–114.

Jaffe, J., and R. Westerfield. 1985. "The Weekend Effect in Common Stock Returns: The International Evidence." *Journal of Finance* 40: 433–454.

Johansen, S. 1988. "Statistical Analysis of Cointegrating Vectors." *Journal of Economic Dynamics and Control* 12: 231–254.

Levy, H., and M. Sarnat. 1970. "International Diversification of Investment Portfolios." *American Economic Review* 60: 668–675.

Roll, R. 1992. "Industrial Structure and the Comparative Behavior of International Stock Market Indexes." *Journal of Finance* 47: 3–41.

Schollhammer, H., and O. Sand. 1985. "The Interdependence Among the Stock Markets of Major European Countries and the United States: An Empirical Investigation of Interrelationships Among National Stock Price Movements." *Management International Review* 25: 17–26.

INTEGRATION AND ANOMALIES IN THE EMERGING MARKETS OF ASIA AND LATIN AMERICA

Reena Aggarwal and Ricardo Leal

ABSTRACT

This study analyzes the recent behavior of some of the largest emerging stock markets. It includes Korea, Malaysia, the Philippines, Taiwan, and Thailand in Asia and Argentina, Brazil, Chile, and Mexico in Latin America. Daily stock market indexes are analyzed between 1982 and 1991. The Latin American markets present a much higher volatility in the period than the Asian markets. The tendency toward day-to-day, linkages between Asian emerging markets and the U.S. markets, between Japan and the United States and between the emerging Asian markets have all increased over time. During the crash period, the linkages between the various markets were very pronounced. The correlations are much higher for volatility of returns than for the mean of returns. The Latin American markets present a lower level of integration relative to the emerging Asian markets. A multivariate regression that includes dummies for the anomalies indicates that the U.S. and Japanese market returns are significant explanatory variables explaining local currency returns in emerging markets. However, the exchange rate variable is not significant in most cases. Four market anomalies are also examined. The average daily returns show that to some extent the Asian markets have a weekend effect of their own and they also have a

Research in International Business and Finance, Supplement 1, pages 75–99.

ISBN: 0-7623-0110-4

"Tuesday effect" which may be driven by the market performance in New York on Monday. In Latin America there appears to be a Monday effect in all four countries. Surprisingly the January effect is not significant in the United States anymore. There is no month-of-the-year, turn-of-the-month, or January effect in most markets although the twist-of-the-Monday effect is found in many countries.

INTRODUCTION

Previous studies have made a strong case for international portfolio diversification in a mean-variance portfolio framework. The co-movement of world exchange indexes and stocks indicates that movements in most Asian and Latin American markets show little similarity with the markets of North America or Europe. Therefore, a strong case has been made for diversifying into these markets (Errunza and Padmanabhan 1988). It has also been documented that if there exists close economic ties between countries, then the relationships between their stock markets will also be strong. With the Economic Monetary Union, for example, it would be expected that the markets of Europe would move closer together. The implications of the North American Free Trade Agreement (NAFTA) should also be similar. Further, the globalization of markets and economies in the last decade should, in general, result in stronger linkages between the markets of the world.

The purpose of this paper is two-fold. First, it examines the extent of integration among nine of the ten largest emerging stock markets according to the International Finance Corporation (1992) during the 1982–1991 period. Market integration is studied by examining the correlations of market returns and also correlations of market volatility. Second, multivariate regression models are estimated with the explanatory variables being dummy variables representing market anomalies, major market returns (U.S. or Japan), and the corresponding exchange rates (dollar or yen). The dependent variable is the country's market daily return. Next, the presence of anomalies is also explored. The presence of the same market anomalies in international markets could be due to spillovers from developed markets or since emerging markets tend to have low correlations of returns with developed markets, the anomalies may be independent effects. The existence of the day-of-the-week, month-of-the-year, turn-of-the-month, and the twist-of-the-Monday effects are investigated. The sample includes daily local and dollar-adjusted returns for Argentina, Brazil, Chile, and Mexico in Latin America and Malaysia, the Philippines, Korea, Taiwan, and Thailand in Asia. Japan and the United States are also analyzed for comparative purposes. The sample is split into two time periods, 1982–1986 and 1987–1991, in order to study whether globalization of world markets has actually brought these stock markets closer together within their regions and outside their regions. International market links are also examined during a crisis period—the crash of October 1987. The financial press maintains that there has been rapid globalization of financial markets. However, despite the casual evidence supporting global linkages, a number of academic studies have found a high degree of independence among the world's stock exchanges.

The rest of the paper is organized as follows: the second section reviews existing literature on market integration and anomalies, the third section provides an overview of the markets being studied, data and methodology are presented in the fourth section, the empirical results are reported in the fifth section, and a summary is provided in the final section.

LITERATURE REVIEW

Roll (1989) points out that prior to the crash of October 1987 direct empirical estimates have found cross-country correlations to be relatively small. Dwyer and Hafer (1988) examine the short-term relations among four major markets: the United States, United Kingdom, Japan, and Germany. The authors do not find that the correlation has increased over time in any significant way. Bennett and Kelleher (1988) document a slight increase in market co-movements during the 1980s relative to the 1970s. Parhizgari, Dandapani, and Bhattacharya (1988) find "bi-directional feedback" between New York, London, and Tokyo with New York being the stronger causative factor. Campbell and Hamao (1992) find increasing long-term integration between the Japanese and the American stock markets. For an earlier review of the literature see Madura (1985).

Roll (1989) reports that the month of October 1987 was the only month during the decade of the 1980s when every major market moved in the same direction. In general, correlations during the crash period are found to be higher than the historical averages (see, for example, Bertero and Mayer 1989; King and Wadhwani 1990). Hillard (1979) finds a very close co-movement among ten major industrial nations during the OPEC embargo period between July 1973 and April 1974.

The number of studies addressing emerging stock markets specifically is limited. Harvey (1993), Divecha, Drach, and Stefek (1992), Errunza and Padmanabhan (1988), Gill and Tropper (1988), and Errunza and Losq (1987), have examined the riskiness and the performance of emerging stock markets. A number of other studies (e.g., Roll 1992; Errunza, Losq, and Padmanabhan 1992) have included a few emerging markets in their sample. One type of anomaly that has been examined more extensively is the abnormal initial returns in IPOs which is also present in many emerging markets (Aggarwal, Leal, and Hernandez 1993; Dawson 1987; Krinsky, Kim, and Lee 1992; Leal 1992).

In general, an examination of the correlations of returns indicates that there could be opportunities to reduce portfolio risk by investing in emerging stock markets. On the other hand, when examining individual companies, Errunza and Padmanabhan (1988) find extreme volatility during the 1976–1984 period. Bruno Solnik suggests that markets volatility may be highly correlated (*Wall Street Journal* 1994).

Many studies examine the interdependence among the major world stock markets (e.g., Dwyer and Hafer 1988; Eun and Shim 1989; Meric and Meric 1989; Roll 1992; Cheung 1993). In general they find that there is not much co-movement among these markets when they are represented by stock market indexes. However, there is a stronger relationship across international industries (Meric and Meric 1989; Roll 1992).

Research addressing the linkages among emerging markets is also limited. Chan, Gup, and Pan (1992) exam the interrelationships between the United States, Japan, South Korea, Taiwan, Hong Kong, and Singapore. They find no evidence of co-integration among these markets. The results suggest that diversification across these markets may be effective. Errunza, Losq, and Padmanabhan (1992) investigate the integration between Argentina, Brazil, Chile, Greece, India, Korea, Mexico, Zimbabwe, and the United States. They conclude that, while markets cannot be considered integrated, they are not completely segmented. An earlier study by Lessard (1973) examines the period between 1958–1968 and finds that the stock markets of Argentina, Brazil, Chile, and Colombia are independent of each other and that returns within each country are due to country specific factors.

Harvey (1993) uses monthly returns from the IFC emerging market indexes between 1976 and 1992 in a number of cross-section regressions to assess market integration. Several measures of market concentration, size, and trading volume are used as independent variables. The results are in general not conclusive. Only asset concentration seems to explain the cross-section volatility. On the other hand, the small number of markets limits a cross-section analysis and, as Harvey notes, the volatility is changing over time. His correlation of returns results are consistent with ours He also examines asset pricing in these markets by using a single-factor model with the excess return of the Morgan Stanley World Index (MSWI) over the Treasury Bill return and a multiple factor model with an exchange rate risk factor and the Morgan Stanley World Index. Both models are not successful in explaining emerging markets returns.

The examination of market anomalies in international markets addresses two issues. It is possible that the anomalies are being generated by U.S. institutions alone and then are spread throughout the world by U.S. investors trading on foreign markets and/or by the fact that markets are somewhat integrated and follow each other's movements. Alternatively, it is also possible that these effects are being generated independently within each country. Most markets being studied in this paper tend to have relatively low correlations with the United States. Therefore, if calendar anomalies are found in these markets it is more likely that they are being generated independently. If all these markets show a similar pattern, it reflects on whether they are integrated or insulated from other markets (Cadsby and Rattner 1992). Seasonal and day-of-the-week patterns have proven to be persistent anomalies in the United States. For a review of calendar anomalies in the United States see Jacobs and Levy (1988), Thaler (1987a, 1987b), and Lakonishok and Smidt (1988).

These calendar anomalies in security returns exist in markets outside the United States as well. Gultekin and Gultekin (1983) present evidence of a January effect in most of the 11 industrialized countries examined. Jaffe and Westeffield (1985) find a Tuesday and a turn-of-the-year effect in the Japanese market. Jaffe and Westerfield (1989) do not find a day-of-the-month pattern similar to the United States in Australia, Canada, Japan, and the U.K. However, there seems to be a country-specific pattern. Jaffe, Westerfield, and Ma (1989) find a twist-of-the-Monday effect for the same four countries.

Agrawal and Tandon (1994) examine anomalies for 18 countries. Brazil, Mexico, Japan, and the United States are common to our sample. The data from Brazil is for the Rio de Janeiro Stock Exchange while our results refer to the São Paulo Stock Exchange which has a greater capitalization and is more diverse. Trading in Rio is more concentrated in a number of state-owned utilities. They examine Brazil and Mexico for an earlier period: 1972–1988. The market proxy for the United States is the Standard and Poor's 500 index (1962–1983) and for Japan the Nikkei index is used (1970–1987). They examine the anomalies in each country in local currency. Their results are consistent with those found by us and reported later. In addition, we also adjust all returns to a dollar basis and use a common time period for all countries.

Turn-of-the-month and pre-holiday effects were also studied by Cadsby and Ratner (1992) for several major international markets. They detected the turn-of-the-month effect in a number of markets. Pre-holiday effects are present for the local holidays. There is no widespread evidence of an influence of the U.S. pre-holiday effects in other international markets.

Many of these anomalies have been studied in other Asian countries, including some emerging markets. Aggarwal and Rivoli (1989) report a small Monday effect and a Tuesday effect for Hong Kong, Malaysia, the Philippines, and Singapore. The returns in January also seem to be higher. Other studies addressing Asia Pacific stock markets also find pervasive day-of-the-week and month-of-the-year effects but the latter are not consistent with tax-loss selling hypothesis (Ho 1990; Lee 1992).

OVERVIEW OF THE EMERGING MARKETS

Emerging Asian markets are attracting considerable attention and interest. The Asian-Pacific economies remain the world's fastest-growing, with strong domestic demand and intra-regional trade helping to offset slumps in U.S. and European export markets. The 1980s have been a decade of enviable growth, and with bright prospects for the future ahead, the region is capturing considerable attention. The Asian Economic Survey conducted by the *Asian Wall Street Journal* (October 12 and November 9, 1992), indicates that economic growth for 12 Asian countries slowed somewhat in 1992, to 5.2% from 5.4% in 1991. But compared to most other parts of the world, Asia's growth looks quite healthy. There is growing feeling that

Asian economies are becoming more self-sufficient. The export-dependent Asia has survived the recession in the United States, Japan, and Europe, due to intra-regional trade and investment, and massive infrastructure projects. Political development has followed economic development in most parts of Asia including the Philippines, Taiwan, and South Korea.

Latin America is also engaged in economic liberalization programs. Chile was the first country among the four analyzed here to open its economy and to carry out massive privatization programs. Its closed-end fund has been among the best performers during 1992 (*Business Week* 1992). Mexico is also among the best performing markets and was the largest emerging market in terms of market capitalization as of August 1992. Argentina has been very successful recently in restructuring its internal debt within the Brady Plan framework. Brazil is by far the largest economy among all the nine markets but has not solved its chronic inflation problem and has just begun its way to restructure its massive external debt.

There is also a movement toward stronger regional integration. In Asia, the Association of Southeast Asian Nations (ASEAN) created its first integrated regional market in January 1993. The ASEAN Free Trade Area (AFTA) is expected to boost trade among its participating countries, including Malaysia, the Philippines, and Thailand, creating a market of 400 million people. The MERCOSUR in Latin America has already brought practical results and boosted trade between Brazil and Argentina in a market of about 200 million people. The free-trade agreements are being implemented gradually and are expected to be fully in place on January 1, 1996. Chile did not join any of two regional economic blocks in Latin America (the MERCOSUR and the Andean Pact), but is seeking bilateral agreements with several countries, including the United States.

The emerging markets are quite small in size when compared to the equity markets in the United States, Japan, and Europe as seen in Table 1. However, the economies of many of these markets have been growing at much higher rates than the rest of the world. Several stock exchange reforms ranging from disclosure requirements, rules for corporate takeovers, structures for establishing futures and options exchanges, to legislation preventing insider trading are underway or have been fully implemented. Several countries have undertaken massive privatization plans.

The dividend yield in the Asian and Latin American countries is much lower than the rest of the world and the United Sates (except for Chile). Price to earnings ratio are also relatively low. There are a number of other interesting characteristics associated with these markets. Individually, the markets tend to be quite volatile, some years appearing among the ten best performing markets in the world and showing up as the worst performers in other years (e.g., Argentina, Brazil, and Taiwan).

The markets also tend to be highly concentrated. A small number of companies account for a large percentage of market capitalization and trading activity. The share of market capitalization held by ten largest stocks, at the end of 1992 was

Table 1. Emerging Markets Profile as of December 1992

	Market Capitalization (in US$ billions)	*Listed Companies*	*P/E Relative to World*	*P/B Relative to World*	*Div. Yield Relative to World*	*Ten Largest Corporations Percent of Capitalization*
Asian Markets						
Malaysia	94	366	.95	1.34	.84	30.9
Philippines	14	170	.61	1.30	.36	52.2
South Korea	107	688	.93	.56	.65	30.5
Taiwan	101	256	.72	1.14	.63	30.2
Thailand	58	305	.61	1.33	.94	28.5
Japan	2399	2118	1.69	.94	.36	16.5
Latin Markets and the U.S.						
Argentina	19	175	1.65	.63	.69	68.8
Brazil	45	565	NM	.20	.24	29.3
Chile	30	245	.56	.90	1.36	53.8
Mexico	139	195	.53	1.05	.35	31.7
U.S.A	4757	7014	.99	1.25	1.04	14.9

Note: NM: Not Meaningful.

Source: *Emerging Markets Factbook,* International Finance Corporation, 1993.

14.9% in the United States and 16.5% in Japan. In contrast the share for this sample of emerging markets varied from a low of 28.5% in Thailand to 68.6% in Argentina.

DATA AND METHODOLOGY

The data consist of daily closing values for the Nikkei Average (Japan), the Bolsa Indice General (Argentina), the BOVESPA São Paulo Stock Exchange Index (Brazil), the IGPA Index (Chile), Seoul Composite Index (Korea), Kuala Lumpur Composite Index (Malaysia), the BMV General (Mexico), the Manila Composite Index (Philippines), Taipei Weighted Price Index (Taiwan), and Bangkok S.E.T. Index (Thailand). All the market indexes are value-weighted (except the Nikkei which is price-weighted) and do not include dividends.

Index data were collected from the *Asian Wall Street Journal* for all the Asian markets except Korea and Taiwan which were provided by the respective stock exchanges. The Brazilian index was collected from the São Paulo Stock Exchange monthly bulletin. The Argentine index was obtained from the daily *La Nacion*. The Chilean and Mexican data were provided by the Santiago and Mexican Stock Exchanges, respectively. The level of the Standard and Poor's 500 (S&P 500) is used as the proxy for the U.S. market. The analysis covers the ten-year period between January 1982 and December 1991. All returns were calculated in local currencies and were also adjusted for U.S. dollar returns.

Table 2. Daily Percent Returns on Country Stock Indexes Local Currency/U.S. Dollar Returns (January 1982–December 1991)

Market	*Mean*	*Median*	*Std. Dev.*	*Minimum*	*Maximum*	*Obs.*
Asian Markets						
Japan	.04/.06	.06/.06	1.14/1.40	–14.90/–16.39	13.24/13.22	2322/2088
Malaysia	.05/.04	.05/.06	.98/1.08	–10.14/–10.39	4.99/10.11	2289/2057
Philippines	.11/.07	.00/.00	2.07/1.81	–12.84/–19.16	10.21/10.41	2330/2118
South Korea	.08/.09	.00/.00	1.25/1.30	–8.04/–7.58	7.78/9.78	2326/2095
Taiwan	.09/.10	.14/.14	2.17/2.22	–12.56/–12.56	13.70/13.70	2288/2075
Thailand	.08/.09	.08/.08	1.40/1.47	–9.99/–13.76	12.03/12.03	2282/2046
Latin America and the U.S.						
Argentina	.81/.27	.37/.24	4.14/4.95	–35.36/–50.91	50.11/50.11	2255/2037
Brazil	.74/.13	.56/.24	3.66/3.81	–25.01/–21.58	33.98/19.97	2339/2102
Chile	.15/.13	.09/.09	1.05/1.80	–9.62/–19.06	8.53/18.48	2389/1985
Mexico	.34/.13	.29/.19	2.34/2.70	–18.33/–27.50	26.60/26.07	2379/1924
U.S.A.	.06	.06	1.08	–20.47	9.10	2448

Descriptive statistics for the markets are presented in Table 2. During the ten-year sample period the Philippines had the highest average daily return of 0.11% among the Asian countries while Japan had the lowest return of 0.04 in local currency. The dollar adjusted daily returns were highest in Taiwan (0.10) and lowest in Malaysia (0.04). All Asian markets except Malaysia had higher volatility, as measured by standard deviation, than the United States. Argentina and Brazil present the highest return and volatility due to their hyper inflationary economies during the late 1980s. Chile and Mexico, despite suffering with inflation problems in the early 1980s, did not see inflation rates nearly as high as those in Argentina and Brazil. Chile and Mexico present a volatility level compatible with the Asian markets in the sample. The returns for each market index are calculated according to equation 1.

$$R_{i,t} = \frac{I_{i,t}/I_{i,t-1}}{X_{i,t}/X_{i,t-1}} - 1 \tag{1}$$

where:

$R_{i,t}$ is the return of index i on day t.
$I_{i,t}$ is the closing index i value on day t.
$I_{i,t-1}$ is the closing index i value on day t–1.
$X_{i,t}$ is the foreign exchange per U.S. dollars on day t.
$X_{i,t-1}$ is the foreign exchange per U.S. dollars on day t–1.

The day-of-the-week effect is examined using the model in equation 2.

$$R_{i,t} = \alpha_{i,1} + \alpha_{i,2}D_2 + \alpha_{i,3}D_3 + \alpha_{i,4}D_4 + \alpha_{i,5}D_5 + \varepsilon_{i,t} \tag{2}$$

where:

$D_2, ..., D_5$ are dummy variables for each day of the week. D_2 is one if the day is a Tuesday and zero otherwise. The same occurs for D_3, D_4, D_5 when the day of the week is a Wednesday, Thursday, or Friday, respectively.

$\varepsilon_{i,t}$ is the error term.

If the returns for each day-of-the-week are the same, one would expect the coefficients α_1, α_2, α_3, α_4, and α_5 not to be significantly different from zero.

The month-of-the-year effect is tested by using the model described in equation 3. To accept the hypothesis that the daily returns in each month of the year are the same, the regression coefficients α_1, α_2, ..., α_{12} cannot be significantly different from zero.

$$R_{i,t} = \alpha_{i},1 + \alpha_{i},2D_2 + \ldots + \alpha_{i},12D_{12} + \varepsilon_{i,t} \tag{3}$$

where:

$D_2, ..., D_{12}$ are dummy variables indicating each month of the year. D_2 is one if the month is February and zero otherwise. The same occurs with $D_3, D_4, ..., D_{12}$ if the month is March, April, and so on, respectively.

$\varepsilon_{i,t}$ is the error term.

Lakonishok and Smidt (1988) test the turn of the month effect. The "turn-of-the-month" is defined as being the four-day period between the last trading day of the month and the first three trading days of the subsequent month. The model used to test the turn-of-the-month effect is described by equation 4. If $\alpha_{2,i}$ is not significantly different from zero, there is no turn-of-the-month effect.

$$R_{i,t} = \alpha_{1,i} + \alpha_{2,i}D_{i,t} + \varepsilon_{i,t} \tag{4}$$

where:

$D_{i,t}$ is the dummy variable that assumes the value one if the day is in the turn-of-the-month period and zero otherwise.

$\varepsilon_{i,t}$ is the error term.

Finally, the twist-of-the-Monday effect is tested by associating the return of a Monday with the previous week returns. The effect is present if the return of a Monday is positively related to the return during the previous week. The previous week return is defined as in Jaffe, Westerfield, and Ma (1989) according to equation 5.

$$R_{i,w} = \frac{F_{i,w} - F_{i,w-1}}{F_{i,w-1}} \tag{5}$$

where:

$R_{i,w}$ is the return of the week w for the index i.
$F_{i,w}$ is the index i closing value for week's w Friday.
$F_{i,w-1}$ is the index i closing value for week's w–1 Friday.

When there was no index or exchange rate for one of the Fridays, regardless of the reason, that week was discarded. If the return of a week was positive, a value of one was assigned to a dummy variable. The variable would be zero otherwise. Using the dummy variables as independent variables, the regression model described in equation 6 is estimated. If the Monday returns are not affected by the previous week returns, the regression coefficient is not significantly different from zero.

$$RM_{i,w+1} = \alpha_i + \beta_i D_{i,w} + \varepsilon_{i,w} \tag{6}$$

where

$RM_{i,w+1}$ is the index i return on the week w+1 Monday as in equation 1.
$D_{i,w}$ is the dummy variable assuming the value one when the return during week w, as in equation 5, is positive and zero otherwise.
β_i is the regression coefficient measuring the intrinsic return on a Monday when the previous week was positive.
$\varepsilon_{i,w}$ is the error term.

EMPIRICAL RESULTS

Day-to-Day Linkages

Table 3 reports correlation coefficients between the daily U.S. returns for two time periods: the first five years of the sample period, 1982–1986, and the second five-year period, 1987–1991. The crash month of October 1987 is not included in the second period and is analyzed separately. Because of the time difference between the United States and Asia, the United States is lagged by one day while obtaining correlations for Asia.

Three facts are clearly evident from the results: correlations between the emerging markets of Asia and Japan have increased over time for all countries; the linkage between Asian markets and the United States has also increased dramatically over time; and the linkages among the emerging Asian countries have also strengthened. Increase in the correlations suggests that financial markets are getting more globalized and integrated. The integration is happening not only with other Asian countries but also with the rest of the world. Many of these markets have been involved in opening up their markets to foreign investors.

Table 3. Correlations Between the Daily Returns in U.S. Dollars for the 1982–1986/1987–1991[a]

	Malaysia	*Philippines*	*S. Korea*	*Taiwan*	*Thailand*	*U.S.A.*
Asian Markets						
Japan	.17*/.33*	.03/.11*	.07*/.08*	.02/.17*	–.03/.27*	.31*/.22*
Malaysia		.03/.22*	.04*/.12*	.10/.18*	.04/.31*	.20*/.35*
Philippines			–.01/.08*	.02/.12*	.05/.21*	.02/.21*
S. Korea				.01/.15*	–.02/.19*	–.01/.05
Taiwan					.01/.25*	.06/.16*
Thailand						.01/.32*
Latin Markets and the U.S.						
	Brazil	*Chile*	*Mexico*	*U.S.A.*		
Argentina	.11*/.04	.05/.06	.08*/.03	.02/.00		
Brazil		–.05/.13*	–.05/.03	–.03/.00		
Chile			–.01/–.01	.02/.03		
Mexico				.01/.05		

Notes: [a]The whole month of October 1987 is not included in the analysis. The U.S. is lagged by one day when calculating correlations for the Asian countries.
*significant at the 5 percent level.

The scenario in Latin America is a different one. The correlations between the Latin American markets is very low in both periods. The same is true about the correlations between the individual markets and the U.S. market. During the 1980s these markets remained mostly closed to foreign investment and suffered with dramatic economic problems. The move toward opening the economies and easing the access of foreign investors started in the late 1980s or early 1990s, depending on the country, and possibly are not reflected in the data yet.

Volatility of daily dollar-adjusted returns for each quarter as seen in Figures 1 and 2 is much higher in the Latin markets than the Asian markets. Brazil and Argentina continue to show high volatility throughout most of the sample period, while Mexican volatility has decreased over time. The volatility of Asian markets moved in a narrow range before the crash, it peaked for all countries (except South Korea) during the crash quarter, after which volatility moved in a much wider range.

It is clear from Table 4 that the correlations between volatilities is very high between the Asian emerging markets and Japan. The volatility correlations are also high between the Asian markets and the United States. These patterns are especially true in the second sub-period (1987–1991). Mexico has high volatility correlations with the U.S. in both the sub-periods, with values of .60 and .62. The other Latin markets also show increased correlations from one sub-period to the next. The results suggest that the volatility may be much more sensitive to spillovers from

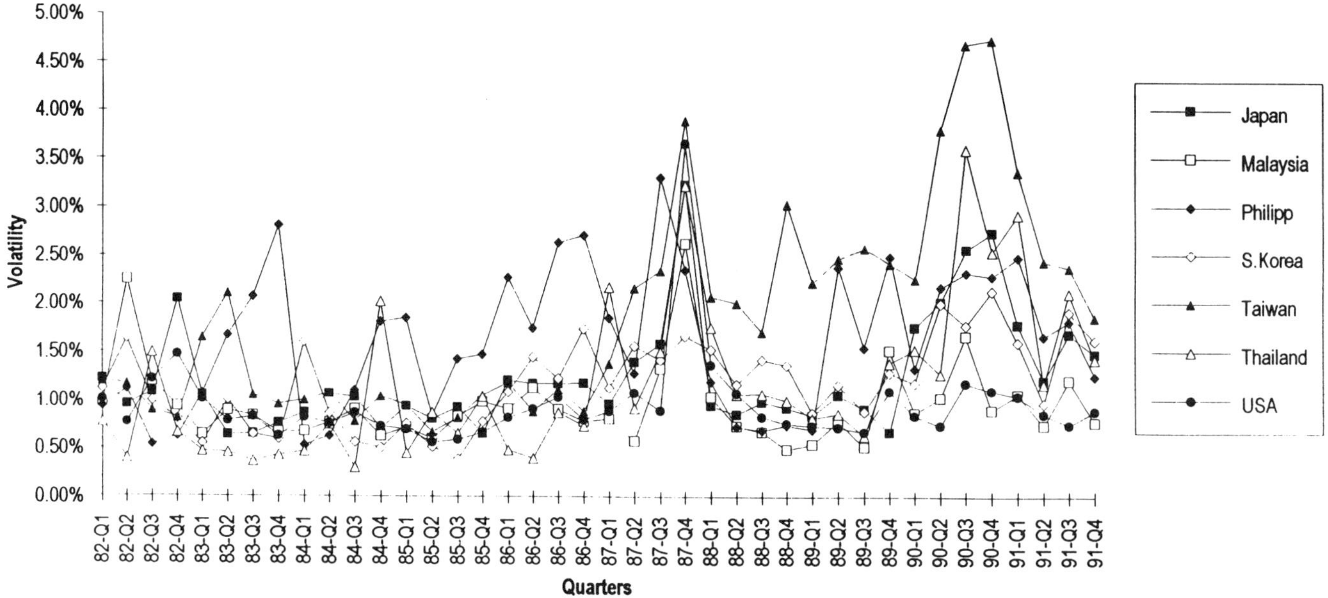

Figure 1. Asian Markets Volatility

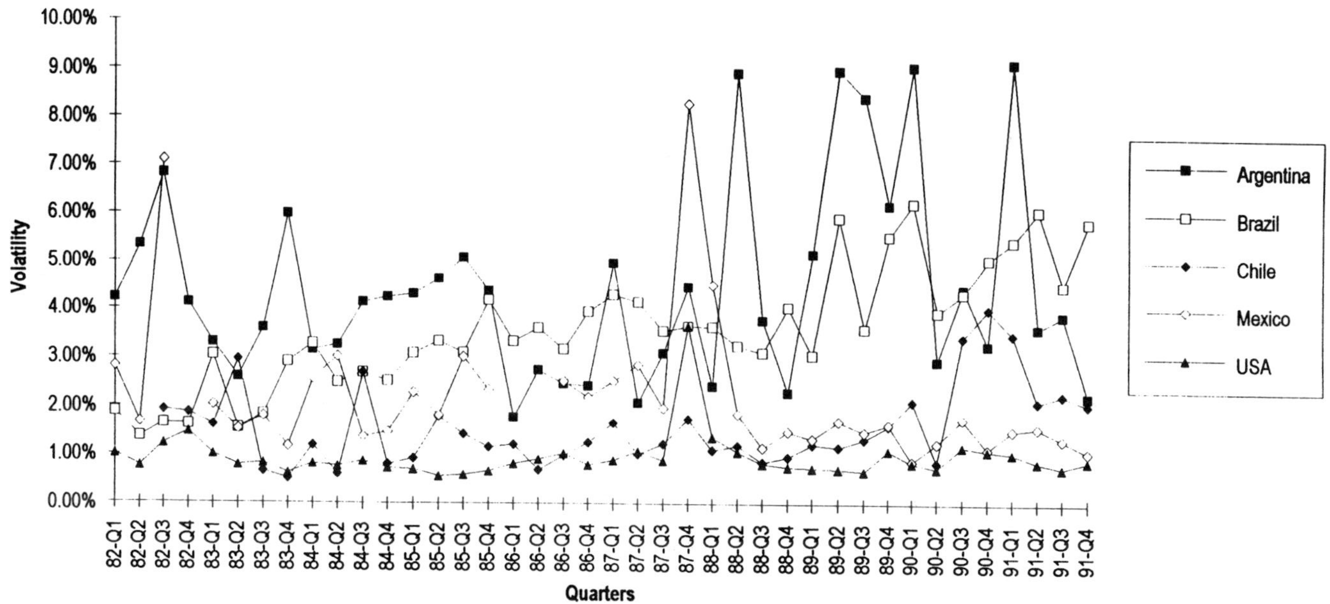

Figure 2. Latin Markets Volatility

Table 4. Correlations Between Volatilities of Returns in U.S. Dollars 1982–1986/1987–1991[a]

	Malaysia	*Philippines*	*S. Korea*	*Taiwan*	*Thailand*	*U.S.A.*
Asian Markets						
Japan	.12/.44	–.22/.46*	.22/.76*	–.26/.79*	–.10/.70*	.79*/.21
Malaysia		–.16/.70*	.49*/.46*	.05/.39	–.14/.67*	.15/.46*
Philippines			.09/.36	.08/.43	–.10/.47*	–.32/.12
S. Korea				.08/.60*	–.19/.57*	.18/.33
Taiwan					–.16/.58*	.03/.21
Thailand						.08/.52*
Latin Markets and the U.S.						
	Brazil	*Chile*	*Mexico*	*U.S.A.*		
Argentina	–.35/.24	.04/.12	.42/–.26	–.03/.15		
Brazil		–.38/.47*	–.20/–.29	–.44*/.01		
Chile			.08/–.27	.26/.36		
Mexico				.60*/.62*		

Notes: [a]The volatility was estimated by the standard deviation of the daily U.S. dollar returns in each quarter in the 1982–1991 period. The whole fourth quarter of 1987 is not included in the analysis due to the October 1987 crash.

*significant at the 5 percent level.

other markets than the average returns. These results are not being driven by the stock markets crash of October 1987. Next, we examine the impact of the crash.

Linkages During the Crash of October 1987

Since the month of October 1987 has been the only month in the last decade when all major stock exchanges moved in the same direction, this period is analyzed separately. It allows an examination of market linkages during a major market event. The results are reported in Table 5. The crash of October 1987 was a very significant event for the whole world and almost all the markets reacted to it. We do not attempt to address the question of what caused the crash. But, during this one-month period the correlations of returns are exceptionally high, most of the correlations more than double at this time. The emerging markets of Asia tend to have stronger linkages with the United States during this period than with Japan or with each other. During the crash period the United States and Japan also have very high return correlations.

The crash was definitely transmitted to almost all the stock exchanges of the world. Taiwan is the only country with a negative correlation with the Tokyo and New York markets during this period. It should be remembered that this was the time when the economy in Taiwan was booming and so was the stock market. On the other hand, the correlation between Chile and the United States was a remark-

Table 5. Correlations Between the Daily Returns in U.S. Dollars during October 1987[a]

	Malaysia	*Philippines*	*S. Korea*	*Taiwan*	*Thailand*	*U.S.A.*
Asian Markets						
Japan	.66*	.53*	.61*	–.01	.14	.75*
Malaysia		.41	.45	–.15	.53*	.73*
Philippines			.45	.43	.53*	.62*
S. Korea				.20	.61*	.66*
Taiwan					–.02	–.04
Thailand						.45
	Brazil	*Chile*	*Mexico*	*U.S.A.*		
Latin Markets and the U.S.						
Argentina	.15	.39	.01	.27		
Brazil		.16	.50*	.24		
Chile			.61*	.89*		
Mexico				.52*		

Notes: [a]The U.S. is lagged by one day in calculating correlations for the Asian countries.
*significant at the 5 percent level.

able 89%. This is the only time during the sample period that the Latin markets showed a high degree of co-movement.

Multivariate Regression Analysis

Table 6 reports results from a multivariate regression that has the dummies representing different anomalies, major market returns (U.S. or Japan), and the corresponding exchange rates (dollar or yen) as independent variables. The returns for each country are first regressed with the dummies, the U.S. returns, and the exchange rate relative to the dollar. For Asian markets the regression is repeated using Japanese returns and the yen exchange rate. The dependent variable is the emerging market daily return in local currency. The purpose is to jointly study the relationship between returns in emerging markets and the returns in developed markets along with the effect of exchange rates and market anomalies. The U.S. returns are lagged by a day when examining Asian countries.

The coefficient on Japanese returns is significant for all five Asian markets. The coefficient on U.S. returns is also significant for most markets. Therefore, in spite of the low correlations found earlier, it appears that after controlling for the anomalies, the U.S. and Japanese markets do seem to be important explanatory variables. For Argentina, Malaysia, and Mexico the U.S. exchange variable is significant. Currencies of Malaysia and Argentina were pegged to the U.S. dollar during most of our sample period. However, the yen is not a significant variable for any of the Asian markets except the Philippines.

Table 6. Regression Analysis for Market Interdependence

Country	*Intercept*	*Monday Dummy*	*January Dummy*	*Turn Dummy*	*Major Market*	*Exchange Rate*	*F (sig.)*
All Markets and the U.S. as the Major Market							
Argentina	1.13*	−1.35*	−.48	−.55*	.08	.06*	9.05*
	(.11)	(.23)	(.32)	(.24)	(.08)	(.02)	(.00)
Brazil	.88*	−1.16*	−.66*	−.15	.18*	.08	7.09*
	(.11)	(.23)	(.33)	(.24)	(.08)	(.04)	(.00)
Chile	.14*	−.09	.19*	.24*	.12*	−.02	10.69*
	(.03)	(.06)	(.09)	(.07)	(.02)	(.02)	(.00)
Malaysia	.06*	−.23*	.14	−.06*	.00	.35*	77.15*
	(.03)	(.05)	(.08)	(.06)	(.05)	(.02)	(.00)
Mexico	.42*	−.69*	.12	−.51*	.24*	.17*	10.21*
	(.09)	(.19)	(.28)	(.21)	(.07)	(.04)	(.00)
Philippines	.09*	−.06	.11	.01	.25*	.06	12.81*
	(.04)	(.09)	(.13)	(.10)	(.03)	(.04)	(.00)
S. Korea	.04	.07	.13	.09	.05*	−.11	1.96
	(.03)	(.07)	(.10)	(.08)	(.03)	(.09)	(.08)
Taiwan	.02	.17	.28	.04	.22*	.08	5.90*
	(.06)	(.12)	(.19)	(.14)	(.04)	(.10)	(.00)
Thailand	.08*	−.02	.03	.04	.32*	−.02	27.32*
	(.04)	(.08)	(.11)	(.09)	(.03)	(.07)	(.00)
Asian Markets and Japan as the Major Market							
Malaysia	.06*	−.23*	.20*	.00	.32*	−.05	60.76*
	(.03)	(.06)	(.08)	(.06)	(.02)	(.03)	(.00)
Philippines	.10*	−.09	.12	.09	.16*	.06*	6.58*
	(.05)	(.10)	(.14)	(.10)	(.03)	(.03)	(.00)
S. Korea	.04	.12	.12	.10	.10*	−.00	4.26*
	(.03)	(.07)	(.11)	(.08)	(.03)	(.04)	(.00)
Taiwan	.01	.18	.28	.00	.26*	.05	8.47*
	(.06)	(.13)	(.20)	(.14)	(.04)	(.06)	(.00)
Thailand	.07	−.04	.01	.06	.28*	−.02	21.43*
	(.04)	(.08)	(.12)	(.09)	(.03)	(.04)	(.00)

Anomalies and Seasonalities

Next, we examine several previously identified anomalies, beginning with the day-of-the-week effect, in order to study patterns and linkages between markets. The U.S. markets clearly have negative Monday returns as seen in Table 7. In most

Table 7. Day-of-the-Week Mean Returns (Standard Deviations) January 1982–December 1991

Country	*Monday*	*Tuesday*	*Wednesday*	*Thursday*	*Friday*	*All Days*
Asian Markets						
Malaysia	–.22	–.03	.13	.09	.17	.04
	(1.38)	(1.12)	(.90)	(.93)	(.98)	(1.08)
Philippines	–.01	.01	.04	.08	.21	.07
	(2.02)	(1.71)	(1.93)	(1.79)	(1.57)	(1.81)
S. Korea	.14	.06	.10	.04	.11	.09
	(1.77)	(1.24)	(1.10)	(1.11)	(1.18)	(1.30)
Taiwan	.13	.22	.03	.09	.04	.10
	(3.06)	(2.07)	(2.00)	(1.97)	(1.87)	(2.22)
Thailand	.05	–.05	.15	.03	.24	.09
	(1.80)	(1.54)	(1.37)	(1.44)	(1.16)	(1.47)
Japan	–.09	–.01	.17	.14	.06	.06
	(1.49)	(1.60)	(1.26)	(1.27)	(1.34)	(1.40)
Latin Markets and the U.S.						
Argentina	–2.14	.29	1.49	1.02	.38	.27
	(6.20)	(4.51)	(4.72)	(4.04)	(4.41)	(4.95)
Brazil	–1.50	.19	.59	.80	.38	.13
	(4.19)	(3.89)	(3.55)	(3.55)	(3.45)	(3.81)
Chile	–.21	.24	.10	.24	.27	.13
	(2.71)	(1.77)	(1.64)	(1.32)	(1.23)	(1.80)
Mexico	–.23	–.17	.31	.32	.38	.13
	(3.02)	(2.51)	(2.68)	(2.70)	(2.49)	(2.70)
U.S.A.	–.04	.09	.11	.04	.07	.06
	(1.43)	(.97)	(.95)	(.97)	(1.02)	(1.08)

Asian markets there appears to be a Monday and a Tuesday effect. This seems consistent with the hypothesis that the Asian markets have their own weekend effect plus they are influenced by what happens in New York. Additionally, all countries but Japan, have the highest volatility on Monday. The strongest Monday effect is in Malaysia. The correlation analysis discussed above also showed that Malaysia, in general, has a very high correlation with the United States. Roll (1992) attributes this to the exchange rate policy used by Malaysia which pegs the ringit to the U.S. dollar.

All Latin American countries have their lowest average daily returns on Monday. Given the low correlations between these markets and the U.S. market it is possible that each one of these countries have their own Monday effects without a strong

Table 8. Regression Model for the Day-of-the-Week Effect with Kruskal-Wallis Statistics Coefficient with Standard Error

Country	α_1 *Monday*	a_2 *Tuesday*	α_3 *Wednesday*	α_4 *Thursday*	α_5 *Friday*	*F (signif)*	*K-W (Chi^2)*
Asian Markets							
Japan	–.09	.08	.26*	.24*	.16	2.50*	11.76*
	(.07)	(.10)	(.10)	(.10)	(.10)	(.04)	(.02)
Malaysia	–.22*	.20*	.35*	.32*	.39*	8.80*	41.25*
	(.06)	(.08)	(.08)	(.08)	(.08)	(.00)	(.00)
Philippines	–.01	.01	.04	.09	.21**	.95	11.62*
	(.09)	(.13)	(.13)	(.13)	(.13)	(.43)	(.02)
S. Korea	.14*	–.07	–.04	–.10	–.03	.37	4.11
	(.07)	(.09)	(.09)	(.09)	(.09)	(.83)	(.39)
Taiwan	.13	.09	–.10	–.04	–.09	.49	2.26
	(.11)	(.16)	(.16)	(.16)	(.16)	(.74)	(.69)
Thailand	.05	–.10	.11	–.02	.20*	2.50*	19.88*
	(.08)	(.11)	(.10)	(.10)	(.10)	(.04)	(.00)
Latin Markets and the U.S.							
Argentina	–2.14*	2.44*	3.64*	3.17*	2.52*	33.30*	146.80*
	(.25)	(.35)	(.34)	(.34)	(.34)	(.00)	(.00)
Brazil	–1.50*	1.69*	2.09*	2.30*	1.88*	24.43*	88.34*
	(.19)	(.26)	(.26)	(.26)	(.26)	(.00)	(.00)
Chile	–.22*	.46*	.32*	.45*	.48*	4.79*	36.45*
	(.09)	(.13)	(.13)	(.13)	(.13)	(.00)	(.00)
Mexico	–.23	.07	.55*	.56*	.62*	4.65*	23.19*
	(.14)	(.20)	(.19)	(.20)	(.20)	(.00)	(.00)
U.S.A.	–.04	.14*	.16*	.09	.11	1.49	1.75
	(.05)	(.07)	(.07)	(.07)	(.07)	(.20)	(.78)

Note: *significant at the 5 percent level.

influence from the United States. All countries present the highest volatility on Monday.

The regression results are presented in Table 8 along with a Kruskal-Wallis non-parametric test for the difference between the days-of-the-week returns. It is important to note that the Kruskal-Wallis test assumes independence among the observations. The only significant models are those for Malaysia, Thailand, Japan, Argentina, Brazil, Chile, and Mexico. In addition, the Kruskal-Wallis test indicates that besides these seven countries, there is a day-of-the-week effect in the Philippines also. Although the average daily returns for each day of the week in Table 7 indicated a pervasive Monday effect for Latin America and a Tuesday effect for

Table 9. Average Daily Returns and Standard Deviation by Month 1982–1991

Country	*Jan*	*Feb*	*Mar*	*Apr*	*May*	*Jun*	*Jul*	*Aug*	*Sep*	*Oct*	*Nov*	*Dec*	*All*
Asian Markets													
Malaysia	.20	.11	.04	.01	.18	.04	.08	–.03	–.20	–.13	–.05	.11	.04
	.92	.85	.80	.86	1.41	.96	.82	1.45	.77	1.70	.77	.98	1.08
Philippines	.23	.21	.17	.03	–.01	.18	.22	–.17	–.11	–.06	.08	.03	.07
	1.54	1.64	1.57	1.54	1.26	1.89	2.03	1.60	2.26	2.53	1.61	1.72	1.81
S. Korea	.18	.17	.27	–.14	.13	.02	.22	–.12	–.06	.12	.13	.18	.09
	1.33	1.15	1.21	1.44	1.28	1.29	1.29	1.34	1.06	1.49	1.22	1.38	1.30
Taiwan	.38	.36	.06	.45	–.02	–.18	.20	.00	.22	–.08	.14	–.20	.10
	2.00	1.89	1.84	1.95	2.31	2.20	2.23	2.39	2.10	2.50	2.42	2.58	2.22
Thailand	.13	.02	.18	.27	.14	.16	.15	.07	–.03	–.13	–.03	.14	.09
	1.23	2.02	1.13	.97	.81	.87	1.18	2.10	1.40	1.89	1.68	1.54	1.47
Japan	.11	.08	.11	.17	–.09	–.09	.06	–.01	–.02	.14	.11	.13	.06
	1.14	1.17	1.30	1.42	1.08	1.06	1.28	1.57	1.28	2.07	1.26	1.43	1.40
Latin Markets and U.S.													
Argentina	–.14	.38	.51	.15	.46	.68	.08	1.12	.46	–.47	–.16	.09	.27
	5.36	5.25	5.39	4.15	4.34	6.84	5.85	4.31	4.35	4.82	3.23	4.75	4.95
Brazil	–.80	.38	.38	.75	.12	–.21	.16	–.11	–.06	.04	–.12	.41	.13
	8.94	4.14	3.30	3.60	4.13	3.70	3.25	3.20	3.51	3.83	4.62	4.17	3.81
Chile	.33	.44	.17	–.03	.06	.09	.18	.11	.16	–.04	–.05	.18	.13
	2.18	1.68	1.50	2.08	.91	1.46	2.13	1.33	2.15	1.75	2.02	1.92	1.80
Mexico	.34	.16	.14	.09	.33	.26	.29	–.04	.32	–.18	–.28	.11	.13
	2.50	2.57	2.48	2.38	1.81	1.91	2.00	3.80	1.85	3.10	4.51	2.21	2.70
U.S.A.	.13	.07	.07	.08	.04	.04	.04	.10	–.07	.00	.03	.14	.06
	1.14	.89	.81	.95	.75	.83	.77	1.06	.88	2.07	1.09	.90	1.08

Asia, the significance of the coefficients in the regression analysis shows mixed results for the Monday effect in Asia.

Table 9 shows the average daily returns for each month for each country. In general, the first few months of the year present a higher average return than the last few months of the year. However, there is no clear January effect. During the period 1982–1991 the highest average daily returns are during the month of December. Table 10 indicates that there is no significant month-of-the-year effect in our sample.

Table 11 presents the average daily returns for the turn-of-the-month days and the remaining days of the month. The results for the regression model specified by equation (4) indicates that only Chile and the United States have a significant turn-of-the-month effect at the 5% level. There is no evidence for the turn-of-the-

Table 10. Regression Model for Month-of-the-Year Daily Returns with Kruskal-Wallis Statistics Coefficients with Standard Errors

Country	*Jan*	*Feb*	*Mar*	*Apr*	*May*	*Jun*	*Jul*	*Aug*	*Sep*	*Oct*	*Nov*	*Dec*	*F/Sig*	*KW Sig*
Asian Markets														
Japan	.11	–.03	.00	.06	–.20	–.20	–.05	–.12	–.13	.03	.00	.03	.73	12.56
	(.11)	(.16)	(.15)	(.15)	(.16)	(.15)	(.15)	(.15)	(.16)	(.15)	(.16)	(.16)	(.71)	(.32)
Malaysia	.20*	–.09	–.16	–.12	–.02	–.16	–.12	–.23*	–.40*	–.33*	–.25*	–.09	2.07*	34.19*
	(.08)	(.12)	(.11)	(.11)	(.12)	(.12)	(.12)	(.12)	(.12)	(.12)	(.12)	(.12)	(.02)	(.00)
Philippines	.23	.06	–.05	–.20	–.23	–.05	.00	–.40*	–.33	–.29	–.15	–.20	1.18	15.07
	(.14)	(.20)	(.19)	(.19)	(.20)	(.19)	(.19)	(.19)	(.19)	(.19)	(.21)	(.20)	(.29)	(.18)
S. Korea	.18	–.15	.08	–.33*	–.05	–.17	.04	–.30*	–.24	–.06	–.05	–.00	2.02*	28.40*
	(.10)	(.14)	(.14)	(.14)	(.14)	(.14)	(.14)	(.14)	(.14)	(.14)	(.14)	(.10)	(.02)	(.00)
Taiwan	.38*	–.02	–.32	.07	–.41	–.57*	–.19	–.38	–.16	–.46	–.24	–.58*	1.64	15.85
	(.18)	(.26)	(.24)	.(25)	(.24)	(.25)	(.25)	(.24)	(.25)	(.25)	(.26)	(.25)	(.08)	(.15)
Thailand	.13	–.11	.05	.13	.01	.03	.02	–.06	–.16	–.26	–.16	.01	.98	9.33
	(.11)	(.17)	(.15)	(.16)	(.17)	(.16)	(.16)	(.15)	(.16)	(.16)	(.16)	.(17)	(.46)	(.59)
Latin Markets and U.S.														
Argentina	–.14	.52	.64	.28	.60	.81	.22	1.25*	.60	–.33	–.02	.22	1.29	25.35*
	(.38)	(.54)	(.52)	(.53)	(.54)	(.56)	(.53)	(.53)	(.54)	(.54)	(.54)	(.56)	(.23)	(.01)
Brazil	–.80*	1.17*	1.17*	1.54*	.92*	.58	.96*	.68	.74	.84	.68	1.21*	1.32	13.45
	(.34)	(.50)	(.48)	(.48)	(.47)	(.48)	(.46)	(.46)	(.48)	(.47)	(.50)	(.47)	(.21)	(.26)
Chile	.33*	.12	–.16	–.35	–.27	–.24	–.14	–.21	–.17	–.36	–.38	–.15	1.08	27.32*
	(.15)	(.20)	(.20)	(.20)	(.21)	(.21)	(.20)	(.20)	(.21)	(.20)	(.20)	(.20)	(.37)	(.00)
Mexico	.34	–.18	–.20	–.25	.01	–.08	–.05	–.38	–.02	–.52	–.62	–.23	.85	5.28
	(.22)	(.31)	(.30)	(.30)	(.31)	(.30)	(.29)	(.29)	(.31)	(.30)	(.33)	(.32)	(.58)	(.92)

Note: *significant at the 5 percent level.

month effect in the remaining emerging markets. Table 12 presents the average returns for the Mondays that followed weeks with negative and positive returns. When there was a negative return on the previous week the next Monday average return was also negative for all countries except Chile and the United States. When the previous week presented a positive return, the next Monday also presents a positive return for the Asian markets. There is a twist-of-the-Monday effect in most countries in the sample. In general, an examination of the anomalies does not reveal any clear pattern that would suggest strong links among the emerging stock markets of Asia and Latin America and the U.S. and Japanese markets.

Table 11. Average Daily Return for the Turn-of-the-Month Days and Other Days of the Month and Regression Analysis for the Turn-of-the-Month Effect

	Statistics Average (Std. Dev.)		*Regression Analysis Coefficient (St. Error)*		
Country	*Other Days*	*Turn of the Month Days*	*Other Days*	*Turn of the Month Days*	*F (signif.)*
Asian Markets					
Japan	.06	.06	.06	.01	.01
	(1.36)	(1.58)	(.03)	(.08)	(.94)
Malaysia	.04	.01	.04	–.03	.16
	(1.11)	(.89)	(.03)	(.07)	(.69)
Philippines	.07	.03	.07	–.05	.19
	(1.77)	(2.00)	(–.05)	(.11)	(.67)
S. Korea	.07	.19	.07*	.12	2.39
	(1.27)	(1.43)	(.03)	(.08)	(.12)
Taiwan	.09	.15	.09	.06	.17
	(2.18)	(2.41)	(.06)	(.14)	(.68)
Thailand	.08	.14	.08*	.06	.48
	(1.46)	(1.51)	(.04)	(.09)	(.49)
Latin Markets and the U.S.					
Argentina	.36	–.14	.36*	–.50	2.95
	(4.98)	(4.78)	(.12)	(.29)	(.09)
Brazil	.10	–.02	.10	–.12	.21
	(4.50)	(3.75)	(.10)	(.26)	(.64)
Chile	.35	.09	.09*	.25*	5.43*
	(1.74)	(1.81)	(.04)	(.11)	(.02)
Mexico	.06	.15	.15*	–.08	.25
	(2.52)	(2.73)	(.07)	(.17)	(.62)
U.S.A.	.21	.02	.02	.18*	9.94*
	(.93)	(1.10)	(.02)	(.06)	(.00)

Table 12. Twist-of-the-Monday Effect Regression Analysis.
Average Monday Returns When the Previous Week Return was Positive or Negative

	Monday Average (St. Dev.)		*Regression Analysis—Coefficient (Std Error)*		
Country	*When Previous Week Positive*	*When Previous Week Negative*	*Intercept (Previous Week Negative)*	*Dummy for Positive Previous Week*	*F (signif.)*
Asian Markets					
Japan	.20	−.51	−.51*	.71*	19.82*
	(1.16)	(1.82)	(.12)	(.16)	(.00)
Malaysia	.03	−.51	−.51*	.54*	12.96*
	(1.42)	(1.31)	(.11)	(.15)	(.00)
Philippines	.30	−.34	−.33*	.63*	8.42*
	(2.07)	(1.97)	(.15)	(.22)	(.00)
S. Korea	.40	−.13	−.12	.52*	7.67*
	(1.77)	(1.80)	(.13)	(.19)	(.01)
Taiwan	.38	−.13	−.13	.51	2.25
	(2.88)	(3.36)	(.25)	(.34)	(.13)
Thailand	.30	−.22	−.22	.52*	6.69*
	(1.53)	(2.16)	(.16)	(.20)	(.01)
Latin Markets and the U.S.					
Argentina	−1.79	−2.88	−2.88*	1.09	2.55
	(6.27)	(6.21)	(.50)	(.68)	(.11)
Brazil	−.70	−2.43	−2.43*	1.73*	16.23
	(3.85)	(4.17)	(.31)	(.43)	(.00)
Chile	−.40	.01	.01	−.41	2.07
	(2.63)	(2.40)	(.22)	(.28)	(.15)
Mexico	.31	−.70	−.70*	1.02*	8.77*
	(2.33)	(3.80)	(.25)	(.34)	(.00)
U.S.A.	−.23	.10	−.23*	.34*	6.18*
	(1.92)	(.93)	(.10)	(.14)	(.01)

SUMMARY AND CONCLUSIONS

The degree of linkage between the world's stock exchanges is an important issue for both investors and researchers. This study demonstrates that the tendency toward day-to-day linkages between Asian emerging markets and the U.S. markets, between Japan and the United States, and between the emerging Asian markets have all increased over time. During the crash period, the linkages between the various markets were very pronounced. The correlations are much higher for volatility of returns than for the mean of returns. The Latin American markets present a lower level of integration relative to the emerging Asian markets.

A multivariate regression that includes dummies for all the tested anomalies indicates that the U.S. and Japanese market returns are significant explanatory variables explaining local currency returns in emerging markets. However, the exchange rate variable is not significant.

Four anomalies were examined. The average daily returns show that to some extent the Asian markets have a weekend effect of their own and they also have a "Tuesday effect" which may be driven by the market performance in New York on Monday. In Latin America there appears to be a Monday effect in all four countries. These effects were found significant in Japan, the Philippines, Thailand, and in all Latin countries. Surprisingly the January effect is not significant in the United States anymore. There is no month-of-the-year effect or January effect in most markets. The small number of monthly observations may have hampered our results. There is no turn-of-the-month effect either. Only Chile and the United States present this anomaly. The twist-of-the-Monday effect is found in many countries.

Connolly (1989) presents several limitations to the traditional statistical tests for the anomalies. We recognize these limitations and the possible violation of the assumptions. By the same token, future research should examine the correlation structure of both returns and volatility more carefully to test for segmentation or integration.

ACKNOWLEDGMENTS

The authors thank Elizabeth Sandoval and Michael Vechery for the data collection, the Taiwan, Seoul, and Mexico Stock Exchanges, and Professors Leonardo Hernandez and Eduardo Walker for the Chilean data.

REFERENCES

Aggarwal, R., and P. Rivoli. 1989. "Seasonal and Day-of-the-Week Effects in Four Emerging Stock Markets." *The Financial Review* 24(4): 541–550.

Aggarwal, R., R. Leal, and L. Hernandez. 1993. "The Aftermarket Performance of Initial Public Offerings in Latin America." *Financial Management* (Spring): 42–53.

Agrawal, A., and K. Tandon. 1994. "Anomalies or Illusions? Evidence from Stock Markets in Eighteen Countries." *Journal of International Money and Finance* 13(1): 83–106.

Asian Wall Street Journal. 1992. October 12 and November 9.

Bennett, P., and J. Kelleher. 1988. "The International Transmission of Stock Price Disruption in October 1987." *Federal Reserve Bank of New York Quarterly Review* 13(2): 17–33.

Bertero, F., and C. Mayer. 1989. "Structure and Performance: Global Interdependence of Stock Markets Around the Crash of October 1987." Discussion Paper No. 30, London, Centre for Economic Policy.

Business Week. 1992. December 28.

Cadsby, C.B., and M. Ratner. 1992. "Turn-of-month and Pre-holiday Effects on Stock Returns: Some International Evidence." *Journal of Banking and Finance* 16: 497–509.

Campbell, J.Y., and Y. Hamao. 1992. "Predictable Stock Returns in the United States and Japan: A Study of Long-Term Capital Market Integration." *Journal of Finance* 47(1) 43–69.

Chan, K.C., B.E. Gup, and M.-S. Pan. 1992. "An Empirical Analysis of Stock Prices in Major Asian Markets and the United States." *Financial Review* 27(2): 289–307.

Cheung, Y.-L. 1993. "A Note on the Stability of the Intertemporal Relationships Between the Asian-Pacific Equity Markets and the Developed Markets: A Non-Parametric Approach." *Journal of Business Finance and Accounting* 20(2): 229–236.

Dawson, S.M. 1987. "Secondary Stock Market Performance of Initial Public Offers, Hong Kong, Singapore, and Malaysia: 1978–1984." *Journal of Business Finance and Accounting* (Spring): 55–76.

Divecha, A.B., J. Drach, and D. Stefek. 1992. "Emerging Markets: A Quantitative Perspective." *Journal of Portfolio Management* (Fall): 41–50.

Dwyer, G.P., and R.W. Hafer. 1988. "Are International Stock Markets Linked?" *Federal Reserve Bank of St. Louis Review* (November/December): 3–14.

Errunza, V., and P. Padmanabhan. 1988. "Further Evidence on the Benefits of Portfolio Investments in Emerging Markets." *Financial Analysts Journal* 44(4): 76–78.

Errunza, V., and E. Losq. 1987. "How Risky are Emerging Markets?" *Journal of Portfolio Management* 14(1): 62–67.

Errunza, V., E. Losq, and P. Padmanabhan. 1992. "Test of Integration, Mild-Segmentation and Segmentation Hypothesis." *Journal of Banking and Finance* 16(5): 949–972.

Eun, C.S., and S. Shim. 1989. "International Transmission of Stock Market Movements." *Journal of Financial and Quantitative Analysis* 24(2): 241–256.

Gill, D., and P. Tropper. 1988. "Emerging Stock Markets in Developing Countries." *Finance & Development* 25(4): 28–31.

Gultekin, M.N., and B. Gultekin. 1983. "Stock Market Seasonality: International Evidence." *Journal of Financial Economics* 12: 469–481.

Harvey, C.R. 1993. "Predictable Risk and Returns in Emerging Markets." Working Paper, Duke University, June.

Hilliard, J.E. 1979. "The Relationship Between Equity Indices on World Exchanges." *Journal of Finance* 34(1): 103–114.

Ho, Y.K. 1990. "Stock Return Seasonality in Asia Pacific Markets." *Journal of International Financial Management and Accounting* 2: 47–77.

Jacobs, B.I., and K.N. Levy. 1988. "Calendar Anomalies: Abnormal Returns at Calendar Turning Points." *Financial Analysts Journal* (November/December): 28–39.

Jaffe, J., and R. Westerfield. 1985. "Patterns in Japanese Common Stock Returns: Day of the Week and Turn of the Year Effects." *Journal of Financial and Quantitative Analysis* 20(2): 261–271.

———. 1989. "Is There a Monthly Effect in Stock Market Returns? Evidence from Foreign Countries." *Journal of Banking and Finance* 13: 237–244.

Jaffe, J., R. Westerfield, and C. Ma. 1989. "A Twist on the Monday Effect in Stock Prices: Evidence from the U.S. and Foreign Stock Markets." *Journal of Banking and Finance* 13: 641–650.

Krinsky, I., J.B. Kim, and J. Lee. 1992. "Motives for Going Public and Underpricing." Working Paper, McMaster University.

King, M., and S. Wadhwani. 1990. "Transmission of Volatility Between Stock Markets." *Review of Financial Studies* 3(1): 5–33.

Lakonishok, J., and S. Smidt. 1988. "Are Seasonal Anomalies Real? A Ninety-Year Perspective." *Review of Financial Studies* 1(4): 403–425.

Leal, R. 1992. "Less Competitive Stock Markets and the Validity of IPOs' Ex Ante Uncertainty Measures." Working Paper, Georgetown University.

Lee, I. 1992. "Stock Market Seasonality: Some Evidence from the Pacific-Basin Countries." *Journal of Business Finance & Accounting* 19(2): 199–211.

Lessard, D.R. 1973. "International Portfolio Diversification: A Multivariate Analysis for a Group of Latin American Countries." *Journal of Finance* 28: 619–633.

Meric, I., and G. Meric. 1989. "Potential Gains from International Portfolio Diversification and Inter-temporal Stability and Seasonality in International Stock Market Relationships." *Journal of Banking and Finance* 13: 627–640.

Parhizgari, A.M., K. Dandapani, and A.K. Bhattacharya. 1988. "Global Market Place and Causality." Working Paper, Florida International University.

Roll, R. 1989. "Price Volatility, International Markets Links, and Their Implications for Regulatory Policies." *Journal of Financial Services Research* 3: 113–147.

———. 1992. "Industrial Structure and the Comparative Behavior of International Stock Market Indices." *The Journal of Finance* 47(1): 3–42.

Thaler, R.H. 1987a. "Seasonal Movements in Securities Prices II: Weekend, Holiday, Turn-of-the-Month, and Intraday Effects." *Journal of Economic Perspectives* 1(2): 169–177.

———. 1987b. "Anomalies—The January Effect." *Journal of Economic Perspectives* 1(2): 197–201.

Wall Street Journal. 1994. "Global Diversification Has Its Downside And May Not Be the Strongest Safety Net." April 14, C1.

PACIFIC BASIN STOCK MARKET LINKAGES

Bala Arshanapalli and John Doukas

ABSTRACT

This paper documents lack of cointegrating structure (vector) among the three major Asian stock exchanges of Japan, Hong Kong, and Singapore using Johansen's (1991) multivariate cointegration testing procedure. The evidence strongly suggests that the three stock markets do not share a common equilibrium relationship and therefore stock market innovations are country-specific without spillover effects over the examination period of this study.

INTRODUCTION

The extent of international capital market linkages has received increasing attention in recent years.[1] However, most of the focus has centered on Japan's integration with the major world stock markets (i.e., U.S. France, Germany, and U.K.). The capital market interaction among Asian stock markets has received far less attention despite their rapidly growing importance.[2] The total Asian capitalization accounts for roughly 47% of the world market capitalization. In this study, we examine the relations among security prices across three major Asian stock markets: Japan,

Research in International Business and Finance, Supplement 1, pages 101–109.

ISBN: 0-7623-0110-4

Hong Kong, and Singapore. We are interested in the extent to which security price innovations in one market influence the opening prices in the next market to trade, using daily open and close prices for the 1991–1992 period.

We use Johansen's (1991) likelihood method for the analysis of co-integration to investigate the extent of integration and asset price interactions among the three Asian equity markets. This procedure allows for a linear determination trend in the data. The theory of cointegration, originally developed by Engle and Granger (1987), implies that a set of asset price series (variables) even when the individual asset series are nonstationary ($I(1)$), they never drift far apart. That is, a linear combination of two or more asset price series is stationary (i.e., $I(0)$). Therefore, the cointegration methodology is used to study how Japan is related to the other two major Asian stock markets. Under the cointegration hypothesis, stock price indexes have a tendency to trend together in the long run even though they may exhibit short-run deviations from this common equilibrium path. Evidence of cointegration among the three major Asian stock markets would imply that there is an underlying cointegrating structure that prohibits any one market to drift too far out from this common equilibrium path for an extended period of time. Adjustments of these short-run deviations and the influence of one market on another are captured through the error correction modeling of asset price changes implied by cointegration. Absence of cointegration would imply lack of capital market integration among the three Asian stock markets. Therefore, this would also suggest that stock market innovations in one market have no impact on the performance of another market(s). Hence, asset price changes cannot be described through an error correction model.

Unlike earlier studies, we use open and close stock market indexes. This enables us to analyze the spillover effects of stock price innovations in one market on the opening price in another market, an issue that has not been empirically addressed while little theoretical work exists.

The remainder of the paper is organized as follows. The next section briefly introduces the concept of cointegration and methodology following Johansen's (1991) work. The next section presents the main results of this study while concluding remarks are provided in the last section.

METHODOLOGY

Testing for stock market linkages using cointegration methodology involves the following two steps. First, it is required to identify the order of integration of each time series (i.e., test for the presence of unit roots in each of the stock market index series). The standard procedure is to apply the Augmented Dickey-Fuller (ADF) tests (see Dickey and Fuller 1979, 1981).[3] Once a common order of integration has been identified in the time series (i.e., $I(1)$), the next step involves Johansen's (1991) multivariate cointegration test. Johansen's test provides maximum likelihood estimates of the cointegration vectors in a model and spans space that encompasses the

Engle and Granger (1987) tests. Johansen's new procedure of deriving the maximum likelihood estimators and likelihood ratio tests for cointegration in Gaussian vector autoregressive models allows for a linear deterministic trend which accordingly ". . . plays a crucial role in the interpretation of the model, as well as in the statistical and the probabilistic analysis" (see Johansen 1991, pp. 1551).[4]

Johansen's procedure can be illustrated with the following general VAR model with Gaussian errors expressed in the error correction form.

$$\Delta X_t = \sum_{i=1}^{p-1} \Gamma_i \Delta X_{t-i} + \Pi X_{t-p} + \mu + \varepsilon_t \quad (t = 1, \ldots, T) \tag{1}$$

where X is an $n \times 1$ vector of stochastic variables, p is the number of lags and ε_t is an independently identically distributed n dimensional vector with zero mean and variance matrix Ω. The first k data points $X_{1-p}, \ldots, X_0$ are considered fixed and the likelihood function is estimated for their given values. The parameters $\Gamma_i, \ldots, \Gamma_{p-1,}\mu$ and Ω are assumed to vary without restrictions, and the hypotheses of interest are formulated as restrictions, on Π. The long-run or cointegrating matrix is given by

$$\Pi = (I - \Pi_1 - \Pi_2 - \ldots - \Pi_p) \tag{2}$$

where Π is an nxn matrix. The number of distinct cointegrating vectors, k, that exist among the X_t variables, will be given by the rank of Π. That is, the rank of Π, k, is the number of linearly independent and stationary linear combinations of X_t that can be found. The objective of tests for cointegration is to test for the rank of Π by testing whether the eigenvalues of $\hat{\Pi}$ are significantly different from zero.[5] Therefore, the main hypothesis considered here is the hypothesis of k cointegration vectors

$$H\text{:} \;\; \Pi = \alpha\beta' \tag{3}$$

where α and β are $n \times k$ matrixes. We can further investigate the relation between the constant term, μ, and the reduced rank matrix Π. If Π is restricted as in equation (3) and $\mu \neq 0$ the nonstationary process X_t has linear trends with coefficients which are functions of μ only through $\alpha\,'\!\perp\!\mu$, where $\alpha\perp$ is a $n \times (n-k)$ matrix of vectors chosen orthogonal to α. Hence, the hypothesis $\mu = \alpha\beta'_{0,}$ or $\alpha'\!\perp\!\mu = 0$, is the hypothesis about the absence of a linear trend in the process.

Johansen has developed the trace test to determine the number of cointegrating vectors. The null hypothesis is that there are k or less cointegrating vectors. The critical values for the trace test are reported in Johansen and Juselius (1990). Letting N denote the number of time periods available in the data, the trace test is estimated as

$$\text{trace test:} \;\; -N \sum_{i=k+1}^{n} \ln\,(1 - \rho_i^2) \tag{4}$$

where ρ's are the canonical correlations ($\rho_1^2 > \rho_2^2 > \ldots > \rho_n^2$) between two sets of residual vectors, R_{0t} and R_{1t}, obtained from

$$\Delta X_t = \sum_{i=1}^{p-1} \Gamma_{0i} \Delta X_{t-i} + R_{0t} \tag{5}$$

$$X_t = \sum_{i=1}^{p-1} \Gamma_{1i} \Delta X_{t-i} + R_{1t} \tag{6}$$

where X_t is the n-vector of variables, Γ_i are matrices of coefficient estimates (i.e., $\Gamma_i = (-\mathrm{I} - \Pi_1 - \ldots - \Pi_i)$, $(i = 1, \ldots, p-1)$). Cointegration among a set of variables holds if k is greater than or equal to one.

Since it is possible to have n–1 cointegrating vectors in a system of a variables and n-k stochastic trends, it is believed that it is better to have many rather than few cointegrating vectors in a given system of variables. This is because cointegrating vectors act as constraints that an economic system imposes on the movement of the variables in the system in the long run. Hence, the greater the presence of cointegrating vectors in a system, the more stable the system. The fewer the number of cointegrating vectors, the less constrained is the long-run relationship. Therefore, *ceteris paribus*, it seems desirable to have many cointegrating vectors since the long-run equilibrium relationship becomes more meaningful.[6]

EMPIRICAL EVIDENCE

Before testing for cointegration, nonstationarity (i.e., $I(1)$) for each individual time series must be established. Engle and Granger (1987) suggest a number of alternative tests for identifying the time series order of integration. The Augmented Dickey-Fuller (ADF) test is used to examine the nature of stationarity of the three Asian stock price indexes. The null hypothesis to be tested is that the index series are nonstationary (i.e., index series have a unit root) against the alternative that they are stationary (i.e., $I(0)$). The results of the unit-root tests are reported in Table 1. The critical values of the ADF test statistics are reported in Engle and Yoo (1987). The results listed in Table 1, show that the null hypothesis of nonstationarity cannot be rejected for all three stock exchange index series. Hence, these results appear to be consistent with the hypothesis that these three national stock index series are uniformly integrated. The order of integration is one, $I(1)$. It should be noted, however, that the nonstationarity hypothesis (i.e., presence of a unit root), in first differences of the stock price index series, is flatly rejected.

Because all three stock price index series were found to be integrated with the same order, cointegration tests can be performed. The results of multivariate cointegration tests for the set of the three Asian stock exchanges are reported in

Table 1. Tests for Unit Roots in Stock Index Series: October 25, 1991–November 24, 1992

Country	*Exchange Index*	*ADF Open*	*ADF Close*
Hong Kong	SEHK All Ordinaries	–0.190	0.045
Japan	Tokyo Stock Price Index (TOPIX)	–1.529	–1.854
Singapore	SES All Share Singapore	–0.558	–0.848

Notes: ADF represents the augmente d Dickey-Fuller test. The ADF test is based on the following regression:

$$Dx_t = a_0 + a_1 X_{t-1} + \sum_{i=1}^{m} b_i Dx_{t-i} + v_t$$

where x_t denotes the stock market index and v_t the error term. In all regressions four (4) lags are used ($m = 4$) since white noise errors, *vt*, are obtained at that lag length. Different lag lengths were used in order to test the robustness of our results. The results remained essentially unchanged.

Table 2. These tests are based on Johansen's (1991) proposed maximum likelihood technique that provides estimates of the cointegrating vectors (k) among a set of variables and offers the test statistics for a number of such cointegrating vectors. The order of autoregressive process used here, p, is four. The use of a higher autoregressive process had no essential impact on the results. Table 2 reports the trace test statistics. According to the trace test, the null hypothesis is that the number of cointegrating vectors is less than or equal to k where k is 0, 1, and 2. In each case the null hypothesis is tested against the general alternative.

Panel A of Table 2 contains the estimated trace test statistic values for the stock market index series of Japan, Hong Kong, and Singapore. It is important to note that for Japan we use the previous day's close index (t–1) while for the other two markets we use today's open index (t). This is motivated mainly because Japan's market is the largest compared to the other two Asian markets and, therefore, interested in the extent to which security price innovations in Tokyo are linked with the opening prices in the next market to trade in the two Asian stock exchanges. The system of the three Asian stock exchanges does not appear to be cointegrated. The null hypothesis that the cointegrating vector is equal to zero cannot be rejected at any conventional level. This implies that there is absence of cointegrating structure among these three stock markets which can be interpreted as evidence against capital market integration among these three major Asian stock markets.

Panel B reports similar results although this time we are using today's open index (t) data for all three exchanges. Japan's stock market, however, begins trading one hour before (i.e., 9:00 a.m. local time) the other two markets. While Japan closes at 3:00 p.m. local time, Hong Kong closes at 3:30 p.m., and Singapore at 4:00 p.m. Finally, Panel C documents no cointegration among the three Asian stock exchanges even when closing prices of the same trading period are considered. This evidence seems to suggest that there is no equilibrium relationship among these

Table 2. Johansen Multivariate Cointegration Tests: October 25, 1991–November 24, 1992

	Trace Test: $-2 \ln Q_k$		
Cointegrating Vector (k)	*Likelihood Ratio*	*5 Percent Critical Value*	*1 Percent Critical Value*
	Panel A: Japan Stock Market Index; Hong Kong Stock Market Index; Singapore Stock Market Index		
	(Close at t–1) (Open at t) (Open at t)		
$k = 0$	24.67604	29.68	35.65
$k \leq 1$	8.98685	15.41	20.04
$k \leq 2$	0.43730	3.76	6.65
	Panel B: Japan Stock Market Index; Hong Kong Stock Market Index; Singapore Stock Market Index		
	(Open at t) (Open at t) (Open at t)		
$k = 0$	18.99843	29.68	35.65
$k \leq 1$	6.84927	15.41	20.04
$k \leq 2$	0.72553	3.76	6.65
	Panel C: Japan Stock Market Index; Hong Kong Stock Market Index; Singapore Stock Market Index		
	(Close at t) (Close at t) (Close at t)		
$k = 0$	21.33278	29.68	35.65
$k \leq 1$	7.02647	15.41	20.04
$k \leq 2$	0.37185	3.76	6.65

Asian stock markets that would keep them from drifting too far apart from each other since October 1991. This result is inconsistent with the results of Arshanapalli and Doukas (1993b) which show evidence of one cointegrating vector in a set of six Asia stock markets including Japan, Hong Kong, and Singapore for the November 1987–December 1992 period. Their results, however, were based on closing stock prices and by considering a broader set of stock markets. It is possible that the cointegrating vector found in their study is associated with the fact that they have considered three more Asian stock exchanges. Overall the results reported in Table 2 suggest that stock price changes in any of the three markets cannot be described with an error-correction model as implied by the theory of cointegration (Engle and Granger 1987).

Finally, Table 3 reports estimates of the trace test statistic values based on bilateral cointegration tests using Johansen's methodology. These results confirm our earlier findings. There is no evidence of cointegration among any of the stock exchange pairs listed in Table 3. These results strongly suggest that the three major Asian

Table 3. Bilateral Cointegration Tests: October 25, 1991–November 24, 1992

		Trace Test: –2 ln Q_k			
Country Pair	*Index Trading Time*	*Cointegrating Vector(k)*	*Likelihood Ratio*	*5 Percent Critical Value*	*1 Percent Critical Value*
Hong Kong	Open	$k = 0$	5.23	15.41	20.04
Singapore	Open	$k \leq 1$	0.81	3.76	6.65
Hong Kong	Close	$k = 0$	6.59	15.41	20.04
Singapore	Close	$k \leq 1$	1.91	3.76	6.65
Hong Kong	Close	$k = 0$	7.36	15.41	20.04
Singapore	Open	$k \leq 1$	0.43	3.76	6.65
Hong Kong	Open	$k = 0$	8.93	15.41	20.04
Japan	Open	$k \leq 1$	0.55	3.76	6.65
Hong Kong	Close	$k = 0$	13.53	15.41	20.04
Japan	Close	$k \leq 1$	0.83	3.76	6.65
Hong Kong	Close	$k = 0$	8.70	15.41	20.04
Japan	Open	$k \leq 1$	1.67	3.76	6.65
Singapore	Open	$k = 0$	5.50	15.41	20.04
Japan	Open	$k \leq 1$	0.78	3.76	6.65
Singapore	Close	$k = 0$	5.45	15.41	20.04
Japan	Close	$k \leq 1$	0.02	3.76	6.65
Singapore	Close	$k = 0$	5.55	15.41	20.04
Japan	Open	$k \leq 1$	0.03	3.76	6.65

stock exchanges do not function in unison and therefore stock exchange innovations in one market do not seem to have any influence in the other two markets. Hence, Japan's influence on the other two Asian stock exchanges does not appear to be an important factor, lending support to the widely held view that Japan's stock market neither influences the other Asian stock markets nor is affected by them. In sum, it appears that Japan's stock market behavior is determined by its own idiosyncratic nature rather than by world[7] or regional stock market developments.

CONCLUSION

This study documents that stock market linkages among the three major Asian stock exchanges (i.e., Japan, Hong Kong, and Singapore) are essentially nonexistent. Using daily open and close stock price index data, we fail to find cointegration among the three Asian stock exchanges as well as for different stock exchange pairs during the recent trading period. This evidence suggests that the degree of the Asian stock market integration is not as strong as might be expected. Our results, based on the most recent developments in the theory of cointegration (Johansen 1991), are very interesting in the sense that they point out that by investing in these three Asian equity markets, investors' portfolio diversification benefits can be enhanced substantially.

NOTES

1. See, for example, Becker, Finnerty, and Gupta (1990), Hamao, Masulis, and Ng (1990), Campbell and Hamao (1989), and Arshanapalli and Doukas (1993a).
2. Arshanapalli and Doukas (1993a, 1993b), and Maliaris and Urrutia (1992) have addressed the issue of integration among Asian markets in the pre- and post-crash period.
3. An alternative unit root test is the Phillips and Perron (1988) test which is robust to a wide variety of serial correlations and time dependent heteroskedasticity. The results of this test, not presented here, are essentially consistent with those reported based on the ADF tests.
4. Johansen's (1991) multivariate cointegration procedure is free of the assumption that the cointegrating vector is unique. Furthermore, it takes into account the error structure of the underlying process. Finally, it allows for several tests regarding the cointegrating vectors and tests for weak exogeneity among variables.
5. If Π is a matrix of zeros, then any linear combination of X_t will be a unit-root process and, hence, nonstationary. For example, let $p = 2$, if $\Gamma_2 = 0$ and $\Gamma_1 = I$, then $(I - \Gamma_1 - \Gamma_2) = 0$. In this case, all the elements of X_t are unit-root processes and $(I - \Gamma_1 - \Gamma_2)$ is rank zero.
6. Alternatively stated, economic models are preferred when they have unique steady-state equilibria.
7. See Arshanapalli and Doukas (1993a) among others.

REFERENCES

Arshanapalli, B., and J. Doukas. 1993a. "International Stock Market Linkages: Evidence from Pre- and Post-October 1987 Period." *Journal of Banking and Finance* 17: 193–208.

———. 1993b. "Asian Equity Markets and the Role of Japan." *Journal of International Securities Markets* 7: 165–172.

Becker, K.G., J.E. Finnerty, and M. Gupta. 1990. "The Intertemporal Relation Between the U.S. and Japanese Stock Markets." *Journal of Finance* 45: 1297–1306.

Campbell, J., and Y. Hamao. 1989. "Predictable Stock Returns in the United States and Japan: A Study of Long-Term Capital Market Integration." Working Paper NBER.

Dickey, A.D., and W.A. Fuller. 1979. "Distribution of the Estimates for Autoregressive Time Series with a Unit Root." *Journal of the American Statistical Association* 24: 427–431.

———. 1981. "Likelihood Ratio Statistics for Autoregression Time Series with a Unit Root." *Econometrica* 49: 1057–1072.

Engle, R.F., and C.W.J. Granger. 1987. "Co-integration and Error Correction: Representation, Estimation, and Testing." *Econometrica* 55: 251–276.

Engle, R.F., and B.S. Yoo. 1987. "Forecasting and Testing In Co-Integrated Systems." *Journal of Econometrics* 35: 143–159.

Hamao, Y., R.W. Masulis, and V. Ng. 1990. "Correlations in Price Changes and Volatility Across International Stock Markets." *The Review of Financial Studies* 3: 281–307.

Johansen, S. 1991. "Estimation and Hypothesis Testing of Cointegration Vectors in Gaussian Vector Autoregressive Models." *Econometrica* 56: 1551–1580.

Johansen, S., and K. Juselius. 1990. "Maximum Likelihood Estimation and Inference on Cointegration—With Applications to the Demand for Money." *Oxford Bulletin of Economics and Statistics* 52: 169–211.

Maliaris, A.G., and J.L. Urrutia. 1992. "The International Crash of October 1987: Causality Tests." *Journal of Financial and Quantitative Analysis* 27: 353–364.

Phillips, B.C.P., and P. Perron. 1988. "Testing for a Unit Root in Time Series Regression." *Biometrika* 75: 335–346.

THE HETEROSKEDASTIC BEHAVIOR OF STOCK PRICES IN AN INTEGRATED GLOBAL MARKET:

EVIDENCE FROM TAIWAN AND KOREA

Thomas C. Chiang, Bang Nam Jeon, and Kap-Soo Oh

ABSTRACT

The paper investigates the time-series properties of stock prices in two emerging Asian stock markets, Taiwan and Korea, for the period January 1975 through December 1990. Although there is little evidence of linear dependence, stock price changes in the two Asian markets exhibit stochastic nonlinear time-dependence properties and substantial autoregressive conditional heteroskedastic (ARCH) effects. Various classes of autoregressive models with (G)ARCH(-M) conditional variance processes were fit to the data. We conclude that the AR(12)-ARCH(3) model can explain a large part of the second-moment nonlinearity and time-varying conditional heteroskedasticity in the data, indicating that the model is an empirically reasonable description of return-generating processes and volatility in the Taiwan and Korea stock exchanges. The AR(12)-ARCH(3) model was further extended to investigate the international linkages between the two Asian stock markets and the major world stock exchanges. Maintaining the weak form efficient-market property and increasing

Research in International Business and Finance, Supplement 1, pages 111–131.

ISBN: 0-7623-0110-4

linkages with the major world stock exchanges seem to be favorable signals toward the further internationalization of the two Asian stock markets in the 1990s.

INTRODUCTION

Two of the fastest growing and the best performing markets among all emerging equity markets, at least until the beginning of 1990, have been the Taiwan and Korea Stock Exchanges. These two Asian markets together accounted for nearly 45% of the world emerging markets' capitalization as of the end of 1990.[1] Though in many ways different from each other, Taiwan and Korea often are lumped together by foreign analysts and investors as Asia's major second-tier economies. Their allegedly closed stock markets, under criticism from foreign investors, further contribute to the perceived similarity.

The Taiwanese and Korean stock markets have been recently sharing two similar, and very significant and meaningful, experiences: liberalization and extreme volatility. Since December 27, 1990 when its securities market-opening plan was finally approved, the Taiwanese government has permitted qualified foreign institutional investors to invest directly in the Taiwan Stock Exchange. The Taiwanese government is expected to take further action toward the final stage of its three-stage plan for opening the securities market in the 1990s. Korea also pledged in 1981 to liberalize its market gradually. The government then, in 1988, set up a timetable for an eventual opening in 1992. The Korean Ministry of Finance recently adopted the two-stage plan of opening up its securities industry. First, in 1991, the government granted branch licenses to qualified foreign securities firms. Second, the bigger breakthrough was realized in January 1992 when foreigners were allowed to invest directly in Korean shares, up to a maximum of 10% in any one company. Internationalization of the two Asian stock markets is expected to provide important benefits to those developing economies: efficient allocation of resources, incremental sources to domestic savings, and improvement of the capital structure of developing country corporations.

Although there are some differences in official attitudes toward market reform in Taiwan and Korea, these two countries have been showing some sluggishness in pledging and scheduling their program of opening markets to foreigners, under the fear that an early opening may shore up share prices with foreign cash. With share prices at extremely low levels after the market's more than 40% plunge in 1990 (down to 566.27 on September 17), Korean policymakers are believed to fear that the country's assets are particularly vulnerable to foreign control. Korea's composite stock price index has recently recovered close to its previous peak level by reaching a 870 level in December 1993. Market fluctuation is more dramatic in the recent history of the Taiwan Stock Exchange. From a 1986 low of 880, the market's weighted index soared by 1,320% to a peak of 12,495 on February 10, 1990. At that time, with turnover passing $6 billion a day, the Taipei market was the world's most heavily traded exchange. After that date Taiwan's weighted stock price index began a drastic losing streak by falling as low as 3,000, a one-forth level of the 1990 peak, by the end of the year. Since then Taiwan's stock prices have recovered gradually, recording a 52.9% increase in Taiwan's weighted stock index during the year of 1993.

Under the increasing pressure to speed the process of opening their doors to foreign investors, Seoul and Taipei have been preparing step-by-step timetables for an eventual opening in the 1990s, although they are expected to be limited ones. By observing the recent volatile movements of stock prices in the two Asian stock markets while opening up their doors to foreign investors, it is natural to raise the following questions. How can we explain the time-varying volatile behavior of stock prices in the Taiwanese and Korean equity markets? Are the return-generating processes in the two Asian equity markets related to those in the major world stock exchanges? Are these two stock exchanges among the most active emerging stock exchanges segmented from or integrated with the world markets, and if so, then to what extent?

The purpose of our paper is as follows. First, we present new evidence about the temporal behavior of stock market returns and investigate the heteroskedastic time-varying volatility behavior of stock prices in the Taiwanese and Korean stock markets. Second, we examine the linkages between these two Asian stock exchanges and the major world markets by using time-series models which incorporate the possibility of nonlinear stochastic dependence in stock prices. The paper is organized as follows. The next section investigates the statistical properties of the rates of change in stock price indexes in the Taiwan and Korea Stock Exchanges. The third section explores the possibility of nonlinear stochastic dependence of stock price changes and performs statistical tests for the fit of various classes of autoregressive conditional heteroskedastic (ARCH) models. The fourth section investigates the international market linkages in the two Asian stock markets by using ARCH. (GARCH) models which account for conditional heteroskedastic, time-varying volatile behavior of stock prices in the Taiwanese and Korean stock markets. The final section provides a summary and concluding remarks.

STATISTICAL CHARACTERIZATION OF STOCK PRICE MOVEMENTS IN THE TAIWANESE AND KOREAN EQUITY MARKETS

Stock prices in industrial countries have been considered to be efficient. Since the publication of Fama's (1965) seminal paper, it has been widely believed that the New York Stock Exchange (NYSE) is an efficient market and that the U.S. stock price is consistent with a random walk process. Several recent studies using the mean reversion test and the variance ratio test have, however, rejected the random walk hypothesis of stock prices (Fame and French 1988; Poterba and Summers 1988; Lo and MacKinlay 1988, 1989).

We, therefore, first investigate whether the random walk theory is appropriate to describe the behavior of stock prices in the Taiwan and Korea Stock Exchanges. We collected the national stock price indexes of Taiwan and Korea for the period from January 1975 to December 1990: the Taiwan Stock Exchange Weighted Stock Index and the Korea Composite Stock Price Index, compiled by the Securities & Exchange Commission, The Republic of China, and the Korea Stock Exchange, respectively. A monthly sampling was conducted from daily national stock price index files by collecting the end-of-the-month closing prices in each market. The sixteen-year period from January 1975 to December 1990 constitutes a sample of 192 observations.

We test the hypothesis that stock price indexes of Taiwan and Korea follow unit-root processes. The presence of a unit root in autoregressive representations indicates that the time series is nonstationary and follows a random walk. The test of the null hypothesis of unit-root nonstationarity will be performed by using the testing procedure proposed by Dickey and Fuller (1979, 1981). Suppose that the time series of the national stock price indexes, ($S_{i,t}$), where i = 1 (Taiwan) and 2 (Korea), have an autoregressive representation with a time trend, t:

$$S_{i,t} = \alpha_{i,0} + \alpha_{i,1}t + \alpha_{i,2}S_{i,t-1} + \varepsilon_{i,t}\,, \tag{1}$$

where $\alpha_{i,0}$ is an intercept, $\alpha_{i,1}$ and $\alpha_{i,2}$ are coefficients, and $\varepsilon_{i,t} \sim NI(0,\sigma_\varepsilon^2)$. The null hypothesis of a unit root, $\alpha_{i,2} = 1$, can be tested through a t-statistic for $\alpha_{i,2}$, denoted

Table 1. Tests for Unit Roots in Stock Prices in the Taiwan and Korea Stock Exchanges, January 1975 through December 1990

	Taiwan		*Korea*	
Statistic	*Normalized*	*Log*	*Normalized*	*Log*
		(levels)		
τ_τ	−1.266	−1.058	−2.145	−1.798
Φ_2	1.857	2.926	1.642	1.918
Φ_3	1.396	0.931	2.326	1.659
		(changes)		
τ_τ	−9.381**	−8.960**	−8.371**	−9.130**
Φ_2	29.333**	26.764**	23.367**	27.795**
Φ_3	43.999**	40.146**	35.047**	41.684**

Notes: All data are monthly (the end of the month): the natural logarithm of and normalized series (January 1975 = 100.0) of the Taiwan Stock Exchange Weighted Stock Index and the Korea Composite Stock Price Index, compiled by the Securities & Exchange Commission, The Republic of China, and the Korea Stock Exchange, respectively. * and ** denote the significance at the 5 and 1 percent levels, respectively. For the critical values, see Fuller (1976, p. 373) for τ_τ, and Dickey and Fuller (1981, p. 1063) for Φ_2 and Φ_3.

as τ_τ. Fuller (1976) and Dickey and Fuller (1979) tabulated empirical percentiles for testing $H_o^{(1)}$: $\alpha_{i,2} = 1$.[2]

In addition to the nonzero drift for the series ($\alpha_{i,0} \neq 0$), stock prices may have nonzero time trends ($\alpha_{i,1} \neq 0$). Under the null hypothesis of a unit root and drift, Dickey and Fuller (1981) suggested an *F*-statistic, Φ_3, for testing the null joint hypothesis $H_o^{(2)}$: $\alpha_{i,0} = \alpha_{i,0}$, $\alpha_{i,1} = 0$, and $\alpha_{i,2} = 1$. The null hypothesis with the test statistic Φ_3 is that the time series is a random walk with drift. Finally, the most restricted form of the joint hypothesis proposed by Dickey and Fuller (1981) is that $H_o^{(3)}$: $\alpha_{i,0} = 0$, $\alpha_{i,1} = 0$, and $\alpha_{i,2} = 1$. The test statistic is denoted by Φ_2. The null hypothesis for the test statistic of Φ_2 is that the time series has a unit root and is a random walk with zero drift and no time trend. Both Φ_3. and Φ_2 can be examined by the asymptotic distribution tabulated by Dickey and Fuller (1981, p. 1063). For instance, under the null hypothesis the 1 and 5% critical values for τ_τ, Φ_3, and Φ_2 ($n = 250$) are –3.43 and –3.99, 6.34 and 8.43, and 4.75 and 6.22, respectively.

The results of tests for unit roots in the natural logarithms and normalized series (January 1975 = 100.0) of stock prices in the Taiwan and Korea Stock Exchanges are reported in Table 1. The *t*-statistics (τ_τ) and *F*-statistics (Φ_2 and Φ_3) from the test equations based on equation (1) fail to reject the null hypothesis of a unit root

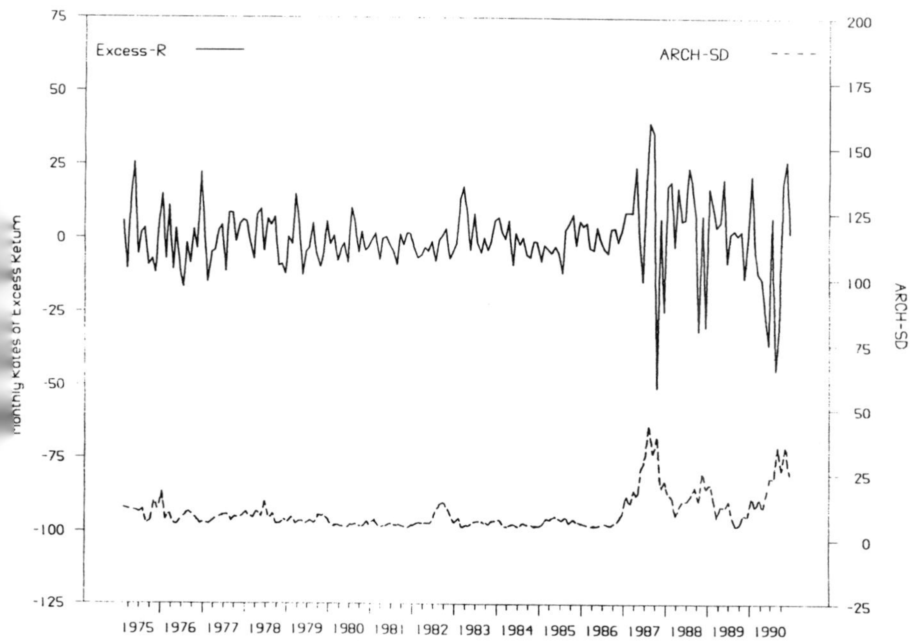

Figure 1. The Excess Return and ARCH-Variance in the Taiwan Stock Exchange January 1975 through December 1990

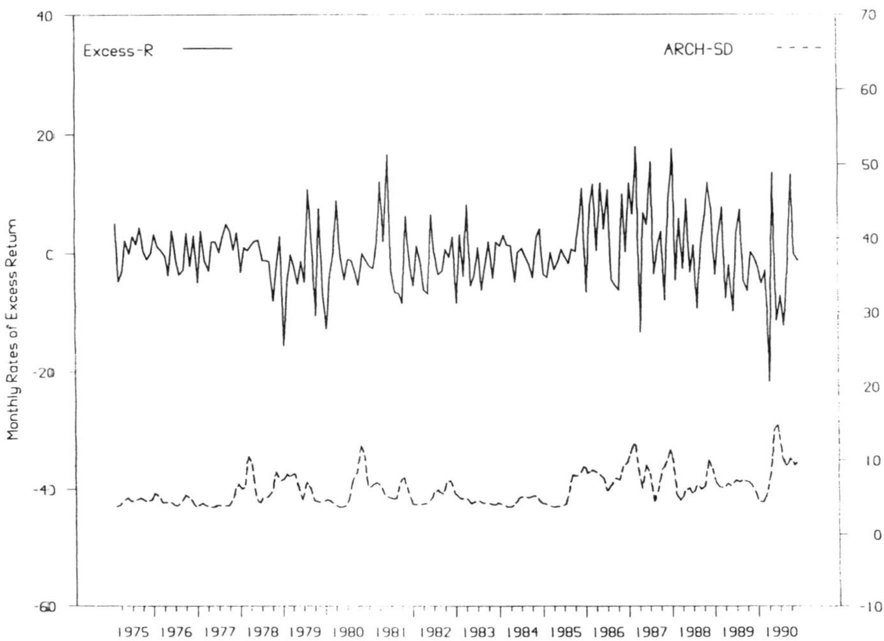

Figure 2. The Excess Return and ARCH-Variance in the Korea Stock Exchange January 1975 through December 1990

for any of the national stock prices at any level. However, the null hypothesis is strongly rejected for the first differenced series of stock prices. In sum, the unit-root tests provide consistent evidence of the notion of the random walk behavior of stock prices (with drift) in the Taiwanese and Korean stock markets. This nonstationarity can be removed by taking the first differences, implying that national stock prices in the two Asian countries are integrated of order one, $I(1)$.[3]

We then investigate the statistical properties of monthly rates of change in stock price indexes of Taiwan and Korea. Table 2 reports sample statistics on the first differences of natural logarithms of stock prices in the Taiwan and Korea Stock Exchanges. The standard deviations of the rates of change in the Taiwanese and Korean stock price indexes during the period from January 1975 to December 1990 were large in both markets, over 11% and 6%, respectively, with the consistently increasing trends throughout the sample period. These two Asian emerging markets are prospering markets, however, with average monthly returns of 1.52% and 1.18% during the last fifteen years in Taiwan and Korea, respectively. For each market, the minimum and maximum rates of change show a range that is consistent with increasing standard deviations throughout the period. A glance at the solid lines in Figures 1 and 2 confirms the changes in variance of stock returns in the Taiwanese and Korean stock markets, respectively.

The distributions of the rates of change in stock price indexes of Taiwan and Korea are strongly leptokurtic, with heavy tails and sharp peaks at the center compared to the normal distribution. The leptokurtic distribution is more conspicuous in the Taiwanese market with significantly negative skewness. The deviation from the normality seems to be well accounted for by nonstationary means and variances in both markets as described in Table 2.

An important implication of the unit-root process of stock prices evidenced earlier is that stock price changes are independent random variables. Ljung-Box tests for lags up to 24 months were conducted to test the hypothesis of independent and identical probability distributions of stock price changes. The null hypothesis of strict white noise cannot be rejected in all cases as reported in Table 2, leading us to conclude that monthly changes in stock prices in Taiwan and Korea are made up of independent variates.

To investigate further the independence hypothesis, we analyze the sample autocorrelation functions.[4] The estimated autocorrelations for the series of monthly stock price changes $\{R_t\}$, squared changes $\{R_t^2\}$, and absolute changes $\{|R_t|\}$ in the Taiwan and Korea Stock Exchanges for the sample period from January 1975 to December 1990 are shown in Figures 3 and 4, respectively. The standard errors (σ) of autocorrelation coefficients were obtained by $1/\sqrt{n-1}$, where n is the number of

Table 2. Sample Statistics on Monthly Rates of Change in Stock Price Indexes of Taiwan and Korea, January 1975 through December 1990[a]

	Taiwan				*Korea*			
Statistic	*1975–79*	*1980–84*	*1985–90*	*1975–90*	*1975–79*	*1980–84*	*1985–90*	*1975–90*
Mean (%)	1.344	0.723	2.464	1.520	0.816	0.503	2.270	1.177
t-stat for mean = 0	(1.14)	(1.03)	(1.23)	(1.78)	(1.47)	(0.80)	(2.44)	(2.68)
Standard deviation	1.344	5.410	16.861	11.814	4.269	4.815	7.850	6.076
Minimum	–15.14	–7.58	–49.34	–49.34	–14.53	–7.37	–20.57	–20.57
Maximum	26.97	18.95	40.64	40.64	11.85	17.74	19.01	19.01
Skewness[b]	0.487	1.048**	–0.740*	–0.524**	–0.778*	1.108**	–0.032	0.253
Kurtosis[b]	0.103	1.608*	1.366*	3.613**	2.244**	2.204**	0.020	1.186**
LB(6)[c]	0.96	3.32	0.85	2.13	5.88	0.69	2.07	1.69
LB(12)	6.84	4.14	1.00	2.29	6.71	3.45	5.35	5.46
LB(24)	12.92	8.21	6.71	10.36	14.36	8.10	12.14	19.74

Notes: [a] The unit of measurement is the change in the natural logarithm of the Taiwan Stock Exchange Weighted Stock Index and the Korea Composite Stock Price Index times 100.

[b] * and ** denote the significance at the 5 and 1% levels, respectively.

[c] LB(n) is the Ljung-Box statistic at lag n, distributed as a chi-squared variate with *n* degrees of freedom.

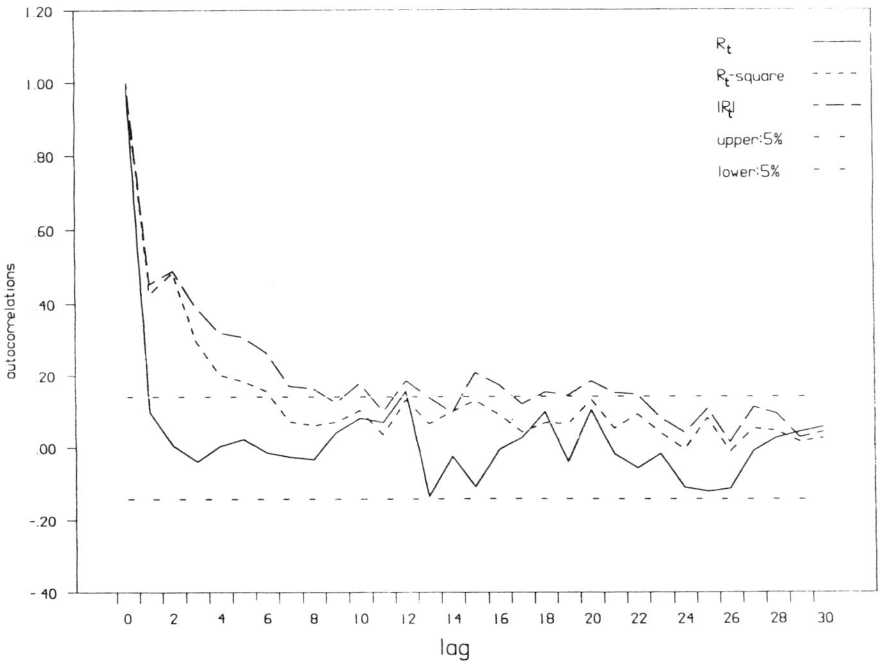

Figure 3. Autocorrelation Functions for Return Series (Taiwan)

observations. The 95% confidence bounds around zero for sample autocorrelation coefficients were set up using the standard errors. The series of stock price changes show insignificant autocorrelations for the first-lag and almost all longer lags. The twelfth-lag autocorrelations are, however, statistically significant for the series of stock price changes both in the Taiwan and Korea Stock Exchanges. The significant twelfth-lag autocorrelations give a reasonable indication of annual seasonality, showing some degree of correlations with the corresponding data points which lead or lag by 12 months. The insignificant autocorrelations of series of stock price changes indicate that not only is the first-differenced series stationary but it appears to resemble white noise. Evidence of unit-root processes of stock price series reported in Table 1 and various Ljung-Box statistics reported in Table 2 also support the conclusion that the differenced series are white noise and the original price series can best be modeled as random walks.

The linear independence is not, however, sufficient to prove statistical independence, in view of the nonnormality of stock price changes. It is possible for stock price changes to be linearly uncorrelated and nonlinearly dependent.[5] The autocorrelation coefficients of the squared stock price changes and the absolute

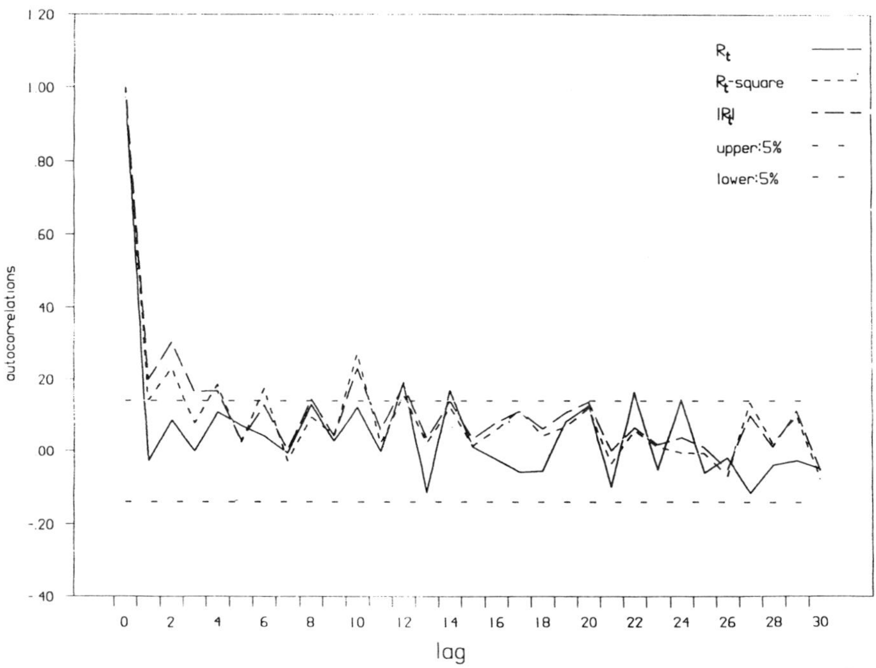

Figure 4. Autocorrelation Functions for Return Series (Korea)

changes can be used to detect nonlinear dependence. The autocorrelations in the squared and absolute stock price change series are larger than those in stock price change series, and they are significantly positive up to long lags, more conspicuously in the Taiwanese stock market. The distributions of the absolute and squared stock price changes seem to depend on their past series. This nonlinear time-dependence property and a leptokurtic distribution of return series should be taken into account when fitting stock price data in the Taiwanese and Korean stock markets.

NONLINEAR DEPENDENCE AND THE ARCH SPECIFICATIONS

One class of models that (1) recognizes the temporal dependence in the second moment of stock returns and (2) exhibits a leptokurtic distribution for the unconditional errors from the stock returns generating process is the autoregressive conditional heteroskedastic (ARCH) model. This model was introduced by Engle (1982) and generalized by Bollerslev (1986, 1987) and Engle, Lilien, and Robins (1987).[6]

We first investigate whether stock prices in the Taiwan and Korea Stock Exchanges have ARCH effects. Tests of ARCH effects in the series of stock price changes in the two Asian stock markets were conducted on the residuals generated by an AR(1, 12) model, which is suitable for the tests of the independence hypothesis and annual seasonality:

$$\text{Taiwan:}\quad (1 - \underset{(1.114)}{0.0821}L - \underset{(2.452)}{0.2048}L^{12})R_{\text{Taiwan}} = \underset{(0.937)}{0.8361} + \varepsilon_t, \tag{2.1}$$

$$R^2 = 0.042,\ D\text{–}W = 1.918,\quad Q(39) = 42.991,$$

$$\text{skewness} = -0.6850^{**},\qquad \text{kurtosis} = 4.3196^{**},$$

$$\text{ARCH}(1) = 24.957^{**},\ \text{ARCH}(2) = 50.583^{**},\ \text{ARCH}(3) = 51.015^{**},$$

$$\text{ARCH}(4) = 53.713^{**}.$$

$$\text{Korea:}\quad (1 - \underset{(0.379)}{0.0279}L - \underset{(2.888)}{0.2324}L^{12})R_{\text{Korea}} = \underset{(1.725)}{0.8260} + \varepsilon_t, \tag{2.2}$$

$$R^2 = 0.046,\ D\text{–}W = 1.943,\quad Q(39) = 41.812,$$

$$\text{skewness} = 0.3185,\qquad \text{kurtosis} = 0.8238^{*},$$

$$\text{ARCH}(1) = 2.032^{**},\ \text{ARCH}(2) = 10.581^{**},\ \text{ARCH}(3) = 11.962^{**},$$

$$\text{ARCH}(4) = 13.082^{**}.$$

where * and ** denote the significance at the 5 and 1% levels.

The LM tests for the ARCH(1 through 4) yield significant test statistics,[7] indicating apparent ARCH effects in the stock price changes in the Taiwan and Korea Stock Exchanges during the sample period. Successive stock price changes in these two markets are not independent because they are related through higher moments. Hence, large values of ε_t are likely to be followed by large values of ε_{t+1} of either sign. As a consequence, we expect a realization of ε_t to exhibit the behavior in which clusters of large observations are followed by clusters of small ones. The plot of the monthly stock price changes in the Taiwan and Korea Stock Exchanges in Figures 1 and 2 illustrates those clustering phenomena shared in both markets. Coefficients of skewness and kurtosis of the error terms, ε_t, indicate their leptokurtic probability distributions. Conventional statistical analysis of stock price changes is not adequate in that the conditional variance is assumed to be constant and normal distributions do not fit the observed data satisfactorily.

An ARMA-(G)ARCH(-M) regression model of orders p and q for stock price changes in the Taiwan and Korea Stock Exchanges, R_t, can be constructed as:

$$R_t \mid \Omega_{t-1} \sim F(\mu_t, h_t) \tag{3.1}$$

$$\mu_t = \phi_0 + \phi_1 R_{t-1} + \phi_2 R_{t-12} + \phi_3 h_t^{1/2} \tag{3.2}$$

$$h_t = \alpha_0 + \sum_{i=1}^{p} \alpha_i e_{t-i}{}^2 + \sum_{j=1}^{q} \beta_i h_{t-j} \tag{3.3}$$

$$e_t = R_t - \mu_t \tag{3.4}$$

where $F(\mu_t, h_t)$ is the conditional distribution of R_t, with conditional mean μ_t and variance h_t; Ω_{t-1} is the set of all information available up to time $t-1$; and $\alpha_0 > 0$, $\alpha_i \geq 0$, and $\beta_i \geq 0$ as the nonnegativity constraints associated with the parameters in the h_t equation are necessary to satisfy regularity conditions associated with the (G)ARCH(-M) model. Note that for $q = \phi_3 = 0$ the process reduces to an ARCH(p) model; for $q = 0$, to an ARCH(p)-M model; and for $\phi_3 = 0$, to a GARCH(p, q) model. Alternatively, for $p = q = \phi_3 = 0$, the conditional variance is constant, as in standard time-series models, and the innovation e_t simply reduces to white noise.[8]

Under the (G)ARCH(-M) process, the conditional mean and variance are time dependent. This specification is suited for fitting the nonlinearly dependent series of stock price changes in the Taiwanese and Korean stock markets showing the heteroskedastic time-varying volatility.

The (G)ARCH(-M) system can be estimated using maximum-likelihood (ML) techniques. For a sample size T, the log-likelihood function is the sum of the conditional log-likelihood for each observation:

$$\mathcal{L}_T(\theta) = 0.5 \sum_{t=1}^{T} l_t(\theta) \tag{4.1}$$

and

$$l_t(\theta) = -\log h_t - \varepsilon_t^2 / h_t. \tag{4.2}$$

This likelihood function can then be maximized with respect to the unknown parameters in θ ($\theta = [\phi_0, \phi_1, \phi_2, \phi_3, \alpha_0, \ldots, \alpha_p, \beta_1, \ldots, \beta_q]$). The log-likelihood function depends on the different parameters in a nonlinear fashion. Furthermore, recursive terms appearing in the first order condition with respect to the conditional variance, h_t, of equation (4.2) require iterative methods. Instead of using analytical derivatives that would require calculating $\partial h_t / \partial \Theta$ recursively, we use numerical derivatives and the Brendt, Hall, Hall, and Hausman (1974) algorithm to obtain ML estimates of the model's parameters.

Maximum-likelihood estimates for the (G)ARCH(-M) model of equation (3) are presented in Table 3 with t-statistics in parentheses. All classes of ARCH-type models show strong ARCH effects. The tests for model specification were also

Table 3. Estimation of ARCH, ARCH-M, and GARCH Models of Monthly Returns in the Taiwan and Korea Stock Exchanges, January 1975 through December 1990

	Taiwan			*Korea*		
Parameter	*ARCH(3)*	*ARCH(3)-M*	*GARCH(1,1)*	*ARCH(3)*	*ARCH(3)-M*	*GARCH(1,1)*
ϕ_0	0.3788	–0.6075	0.8998	0.9036	0.2922	0.8797
	(0.76)	(0.56)	(1.40)	(2.12)	(0.20)	(2.08)
ϕ_1	0.1125	0.0996	0.0549	0.0157	0.0124	–0.0225
	(1.36)	(1.19)	(0.65)	(0.20)	(0.16)	(0.26)
ϕ_2	0.0749	0.0678	0.0744	0.2214	0.2237	0.1814
	(1.55)	(1.53)	(1.13)	(3.60)	(3.58)	(2.87)
ϕ_3	—	0.1318	—	—	0.1184	—
		(0.90)			(0.44)	
α_0	17.8558	18.0161	14.4063	12.3664	12.5620	1.9766
	(2.46)	(2.59)	(3.99)	(3.91)	(3.89)	(2.04)
α_1	0.3796	0.4184	0.4099	0.0862	0.0916	0.1370
	(2.57)	(2.64)	(3.25)	(0.80)	(0.84)	(2.12)
α_2	0.1874	0.1813	—	0.4099	0.3815	—
	(1.56)	(1.61)		(3.22)	(3.02)	
α_3	0.4408	0.4767	—	0.2789	0.2838	—
	(2.56)	(2.73)		(2.26)	(2.27)	
β	—	—	0.5000	—	—	0.8261
			(6.14)			(12.71)
Log-likelihood	–469.25	–469.74	–481.24	–393.09	–393.02	–397.42
LR(3)[a]	98.32			27.44		
LR(4)[b]		97.33			27.58	
LR(2)[c]			74.32			18.78

Notes: Numbers in parentheses are t-statistics.

[a] The log-likelihood ratio test for H_0: $\alpha_1 = \alpha_2 = \alpha_3 = 0$. The statistic is distributed as a chi-square with three degrees of freedom. The 95 percent and 99 percent quantiles in the distribution of the test statistic, $\chi^2(3)$, are 7.81 and 11.34, respectively.

[b] The log-likelihood ratio test for H_0: $\phi_3 = \alpha_1 = \alpha_2 = \alpha_3 = 0$. The statistic is distributed as a chi-square with four degrees of freedom. The 95 percent and 99 percent quantiles in the distribution of the test statistic, $\chi^2(4)$, are 9.49 and 13.28, respectively.

[c] The log-likelihood ratio test for H_0: $\alpha_1 = \beta = 0$. The statistic is distributed as a chi-square with three degrees of freedom. The 95 percent and 99 percent quantiles in the distribution of the test statistic, $\chi^2(2)$, are 5.99 and 9.21, respectively.

conducted by estimating different likelihood ratio statistics. The statistic is distributed as a χ^2 with appropriate degrees of freedom, determined by the number of restrictions. The likelihood ratio tests soundly rejected all hypotheses of homoskedasticity (LR(3)), non-ARCH mean effects (LR(4)), and non-GARCH effects (LR(2)) both in the Taiwanese and Korean stock price series. The order p and q of the (G)ARCH(-M) processes were determined by applying likelihood ratio tests successively until the improvement in the log-likelihood function becomes insignificant. A maximum of three lags seems to fit series of stock price changes in Taiwan and Korea satisfactorily.

The estimates of ϕ_1 and ϕ_2 are comparable with those obtained by OLS in the AR(1) with annual seasonality as reported in equations (2.1) and (2.2). Annual seasonality is confirmed in Korea, but coefficients on AR(1) term are not significant in both markets, as expected. Conditional mean effects in the ARCH(3)-M model are not statistically significant in both markets. The estimates of α_0 are all positive and considerably smaller than the sample variances (squared standard deviations) shown in Table 2. This is due to changing conditional variances over time, and significant portions of the sample variances are explained by ARCH terms in both markets. In the GARCH(1, 1) estimation, the sums of the coefficients of α_1 and β are found to be close to unity.[9] These sums are dominated by β, especially in Korea, indicating that changes in market volatility tend to be persistent.[10] The number of parameters in the GARCH(1, 1) model is smaller than that in the ARCH(3) model. However, the log-likelihood function values for various classes of (G)ARCH(-M) models indicate that the ARCH(3) process is the reasonable specification which picks up the best fit.

The fit of the ARCH(3) model is further investigated by performing various diagnostic tests. As reported in Table 4, we examine the possibility of remaining ARCH effects, heteroskedasticity, and serial correlation in the errors. The test for remaining ARCH effects is carried out by regressing $(\hat{\varepsilon}_t^2 - \hat{h}_t)/\hat{h}_t$ on one to three lags of the dependent variable, where $\hat{\varepsilon}_t$ is the residual obtained from the mean equation of the ARCH(3) regression and $\hat{h}_t$ is the conditional variance evaluated at the maximum-likelihood estimates. The results are reported under ARCH(1) through ARCH(3). The statistics are distributed as a χ^2 with one, two, and three degrees of freedom. Percentiles of the χ^2 distribution are reported in parentheses. The null hypothesis of no remaining ARCH effects in the errors of the ARCH(3) model cannot be rejected at high significance levels in either Taiwan or Korea. A White-type test (1980) for heteroskedasticity for the residuals using χ^2-statistic with four degrees of freedom also shows that the null hypotheses of homoskedasticity in the standardized residuals cannot be rejected at any level of significance.

The results of Lagrangian multiplier tests for serial correlation of orders 1 and 12 are reported under Serial 1 and Serial 12 in Table 4. The test statistics of the $T{\cdot}R^2$, distributed as a $\chi^2(1)$ and a $\chi^2(12)$, were obtained by regressing the standardized residuals $(\hat{\varepsilon}_t/\sqrt{\hat{h}_t})$ on one and twelve lagged values of the variable. The null hypothesis of no serial correlation in the errors cannot be rejected at any conven-

Table 4. Diagnostic Tests on Standardized Residuals Obtained from ARCH(3) Estimations

	Taiwan	*Korea*
ARCH(1)	0.3937 (0.530)	0.3025 (0.582)
ARCH(2)	0.5726 (0.751)	0.5441 (0.762)
ARCH(3)	0.9584 (0.811)	0.5665 (0.904)
White	2.2274 (0.694)	5.6430 (0.227)
Serial 1	1.0905 (0.296)	0.0305 (0.861)
Serial 12	10.7329 (0.552)	3.6356 (0.989)
Skewness	0.1885 (0.316)	0.0330 (0.860)
Kurtosis	0.3914 (0.303)	0.8478 (0.026)

Notes: Numbers in parentheses are significance levels.

tional significance level. As evidenced by coefficients of skewness and kurtosis, the standardized residuals approach a normal distribution apart from a leptokurtic probability distribution of original data series.

In sum, (G)ARCH(-M) type models, especially the ARCH(3) specification, provide various supporting evidence of the best fit to data. The time-varying volatile behavior of stock prices in the Taiwan and Korea Stock Exchanges can be described satisfactorily by using ARCH(3) processes. In these two Asian markets, although there is little linear dependence in the data, we detect strong nonlinear dependence. This nonlinearity is likely to enter through variances. This is consistent with the presence of conditional heteroskedasticity. The fitting performance and diagnostic tests show that the ARCH(3) model can account for most of the nonlinearity in the data. In both Asian markets, the inherent uncertainty and volatility seem to vary widely over time. Large and small errors tend to cluster together. As shown in Figures 1 and 2, large returns of either sign are more frequently observed in periods of high volatility and vice versa. The estimated ARCH-standard deviations, $\sqrt{\hat{h}_t}$, in the Taiwanese and Korean stock markets are plotted in the lower part of the Figures 1 and 2, respectively. The time-varying volatile behavior of stock prices with changing variances is well reflected in the estimated ARCH-standard deviations obtained from the maximum-likelihood estimates of ARCH(3) models in each market. The second half of the 1980s shows substantially larger volatility than the earlier period, although there are several earlier episodes of increased volatility, especially in Korea.

LINKAGE BETWEEN THE TWO ASIAN STOCK MARKETS AND THE MAJOR WORLD STOCK EXCHANGES

As capital controls have been relaxed, world financial markets have become more closely linked in recent years. The large degree of international co-movements in

Table 5. Correlation Matrix of Stock Price Changes in World Stock Exchanges, January 1975 through December 1990

	U.S.	*U.K.*	*Japan*	*Taiwan*
U.K.	0.582			
	(9.84)			
Japan	0.440	0.412		
	(6.74)	(6.22)		
Taiwan	0.282	0.303	0.357	
	(4.04)	(4.37)	(5.25)	
Korea	0.210	0.188	0.311	0.103
	(2.95)	(2.63)	(4.50)	(1.42)

Note: All data are monthly (the end of the month): the S&P 500 for the United States, the FT-500 Share Index for the United Kingdom, the Nikkei 225 for Japan, the Taiwan Stock Exchange Weighted Stock Index for Taiwan, and the Korea Composite Stock Price Index for Korea. Numbers in parentheses are t-statistics which are obtained by $t = r\sqrt{n-2}/\sqrt{1-r_2}$, where r is a sample correlation coefficient and n is the number of observations ($n = 191$).

stock prices in the Taiwan and Korea Stock Exchanges is a favorable and promising precondition suggesting that the scheduled stock market opening to foreign investors in the 1990s can be carried out successfully.

Table 5 reports cross-correlations between rates of monthly change in national stock price indexes during the period from January 1975 to December 1990. Correlation coefficients between the major world markets, the United States, United Kingdom, and Japan, are in the range of 0.41 to 0.58. Cross-correlations between the two Asian markets and the major world markets are smaller: a range of 0.28 to 0.36 for Taiwan and a range of 0.19 to 0.21 for Korea. The bilateral relationship between Taiwan and Korea seems to be not strong, showing a low correlation coefficient, 0.103. Japan seems to be the most influential market to Taiwan and Korea, followed by the United States and the United Kingdom.

Further investigation of the linkage of stock returns in Taiwan and Korea with those in the major world stock exchanges was conducted by including foreign variables in the conditional mean equation of ARCH(3) models. The national stock price indexes in foreign markets are the S&P 500 composite index for the United States, the FT-500 share index for the United Kingdom, and the Nikkei 225 for Japan. The ARCH error process is incorporated in a regression framework by assuming that the distribution of R_t conditional on the information at time t–1, Ω_{t-1}, is normal with mean $R_t'\beta$ and variance, h_t, where h_t depends on past disturbances. Estimation results of the regression parameters and the ARCH parameters are reported in Table 6. To account for the annual seasonality found earlier, a twelfth-lag term was included in each equation. Significant ARCH effects were detected in all estimation equations. Specification tests using likelihood ratio (LR) statistics were undertaken to justify the regression models for stock price changes

Table 6. Linkages of Stock Prices in Taiwan and Korea with Stock Prices in the Major World Stock Exchanges, the United States, the United Kingdom, and Japan, January 1975 through December 1990

Independent Variable	*Taiwan*				*Korea*			
	1	*2*	*3*	*4*	*5*	*6*	*7*	*8*
Constant	0.199	0.249	−0.097	0.479	0.775	0.836	0.596	0.771
	(0.38)	(0.47)	(0.21)	(1.00)	(1.80)	(2.03)	(1.19)	(2.03)
U.S.	0.336				0.193			
	(2.96)				(2.42)			
U.K.		0.290				0.147		
		(3.80)				(2.38)		
Japan			0.350				0.275	
			(3.09)				(2.43)	
Korea				0.046				
				(0.64)				
Taiwan								0.107
								(2.79)
Taiwan(−12)	0.117	0.087	0.084	0.087				
	(2.26)	(1.68)	(1.92)	(1.79)				
Korea(−12)					0.248	0.234	0.210	0.205
					(4.21)	(4.05)	(3.17)	(3.29)
ARCH effects								
Constant	17.469	19.215	14.209	17.477	10.710	10.368	15.560	8.805
	(2.35)	(2.62)	(1.94)	(2.24)	(3.37)	(3.32)	(5.57)	(3.13)
ε^2_{t-1}	0.394	0.387	0.474	0.417	0.072	0.100	0.058	0.214
	(2.74)	(2.78)	(3.59)	(2.80)	(0.61)	(0.87)	(0.68)	(1.44)
ε^2_{t-2}	0.271	0.299	0.207	0.218	0.428	0.406	0.294	0.358
	(1.65)	(1.85)	(1.85)	(1.62)	(3.36)	(3.40)	(2.23)	(2.84)
ε^2_{t-3}	0.322	0.249	0.418	0.395	0.337	0.338	0.250	0.333
	(2.11)	(1.86)	(2.52)	(2.38)	(2.21)	(2.42)	(2.07)	(2.42)
Log-likelihood	−465.66	−465.95	−466.28	−470.14	−389.84	−390.12	−389.77	−389.66
LR(1)[a]	9.34	8.76	8.10	0.38	6.55	5.99	6.69	6.90
LR(4)[b]	107.22	106.64	105.98	98.26	34.08	33.52	34.22	34.44

Notes: Numbers in parentheses are *t*-statistics.

[a] The log-likelihood ratio test for H_0: A coefficient of U.S., U.K., Japan, Korea, or Taiwan is 0 in each estimation equation. The statistic is distributed as a chi-square with one degrees of freedom. The 95 percent and 99 percent quantiles in the distribution of the test statistic, $\chi^2(1)$, are 3.84 and 6.63, respectively.

[b] The log-likelihood ratio test for H_0: A coefficient of U.S., U.K., Japan, Korea or Taiwan is 0, and there are no ARCH effects in each estimation equation. The statistic is distributed as a chi-square with four degrees of freedom. The 95 percent and 99 percent quantiles in the distribution of the test statistic, $\chi^2(4)$, are 9.49 and 13.28, respectively.

in Taiwan and Korea combined with the ARCH(3) errors. The log-likelihood ratio tests reported under LR(4) soundly rejected the null hypothesis that coefficients of stock price changes in foreign markets are zero *and* there are no ARCH effects in each estimation equation.

The estimation results lead to the implications that follow. There is evidence that stock price changes in the Taiwan and Korea Stock Exchanges are significantly influenced by stock price movements in the major world stock exchanges. The impact of the major world stock markets on the movements of stock prices seems to be greater in the Taiwanese market than in the Korean market.[11] Sizes of the coefficients on the major world stock exchanges in the estimation equations for Taiwan are in the range of 0.29–0.35, while those for Korea are in the range of 0.15–0.28.

The magnitudes of the coefficients on foreign variables suggest that the degree of co-movements of stock prices in the two Asian markets seems to be the greatest with the Japanese market, followed by the U.S. market and UK market. The market linkage between Taiwan and Korea seems to be not strong and statistically not significant. The log-likelihood ratio tests, reported under LR(1), for the null hypothesis that there is no linkage of stock prices in the Taiwanese and Korean markets with stock prices in the major world stock exchanges, the United States, the United Kingdom, and Japan, can be rejected at the conventional significant level.[12]

A number of macroeconomic factors may have contributed to the role of the major world stock exchanges in determining stock prices in the two Asian markets during the last two decades. A trend toward growing interaction and dependence of the Taiwanese and Korean economies on Japan, the United States, and the United Kingdom in this descending order during the sample period can justify the significant regression coefficients, even though opportunities of investment by foreign investors were limited during the sample period and are scheduled to be greatly extended in the 1990s in the two Asian stock markets. Evidence of annual seasonality remains strong in this regression-ARCH model, more conspicuously in Korea.

CONCLUSION AND POLICY IMPLICATIONS

This paper shows that monthly stock price changes in the Taiwan and Korea stock exchanges during the period from January 1975 to December 1990 exhibit significant levels of stochastic nonlinear time-dependence properties. Although there is little indication of linear dependence in the data, evidenced by unit-root nonstationary processes of stock prices and the quickly falling-off autocorrelation functions of their differences, the autocorrelations of the squared and absolute stock price changes detect evidence of nonlinear dependence.

The time-varying volatility behavior of stock prices in the two Asian stock markets was investigated to explain nonlinear dependence by detecting the presence of conditional heteroskedasticity in the data series. Various classes of autoregressive models with (G)ARCH(-M) conditional variance processes were fit to the data. Based on the values of log-likelihood function and various specification tests, we conclude that the AR(12)-ARCH(3) model best fits stock price data in the two Asian markets. The model was shown to account for most of the second-moment nonlinearity and time-varying conditional heteroskedasticity in the data. The insignificant coefficients of conditional-variance variables in the mean equation of the ARCH-M model indicate that nonlinearity enters through variances rather through means in the behavior of stock prices in the Taiwanese and Korean stock markets.

The AR(12)-ARCH(3) model was extended to investigate the degree of the international linkages between the two Asian stock exchanges and the major world stock exchanges by including foreign market variables in the mean equation of the model. The regression-ARCH(3) model provided evidence that the Taiwanese and Korean stock markets have shared long-run co-movements with the major world stock exchanges. The market most influential on the two Asian markets seems to be the Japanese market, followed by the U.S. market and the UK market during the sample period. Taiwan seems to have been more influenced by, and linked to, the world markets than Korea does, while the market linkage between the two Asian markets is rather weak or statistically insignificant. Because of the limited opportunities of investing directly by foreign investors, evidence of long-run co-movements may be attributed to various indirect channels of linkages including macroeconomic factors in the highly open economies of Taiwan and Korea, and their increasing dependence on and interaction with industrial economies as foreign sourcing and markets for Taiwanese and Korean exports. Maintaining the weak form efficient-market property and increasing linkages with the major world markets seem to be favorable signals toward the further internationalization of the two Asian stock markets in the 1990s.

The ARCH class models, as nonlinear time-series models fitting time-varying conditional heteroskedasticity, do not require knowledge of the general structure of the economy. Instead, they postulate that if past errors are large, so will the conditional variances be. In the ARCH model, changes in variances are, therefore, predictable based on past changes. This type of conditional heteroskedasticity arises *endogenously* and persists over time, which can be described reasonably well by the ARCH specifications as adopted in this study.

An alternative source of heteroskedasticity may be an exogenous one to the system. An exogenous shift in policy regime or unexpected government regulations can lead to the anecdotal changes in variance of stock prices. This type of *exogenous* heteroskedasticity is expected to occur more often than not, especially in underdeveloped equity markets. The successful modeling of exogenously changing variances requires exact knowledge of, and the quantification of, the volatility-generating exogenous variables. Furthermore, changes in variances are unpredictable based on past changes in stock prices. This alternative source of heteroskedasticity is, therefore, left to future research.

ACKNOWLEDGMENTS

They are grateful to Jongmoo Jay Choi for helpful comments and discussion and to Sangjun Bak and Cheng-Yu Yan for their help with data collection and research assistance. Jeon acknowledges research support from the University Research Scholar Award, Drexel University.

NOTES

1. Between 1984 and 1990, according to the International Finance Corporation (IFC), the capitalization of equity markets quintupled in the 32 developing countries whose markets are monitored by the IFC. Total capitalization amounted to about $470 billion as of the end of 1990. The share of emerging markets in the world market capitalization is only still 4.9%. The potential growth of the emerging markets, however, seems to be large, considering that the aggregate GNP of emerging stock-market countries is about 12% in the world GNP.

2. By reparameterizing equation (1), we can write:

$$\Delta S_{i,t} = \alpha_{i,0} + \alpha_{i,1}t + \alpha'_{1,2}S_{i,t-1} + \varepsilon_{i,t},$$

where testing H_0: $\alpha_{i,2} = 1$ is equivalent to testing H_0: $\alpha'_{i,2} = 0$.

3. Stock prices following a random walk with a drift term, that is, $S_{i,t} = \mu + S_{i,t-1} + \varepsilon_t$, can be rewritten as $S_{i,t} = \mu t + \Sigma_{j=0}^{t}\ \varepsilon_{t-j}$ with the initial condition $S_{i,0} = 0$. We can see in this case that stock prices follow the joint process of a linear trend and a drift-free $I(1)$ process (or random walk) whose variance is $t\sigma^2$.

4. The pattern of serial correlations may provide valuable insight into the asset pricing process. Positive first-order serial correlations may result from slow adjustment to new information, insider information, or infrequent trading, while negative first-order correlations may arise from thin markets, measurement errors in prices, or overreaction in price adjustment creating reversals in return series. For further discussion about serial correlations in stock prices with empirical investigations on LDC securities markets, see Errunza and Losq (1985).

5. Linear independence of stock prices in less developed country stock markets have been reported by several empirical studies, for example, Errunza (1979), Errunza and Losq (1985), and Laurence (1986). A study by Errunza and Losq (1985) concluded that on the basis of serial correlation coefficients and runs tests, LDC markets, even though not as efficient as major industrialized country markets, are quite comparable to the smaller European markets.

6. French, Schwert, and Stambaugh (1987) found that the GARCH-M model was an attractive representation of the behavior of daily stock returns in the United States, successfully capturing the impacts of time-varying volatility on a stock's expected return. Akgiray (1989), on the other hand, found that GARCH (1, 1) processes showed the best fit and forecast accuracy in daily U.S. stock price indexes.

7. The test statistic is $T{\cdot}R^2$ which is distributed as $\chi^2(p)$, where T is the number of observations, $R2$ is the R-square obtained from the regression:

$$\varepsilon_t^2 = \beta_0 + \sum_{i=1}^{p} \beta_i \varepsilon_{t-i}{}^2,$$

and p is the order of the ARCH process and the number of lags in the above regression.

8. Conditional variance models do not force the probability distribution of variables to be normal. Several studies which investigated the statistical properties of ARCH processes have reported that the empirical distribution of variables generated by these processes were heavy tailed, compared to the normal distribution (see, for example, Bollerslev 1986; Hsieh 1989).

9. Bollerslev (1986) showed that a sufficient condition for the GARCH(*p*, *q*) process to be wide-sense stationary is that $\alpha_1 + \beta < 1.0$.

10. The estimated half-lives of volatility shocks are 7 months and 18 months for Taiwan and Korea, respectively. The half-life of a volatility shock is computed as $\ln 0.5/\ln(\alpha_1 + \beta)$.

11. We conducted the multivariate tests for unit roots and cointegration proposed by Johansen (1988), using stock price series rather than return data, in a system of national stock prices in the Taiwanese and Korean stock markets along with the world's major stock exchanges. Testing at the 5% level of significance, we could not reject the hypothesis that there was at least one independent cointegrating vector in the system of stock prices of the United States, the United Kingdom, Japan, and Taiwan. This implies that the Taiwanese stock prices have shared one long-run equilibrium relationship with the three other national stock prices since the mid-1970s. However, the Korean stock market did not show significant evidence of sharing a common stochastic trend with the major world stock exchanges. For empirical investigations of the short-run and long-run international stock market linkages, see Eun and Shim (1989), von Furstenberg and Jeon (1989), Jeon and von Furstenberg (1990), and Jeon and-Chiang (1991).

12. Studies on the fitness tests for ARCH specifications such as Gallant (1987) report that in general, especially for small samples, the Lagrangian multiplier test and the likelihood ratio test are preferred over the Wald test (*t*-test), even though all the tests have similar asymptotic power.

REFERENCES

Akgiray, V. 1989. "Conditional Heteroscedasticity in Time Series of Stock Returns: Evidence and Forecasts." *Journal of Business* 62: 55–80.

Bollerslev, T. 1986. "Generalized Autoregressive Conditional Heteroskedasticity." *Journal of Econometrics* 31: 307–327.

———. 1987. "A Conditionally Heteroskedastic Time Series Model for Speculative Prices and Rates of Return." *Review of Economics and Statistics*: 542–547.

Brendt, E.K., B.H. Hall, R.E. Hall, and J.A. Hausman. 1974. "Estimation and Inference in Nonlinear Structural Models." *Annuals of Economic and Social Measurement*: 653–665.

Dickey, D.A., and W.A. Fuller. 1979. "Distribution of the Estimators for Autoregressive Time Series with a Unit Root." *Journal of the American Statistical Association* 74: 427–431.

———. 1981. "Likelihood Ratio Statistics for Autoregressive Time Series with a Unit Root." *Econometrica* 49: 1057–1072.

Engle, R.F. 1982. "Autoregressive Conditional Heteroskedasticity with Estimates of the Variance of United Kingdom Inflation." *Econometrica* 50: 987–1007.

Engle, R.F., D. Lilien, and R. Robins. 1987. "Estimating Time Varying Risk Premia in the Term Structure: The ARCH-M Model." *Econometrica* 55: 391–407.

Errunza, V.R. 1979. "Efficiency and the Programs to Develop Capital Markets: The Brazilian Experience." *Journal of Banking and Finance* 3: 355–382.

Errunza, V.R., and E. Losq. 1985. "The Behavior of Stock Prices on LDC Markets." *Journal of Banking and Finance* 9: 561–575.

Eun, C.S., and S. Shim. 1989. "International Transmission of Stock Market Movement." *Journal of Financial and Quantitative Analysis* 24: 241–256.

Fama, E.F. 1965. "The Behavior of Stock Market Prices." *Journal of Business* 38: 34–105.

Fama, E.F., and K.R. French. 1988. "Permanent and Temporary Components of Stock Prices." *Journal of Political Economy* 96: 246–273.

French, K.R., G.W. Schwert, and R.F. Stambaugh. 1987. "Expected Stock Returns and Volatility." *Journal of Financial Economics* 19: 3–29.

Fuller, W.A. 1976. *Introduction to Statistical Time Series*. New York: John Wiley.

Gallant, R.A. 1987. *Nonlinear Statistical Models*, volumes 1 and 2. New York: John Wiley.

Hsieh, D.A. 1989. "Testing for Nonlinear Dependence in Daily Foreign Exchange Rates." *Journal of Business* 62: 339–368.

International Finance Corporation. 1990. *Emerging Stock Markets Factbook.* Washington, DC: IFC.

Jeon, B.N., and T.C. Chiang. 1991. "A System of Stock Prices in World Stock Exchanges: Common Stochastic Trends for 1975–1990?" *Journal of Economics and Business* 43: 329–338.

Jeon, B.N., and G.M. von Furstenberg. 1990. "Growing International Co-movement in Stock Price Indexes." *Quarterly Review of Economics and Business* 30: 15–30.

Johansen, S. 1988. "Statistical Analysis of Cointegrating Vectors." *Journal of Economic Dynamics and Control* 12: 231–254.

Kaminsky, G., and R. Peruga. 1990. "Can a Time-Varying Risk Premium Explain Excess Returns in the Forward Market for Foreign Exchange?" *Journal of International Economics* 28: 47–70.

Laurence, M.M. 1986. "Weak-Form Efficiency in the Kuala Lumpur and Singapore Stock Markets." *Journal of Banking and Finance* 10: 431–445.

Lo, A.W., and A.C. MacKinlay. 1988. "Stock Market Prices Do Not Follow Random Walks: Evidence from a Simple Specification Test." *Review of Financial Studies* 1: 41–66.

———. 1989. "The Size and Power of the Variance Ratio Test in Finite Samples: A Monte Carlo Investigation." *Journal of Econometrics* 40: 203–238.

Mistry, P.S. 1987. "Globalization of Financial Markets: Implications for Asian Developing Countries." *International Journal of Development Banking* 5: 3–20.

Poterba, J.M., and L.H. Summers. 1988. "Mean Reversion in Stock Prices: Evidence an Implications." *Journal of Financial Economics* 22: 27–59.

von Furstenberg, G.M., and B.N. Jeon. 1989. "International Stock Price Movements: Links and Messages." *Brookings Papers on Economic Activity* (1): 125–179.

White, H. 1980. "A Heteroskedasticity-consistent Covariance Matrix Estimator and a Direct Test for Heteroskedasticity." *Econometrica* 48: 817–838.

OIL AND WORLD STOCK MARKETS' REACTION TO THE GULF CRISIS

A.G. Malliaris and Jorge L. Urrutia

ABSTRACT

This paper uses two methodologies to empirically investigate the economic significance of the Gulf Crisis on the oil and world equity markets. The first methodology is an event study based on the market and risk-adjusted return. Daily and cumulative abnormal returns are calculated for selected multi-day intervals for 12 world equity markets. The results indicate that significant negative abnormal returns materialized on the third day after the Iraqi invasion of Kuwait, while significant positive abnormal returns were observed two days after the war began. Furthermore both of these findings are stronger for portfolios of national markets of countries that are oil importing. The second methodology uses Granger causality between oil and world equity markets to confirm the importance of oil. While little causality is detected between oil and world equity markets prior to the invasion of Kuwait, strong contemporaneous causality and an increase in lead-lag and feedback is present between these markets during the Gulf Crisis period.

Research in International Business and Finance, Supplement 1, pages 133–153.

ISBN: 0-7623-0110-4

INTRODUCTION

From early August 1990 to January 1991, the world news was dominated by the Persian Gulf Crisis. The financial press, in particular, attempted to assess the impact of the crisis on world equity and oil markets. Furthermore, because of the significance of the crisis, various assertions were made that this world event had triggered the U.S. macroeconomic recession. It is the purpose of this paper to subject daily data of 12 national stock markets and the oil market to two rigorous methodological analyses which would enable us to obtain specific statistical evidence of what actually the data show. The first methodology is the market and risk-adjusted return event-study approach and the second is the Granger causality approach.

These two methodologies are selected because of the issues we wish to explore. First, motivated by Roll (1988) who suggested that the October 1987 world stock market crash was caused by some "unnamed worldwide triggering variable," we wish to confirm that the Persian Gulf Crisis was an identifiable global event that generated declines in world equity markets. Obviously, declines were both observed and reported in the financial press. However, such casual evidence is not sufficient to confirm the impact of the Gulf Crisis. A rigorous event methodology is needed to evaluate the effect of the Iraqi invasion of Kuwait.

In conducting such an event methodology, one needs to be aware of the joint hypothesis of market efficiency according to which returns of world equity markets continuously adjust to the flow of new information concerning developments in the Persian Gulf during the period of August 1990 to January 1991. In other words, under the grand umbrella of the Persian Gulf Crisis, examination of daily data can be used to reveal the response of aggregate returns to the release of relevant information. For example, while the news of Iraq's invasion of Kuwait was announced early on August 2, 1990, the strong opposition, first, by the United States and almost subsequently by numerous other countries, intensified what was a local conflict between two neighboring Gulf countries into a worldwide major political event. The further escalation, three days after the invasion by the government of Iraq, induced investors worldwide to assess these developments seriously. Similarly, investors daily assessed the eventual resolution of this conflict as the Allied forces prepared to liberate Kuwait and correctly anticipated a quick and successful ground attack by the Allied forces. These issues are discussed in Malliaris and Urrutia (1995).

Embedded in our event methodology is the significance of oil in the world economy. Obviously, Kuwait's invasion disrupted oil production and caused world oil prices to increase dramatically. To investigate the specific impact of oil on world equity markets we use Granger's causality methodology. We hypothesize that the Gulf Crisis with both its actual and potential disruption of world oil output affected world equity returns and, conversely, such equity returns, by the efficiency of world equity markets correctly anticipated the evolution of oil prices.

The next section briefly presents the data used while the third section describes the event study methodology. The Granger causality methodology is the topic of the fourth section. The last two sections are devoted to an analysis of our results and our conclusions, respectively.

DATA DESCRIPTION

Daily closing price indexes for the time period October 1, 1989 through January 31, 1991, are collected from the *WSJ*, for the World Index and 12 national markets: New York S&P 500, Toronto 300 Composite, London FT-100, Frankfurt DAX, Zurich Credit Swisse, Paris CAC40, Milan Stock Index, Amsterdam ANP-CBS General, Australia All Ordinaries, Hong-Kong Hang Seng, Singapore Straits Times, and Tokyo Nikkei Average.

Daily returns are computed as $R_t = 100 * [\ln(P_t/P_{t-1})]$, where P_t and P_{t-1} are daily price indexes for days t and t–1, respectively. The data sample is divided into an "Estimation Period" from October 1, 1989 through June 30, 1990 ($t = -206$ to $t = -23$), and an "Event Period," from July 1, 1990 to January 31, 1991 ($t = -22$ to $t = +119$). The event day ($t = 0$) corresponds to August 2, 1990, the day Iraq invaded Kuwait. Other important dates in the data sample are January 16, 1991 ($t = +112$) the day the Allied Forces - Iraq war began, and January 24, 1991 ($t = +118$), the day the International Coalition launched the ground attack.

EVENT-STUDY METHODOLOGY

In order to determine if an asset's returns are abnormal, it is necessary to compare them to a benchmark. This paper uses the market and risk-adjusted return method which takes into account both the market-wide factors and the systematic risks of each security. This method seems to be the favorite procedure of event-study researchers. It presumes that the CAPM generates expected returns and uses a regression model to predict the security's expected returns. This OLS regression procedure, known as the market model, consists of regressing the security's returns on the market's returns. The security's excess return is equal to the difference between the observed return during the event period and the return predicted by the OLS regression.

Let $R_{i,t}$ designate the observed return for national market i at time t. Define $AR_{i,t}$ as the excess or abnormal return for national market i at day t. For every national market, the excess or abnormal return for each day in the event period is estimated using the following formula:

$$AR_{i,t} = R_{i,t} - [\hat{\alpha}_i + \hat{\beta}_i R_{w,t}] \tag{1}$$

where $R_{w,t}$ is the observed return for the World Index at day t of the event period, ($t = -22, +119$), and $\hat{\alpha}_i$, $\hat{\beta}_i$ are the OLS values obtained by running regression (2) for the estimation period ($t = -206, -23$)

$$R_{i,t} = \alpha_i + \beta_i R_{w,t} + \varepsilon_{i,t}\,. \tag{2}$$

The standardized daily abnormal returns for national market i, $SAR_{i,t}$, are given by:

$$SAR_{i,t} = \frac{AR_{i,t}}{S_{i,t}} \tag{3}$$

where $S_{i,t}$ is the square root of national market i's estimated forecast variance, calculated as

$$S_{i,t} = \sqrt{S_i^2\left[1 + \left(\frac{1}{184}\right) + \frac{(R_{w,t} - \overline{R}_w)^2}{\sum_{k=-206}^{-23} (R_{w,k} - \overline{R}_w)}\right]}\,. \tag{4}$$

In equation (4), $R_{w,t}$, $R_{w,k}$ denote observed returns for the World Index at day t of the event period and day k of the estimation period, respectively and $\overline{R}_w$ is the average return of the World Index for the estimation period, computed by

$$\overline{R}_w = \frac{1}{184}\sum_{k=-206}^{-23} R_{w,k}\,. \tag{5}$$

Finally, S_i^2 is the residual variance for national market i, that corresponds to the mean-squared error of the OLS regression (2) and the number of observations in the estimation period is 184.

The cumulative abnormal returns for national market i, $SCAR_i$, over a multi-day period (t_1, t_2), are computed by

$$SCAR_{i,t_1,t_2} = \sum_{t=t_1}^{t_2} SAR_{i,t}\,. \tag{6}$$

The cross-sectional average standardized daily abnormal return for a portfolio of national markets, at day t of the event period, $ASAR_t$ is given by:

$$ASAR_t = \frac{1}{N}\sum_{i=1}^{N} SAR_{i,t} \tag{7}$$

where N is the number of national markets in the portfolio.

The $ASAR_t$'s can be accumulated over selected multi-day intervals of the event period using

$$ASCAR_{t_1,t_2} = \sum_{t=t_1}^{t_2} ASAR_t\,. \tag{8}$$

In equation (8), $ASCAR_{t_1,t_2}$ denotes the average standardized cumulative abnormal return for a portfolio of national markets during the (t_1, t_2) interval of the event period.

The null hypotheses to be tested are that the mean excess return for the day t of the event period, and the mean cumulative excess return over a multi-day interval of the event period are equal to zero.

The Z-statistic for the average standardized daily abnormal returns for any event day t is computed as

$$Z_{i,t} = SAR_{i,t}\ ,\ Z_t = ASAR_t\sqrt{N} \tag{9}$$

for an individual national market and for a portfolio of national markets, respectively. The Z-statistic for the average standardized cumulative abnormal returns over a multi-day interval (t_1,t_2) of the event period is calculated as:

$$Z_{i,t_1,t_2} = \frac{SCAR_{i,t_1,t_2}}{\sqrt{t_2 - t_1 + 1}}\ ,\ Z_{t_1,t_2} = \frac{ASCAR_{t_1,t_2}\sqrt{N}}{\sqrt{t_2 - t_1 + 1}} \tag{10}$$

for an individual national market and for a portfolio of national markets, respectively.

These statistics are widely used in event studies, as in Patell (1976), Masulis (1980), Dodd (1980), Dann (1981), Holthausen (1981), Leftwich (1981), Dodd and Warner (1983), and Brown and Warner (1980, 1985).

GRANGER CAUSALITY TESTS

The lead-lag tests used in this paper are based on the Granger tests of causality. The causal test of Granger is essentially a test of the predictive ability of time-series models. A time series $\{Y_t\}$ causes another time series $\{X_t\}$, if present X can be predicted better by using past values of Y than by not doing so, other relevant information, including the past of X, being used in either case. More formally, let $\sigma^2(X/U_t)$ be the variance of X given the information in the universe accumulated since (t-1) and let $\overline{U}(\overline{U} - \overline{Y})$ be the information in the universe with past values of Y included and excluded, respectively. The following definitions of causality are of interest.

1. Unidirectional causality: if $\sigma^2(X/\overline{U}) < \sigma^2(X/\overline{U} - \overline{Y})$ then Y is causing or leading X, denoted by $Y \rightarrow X$.
2. Bidirectional causality or feedback: if $\sigma^2(X/\overline{U}) < \sigma^2(X/\overline{U} - \overline{Y})$, and $\sigma^2(Y/\overline{U}) < \sigma^2(Y/\overline{U} - \overline{X})$ then feedback is occurring, denoted by $Y \leftrightarrow X$.

A description of the several testable forms of Granger causality can be found in Pierce and Haugh (1977), Geweke, Meese, and Dent (1983), and Guilkey and Salemi (1982). In this paper we use the following version of the Granger causal model:

$$\ln Y_t = \alpha_0 + \sum_{i=1}^{m} \alpha_i \ln X_{t-i} + \sum_{j=1}^{m} \beta_j \ln Y_{t-j} + \varepsilon_t \tag{11}$$

$$\ln X_t = a_0 + \sum_{i=1}^{m} a_i \ln Y_{t-i} + \sum_{j=1}^{m} b_j \ln X_{t-j} + \mu_t \,. \tag{12}$$

The definition of causality given above implies that X is causing (leading) Y provided some α_i is not zero in equation (11). Similarly, Y is causing (leading) X if some a_i is not zero in equation (12). If both of these events occur, there is feedback. The statistic is calculated by estimating the above expressions in both unconstrained (full model) and constrained (reduced model) forms, and may be written as:

$$F_1 = \frac{(SSE_r - SSE_f)/m}{SSE_f/(T - 2m - 1)} \tag{13}$$

where SSE_r, SSE_f denote residual sum squares of the reduced and full models, respectively, T is the total number of observations, and m is the number of lags.

Engle and Granger (1987) show that if two nonstationary variables are cointegrated, the Granger causality tests are misspecified and an error correction term model is necessary. If variables X_t and Y_t are both nonstationary in levels but the first differences of the variables are stationary, it is said that X_t and Y_t are both integrated of order one, and denoted as $I(1)$. If variables X_t and Y_t are both $I(1)$, their linear combinations of the form $Z_t = X_t - \alpha Y_t$ are also $I(1)$. However, if there is an α such that Z_t is $I(0)$, the linear combination of X_t and Y_t is stationary and it is said the two variables are cointegrated. If cointegration is present, regressions (11) and (12) are misspecified because they exclude an error correction term that can capture the long-term relationship between the two variables.

Before testing for the presence of cointegration, it is necessary to establish that the two time series are $I(1)$. The tests of stationarity are conducted by means of the Augmented Dickey and Fuller (1981) test, ADF, regression:

$$\ln X_t - \ln X_{t-1} = b_0 + b_1 \ln X_{t-1} + \sum_{i=1}^{m} b_i (\ln X_{t-i} - \ln X_{t-i-1}) + \varepsilon_t \,. \tag{14}$$

The null hypothesis of nonstationarity is H_0: $b_1 = 0$ in equation (14).

Engle and Granger (1987) propose several ways of testing for cointegration. This paper uses the ADF test of cointegration consisting of running first the cointegration regression

$$\ln X_t = \alpha_0 + \alpha_1 \ln Y_t + \varepsilon_t \, . \tag{15}$$

and then running the following ADF regression on the residuals of (15)

$$\varepsilon_t - \varepsilon_{t-1} = b_0 - b_1\varepsilon_{t-1} + \sum_{i=1}^{m} b_i(\varepsilon_{t-i} - \varepsilon_{t-i-1}) + \mu_t \, . \tag{16}$$

The null hypothesis of no cointegration is $H_0 : b_1 = 0$ in equation (16). If the null is rejected the variables X_t and Y_t are cointegrated and the error correcting models in equations (17) and (18) are needed in testing for causal relationships

$$\ln Y_t = \alpha_0 + \sum_{i=1}^{m} \alpha_i \ln X_{t-i} + \sum_{j=1}^{m} \beta_j \ln Y_{t-i} + \delta\varepsilon_{t-1} + \phi_t \tag{17}$$

$$\ln X_t = a_0 + \sum_{i=1}^{m} a_i \ln Y_{t-i} + \sum_{j=1}^{m} b_j \ln X_{t-j} + c\varepsilon_{t-1} + \mu_t \, . \tag{18}$$

In the above regression equations, the error correction term ε_{t-1} corresponds to the lagged residuals of regression (15).

ANALYSIS OF EMPIRICAL RESULTS

This section of the paper empirically analyzes the response of the equity market prices to the Persian Gulf Crisis by, first, estimating excess returns for each individual national stock market and second, by computing abnormal returns for selected portfolios of national equity markets. Since an event such as the Persian Gulf Crisis could produce changes in the alpha and beta coefficients, we proceed first to test for alpha and beta shifts by means of a procedure suggested by Ruback (1982) and Alexander, Benson, and Kampmeyer (1984). We test for alpha and beta shifts between the pre-event and post-event estimation periods using the following regression model

$$R_{i,t} = \alpha_{i,0} + \alpha_{i,1} D_t + \beta_{i,1} R_{w,t} + \beta_{i,2}(D_t R_{w,t}) + \varepsilon_{i,t}, \tag{19}$$

where $R_{i,t}$ is the observed return for national market i on day t, $R_{w,t}$ is the observed return for World Index i on day t, and D_t is the dummy variable that takes a value of zero for the pre-event estimation period and one for the post-event estimation period.

Table 1. Tests of Alpha and Beta Shifts Between the Pre-Event and Post-Event Periods (*t*-statistic in Parenthesis)

Market	$\alpha_{i,1}$	$\beta_{i,1}$
New York	–0.038 (–0.28)	0.305 (2.63)*
Toronto	–0.004 (–0.05)	0.191 (3.13)*
London	–0.096 (–0.80)	0.230 (2.28)*
Frankfurt	–0.298 (–1.52)	–0.054 (–0.33)
Zurich	–0.261 (–1.81)	0.037 (0.30)
Paris	–0.886 (–1.09)	0.336 (0.49)
Milan	–0.037 (–0.15)	–0.220 (–1.08)
Amsterdam	–0.117 (–0.95)	0.900 (0.86)
Australia	–0.037 (–0.31)	0.046 (0.46)
Tokyo	–0.178 (–0.86)	0.199 (1.13)
Hong-Kong	–0.108 (–0.76)	–0.125 (–1.04)
Singapore	–0.210 (–1.26)	0.080 (0.57)

Note: * Statistically significant at the 5% level.

Generally, the results reported in Table 1 indicate that the shifts in alphas and betas are insignificant and thus are not expected to have an important impact in the computation of abnormal returns. Therefore, the results reported in this paper correspond to those obtained by estimating alphas and betas from the pre-event estimation period containing observations from –206 through –23.

Table 2 reports the abnormal returns, *SAR*s, for the individual national markets. Before the invasion of Kuwait the *SAR*s are more negative than positive but statistically insignificant. For the day $t = +1$ and day $t = 0$ (the day of the invasion of Kuwait) the *SAR*s are negative or positive but insignificant in a statistical sense. All *SAR*s, except Toronto, are negative and statistically significant for day $t = +3$ (three days after the invasion of Kuwait). Most *SAR*s are insignificant on day $t = +112$ that is the day the Allied Forces-Iraq war began. However, on day $t = +114$, (two days after the initiation of the air attack) all national markets, except Toronto, exhibit statistically significant positive excess returns. On day $t = +118$ (the day the Allied Forces launched the ground attack) most *SAR*s are negative but insignificant.

In analyzing the reaction of the world equity markets to the Iraqi invasion of Kuwait, one needs to comment on the synchronization problem discussed in detail in Malliaris and Urrutia (1992). This problem has to do with the wide range of global time zones. For example, when the Iraqi army crossed the borders of Kuwait early in the morning (local Iraqi time) of August 2, 1990, the Tokyo stock market was half-way through its trading session for that day, while the New York stock market had not yet opened. The Tokyo market had negative returns for the day but were statistically insignificant. When stocks began trading in New York on the same day, August 2, 1990, the Iraqi invasion was already near its completion, and the closing S&P Index was down with negative daily returns, which were also statisti-

Table 2. Daily Standardized Abnormal Returns (SAR) for National Stock Markets for the Event Period : July 1, 1990 through January 31, 1991. ($t = -22$ to $t = +119$) Event day $t = 0$, August 2, 1990 : Iraqi invasion of Kuwait; Day $t = +112$, January 16, 1991: war started Day $t = +118$, January 24, 1991: Ground attack began

	New York	*Toronto*	*London*	*Australia*	*Frankfurt*	*Zurich*
–10	–0.6975	–1.2944	–0.6468	–0.4127	1.1011	–0.3720
–9	0.4462	0.1183	–0.4234	–0.3534	–0.3669	–0.1905
–8	–0.5060	0.5882	0.8086	–0.2121	–0.4095	0.2974
–7	–1.3127	–1.1030	–1.6249	–0.0916	–0.3687	–0.9830
–6	0.0886	0.0610	–0.0297	–0.5910	–0.5974	–0.8092
–5	0.4659	0.6314	0.1370	0.3711	–0.1178	0.0826
–4	–0.1124	–0.1874	–0.6297	0.0642	0.3174	–0.3874
–3	–0.6173	–0.0531	–0.5879	–0.6993	–0.4696	–0.4671
–2	0.1402	–0.3526	–0.5379	–0.7343	–0.2755	–0.5844
–1	2.1326*	1.0594	0.4146	0.6019	0.1677	0.5261
0	–1.5434	1.0860	0.9721	0.9317	–0.9588	0.0507
1	–0.5445	–0.4249	–1.9546	1.8771	–0.8696	–0.8947
2	–0.7786	–0.3453	–0.3218	–1.3401	–1.0593	–1.1828
3	–2.3350*	0.1949	–3.5192*	–2.3809*	–3.4958*	–4.8122*
4	–0.0009	–2.0759*	0.8925	0.0068	0.9748	1.6702
5	0.7973	0.3197	–0.0066	1.3414	–1.6965	–1.8079
6	0.5520	0.3800	0.4497	–0.2225	1.0329	0.3998
7	–0.8846	0.2685	–0.4279	0.4814	–0.3026	0.2587
8	0.5917	–0.0335	–0.8096	–0.7882	–1.5710	–2.1509*
9	–0.4414	0.2151	0.0420	0.4902	0.3320	0.0490
10	0.5148	1.0318	0.7019	0.0847	0.8383	1.0585
20	0.6245	–0.6523	0.0354	–1.3869	0.6903	0.1101
40	–0.9570	–0.7496	1.1474	0.6103	–1.3270	0.3142
60	–0.1861	0.9905	–0.9074	0.0596	0.0306	–0.7040
110	0.4296	–0.2130	0.0004	0.8870	–0.1495	–0.5499
111	–0.6745	–0.6674	–1.1219	–0.8686	–2.5290*	–2.2277*
112	0.4790	0.0439	–0.3011	–0.8006	–0.1877	0.0079
113	–0.4848	–1.0986	–1.8528	–1.1707	–0.0358	0.1846
114	2.5903*	1.5816	2.4730*	2.5563*	4.4182*	4.0501*
116	–0.2783	–0.1513	–1.0075	0.3451	–0.7151	–1.0788
117	–0.5425	–0.1653	–0.39	0.0989	–0.7468	0.5522
118	0.0838	–0.6521	–0.5074	–0.4512	–0.7380	0.8078
119	0.9429	1.0109	0.7711	0.4028	0.6898	1.7633

(continued)

cally insignificant. The closing times of the other ten markets fall approximately between Tokyo and New York, with Australia being the first stock market to trade.

On August 3, 1990 when Tokyo, Australia, Hong-Kong, and Singapore started trading, it was known that the invasion had been completed and that the United States had warned Iraq to withdraw. As the hours passed and the markets, first in

Table 2. (Continued)

	Paris	*Milan*	*Amsterdam*	*Tokyo*	*Hong Kong*	*Singapore*
–10	–0.1037	1.0422	–0.3437	–0.2179	1.6269	2.2583*
–9	–0.8662	–0.1863	–0.0011	0.1927	–0.3214	0.0875
–8	–0.2359	–0.1047	0.5802	–1.1659	0.2090	–0.1990
–7	–2.4764*	–0.9020	–0.9308	–1.0964	0.3891	0.1528
–6	–0.3103	–0.9964	–0.2342	–0.4000	–1.7841	–0.6161
–5	–0.4345	–0.3063	0.4732	0.1554	0.4747	0.3374
–4	–1.2461	0.4796	–0.3043	–0.6210	–1.1514	–0.1504
–3	–1.4599	0.0067	–0.6183	–1.1716	0.0023	0.2856
–2	–1.0641	–0.0271	–0.2474	–1.1335	–1.0155	–0.5053
–1	–0.0829	0.4103	0.3957	1.4682	–0.3037	–0.1349
0	–0.8258	–1.2741	0.3683	–0.0960	0.4593	0.2191
1	–2.5759*	–2.3892*	0.1996*	–1.1320	–1.7014	–1.1274
2	–2.9116*	–0.9145	–1.9668*	–1.2518	–1.9668*	–0.8603
3	–5.5254*	–3.6662*	–2.2503*	–2.1868*	–7.3418*	–4.7749*
4	1.4278	–0.2909	1.3896	–2.4402*	–0.3261	–2.9078*
5	–3.4674*	0.5763	–1.3550	2.2365*	1.3247	0.7611
6	0.6362	–0.9412	–0.0573	–2.1320*	–1.8150	0.0058
7	–0.5761	0.0076	–0.0291	–0.6189	–0.5295	–1.7102
8	–0.5708	–1.0897	–1.3832	–3.1688*	–1.1862	–3.0904*
9	–4.1186*	–0.1982	0.3928	1.0227	1.0043	0.1402
10	–0.5716	–0.2230	0.6821	4.0235*	3.0139*	1.9959*
20	0.4357	–0.5809	0.4425	–2.3229*	–1.9955*	–0.2102
40	0.9700	0.9534	–0.1928	–1.4614	–0.5059	0.1683
60	–1.7621	–0.2604	0.0959	1.6498	–0.0308	–0.0201
110	–1.3326	–0.0762	–0.1012	0.8051	0.4790	0.5798
111	–4.0285*	–2.3221*	–1.1149	–0.0332	–0.7351	0.0964
112	0.4705	0.0626	0.0168	0.1511	–1.3152	–1.0472
113	–0.4819	0.5982	–0.7139	–2.8133*	–0.0501	–0.9468
114	5.8185*	3.6398*	1.9894*	3.0303*	3.2259*	3.7073*
116	–0.9798	–1.0850	–0.8667	–1.3511	–0.2501	–0.5333
117	–0.8740	–1.4057	–0.0995	–0.1903	–0.2968	0.2548
118	–2.1601	–0.6337	–0.2443	–0.8043	0.9419	–0.6991
119	1.3499	0.1176	0.5137	0.6483	1.4776	0.4705

Note: * Significant at the 5% confidence level or better.

the Far East, then in Europe and finally in Canada and the United States closed, once again, almost all had negative but statistically insignificant returns. By August 5, 1990, three days after the completion of Kuwait's invasion and the strong warning by the United States and the U.N. Security Council, it became clear to the financial community that such an invasion was no longer a local dispute between two oil-producing Arab neighbors, but rather a global event with the U.S.-Allied Forces taking a strong position against Iraq. When Iraq failed to withdraw from Kuwait on August 5, 1990, early that day Kuwaiti time, first the Far Eastern stock markets followed by the European and finally by New York sold off with negative and statistically significant abnormal returns. Only Toronto did not react on August 5, and instead reacted the following day.

In sum, only five out of twelve national markets exhibit negative abnormal returns in the day of the invasion of Kuwait ($t = 0$) and the day the war started ($t = +112$). However these *SAR*s are statistically insignificant. The significant negative abnormal returns of day $t = +3$ suggest that the national equity markets reacted to the Iraqi invasion of Kuwait with three-days lag. The highly significant negative abnormal returns of day $t = +3$ reflect an increase in uncertainty and an anticipation of a long war. On the other hand, the statistically significant abnormal returns of day $t = +114$ suggest investors' expectations of a quick end to the armed conflict in the Middle East and, therefore, a dramatic reduction in uncertainty about the outcome of the conflict.

The standardized cumulative abnormal returns for individual national markets, *SCAR*s, constructed for several multi-day intervals, are presented in Table 3. Most *SCAR*s for the (–1,0) interval are positive but insignificant. Most *SCAR*s are negative but significant only for Australia, Paris, and Milan for the (0,+1) interval. However , most *SCAR*s are negative and statistically significant for the (0,+3) interval. All *SCAR*s are negative but insignificant for the (+111,+112) and (+117,+118) intervals. The *SCAR*s of Table 3 reinforce the conclusion drawn from the *SAR*s of Table 2, in the sense that national equity markets reacted with several-day lags to the invasion of Kuwait and that the event of August 2, 1990, had a bigger impact on stock prices that the initiation of the war and the ground attack.

In order to get more insights about the impact of the Gulf Crisis on equity prices, countries have been grouped in portfolios according to the degree of their dependence on oil imports as follows:

1. Partial dependence or oil exporters portfolio, composed of New York, Toronto, London, and Australia,[1]
2. European oil importers portfolio, composed of Frankfurt, Zurich, Paris, Milan, and Amsterdam; and,
3. Asian oil importers portfolio, composed of Tokyo, Hong-Kong, and Singapore.

There are other reasons for putting the UK and U.S. markets in the same portfolio. In effect, the major initiative of Operation Desert Shield was taken by these two countries. Therefore, it is expected that defense related companies in the UK and United States benefitted from the Gulf Crisis. Also, big corporations in the United States and UK often hedge against oil price fluctuations through forward and future markets.

Table 3. Standardized Cumulative Abnormal Returns (SCAR) of National Stock Markets for the Event Period : July 1, 1990 through January 31, 1991 ($t = -22$ to $t = +119$). Event Day $t = 0$, August 2, 1990: Iraqi invasion of Kuwait; Day $t = +112$, January 16,1991: war started Day $t = +118$, January 24, 1991: Ground attack began.

	(–1,0)		*(0,1)*		*(0, +3)*		*(+111,+112)*		*(+117,+118)*	
	SCAR	*Z*	*SCAR*	*Z*	*SCAR*	*Z*	*SCAR*	*Z*	*SCAR*	*Z*
New York	0.5892	0.4166	–2.0878	–1.4763	–5.2021	–2.6011*	–0.1955	–0.1382	–0.4588	–0.3244
Toronto	2.1454	1.5170	0.6612	0.4675	0.5107	0.2554	–0.6234	–0.4408	–0.8174	–0.5780
London	1.3867	0.9805	–0.9825	–0.6947	–4.80235	–2.4118*	–1.4230	–1.0062	–0.8975	–0.6346
Australia	1.5336	1.0844	2.8088	1.9861*	–0.9122	–0.4561	–1.6692	–1.1803	–0.3523	–0.2491
Frankfurt	–0.7910	–0.5593	–1.8283	–1.2928	–6.3835	–3.1918*	–2.7167	–1.9210	–1.4849	–1.0500
Zurich	0.5768	0.4079	–0.8440	–0.5968	–6.8390	–3.4195*	–2.2198	–1.5696	1.3600	0.9617
Paris	–0.9087	–0.6426	–3.4017	–2.4053*	–11.8387	–5.9194*	–3.5580	–2.5159*	–3.0341	–2.1454*
Milan	–0.8639	–0.6109	–3.6633	–2.5904*	–8.2440	–4.1220*	–2.2595	–1.5977	–2.0393	–1.4420
Amsterdam	0.7640	0.5403	0.5679	0.4016	–3.6492	–1.8246	–1.0981	–0.7765	–0.3437	–0.2431
Tokyo	1.3721	0.9702	–1.2281	–0.8684	–4.6666	–2.3333*	–0.1179	–0.0834	–0.9946	–0.7033
Hong Kong	0.1556	0.1100	–1.2422	–0.8783	–10.5507	–5.2754*	–2.0502	–1.4497	0.6452	0.4562
Singapore	0.0842	0.0595	–0.9083	–0.6423	–6.5435	–3.2718*	–0.9509	–0.6724	–0.4443	–0.3142

Note: * Significant at the 5% confidence level or better.

Table 4 shows the daily average standardized abnormal returns, *ASARs*, for the three portfolios. The Iraqi invasion of Kuwait had a global negative effect on all three portfolios of national markets. In effect, the abnormal returns on day $t = +3$ are all negative and significant. However, the *ASARs* are much larger for the oil

Table 4. Daily Average Standardized Abnormal Returns (ASAR) for Portfolios of National Stock Markets for the Event Period: July 1, 1990 through January 31, 1991 ($t = -22$ to $t = +119$). Event Day $t = 0$, August 2, 1990 : Iraqi invasion of Kuwait; Day $t = +112$, January 16, 1991: war started Day $t = +118$, January 24, 1991: Ground attack began.

	Exporters		*European - Imp.*		*Asian - Imp.*	
Event Day	*ASAR*	*z-Score*	*ASAR*	*z-Score*	*ASAR*	*z-Score*
–10	–0.7629	–1.5257	0.2648	0.5920	1.2224	2.1173*
–9	–0.0531	–0.1061	–0.3222	–0.7205	–0.0137	–0.0238
–8	0.1697	0.3394	0.0255	0.0570	–0.3853	–0.6673
–7	–1.0330	–2.0661*	–1.1322	–2.5317*	–0.1849	–0.3202
–6	–0.1178	–0.2356	–0.5895	–1.3181	–0.9334	–1.6167
–5	0.4013	0.8027	–0.0606	–0.1354	0.3225	0.5586
–4	–0.2164	–0.4327	–0.2282	–0.5102	–0.6409	–1.1101
–3	–0.4894	–0.9788	–0.6017	–1.3453	–0.2946	–0.5102
–2	–0.3712	–0.7423	–0.4397	–0.9832	–0.8847	–1.5324
–1	1.0521	2.1042*	0.2834	0.6337	0.3432	0.5945
0	0.3616	0.7232	–0.5279	–1.1805	0.1941	0.3362
1	–0.2617	–0.5234	–1.3059	–2.9202*	–1.3203	–2.2868*
2	–0.6964	–1.3929	–1.6070	–3.5934*	–1.3596	–2.3549*
3	–2.0101	–4.0201*	–3.9500	–8.8325*	–4.7678	–8.2581*
4	–0.2944	–0.5888	1.0343	2.3128*	–1.8914	–3.2760*
5	0.6129	1.2259	–1.5501	–3.4661*	1.4408	2.4955*
6	0.2898	0.5795	0.2141	0.4787	–1.3137	–2.2755*
7	–0.1407	–0.2813	–0.1283	–0.2869	–0.9529	–1.6504
8	–0.2599	–0.5198	–1.3531	–3.0256*	–2.4818	–4.2986*
9	0.0765	0.1529	–0.7086	–1.5844	0.7224	1.2513
10	0.5833	1.1666	0.3568	0.7979	3.0111	5.2154*
20	–0.3448	–0.6897	0.2195	0.4909	–1.5096	–2.6146*
40	0.0128	0.0256	0.1436	0.3210	–0.5997	–1.0387
60	–0.0109	–0.0217	–0.5200	–1.1627	0.5330	0.9231
110	0.2760	0.5520	–0.4419	–0.9881	0.6213	1.0761
111	–0.8331	–1.6662	–2.4444	–5.4659*	–0.2240	–0.3879
112	–0.1447	–0.2894	0.0740	0.1655	–0.7371	–1.2767
113	–1.1517	–2.3035*	–0.0898	–0.2008	–1.2701	–2.1998*
114	2.3003	4.6006*	3.9832	8.9067*	3.3212	5.7524*
116	–0.2730	–0.5460	–0.9451	–2.1133*	–0.7115	–1.2324
117	–0.2498	–0.4995	–0.5147	–1.1510	–0.0774	–0.1341
118	–0.3817	–0.7635	–0.5936	–1.3274	–0.1872	–0.3242
119	0.7819	1.5638	0.8868	1.9831*	0.8655	1.4991

Note: * Significant at the 5% confidence level or better.

Table 5. Average Standardized Cumulative Abnormal Returns (ASCAR) of Portfolios of National Stock Markets for the Event Period : July 1, 1990 through January 31, 1991 ($t = -22$ to $t = +119$). Event day $t = 0$, August 2, 1990 : Iraqi invasion of Kuwait; Day $t = +112$, January 16, 1991: war started Day $t = +118$, January 24, 1991: Ground attack began.

	(–1,0)		*(0,1)*		*(0,+3)*		*(+111,+112)*		*(+117,+118)*	
	SCAR	*Z*	*SCAR*	*Z*	*SCAR*	*Z*	*SCAR*	*Z*	*SCAR*	*Z*
Exporters Portfolio	1.4137	1.9993*	0.0999	0.1413	–2.6066	–2.6066*	–0.9778	–1.3828	–0.6315	–0.8931
Europe Importers Portfolio	–0.2446	–0.3867	–1.8339	–2.8996*	–7.3098	–8.2629*	–2.3704	–3.7480*	–1.1084	–1.7525
Asian Importers Portfolio	0.5373	0.6581	–1.1262	–1.3793	–7.2536	–6.2816*	–0.9611	–1.1771	–0.2646	–0.3241

Note: * Significant at the 5% confidence level or better.

importer portfolios than for the oil exporter portfolio. The *SAR*s are all negative for day $t = +111$ (one day before the war began), but are statistically significant only for the European importer portfolio. However, for day $t = +114$ (two days after the air attack started), all *SAR*s are positive and significant, but again, larger for the oil importer countries. For day $t = +118$ (the day the ground attack began) all *SAR*s are negative but not statistically significant.

The results of Table 4 indicate that the capital markets of oil importing countries were more affected than those of oil exporting countries by the Gulf Crisis. The abnormal returns for the portfolio of national markets also indicate that the negative impact of the conflict on stock prices was stronger on the days following the invasion of Kuwait than around the actual war.

The portfolios' cumulative abnormal returns (*ASCAR*s), presented in Table 5, indicate that the three portfolios experienced significant negative abnormal returns in the (0,+3) interval. Again, the negative impact is stronger for oil importing countries. The *ASCAR*s are also negative around the initiation of the war, the (+111,+112) interval, but they are significant only for the European oil importing portfolio.

The empirical findings for the portfolios of exporting and importing countries confirm the results reported for the individual national markets. That is, large

Table 6. Augmented Dickey-Fuller Tests of Stationarity for Oil Prices and Selected Equity Prices

Market	b_0	b_1	b_2	b_3	b_4	R^2
New York	0.167	–0.029	–0.068	–0.028	–0.076	0.028
	(0.082)	(0.014)	(0.056)	(0.056)	(0.056)	(2.26)
	(2.043)*	(–2.046)	(–1.211)	(–0.493)	(–1.352)	
Frankfurt	0.055	–0.007	–0.041	0.004	0.056	0.007
	(0.063)	(0.008)	(0.056)	(0.056)	(0.056)	(0.575)
	(0.877)	(–0.885)	(–0.724)	(0.070)	(0.993)	
Tokyo	0.028	–0.0029	0.062	–0.146	–0.005	0.026
	(0.059)	(0.006)	(0.056)	(0.056)	(0.056)	(2.078)
	(0.476)	(–0.500)	(1.095)	(–2.623)	(–0.081)	
Oil	0.029	–0.010	0.099	–0.202	0.023	0.051
	(0.024)	(0.008)	(0.056)	(0.056)	(0.057)	(4.286)*
	(1.196)	(–1.196)	(1.755)	(–3.636)*	(0.410)	

Notes: Model:

$$\ln P_t - \ln P_{t-1} = b_0 + b_1 \ln P_{t-1} + b_2(\ln P_{t-1} - \ln P_{t-2}) + b_3(\ln P_{t-2} - \ln P_{t-3}) + b_4(\ln P_{t-3} - \ln P_{t-4}) + \varepsilon_t$$

The null hypothesis is $b_1 = 0$ (prices are non-stationary).

The critical *t*-statistic for the b_1 coefficient at the 5% confidence level is –2.88 (from Dickey and Fuller 1981).

An asterisk * indicates significant at the 5% level.

Standard errors and *t*-statistics in parentheses.

negative abnormal returns in the days immediately following the invasion of Kuwait, reflecting an increase in market uncertainty and investors' expectations of a long armed conflict. The lesser impact on equity prices of the initiation of the war and the final ground attack suggest a decrease in uncertainty and investors' expectations of a quick end to the war. Finally, the negative impact of the Gulf Crisis was more dramatic in the equity markets of European and Asian importer countries than in those of in oil exporter countries.

Granger causality tests have also been conducted in order to examine the changes produced by the Gulf Crisis in the relationships between the oil market and the equity markets. Daily closing prices for the Arab lite oil spot have been collected from the *Wall Street Journal* for the time period October 1, 1989 through January 31, 1991. Causality tests have been conducted for two time periods, the pre-event period from October 1, 1989 through June 30, 1990; and the event-period from July 1, 1990 through January 31, 1991. Three representative national equity markets have been selected: New York (an oil exporter), Frankfurt (a European oil importer), and Tokyo (an Asian oil importer).

Table 7. Augmented Dickey-Fuller Tests of Stationarity for Oil Returns and Selected Equity Returns

Market	b_0	b_1	b_2	b_3	b_4	R^2
New York	−0.001	−1.242	0.157	0.114	0.024	0.542
	(0.001)	(0.124)	(0.104)	(0.083)	(0.056)	(93.576)*
	(−0.355)	(−10.042)*,a	(1.510)	(1.377)	(0.421)	
Frankfurt	−0.001	(−1.031)	(−0.014)	(−0.016)	(0.034)	0.525
	(0.001)	(0.115)	(0.100)	(0.081)	(0.056)	(87.174)*
	(−0.518)	(−8.976)*,a	(−0.139)	(−0.191)	(0.605)	
Tokyo	−0.001	−1.113	0.172	0.022	0.016	0.485
	(0.001)	(0.116)	(0.098)	(0.077)	(0.056)	(74.481)*
	(−1.398)	(−9.608)*,a	(1.751)	(0.281)	(0.288)	
Oil	0.001	−1.117	0.212	0.001	0.022	0.485
	(0.003)	(0.115)	(0.098)	(0.077)	(0.057)	(74.451)*
	(0.139)	(−9.669)*,a	(2.152)*	(0.007)	(0.395)	

Notes: Model:

$$R_t - R_{t-1} = b_0 + b_1 R_{t-1} + b_2(R_{t-1} - R_{t-2}) + b_3(R_{t-2} - R_{t-3}) + b_4(R_{t-3} - R_{t-4}) + \varepsilon_t$$

where

$$R_t = 100\ln(P_t/P_{t-1})$$

The null hypothesis is $b_1 = 0$ (returns are non-stationary)

The critical t-statistic for the b_1 coefficient at the 5% confidence level is −2.88 (from Dickey and Fuller 1981, Table 8.5.2).

An "a" indicates rejection of the null hypothesis at the 5% of significance level.

An asterisk * indicates significance at the 5% level.

Standard errors and t-statistics in parentheses.

Prior to the implementation of the Granger causality tests, it is necessary to check first, if prices are integrated of order one, denoted by $I(1)$, and second, if they are cointegrated. The results of the Augmented Dickey and Fuller, (ADF), tests of stationarity for the price levels and the price first differences or returns are presented in Tables 6 and 7, respectively.[2] The null hypothesis of nonstationarity cannot be rejected for price levels but it is rejected for returns. Therefore prices are $I(1)$, and tests of cointegration are appropriate. Table 8 indicates that the null of no-cointegration cannot be rejected in all cases, except for New York stock prices and oil prices. Therefore, Granger causality tests are conducted by running regressions (11) and (12), but for New York-oil we run regressions (17) and (18) which incorporate an error correction term to correct for cointegration. The results presented in Table 9 show[3] contemporaneous causality and strong lead-lag relationships between oil markets and the selected national equity markets. Contemporaneous causality and feedback suggest that oil markets and equity markets reacted simultaneously to the Persian Gulf Crisis and they affected each other during the conflict.

Table 8. Tests Of Cointegration Between Oil Prices And Selected Equity Prices

Independent Variable	*Dependent Variable*	b_1	R^2
New York	Oil	–0.0954	0.073
		(–3.48)[b]	(6.21)*
Oil	New York	–0.072	0.07
		(–2.94)[c]	(5.93)*
Frankfurt	Oil	–0.012	0.032
		(–0.89)	(2.62)*
Oil	Frankfurt	–0.014	0.034
		(–1.12)	(2.79)*
Tokyo	Oil	–0.006	0.02
		(–0.53)	(1.35)
Oil	Tokyo	–0.013	0.023
		(–1.08)	(1.82)

Notes: The model used to test for cointegration is the following:

$$\ln P_{1t} = \alpha_0 + \alpha_1 \ln P_{2t} + \varepsilon_t \qquad \text{(a)}$$

$$\varepsilon_t - \varepsilon_{t-1} = b_0 + b_1\varepsilon_{t-1} + b_2(\varepsilon_{t-1} - \varepsilon_{t-2}) + b_3(\varepsilon_{t-2} - \varepsilon_{t-3}) + b_4(\varepsilon_{t-3} - \varepsilon_{t-4}) + \mu_t \qquad \text{(b)}$$

The null hypothesis of no-cointegration is $H_0 : b_1 = 0$ (in equation *b*).

The *t*-critical at the 5% and 10% of significant levels are 3.17 and 2.84, respectively (from Engle and Granger 1987).

An "b" or a "c" indicate rejection of the null of no-cointegration at the 5% or 10%, respectively.

An asterisk * indicates the individual regression coefficient is different from zero at the 5% level.

t-statistics in parentheses.

Table 9. Granger Causality Test Between Oil Market And Selected National Equity Markets

Independent Variable	*Dependent Variable*	b_0, β_0	b_1, β_1	b_2, β_2	b_3, β_3	*F*
Oil	Frankfurt	–0.7537	–0.3789	–0.2322	–0.2961	10.26[a]
		(0.1384)	(0.1441)	(0.1454)	(0.1445)	
		(–5.445)*	(–2.629)*	(–1.597)	(2.050)	
Frankfurt	Oil	–0.1145	–0.048	0.017	–0.027	10.14[a]
		(0.0210)	(0.0219)	(0.0222)	(0.0221)	
		(–5.445)*	(–2.186)*	(0.767)	(–1.229)	
Oil	Tokyo	–0.4720	–0.0691	0.1020	0.1070	3.40[a]
		(0.1431)	(0.1440)	(0.1445)	(0.1406)	
		(–3.299)*	(–0.480)	(0.706)	(0.761)	
Tokyo	Oil	–0.0710	–0.0928	0.0239	–0.0617	9.43[a]
		(0.0225)	(0.0220)	(0.0226)	(0.0227)	
		(–3.299)*	(–4.219)*	(1.061)	(–2.723)*	
Oil	New York	–1.1641	–0.6841	–0.3958	0.1934	12.30[a]
		(0.1954)	(0.2062)	(0.2080)	(0.2067)	
		(–5.975)*	(–3.318)*	(–1.903)	(0.935)	
New York	Oil	–0.0840	0.0140	–0.0116	0.0077	11.16[a]
		(0.0147)	(0.0160)	(0.0158)	(0.0156)	
		(–5.724)*	(0.877)	(–0.732)	(0.496)	

Notes:

$$\ln Y_t = \alpha_0 + \sum_{i=1}^{m} \alpha_i \ln X_{t-i} + \sum_{j=1}^{m} \beta_j \ln Y_{t-j} + \delta\varepsilon_{t-1} + \phi_\tau \quad (X_t \rightarrow Y_t)^b \qquad \text{(I)}$$

$$\ln X_t = \alpha_0 + \sum_{i=1}^{3} \alpha_i \ln Y_{t-i} + \sum_{j=1}^{3} b_j \ln X_{t-j} + c\varepsilon_{t-1} + \mu_t \quad (Y_t \rightarrow X_t)^b \qquad \text{(II)}$$

An asterisk * indicates significant at the 5% confidence level or better.
An "a" indicates rejection of the null hypothesis of no-causality at the 5% level or better.
A "b" means that $c = 0$, $\delta = 0$ if no cointegration (cointegration is present only for oil prices and New York stock prices).
Equation I and II are Granger test of causality. Equation I tests if X is leading Y, and equation II tests if Y is leading X. If both events occur there is a feedback, Coefficients b_0 or β_0 statistically different from zero implies contemporaneous causality. The variable ε_{t-1} corresponds to the error correcting term if cointegration is present. The null hypotheses of no-causality are $\Sigma\beta_j = 0$ or $\Sigma b_j = 0$ for equations I and II, respectively.

SUMMARY AND CONCLUSIONS

The purpose of this paper is to empirically investigate the impact of the Gulf Crisis on national equity markets and the changes in causality relationships between the oil and equity markets during the Iraq-Kuwait conflict. The data consist of daily closing prices for the time period October 1, 1989 through January 31, 1991 for the World Index, Arab light oil and the following national equity markets: New York S&P 500, Toronto 300 Composite, London FT-100, Frankfurt DAX, Zurich Credit

Swisse, Paris CAC40, Milan Stock Index, Amsterdam ANP-CBS General, Australia All Ordinaries, Hong-Kong Hang Seng, Singapore Straits Times, and Tokyo Nikkei Average. The data are divided into an "Estimation period from October 1, 1989 to June 30, 1990 ($t = -206$ to $t = -23$), and an "Event period" from July 1, 1990 to January 31, 1991 ($t = -22$ to $t = +119$). The event day t=0 corresponds to August 2, 1990, the day the Iraqi army invaded Kuwait. Two other important dates in the event period are January 16, 1991 ($t = +112$), the day the war started, and January 24, 1991 ($t = +118$), the day the Allied Forces initiated the ground attack.

Daily and cumulative abnormal returns for selected multi-day intervals are calculated for the individual national markets. Half of the national markets exhibit negative abnormal returns in the day of the invasion of Kuwait ($t = 0$) and the day the war began ($t = +112$). The significant negative abnormal returns on day $t = +3$ indicate that the national markets reacted to the Iraqi invasion of Kuwait after it became clear that the crisis took a global perspective and President Bush committed to use force to liberate Kuwait. The highly negative abnormal returns of day $t = +3$ reflect an increase in uncertainty and anticipation of a long war. On the other hand, the statistically significant positive abnormal return of day $t = +114$ (two days after the war began) suggest that investors correctly anticipated a quick end to the war. Cumulative abnormal returns for individual national indexes reinforce the conclusion that the invasion of Kuwait had a bigger negative impact on stock prices that the initiation of the war and the ground attack.

Daily and cumulative abnormal returns are also computed for the following three portfolios of national markets: oil exporters portfolio composed of New York, Toronto, London, and Australia; European oil importers portfolio composed of Frankfurt, Zurich, Paris, Milan, and Amsterdam; and Asian oil importers portfolio composed of Tokyo, Hong-Kong, and Singapore. It is found that the negative abnormal returns of day $t = +3$ are much larger for the oil importing countries than for the oil exporters. For day $t = +114$ all abnormal returns are positive and significant but larger for the oil importing countries. The empirical findings for the portfolios reinforce the conclusions drawn for individual equity markets. Thus, we confirm large negative abnormal returns in the days following the invasion of Kuwait and a lesser impact caused by the initiation of the war and the ground attack. Finally, the equity markets of European and Asian oil importing countries were more affected than those of oil exporting countries. Our findings suggest a dramatic increase in market uncertainty around the invasion of Kuwait and investors' expectations for a long armed conflict. The lesser effect of the war suggests a reduction of uncertainty after the war started and investors' expectations of a quick end to the armed conflict.

Finally, causality tests are conducted to examine the changes produced by the Persian Gulf Crisis in the lead-lag relationships between the oil market and the equity markets. Little causality is detected for the period before the invasion of Kuwait. However, strong contemporaneous causality and an increase in lead-lag relationships and feedback between oil and equity markets are found for the period during the Persian Gulf Crisis. Thus, oil and stock markets reacted simultaneously to the conflict and they affected each other during the Gulf War.

ACKNOWLEDGMENT

We are thankful to Chirag Patel, Wichai Saenghirunwattana and Henry Wen-Herng King for data collection and extensive computational assistance.

NOTES

1. For brevity of presentation, the tables and analysis describe this as a portfolio of oil exporters.
2. The results of the tests of stationarity and cointegration tests are presented only for the event-period. Prices are also found to be $I(1)$ for the pre-event period. No-cointegration is found for the pre-event period.
3. The results of the Granger causality test are reported only for the event-period. Little lead-lag relationship was detected for the pre-event period.

REFERENCES

Alexander, G., P.G. Benson, and J.M. Kampmeyer. 1984. "Investigating the Valuation Effects of Announcements of Voluntary Corporate Selloffs." *Journal of Finance* 39: 503–517.

Brown, S.J., and J.B. Warner. 1980. "Measuring Security Price Performance." *Journal of Financial Economics* 8: 205–258.

———. 1985. "Using Daily Stock Returns: The Case of Event Studies." *Journal of Financial Economics* 14: 3–32.

Dann, L. 1981. "Common Stock Repurchases: An Analysis of Returns to Bondholders and Shareholders." *Journal of Financial Economics* 9: 113–138.

Dickey, D., and W. Fuller. 1981. "Likelihood Ratio Statistics for Autoregressive Time Series with a Unit Root." *Econometrica* 49: 1057–1072.

Dodd, P. 1980. "Merger Proposals, Management Discretion and Stockholder Wealth." *Journal of Financial Economics* 8: 105–137.

Dodd, P., and J.B. Warner. 1983. "On Corporate Governance: A Study of Proxy Contests." *Journal of Financial Economics* 11: 401–438.

Engle, R.F., and C.W.J. Granger. 1987. "Cointegration and Error correction: Representation, Estimation, and Testing." *Econometrica* 55: 251–276.

Geweke, J., R. Meese, and W. Dent. 1983. "Comparing Alternative Tests of Causality in Temporal Systems." *Journal of Econometrics* 21: 161–194.

Guilkey, D.K., and M.K. Salemi. 1982. "Small Sample Properties of Three Tests for Granger Causal Ordering in a Bivariate Stochastic System." *The Review of Economics and Statistics* 64: 668–680.

Holthausen, R. 1981. "Evidence on the Effect of Bond Covenants and Management Compensation Contracts on the Choice of Accounting Techniques: The Case of the Depreciation Switchback." *Journal of Accounting and Economics* 7: 73–109.

Leftwich, R. 1981. "Evidence on the impact of Mandatory Changes in Accounting Principles on Corporate Loan Agreements." *Journal of Accounting and Economics* 3: 3–36.

Malliaris, A.G., and J. Urrutia. 1992. "The International Crash of October 1987: Causality Tests." *Journal of Financial and Quantitative Analysis* 27: 353–364.

———. 1995. "The Impact of the Persian Gulf Crisis on National Equity Markets." *Advances in International Banking and Finance* 1: 43–65.

Masulis, R.W. 1980. "The Effect of Capital Structure Change on Security Prices: A Study of Exchange Offers." *Journal of Financial Economics* 8: 139–178.

Patell, J.M. 1976. "Corporate Forecasts of Earnings per Share and Stock Price Behavior: Empirical Tests." *Journal of Accounting Research* 14: 246–276.

Pierce, D.A., and L.D. Haugh. 1977. "Causality in Temporal Systems: Characterizations and a Survey." *Journal of Econometrics* 5: 265–293.

Roll, R. 1988. "The International Crash of October 1987." *Financial Analysts Journal* pp: 19–35.

Ruback, R.S. 1982. "The Effect of Discriminatory Price Control Decisions on Equity Values." *Journal of Financial Economics* 10: 83–105.

WHY STOCK VALUATION RATIOS DIFFER INTERNATIONALLY

Jongmoo Jay Choi and Michael G. Papaioannou

ABSTRACT

An essential step in international investment decisions is the valuation of national stock markets. This paper examines the stock market valuation of five major countries relative to the United States within a simple comparative valuation model. The effects of fundamental economic variables are estimated on a broad range of relative valuation ratios such as the price-earnings, the price-cash flow, and the price-book value ratios. Among the most notable findings is the significance of exchange rates, as well as the role of the cost of equity capital variable, in determining the relative stock valuation. Earnings growth is insignificant while dividends are important for select countries. Evidence also exists for changes in structural coefficients over time due to changing market environments in the 1980s as opposed to the 1970s.

The essence of security analysis is stock valuation. In an international context, stock valuation, however, is confounded by the persistent disparity that exists in the valuation of national markets. As shown in Table 1, the average price-earnings ratio (P/E) is almost three times higher in Japan (27.0) than in the UK (9.7) during the period between January 1974 and December 1988. Similar disparity is seen in other

Research in International Business and Finance, Supplement 1, pages 155–169.

ISBN: 0-7623-0110-4

valuation ratios such as the price-cash flow ratios (P/C) or the price-book value ratios (P/B). For the six major industrial countries included in Table 1, the average P/C ratio ranges from 8.9 for Japan to 3.6 for France, while the average P/B ratio is 2.51 for Japan but only 1.07 for France.

Fundamentally, this persistent international disparity in stock valuation ratios portends partially segmented international capital markets. Conditional on these market environments, two approaches, however, have been forwarded toward providing more specific explanations for valuation disparities. The first explanation is based on institutional and accounting factors. French and Poterba (1990), for instance, attribute a portion of the U.S.-Japanese valuation differences to the Japanese accounting practices and cross-ownership of Japanese corporations. The second explanation is based on economic fundamentals. Ando and Auerback (1988) and Frankel (1991) document significant differences in the costs of capital of Japanese and U.S. corporations. Duke and Papaioannou (1993) show relatively lower size-adjusted trading volumes and concentrated investments in larger firms in Japan, suggesting a higher risk premium in Japan relative to other advanced countries. Choi (1995) estimates the effect of macroeconomic factors in the relative valuation of the U.S.–Japanese stock markets.

This paper follows the second approach and examines the effect of economic fundamentals in the relative valuation ratios of six major stock markets (Canada, France, Germany, Japan, the UK, and the United States). A simple comparative valuation model is developed to examine the relative stock valuation of five of these countries using the United States as a reference country. The comparative valuation model identifies the cost of capital, earnings growth rates, exchange rates, and dividend payout ratios as potential explanatory variables.

Estimation results indicate that exchange rate changes are the most consistently significant variable affecting relative levels of all three valuation ratios included in Table 1. This finding suggests the presence of an economic exposure effect even when currency translation effects are ostensibly absent. The cost of capital is less prominent but still an important determinant of relative stock valuation ratios for most countries. Earnings growth rates are shown to be generally insignificant, while dividend payments are important for select countries. Another important variable is a dummy variable which measures the intertemporal changes in regulatory market environments over time. The coefficient on this variable shows the sensitivity of the valuation ratios to underlying market environments.

This paper is organized in four sections. The first section presents a basic comparative valuation model. The second section describes the data and examines correlation patterns among independent variables. The third section reports estimation results of the basic model. The fourth section examines the effect of changing market environments over time. The final section contains a summary and conclusions.

Table 1. Valuations of International Stock Markets (January 1974–December 1988)

	Canada	*France*	*Germany*	*Japan*	*U.K*	*U.S.A.*
Price-Earnings Ratio						
High	45.4	252.4	17.7	64.0	17.3	20.3
Low	7.6	4.2	7.1	15.1	4.7	7.0
Average	13.9	19.8	11.7	27.0	9.7	10.9
Price-Cash Flow Ratio						
High	11.6	7.2	6.4	18.1	10.5	9.5
Low	4.1	1.6	2.9	5.2	3.0	4.2
Average	6.5	3.6	4.0	8.9	5.7	6.0
Price-Book Value Ratio						
High	2.08	2.40	2.83	5.2	2.45	2.32
Low	0.77	0.54	1.06	1.57	0.66	0.98
Average	1.39	1.07	1.61	2.51	1.23	1.44
Capital Gains (%)						
High	77.6	88.5	81.8	78.5	136.2	51.5
Low	–42.4	–39.9	–39.7	–13.7	–29.2	–21.5
Average	10.8	14.5	9.3	16.7	18.6	9.1
Dividend Yield (%)						
High	6.1	9.9	6.5	2.9	7.5	6.6
Low	2.3	2.3	2.6	0.5	3.2	2.8
Average	3.9	5.4	4.4	1.6	5.3	4.6

Note: Capital gain ratios are based on 12-month holding period.

Source: Morgan Stanley, *Capital International Perspectives.*

A COMPARATIVE VALUATION MODEL

Specification of a market valuation model requires assumptions on international capital markets. Due to capital controls and other constraints, many researchers believe that even the capital markets of advanced countries are not totally integrated with other world capital markets.[1]

Following this view, we assume an *N*-asset, *N*-country model, with one composite asset for each of the *N* countries, in an environment of partially segmented international capital markets. With market segmentation, assets are not perfect substitutes and their values are partly or exclusively determined by their national economic variables. This simple *N*-asset, *N*-country model is useful for comparative valuation purposes, and differs from an asset pricing model that purports to value assets in the context of portfolios in a given market environment.

A parsimonious model of stock valuation utilizes the discounted cash flow model. It is assumed that the value of stock of country i, P^i, equals the present value of a respective stream of dividends per share, D_t^i, discounted at a capitalization rate, r^i, for each country, and measured in the respective country's currency units. If one assumes a constant growth of dividends at a rate of g^i, we have the Gordon model:

$$P^i = \frac{D_1^i}{(r^i - g^i)};\ r^i > g^i \tag{1}$$

where time subscripts are dropped for contemporaneous values for notational convenience and the subscript "1" indicates one-period lead values. If needed, the dividend payout ratio can also be introduced in equation (1) by writing:

$$D_1^i = d^i E_1^i \tag{2}$$

where E_1^i is earnings per share at time one and d^i is the dividend payout ratio.

Note that P^i in the above is expressed in country i's currency units. Hence, no currency translation is necessary. However, the concept of economic exchange exposure suggests that, quite apart from translation effects, exchange rate changes can still affect the firm's operating earnings and asset values in that country due to economic channels that operate through revenues and expenditures. That is, exchange rate changes cause changes in relative prices of outputs, which in turn affect revenues depending on the market demand elasticity for the firm's outputs. Similarly, changes in input prices caused by exchange rate changes influence the expenditures depending on the firm's dependence on local supply of inputs.

The effect of economic exchange exposure in country i can be expressed as:

$$E_t^i = f(e_t^i, \beta_t^i) \approx h_t^i e_t^i + s_t^i E_t^i \tag{3}$$

where e_t^i is the spot value of country i's currency value against U.S. dollars, the numeraire currency, β_t^i is a vector of other variables affecting country i's cash flows, and h^i and s^i are arbitrary parameters. Earnings therefore consist of a component that is subject to economic exchange exposure and a component that is independent of it. The economic exposure stems from the fact that exchange rate changes affect the relative prices and costs and, hence, the revenues and expenditures of the firm's overseas operations. At the level of the firm, the direction of the economic exposure effect depends on market demand elasticities for the firm's outputs and the firm's dependence on local inputs (Choi 1986). For an aggregate economy, $h_t^i < 0$ if the Marshall-Lerner condition concerning the domestic and foreign demand elasticities hold.

We may express the relative valuation of any pair of stock markets in terms of their relative valuation ratios, using the United States as the numeraire country. Equations (1) through (3) can be combined to yield:

$$P^i/E^i = d^i_1(h^i_1 e^i_1 + s^i_1 E^i_1) \,/\, (r^i - g^i)E^i \tag{4}$$

for country i, and, for the numeraire country:

$$P^{US}/E^{US} = d^{US}_1(h^{US}_1 e^{US}_1 + s^{US}_1 E^{US}_1) \,/\, (r^{US} - g^{US})E^{US}. \tag{5}$$

On the surface, these P/E ratios are neutral with respect to the monetary unit and hence are free of direct currency translation impact; the dimensions are either currency i over currency i or the U.S. dollar over the U.S. dollar. However, they are not completely free of exchange rate influences for two reasons. First, to the extent that reported national earnings include earnings from firms' overseas operations, the reported earnings are subject to some translation effects as well as economic impacts arising from foreign operational earnings. Second and perhaps more importantly, domestic operation also has an exchange exposure in an economic sense due to the effect of exchange rates on relative prices and relative competitive positions. These effects of exchange rates are summarized in h^i_1 and h^{US}_1 in equations (4) and (5).

Subtraction of equation (5) from (4) yields a model of relative P/E ratios between country i and the United States. It is also possible, *mutatis mutandis*, to derive similar models for the price-cash flow ratios (P/C) or the price-book value ratios (P/B). Equations for these alternative ratios are obtained if we assume that, ceteris paribus, cash flows and book values are positively related to earnings. Linear approximation to equations (4) and (5) enables us to express the relative valuation equation in terms of all three ratios:

$$\ln(P^i/x^i) - \ln(P^{US}/x^{US}) = a_0 + a_1(r^i - r^{US}) + a_2(g^i - g^{US})$$

$$+ a_3 \ln e^i + a_4 \ln d^i \,,$$

$$x^i = E^i, C^i, B^i;\; x^{US} = E^{US}, C^{US}, B^{US} \tag{6}$$

where E, C, and B respectively denote earnings, cash flows and book value of equities. Thus, the relative valuation ratios of country i vis-*à*-vis the United States is expressed as a function of relative economic fundamentals of the two countries. The use of bilateral exchange rates here abstracts from any effects of misaligned multilateral cross exchange rates.

It is possible that an equilibrium in the world money markets establishes some connection between explanatory variables in equation (6). In an environment of perfectly integrated money markets as well as completely flexible foreign exchange markets, the international interest rate parity, for example, would indicate a close correlation between the interest rate differential and exchange rate changes. Existence of capital controls and other frictions in segmented international markets, however, would preclude such an equilibrium.

DATA AND CORRELATION PATTERNS

Empirical estimation utilizes monthly data for Canada, France, Germany, Japan, the United Kingdom, and the United States for the period of January 1974 to December 1988. This period represents a period of flexible exchange rates after the turbulence following the 1973 oil shock had subsided. It excludes the recent period of asset price deflation in Japan started in 1989. Data definitions are: P^i = the stock price index of country i; E^i = expected corporate earnings; r^i = the cost of equity capital measured by the annualized rate of monthly price changes and dividend yields; d^i = dividend payout rate; g^i = the annualized growth rate of monthly expected corporate earnings; and e^i = the U.S. dollar per one foreign currency unit. The United States is used as the numeraire country. All variables are measured based on end-of-the-month data for the entire sample period of January 1974 to December 1988.

Consistent with the assumption of the discount cash flow model, earnings and cost of equity capital are defined as expected values rather than actual values. Expected values were estimated by ARIMA (1,1,1) with in-sample data.[2] The expected growth rates used are also the rates of changes in ARIMA estimates of corporate earnings levels; alternatively, ARIMA was applied directly on growth rates of actual earnings, but with no appreciable differences.

The data source for capital market data is *Capital International Perspectives* published by Morgan Stanley. The three valuation ratios—P/E, P/C, and P/B—were calculated by Morgan Stanley. These ratios are based on broad market aggregate measures; see *Capital International Perspectives* for exact definitions. The exchange rate series was provided by Wharton Econometric Forecasting Associates, Inc., Pennsylvania.

Table 2 provides correlations among independent variables used in regressions. The correlation of particular interest is the one between the cost of capital differential (country i minus the United States) and exchange rates against the U.S. dollar. The international interest rate parity specifies a relation between the interest rate differential and exchange rate changes. To the extent that the cost of equity capital can be measured by the risk-free interest rate plus the market risk premium, a significant correlation is expected between $r^i - r^{US}$ and $\ln e^i$. However, the correlation is significant at the five percent level between these variables only for Japan and France in Table 2, and the magnitudes are generally low (all less than 0.4 in absolute values). No significant correlation is observed between these two variables for the rest of the countries, indicating either deviations from interest rate parity or time-varying relative risk premiums, or both.

Another interesting point is that the correlation between the cost of capital differential and the dividend payout rate is statistically significant for all countries considered, although the signs are different (negative for Canada and Germany and positive for the rest). Furthermore, exchange rate changes have statistically significant and negative correlations with the dividend payout rate for all countries except

Table 2. Correlation Among Independent Variables

	Canada	*France*	*Germany*	*Japan*	*U.K.*
corr (r^i-r^{US}, g^i-g^{US})	–0.057	–0.005	0.032	–0.072	0.038
corr (r^i-r^{US}, ln e^i)	0.032	–0.299*	–0.084	–0.408*	0.009
corr (r^i-r^{US}, d^i)	–0.272*	0.223*	–0.413*	0.561*	0.187*
corr (g^i-g^{US}, ln e^i)	–0.056	0.048	–0.001	0.009	–0.062
corr (g^i-g^{US}, d^i)	0.019	–0.130	0.045	–0.008	0.055
corr (ln e^i, d^i)	–0.322*	–0.275*	–0.002	–0.646*	–0.615*

Notes: * Significant at 5%.

Data definitions: r^i = the cost of equity capital measured by the annualized rate of monthly price changes and dividend yields, g^i = expected corporate earnings growth rates, d^i = dividend payout rate, ln e^i = natural logarithm of the exchange rate of the U.S. dollar per one unit of the country *i*'s currency. Superscript "*i*" refers to the variable of country *i*, and "*US*" to the U.S. variable.

Germany. The negative correlation between exchange rate changes and dividend payout rates means that a depreciation of the respective country's currency against the U.S. dollar is associated with a higher rate of dividend payments domestically. This supports a notion that since a depreciating currency indicates inflationary pressures dividends will have to remain high to induce equity investments (or, conversely, in an economy with an appreciating currency and low inflation such as Japan, dividend payments can be low).

ESTIMATION RESULTS

This section reports estimation results of equation (6) for three relative valuation ratios—the price-earnings ratio (P/E), the price-book value ratio (P/B), and the price-cash flow ratio (P/C)—for five major industrial countries (Canada, France, Germany, Japan, and the UK) relative to the United States.

Table 3 reports the time-series estimation results of P/E ratios with and without the dividend payout rate. Estimation was done by an ordinary least square; the Cochrane-Orcutt method was also tried but was not fruitful. However, to examine the effect of changing market environments, a time dummy will be included later in the form of both intercept and slope dummies. The estimation results of the basic model indicate that, in both equations with and without dividends, the cost of equity capital variable is significant and negative for Canada, Germany, and the UK. For France and Japan, however, the cost of capital is not statistically significant, although the signs are negative for all cases confirming a familiar negative relation between the discount rate and stock valuation.

Terms indicating the expected corporate earnings growth, $g^i - g^{US}$, are all insignificant at the five percent level (two-tailed test). Even at the ten percent level, the coefficient is significant only for Japan.

The variable of most significance is the exchange rate. The exchange rate coefficients are significant for all countries for all model specifications. The signs of the exchange rate coefficient are negative for all countries except Japan, indicating that a rise in the value of the country's currency against the U.S. dollar lowers the P/E ratio of that country relative to the United States. This result offers evidence that an appreciation of the currency value leads to a faster decrease in the country's stock prices relative to corporate earnings. This is consistent with the view that the financial markets (stocks) adjust faster than the real markets (earnings). In Japan, however, a strong yen is associated with a rise in stock prices, which is consistent with the translation effect of net assets or net cash inflows from the U.S. standpoint.

The relative P/E ratios are also shown to be affected by dividend payout ratios. The effects of dividend payout ratios are significantly positive for all countries but Japan. This indicates that, except in Japan, high dividend payments are viewed

Table 3. Estimation of the Price-Earnings Ratios

	Constant	$r^i - r^{US}$	$g^i - g^{US}$	$\ln e^i$	d^i	R^2	F
Canada	0.050	–0.092*	–0.0002	–1.759*		0.39	35.4
	(0.87)	(–5.17)	(–0.07)	(–8.74)			
	–0.563*	–0.033*	0.0001	–0.955*	1.243*	0.88	301.2
	(–16.19)	(–3.95)	(0.22)	(–10.04)	(25.92)		
France	–1.244*	0.019	–0.003	–0.857*		0.16	10.6
	(–4.09)	(0.90)	(–1.43)	(–4.80)			
	–0.787*	–0.015	–0.0003	–0.448*	0.328*	0.68	88.6
	(–4.14)	(–1.12)	(–0.24)	(–3.96)	(16.5)		
Germany	–0.306*	–0.033*	0.0006	–0.379*		0.24	18.0
	(–5.37)	(–4.77)	(1.16)	(–5.87)			
	–0.927*	–0.011#	0.0004	–0.361*	1.407*	0.47	36.6
	(–10.50)	(–1.67)	(0.84)	(–6.63)	(8.38)		
Japan	5.114*	–0.005	0.001#	0.795*		0.65	99.2
	(17.98)	(–1.30)	(1.64)	(15.25)			
	5.162*	–0.0058	0.001	0.810*	0.082	0.69	74.1
	(16.92)	(–1.36)	(1.62)	(13.06)	(0.44)		
U.K	0.197*	–0.022*	0.0006	–0.471*		0.42	33.0
	(6.09)	(–5.82)	(1.18)	(–9.02)			
	–0.136	–0.025*	0.0006	–0.355*	0.563*	0.44	39.6
	(–1.12)	(–6.45)	(1.17)	(–5.41)	(2.83)		

Notes: Numbers in parentheses are *t*-values.

* Significant at 5% (two-tailed test)

Significant at 10% (two-tailed test)

Data definitions: r^i = the cost of equity capital measured by the annualized rate of monthly price changes and dividend yields, g^i = expected corporate earnings growth rates, d^i = dividend payout rate, $\ln e_i$ = natural logarithm of the exchange rate of the U.S. dollar per one unit of the country *i*'s currency. Superscript "*i*" refers to the variable of country *i*, and "*US*" to the U.S. variable.

Table 4. Estimation of the Price-Book Value Ratios

	Constant	$r^i - r^{US}$	$g^i - g^{US}$	*ln* e^i	d^i	R^2	*F*
Canada	0.013	–0.036*	0.0006	–0.143		0.09	5.3
	(0.42)	(–3.60)	(0.74)	(–1.26)			
	0.147*	–0.049*	0.0005	–0.317*	–0.270*	0.20	10.2
	(3.57)	(–4.99)	(0.72)	(–2.82)	(–4.77)		
France	–1.415*	–0.058*	0.0008	–0.662*		0.37	33.4
	(–11.38)	(–6.66)	(1.01)	(–9.10)			
	–1.477*	–0.053*	0.0005	–0.717*	–0.044*	0.42	29.7
	(–12.12)	(–6.26)	(0.61)	(–9.92)	(–3.45)		
Germany	–0.128*	–0.006	0.0001	–0.250*		0.08	5.0
	(–2.21)	(–0.85)	(0.19)	(–3.83)			
	0.141	–0.016*	0.0002	–0.258*	–0.609*	0.13	6.3
	(1.36)	(–2.08)	(0.39)	(–4.04)	(–3.09)		
Japan	42.81*	–0.013*	0.0007	0.705*		0.78	198.7
	(22.3)	(–4.52)	(1.42)	(20.0)			
	3.878*	–0.005#	0.0007#	0.577*	–0.751*	0.82	190.0
	(20.7)	(–1.91)	(1.76)	(15.0)	(–6.05)		
U.K.	0.138*	–0.017*	0.0003	–0.510*		0.32	25.8
	(3.49)	(–3.51)	(0.05)	(–8.01)			
	0.056	–0.017*	0.0003	–0.481*	0.138	0.32	19.3
	(0.37)	(–3.53)	(0.04)	(–5.88)	(0.55)		

Notes: Numbers in parentheses are *t*-values.
* Significant at 5% (two-tailed test).
\# Significant at 10% (two-tailed test).
Data definitions: r^i = the cost of equity capital measured by the annualized rate of monthly price changes and dividend yields, g^i = expected corporate earnings growth rates, d^i = dividend payout rate, ln e^i = natural logarithm of the exchange rate of the U.S. dollar per one unit of the country *i*'s currency. Superscript "*i*" refers to the variable of country *i*, and "*US*" to the U.S. variable.

positively by the market; in Japan, high retention is a primary vehicle for internal growth and future capital gains. This combination of relatively lower dividends and higher capital gains in Japan was evident in the descriptive statistics given in Table 1. Finally, it should be noted that the inclusion of the dividend payout rate as an additional explanatory variable does not materially alter the effects of other explanatory variables for most countries.

Tables 4 and 5 provide the estimation results of the price-book value (P/B) ratios and the price-cash flow (P/C) ratios, respectively. Compared to the P/E ratios reported in Table 3, the signs of individual coefficients are generally more consistent, and the levels of significance are higher in Tables 4 and 5. Between the two latter ratios, the significance of coefficients is more uniform and robust for P/C than P/B. This suggests that cash flows, rather than earnings or book values, are the most direct subject of market capitalization.

Table 5. Estimation of the Price-Cash Flow Ratios

	Constant	$r^i - r^{US}$	$g^i - g^{US}$	$\ln e^i$	d^i	R^2	F
Canada	–0.048	–0.048*	0.0005	–1.172*		0.50	54.6
	(–1.64)	(–5.28)	(0.75)	(–11.38)			
	–0.242*	–0.029*	0.0006	–0.918*	0.393*	0.65	77.0
	(–7.27)	(–3.70)	(1.03)	(–10.08)	(8.57)		
France	–1.449*	–0.034*	0.0004	–0.560*		0.32	26.8
	(–13.25)	(–4.48)	(0.65)	(–8.75)			
	–1.436*	–0.035*	0.0005	–0.548*	0.009	0.33	20.2
	(–12.98)	(–4.54)	(0.75)	(–8.34)	(0.81)		
Germany	–0.563*	–0.026*	0.0003	–0.119*		0.12	7.8
	(–11.6)	(–4.43)	(0.74)	(–2.17)			
	–0.600*	–0.025*	0.0003	–0.118*	0.085	0.12	5.9
	(–6.71)	(–3.81)	(0.70)	(–2.15)	(0.50)		
Japan	4.593*	–0.018*	0.0005	0.793*		0.81	231.3
	(22.2)	(–5.92)	(1.03)	(21.0)			
	4.375*	–0.014*	0.0006	0.724*	–0.406*	0.81	182.7
	(20.2)	(–4.26)	(1.15)	(16.3)	(–2.82)		
U.K.	0.288*	–0.022*	0.0006	–0.521*		0.36	31.0
	(7.36)	(–4.70)	(0.99)	(–8.25)			
	–0.082	–0.025*	0.0006	–0.392*	0.624*	0.38	25.7
	(–0.55)	(–5.27)	(0.98)	(–4.92)	(2.59)		

Notes: Numbers in parentheses are *t*-values.

* Significant at 5% (two-tailed test).

Significant at 10% (two-tailed test).

Data definitions: r^i = the cost of equity capital measured by the annualized rate of monthly price changes and dividend yields, g^i = expected corporate earnings growth rates, d^i = dividend payout rate, $\ln e^i$ = natural logarithm of the exchange rate of the U.S. dollar per one unit of the country *i*'s currency. Superscript "*i*" refers to the variable of country *i*, and "*US*" to the U.S. variable.

For individual coefficients, the cost of capital term has a significant negative effect at the five percent level on both the relative P/B and P/C ratios for all countries for 18 out of 20 times. This is consistent with the previous finding in Table 3 that the relative cost of capital and the relative P/E ratios are negatively related. As in the case of the P/E in Table 3, the effects of corporate earnings growth are generally insignificant on both P/B and P/C ratios.

The dividend payout rate has a divergent impact depending on the ratios and countries. For P/B, it has a significant negative effect for all countries except the UK; and for P/C, it is significantly positive for Canada and the UK, but negative for Japan. These results are in contrast with the previous result on P/E that the effects are significant and positive for all countries except Japan. These differential results of dividends mirror the controversy in the literature: dividends can have a positive effect on stock prices because of information signalling and uncertainty, a negative effect due to taxes and growth opportunities, or a zero effect when the two effects exactly offset each other.

It is not exactly clear why these different arguments apply differently for different countries. One important underlying factor, though, is time horizon of management and society. In a society with long time horizon, retention of earnings for future growth may be viewed more positively than immediate cash dividends and consumption. With short time horizon, cash dividends may be in greater demand. Hence, the negative effect of dividends on stock valuation in Japan relative to the United States may be understood by long-term orientation of the Japanese management compared to their U.S. counterpart.

Exchange rates have a highly significant effect on both the P/B and P/C ratios. This finding is similar to that of the P/E ratio and indicates a high association between the country's currency rate against the dollar and the respective relative valuation ratios. In particular, an exchange rate appreciation relative to the U.S. dollar leads to a decrease in the relative valuation ratios of the country. The notable exception, however, is Japan, where a strong yen against the dollar results in an increase in the Japanese P/B and P/C ratios relative to the United States.

For all three valuation ratios and for all countries except Japan, an appreciation in the value of the country's currency relative to the U.S. dollar is associated with a *decline* in the country's valuation ratios relative to those of the United States. This finding makes sense if higher currency values lead to higher real export prices and to lower international demand for the country's products. If that is true, one would expect higher valuation effects to occur with an appreciating currency in a country whose trade balance with the United States is improving assuming an elastic world market demand. The Japanese case, however, is an exception because an appreciation of the yen is associated with an *increase* in the relative valuation of the Japanese stock markets. This finding on Japan is not consistent with the trade-worsening effects of a strong yen expected with an elastic market demand. However, this is consistent with the existence of the J-curve phenomenon as well as the intervening effect of a third variable such as higher saving rates of Japan than in the United States.

THE EFFECT OF CHANGING MARKET ENVIRONMENTS

The above analysis is subject to qualifications due to changing market environments over time during the sample period. The sample period is marked with major decontrol of capital flows and financial markets occurring in the United States, Japan, and Europe around 1981. In the United States a law concerning deregulation of depository institutions was enacted; in Japan, international capital flows were decontrolled; in the UK and elsewhere in Europe, measures were taken to remove barriers to international movements of capital and labor. To address the issue of intertemporal stability of the underlying structural model, time is added in the basic model in the form of an intercept and an augmented regression including both the

Table 6. The Effect of Time on P/E Ratios

	Canada		France		Germany		Japan		U.K.	
constant	0.189*	–0.249*	–3.081*	–3.491*	–0.364*	0.115	4.928*	2.499*	0.219*	0.485*
	(3.43)	(–3.05)	(–6.88)	(–2.29)	(–6.57)	(1.03)	(16.0)	(2.85)	(3.73)	(5.58)
$r^i – r^{US}$	–0.127*	0.015	–0.0005	–0.058*	–0.034*	–0.021*	–0.0029	–0.016*	–0.024*	–0.013*
	(–7.53)	(0.58)	(–0.026)	(–2.14)	(–5.13)	(–2.43)	(–0.71)	(–2.34)	(–5.60)	(–5.69)
$g^i – g^{US}$	–0.0007	0.0006	–0.0024	0.001	0.0006	0.001#	0.0011#	0.0011	0.0006	–0.0003
	(–0.06)	(0.36)	(–1.30)	(0.46)	(1.27)	(1.68)	(1.68)	(1.27)	(1.31)	(–0.48)
$\ln e^i$	–0.0052	–1.943*	–2.195*	–2.533*	–0.478*	0.109	0.765*	0.325*	0.494*	–0.843*
	(–0.02)	(–4.54)	(–7.29)	(–2.46)	(–7.39)	(0.84)	(13.73)	(2.04)	(–6.83)	(–7.17)
T	0.449*	1.166*	0.807*	–0.178	–0.056*	–0.577*	0.42	3.358*	–0.0129	–0.409*
	(6.77)	(8.30)	(–5.28)	(–0.11)	(–2.53)	(–4.50)	(1.54)	(3.62)	(–0.45)	(–4.18)
$(r^i – r^{US})T$		–0.206*		0.152*		0.0006		0.004		0.021*
		(–6.23)		(3.71)		(0.04)		(0.43)		(2.71)
$(g^i – g^{US})T$		0.0002		–0.007*		–0.001		–0.0004		0.002*
		(0.11)		(–2.17)		(–1.24)		(–0.35)		(2.19)
$(\ln e^i)T$		2.526*		0.566		–0.698*		0.610*		0.584*
		(4.27)		(0.53)		(–4.65)		(3.61)		(4.07)
R^2	0.52	0.61	0.29	0.36	0.32	0.35	0.69	0.73	0.43	0.50
F	44.4	36.6	16.2	13.3	18.9	12.5	75.6	63.9	29.9	22.9

Notes: Numbers in parentheses are *t*-values.
* Significant at 5% (two-tailed test); # Significant at 10% (two-tailed test).
T = time dummy (1 for post-January 1981 period and 0 for pre-January 1981).

intercept and slope dummies (one for the post-January 1981 period and zero before).

Table 6 examines the impact of time on the relative P/E ratio in the context of an augmented regression to capture the effects of possible government measures or other changes in policy regimes. The estimation results show a significant intercept dummy for seven out of ten equations, suggesting that an important structural shift has occurred. The effect of time is positive for Canada and Japan, and negative for all European countries considered. In particular, the relaxation of capital controls in Japan and monetary deregulation contained in the Depository Institution Deregulation and Monetary Control Act in the United States in 1981 appear to have contributed to a rise in the Japanese P/E ratio versus the United States. It is interesting that these measures appear to have benefitted the Japanese stocks more than the U.S. stocks, possibly because of the outburst of outward direct investments by the Japanese firms since the decontrol.

The effects of slope time dummies in the cost of capital term are significant only for Canada, France, and the UK. Since the time-invariant static coefficient of the cost of capital term has a relatively high significance for France and the UK in the augmented regression, its impact appears to have been influenced by static policy changes as well as the dynamic changes in market environments that work through time-slope coefficients. For Canada, the impact of the cost of capital term appears to be influenced only by the slope time coefficients. For Japan and Germany, the static time-invariant coefficients of the cost of capital term are shown to be significant, while the effect of the slope dummies is insignificant, indicating that the effect of the cost of capital is more intertemporally stable in these countries.

For earnings growth, the slope dummies are significant for France and the UK at the 5% level. Since the time-invariant static coefficients are insignificant for all countries including Japan and Germany, the effect of the growth term on the relative P/E ratios of these two countries appears to have been influenced by gradual changes in their slope coefficients rather than a one-shot shift in January 1981. Exchange rates, in contrast, are mostly significant not only in time-invariant static coefficients but also in time-varying slope coefficients.

Finally, it is interesting that the slope-time coefficients of the exchange rate term are significant and positive for Canada, Japan, and the UK, and negative for Germany. The positive sign for three countries indicates a time trend that an appreciation of the respective national currency against the U.S. dollar exerts a positive influence on the relative P/E ratios between the country and the United States. The negative sign for Germany indicates that an appreciation of the Deutsche mark against the dollar exerts a negative influence on German-U.S. relative P/E ratios. That is, the negative effect of a strong mark is felt more quickly by share prices than by expected earnings of German firms, relative to the similar impact in the United States.

CONCLUSIONS

This paper examines the determinants of relative stock valuation ratios of Canada, France, Germany, Japan, and the UK relative to the United States within a simple comparative market valuation model. The basic model includes economic fundamentals such as the relative cost of equity capital, relative expected earnings growth, currency values, and dividend payout ratios. Estimation results show exchange rate changes as the most significant and consistent determinant of the relative stock market valuations for all countries considered and throughout alternative model specifications. The relative cost of equity capital also has a strong explanatory power with the possible exception of Japan. The effect of expected earnings growth is insignificant. There is also evidence of a structural shift both in the form of intercept shift and through changes in the slope coefficients of exchange rates and other variables.

It should be noted that the present study provides only a partial explanation for relative market valuation disparity. It focuses on economic fundamentals in a comparative time-series context to the neglect of institutional and accounting differences. A complete analysis requires simultaneous consideration of both the fundamental and institutional factors.

NOTES

1. For a recent empirical test of market segmentation for various industrial countries, see Harvey (1991).
2. ARIMA (1,1,1) uses the first-difference equation of the following form:

$$(X_t - \mu) - \phi_1(X_{t-1} - \mu) = e_t - \theta_1 e_{t-1}$$

where X is the variable concerned, μ is mean of X and e is the error term, ϕ_1 is AR(1) estimate, and θ_1 is MA(1) estimate.

ACKNOWLEDGMENTS

We would like to thank Larry Duke and George Tsetsekos for helpful comments on an earlier draft. The views expressed in this paper are those of the authors and do not necessarily represent those of the I.M.F. or the Bank of Greece.

REFERENCES

Ando, P., and A. Auerbach. 1988. "The Cost of Capital in the United States and Japan: A Comparison." *Journal of the Japanese and International Economics* 2: 134–58.

Campbell, J.Y., and R.J. Shiller. 1987. "Cointegration and Tests of Present Value Models." *Journal of Political Economy* 95: 1062–88.

———. 1988. "Stock Prices, Earnings, and Expected Dividends." *Journal of Finance* 43: 661–76.

Chen, N.-F., R. Roll, and S.A. Ross. 1986. "Economic Forces and the Stock Market." *Journal of Business* 59: 383–404.

Choi, J.J. 1986. "A Model of Firm Valuation with Exchange Exposure." *Journal of International Business Studies* 17: 153–60.

Choi, J.J. 1989. "Diversification, Exchange Risk, and Corporate International Investment." *Journal of International Business Studies* 20: 145–155.

———. 1995. "The Japanese and US Stock Prices: A Comparative Fundamental Analysis." *Japan and the World Economy* 7: 347–360.

Duke, L.K., and M.G. Papaioannou. 1993. "Accessing Emerging Stock Markets: Prerequisites for International Investors." *Journal of Investing* 2: 18–25.

Fama, E.F., and K.R. French. 1988. "Permanent and Temporary Components of Stock Prices." *Journal of Political Economy* 96: 246–73.

Frankel, J.A. 1991. "The Japanese Cost of Finance: A Survey." *Financial Management* 2O: 95–127.

French, K., and J. Poterba. 1990. "Are Japanese Stock Prices Too High." NBER Working Paper, No. 3290.

Harvey, C.R. 1991. "The World Price of Covariance Risk." *Journal of Finance* 46(1): 111–158.

Hawkins, D. 1977. "Toward an Old Theory of Equity Valuation." *Financial Analysts Journal* 33: 48–53.

Hodder, J., and A. Tschoegel. 1985. "Some Aspects of Japanese Corporate Finance." *Journal of Financial and Quantitative Analysis* 20: 173–190.

Miller, M., and F. Modigliani. 1961. "Dividend Policy, Growth and the Valuation of Shares." *Journal of Business* 34(4): 411–33.

Roll, R. 1992. "Industrial Structure and the Comparative Behavior of International Stock Market Indices." *Journal of Finance* 47: 3–41.

Summers, L.H. 1986. "Does the Stock Market Rationally Reflect Fundamental Values?" *Journal of Finance* 41: 591–601.

PART II

FINANCIAL ISSUES IN EMERGING MARKETS

FINANCIAL LIBERALIZATION AND BANK SOLVENCY: A MULTI-COUNTRY STUDY

Jacqueline Chavez, Klaus P. Fischer, and Edgar Ortiz

... a liberalization is a serious macroeconomic shock.

—Sussman (1992)

few monetary authorities are prepared to accept as reasonable any interest rate level that is market determined.

—Pereira Leite and Sundararajan (1990)

ABSTRACT

The purpose of the paper is twofold: (1) to evaluate and measure the effect of financial liberalization (FL) processes on bank risk exposure; (2) to provide policy tools for bank regulators and supervisors that must oversee an FL process. Thus, this research has policy implications in the sense that it can help regulators safely steer a banking system through an FL.

We pursue these questions by assessing the changes in market-based asset values and risk exposure measures for commercial banks (CB) before and during an FL program. We do this for a sample of four countries: Brazil, Greece, Mexico, and Thailand. We use a model based on the options pricing theory. This model uses the

Research in International Business and Finance, Supplement 1, pages 173–198.

ISBN: 0-7623-0110-4

first and second moment of bank stock returns and bank accounting data to obtain first and second moments of banks asset values and certain measures of bank risk. Option theory suggests that stock issued by banks are claims whose value is contingent upon the value of the underlying assets and liabilities of the bank. Thus, changes in the prices of bank stocks (observable) provide the researcher or regulator a window into the implied market's assessment of the expected performance of the bank (not observable) given a portfolio of loan assets. We obtain estimates of the first and second moment of bank returns using a conditional asset pricing model. Once the value of assets has been found using the options model, we go on to compute theoretical probabilities of bank failure. This approach has the advantage of assessing indirectly a variable (bankruptcy risk) that, although critical to monitor the solvency of banks, cannot be inferred directly from the accounting data generated by banks.

The analysis and statistical test suggest that risk exposure of banks increases following an FL program. The effect is most marked in the standard deviation of bank asset values. This is so even for banks operating in countries that have undertaken very cautious FL processes such as Thailand. The results obtained corroborates casual observations of financial crisis in Latin America and Asia following FL. We draw policy implications of these results at the end of the paper.

INTRODUCTION

Assume you are a regulator or banking authority (BA) who receives instructions by the government to steer the banking system through a financial liberalization (FL) process. In particular, you are responsible for ensuring that the banking system rides through the FL process, suitably transformed, but in good health. Under the circumstances, institutional failures are to be avoided. How do you measure the risk exposure of banks or the probability of institutional failure as they go through the FL process? This is hard to do given the range of factors that can affect the solvency of a bank, including: managerial factors; the solvency of the bank's major borrowers; the limited value of accounting information under changing conditions; macroeconomic factors; and so forth.

The issue is important for a successful execution of FL programs. The best laid plans for a structural reform program that seeks to encourage capital flows, savings, and investment in a country, can stumble when one or more financial institutions face solvency problems provoking a panic in the system. The effects of such panics can be devastating, ranging from sudden monetary contraction to widespread financial difficulties in the productive sector and surges in unemployment. Bank solvency problems may originate from a number of sources: increased corporate failure by nonfinancial bank customers, run on deposits, imprudent lending activity by the banks, are just a few examples.[1] It is not unusual for economists planning and supervising national economic reform programs, to ignore the microeconomic effects of such programs, specially in terms of risk exposure of business of all sort. This is not surprising considering that the change in risk exposure is generally absent of most economic planning models guiding these programs. The link between some aspects of FL and solvability of the banking sector has been addressed by some researchers. Pereira Leite and Sundararajan (1990) address the issue of interest rates liberalization and bank "soundness" in a study that proposes a set of policy tools for a safe FL process. However, nowhere in the literature do we find an effort to *measure* bank risk exposure under FL.

Although it is true that several FL processes came and went without large-(or small-) scale bank failures, the risk exists. Outright institutional debacles have occurred following FL. Examples of this are Colombia, Argentina, and Indonesia. In effect, many FL processes have ended, and were terminated, with a major crisis in the banking sector. These crises sometimes represent huge losses to governments, like Venezuela in 1994. There the government was forced to come up with a rescue package with a value equivalent to 13% of GDP of Venezuela (Sundararajan 1995). In Argentina, in the period of six years following an FL initiated in 1977, almost 32% of the registered banking institutions disappeared.[2] As of 1994, following the FL program and before the so-called financial crisis, bad debts of the Mexican banking system exceeded the book value of risk capital (Colosio 1994) with two major banks' bad loan portfolios near 10% of assets, up from 3% in 1990. Often the absence of institutional failure results from the *conjectural government guarantees* (CGG) or *forbearance* extended by the state to ensure the solvency of the financial system throughout the FL process. This CGG may not have been removed as part of the FL process, or may have been reinstated when authorities perceived that the FL process puts the banking system in danger. Chile and Colombia are two examples in which the FL processes have been managed in different ways to guarantee the survival of banks.[3]

It is not our intention to question the legitimacy of FL ("the only game in town," [McKinnon 1989]). Rather, we seek to study the effect of these reforms on the functioning of the banking system and to develop instruments that allow a better monitoring of banks under conditions of FL. The exhaustion of the controlled import-substitution model of economic growth left many countries with no option but to engage markets to resume growth or escape recession. Many are doing this in a radical way. It is by no means evident that, despite the wave of FL observable in almost every continent, many forms of controls on credit and interest rates may be very useful to promote economic growth and social justice. Recently Vittas and Cho (1994) have reviewed the practices of directing credit allocation, a prominent form of financial repression, and found that some experiences (such as Korea and Japan) suggest that these credit programs can promote investment and growth.

To get a better grip of the issue we make, as Kryzanowski and Roberts (1993) and King (1992), a distinction between economic insolvency and institutional failure. More specifically we approach Demirgüc-Kunt's (1989) definition of market value insolvency focusing on the probability that the market value of assets exceeds the market value of liabilities.[4] We view the methodology used more as part of an "early warning system" (EWS) to anticipate hazardous situations rather than to obtain point estimates of bankruptcy risk. The model we use draws from the options pricing theory. It exploits the information contained in both, the bank accounting data and the public information pool contained in the price index of banks, about the banking system's performance. In the option pricing context securities issued by the banking sector are claims whose value is contingent upon the value of assets and liabilities of the bank. Thus, changes in the prices of bank stocks (observable) provide the researcher a window into the market's assessment of both the expected performance of the bank and the value of the portfolio of loan assets (both not observable). We go further to investigate the even more pertinent question of the change in risk of failure that these fluctuations suggest. Thus, we go on to compute probabilities of bank failure that results from comparing the value of bank's assets and liabilities. Insolvency risk is generally considered by bank supervisors and in Basel directives to be a key measure of bank performance (in contrast, for example, with the securities industry where liquidation risk is considered of more importance). Bank insolvency risk is also the central point of concern in the 1993 bank capital adequacy directive (CAD) of the European Union that seeks to harmonize bank regulation across member states.

FROM *FINANCIAL REPRESSION* TO *FINANCIAL LIBERALIZATION*: WHAT DOES IT DO TO COMMERCIAL BANKS?

Many authors regard FL as a key mechanism to promote economic growth and development of the financial sector in economies previously "financially repressed." The original theoretical analysis that supports this hypothesis was presented by McKinnon (1973) and Shaw (1973). It has since been recognized (e.g., McKinnon 1989) that FL is a more complex process than originally thought. This has led to a sequel of studies that attempt to evaluate empirically actual FL experiences in a number of countries (see Gibson and Tsakalotos 1994 and Warman and Thirlwall 1994 for a detailed review of this literature). In these studies, researchers focused mostly on the overall incentives to savings and investment (e.g., Morisset 1993; Cho 1989; Warman and Thirlwall 1994), the new mechanisms of interest rate determination (e.g., Gochoco 1991), the linkage between FL and inflation (e.g., Corsepius 1992), and so on. Lately, Gibson and Tsakalotos (1994) and others have examined the effect of FL combined with macroeconomic stabilization programs within both closed and open economy models. Since the ultimate goal of any FL process is to promote economic development, some authors have focused on the link between economic development and financial intermediaries (e.g., King and Levine 1993). Generally researchers have focused on the macroeconomic effects of FL. The microeconomic effect of FL, that is, the impact on the functioning of individual institutions (e.g., financial intermediaries and nonfinancial enterprises) has largely been ignored.

FL is a complex process and its effect on the banking sector is only partially understood. In this section we will attempt to analyze the link between a "typical" FL and some measures of commercial banks' performance. FL can change considerably the business environment of financial intermediaries. This is so because it changes radically the macroeconomic and regulatory framework under which banks operate. For example, FL may imply: elimination of interest rate controls; modification or elimination of credit allocation quotas and policies; elimination of interest rate subsidies and government financed funding schemes; opening of the capital account to international flows; and so on. Obviously the sector that is most affected by FL is the commercial banking sector. Commercial banks can be affected directly or indirectly. Directly because commercial banks are often the immediate targets of the liberalization process. Indirectly, because liberalization usually modifies the decision parameters used by both banks and nonfinancial bank customers to make financing decisions. Liberalization may also modify the type and amount of credit intermediated by commercial banks or other financial institutions.

FL can be understood simply as removal of financial repression (FR). FR consists of a set of restrictions on market competition that yields a protected environment for financial intermediaries. The most common restrictions are: (1) guaranteed intermediation margin through fixation of lending and deposit rates or direct subsidy programs (see, for example, Gibson and Tsakalotos 1994); (2) controls on international capital flows and foreign competition; (3) barriers to exit for financial intermediaries often accompanied by unlimited (conjectural) deposit insurance; (4) barriers to exit for major industrial clients of financial intermediaries, that is, conjectural loan insurance for the largest loans in the portfolio; (5) guaranteed business activity through government funded credit allocation programs to key economic sectors. An FL program consists of the simultaneous removal of all or part of these restrictions. Of all restrictions, the one that is central to FR is fixation of interest rates. Therefore, as Galbis (1986)[5] we take relaxation or lifting of controls on interest rates as the central event of FL. This is obviously a simplification of the complex reality of FL. However it allows us to focus on specific dates in the statistical analysis.

Now, to see the impact of FL, consider the following list of measures and the consequences they may have on bank profitability and risk exposure.

Elimination of Deposit and Lending Rate Controls

Description

This regulatory change has four separate effects on banks.

Interest rate risk. The immediate result of lifting controls is often an increase in the level and volatility of deposit and lending rates that can now float freely according to market conditions. This increase in volatility may be caused by several factors of which we emphasize two: portfolio shifts and competition for funds.

Portfolio shifts follow the elimination of rate controls, a form of market segmentation. These shifts occur when borrowers and lenders readjust their positions to the new market conditions. Competition for funds is likely to be intense following an FL. Deregulation of rates often leads to price wars as banks seek to capture market shares in a phenomenon similar to the one observed following the deregulation of the U.S. airline industry. These wars may be encouraged by the existence of an oligopolistic structure in the banking sector, a phenomena that is quite common among EM. The enhanced volatility can persist over a relatively long transition period until the market settles into an equilibrium point where speculation in, and arbitrage between, different market segments becomes less profitable.

Intermediation margin. Removal of controls (of borrowing and lending rates) eliminates an implicitly guaranteed intermediation margin (IM) and bank profitability. Under the new environment, banks may be forced to compete for deposits and loan costumers, squeezing their profit margins. The presence of oligopolistic power in the financial sector could imply that while some banks strive using their relative market power position, others may find the new competitive environment difficult to endure. Further, if banks accomplish any maturity transformation at all, an increase in deposit rates will not result in an automatic increase in rates of outstanding assets. The now almost-forgotten wave of American S&LA failures in the early 1980s due to the rise (quite moderate by emerging-markets' standards) of deposit rates following President Carter's Depository Institutions Deregulation and Monetary Control Act (DIDMCA) of 1980, is a stark reminder of the effect such an unilateral shift in rates may have on bank performance.

Risk-taking. Elimination of ceilings on deposit and lending rates changes the incentives for risk-taking activities by banks. More concretely, it encourages risk-taking and expands the opportunities for doing so.[6] Controlled lending rates encouraged banks to seek projects with low risk, as lending rates cannot be adjusted to account for risk and moral hazard. With liberation of interest rates, increases in deposit rates practically forces banks to seek lending at higher rates in projects that are likely to be riskier. Lifting of lending-rate controls also reinforces the incentives for banks to seek to finance borrowers willing to pay higher rates-higher risk projects. If deposit rates would be fairly priced according to the asset risk exposure of each bank, no benefit would accrue to bank shareholders. However, in absence of such a fair pricing, given a cost of deposits (or unlimited CGG), agency theoretic arguments suggest that bank shareholders gain by seeking projects of higher risk. A fair pricing mechanism will surely not exist in the presence of a deposit insurance scheme (conjectural or explicit) at fixed rates. Reduction of the intermediation margin resulting from competition will also encourage banks to engage in lending to more risky customers to increase returns on funds placed. The phenomena of bank risk-taking has also been analyzed in the context of DIDMCA of 1980 and the Garn-St. Germain Depository Institutions Act of 1982 (see, e.g., Pantalone and Platt 1987; Keeton 1984).[7]

Quality of asset portfolio. Volatility (usually with a marked increase) in interest rates will increase both financing costs and failure risk of bank nonfinancial costumers. The quality of bank assets will deteriorate accordingly.

Effect

The overall result of the elimination of deposit and lending rates controls is that banks may face increased profit-making opportunities. However, they will also be exposed to a considerable increase in interest rate and asset portfolio risk. The effect will generally not be uniform for banks of different size. The new ability of banks to compete for deposits may cause an accelerated growth of the bank's liabilities. This growth may or may not be used to finance loans to the business sector. As we will see, under certain conditions banks may be encouraged to invest increasingly in marketable securities, mostly government issued.

Deregulation and/or Re-regulation of Financial Markets

Description

These measures consist mostly of elimination of regulated specialization of financial institutions and promotion of new financial instruments and markets (e.g., bonds and stock markets, financial derivatives, etc.). This process can create strong incentives for market participants to engage in alternate forms of financial intermediation, in particular through securitized markets (disintermediation).[8] Diversification of financial instruments in the economy is generally considered a desirable effect in a global sense, since it has the effect of "completing the markets." However, the consequences of disintermediation on individual banks must be considered. On the liability side, availability of new financial instruments encourage the reallocation of funds to more competitive markets. Again, DIDMCA is a good example. Massive amounts of funds shifted out of the American banking sector into, mainly, a booming mutual fund sector. Under deregulation, mutual funds could provide bank-like services to depositors. Banks are thus forced to compete for deposits increasing the costs of funds. On the asset side, nonfinancial enterprises find it advantageous to raise funds through alternative mechanisms such as domestic stocks or bonds, or quite often, in the international bond and stock markets. Major borrowers, usually those with the highest credit rating, may thus reduce their demand for bank originated funds. Banks are forced to shift their loan portfolio to smaller customers, often more risky and with higher information asymmetry. In some emerging markets banks are given the chance to operate as universal banks (e.g., Mexico and Thailand) thus enabling them to profit from these new opportunities. But, even if universal banking is allowed, this is often a new line of business in which bankers may possess little or no experience. With or without the possibility of universal banking, deregulation adds to the uncertainty of the banking business environment. Even under the most liberal bank regulation regime, some of the funds that are no longer intermediated by the traditional banking sector, cannot be recaptured by universal banking institutions.

Effect

The overall effect may be a fall in the relative importance of the commercial banking sector in the process of financial intermediation. In a rapidly expanding economy, the growth in assets may compensate for this loss. However, if FL is not accompanied by adequate growth, the effect would be a shrinking of the banks' balance sheet with reduction on both the assets and liabilities. Further, intermediation margins could fall while the credit-risk exposure on the portfolio of asset would increase.

Economic Reform

Description

Most FL programs are not undertaken in isolation. On the contrary, usually they are part of a larger package of economic reforms that include liberalization of the domestic good and international trade markets, cuts and shifts in government spending, changes in monetary and exchange rates policies, elimination of industrial subsidies, and so forth. Often, the package of FL is part of a "structural adjustment program" sponsored by the International Monetary Fund (IMF), that contains provisions for international trade, monetary, and fiscal policies. The consequences of these reforms on the performance of firms can be quite varied. This, in turn, affects the credit quality of the banks' portfolios. Some bank customers may indeed succeed and flourish in this new competitive environment. Those firms unable to adapt or those that exist for the sole purpose of exploiting the rents resulting from a particular form of market segmentation, may suffer. While the success of the winners will not improve much portfolio performance (because of the non-residual nature of loan assets), the failure of the looser will reflect negatively on the performance of assets. In particular this will reflect on the non-performing portfolio of banks. Under these circumstances, banks often see the need to charge higher risk premiums on (now liberalized) loan rates charged to customers. While this may increase the profitability of banks in the short term, these higher premiums only augment the already high credit risk created by economic reforms.[9] Roe (1991) is one author who has emphasized this relationship in what he calls "the macro-micro feedback process" although in the context of highly controlled markets rather than FL.

Effect

The resulting effect should be a short-term increase in intermediation margins obtained from higher risk customers accompanied by a relative increase of non-performing loans in the long run.

Elimination of Barriers to Entry and Exit

Description

Under FR, the survival of banks *and* major nonfinancial enterprises is conjecturally but effectively guaranteed by the state.[10] Elimination of barriers to exit (removal of CGG)—as occurred, for example, in the early 1980s in Argentina and Brazil—changes considerably both the liquidity of the banks and the credit quality of the banks' loan portfolios. This effect can be particularly severe in the absence of a deposit insurance scheme in place, a situation that is quite common in EM. Further, if FL also opens the market to domestic and foreign competition, elimination of barriers to entry increases competitive pressure on the banking system.

Effect

The effect of this particular measure can be quite complex. On the liabilities side of the balance sheet, removal of CGG reduces savers confidence in the solvability of the bank and discourages deposit—or shifts them from smaller or less solvable banks to larger or "too-big-to-fail" banks. Thus, one effect could be a relative shrinking of deposits with smaller banks. On the asset side, elimination of barriers to exit of industrial customers could affect negatively the non-performing portfolio.

Adoption of International (BIS) Capital Standards

Description

The adoption of the BIS or similar capital standards often accompanies FL. It has been argued (see Berger and Udell 1994 among others) that risk-based capital standards (RBCS) can be viewed as a regulatory tax that is higher for asset items that are assigned a higher risk rating. Since equity capital is more expensive than any other source of fund, RBCS encourage substitution of risky assets for low risk assets, predominantly treasury securities. This leads to a *credit crunch* or reduction in the supply of credit to the business sector. This credit crunch, juxtaposed to the increase in interest rates, complicates the financing picture of business enterprises and, consequently, the value of the bank's loan portfolio.

Effect

The effects of these measures are hard to detect in the banks' balance sheet. However, one observable effect should be a relative increase of holdings in government securities.

Bank Supervision and Enforcement Powers

Elimination of unlimited conjectural government guarantees on deposits and controls over the financial system price setting and allocation mechanisms is often accompanied by increased supervision of banks to guarantee the safety of the system. This is so because FL introduces many incentives and opportunities for profit-and risk-taking thus reducing the safety of the banking system. There exists a reciprocal relation between the value of the deposit insurance on one side and covenant rights to surveillance and seize bank assets on the other, if one wishes to keep the safety of the system relatively constant (see, e.g., Merton and Bodie 1992). Now, the essential components of a financially repressed system can often be eliminated quite easily given a reasonable political will. This, as we have seen, introduces considerable uncertainty into the banking system. For example, control on interest rates (deposit and lending), controls on international capital flows, economic reforms, and so on, can usually be eliminated by a simple decree. However, the same thing cannot be said of bank supervision. Often, central banks or bank superintendents of developing countries must perform the supervision duty using company laws that apply to standard industrial enterprises. These company laws may not provide bank supervisory bodies with the power and flexibility in terms of disclosure requirements, ability of taking over the control of the bank, and so on available to bank regulators of most industrialized countries. The case of a single insolvent bank can languish over years in court putting into question the safety of the whole banking system. Thus, an FL process that is undertaken without empowering the supervisory body to take rapid control of a critical situation through changes in company laws, adds considerably to the already inherently high uncertainty associated to the program.

Although it is unlikely that all these developments will be felt simultaneously, it is very likely that several of these scenarios may present themselves concurrently in most FL processes. The overall effect of the set of measures that accompany FL is to create incentives for banks to increase profit-making while increasing interest rate and asset risk.

THE MODEL[11]

The model is based on the option's principle that a bank's equity can be viewed as a derived asset (a call option) whose value depends on the value of the bank's asset, mostly the portfolio of loans. For the latter there is usually no observable market value. Book values are imperfect estimators of the true value of these assets. As is usually the case in adapting the options pricing model to corporate finance, we assume that the bank's assets follow a Wiener process,

$$dA/A = \mu_A dt + \sigma_A d\tilde{w}$$

where $\mu_A\, dt$ represents the instantaneous expected change in asset value, σ_A is the instantaneous standard deviation of asset values change, and dw is a white noise. If we add the standard "frictionless" market assumption two major results follow. First, if the bank's stock represents a call option on the bank's assets the following relation between the value of stock, V, and the value of assets, A, σ_A, and the value (exercise price) of liabilities, D, including deposits and preferred stock (usually absent in emerging markets) can be established:

$$V = AN(d_1) - DN(d_1 - \sigma_A\sqrt{T}) \tag{1}$$

where $N(.)$ represents the standard normal cumulative distribution, T represents the expiration date of liabilities,[12] and

$$d_1 = \left[\ln\left(\frac{A}{D}\right) + (0.5\sigma_A^2 T\right]/\sigma_A\sqrt{T} \tag{2}$$

In contrast to Black and Scholes, in our context, as in that of Ronn and Verma (1986) and Giammarino, Schwartz, and Zechner (1989), the nominal value of liabilities is the present value of the exercise price of the option. Thus the risk-free interest rate does not appear in the equation. Second, applying Ito's lemma, the standard deviation of the stochastic process dA/A can be represented as

$$\sigma_A = \frac{V\sigma_v}{A\,(\partial V/\partial A)} = \frac{V\sigma_v}{AN(d_1)} \tag{3}$$

where σ_v is the instantaneous standard deviation of the process dV/V. In this system of two equations (1) and (3), only the value of equity, V, and the current face value of liabilities, D, can be observed directly. The variable σ_v can be observed only indirectly. It represents the market's estimate, at time T–1, of the instantaneous standard deviation of the process dV/V over the period until expiration of the option, given the current information set. It is, thus, a conditional standard deviation, conditioned upon the information set $\mathcal{F}_{t-1}$. We will have more to say about the estimation of σ_v later. This leaves a system of two equations with two unknown variables, A and σ_A, that can be solved simultaneously. Given the nonlinear character of the system, numerical methods must be used.

Measuring Insolvency Risk[13]

Insolvency occurs when the value of liabilities (excluding capital) exceeds the value of assets. We focus not on the ex post bankruptcy states but rather on the ex ante of bankruptcy probability as implied in the market's value assessment of bank stocks. Presumably, if the probability of insolvability is high enough, BA or the state will intervene to take remedial action. More often than not, remedial action does not imply orderly liquidation of assets, but rather an injection of liquidity to guarantee the survival of the bank. Assume that at the beginning of a planning period $t-1$, the expected value of assets at time t can be represented by $E_{t-1}(A_t)$. Then, given an outcome A_t, the probability that the value of assets is insufficient to cover liabilities, $P(A - D \leq 0)$ can be represented as follows:

$$P(A - D \leq 0) = P(\tilde{A} \leq D) = P(\tilde{z} \leq X)) \tag{4}$$

where

$$\tilde{z} = \frac{\tilde{A} - E(\tilde{A})}{\sigma_A'}, \quad X = \frac{D - E(\tilde{A})}{\sigma_A'} \tag{5}$$

and the variance of the value of assets, $\sigma_A' = |\,\sigma_A E(A)|$. If $\tilde{A}_t \sim N(E(A), \sigma_A')$, the probability of insolvency can be written

$$P(\tilde{A} \leq D) = P(\tilde{z} \leq X)) = \int_{\infty}^{x} \frac{1}{\sqrt{2\Pi}} \; e^{-(z^2/2)} dz \tag{6}$$

Given an appropriate proxy of $E_{t-1}(A_t)$, this probability can be computed once we obtain estimates A_t and σ_A using equation (6).

It is important to note here that the actual probability of institutional failure is a function of many other factors besides the market's implicit assessment A and/or $P(X)$.[14] In this study we are less interested by the actual institutional liquidation probability than by the evolution of bank risk exposure that accompanies an FL process. Thus, we will focus on the relative change of $P(X)$ with the passage of time and the application of FL.

DATA

We use data from three sources. Two sources provide aggregated data of a group of banks, the third set is a bank of information on significant events in a sample of 23 EM, including FL events. These are the details: (1) the source of aggregate balance sheet is the IMF's *International Financial Statistics (IFS)*. The choice of aggregate data allows us to work with reasonably long periods of time. We use consolidated balance sheet data for Depository Institutions reported in the *IFS* under the heading of Monetary Statistics, items 20 to 27A. Although it would be convenient from the econometric point of view to use the highest frequency of observations possible, it appeared to us that monthly observations provide a fictitious level of detail in information. Thus, we use quarterly data. (2) The source of stock market returns of a portfolio of domestic banks is the World Bank's

Emerging Markets Data Base (EMDB). This data is available starting from January 1976 for the sample of countries used in this study. The returns on the portfolios are value-weighted returns of all constituents in sector 60 (Commercial Banks) of the database. (3) The dates and descriptions of FL events for a sample of 23 candidate countries. This data was collected from a wide range of printed and electronic sources that include every possible scientific and journalistic publications to which we had access and time to research, including World Bank working papers, economic journals, the *Financial Times, OECD Economic Studies, World Bank Country Studies,* and all publications listed in the *ABI Reference Index* (that lists among others *The Economist, Euromoney, Banker,* and several regional business reviews such as *Asia Business,* etc.). The countries covered in the study are Brazil, Greece, Mexico, and Thailand.

The choice of aggregated data forced us to make some assumptions. First, clearly there is not a one-to-one correspondence between stock market returns and balance sheet data. Both are consolidated data of groups of banks. Although we have no information on the institutional overlapping of the two subsets, both sources report data of the largest banks.[15] Thus a reasonable overlapping can be expected. The implication is that the bank portfolio returns obtained from the *EMDB* are only an imperfect estimator of the change in equity value of the group of banks included in the *IFS*. Further, when using desegregated data it is possible to establish the capitalization value, V, of a bank stock and its corresponding book value of debt, D. This correspondence disappears at the aggregated level. We bypass this latter problem by standardizing all data to a base of 1.0 in January 1976—or alternative dates when applicable—and focus on the *changes* in market value of stock, V, and book value of liabilities (exercise price), D, the two inputs in equations (1) and (3). Second, we assume that the proportion of book value of risk capital with respect to total assets remains constant throughout the study period at the level of the first period of observation.

The use of aggregated data also means that the results are only indicative of the change in economic insolvency of the system as a whole. It does not imply that every bank in the sample is in the same situation. It is also possible that the state—of financial health or difficulty—of particular banks may be over- or underrepresented with respect to their relative importance in the economy. However, we cannot identify any systematic bias in the data. Thus possible distortions should be viewed as noise.

STATISTICAL METHODOLOGY

The statistical procedure consist of three distinct steps: (i) estimation of conditional variances of stock returns, σ^2_{Vt}; (ii) solution of the system of nonlinear equations (1) and (3) for the value of the bank's assets, A, and conditional variances of asset returns, σ^2_{At}; (iii) estimation of stock price implied probability of bank bankruptcy. Now the details.

1. Estimation of Conditional Expected Returns $E[r_{jt}/\mathcal{F}_{t-1}]$ and Variances of Stock Returns ($\sigma^2_{Vt}/\mathcal{F}_{t-1}$)

The first step is to obtain an estimate of the conditional variance of returns of bank stocks. The standard procedure used in the literature is to compute the variance over a moving window of past returns that varies from 12 months (on a monthly basis, Noah and Roy 1994; Furlong 1988; or on a daily basis, Giammarino, Schwartz, and Zechner 1989). We do not adopt this procedure because it supposes that the historical standard error is equal to the conditional standard error at each point in time. We adopt an alternative methodology that makes use of recent theoretical and empirical developments in asset pricing technology. We model conditional returns assuming a model that has become quite standard in the finance literature seeking to measure stock price volatility.[16]

$$E[r_{jt}|\mathcal{F}_t] = a + br_{jt-1} + c\sigma^2_{jt} + \varepsilon_t$$

where $\mathcal{F}_{t-1}$ represents the set of conditioning variables, not including r_{jt} but containing its past history. That is, the return on the stock, conditional upon the information set $\mathcal{F}_{t-1}$ is equal to an expected value plus a random error. See Nelson (1991), Hsieh (1993), and Glosten, Jagannathan, and Runkle (1993) for theoretical supports of this choice of model. The error, ε_t, can be assumed to be conditional on the same information set, $\mathcal{F}_{t-1}$, and normally distributed, that is $(\varepsilon_t|\mathcal{F}_{t-1})\sim N(0,h_t)$, or t-distributed, where h_t represents the conditional variance at time t. We choose to give this conditional variance an EGARCH (exponential generalized autoregressive conditional heteroscedastic) parametrization. The complete model can thus be written as follows:

$$r_{jt} = b_0 + b_1 r_{jt-1} + b_2 h_t + \varepsilon_t$$

$$\varepsilon_t|\mathcal{F}_{t-1} \sim t(0,h,v)$$

$$\ln(h_t) = \alpha_t + \delta LIB + \lambda INF + \beta \ln(h^2_{t-1}) + \theta g(\varepsilon_t)$$

$$g(\varepsilon_t) = \left(\left| \frac{\varepsilon_t}{\sqrt{h_t}} \right| - \frac{\sqrt{2.0}}{\Pi} - \gamma \frac{\varepsilon}{\sqrt{h_t}} \right) \tag{8}$$

We augmented the conventional EGARCH to incorporate two dummy variables: one for periods of financial liberalization and one for periods of high inflation. The parameters of the system were estimated using an FIML estimation procedure assuming (and testing) a t-distributed vector of errors.[17] A t-test on the statistic representing degrees of freedom on the t-distribution is a sufficient statistic to test the restriction that the distribution is normal. Other specification of a GARCH-M with leverage (e.g., Giammarino, Schwartz, and Zechner 1993) where also tested.[18]

The periods of liberalization identified for each of the four countries are the following:

Financial Liberalization Periods

Country	*FL Period*
Brazil	1. 1976:01 to 1979:8
	2. 1981:03 to 1986:03
	3. 1991:10 to present
Greece	1. 1987:2 to present
Mexico	1. 1989:04 to present
Thailand	1 1989:12 to present

For these periods the dummy variable *LIB* was given the value of 1.0 and 0.0 otherwise. The central commonality of these FL periods is that they are characterized by the absence of—or highly diminished—controls on interest rates. While certainly not being the only feature of an FL process, it is a trademark of any process of de- and reregulation of the financial system. The three periods of FL of Brazil are quite characteristic of the on and off nature of the process in the Souther Cone. In fact, the current "wave" of FL initiatives in Latin America has come to be known as the "second FL wave," that follows that of the late 1970s and early 1980s. Asian and southern European countries are experiencing their "first" (and last?) liberalization wave.

2. Solution of the System of Contingent Claims Equations for the Value of Assets and Variances of Asset Returns

The system of equations (1) and (3) was solved for *E[A], A* and σ_A once for each quarter from January 1976 to April 1992, or depending upon data availability. The solution of the system of equation was accomplished using numerical methods. The computer implementation of the procedure is based on a *Mathematica* routine that searches for the roots of a system using the secant method. The roots were robust for initial values within a very limited interval, but we never encountered the problem of finding more than one real root. Outside of the interval, the procedure would simply not converge even after large numbers of iterations, or would jump to imaginary roots. Thus we were forced to approach the interval within which we could find the solution using the logic implicit in options model and by trial and error. Once in the useful interval, we observed a clear consistency between the sequence of numerical results obtained and the intuition suggested by the derivatives of the options pricing model.

Computation of Probabilities of Insolvency

One problem encountered in this step is the identification of an appropriate proxy of expected value of assets, $E(\tilde{A})$. As indicated earlier, we used expected conditional means returns to compute at each point in time the expected value of stock. Then we used the system of equations (1) and (3) to compute the implicit expected value of bank assets, $E[A]$. Probabilities of insolvency were then computed using a numerical integration procedure on equation (6).

RESULTS

We report the results for each of the three steps described above, as follows. The use of an EGARCH model to estimate conditional variances implies that we are assuming that returns of bank stocks are heteroscedastic. We test this assumption explicitly performing the Gauss-Newton regression suggested by Engle (1982).[19] The statistic n times the *centered* R^2 is a test of heteroscedasticity distributed $\chi^2(p)$. We used $p = 6$ and obtained statistics with significance level of at least 5% ($\chi^2(6) = 12.6$) for Brazil (12.7), Greece (25.4), and Thailand (39.3) and nonsignificant for Mexico (2.08). The results of the estimation of h_t are reported in Table 2. There we present the parameters, of system (8) with related statistics. All estimations were performed in real terms. The purpose of this table is to emphasize the validity of the model chosen for the estimation of h_t and to observe bank stock volatility during periods of financial liberalization. It is quite clear that the EGARCH(1,1) formulation, used frequently in the finance literature, is appropriate for our purposes. We tested, as an alternative, specifications of the leveraged models of volatility of Giammarino, Schwartz, and Zechner (1993). This latter model was difficult to estimate and sensitive to initial values of the coefficients. Further, the coefficients were often outside of their expected range. Thus we continued working with the EGARCH model despite the critic of Engle and Ng (1993).

With these statistical results we can feel comfortable that the conditional variance, h_t, obtained from this simple form of the asset pricing model, appears to be quite appropriate. From Table 1 it becomes clear that the choice of a t-distribution for the residues is fully supported by the data, with the only exception of the second period for Mexican data. In this latter case, both the coefficient corresponding to degrees of freedom and the sampling statistics of the errors (in Table 2) suggest normally distributed errors. In Figure 1 we present a plot of h_t. In the plot we have indicated through a grey area the periods of interest rate liberalization. These dates were established through the research done on the FL events using bibliographical data. Thus the event-dates reported were *not influenced by the observed variations in the value of* h_t. The plot is rather remarkable. It is surprising that the FL processes could have such distinct effect on the volatility of bank stock returns.

Table 1. Conditional Variances of Bank Stock Returns

In this table we report for each country in the sample, the value of coefficients and related statistics for the system

$$r_{jt} = b_0 + b_1 r_{t-1} + b_2 h_t + \varepsilon_t \quad \varepsilon_t \sim t(0, h_t, v)$$

$$\ln(h_t) = \alpha + \delta LIB + \lambda INF + \beta \ln(h_{t-1}) + \theta\left(\left|\frac{\varepsilon_t}{\sqrt{h_t}}\right| - \sqrt{\frac{2.0}{\Pi}} - \Upsilon\frac{\varepsilon}{\sqrt{h_t}}\right)$$

obtained from a FIML estimation procedure. We report the results for a model based on nominal returns and for a model based on real returns. The values in parentheses are *t*-statistics.

	Mean Equation $r_{jt} = b_0 + b_1 r_{t-1} + b_2 h_t + \varepsilon_t$			Variance Equation $\ln(h_t) = \alpha + \delta LIB + \lambda INF + \beta \ln(h_{t-1}) + \theta\left(\left\|\frac{\varepsilon_t}{\sqrt{h_t}}\right\| - \sqrt{\frac{2.0}{\Pi}} - \Upsilon\frac{\varepsilon}{\sqrt{h_t}}\right)$						
Country	b_0	b_1	b_2	α	δ	λ	β	θ	Υ	v
Brazil	–0.0388	0.001	1.1728	–0.0834	–0.0390	–0.0469	0.9566	0.2460	0.4811	5.2497
	(–1.480)	(0.0135)	(1.581)	(–0.592)	(–0.819)	(–0.685)	(22.47)	(2.076)	(1.942)	(2.382)
Mexico (1)	–0.0704	–0.0387	4.7654	–9.535	—	—	–0.9745	0.4807	0.0241	6.0993
(1976:02–1982:07)	(–1.9327)	(–0.5429)	(1.708)	(–106.507)	—	—	(–51.741)	(3.983)	(–0.124)	(1.600)
Mexico (2)	0.0079	0.0009	2.3164	–4.683	—	—	–0.1586	–0.9747	0.232	—
(1988:06–1992:12)	(0.2166)	(0.0107)	(0.8431)	(–2.2014)	—	—	(–0.3027)	(–1.8897)	(0.9031)	—
Greece	–0.0122	0.1119	0.4229	–9.2936	2.5118	—	–0.7873	–0.2218	–0.1048	3.723
	(–1.480)	(2.569)	(0.427)	(–8.225)	(4.419)	—	(–4.058)	(–1.327)	(0.166)	(3.383)
Thailand	0.0037	0.1132	0.2515	–0.7557	0.4516	—	0.8344	0.7469	–0.3540	3.1682
	(1.008)	(1.433)	(0.808)	(–1.989)	(2.325)	—	(13.94)	(2.707)	(–1.611)	(3.187)

Table 2. Sample Statistics

Country		Non-liberalization				Liberalization			
		Mean	*StdDev*	*Skewness*	*Kurtosis*	*Mean*	*StdDev*	*Skewness*	*Kurtosis*
Brazil	Conditional Mean	0.0498**	0.0481	0.6926**	0.0256	–0.0022	0.0207	2.187**	5.3055
	Conditional Variance	0.0755**	0.0410	0.695**	0.0377	0.0304**	0.0157	2.146**	5.507**
	Residues	–0.0152	0.2514	0.3745	1.0558*	0.0387**	0.1643	1.126**	1.972**
	Actual Returns	0.0328	0.2579	0.5327*	1.1571**	0.0355**	0.1673	1.1939**	1.959**
Greece	Conditional Mean	–0.0106**	0.007	0.3046	–0.0985	0.0021	0.0189	1.5181**	3.3954**
	Conditional Variance	0.0057**	0.0013	1.811**	9.424**	0.0239**	0.0085	1.966**	7.847**
	Residues	0.0044	0.0722	0.8400**	1.915**	0.0185	0.1693	1.821**	4.859**
	Actual Returns	–0.0057	0.0678	1.0561**	3.0499**	0.0337	0.1749	1.9332**	5.0013**
Mexico	Conditional Mean	0.0030	0.0300	0.6536	1.9977**	0.0546**	0.0211	0.4805	–0.4060
	Conditional Variance	0.0101**	0.0068	1.927**	5.725**	0.0201**	0.0091	0.4806	–0.4077
	Residues	0.0129*	0.0865	0.5431**	10.373**	0.0235	0.1310	0.7024*	–0.2464
	Actual Returns	0.0004	0.1148	1.3766**	5.7932**	0.0682**	0.1338	0.8228**	0.2601
Thailand	Conditional Mean	0.0089**	0.0135	1.7267**	4.9713**	0.0647**	0.0844	2.1131**	4.8147**
	Conditional Variance	0.0121**	0.0184	2.840**	8.304**	0.1875**	0.2126	2.051**	4.646**
	Residues	0.0094**	0.0929	–0.905**	11.263**	0.0633	0.3393	0.6159	0.786
	Actual Returns	0.0183**	0.0938	–0.2729	8.9014**	0.1281**	0.3416	1.0308**	1.1896

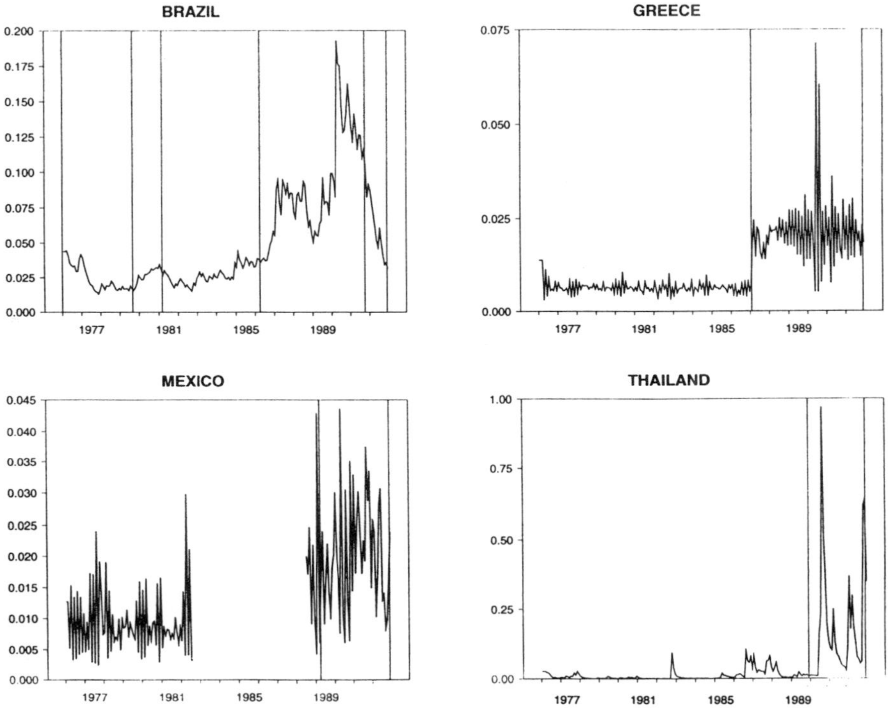

Figure 1. Conditional Variances of Bank Stock Returns

To provide the reader with an impression of the source of changes in the conditional variance we also present graphs of actual (real) returns on stocks (Figure 2) and a (real) stock price index with a base in January 1976 of 1.0.

The numerical solutions, A and $P(A \leq D)$, are plotted in Figures 4 and 5, respectively. These two plots provide a perspective of the historical evolution of the value of assets and probabilities of failure before, during, and after FL.

The overall picture one obtains from observing these figures and tables is that financial liberalization introduces a substantial amount of uncertainty into the banking sector. This conclusion is supported by the observed increased volatility of stock market returns and the signs of the liberalization dummy variables in the conditional variance regressions. However, this uncertainty is accompanied by a substantial increase in stock prices. The increased volatility has also an effect on implied asset values. These also become quite volatile while showing a strong growth. A similar conclusion can be drawn from the implied values of bankruptcy probability. Both, implied values of assets and implied probabilities fluctuate enormously during the liberalization period. In the case of Thailand these implied probability values attain the value of 0.85 shortly after the initiation of the liberalization process.

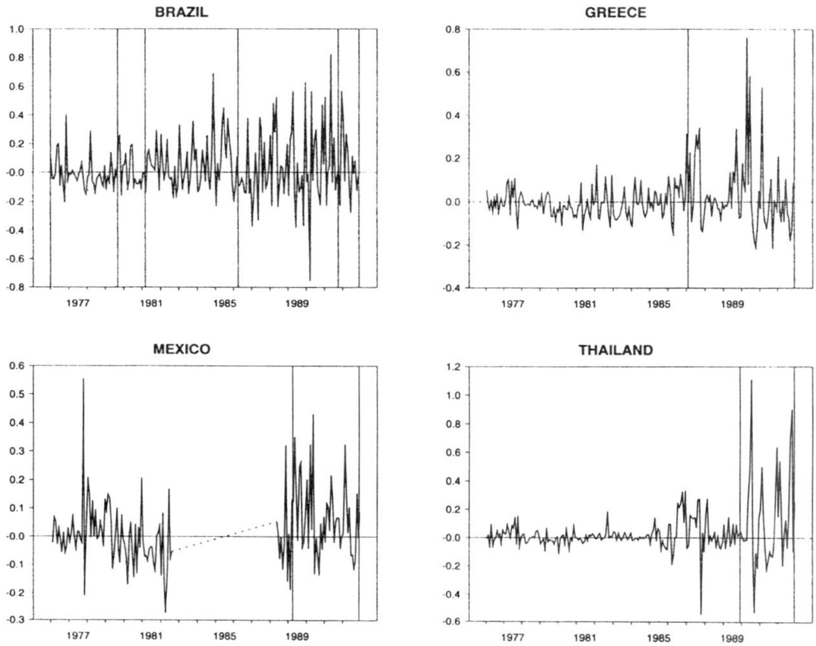

Figure 2. Real Returns of Bank Stocks

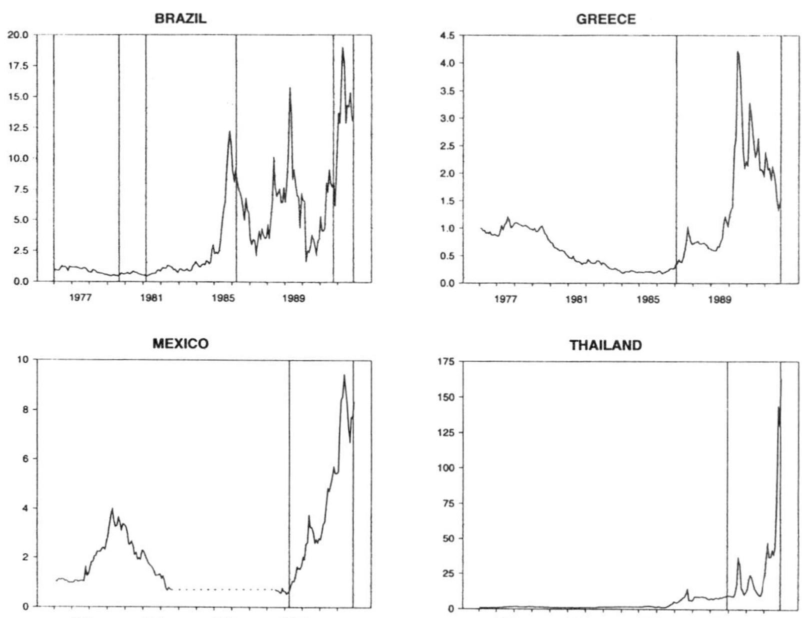

Figure 3. Index of Real Bank Stock Prices (Base, 1/1976 = 1.0)

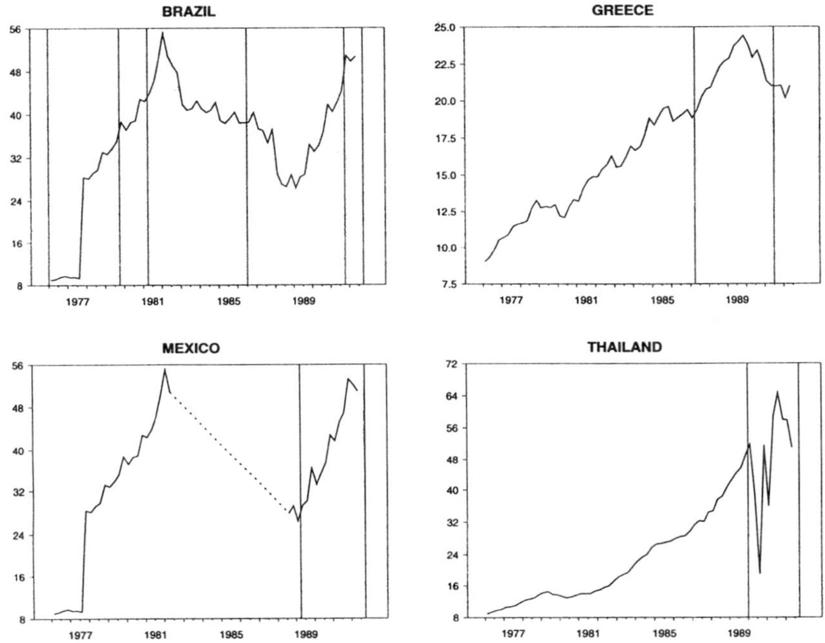

Figure 4. Stock Price Implied Value of Assets

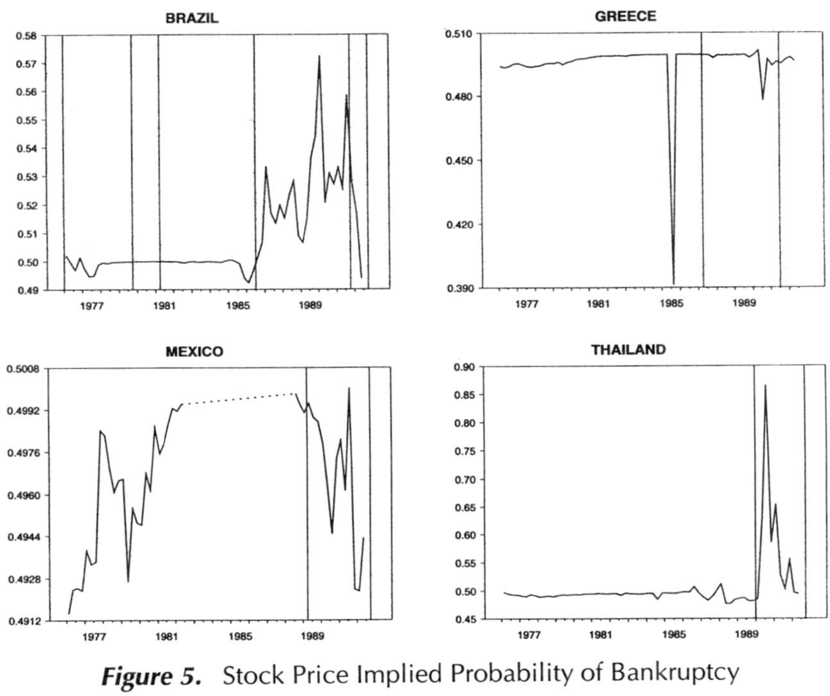

Figure 5. Stock Price Implied Probability of Bankruptcy

CONCLUSIONS AND POLICY RECOMMENDATIONS

The evidence provided by the empirical analysis carried out in this paper suggests the following conclusions and policy recommendations:

1. The stock market in which bank shares are traded is an additional instrument to gage the evolution and health of the banking system in the context of financial liberalization. The market is sensitive to the impact of the FL process on the value of bank assets (in itself a thermometer of health in the economy) and its solvency situation. Thus, the market price can be used as an indicator of the impact of the whole liberalization process or of specific measures on commercial bank performance. It is of course an open question whether the "smart economists" of the ministry of economic affairs are ready to concede that prices and implicit valuations reflect the aggregated wisdom of market participants and not just volatile scare-rabbit response by uninformed investors.
2. The data of the four countries studied, suggest that banks are subject to a substantial increase in risk under financial liberalization, however measured. Conditional volatility of stock market returns increase, but so do the volatility of market value of assets and implied probabilities of bankruptcy. Thus, supervisory authorities need to perform a particularly intense scrutiny of all critical variables associated to bank performance during periods of financial liberalization.

ACKNOWLEDGMENTS

This research was completed with the support of the program of economic analysis and research applied to international development (PARADI), financed by the Canadian International Development Agency (CIDA). The institutions affiliated to the PARADI program are the Montreal University's Centre de recherche et de développement en économique (CRDE) and Laval University's Centre de recherche en économie et finance appliquées (CREFA). The purchase and installation of the data needed for this research was financed by PARADI, SSHRC and FCAR research grants.

NOTES

1. The 1995 Argentina financial crisis is a case in point. It was predominantly—if not only—a crisis of confidence in the banking sector. In the four months following the Mexican crisis, over 4 billion dollars (around 10% of the total deposit base in the country) left the banking sector, most of it not to leave the country, but—as the minister of economy D. Cavallo remarked—to be stuffed "under the mattress." The international financing package obtained by Argentina in the following months was largely used to establish an emergency deposit insurance scheme. The only purpose of this action was to restore domestic savers confidence in the banking system. The whole long-term restructuring program of the Argentina economy was in danger following this banking crisis.

2. In 1980, following a liberalization of several aspects of the Argentina banking sector initiated in 1977 (including the liberalization of interest rates) the Banco de Intercambio Regional was liquidated for reasons of insolvency. Shortly after, when the authorities perceived that the BIR will not be the exception, the decree 22.267 was issued giving the central bank the tools to come to the rescue of the banks Los Andes, Oddone, and Internacional. However, even with these tools in hand the central bank could not avoid the liquidation, during the six-year period following the crisis of 1979, of almost 32% of the registered banking institutions (Casas 1989).

3. In these two countries financial liberalization led to a major banking crisis that forced the respective BA to reverse important aspects of the liberalization drive, sometimes at a huge social cost (e.g., Colombia), or introduce emergency measures to ensure the liquidity of the baking system (e.g., Chile). In the case of Colombia the liberalizations process has been extremely bumpy with several policy reversals over the years accompanied by massive bail outs of the banking system that in terms of percentage of GDP can be compared to the U.S.-based S&L bail out of the 1980s.

4. In her classification of failure definitions, Demirgüc-Kunt identifies four different concepts of bank failure: book-value insolvency, market-value insolvency, official (de jure) insolvency, and de facto failure (see Demirgüc-Kunt 1989, table 2, for details).

5. This author goes as far as defining "FL is the elimination of FR, that is, increase of interest rates to an efficient equilibrium level that promotes optimal saving rates and avoids misallocation of real and financial resources."

6. It is remarkable that, in one of the most thorough and candid analysis of the Mexican banking crisis made by a Mexican public figure, Miguel Mancera-Aguayo (1995), the governor of the Bank of Mexico, fails to even mention as a problem the shift in risk taking activities of commercial banks following the FL in that country. It is worth noting that the huge loan default rate was one important element in the crisis that lead to the establishment by the government of a rescue package. This package consisted of over 11 billion dollars of taxpayer's money in direct financing to commercial banks. In addition, parallel Support to Non-performing Borrowers' Program (*Acuerdo para el Apoyo de Deudores, ADE*) with loan restructuring facilities of up to 30 years was also put in place. We do not have information about the cost of this program.

7. For many years following World War II, only four or five banks failed each year. By contrast, in 1986 alone following the deregulation process, 138 banks failed. See also Corbo, de Melo, and Tybout (1985) for some details of bank risk-taking practices during the FL experiences in Argentina, Chile, and Uruguay.

8. See Merton (1995) for an interesting discussion on the competitive interaction between financial intermediaries and financial markets in a secular as well as a deregulatory context.

9. It is now a fairly established belief among Mexican economists that the current peak of non-performing bank portfolios is largely self-induced. Firms were facing two simultaneous shocks, the high risk associated with the sudden and almost total liberalization of international trade, and the high risk-adjusted loan rates charged by banks.

10. It is by no means unusual in repressed economies for the state to step in and rescue an enterprise whose insolvency would endanger the liquidity of a bank or an important number of jobs.

11. The model draws on the original work of Mertont (1977) and later contributions by Ronn and Verma (1987), Furlong (1988), Giammarino, Schwartz, and Zechner (1989), Kormendi, Bernard, Pirrong, and Snyder (1989), Noah and Roy (1994). There are, of course, a number of assumptions that must be made to make the direct application of the option's framework to corporate finance and bank asset valuation. For an illuminating discussion of these issues we refer the reader to Giammarino, Schwartz, and Zechner (1989).

12. In most of the literature on bank solvency risk (e.g., Giammarino, Schwartz, and Zechner 1989), T represents the time to the next audit of the bank. See the same reference for a discussion about this and other assumptions regarding the boundary conditions of equation (.) when used in the context of bank solvency questions.

13. Since our data consists of balance sheet items, this section builds upon the model of Ronn and Verma (1986), an approach based on comparing the value of assets and liabilities (both stock data). This approach contrasts with that of, for example, Furlong (1988) that compares the value of risk capital with current income (a flow item).

14. This observation has lead Giammarino, Schwartz, and Zechner (1989) to modify the exercise price of the equity option, D, in equation (1) and (2) to ρD, where $\rho < 1$. Thus ρD represents the critical asset value below which BA finds it optimal to force liquidation of assets. The size of ρ will be a function of the transactions costs—and we might add social and political cost—of institutional liquidation.

15. Not surprisingly, the number of banks included in the *IFS* is larger than that included in the *EMDB* as many banks are closely held, state controlled, or of foreign ownership.

16. It appeared to us that the additional accuracy (in estimating conditional variances) that would be obtained from adding complexity to the formulation of the asset pricing model, would be misplaced in our context. This is especially true if we consider the somewhat heroic assumptions that are standard in the literature when applying the options pricing model to the bank insolvency risk problem.

17. The assumption of normality can be justified by the fact that returns are observed on a monthly basis. It is a well-known fact that stock returns are less and less leptokurtosic as one reduces the frequency of observation from a daily to a weekly to a monthly basis.

18. This specification tests were considered important in the light of results recently reported by Engle and Ng (1993). These authors find that the variability of the conditional variance estimated using an EGARCH specification is too high. The Giammarino, Schwartz, and Zechner (1993) appears to be the best parametric model.

19. The Gauss-Newton regression takes the form

$$\mu_t^2 = a + \sum_{j=1}^{p} c_1 \mu_{t-j}^2 + residual$$

where μ_t^2 is the residue of the regression.

$$r_t = b_0 + b_1 r_{t-1} + \mu_t$$

REFERENCES

Berger, A.N., and G.F. Udell. 1994. "Did Risk-Based Capital Allocate Bank Credit and Cause a Credit Crunch in the United States?" *Journal of Money Credit and Banking* 26: 585–633.

Casas, J.C. 1989. *Saneamiento de Bancos*. Buenos Aires: Ediciones El Cronista Comercial.

Cho, Y.J. 1988. "The Effect of Financial Liberalization on the Efficiency of Credit Allocation." *Journal of Development Economics* 29: 101–110.

Colosio, L.D. 1994. "La Vulnerabilidad del Sistema Bancario Mexicano, su Liberalización, Regulación y Supervisión." *El Mercado de Valores* 54: 7–11.

Comisión Nacional de Valores. Iinforme Anual de la Comisión Nacional de Valores, 1991. *El Mercado de Valores* 12: 24–31.

Corbo, V., J. de Melo, and J. Tybout. "Por que fracasaron las recientes reformas en el Cono Sur." Pp. 403–443 in *Estabilización y ajuste estructural en Améerica Latina*, edited by S. Roca. Lima, Peru: Escuela de Administración de Negocios (ESAN).

Corsepius, U. 1992. "Financial Reform, Inflation, and Investment Behaviour in Developing Countries: Evidence from Peru. Pp. 251–261 in *Business Finance in Less Developed Capital Markets*, edited by K.P. Fischer and G. Papaioannou. Westport, CT: Greenwood Press.

Demirgüc-Kunt, A. 1989. "Deposit- Institution Failure: A Review of Empirical Literature." *Economic Review*, FRB of Cleveland 25: 2–18.

Engle, R.F., and V.K. Ng. 1993. "Measuring and Testing the Impact of News on Volatility." *Journal of Finance* 48: 1749–1778.

Engle, R.F. 1982. "Autoregressive Conditional Heteroscedasticity with Estimates of the Variance of United Kingdom Inflation." *Econometrica* 50: 987–1007.

Furlong, F.T. 1988. "Changes in Bank Risk-Taking." *Economic Review*, Federal Reserve Bank of San Francisco (Spring): 45–56.

Galbis, V. 1986. "Liberalización del Sector Financiero Bajo Condiciones Oligopólicas y la Estructura de los Holding Bancarios." Pp. 289–315 in *Estabilización y ajuste estructural en Améerica Latina*, edited by S. Roca. Lima, Peru: Escuela de Administración de Negocios (ESAN).

Giammarino R., E. Schwartz, and J. Zechner. 1989. "Market Valuation of Bank Assets and Deposit Insurance in Canada." *Canadian Journal of Economics* 22: 109–127.

Gibson, H.D., and E. Tsakalotos. 1994. "The Scope and Limits of Financial Liberalization in Developing Countries: A Critical Survey." *Journal of Development Studies* 30: 578–628.

Glosten, L.R., R. Jagannathan, and D.E. Runkle. 1993. "On the Relationship between the Expected Value and Volatility of the Nominal Excess Return on Stocks." *Journal of Finance* 48: 1779–1801.

Gochoco, M.S. 1991. "Financial Liberalization and Interest Rates Determination: The Case of the Philippines, 1981–1985." *Journal of Macroeconomics* 13: 335–350.

Hsieh, D.A. 1993. "Implications of Nonlinear Dynamics for Financial Risk Management." *Journal of Financial and Quantitative Analysis* 28: 41–66.

Kaen, F.R., and D. Michalsen. 1994. "The Effects of the Norwegian Banking Crisis on Norwegian Bank and Non-bank Stocks." *Journal of Financial Services Research*, forthcoming.

Keeton, W.R. 1984. "Deposit Insurance and the Deregulation of Deposit Rates." *Economic Review*, Federal Reserve Bank of Kansas City (April): 28–47.

King, K.K. 1992. "Deposit Insurance as a Put Option: Alternative Approaches to Modelling Regulatory Forbearance." Board of Governors of the Federal System, September.

King, R.G., and R. Levine. 1993. "Financial Intermediation and Economic Development. Pp. 156–196 in *Capital Markets and Financial Intermediation*, edited by C. Mayer and X. Vives. New York: Cambridge University Press.

Kumar, P.C., and G. Tsetsekos. 1992. "Securities Market Development and Economic Growth." Pp. 55–65 in *Business Finance in Less Developed Capital Markets*, edited by K.P. Fischer and G. Papaioannou. Westport, CT: Greenwood Press.

Kormendi, R.C., V.L. Bernard, S.C. Pirrong, and E.A. Snyder. 1989. "The Origins and Resolution of the Thrift Crisis." *Journal of Applied Corporate Finance* 2: 85–99.

Kryzanowski, L., and G.S. Roberts. 1993. "Canadian Banking Solvency, 1922–1940." *Journal of Money, Credit and Banking* 25: 361–376.

Mancera-Aguayo, M. 1995. "Ajustes de Politica Frente a Turbulencias Financieras." *El Mercado de Valores* 10: 19–25.

McKinnon, R.I. 1989. "Financial Liberalization and Economic Development: A Reassessment of Interest-rate Policies in Asia and Latin America." *Oxford Review of Economic Policy* 5.

———. 1973. *Money and Capital in Economic Development.* Washington, DC: Brookings Institution.

Merton, R.C. 1977. "An Analytic Derivation of the Cost of Deposit Insurance and Loan Guarantees: An Application of Modern Option Pricing Theory." *Journal of Banking and Finance* 1: 3–11.

Merton, R.C., and Z. Bodie. 1992. "On the Management of Financial Guarantees." *Financial Management* 21: 87–109.

Morisset, J. 1993. "Does Financial Liberalization Really Improve Private Investment in Developing Countries?" *Journal of Development Economics* 40: 133–150.

Nelson, D.B. 1991. "Conditional Heteroscedasticity in Asset Returns: A New Approach." *Econometrica* 59: 347–370.

Noah, C., and J. Roy. 1994. "La Probabilité de l'Insolvabilité des Banques Canadiennes." Proceedings *FINANCE* of the ASAC Conference, Halifax.

Pantalone, C.C., and M.B. Platt. 1987. "Predicting Commercial Bank Failure Since Deregulation." *New England Economic Review* (July/August): 37–47.

Pereira Leite, S., and V. Sundararajan. 1990. "Issues in Interest Rate Management and Liberalization." *IMF Staff Papers* 37 (December): 735–752.

Roe, A. 1991. "Financial Systems and Development in Africa." Pp. 5–28 in *Financial Systems and Development in Africa*, edited by P. Callier. Washington, DC: The World Bank.

Ronn, E.I., and A.K. Verma. 1986. "Pricing Risk-Adjusted Deposit Insurance: An Option Based Model." *Journal of Finance* 41: 871–895.

Shaw, E. 1973. *Financial Deepening in Economic Development*. New York: Oxford University Press.

Sundararajan, V. 1995. "Banking Restructuring and Transitions to Indirect Instruments of Monetary Policy." Working Paper, Symposium on Business Finance in Emerging Markets, Laval University, Québéc, September.

Sussman, O. 1992. "Financial Liberalization: The Israeli Experience." *Oxford Economic Papers* 44: 387–402.

Vittas, D., and Y.J. Cho. 1994. "The Role of Credit Policies in Japan and Korea." *Finance and Development* (March): 10–12.

Warman, F., and A.P. Thirlwall. 1994. "Interest Rates, Savings, Investment and Growth in Mexico 1960–1990: Test of the Financial Liberalization Hypothesis." *The Journal of Development Studies* 30: 629–649.

THE EFFECT OF DEPOSIT VARIABILITY ON THE PORTFOLIO BEHAVIOR OF COMMERCIAL BANKS IN AN EMERGING FINANCIAL MARKET

Imad A. Moosa and Nabeel E. Al-Loughani

ABSTRACT

This paper investigates the effect of deposit variability on the portfolio behavior of commercial banks in the emerging financial market of Kuwait. We demonstrate, on the basis of cointegration tests, that domestic credit is inversely related while the acquisition of foreign assets is positively related to deposit variability in the long run. Causality testing also shows that the variability of certain deposit categories has a short-run effect on domestic credit and on commercial banks' tendency to borrow from international financial markets.

INTRODUCTION

Deposit variability, which refers to the uncertainty surrounding the future level of deposits, arises due to an imperfect synchronization of deposit inflows and out-

Research in International Business and Finance, Supplement 1, pages 199–212.

ISBN: 0-7623-0110-4

flows. This variability has been established as a major problem facing banks because it weakens their ability to predict changes in the level of deposits. Banks normally operate on the insurance principle of offsetting risk by matching withdrawals by one customer by deposits from another. However, banks facing higher risk of withdrawal would hold relatively higher proportions of cash and assets with short maturities in their portfolios. They would also rely more heavily on borrowing from the central bank and from the interbank market.

Although deposit variability attracted the interest of financial economists in the 1960s and the 1970s, it has received little attention recently.[1] This may be attributed to the proposition that the risk arising from deposit variability has been overshadowed by interest rate and exchange rate risk. Nevertheless, deposit variability remains an important issue, not only for banks themselves but also for the monetary authorities and the economy at large. It is important for banks because it affects their portfolio behavior and impinges on their asset composition. For example, the more volatile a bank's deposits the more liquid its assets will be (Kane and Malkiel 1965; Hester 1962). Moreover, since deposit variability affects the asset composition and the frequency of engaging in costly reserve adjustment, variability affects profitability (Shull 1968; Kane and Malkiel 1965; Dewald and Dresse 1970). Monetary authorities are also concerned with deposit variability because it affects the holdings of cash and excess reserves which have some implications for the path and speed of monetary policy actions. Furthermore, since it is a determinant of borrowing from the central bank, deposit variability should have some implications for the administration of the discount window (Dewald and Dresse 1970). Another aspect of the effect of deposit variability on the macroeconomy is that it affects (via the composition of the asset portfolio) the availability of funds for loans and, therefore, the loan rate (Shull 1968).[2]

Studies of deposit variability have been conducted for a number of distinct purposes using various methods, different data sets and a diversity of measures of deposit variability (see, for example, Chairnoff 1967; Gramley 1962; Murphy 1968; Rangarajan 1966; Struble and Wilkerson 1967; Morrison and Selden 1965). Most of the studies are based on cross-sectional data on individual banks and are generally concerned with three aspects of deposit variability. First, they are concerned with a comparison of the variability of different categories of deposits and, therefore, the contribution of each category to overall variability (e.g., Pattison 1974; Melnik 1979). Second, the concern is with the factors affecting deposit variability such as bank size,[3] branching,[4] and company affiliation.[5] The third concern is with the effect of deposit variability on the portfolio behavior of commercial banks (Bond 1971; Melnik 1970; Hester and Pierce 1975; Kane and Malkiel 1965; Barth and Bennett 1975; Dewald and Dresse 1970).[6]

This paper deals with the third aspect, the effect of deposit variability on portfolio behavior. The distinguishing features of this study are the following: (1) it examines the issue in the emerging financial market of Kuwait;[7] (2) it uses aggregated time-series data; (3) it employs a new measure of deposit variability, the conditional variance of the detrended level of deposits; and (4) it is based on cointegration and causality testing. We start with a theoretical and analytical background, then we present an outline of the econometric methodology, and this is followed by a presentation of the empirical results. We end up with some concluding remarks.

THEORETICAL AND ANALYTICAL ISSUES

This section deals with some theoretical and analytical issues pertaining to (1) the effect of deposit variability on the portfolio behavior of commercial banks, and (2) the measurement of deposit variability. We will begin with the first issue.

Theoretical modeling of the role played by deposit variability in determining the portfolio behavior of commercial banks, the composition of their balance sheets, and their profitability can be based on a modification of the Tobin-Markowitz portfolio model to incorporate the effect of deposit variability. The earliest attempt of this kind was, perhaps, made by Porter (1961) who developed a bank portfolio management model in which deposit variability is expressed explicitly. We will illustrate the basics of these models by reference to the Kane-Malkeil (1965) model. This model is neoclassical in spirit: a bank maximizes an objective utility function (with expected profit and risk being the arguments) subject to market and balance sheet constraints. The utility function is given by

$$u = u[E(\pi), \sigma^2(\pi)] \tag{1}$$

where u is utility, E is the expected value operator, π is profit and σ^2 is its variance. It is normally assumed that $\partial u/\partial E(\pi) > 0$ and $\partial u/\partial\sigma^2(\pi) < 0$. The balance sheet constraint is given by

$$X_0 + L_0 = D_0 \tag{2}$$

where D is deposits, L is loans, X is other assets, and the subscript 0 denotes the initial period. The expected value and the variance of profit are given by

$$E(\pi) = LE(r) + XE(g) \tag{3}$$

$$\sigma^2(\pi) = L^2G_r^2 + L^2\sigma_r^2LX\rho_{r,g}\sigma_r\sigma_g + X^2\sigma_g^2 \tag{4}$$

where r and g are the holding period rates of return on loans and other assets. The model assumes that the maturities of X and L are equal and extend beyond the bank's short-term planning horizon, that loans are nonmarketable and that borrowing from the central bank is not permitted. Moreover, the model assumes that deposit drains during the holding period are met by sales of other assets and that all deposit inflows during the period are used to augment the holdings of other assets, not to increase loans. On the basis of this model, Kane and Malkiel show that bankers wish to minimize deposit variability, that an increase in volatility worsens the bank's opportunity set because deposit variability increases risk exposure. By allowing for costs of asset acquisition and sale, or by assuming that deposit flows and asset yields are inversely related, they also show that deposit variability causes a decrease in profit. Using a similar methodology, but a more disaggregated balance sheet, Melnik (1970) shows that the various components of the investment portfolios are sensitive to changes in wealth, relative yields, and deposit variability. He also demonstrates that an increase in deposit variability will, *ceretis paribus*, induce banks to shift more funds to highly liquid assets.

Barth and Bennett (1975) used the Miller-Orr (1966) model to show the effect of deposit variability on cash holdings by banks. The model is based on the standard hypothesis in inventory theory of minimizing expected costs associated with managing a cash balance. The underlying assumption is that cash holdings fluctuate between an upper and a lower limit. When the upper (lower) limit is reached, other assets are acquired (sold) in sufficient amounts to reduce (increase) cash to a "return-to" point. This point, z, and the upper limit, h, can be determined by minimizing the expected cost function

$$E(k) = \frac{\gamma\sigma^2}{zf} + \frac{g(f + 2z)}{3} \tag{5}$$

where $f = h - z$, k is the cost of managing cash, γ is the cost per transfer between cash and other assets, σ^2 is the variance of changes in cash balances, and g is deposit earnings per unit of assets. When the model is solved, it produces the optimal values of z, f, and h which are given by

$$z^* = \left(\frac{3\gamma\sigma^2}{4g}\right)^{1/3} \tag{6}$$

$$f^* = 2z^* \tag{7}$$

$$h^* = 3z^* \tag{8}$$

It is obvious from equation (6) that the optimal return-to point is a function, *inter alia*, of the variance of cash flow. In an empirical form, the model can be represented by the cross-sectional regression

$$\log z_i = a + b \log\sigma_i^2 + \xi_i \tag{9}$$

where z_i is excess reserve plus due-from balances.

We will now consider the second issue, the measurement of deposit variability. The conventional measures used in cross-sectional studies are based on the variance of the level of deposits, including the standard deviation and the coefficient of variation; these are calculated over the sample period. The coefficient of variation is conceived to be far from a perfect measure of deposit variability (e.g., Morrison and Selden 1965; Murphy 1968). One of the most important criticisms raised against these measures is based on the distinction between anticipated and unanticipated cash withdrawals and, therefore, between anticipated and unanticipated (random) variability. For example, Barth and Bennett (1975) point out that since deposit flows are assumed to be completely stochastic, the variance of total deposits may be an inappropriate measure, for not all deposit withdrawals are unanticipated. To separate out random variability, they regressed total deposits on seasonal dummies and a trend and used the variance of the residuals of this regression as a measure of variability. Likewise, Dewald and Dresse (1970) define random variability as the variability "that is not readily accountable to seasonal variation and trend in deposit growth." They argue that portfolio behavior is not related to overall variability but to random variability, and propose to measure random variability by the ratio of the standard error of the estimate to the mean, where the standard error is associated with the regression of total deposits on seasonal dummies and a trend. They show that this measure explains short-term reserve adjustment better than the coefficient of variation.[8] Murphy (1968) also uses the standard error but he only adjusts for a deterministic trend.

On a similar line of reasoning, Melnik (1979) argues that in the context of uncertainty about the future deposit levels, a deposit series, D_t, may be viewed as composed of a permanent component, D_t^P, and a transitory component, D_t^T. Starting with an ARIMA model of the form

$$D_t = D_{t-1} + \varepsilon_t - \theta\varepsilon_{t-1} \tag{10}$$

Melnik shows that

$$D_t = D_{t-1} + D_t^T - \theta D_{t-1}^T \tag{11}$$

and

$$D_t^P = D_{t-1}^P + (1-\theta)D_{t-1}^T \tag{12}$$

where the term $(1-\theta)D_{t-1}^T$ gives the amount of the preceding period's transitory component which is absorbed into the current period's component. Thus, the smaller the value of θ, the more rapid is the pace in which the permanent component is revised and the more difficult it is to predict the level of deposits. Hence, θ is a measure of variability such that smaller values of θ imply higher variability. Another aspect of deposit variability was discussed by Kaufman (1972), who emphasized the importance of the length of period over which deposit variability is measured. He argues that a finding of an inverse relationship between variability and bank size is obtained only because of incorrectly measuring variability. He shows that deposit variability is positively correlated with size for very short-term variability, the correlation becomes less positive and turns negative for long periods.

DATA AND METHODOLOGY

In this study we do not attempt to build a structural model but rather test, on the basis of the findings of previous studies, some hypotheses specified as reduced form equations. The empirical results of this study are based on a sample of monthly observations covering the period February 1980–June 1990.[9] The data are time series on items of the consolidated balance sheet of commercial banks as published by the Central Bank of Kuwait. Three major balance sheet items are considered: on the asset side we consider domestic credit (loans), *DC* and foreign assets, *FA*, while on the liabilities side we consider foreign liabilities, *FL*. For the purpose of empirical testing these items are measured as (logarithms of) their ratios to total assets. From the previous discussion, we may expect the following: when deposit variability is high, banks will take one or a combination of these actions: (1) reduce domestic credit, (2) increase foreign assets (since they are mostly short-term liquid assets), and (3) increase foreign liabilities by borrowing from international financial markets.

In order to take account of difference in the variability of different deposit categories, we consider the variability of 14 deposit categories classified according to maturity (e.g., demand versus time deposits), currency of denomination (e.g., domestic versus foreign currency deposits), and holders (e.g., private sector versus government deposits). The definitions of deposit categories are given in Table 1.[10]

Variability is measured by the conditional variance of the detrended (first difference of) log level of deposits. Thus, if X is the log level of any of the categories above, a GARCH-M(1,1) may be written as

Table 1. Definitions of Deposit Categories

Symbol	*Definition*
PM	Private sector demand deposits
PT	Private sector time deposits
PS	Private sector saving deposits
PC	Private sector certificates of deposit
FD	Private sector foreign currency deposits
PD	Private sector total deposits
GM	Government demand deposits
GT	Government time deposits
GD	Government total deposits
TD	Total (private sector and government) deposits
KD	Domestic currency (Kuwaiti dinar) deposits
TT	Total (private sector and government) deposits
ND	Total non-interest bearing deposits
ID	Interest bearing deposits

$$\Delta X_t = a_0 + a_1 h_t^2 + \varepsilon_t \tag{13}$$

$$h_t^2 = b_0 + b_1 h_{t-1}^2 + b_2 \varepsilon_{t-1}^2 \tag{14}$$

where h_t^2 is the conditional variance and $\varepsilon_t \sim N(0,h_t^2)$. Thus $V(PM) \equiv h^2(PM)$, that is, the conditional variance of private sector deposits, and so on.

We start by testing for unit root. This is carried out on the basis of the Dickey-Fuller (1979) ADF statistic as well as the $\hat{Z}_\alpha$ and $\hat{Z}_t$ statistics proposed by Phillips (1987) and Phillips and Ouliaris (1990). For any variable, x_t, the ADF statistic is the t-ratio of α in the regression

$$\Delta x_t = \kappa + \alpha x_{t-1} + \gamma t + \sum_{i=1}^{m} \delta_i \Delta x_{t-i} + \varepsilon_t \tag{15}$$

The $\hat{Z}_\alpha$ and $\hat{Z}_t$ statistics are derived from the regression

$$x_t = \alpha x_{t-1} + \nu_t \tag{16}$$

The $\hat{Z}_\alpha$ statistic is then given by

$$\hat{Z}_\alpha = N(\hat{\alpha} - 1) - (1/2)(s_T^2 - s_V^2)\left(N^{-2} \sum_{2}^{N} \nu_{t-1}^2\right)^{-1} \tag{17}$$

where N is the sample size, $\hat{\alpha}$ is the estimated value of α and

$$s_V^2 = N^{-1} \sum_{1}^{N} \nu_t^2 \tag{18}$$

$$s_T^2 = N^{-1} \sum_{1}^{N} \nu_t^2 + 2N^{-1} \sum_{s=1}^{k} w_{sk} \sum_{t=s+1}^{N} \nu_t \nu_{t-s} \tag{19}$$

for some window size such as $w_{sk} = 1 - s/(k+1)$. The $\hat{Z}_t$ statistic is given by

$$\hat{Z}_t = \left[\sum_{2}^{N} \nu_{t-1}^2\right]^{1/2} (\hat{\alpha} - 1)s_T - (1/2)(s_T^2 - s_V^2)\left[s_T (N^{-2} \sum_{2}^{N} \nu_{t-1}^2)^{1/2}\right]^{-1} \tag{20}$$

Phillips and Ouliaris (1990) have demonstrated that these two test statistics have limiting distributions that are free of nuisance parameters.

To test for cointegration the ADF, $\hat{Z}_\alpha$ and $\hat{Z}_t$ statistics are applied to the residuals of the cointegrating regression

$$X_t = \beta_0 + \beta_1 V(Y)_t + \varepsilon_t \tag{21}$$

where $X_t' = (CR \;\; FA \;\; FL)$. If X and $V(Y)$ are cointegrated then according to Granger's Representation Theorem, there is a valid error correction model of the form

$$\Delta X_t = \alpha + \sum_{i=1}^{m} \gamma_i \Delta X_{t-i} + \sum_{i=0}^{k} \delta_i \Delta V(Y)_{t-i} + \theta \hat{\varepsilon}_{t-1} + \xi_t \tag{22}$$

If, on the other hand, X and $V(Y)$ are not cointegrated, we can test for (short-run) causality using unrestricted VAR specification. If $V(Y) \sim I(1)$, the VAR is specified as

$$\Delta X_t = \alpha + \sum_{i=1}^{m} \gamma_i \Delta X_{t-i} + \sum_{i=0}^{k} \delta_i \Delta V(Y)_{t-i} + \xi_t \tag{23}$$

If $V(Y) \sim I(0)$, the model is specified as

$$\Delta X_t = \alpha + \sum_{i=1}^{m} \gamma_i \Delta X_{t-i} + \sum_{i=0}^{k} \delta_i V(Y)_{t-i} + \xi_t \tag{24}$$

The null hypothesis of no causality from deposit variability to the asset/liability item ($V(Y) \rightarrow X$), is given by $H_0{:}\delta_i = 0, \forall i$.

EMPIRICAL RESULTS

The results of unit-root tests are presented in Table 2. These results show that the three asset/liability items (DC, FA, and FL) are integrated of order one, and that all deposit variabilities are integrated of order one except $V(TT)$, $V(PT)$, $V(PC)$, and $V(TD)$ which turned out to be integrated of order zero.

The results of testing for cointegration are presented in Table 3. These results show that domestic credit is cointegrated with the variability of private sector demand deposits and total non-interest bearing deposits, $V(PM)$ and $V(ND)$. The cointegrating regression between domestic credit and the variability of private sector demand deposits turned out to be

$$\underset{}{DC_t} = \underset{(-38.46)}{-0.640} - \underset{(-2.23)}{0.591} V(PM)_t$$

where the figures in parentheses are the t-statistics corrected along the lines proposed by West (1988).[11] The parsimonious error correction model is given by

$$\Delta DC_t = \underset{(0.34)}{0.001} + \underset{(3.16)}{0.271} \Delta DC_{t-12} + \underset{(1.52)}{0.208} \Delta V(PM)_{t-2} - \underset{(-2.50)}{0.124} \hat{\varepsilon}_{t-1}$$

$$R_2 = 0.16$$
$$DW = 1.75$$
$$SC(12) = 15.10$$
$$FF(1) = 2.64$$
$$NO(2) = 8.22$$
$$HS(1) = 5.97$$

In this case the conventional t-statistics are given in parentheses since all of the variables are stationary. The model passes the diagnostic tests for serial correlation, *SC*, functional form, *FF*, normality, *NO*, and heteroscedasticity, *HS*. All of these test statistics are distributed as χ^2 with the degrees of freedom given in parentheses.

The cointegrating regression between domestic credit and the variability of non-interest bearing deposits is given by

$$\underset{}{DC_t} = \underset{(-38.01)}{-0.640} - \underset{(-2.22)}{0.490} V(ND)_t$$

and the corresponding error correction model is given by

$$\Delta DC_t = \underset{(3.50)}{0.001} + \underset{(3.10)}{0.264}\Delta DC_{t-12} + \underset{(1.88)}{0.299}\Delta V(ND)_{t-2} - \underset{(-2.54)}{0.125}\hat{\varepsilon}_{t-1}$$

$$R^2 = 0.17$$
$$DW = 1.75$$
$$SC(12) = 14.42$$
$$FF(1) = 0.96$$
$$NO(2) = 6.68$$
$$HS(1) = 6.83$$

The evidence provided by these estimates indicates that in the long run, increased variability of demand deposits (non-interest bearing deposits) puts pressure on banks to reduce the ratio of domestic credit to total assets, that is, they shift out of the less liquid, high yielding assets.

The results also show that foreign assets are cointegrated with the variability of government demand deposits. The cointegrating regression is given by

$$FA_t = \underset{(-32.39)}{-1.403} + \underset{(2.00)}{0.198} V(GM)_t$$

and the corresponding error correction model is given by

$$\Delta FA_t = \underset{(-1.41)}{-0.004} - \underset{(-2.17)}{0.190}\Delta FA_{t-6} + \underset{(1.96)}{0.175}\Delta FA_{t-11} - \underset{(-2.41)}{0.037}\Delta V(GM)_{t-6} - \underset{(-2.91)}{0.076}\hat{\varepsilon}_{t-1}$$

$$R^2 = 0.16$$
$$DW = 2.15$$
$$SC(12) = 10.82$$
$$FF(1) = 0.02$$
$$NO(2) = 0.58$$
$$HS(1) = 0.01$$

Table 2. Testing for Unit Root

Variable	*Level*	*First Difference*
DC	−2.30	−9.51*
FA	−2.11	−11.99*
FL	−2.99	−11.91*
V(PM)	−1.61	−4.84*
V(PT)	−5.33*	
V(PS)	−2.69	−10.39*
V(PC)	−3.02*	
V(FD)	−2.01	−11.87*
V(PD)	−1.56	−10.55*
V(GM)	−3.13	−11.09*
V(GT)	−0.12	−4.38*
V(GD)	−0.88	−5.32*
V(TD)	−3.61*	
V(KD)	−1.37	−9.71*
V(TT)	−4.73*	
V(ND)	−1.71	−4.52
V(ID)	−1.54	−4.98*

These results indicate that in the long run, increased volatility of government demand deposits induces banks to increase their acquisition of foreign assets, that is, they shift to more liquid, low yielding assets.[12] This finding is consistent with the hypothesis put forward by Melnik (1970, p. 642) that banks hold liquid assets

Table 3. Testing for Cointegration

	DC			*FA*			*FL*		
	ADF	$\hat{Z}_\alpha$	$\hat{Z}_t$	*ADF*	$\hat{Z}_\alpha$	$\hat{Z}_t$	*ADF*	$\hat{Z}_\alpha$	$\hat{Z}_t$
V(PM)	−3.46*	−18.05*	−3.19*	−2.52	−7.54	−2.50	−2.80	−12.81	−2.73
V(PS)	−2.26	−11.51	−2.50	−2.04	−5.24	−1.99	−2.30	−8.71	−2.21
V(FD)	−2.96	−10.85	−2.44	−2.04	−5.21	−1.99	−2.29	−8.65	−2.20
V(PD)	−2.63	−10.93	−2.38	−1.92	−6.06	−1.96	−2.33	−9.68	−2.27
V(GM)	−2.75	−12.25	−2.57	−3.67*	−22.63*	−3.76*	−3.07	−16.67	−3.07
V(GT)	−2.30	−10.58	−2.38	−1.90	−5.81	−1.95	−2.48	−12.31	−2.47
V(GD)	−2.29	−10.58	−2.38	−1.88	−5.73	−1.94	−2.39	−11.50	−2.38
V(KD)	−2.50	−11.55	−2.54	−2.03	−5.47	−2.02	−2.36	−9.79	−2.31
V(ND)	−3.41*	−17.25*	−3.12*	−2.49	−7.40	−2.48	−2.76	−12.38	−2.69
V(ID)	−3.12	−14.56	−2.84	−2.38	−6.98	−2.38	−2.72	−12.02	−2.64

Note: *significant at the 5% level.

to cover possible deposit withdrawals because of the high alternative costs (e.g, those resulting from reserve deficiency).

The results of testing for causality are presented in Table 4. These results show the following:

1. There is short-run causality to domestic credit from two out of eight $I(1)$ deposit variabilities that do not cointegrate with it: these are $V(PD)$ and $V(ID)$. This evidence suggests that banks adjust their domestic loan portfolios in response to the variability of interest bearing deposits.
2. None of the nine $I(1)$ deposit variabilities that do not cointegrate with foreign assets cause this item in the short run. This evidence indicates that banks do not take into consideration short-run variability when they determine the size of funds that are used to acquire foreign assets.
3. Only one of the ten $I(1)$ deposit variabilities that do not cointegrate with foreign liabilities cause this item in the short run: this is $V(GT)$. This evidence suggests that in the short run, banks alter the extent of their reliance on international financial markets for borrowed funds when the variability of the government time deposits rises.
4. There is no short-run causality from any of the four $I(0)$ variabilities to any of the three balance sheet items.

Table 4. Testing for Short-Run Causality ($V(Y) \rightarrow X$)

	DC	*FA*	*FL*
V(PM)		1.25	0.97
V(PT)	1.35	1.26	0.35
V(PS)	1.18	1.03	0.07
V(PC)	0.10	0.12	0.14
V(FD)	0.07	0.81	1.54
V(PD)	3.44*	1.00	2.14
V(GM)	1.38		0.56
V(GT)	1.53	0.95	4.40*
V(GD)	2.05	0.84	1.63
V(TD)	0.79	0.38	0.34
V(KD)	0.18	1.04	1.75
V(TT)	0.74	0.47	0.47
V(ND)		1.22	1.01
V(ID)	2.74*	0.47	0.65

Note: *significant at the 5% level.

CONCLUSIONS

The empirical evidence presented in this study suggests the following conclusions: first, banks adjust their asset portfolios in the light of deposit variability of demand deposits in the long run. Second, what matters to banks in determining the size of the loan portfolio in the short run is the variability of interest-bearing deposits. Third, in the short run, deposit variability does not play a role in determining the size of foreign assets. Finally, the variability of government time deposits leads banks to increase their borrowing from international financial markets in the short run.

One final remark must be made. The results presented in this study are based on reduced form equations, and so may not provide an explanation for the mechanism whereby the effect is transmitted from deposit variability to the portfolio composition. This is a task that can be accomplished by specifying a parameterized structural model. The results presented here may provide some guidance for the specification of such a model.

ACKNOWLEDGMENT

We gratefully acknowledge a grant from Kuwait University to finance work on this paper (project number CB003). We are also grateful to Lee Smith who read the draft and came up with some useful suggestions.

NOTES

1. Apart from Zarruk (1989) little work was done on deposit variability in the 1980s and the 1990s.
2. In this sense the interest rate risk facing bank customers is related to deposit variability.
3. Studies addressing the issue of size test the hypothesis of negative correlation between size and deposit variability (see Struble and Wilkerson 1967; Kaufman 1972).
4. Studies dealing with branching test the hypothesis of the "portfolio effect" which is the reduction in the overall deposit variability through the addition of sets of branches (see Anderson, Haslem, and Leonard 1976 p. 455 for a survey).
5. These studies investigate the hypothesis that affiliated banks exhibit less deposit variability for a given rate of deposit growth, *ceteris paribus* (Herzig-Marx 1979).
6. In general, these studies are concerned with the hypothesis that banks' portfolio composition depends on the probability that total deposits will be reduced in the future. In this context, banks will find it more convenient to purchase assets yielding relatively low returns in order to reduce the probability of reserve deficiency (Melnik 1970, p. 642).
7. There are several studies of the behavior of commercial banks in emerging financial markets, but these do not take explicit account of the role of deposit variability (see, for example, Arjoon 1994).
8. Kaufman (1972) asserts that the argument put forward by Dewald and Dresse (1970) that bank total asset management is more strongly affected by unpredictable deposit variability does not necessarily imply that total asset management is also more strongly affected by unanticipated than by total variability. Alternatively, he argues that banks consider both predictable and unpredictable variability in determining their asset mix, although the elasticities are likely to be different.
9. The reason why the sample period ends in June 1990 is the discontinuity created by the Iraqi invasion of Kuwait.

10. The importance of measuring the variabilities of different deposit categories can be seen from the procedure adopted by some economists to use the deposit mix itself as a proxy for deposit variability. Morrison and Selden (1965) used this proxy and found the ratio of demand deposits and total deposits to be positively correlated with deposit variability.

11. The t-statistics are corrected because the conventional standard errors and t-statistics cannot be used to make inference, given that the underlying variables are nonstationary. The objective of the correction is to make the t-statistics asymptotically normal and thus valid for making inference.

12. The role played by the variability of government deposits was referred to by Robinson (1962, p. 88) who described what he called "the balances of public funds" as being "notoriously unstable." In the case of Kuwait, this factor should be of greater importance, given the big role played by the government in (financing) the economy.

REFERENCES

Anderson, R.N., J.A. Haslem, and J.B. Leonard. 1976. "An Empirical Analysis of the Impact of Branching on Demand Deposit Variability." *Journal of Financial and Quantitative Analysis* 11: 455–464.

Arjoon, S. 1994. "The Portfolio Behavior of Commercial Banks in the Commonwealth Caribbean." *Applied Financial Economics* 4: 413–422.

Barth, J.R., and J.T. Bennett. 1975. "Deposit Variability and Commercial Bank Cash Holdings." *Review of Economics and Statistics* 57: 238–241.

Bond, R. 1971. "Deposit Composition and Commercial Bank Earnings" *Journal of Finance* 26: 39–50.

Chairnoff, H. 1967. "Deposit Variability: A Banker's Headache." *Federal Reserve Bank of Philadelphia Business Review* (September): 9–15.

Dewald, W.G., and R. Dresse. 1970. "Bank Behavior with Respect to Deposit Variability." *Journal of Finance* 25: 869–879.

Dickey, D.A., and W.A. Fuller. 1979. "Distribution of the Estimators for Autoregressive Time Series with a Unit Root." *Journal of the American Statistical Association* 74: 427–431.

Gramley, L.E. 1962. "Deposit Variability at Individual Banks." *Essays on Commercial Banking*, Federal Reserve Bank of Kansas City: 41–53.

Herzig-Marx, C. 1979. "Holding Company Affiliation and Long-run Deposit Variability." *Journal of Economics and Business* (Winter): 111–118.

Hester, D.D. 1962. "An Empirical Examination of a Commercial Bank Loan Offer Function." *Yale Economic Essays* 2: 3–57.

Hester, D.D., and J.L. Pierce. 1975. *Bank Management and Portfolio Behavior*. New Haven: Yale University Press.

Kane, E.E., and B.G. Malkeil. 1965. "Bank Portfolio Allocation, Deposit Variability and the Availability Doctrine." *Quarterly Journal of Economics* 79: 113–134.

Kaufman, G.G. 1972. "Deposit Variability and Bank Size." *Journal of Financial and Quantitative Analysis* 7: 2087–2096.

Melnik A. 1970. "Short-run Determinants of Commercial Bank Investment Portfolios." *Journal of Finance* 25: 639–649.

———. 1979. "Demand Deposit Variability in Banks: A Time Series Analysis." *Journal of Bank Research* (Summer): 97–101.

Miller, M., and D. Orr. 1966. "A Model of the Demand for Money by Firms." *Quarterly Journal of Economics* 80: 413–435.

Morrison, G.R., and R.T. Selden. 1965. *Time Deposits Growth and the Employment of Bank Funds*. Chicago: Association of Reserve City Bankers.

Murphy, N.B. 1968. "A Cross-section Analysis of Demand Deposit Variability." *Journal of Financial and Quantitative Analysis* 3: 87–95.

Pattison, J.C. 1974. "Bank Deposit Variability: Some Further Evidence." *Journal of Bank Research* (Winter): 308–310.

Phillips, P.C.B. 1987. "Time Series Regression with a Unit Root." *Econometrica* 58: 277–301.

Phillips, P.C.B., and S. Ouliaris. 1990. "Asymptotic Properties of Residual Based Tests for Cointegration." *Econometrica* 58: 165–193.

Porter, R.C. 1961. "A Model of Bank Portfolio Selection." *Yale Economic Essays* 1: 325–359.

Rangarajan, C. 1966. "Deposit Variability in Individual Banks." *National Banking Review* 4: 61–71.

Robinson, R.I. 1962. "The Management of Bank Funds." New York: McGraw Hill.

Shull, B. 1968. "Report on Research Undertaken in Connection with a System Study." *Reappraisal of the Federal Reserve Discount Mechanism*, U.S. Board of Governors of the Federal Reserve System.

Struble, F.M., and C.H. Wilkerson. 1967. "Bank Size and Deposit Variability." *Federal Reserve Bank of Kansas City Monthly Review* (November–December): 3–9.

West, K.D. 1988. "Asymptotic Normality when Regressors have a Unit Root." *Econometrica* 56: 1397–1418.

Zarruk, E.R. 1989. "Bank Spread with Uncertain Deposit Level and Risk Aversion." *Journal of Banking and Finance* 89: 797–810.

THE KOREAN STOCK MARKET: THE ROAD TO GLOBALIZATION AND LIBERALIZATION

Young-Kwon Cho and Steven R. Cunningham

ABSTRACT

This paper details the institutional and regulatory development of the Korean stock market from 1953. We focus primarily on the characteristics of the secondary market and economic policy issues. We discuss the past and present developments of the market—history, market liberalization efforts, microstructure, the main policy tools used to dampen volatility, the role of investment trusts, the status of the securities industry, stock ownership, and the real-name system reforms. Finally, we suggest some policy recommendations for the Korean stock market as it faces complete liberalization and globalization.

INTRODUCTION

Now well past its critical early years, the growth of the Korean stock market has been accelerating since the second half of 1985. Riding on a wave of dreams, the market has captured the popular imagination; even small-plot, private farmers

Research in International Business and Finance, Supplement 1, pages 213–239.

ISBN: 0-7623-0110-4

speculate daily, standing shoulder to shoulder with powerful institutional investors. Before the Korea Fund was listed on the New York Stock Exchange (NYSE) in August 1984, the Korean equity market did not get much attention even from Korean investors or Korean firms seeking financial capital. It was not until January 1992 that the market began to open to foreign investors, and then only in stages.[1] But by the end of December 1994, the market's capitalization was 151 trillion won (US$191 billion) with 699 companies listed, and by 1997 the market will be the second largest market in Asia after the Tokyo Stock Exchange (TSE) in terms of market capitalization.

Despite its growth in the last 10 years, language, distance, and the closed nature of Korean financial circles have precluded interested parties outside Korea from having much opportunity to be introduced to the particulars of the Korean equity market. This paper provides that introduction, focusing primarily on the attributes of the secondary market. The story is one of gradual liberalization and globalization in response to the growing capital needs of the developing Korean economy, the desire of foreign investors to participate, and the willingness of domestic interests to accept foreign competition in its various forms. The implications out of this study will be useful to the newly emerging markets in Eastern European countries and other new markets.

This paper proceeds as follows. In the next section, we review the history of the Korean stock market and its institutional features from the Korean War through 1979. The third section follows with a discussion of the developments of the market since 1980. Additional elements of the institutional structure of the market are considered in the fourth section. The fifth and sixth sections discuss the efforts to control market volatility, as well as the ways in which the securities industry in general, and investment trust companies in particular, developed and continue to influence the capital markets; the distribution of stock ownership will be discussed. Finally, we offer a brief summary and concluding statements.

THE KOREAN EQUITY MARKET—BIRTH AND EARLY DEVELOPMENT

Before 1956 an informal equity market existed in the form of a private investor's club that became the Korea Securities Dealers Association (KSDA) in late 1953. The KSDA assumed the responsibility of operating the equity market until the Korea Stock Exchange (KSE) was established in March of 1956. At that time, 49 securities companies engaged in trading the 13 companies and three government bonds that were listed. From 1956 to 1961 81% of the trading was in government bonds that were issued to raise funds to rebuild the nation after the Korean War. In 1956 the government tried to introduce a new Securities Act to replace the 1943 Decree on the Chosun Stock Exchange written during the Japanese takeover period. When the Securities Act failed to pass the National Assembly, the government was obligated to implement the older decree, giving the government nearly complete power in supervising the new exchange.

The stock market crash of 1958 was a source of much concern for the authorities because of the enormous public outrage it brought against the KSE. The public saw the KSE as a "playground of irrational speculators." In an attempt to boost the market, the government passed the Asset Revaluation Act in 1958. The act allowed for the inflation-adjusted revaluation of the book value of company assets, effectively permitting companies to issue new shares by conversion. The act also encouraged state-owned enterprises to have generous dividend policies, and to offer their shares on the KSE.

In January 1962, having faced another market crash in 1959, the government introduced a new Securities and Exchange Law (SEL), at last replacing the 1956 Decree on the Chosun Stock Exchange. The new SEL was modeled after the new Japanese Securities and Exchange Law. By adopting the new SEL, the government tried to provide companies easy access to financing through the stock market. In line with the new SEL, the government gave more flexibility to companies by enhancing the discretionary power of boards of directors in issuing new shares, and by permitting new shares to be issued below par value. Following the adoption of these measures, the volume of stock trading began to surpass the volume of bond trading. During the period from July 1961 to May 1962, the monthly transaction value of stock trading increased dramatically, from 13 million won to about 25 billion won.

This bullish phase, however, was not sustained. Two explanations are usually given, the second seeming more plausible than the first. (1) Settlement was not required until two months after the trading date. Speculations during the float often made settlements impossible, or at least risky. (2) Securities companies speculated and manipulated the market with their holdings of shares in the KSE (securities companies furnished the capital of the KSE). These two practices disturbed the market so badly that in May 1962, during the so-called May Securities Incident, there were insufficient funds (about 3.5 billion won) to settle the transactions of the KSE shares. Responding to this incident, the government financed enough money to settle 2.8 billion won of the transactions. In addition, the government exempted the buyers' responsibilities to settle the transactions, resulting in major losses for many investors.[2] The government actions precipitated a series of incidents each culminating in a market closing. Finally, in desperation, the Ministry of Finance (MOF) closed the KSE from February 25 to May 9 of 1963 to await major reforms.

Before reopening the KSE, the MOF initiated several measures to stabilize the market, and amended the SEL (April 1963). The initiatives were as follows: (1) the KSE was reformed as a government operated nonprofit organization,[3] (2) the Korea Securities Financial Corporation (KSFC) was assigned full responsibility for clearinghouse operations and securities financing for the exchange, and (3) a *daily price fluctuation limit* (DPFL) was established. Following these initiatives, much to the surprise of the government, the market did not improve but rather worsened.

In fact, the market turned broadly bearish. Manufacturing companies, choosing to avoid equity market financing, turned increasingly to financing through the banking sector, the unorganized private fund market, and foreign sources. Many companies struggled to avoid bankruptcy after overleveraging. From March 1956 to 1967 the number of securities companies fell from 47 to 25. The securities market was failing its primary market function of channeling funds to productive investments to support economic growth. The government had to find a way to revive the capital market, a key objective of its Second Five-Year Economic Development Plan (1968–1972).

Appreciating the importance of the equity market to the economy, the government introduced in 1968 the Capital Market Promotion Act (CMPA). The main purpose of the CMPA was to encourage public investors to hold stocks, hopefully improving the stock market climate. The major contents of the CMPA were as follows: (1) shareholders were guaranteed to receive an annual dividend at least equal to the one-year time deposit interest rate; (2) the MOF was given discretion to offer state-owned stocks with no restrictions regarding price and volume; (3) shareholders of listed companies were exempted from capital gains taxation; (4) a shareholder and his or her affiliates were permitted to obtain up to 51% of the issued voting shares; and (5) the Korea Investment Corporation (KIC) was established in December 1968 with the formal responsibility for the issuance, distribution, and underwriting of securities. The KIC also was assigned the role of stabilizing securities prices in the market.

Another landmark in the development of the Korean equity market happened in the same year (1968)—the Securities and Exchange Law (SEL) was amended, dividing the securities industry into two business areas. To be allowed to enter into the two main securities businesses—brokerage/dealing and underwriting—a company was required to have a capitalization of at least 50 million won. A company with a capitalization in the range of 30 to 50 million won was permitted to engage in brokerage and dealing businesses only. The amended SEL also shortened the clearing period between trading and settlements. Previously, the common practice was for settlement within two months after the trading day. In February 1, 1969, next-day settlements, often called "regular way transactions," began. To give additional flexibility to investors, by paying additional charges the settlement date could be extended up to 60 days. Hence, speculative factors were present even in the new "regular way" transactions.

Despite all this, only 234 companies were listed on the KSE by 1968. Company executives tended to dismiss the virtues of going public. The widespread notion was that it was almost impossible to declare annual dividends equivalent to the one-year time deposit rate, then 23%. Companies also worried about the possibility of losing control of companies to investors. Moreover, the financial institutions, still relatively inexperienced, suffered severe limitations in their abilities to underwrite new stock offerings. The final stroke was when the government decided to conduct a tight monetary policy in late 1969. Companies, seeing little alternative, looked to the "unorganized loan market" for external funding, and the stock market took another big drop in 1970.

The devastation that followed in the capital markets over the next two years forced the government to pass the August 3 Emergency Decree in 1972. The decree was designed to eliminate the "unorganized loan market." By the decree, all companies were required to report to the government the details of debits and credits to the "unorganized loan market." Companies were allowed to repay only 1.35% per month out of the principal amount of the private debt, an extremely low interest rate in terms of loan practices in the early 1970s. At the same time, the government introduced the Going Public Encouragement Act in December 1972. The act gave the MOF the authority to ask companies to go public. It also allowed employees to subscribe to up to 10% of the newly issued stocks.

Perhaps due to the government efforts, the stock market started to advance in 1973. The government not only forced companies to go public but also engaged in securities analysis and the pricing of new issues (usually underpricing). The demand for securities started to surpass the supply of securities.[4] Investment trust funds grew fast enough to establish the Korea Investment Trust Company in August 8, 1974. Investment trust funds grew to the level of 40 billion won in 1976 from the initial fund of 4.6 billion won. In February 1977 the newly established Daehan Investment Trust Company assumed the role of the KIC, and the KIC was dissolved.

This expansion of the equity market caused several regulatory problems due to the coexistence of the several government agencies with conflicting jurisdictions. Inefficiencies arose because of redundant supervision. Recognizing the problem, the government revised the Securities and Exchange Law (SEL) dramatically in February 1977, creating the Securities and Exchange Commission, establishing it as a major policy making body. It also established the Securities Supervisory Board as a policy implementing agency.[5] The SEL also broke down the securities business licenses into three areas. That is, the paid-in capital amount of the securities companies became a benchmark to get each license for "dealer," "broker," or "underwriter." It also introduced the system of takeover bids. To decrease the possibility of hostile takeovers, individual shareholders were not permitted to hold shares in excess of a certain limit. In return, a controlling shareholder was induced to lower his or her ownership to 35% or less. It also required the companies to file their annual and semiannual reports with the MOF and the KSE. Disclosure requirements were toughened; companies were required to file financial statements with the SEC, and regulations regarding insider trading was also consolidated. Hence, by these fundamental changes in the SEL, the Korean equity market became well-poised to enter the 1980s.

THE POST-1980 PERIOD—THE ERA OF THE MARKET LIBERALIZATION

Setting the Stage for the Globalization

In January 14, 1981 the MOF announced a four-step plan for the globalization of the Korean capital market. The general theme of the plan was to give foreign investors opportunities to invest in the Korean capital market. The four-step plan was established with the following features. During Stage I (1981–1984), planning for the opening of the market to foreign investors was to be completed, and an international investment trust fund was to be authorized. During Stage II (1985–1987), foreign investors were to be allowed limited participation in the securities market. The restrictions on foreign investors were to be gradually lifted, and limited foreign offerings by domestic securities companies were to be permitted in Stage III (1988–1990). Stage IV, in the early 1990s, would bring complete liberalization of the market, including domestic investors participating directly in foreign securities markets.

In 1981 in accordance with Stage I of the plan, the Korea International Trust (KIT) and the Korea Trust (KT) were established for foreign investors. The actual sale of *beneficial certificates* (BC) began abroad. Meanwhile, the Securities and Exchange Law (SEL) was again amended in April 1982. One noticeable provision in the SEL was to require an approval from the MOF for domestic and foreign securities companies seeking business in the foreign and domestic market, respectively. In October 1982 the MOF permitted financial institutions to engage in bond transactions with repurchase agreements, which might include issued bonds. On July 1983 the MOF announced the Measures for the Reinforcement of Capital Market Function. The measures included the "issue-at-market" price system, and allowed big securities companies to expand their business areas (e.g., payments guarantees on corporate bonds, underwriting and distribution of commercial papers, and business expansion to the foreign capital markets). The culmination of the first stage of the plan was the listing of the Korea Fund (KF) on the New York Stock Exchange (NYSE) on August 1984.[6]

During Stage II of the plan (1984–1987), the MOF announced the Guidelines for the Overseas Floatation of Securities in November 1985. The guidelines specified requirements for qualifications for domestic companies issuing securities (convertible bonds) abroad, including conversion price and conversion period rules. Following the guidelines, the MOF allowed Samsung Electronics Company for the first time to issue convertible bonds (Samsung CB) worth US$20 million in the Euro-Bond market on November 1985.

During the second stage of the plan for globalization, one of the debates was regarding the "consolidation of shares." Domestic market participants were concerned that the 500 won (US$0.60) face value of shares was too inexpensive in terms of the purchasing power of foreign exchanges. Koreans worried that the lion's share of the domestic capital would fall into hands of foreign speculators. Hence, the face value of a share was raised to 5,000 won (US$6.40). Unfortunately, this had the secondary effect of adding more downside risk for investors. To offset some of the added risk, the SEC amended the daily price fluctuation limit (effective September 1986), according to the market experience since December 1985.[7]

During the second stage of the plan, the Korean equity market did not fulfill the original objective of opening the market to limited foreign investment. Attempting to rectify this, the MOF overhauled the original globalization plan of 1981 in December 1988. Under this new plan, foreign investors were to be permitted to make limited direct investment through the stock market as early as January 1992.

Despite the unceasing efforts by the government and securities industry, the market remained sluggish because of the worries over the prospects of the domestic economy and a sharp increase in crude oil prices due to the crisis in the Gulf.[8] Attempting to address the weak domestic market performance, the government launched another initiative. Guidelines for the Securities Industry Opening were laid out in November 1990. The guidelines provided for the expansion of the international business activities of the securities industry through the opening of branch offices or subsidiaries abroad. The foreign securities companies were also allowed to open Korean branches or to form joint ventures with domestic companies. Beginning January 1991 the government began to accept applications from the domestic securities companies for the opening of foreign business offices. In March 1991, pursuant to the November 1990 guideline, the government allowed foreign securities companies to open their branches in Korea.

As globalization efforts continued, the stock market remained sluggish mainly due to the weak economy and high interest rates, among other reasons.[9] The government was pressured to take action to rescue the stock market and responded by allowing a complete liberalization of the discount rate on the "issue-at-market" price system at the time equity shares are issued. In addition, the state temporarily halted its sales of state-owned securities and permitted the issuance of 1 trillion won of "exchangeable bonds" by securities companies.[10]

Beginning the New Era of Market Globalization

At last, in January 1992 the stock market opened to foreign investors.[11] Even with the new flow of funds from foreign investors, the stock market showed no clear signs of improvement. In an effort to shore up confidence, the government announced the 3-18 Stock Market Stabilization Measures on March 18, 1992. The main focus of the 3-18 Measures was on creating more demand in the market. It opened the door to a more extensive range of foreign investors such as foreign securities companies and contractual-type investment trusts. It also permitted the increase in capital of the Korean funds abroad, notably the KF, KEF, and Korea Asia Fund (KAF), by US$1.5 billion. And, it permitted the two Korean investment trust companies (Deahan and Citizen) to issue beneficiary certificates (backed 80%

by stocks) worth 400 billion won. As a result, about 600 billion won in investment funds were expected to be made available to purchase stocks. Thus, the 3-18 Measures helped ease the continuing sluggishness in the market, but they lacked the power to turn the market in the face of the weakness of the real economy and the existing market liquidity problems.[12]

Meanwhile, after the market liberalization, the Korean stock market started to experience two extreme, divergent movements in stock prices. The share prices of the "blue chips" and the financial industry were down by 8.77% from January 4, 1992 to May 26, 1992. Stock prices of the medium-sized firms (with paid-in capital of 5 to 15 billion won) and small-sized firms (with paid-in capital of less than 5 billion won), however, increased by 37.1% and 54.6%, respectively. That makes market index readings unreliable; the KOSPI is weighted more in favor of the large capitalization stocks. The popular wisdom was that the extreme movements of the stock prices were the result of the trading patterns of the foreign investors; the more likely cause was the depressed economy. The yield of three-year corporate bonds moved from 18.2% in October 1990 to 17.1% in May 1992, and the current account balance still showed a negative US$233.2 million in May 1992. This was the first time the current account balance had been in deficit since 1986.

During economic downswings Korean investors stick to stocks that have high asset values or high yields. These investors are also reluctant to hold the relatively expensive shares of the "blue chips" or the financial industry (which also have more outstanding shares than small- or medium-sized firms). Thus, it was hard for the MOF to accept the extreme movements as "natural" phenomena. More important, the poor performance of the market was beginning to concern the institutional investors, especially the investment managers in investment trust companies.

On June 11, 1992 the DOF allowed Japanese brokerage firms to open branches. Previously, Japanese securities companies were restricted in conducting business in Korea. The DOF also increased the foreign investment limit to 25% of the total outstanding shares of joint venture companies and companies issuing securities (CB, BW, or DR) abroad.[13] The increases of the investment limit of certain companies were designed to attract more foreign money to the stock market. Unfortunately, this ad hoc measure, not formally part of the guidelines, did not cause any significant money inflows into the market.

Despite efforts by the government, the stock market did not perform to the expectations of market participants. On August 24, 1992 the MOF announced another market-boosting measures to induce lower market interest rates to expand the demand base for the stocks, and to permit securities companies to sell large denomination Repurchase Agreements (RPs) to individual investors to ease the cash flow of the securities industry. To lower interest rates, the MOF initiated (1) flexible targeting and an increased growth rate of monetary aggregate (18.5% growth rate for M2), (2) a recommendation for the lowering of corporate bond rates on the benchmark three-year maturity, and (3) a reduction of the spread between the deposit rate and the loan rates of the commercial banks. To stimulate stock market demand, the MOF (1) allotted the trust accounts of commercial banks and insurance companies 2 trillion 200 billion won in stock purchasing funds, (2) increased the Securities Market Stabilization Fund (SMSF) by an additional 500 billion won, (3) required financial institutions to be net buyers of stocks, and (4) allowed foreigners to buy shares of POSCO and KEPCO earlier than planned, with the investment limit for one foreign investor at 1% of the total outstanding shares of the POSCO or KEPCO.

In short, the main objective of the government's actions taken on August 24, 1992 was to create a larger demand base (worth 3 trillion 900 billion won) for the stock market. Unfortunately, market conditions were not favorable enough to increase demand by that much. For example, the additional SMSF was to be raised through contributions (140 billion won) from the newly established securities companies. The rest of the 360 billion won was to be raised from the contributions of newly listed companies and companies increasing their capital during the next year. The bear market, however, kept the companies from financing through the stock market. The other measures also required strong governmental administrative "guidance." It was hard for the government to pursue these other measures in the depressed market environment.

Remarkably, in October 1992 the MOF lifted the ban on foreign purchases of the POSCO shares. The restriction was that a foreign investor could buy 1% of the total outstanding shares, but no more than 8% of the total outstanding shares could be purchased by foreigners. The same rule applied to the shares of the KEPCO from November 1992.[14] By lifting these restrictions the MOF broke with the earlier established "principles" of the market opening. As noted before the purchase of shares in the companies by foreign investors was not allowed because those companies were regarded as "key industries." As a result of lifting the bans foreign investment increased to US$2 billion by December 1992.

In the less than seven years since its opening in December 1988, the market has been criticized by market professionals and foreign investors. To them, it appears that the government's only real interest in "globalization" is to "pump up" its sagging domestic stock market. They argue that frequent government involvement can undermine the efficiency of the stock market. In fairness, the seemingly odd timing of the introduction of market reforms is more likely to stem from the fears regarding the market liberalization among some government officials and some domestic market participants. They fear foreign participation in the Korean markets, the lack of stock market stability, and the lack of international competitiveness in the Korean securities industry. These fears are unfounded. Most foreign securities companies in Korea are licensed only for the brokerage business. Thus, the Korean securities industry has a competitive edge on the Korean stock market. The domestic investors still favor domestic brokerage houses. Foreign investors can provide the market stability by being a source of a broad base of liquidity. As the market size grows with more market opening, however, the market dominance by the domestic securities industry could not be guaranteed. There exists a possibility that "hot money" from foreign speculators can disturb the market as well as the linkage of the market with foreign interest rates volatility. Several tasks are left for the Korean securities industry, including the development of financial derivatives such as futures and options.[15]

FURTHER INSTITUTIONAL DETAIL OF THE KOREAN STOCK MARKET

The KSE Structure

The KSE's trading floor is composed of the stock trading section, the bond trading section, and the beneficiary certificates (BC) trading section. For the stock trading section, the KSE has three trading sections: the First, Second, and Administrative Trading Sections. To be listed on the KSE, applicants have to fulfill listing requirements stipulated by the Listing Regulation (amended in November 1991) of the KSE. To be listed in the First Trading Section, a company is required to have more than 5 billion won in paid-in capital, the controlling shareholder has to have less than a 51% stake, and more than 40% of the outstanding shares have to be held by minority shareholders. A newly listed issue has to be traded in the Second Trading Section for at least one year. After the newly listed shares are traded for a year without problem, then they can be transferred to the First Trading Section. If a company's stock shows a peculiar trading volume or price movement, for example, the stock price moves up by more than five times or eight times its own daily price fluctuation limit (DPFL) during the last six or twelve trading days, respectively, then the KSE designates it as a "surveillance issue" for the purpose of maintaining market stability. If a company's stock is to be delisted, or if the company is facing bankruptcy, it is moved down to the Administrative Trading Section, and is traded with a reduced DPFL.

The stocks listed in the First Trading Section can be regarded as "blue chip" shares. During the period 1990 to 1991, 126 companies have been transferred to the First Trading Section from the Second Trading Section. After the KSE amended the listing requirements in November 1991, only 10 companies were transferred to the First Trading Section during 1992. On the other hand, 20 companies were moved to the Second Trading Section during 1990 to 1991, while only three companies moved during 1992. The prices of stocks that are moved to the Second Trading Section have a high probability of taking a nosedive. Margin transactions are only allowed on shares in the First Trading Section, so that investors who purchased stocks that are transferred to the Second Trading Section have enormous selling pressure to repay margin loans.

The KSE has two trading sessions a day from Monday through Friday, but only one morning session on Saturday. The morning trading session runs from 9:20 to 11:20 am, and the afternoon trading session runs from 1:30 to 3:30 pm. Thus, total trading time is 22 hours per week. This is 10.5 hours shorter than the NYSE, but only 30 minutes shorter than the Tokyo Stock Exchange (TSE). Additionally, the first trading day of the year (January 3rd) and the last trading day of the year have only morning trading sessions.

To handle the ever-increasing trading volume and the needed dissemination of information to the market, the KSE started a computerized trading system. On March 2, 1988, the KSE started the Stock Market Automated Trading System (SMATS). Initially, it handled only 7% of the total trading volume, with the rest of the volume traded by the traditional manual handling of orders. In 1992 the SMATS handled 96.5% of total volume. Member firms get the trading results from the SMATS automatically, thus the introduction of the SMATS to the exchange has contributed to fast and accurate matching, price determination, and settlement.

Trading Procedure

Whether the securities are actively traded or not, the KSE conducts the order execution by one of the following order-driven systems: (1) a call auction method (a periodic system) or (2) a continuous auction system. The call auction method is a periodic auction where orders are batched for execution at a single price. For the continuous auction, orders are made continuously and trading occurs whenever orders match. The call market methods are used on the following occasions: (1) opening time (9:40 am) of the morning trading session, (2) opening time (1:20 pm) of the afternoon trading session, and (3) closing time (3:20 pm) of the afternoon trading session. The rest of the time the continuous auction method is used to match the prices including the morning trading session's closing price.[16] For the call market method, also called the "simultaneous bids and offer method" or "single price execution method," orders are batched for trading at a single price in the following cases: (1) orders taken during last 100 minutes before the morning and afternoon trading session opens, (2) initial price determination for the orders taken during the 10 minutes immediately following the resumption of trading after a "halt in trading," and (3) orders taken 10 minutes before closing (since December 1989 for the stocks traded by the SMATS).

The orders are executed under the competitive trading principles with the priority given to price, time, and volume, in that order. Trading priority is given to the highest bid and lowest offer prices. When an order coincides with other orders in price and time, larger volume can take precedence. Also, individual investor orders are given priority over securities firm's dealing account orders.

For example, as in Table 1, the bids/offers for company A's stock are submitted as follows: (1) sell at 20,000 won, 4,000 shares from brokerage house 1, (2) sell at 18,000 won, 3,000 shares from brokerage house 2, (3) buy at 21,000 won, 3,000 shares from brokerage house 3, and (4) buy at 20,000 won, 2,000 shares from brokerage house 4. Then the single matched price is 20,000 won which equalizes the quantity below 20,000 won for selling and quantity above 20,000 won for

Table 1. Price Matching of Company A stocks

Member Firms	*Selling*	*Buying*
Member #1	20,000 won; 4,000 Shares	
Member #2	18,000 won; 3,000 Shares	
Member #3		21,000 won; 3,000 Shares
Member #4		20,000 won; 2,000 Shares

buying. The rest of 2,000 shares for selling is not traded. Thus, this call market method fulfills the property of the classic demand and supply analysis.

A special case (honoring the quotation which is closer to the previous prices) exists for the call market method. For instance, if the selling/buying order for company A's stock is taken as follows: sell at 20,000 won, 2,000 shares from brokerage house 1, and buy at 21,000 won, 2,000 shares from brokerage house 2. If the previous clearing price (including yesterday's closing price) is 21,200 won, then 21,000 won is the matched single price since it is closer to the previous price. On the other hand, if the previous price fell in-between, like 20,600 won, then the matched single price is 20,600 won. If the previous clearing price was 19,600 won, then 20,000 won is the settled price.

The continuous auction method is used throughout the two trading sessions after the single matched price is determined by the call market method. This continuous auction method is called "post trading." When the highest bid and lowest offer prices are falling into the possible matching range, then transaction occurs following the quoted prices submitted earlier, whichever (bid or offer) is submitted first. For example, when investor A submitted a selling order of 4,000 shares of company A at 21,000 won first and investor B gave buying order of 2,000 shares of the company at 22,000 won later, then the transaction occurs at the 21,000 won which was submitted first. On the other hand, if the bid price is 22,000 won with 5,000 shares first and the offering price is 21,000 won with 3,000 shares later, then the price is determined at 22,000 won.

The NYSE uses a periodic auction system in the order-driven system for the opening and changes to a continuous dealership market with market makers. Amihud and Mendelson (1987) compare the two different trading mechanisms in the NYSE with regard to stock price behavior. They find high return variance and more divergence from the "random walk" hypothesis when using the opening call auction method. But the main cause of this phenomenon is due to the preceding non-trading time. In a theoretical model, Madhavan (1992), however, argues that a periodic auction method causes higher costs of collecting information for investors and a loss of trading continuity, but that it can give better price efficiency in the process of price discovery. The continuous auction method, however, causes informational asymmetry in the market. The price that ultimately eventuates may not be the theoretical "equilibrium" price.

The KSE does not have specialists to act as market makers so that these studies may not be directly applicable, but it is interesting to compare the two trading procedures in terms of stock return behavior in the Korean stock market.

Clearing and Settlement

As noted in the previous section, the Korea Securities Settlement Corporation (KSSC) was established in December 1974 to provide centralized clearing and settlement. Two typical transactions exist, spot transactions and regular-way transactions. Regular-way transactions have a three-day settlement period including the trade date ($T + 2$) with two side matching. This applies to all listed shares except for the shares in the Administrative Section. Spot transactions have to be settled on the trading day ($T + 0$), as do all transactions with stocks in the Administrative Section. Bond trading uses both transaction types. For the regular-way transactions, 2:00 pm is the "time limit for clearing" (TLC) for weekdays. The TLC for Saturday is 12:00 pm. For spot transactions, 1:00 pm is the TLC for transactions made in the morning trading session, and 4:00 pm is the TLC for transactions made in the afternoon trading session.

Good-faith deposits or entrustment guaranty deposits (currently 40% of the trading value) have to be deposited to insure that the shares are purchased within the settlement date. Otherwise, the shares purchased with no good-faith deposit will be sold automatically. The KSSC centrally conducts custodian services to settle the transaction by the book entry clearing system. It also utilizes multilateral netting (net balance delivery) to clear the securities transactions involved. Securities lending or borrowing are not permitted to settle the transaction.

To protect investors and securities companies from incurring losses due to unsettled transactions, the KSE has established the Joint Compensation Fund. Each member of the KSE is required to deposit 1/100,000 of its own trading value into the fund. The minimum contribution from each member will be the bigger amount from either of the following two: (1) 2/300 of its own trading value last year, or (2) the total deposit amount made last year divided by the number of total members. Once its contribution limit is reached, members no longer need to contribute to the fund.[17]

POLICY TOOLS CURBING STOCK MARKET VOLATILITY

Daily Price Fluctuation Limits (DPFL)

The DPFL has been used since April 1963 to reduce excessive price fluctuations and to protect investors from exposure to market instability. The DPFL are applied to stocks, beneficiary certificates (BC), and equity-related debt securities such as

Table 2. DPFL for Shares and Beneficiary Certificates (unit: won)

Share Prices	*General Issues*
20,000–21,600	±1,200
30,000–31,600	±1,800
40,000–41,600	±2,400
50,000–51,600	±3,000
60,000–61,600	±3,600
70,000–71,600	±4,200
80,000–81,600	±4,800
90,000–91,600	±5,400
99,000–99,900	±5,900
above 100,000	±6%

Source: Korean Securities Dealers Association

convertible bonds (CB) and bonds with stock purchase warrant (BW). As shown in Table 2, the DPFL of stocks and BC is 6%.[18]

A unique attribute of the DPFL is no flexibility in the price limit. Thus, contrary to the main purpose advocated by the authorities, the DPFL could distort and delay the price adjustment process in the market. It could give false signals to the investors. In the U.S. stock market, a big price change such as the October crash in 1989 can occur in a day. A similar price change on the KSE might take several days.

Margin Regulation

The primary purpose of margin regulation is to reduce price fluctuations (Goldberg 1985). In the United States, the Fed has changed the margin requirement on 22 different occasions since 1934. From January 1974 to the present, the U.S. margin requirement has not changed, remaining at 50%. The Korea Stock Exchange (KSE) has, in contrast, changed margin requirements 18 times from 1977 to 1992 ranging from 40 to 100%.[19] The initial margin requirement is applied to both stock purchases and short sales. (The transaction volume of short sales has been insignificant on the KSE.) Margin transactions represent from 30 to 40% of the total trading volume on the KSE in recent years. In Korea, as in the United States, margin requirements have been used as a policy instrument to control speculation and to reduce price fluctuations.

The effects of margin requirements on market volatility is an ongoing question. There are two competing views. Moore (1966), Officer (1973), Schwert (1989), Salinger (1989), and Hsieh and Miller (1990) argue that the margin requirement is not an effective instrument for dampening market volatility. On the other side of the argument is Hardouvelis (1988, 1990), who argues that a negative relationship exists between margin requirement and stock market volatility.

Margin regulation in the Korean stock market is similar to the U.S. stock market, but possesses some unique attributes. Investors open a margin account by depositing 1,000,000 won (about US$1,300) and pay the quoted interest rate of 13% per annum on margin loans from the securities company.[20] For short-selling, brokers hold the proceeds from securities sales on behalf of their clients until they repay the borrowed stocks. Customers receive interest payment, usually 4% per annum, from the proceeds.

The Securities and Exchange Commission (SEC) is controlled by the Ministry of Finance. The SEC can change the margin requirement ratio whenever it feels that it is necessary to do so between 40 and 100%. To fulfill margin requirements, an investor can deposit cash or securities. The investor is required, however, to carry more securities in his or her account relative to cash itself. The value of the securities, called the "loan value," is discounted by an assessment rate. Cash loans or stock loans must be repaid within 150 days with no extension.

Margin trading is allowed only on the shares listed on the First Trading Section of the KSE.[21] The shares cannot be "surveillance issues." In addition, foreign investors cannot use margin trading. Brokers can make loans to their customers either by using their own proceeds or by financing from the Korea Securities Finance Corporation (KSFC). A securities company can lend single investors up to 50 million won as a cash loan and up to 20 million won as a stock loan. As a whole, a securities company cannot loan more than 60% of its own paid-in capital in margin cash loans and more than 50% of its own paid-in capital in stock loans. The margin buying position in a company share is allowed up to 20% of its outstanding shares. But, maximum 10% of a company's outstanding shares is allowed for the short-sale position.

The investor engaged in margin trading has to keep a "maintenance required rate of collateral" (MRMC) of 130% of the amount of the margin loan extended. If the investor falls below this MRMC, he will receive a margin call from his or her broker asking for additional collateral to restore the MRMC. If an investor fails to maintain the MRMC, he or she is prohibited from making any additional market transactions. From the securities industry's point of view, it is difficult to ask for additional collateral from the investor. Many margin accounts did not satisfy the MRMC during the bearish phases in the period of 1989 and 1990. These accounts were called "empty-can accounts." On October 10, 1990 the government asked the securities industry to eliminate the "empty-can accounts" by "covering," where covering is when the securities industry forcefully sells the securities in the margin loan accounts and buys securities in the stock-loaned accounts. These "empty-can accounts" still exist, however, due to brokerage houses' competition for stock market shares. They have become a significant burden for the Korean securities industry.

In addition to the margin regulation, both domestic and foreign investors are required to make an "entrustment guaranty deposit" (EGD), or good-faith deposit to the securities company whenever an order is placed. Currently, the EGD is 40% (cash) of the trading value, but foreign financial institutions can be exempted in case of approval of the KSE. "Surveillance" and "administrative" stocks are required to have 100% of EGD.

Pseudo-Circuit Breakers

The Korean stock market has an indirect method of supporting the market in case of a decline in stock prices. Financial institutions and listed companies formed the Securities Market Stabilization Fund (SMSF) on May 4, 1990 to maintain market stability. Generally, in a bear market selling pressure is high; in bull markets buying pressure increases. To counter dramatic swings in buying and selling pressure the Fund was created with no government involvement. Within four days of its inception, the SMSF held 4 trillion won, about 4% of the KSE's total market capitalization. The SMSF is regarded as funds formation within the market, an outside pool of funds, but it is highly regarded as a self-regulatory tool for dampening market volatility. It can function as a "pseudo-circuit breaker" to avert a runaway bear market.

After three years of operation (as of May 4, 1993), the size of the SMSF has increased to 5 trillion won (with capital of 4 trillion 600 billion won and the rest in income from interest and dividend payments). Currently, about 87.5% of the fund has been used to purchase stocks. Due to its success, its members have decided to extend the SMSF for three more years.

CURRENT DEVELOPMENTS IN THE KOREAN STOCK MARKET

Securities Industry

Until late 1990 the securities industry consisted of only 25 companies.[22] In late 1990 the MOF allowed short-term finance companies to convert to the securities business. As a result of these initiatives five short-term finance companies located in Seoul shifted into securities companies in July 1991. Also, the Korea Development Bank was permitted to open a securities subsidiary with paid-in capital of 150 billion won. In July 1992 for the first time, the DOF allowed Dong-Bang Corporation to have a joint venture securities company with a Hong Kong based Peregrine securities company. Currently, all 32 companies are allowed to conduct business in the three main areas: dealing, brokerage, and underwriting.[23]

In terms of the market share of the brokerage business, no distinctive leader exists such as the "Big Four" in the Japanese market (Takagi 1989). The top-ten member firms had a 67.1% market share of stock and bond trading during 1991. From January 1993 to December 1993 the top-ten member firms had a market share of 62.4% of stock and bond trading. From January 1994 to December 1994, however, the market share of the top ten decreased to 58%.

The 32 securities companies have total paid-in capital of 3 trillion 815 billion won, and a total of 792 branches (402 branches in Seoul and 390 in the rest of the country) throughout the country at the end of December 1994. The top ten securities companies account for 405 branches, or 51%. Thus, the market share and the number of branches of the top ten almost matched each other. That is, the large number of branches can capture a bigger market share. Even though member firms exert effort to obtain permission to open branches from the MOF, the top ten, for the time being, will be fighting to maintain their current status of market dominance.

Korea, however, is a small but highly populated country. Possibilities exist for the other member firms or experienced foreign securities companies to capture a good market share. Currently, eleven foreign securities companies, including Citi Corp, Merrill Lynch, and Daiwa, have memberships in the Korea Stock Exchange. In 1994 the market share of the eleven foreign companies was 2% and was expected to increase.[24] Also, other newly established local securities companies are increasing their market shares.

From December 1994 the KSE imposed a 12% ceiling on foreign investment for all listed shares. The top-ten firms face more competition from foreign brokerage houses should the ceiling be lifted. Also, despite a recommendation from the government-commissioned Financial Industry Development Committee to end the legal separation of investment and commercial banking by year 2005, Korean financial markets will have clear divisions of the banking, securities, and insurance industry, with some possible mergers and government guidance. Only then will the current, relatively weak dominance of the market by the top ten be weakened. Rather, a few big firms with possible mergers could emerge as new leaders in the market.

Investment Trust Companies

Investment trust companies were formed as early as 1974 by the securities companies and commercial banks. The Securities Investment Trust Business Law in 1969 set the stage for investment trusts in Korea. Currently 14 management companies exist. While eight are engaged mostly in investment trusts, the rest are merchant banking corporations specializing in bond funds. The three major investment trust companies control more than 90% of the market in the investment trust industry. Five regional investment trust companies and the six merchant banks together take less than 10% of the market. Thus, three major investment trust companies literally represent the industry.[25]

During a bullish phase of the market the KOSPI hit a record high of 1,007.77 on April 1, 1989. In August 1989 the MOF allowed foreign investors with CBs of domestic companies to keep the converted shares up to 3% of outstanding shares of the companies. The stock market after April 1 did not perform to the high expectation of the investors, however. Investors became pessimistic about the economy and uneasy about labor relations in the country. Institutional investors also were facing a liquidity constraint due to the huge new supply of the government's Monetary Stabilization Bonds (MSB), designed to control monetary growth and inflation. During the third quarter of 1989 investors began to feel that the sluggish economy was not a temporary phenomenon. An enormous selling pressure began to mount on the stock market. The KOSPI fell to 844.75 in December 1989. In response to this bearish sentiment, the MOF announced a famous scheme called the 12-12 Government Actions of December 12, 1989. In fact, to give stimulus to the equity market the MOF has tried several initiatives. But, it did not succeed in turning the market around.

The enactment of the 12-12 Government Actions was like an massive injection of medicine.[26] The actions allowed investment trust companies to receive support funds from the Bank of Korea (BOK). The 12-12 Government Actions had several problems contrary to its own intended objectives.[27] One of the major problems was that the relatively unlimited supply of funds to the three major investment trust companies from the BOK let them engage in a massive buying spree.

Initially, the 12-12 Actions were welcomed by most investors and market professionals, who thought it would ease the excess supply of stocks. The measure boosted the market temporarily, resulting in a three-day increase of 9.9% of the KOSPI. Stock market rallies, if they are to survive, must eventually be buttressed by real economic progress. From 1985 to 1988 the Korean economy enjoyed a surging current account surplus due to the unprecedented favorable economic environment. That is, the economy benefitted from the so-called "three lows," which are the depreciated won relative to the Japanese yen, the low interest rates abroad, and low oil prices. The surplus of the nation's current account was one of the major sources of money inflow to the market until 1988. After 1989 the surplus shrank and deteriorated into deficit by 1990.[28] While productivity rose only 10% a year average wages rose by more than 18% a year from 1987 to 1992.

As the KOSPI fell to 566.27 on September 17, 1990 investors and the policy-makers were getting nervous. Investors were dumping stocks and investment trust companies also did little to help. During this quagmire the MOF, on September 18, 1990, announced a plan for issuing beneficiary certificates (BC) that guaranteed a minimum 10% rate of return.[29] By allowing the eight investment trust companies to sell the 10% return guaranteed BC (worth 2 trillion 600 billion won) and list them on the KSE, the MOF tried to ease the financial difficulties of the investment trust industry. Hence, the eight investment trust companies could play a role as institutional investors.

The action taken by the MOF on September 18, 1990 might have had the desired effect on the stock market if the BC had sold as intended. The investment trust industry would be able to purchase about 3.2% of the stocks in the market (total market capitalization was about 66 trillion won). But, as is so often the case, the market conditions did not cooperate. The pension funds in Korea are required to invest in financial products that guarantee at least the interest rates reflecting real economic activity, such as corporate bond rates or time-deposit rates. Before September 18, 1990 pension funds were not allowed to purchase existing BCs (which give returns less than the above interest rates). They could participate, however, by purchasing new BCs. The three-year maturity corporate bond rate was, however, around 17%.[30] Investors could also switch from the existing BCs to these new high-yield BCs, lessening the impact. Also, the new BCs were not redeemable for three years, making them less liquid relative to other high-yield products such as the CMA (cash management accounts), the BMF (bond management fund), or CDs (certificate of deposit).

Ongoing declines in the stock market did not stop despite the extensive efforts of government and industry. Investment trust companies were on the brink of bankruptcy. On May 27, 1992 the government took strong actions to boost the stock market and bail out the investment trust industry. Despite opposition from the BOK,[31] a special loan (worth 3 trillion won) was given to the industry from the BOK at a 3% annual interest rate. And, the government also provided the industry with 300 billion won in loans at a 3% annual interest rate. As a result of the 12-12 Actions (which allowed investment trust companies to purchase stocks to support the market by using the loans from the BOK) and the depressed stock market, investment trust companies incurred an enormous debt (6 trillion 59 billion won). The investment trust companies lost investor confidence, resulting in huge withdrawals of deposits. In the midst of the depressed stock market, the investment trust companies had no choice but to sell the purchased stocks to lessen the liquidity problem. Since the 12-12 Actions, the three major investment trust companies (Korea, Daehan, and Citizen) had the additional burden of annual interest payments of 600 billion won. Hence, the 5-27 Actions were important because they helped rescue the investment trust industry and financial markets altogether.

Due to the stagnant economy and uncertain political climate in the ruling Democratic Liberal Party, however, the 5-27 Actions did not help turn around the market. The government again attempted to stabilize the market.[32] Thus, even after receiving tremendous financial help from the BOK, the investment trust industry suffered big losses from April 1992 to March 1993. The industry still has a debt of about 6.4 trillion won as of June 1993 from the BOK, commercial banks, and short-term financing companies. Even though the industry started to make modest profits in the fiscal year of 1993 and 1994 mainly due to the upbeat stock market, new products, and belt tightening, it will take time to reestablish themselves as solid institutional investors.

Real-Name System Reform

From stock trading to bank accounts, three types of accounts have been used: real-name accounts, alias accounts (with false names and false identification numbers), and borrowed-name accounts (real identification numbers but other persons' names). The main reasons to have alias or borrowed-name accounts are as follows: (1) to avoid the various taxes when passing assets to third parties, (2) to guarantee anonymity, and (3) to quietly take controlling interest in a company.

Alias account holders cannot use margin transaction and cannot purchase stocks in public offering. These disadvantages do not matter to alias account holders. The main advantage of alias accounts is that they can use their inside information to take profits or protect their interests. For tax purposes, the borrowed-name and real-name accounts are treated equally.

To eliminate alias accounts the government has taxed alias accounts three times higher than real-name accounts since 1989. Real-name account holders pay an income tax of 21.5% of the dividend payment as compared with 64.5% for alias account holders. While alias accounts have been about 1 to 3% of the total accounts in the stock market, the potential effects on the market have been more significant than is suggested by this small number. Accordingly, the government proposed "real-name accounts reform" to put an end to the economic injustice that the accounts imply. The alias accounts have been isolated as possible sources of disruption in the market, they distort the distribution of stock ownership, and they likely play a role in political corruption.

Currently, capital gains on the KSE are exempt from taxes to direct more funds to capital markets. Households that rely mainly on fixed labor income, however, were destined to pay higher taxes relative to financial or real asset holders, who can use alias accounts. Thus, it has been difficult for the government to implement a global income tax or integrated income tax (expected to be introduced in 1996). Alias or borrowed-name accounts with no integrated income tax system contributed to the worsening of the income distribution as well as the disruption in financial markets.

The new administration implemented the reform in a dramatic stroke with the announcement of the August 12 Decree ordering investors under aliases to replace their accounts with real name accounts by October 12, 1993. The real-name accounts reform requires the sacrifice of a privilege enjoyed by a few people (less than 3% of the population). A strong uproar, or perhaps silent resistance in the form of a monetary overhang or speculation in real assets, was expected after the August 12 Decree. Once done, however, it will help the economy adjust to a more desirable path with a more equal distribution of wealth, fewer loopholes in the tax system, more transparency of the workings of the economy, and a more efficient stock market.[33]

During the two-month transition from August 12 to October 12, 1993 more than 90% of the alias accounts were converted to real-name accounts. The borrowed-name accounts, estimated to be about 10% of the total accounts in the market (about 4.6 million accounts), showed no significant evidence of conversion to real-name accounts (about 0.4%). It is not hard to see why this happened: there are no obstacles to conducting transactions from borrowed name accounts.

In implementing real-name system reform one of the biggest hurdles was keeping funds from fleeing the (legal) financial market, creating shortages of desperately needed funding for capital projects. The government attempted to capture these funds by permitting a special issue of 10-year industrial bonds, available only to alias account holders converting to real-name accounts. Two kinds of bonds were issued: for accounts with balances below 3 billion won the bonds pay 3% per annum, for all other accounts the rate is 1% per annum.

Given the low debt load of the Korean government, an approach might be for the government to directly sponsor capital projects financed by budget deficits. Not only does this provide a solution to capital flight, but may also provide greater flexibility to the Korean central bank in the conduct of monetary policy. Currently, because the market for government debt is so "thin," the central bank must discern money market conditions from estimates of monetary aggregates, particularly M2. Moreover, government capital projects are sorely needed: the infrastructure has badly deteriorated from years of neglect, and has not been expanded to handle the increasing demands on it. Finally, expanding and upgrading the debt market will pave the way for the introduction of a well-founded derivative market later.

Distribution of Stock Ownership

As shown in Table 3 accompanying the expansion and boom in the market during the 1980s individual investors accounted for more than 50% of total stock ownership. After the market opened to foreign investors in 1992 foreign investors and financial institutions increased their stock ownership.[34] Currently, most blue-chip stocks in the First Trading Section have reached their limit of foreign ownership (10% of listed companies stocks). Overall, by the end of December 1993 foreign ownership had reached 8.8% of all listed stocks, up by 4.37% from December 1992. Meanwhile, the MOF, worrying about possible monetary expansion from the influx of foreign funds, does not have an explicit proposal on raising the foreign ownership limit. On June 28, 1993 the MOF announced (as a part of the Second-Stage of the Financial Markets Liberalization and Internalization Plan) its plan of raising the current foreign stock ownership limit by 1994, but without specifying the limit level.[35] This lack of specific information regarding the foreign ownership limit causes unnecessary uncertainty for the market. It might force investors to guess

Table 3. Distribution of Stock Ownership

	75	*80*	*86*	*89*	*90*	*91*	*92*	*93*	*94*
Government	13.90	14.45	0.12	11.84	0.12	0.1	0.03	0.0	0.0
Financial Institutions	8.14	5.92	12.39	5.84	13.42	15.5	16.16	18.8	19.29
Securities Companies	6.29	2.24	6.72	5.07	5.36	5.56	5.8	5.3	4.0
Investment Trusts			0.76	2.67	9.34	8.53	8.09	6.6	7.31
Judicial Persons	17.70	19.39	24.53	17.85	17.99	17.18	20.91	19.2	20.08
Individuals	52.93	56.01	52.43	54.62	51.63	50.24	44.57	41.3	40.18
Foreigners	1.04	1.99	3.01	2.13	1.97	2.89	4.43	8.8	9.12

Source: KSE and Monthly Review of Securities Supervisory Board. Units are percentages based on the number of shares owned. Note: From 1986, financial institutions include not only banking firms, but also insurance companies and short-term finance companies.

about future limits and force stock prices away from the fundamental values due to the uninformative posture of the authorities. Thus, it should have a transparent policy toward foreign ownership of stocks as well as other matters.

Under the current SEL, however, individual investors have to notify and obtain permission from the SEC to obtain more than 10% of the outstanding shares of a listed company. On March 16, 1993 the DOF announced its plan to eliminate this proposition from the SEL (expected to be implemented next year). Responding to this announcement, several effects are expected to emerge. By lifting the 10% ceilings it might enhance stock market stability by keeping controlling shareholders from selling and solidifying their stakes in the company. Small and medium sized companies (paid-in capital below 15 billion won) are being considered as possible M&A targets. Controlling shareholders are reluctant to sell stock to avoid the possible takeover. From these developments it is expected that the securities companies will develop the business area of mergers and acquisition (M&A). Second, more price divergence between the preferred stocks (no voting rights) and common stocks (with voting rights) will emerge.

CONCLUSIONS

During a relatively short time the Korean stock market has grown remarkably. The new administration is trying to upgrade the market by fostering more deregulation of financial markets. The new measures include interest liberalization, and the deregulation of securities markets.[36] Still, several things may have to be changed to guide the market more efficiently. First, the government may have to keep a "hands-off" policy toward the market. The government has constantly used measures to boost the market. The government should avoid such discretionary policy

This is the only way that the stock market can become self-sufficient over the long run.

From the price adjustment mechanism, it might be desirable to increase (or give more flexibility) to the range of the DPFL to allow the market to adjust to disturbances quickly. Thus, the market can increase its informational efficiency. It is, of course, hard for the authorities to discard the DPFL (being used as a "circuit breaker"). As a result of the lack of flexibility in the DPFL investors have to pay higher information costs.

The market for the stock index futures is planned for the second half of 1995. One of possible disputes among the concerned parties is regarding who is going to supervise or oversee the new market. Considering the coordination problem among the markets, the current format of the Securities Supervisory Board (one agency) might be the most desirable approach. The adoption of one agency supervision or oversight may dampen market volatility. Furthermore, margin regulation is heavily used under the slogan of reducing market volatility. A study needs to be done on the relevance of margin regulation in Korea. This history represents only the first steps in a long journey for policy makers in Korea.

ACKNOWLEDGMENTS

The authors would like to express their appreciation to Sung-Kwan Cho of Coryo Securities Corporation of Seoul, Korea, for his invaluable assistance in this study and Stephen M. Miller, Mark S. Chandler, and Jack O'Meara for their comments.

NOTES

1. Elaborate restrictions remain on the fraction of a company's outstanding stock that may be purchased by foreign investors. The foreign institutional investor limit has been 10% of a company's total outstanding shares, and an individual foreign investor is restricted to 3% of a company's total outstanding shares. Overall, before December 1, 1994, the total foreign investment limit has been 10% of the total outstanding shares of a listed company on the Korea Stock Exchange (KSE). All major restrictions are scheduled to be eliminated by the end of 1997. From July 1, 1995 the investment limit has been expanded to 15%.

2. The second half of 1962 was marked by four consecutive KSE closings. The KSE closed from June 1 to June 6, due to a walk out of "floorbrokers" protesting against the government's exemption of the buyers' responsibilities in settling the transactions. The Monetary Reform of June 10, 1962 caused the KSE closing from June 11 to July 12. From August 31 to September 3 it was a Taeyang Securities Company refusal to settle transactions that closed the market. Finally, December 4 to December 7 the market closed due to another protest against government regulations on the KSE (see *Securities Market in Korea* 1992 for more details).

3. The KSE reorganized into a membership organization in March 1, 1988.

4. The excess demand for securities resulted in an underwriting method change from the "best efforts (stand-by)" to the "firm commitment" method. Despite this change, however, the MOF raised the minimum number of shares to the public to 40% from 30% to meet the surging demand.

5. Both agencies were controlled by the MOF. Before February 1977 the MOF, the KIC, and the KSE all supervised the market.

6. On January 4, 1983 a new benchmark stock index called the Korean Composite Stock Price Index (KOSPI) was created to measure market performance in terms of market capitalization. The starting-base date (January 4, 1980) KOSPI was set to 100.

7. In the following April non-listed stocks started to trade on the Over the Counter (OTC) Market. Small firms (with less than 0.2 billion won in paid-in capital) have to be traded on the OTC before being listed on the KSE. The shares of the OTC are traded through the KSDA. As of April 1993 the shares of 130 firms are traded on the OTC. The brokerage commission is 0.4% of the trading value. Still the lack of liquidity is a problem due to riskness of the small firms.

8. In March 1988 the KSE was reorganized as a membership organization, jointly managed by 25 securities companies. When the 12-12 Government Actions, which will be discussed later, failed to give the stock market the boost it needed, the government again acted upon the depressed market on March 2, 1990. These actions (1) lifted the ban on margin transactions for the shares of securities companies and (2) formed a US$300 million "Matching Fund" to be established in June 1990. The fund was to be raised from domestic and foreign markets, and with 40% of the fund to be invested in the domestic market and 60% in foreign markets. The three major investment trust companies were each allocated US$100 million.

9. The benchmárk corporate bond rate (three-year maturity) increased to 18.6% in May of 1991 from 14.3% in April 1989 (when the KOSPI hit a record high of 1007).

10. The DOF laid out details of the Korean stock market opening on September 1991. On October, 1991, the DOF permitted foreigners (who have CB of domestic firms) to reinvest in the Korean stock market with the proceeds from the sale of converted shares.

11. Foreign investors are defined as follows: foreign residents in Korea, Korean residents abroad, and foreign financial institutions branches and offices in Korea.

12. The DOF, on March 27, 1992, finally came up with First Stage Plan of Financial Market Opening. According to the Plan, the foreign financial institutions participating in the market would have the status of domestic residents starting July, 1992. The plan also allowed foreign financial institutions to do business in the Over The Counter (OTC) market starting July, 1992.

13. According to the originally planned *Guidelines for the Stock Market*, foreign investors were allowed to buy up to 10% of the total outstanding shares of a listed company. Foreign investors, however, could buy a maximum of 8% of the total outstanding shares in industries such as communications, transportations, utilities, insurance, and securities. Moreover, the share holdings of Pohang Iron and Steel company (POSCO) and Korea Electric Power Corporation (KEPCO) were completely forbidden to foreign investors. In the last quarter of 1992, however, these restrictions were loosened as a result of the poor performance of the market (see Jookan Coryo Securities 1992).

14. The Shares of POSCO and KEPCO has been listed on the NYSE in the form of ADR (American Depository Receipts) from November 1994.

15. On April 16, 1993 the Korea Financial Futures Association was established, under the control of the MOF. Under the current plan of the MOF the opening of the stock index futures market is expected for the second half of 1995. One of the debates is whether the financial futures and commodity futures market should be separated or integrated.

16. On the KSE, the basic trading unit is 10 shares of stocks and beneficiary certificates (BC). Odd lots trading (orders less than a trading unit) take place on the OTC market through the securities companies self-dealing accounts. The basic quotation unit is 100 won for the stocks above 10,000 won but a multiple of 10 won for the stocks below 10,000 won. For bonds, 100,000 won is the par value.

17. For additional protection, members are encouraged to contribute to the Fidelity Guarantee Money up to a maximum of 50 million won (US$64,102). Securities companies are encouraged to keep total liabilities at a level less than 10 times net assets.

18. Before April 1995 the DPFL of stocks and BC ranged from 2 to 6.6% depending on the price ranges. The DPFL for shares (regardless of the price range) listed on the KSE was increased to a 6% range in April 1995 and is scheduled to reach an 8% range by 1997.

19. In Korea the official margin transaction was adopted in June 1971.

20. Before November 25, 1992 the required deposit to open the margin account was 100,000 won (about US$130).

21. Margin trading in the shares of securities companies was not allowed until March 2, 1990.

22. Due to stock market booms in the 1980s the securities industry enjoyed soaring profits through 1990. From April 1991 to March 1992, however, the securities industry (11 securities companies, among others), for the first time since 1980 incurred a negative net income of 108 billion won due to the poor performance of the market. But due to reductions in interest rates and a decent performance of the market from April 1992 to March 1993, all 32 securities companies were profitable, jointly making a net income of 450 billion won, which is about 30 times more than previous fiscal year of 15.7 billion won net income.

23. The DOF permits a securities company that has more than 3 billion won of capital stock to enter the three main business areas. A securities company with more than 20 billion won is allowed to get a license for foreign market operation, and can invest up to US$50 million abroad.

24. Until 1993 most foreign investors traded securities through nonmember foreign securities firms operating in Korea. These nonmember foreign firms did not hold KSE membership, possibly due to the high fees involved. Because of the nonmember status, the foreign brokerage houses could not make direct transactions. Thus, when they take trading orders from investors (mostly foreign investors), the nonmember foreign firms place an order through domestic member firms. The member firms act as "standing agents" to do all the services involved in the transactions.

25. Contractual investment trust funds (which are similar to the British unit trust rather than the American type mutual fund) are only authorized. The contractual-type requires three parties to be involved: a management company (a fund manager), a trustee (a custodian bank), and beneficiaries (investors). To establish a fund, the trust deed agreed upon by the management company and trustee requires an approval from the MOF. The management company issues beneficiary certificates (BC) which represent the rights of investors. Moreover, open-end type funds are more popular than closed-end type funds. With the open-end funds, investors have the right to sell BCs at any time. The fund's net asset value (NAV) determines the price. Open-end type funds allow for additional issues and redemption. Closed-end type funds, however, can be redeemed under certain circumstances. The funds will not redeem BC at their NAV.

26. The major contents of the 12-12 Government Actions were as follows: (1) increasing discounts up to 30% from previous "within 10%" of the market price at the time of issuing new stocks, (2) allowing the use of securities as a substitute for cash in the "good-faith deposit (40%)" in the time of purchasing securities (previously 40% cash was required), and (3) increasing the capital of Korea Euro-Fund (KEF) by US$50 million in the first quarter of 1990 (previously planned by US$30 million) (see Jookan Hanyang Securities 1992).

27. One of the main provisions of the 12-12 Actions was that an offering company can have flexible application of up to 30% discount rate from the current share price. This was against the principle of "issue-at-market price system." The "issue-at-market price system" was introduced in December 1983 to reinforce the market function. The merits of this system are to improve the health of firms financial structure and to stabilize the stock market without disturbing prices divergence in the time of new offerings. Thus by violating the principle of the "issue-at-market price system," the actions also distorted market pricing. In 1991 the government completely liberalized the discount rate of the "issue-at-market price system."

28. To sterilize the external surplus during 1986 to 1989 the BOK sold more Monetary Stabilization Bonds (MSB).

29. The guaranteed BC was designed to give investors at least the return of the three-year time deposit rate. The interest rate on three-year time deposits was 33.1% at that time. The maturity of this guaranteed BCs was determined to be three years (which was September 1993). Because of poor market performance during the last three years, the investment trust industry faced a severe liquidity problem. Recently, on May 13, 1993 the government extended the maturity of the BCs three more years until September 1996. The main reason was to ease the liquidity problem for the investment trust companies that should repay the principal of the BCs. Individual investors, however, can choose to get repaid the principal or extend the redemption period. Contrary to the Securities Market Stabilization Fund, the BC was expected to induce more money influx from outside the market, such as individual investors and pension funds (see Jookan Daewoo Securities 1990).

30. The actual sales of the BCs was about 1 trillion 850 billion won. The pension funds and institutional investors purchased 920 billion won of the BCs. The rest (660 billion won) were sold to individual investors.

31. On the economic front, the BOK worried about resulting monetary expansion. On the political front, the BOK was concerned that the special loan might be viewed as "special treatment" for the financial industry relative to other industries (see Jookan Korea Development Securities 1992).

32. From October 1985 to April 1989 the KOSPI increased from 130 to 1007.77. However, after 1988 the stagnant economy, labor disputes, and Current Account deficits became a burden to the fast growing stock market. In response the government found it necessary to take action to stabilize the market. Interventions have become particularly common in conjunction with government announcements.

33. The implementation of the real-name accounts reform should improve the central bank's ability to manage monetary policy due to increased stability in the long-run velocity of money. The central bank is currently under criticism for targeting M2, which only accounts for about 31% of total liquidity available to the economy.

34. This implies a reduction in the direct ownership of stocks by individual investors. This has been offset, to some extent, by the increased indirect ownership by individual investors by purchasing other financial products such as BCs.

35. Fortunately the MOF finally increased the foreign limit to 12% from December 1, 1994 and then to 15% from July 1, 1995. According to the "Blue Print," the foreign ownership limit will be removed by 1997.

36. Those are including a repeal of restrictions on seasoned offerings and issuing corporate bond for the small and medium sized companies. The MOF also announced its Three-Stage Plan of Financial Markets Liberalization and Internalization on June 28, 1993, which will be completed by 1997.

REFERENCES

Amihud, Y., and H. Mendelson. 1987. "Trading Mechanisms and Stock Returns: An Empirical Investigation." *Journal of Finance* 42: 533–553.

Goldberg, M. 1985. "The Relevance of Margin Regulations." *Journal of Money, Credit, and Banking* 17: 521–27.

Hardouvelis, G. 1988. "Margin Requirements and Stock Market Volatility." *Federal Reserve Bank of New York Quarterly Review* (Summer): 80–89.

———. 1990. "Margin Requirements, Volatility, and the Transitory Component of Stock Prices." *American Economic Review* 80: 736–62.

Hsieh, D., and M. Miller. 1990. "Margin Regulation and Stock Market Volatility." *Journal of Finance* 45: 3–29.

Jookan Coryo Securities. 1992. Coryo Securities Corporation (June).

Jookan Daewoo Securities. 1990. Daewoo Securities Company (September).

Jookan Hanyang Securities. 1992. Hanyang Securities Company (June).

Jookan Korea Development Securities. 1990. Korea Development Securities Company (September).

Madhavan, A. 1992. "Trading Mechanisms in Securities Markets." *Journal of Finance* 47: 607–642.
Monthly Review. 1993. Korea: Securities Supervisory Board.
Moore, T.G. 1966. "Stock Market Margin Requirements." *Journal of Political Economy* 34: 158–167.
Officer, R.R. 1973. "The Variability of the Market Factor of the New York Stock Exchange." *Journal of Business* 46: 434–53.
Salinger, M. 1989. "Stock Market Margin Requirements and Volatility: Implications for Regulation of Stock Index Futures." *Journal of Financial Services Research* (December): 121–39.
Schwert, G.W. 1989. "Margin Requirements and Stock Volatility." *Journal of Financial Services Research* 3: 153–64.
Takagi, S. 1989. "The Japanese Equity Market: Past and Present." *Journal of Banking and Finance* 131: 537–570.

CAPITAL MARKET INTEGRATION AND EMERGING MARKETS

Alan Alford and Jacques Lussier

ABSTRACT

Recent studies have shown that the gains from international portfolio investment have been decreasing over time. Simultaneously, emerging economies have changed the characteristics of their capital markets. As the gains from developed markets have declined, investors have focused their energies on these emerging markets. This paper examines how the price of risk has changed in these markets from 1989 through 1992. The statistical analysis indicates that the price of risk is volatile and finds minimal evidence of a change in the available segmentation gains.

International diversification has been shown to provide investors with greater returns for less risk. These gains for investors emanate from two sources. First, investors gain as they reduce the systematic risk of their portfolios. Since no two countries are perfectly correlated, the purchase of foreign shares reduces country-specific risk from a portfolio. The traditionally low correlation between countries has provided a greater chance for risk diversification. Second, investors have gained from the mispricing of assets due to capital market segmentation. These gains exist because of barriers to the mobility of capital between countries. Markets then have

Research in International Business and Finance, Supplement 1, pages 241–255.

ISBN: 0-7623-0110-4

different prices of risk because there exist only limited mechanisms to permit the elimination of arbitrage situations. Investors are unable to reallocate savings to take advantage of higher returns.

Within developed markets evidence exists that the capital markets are moving toward a more integrated pricing of assets. Alford and Folks (1996) demonstrate that the gains from international investment across markets are indeed a declining function of time. They suggest that the risk-adjusted returns around the world are collapsing toward a common price of risk. Further, economic linkages between these countries have strengthened. The increased linkages translate into an increased correlation between the movement of these countries' capital markets which, in turn, leads to a diminished diversifiability of risk.

Emerging markets may not have experienced these changes. Traditionally, these countries' economies have been more isolated and have followed policies of import substitution. Therefore, they have been more insulated from international shocks that may affect more global economies. These markets may also provide greater gains due to the mispricing of their assets. Divecha, Drach, and Stefek (1992) confirm that the emerging markets tend to be uncorrelated with each other and with the developed markets. Lessard (1973), using factor analysis, finds that the returns from four South American countries are generated by individual market factors, not by any regional factor representing systematic risk of the four countries. Errunza (1977) finds that an optimal portfolio would include Spanish equities due to the negative correlation of Spain with other markets. Errunza and Losq (1985) conclude that emerging markets are mildly segmented. They find that there are different processes generating asset returns across the countries that they study, but these processes are somewhat related to the international price of risk. Therefore, the possibility exists that the gains from international diversification will still tend to be strong in these markets. Further, these excess gains emanated from both sources of returns in international investment—increased diversification of risk and mispricing of assets, the segmentation of these markets.

However, the effects of capital market segmentation go beyond portfolio effects. The cost of capital for companies and the effectiveness of a government's monetary and fiscal policy are also determined by the level of capital market integration. The restricted mobility of capital, for investors and for corporations, creates a situation where the risk-adjusted returns deviate from the risk-adjusted return in integrated markets. Some investors can earn excess profits to which other investors do not have access while some corporations obtain cheaper sources of financing than do others. For economic policy, the degree of capital mobility effects the dimension of overshooting in the exchange rate as well as the probability of "crowding out" of net exports and of investments in the economy due to changes in fiscal policies.

This study examines the magnitude of mispricing in emerging markets and how this has changed over time. We replicate the study of Alford and Folks to examine the price of risk in these markets and to determine if, as with developed markets, these prices are collapsing toward a common value. Our tests consolidate, and update, many of the tests performed previously on emerging markets and provide a comparison to the existing research on developed capital markets. They yield an analysis of the benefits of including emerging markets in a diversified portfolio.

DETECTING CHANGES IN THE LEVEL OF INTEGRATION

Alford and Folks develop a model based on the existence of ownership barriers between countries that distort the required rates of return. They base their model on the assumption that investors concern themselves only with the first two moments of an asset's return. Further, they assume that investors form their portfolios in the same numeraire and, thus, asset returns contain both the risk of the assets as well as any exchange rate risk. Finally, they assume that there exist ownership barriers that restrict investors. From these three basic assumptions, they then derive a closed-end model that describes the relationship between assets in segmented markets:

$$\frac{R_i - R_f}{\sigma_{im}} = \frac{R_m - R_f}{\sigma_m^2} \left(\frac{\left(1 - \frac{\lambda_i}{\sigma_{im}}\right)}{\left(1 - \frac{\lambda}{\sigma_m^2}\right)} \right). \quad 1$$

Alford and Folks define the coefficient $(1 - \lambda_i/\sigma_{im})/(1 - \lambda/\sigma_m^2)$ as the coefficient of integration. Their model asserts that the price of risk across markets should be proportional to the price of risk for the global market portfolio. The ratio of these two components provides a scale-free coefficient of the relative mispricing of risk. Their analysis indicates that if a market is integrated, this coefficient should have a value of one. Thus the ratio indicates whether a given country portfolio, or security, is mean-variance efficient. Jorion and Schwartz (1986) observe that integrated markets should be mean-variance efficient. Alford and Folks define the deviation from a value of one as the coefficient of segmentation for an asset. Their analysis indicates that this coefficient reflects the degree of segmentation inherent in a market. The coefficient of segmentation, beyond determining the degree of mispricing inherent in the markets, also infers how investors would shift their portfolios if the barriers did not exist. A positive coefficient of segmentation would imply that investors would have preferred that security over the market portfolio due to its greater return given the level of risk it offers. Correspondingly, an asset with a negative coefficient indicates that its risk level was too high given its expected return and that investors would prefer to hold the market portfolio.

The application of this model is dependent on the assumption that investors quantify risk as the covariance of an asset with a benchmark portfolio. Alford and Folks note that their model is robust to all sources of capital market segmentation, not just ownership barriers, when tested empirically. However, it is reasonable to suspect that the risk in emerging markets is not fully captured by this measure. Alford (1993b) asserts that emerging markets exhibit risks alien to developed markets. First, these markets may require a substantial liquidity premium due to their thinness. Investors value the ability to be able to buy and to sell securities quickly and with a minimum influence on prices. With smaller markets this characteristic may be more problematic. The indicated price of an asset may not be the price at which it will trade. This misstates the returns available in a market and may induce a bias into an empirical analysis of asset prices. Alford also indicates that emerging markets suffer from thin economies. Thinness, either in the economy or in the capital market, exacerbates the effect of shocks. The volatility results largely from these stimuli that provide new information to a market.

Second, the estimated covariance risk may not fully capture the political uncertainty that is present in many of these countries. Political risk is often discussed within direct investment as an exposure with which multinationals must deal. It is a risk that may be minimized in areas with stable, predictable political processes. The assessment of this risk can be quite difficult even for the most prepared investors. New governments may have drastically new policies that change the direction of the local economy. On a more basic level, governments can radically influence the returns that may be obtained in the market. By changing tax policy or even exchange rate policy, a government alters the return that all investors enjoy. These actions can occur very capriciously and unpredictably. Thus, emerging markets may be forced to provide an extra premium to entice foreign investment, both direct and portfolio.

Third, Maldonado and Saunders (1981) indicate that gains from international investment may be overstated if the estimated variance-covariance matrix is not stable over time. Their argument is that the efficient frontier may not be a constant point of reference causing an overestimation of the achievable diversification gains from investing in these markets. An overestimation of these gains would increase the observed segmentation coefficient for the emerging markets. Errunza finds a comparable problem in his analysis. He notes that a bias exists in his test that increases as he includes more countries, but decreases as he uses more time periods. Thus, this aggravates the possibility of finding changes in market segmentation.

These sources of risk differentiate between the developed and the emerging markets. If developed markets are mean-variance efficient and the emerging markets are not, then their returns would be determined by different processes. Applying a mean-variance analysis, in the presence of these risks, would indicate the potential for returns different from those required by the Capital Asset Pricing Model. However, this is consistent with a definition of market segmentation as there would not exist a common pricing of assets between the two groups of markets. Returns would then be generated by different processes in the emerging markets than in the developed markets. The error terms from a cross-sectional regression would still be related to the total risk of the specific market and would not be a decreasing function of time. The risk-return relationship would still differ from the developed markets and an empirical estimation of the Alford-Folks model would capture that divergence.

TESTING THE HYPOTHESIS OF INCREASED CAPITAL INTEGRATION

To test the hypothesis of emerging capital market integration, we examine the Emerging Market Database from the International Financial Corporation. We calculate returns using the monthly database. Our analysis is limited by the data contained in the database. The tests comprise ten countries for which returns are completely available from January 1985 to December 1992.[2] The analysis begins in January 1985 since this is the first reported return of the composite index that represents the market return in this analysis. Since all returns are calculated using the U.S. dollar as the numeraire, our proxy for the risk-free rate will be the same as that for Alford and Folks, the short-term U.S. interest rate reported by the OECD's *Primary Economic Indicators*.

Using the annual estimation of segmentation coefficients proposed by Alford and Folks, this would allow only to calculate the coefficients for 1990 and 1991. Instead, we estimate the coefficients on a monthly basis with the variance-covariance matrix for the preceding 48 months also being updated monthly. This change in methodology provides for the possibility of greater volatility in the estimated segmentation coefficients as the effects of surprises on the estimates may overstate the volatility of the price of risk in these markets. The movement toward capital market integration can be underestimated by this redesign of the study. However, as noted by Errunza, the inclusion of more time periods reduces the bias of an unstable variance-covariance matrix.

ASSESSMENTS OF PRICING DIFFERENCES FOR EMERGING MARKETS

The resulting coefficients listed in Table 1 are still extremely volatile. Table 2 provides the summary statistics for the coefficients. Six of the markets have positive medians, insinuating that, on average, investors would have been substantially overcompensated for the covariance risk borne. Four of these six also have positive means showing the magnitude of the overcompensation available through these markets over the time period studied.

These benefits, however, are tempered by high volatility in the price of risk. Overall, the data shows a variance of 10,934.86. Individually, this statistic ranges from 60.28 for Mexico to over 59,016.05 for Jordan. Therefore, realized returns depend on when securities are purchased. This indicates that the price of risk in these countries has a very wide distribution. The benefits from the purchase and from issuance of securities in these markets would be tenuous at best. These markets are not for short-term investment strategies. An investor never knows where a peak

Table 1. Scaled Segmentation Coefficients on Monthly Basis Relative to Emerging Market Index

Month	*Argentina*	*Brazil*	*Chile*	*Greece*	*Jordan*
January 1989	−1.89269	−4.23341	2.630571	−11.0265	43.13552
February 1989	−3.6199	4.506305	1.365565	−1.36478	−68.2917
March 1989	2.597557	2.307509	−1.06287	−3.46824	−988.204
April 1989	−3.03195	5.46055	2.004821	2.976233	−73.2782
May 1989	3.412207	−1.73269	−0.39992	10.55667	−51.3228
June 1989	−37.2148	4.966288	1.403922	0.34916	196.0438
July 1989	−280.323	4.977612	−9.4822	48.17321	−260.196
August 1989	191.6051	−5.58167	−6.24334	39.28653	205.0068
September 1989	405.1559	0.597057	1.704109	77.40754	19.17191
October 1989	102.7187	−18.6409	−25.59	11.98589	107.5348
November 1989	10.62955	2.06172	−1.61498	2.221457	−1.52212
December 1989	−1.92866	2.015452	1.702549	−0.81963	4.511972
January 1990	5.857485	−0.49536	1.74891	2.106205	−2.35908
February 1990	4.861195	−0.31212	3.347081	1.24661	−105.364
March 1990	−4.65615	11.93217	−0.99334	−2.13542	−2.49162
April 1990	2.526148	31.0395	−1.68636	29.59007	19.64049
May 1990	−1.67039	−3.08284	−1.28047	−0.37098	9.206476
June 1990	−1.30308	0.440046	−0.26216	14.71606	20.8179
July 1990	0.85088	4.118432	−0.91935	−0.89233	−16.3865
August 1990	0.463756	0.761448	−0.40509	0.485529	56.86128
September 1990	−1.88198	0.829069	−0.85082	0.682774	−0.56194
October 1990	14.20168	44.07609	1.639247	26.77849	7.948658
November 1990	−1.68042	−2.51292	−3.14634	1.677145	−2.93893
December 1990	−5.14605	−7.88712	5.485348	2.2402	36.15132
January 1991	143.6849	492.2661	149.747	−29.1211	−1209.84
February 1991	−0.24592	2.521267	0.916694	3.340952	14.64892
March 1991	54.22888	−11.7504	0.714111	−13.12	74.25665
April 1991	17.01001	8.494211	−0.30604	−61.5391	182.3961
May 1991	−0.71312	12.70801	0.24514	−6.16517	−19.4565
June 1991	1.957361	−6.63514	−4.81448	2.615383	5.355149
July 1991	0.983338	3.659497	3.739612	0.68042	−40.4457
August 1991	64.63402	−4.2358	3.462529	3.978494	−45.8602
September 1991	−4.3108	3.410046	−3.15246	3.941679	−23.0744
October 1991	2.805608	0.256349	−2.31534	−0.72342	−6.64539
November 1991	84.50648	88.3972	24.85168	−15.7989	60.70912
December 1991	1.508128	4.80871	−1.08625	−0.85496	6.168124
January 1992	−0.71565	2.243793	−0.92941	0.489887	−0.55638
February 1992	−2.89635	−1.1997	7.186742	−3.3643	7.45562
March 1992	−16.5547	−9.57668	−9.72361	10.32858	44.40452
April 1992	43.90907	7.347567	3.243759	3.663438	346.4995
May 1992	−7.3848	2.169685	−2.48324	12.3013	24.46058
June 1992	1.320104	1.956415	−1.28917	−3.04245	−3.54613
July 1992	21.88276	−15.0476	1.000947	8.918212	93.51869
August 1992	1.785441	−0.94822	1.079011	0.044459	−3.11506
September 1992	3.080036	−3.27174	2.411547	8.008256	−28.6753
October 1992	−2.83377	−3.83052	1.188823	−6.61401	−7.12268
November 1992	7.420673	10.66794	7.830469	−5.50604	−30.9468
December 1992	5.699712	3.100867	−0.21919	−0.32518	28.12576

(*continued*)

Table 1. (Continued)

Month	*Malaysia*	*Mexico*	*Philippine*	*Thailand*	*Venezuela*
January 1989	1.796964	–1.11947	–5.06928	2.033262	–83.4226
February 1989	–1.35038	–1.59835	0.427745	–1.19005	1009.022
March 1989	–0.84455	–0.21171	–9.64431	–1.02267	–24.4067
April 1989	1.760984	0.351013	–29.9461	2.432577	167.4591
May 1989	–0.65316	0.140112	–8.10562	0.120314	13.20584
June 1989	–0.09299	–2.81176	–7.44052	–2.57389	–6.32241
July 1989	5.393637	–0.63768	–290.19	–1.03715	2.8996
August 1989	–3.97036	3.962635	55.37787	7.58937	–86.9492
September 1989	1.960812	0.583252	–30.4982	–0.07512	–2.29436
October 1989	16.11522	4.704283	137.5321	–4.54013	77.32288
November 1989	–2.40546	–0.45019	3.982042	–3.93282	–18.6376
December 1989	2.663714	–0.15032	65.12391	1.2053	5.654554
January 1990	–0.31587	0.081931	–21.1236	1.248821	–1.27928
February 1990	5.346633	0.140371	–1.41224	–2.785	–29.6154
March 1990	1.94643	–0.79715	–0.81393	–1.33344	174.7111
April 1990	–12.2209	0.399772	–5.04577	–1.31138	–104.122
May 1990	3.396402	0.395396	–1.85861	1.091464	–9.56024
June 1990	–1.96239	–1.69023	0.708683	–0.67648	3.532438
July 1990	1.815205	–0.19623	–1.23894	0.106552	–13.3964
August 1990	2.188716	–0.10906	0.366136	0.539769	44.73523
September 1990	2.18774	–0.27495	2.166812	0.840986	9.570555
October 1990	–17.1039	–16.0005	28.89522	2.726466	139.2485
November 1990	1.079107	–1.44071	–4.26636	1.066335	6.002287
December 1990	8.486488	–1.05121	–0.04345	3.532728	–4.33308
January 1991	–47.5524	–16.6343	–51.4773	87.48836	237.3681
February 1991	1.105408	–0.71587	0.873037	0.044468	2.039738
March 1991	4.872134	11.93397	11.55253	7.279943	9.329136
April 1991	1.892425	38.03009	17.78322	–10.0695	–3.42629
May 1991	1.546962	2.928642	1.946968	–3.09935	1.337503
June 1991	1.532623	–0.06684	0.594892	1.371861	–9.91074
July 1991	–3.67251	2.616714	–1.28259	–2.00891	–0.20396
August 1991	–12.3816	1.067976	–1.97804	–3.106	1.611982
September 1991	1.434527	–0.48924	1.903332	–0.14543	20.54642
October 1991	0.022174	0.345861	0.651663	–1.77467	–35.7456
November 1991	–2.58221	–8.91681	–33.8282	–28.6343	0.113745
December 1991	0.593736	–0.69309	–0.32217	–0.00279	–5.88543
January 1992	0.247522	–0.06659	–0.24256	–0.12248	–10.419
February 1992	8.063029	4.65278	0.32085	–0.76226	15.75261
March 1992	8.35946	3.382143	3.124468	–7.72115	–253.259
April 1992	10.94362	–21.0775	17.73705	–40.4491	–510.58
May 1992	3.68211	–0.3968	–16.282	6.662557	–87.6121
June 1992	–1.29175	0.595351	–1.92992	–1.93624	–6.36797
July 1992	–8.08251	–2.6102	–0.74861	7.651739	244.9879
August 1992	1.264689	0.467007	0.164756	–1.19478	33.2878
September 1992	–8.23119	1.030959	–0.25549	–7.18729	–148.923
October 1992	4.742683	3.072463	–1.28483	2.359489	25.52202
November 1992	–6.7399	–7.88484	6.009418	6.154834	–234.498
December 1992	–5.31495	0.247505	–2.99877	0.261182	–26.0734

Table 2. Descriptive Statistics

	Argentina	*Brazil*	*Chile*	*Greece*	*Jordan*
Median	1.414116	1.985934	0.012973	0.681597	1.977797
Maximum	405.1559	492.2661	149.747	77.40754	346.4995
Minimum	−280.323	−18.6409	−25.59	−61.5391	−1209.84
Mean	17.4743	14.10898	3.199868	3.500814	−29.3228
Variance	6721.242	5226.86	505.2402	365.5832	59016.05
Skewness	1.619254	6.449832	6.12075	0.785125	−3.79202

	Malaysia	*Mexico*	*Philippines*	*Thailand*	*Venezuela*	*All Countries*
Median	1.185049	−0.08795	−0.28883	−0.0988	−0.74162	0.24751317
Maximum	16.11522	38.03009	137.5321	87.48836	1009.022	1009.02239
Minimum	−47.5524	−21.0775	−290.19	−40.4491	−510.58	−1209.84027
Mean	−0.64527	−0.14811	−3.66137	0.321616	11.23442	1.57606240
Variance	82.09372	60.28346	2513.53	227.7369	35254.08	10934.8614
Skewness	−3.06531	1.849796	−3.58102	3.679998	2.835174	−3.03250985

or a valley is to be found. The same holds for companies issuing securities in these markets. In one month, it is possible to sell a company's securities at a price below its intrinsic value based solely on the volatile market conditions. In the next month, the same security could be sold well above its intrinsic value.

If these emerging markets are integrating, the price of risk should be collapsing toward a common value. Thus, the smallest deviations from the common price of risk should be found in the last year. Four of the countries have their least extreme segmentation coefficient in the final year. Of these, Chile is the only country to exhibit its least extreme value in December 1992, the final month of the study. However, the other six countries demonstrate their least extreme value in 1991. At the other extreme, four countries provide their most extreme coefficient in 1989. However, five countries render their most extreme result in January 1991. For the other five, this is also an extreme month. January 1991 provides a spike in the coefficients. In this month, there seems to be a strong diversification influence. The price of risk in the index is just over eight percent while the countries have a significantly more extreme price of risk. In short, the markets are moving in different directions, at different speeds, from the index. Thus, there is a certain fragility inherent within the markets. The question is how this fragility has changed over time and if this fragility impedes increased capital market integration among these markets.

To test the hypothesis of increased capital market integration, like Alford and Folks, we take the absolute value of the coefficients and apply the Page Rank Test for Ordered Alternatives.[3] In both cases, the null hypothesis is that the coefficients of segmentation for these ten countries are declining functions of time; the alternate is that the order of the coefficients is random. Our tests explore any movement of the price of risk in these emerging markets toward a common price of risk for emerging markets. The test results in a Page statistic of 288,045. In this test we have 10 countries and 48 months. For a test of this size, the expected value of the Page Statistic is 288,120 with a standard deviation of 4249.1787. Applying a large sample approximation to the observed statistic yields a normalized statistic of –0.0176505 which provides a *p*-value of 50.70%. The statistical test shows that the ordering of the coefficients of segmentation is nearly random. We find that there is no movement toward integration of these markets with each other.

These emerging markets do not appear to be collapsing toward a common price of risk. Rather, there appears to be no movement whatsoever. The price of risk is not being homogenized between the countries. This should not be surprising as there still is limited interaction between these countries. However, this measurement does not examine how the prices of risk in these markets are changing relative to the more developed capital markets. There has been a definite increase in the economic interaction between these countries individually and developed economies. This would support the hypothesis that the price of risk has changed between these markets. Thus, we replicate these tests using Morgan Stanley Capital International's world market index with no dividends and with the U.S. dollar as the numeraire.

Table 3 reports the scaled segmentation coefficients using the world market portfolio as a point of reference. Nine of the countries have a negative median. This has definite corporate effects. Companies in these countries should be utilizing more equity financing since it would lead to a wealth transfer to current shareholders. The relatively lower cost of equity would provide these companies with comparative advantages over their developed economy competition. Yet, Mullin (1993) implies that this type of financing is not used till later in the economic development of a country. Examining the means, however, leads to a different picture of the markets. Six of the markets have positive means, insinuating that, on average, investors would have been substantially overcompensated for the covariance risk borne.

As should be expected, the scaled segmentation coefficients are even more volatile. The variance for the four years is 38,562.72. Now, Brazil owns the most volatile coefficients. Interestingly, it is the only country with a positive median coefficient. The most volatile coefficients occur in 1990 which has a variance of 151,375.22. Each of the ten countries has high volatility in this year. Unlike the previously estimated coefficients, when using the world market portfolio as a point of reference, the coefficients have a definite, positive skewness. This reinforces the overpricing of assets in these markets as most of the observed coefficients occur below the mean. This also denotes that the extreme overcompensation is much less likely than other risk-adjusted returns.

As with the coefficients calculated relative to the IFC index, one month demonstrates extreme results. Eight countries have their most extreme segmentation

Table 3. Scaled Segmentation Coefficients on Monthly Basis Relative to the World Market Portfolio

Month	*Argentina*	*Brazil*	*Chile*	*Greece*	*Jordan*
January 1989	12.51193	–24.4039	5.910871	–7.18372	–31.1106
February 1989	95.39463	39.32323	4.526977	–1.22283	77.78599
March 1989	174.5977	–50.0296	–0.67218	1.998353	–39.1686
April 1989	58.03284	94.1536	10.96806	2.309885	–22.1954
May 1989	45.92138	8.153319	–2.80308	–8.53322	–14.4927
June 1989	292.0298	63.49039	5.877208	0.264625	38.48517
July 1989	6.658461	1.449034	–2.27613	1.567261	–21.4391
August 1989	9.239273	4.023125	2.156107	–6.53194	54.99829
September 1989	–35.3839	4.725729	4.558561	40.75505	–11.7239
October 1989	–2.56151	–7.16711	–5.94397	–0.15018	–7.96296
November 1989	2.98038	–16.4592	0.548304	–3.71448	–2.05303
December 1989	–0.53785	18.9196	6.76977	–0.79827	–13.3801
January 1990	–13.7356	12.55731	36.4008	14.27626	14.26051
February 1990	4.327887	–1.54695	–4.22267	–2.00336	10.57526
March 1990	4.010545	12.4404	–0.99199	–1.72964	–1.14869
April 1990	6.272859	–47.9542	0.295239	–28.266	–4.57373
May 1990	–0.15423	–3.94435	–1.34807	–0.54951	–0.17187
June 1990	–2.31067	–11.0318	–4.64825	–44.8905	–9.88706
July 1990	–883.938	3663.395	41.93493	36.10701	–745.767
August 1990	–3.47671	3.882767	0.11503	0.791312	7.519904
September 1990	1.431602	1.695774	–0.78669	0.561576	–0.9356
October 1990	1.768051	–6.43111	–1.3365	–3.01689	–1.12994
November 1990	1.412384	–7.0012	–7.95724	4.524666	–1.66766
December 1990	9.654596	–17.6987	14.37554	3.34345	7.989031
January 1991	–11.7334	33.97699	9.558925	–2.10448	–9.63594
February 1991	–2.43663	3.664851	2.839494	6.371808	2.397648
March 1991	27.08668	2.244207	–1.81762	3.394494	–5.91746
April 1991	–60.4778	18.50562	1.326567	–172.233	92.16606
May 1991	–1.87087	23.11069	2.502076	–12.908	–9.00747
June 1991	–3.06371	–3.30782	–3.52559	1.006099	–0.35541
July 1991	–2.67862	1.09744	2.523037	–0.09328	–5.24509
August 1991	191.3013	3.669807	–11.4013	–9.59411	15.9313
September 1991	–10.2929	–8.49767	5.785969	–12.6251	9.129662
October 1991	–33.1451	5.421493	–12.6342	0.669062	–7.75181
November 1991	–3.43969	2.399633	1.054975	–1.65102	–0.56256
December 1991	–3.71771	5.960928	–1.23287	–0.77086	0.806407
January 1992	0.169104	–12.3017	–1.71262	–9.43875	–1.4495
February 1992	–2.55779	–0.85264	–16.6914	1.728928	–2.65842
March 1992	1.379835	–2.00032	–4.08199	1.113482	0.502134
April 1992	–11.7957	0.63279	1.396788	0.26589	16.68662
May 1992	–2.60928	–1.64753	–0.11832	–4.80263	–2.35939
June 1992	–7.20582	5.308279	–2.85487	–7.67761	–2.46122
July 1992	–49.3426	–20.166	7.110836	21.46925	32.92084
August 1992	6.45707	–1.09493	–12.1529	–4.13052	0.051999
September 1992	–8.48555	–4.06984	12.1695	19.45056	–11.6752
October 1992	–3.64471	1.978189	–7.24308	8.392331	0.801073
November 1992	7.231313	–7.32497	–14.126	2.969462	3.406003
December 1992	–93.5117	28.16313	14.83797	6.567893	53.40857

(continued)

Table 3. (Continued)

Month	*Malaysia*	*Mexico*	*Philippine*	*Thailand*	*Venezuela*
January 1989	2.806023	−1.27699	0.472217	6.249142	−76.1855
February 1989	−1.58257	−2.53378	−1.55669	−1.5028	237.5811
March 1989	−1.55997	−5.35867	−11.6182	−0.86954	97.40871
April 1989	6.829971	4.886313	27.04952	14.33454	184.0126
May 1989	−1.74826	−4.72256	−5.75415	−4.76958	−29.9157
June 1989	0.921024	−6.90115	3.204255	−6.33778	−24.3279
July 1989	−0.2813	−0.93885	4.138492	−1.00656	−0.04264
August 1989	0.009628	−3.82045	1.483624	−6.1124	67.46064
September 1989	2.736764	2.301773	3.244587	1.20316	−3.04886
October 1989	1.053065	0.276698	−3.34125	−1.91798	12.69748
November 1989	0.962816	−2.43539	−0.14886	7.838623	29.11454
December 1989	4.143198	1.563582	−10.5607	5.428412	3.949476
January 1990	2.869853	12.89784	28.73096	25.22884	−12.0122
February 1990	−2.57514	−1.64103	−0.78792	0.165838	26.01295
March 1990	−0.02024	−0.85113	−0.85266	−1.2794	1418.128
April 1990	4.330034	−2.42434	4.119101	−0.62737	39.33917
May 1990	0.348397	−0.05199	−1.69414	0.651767	−2.7769
June 1990	0.082405	0.7335	−6.74172	−1.92198	−5.13291
July 1990	333.0511	205.3542	−91.5306	325.6475	−1026.2
August 1990	0.373366	−0.18766	0.805649	0.620595	11.15078
September 1990	0.232453	−0.45113	2.302388	0.560273	1.545273
October 1990	−0.44815	−0.01529	−3.1352	−1.25669	−4.06022
November 1990	0.602835	−1.67108	−7.35344	2.492121	3.297632
December 1990	3.823765	−1.05419	0.326329	4.175024	−2.45119
January 1991	−1.69211	−1.48518	−3.06214	1.964028	2.024052
February 1991	0.027396	−0.7106	1.557719	0.036044	0.042799
March 1991	−1.77717	−4.64045	−5.26803	−3.16517	−1.96234
April 1991	1.784537	84.80629	49.02951	−19.1305	−2.69709
May 1991	1.080103	6.482861	5.84306	−4.59211	0.373126
June 1991	−0.51443	−0.58584	−0.13583	−0.04053	−2.24275
July 1991	−1.53166	0.652909	−1.15308	−1.41388	−0.88098
August 1991	6.151338	−3.95735	0.70276	1.836516	−2.18884
September 1991	−2.89326	−1.94342	−7.1196	−2.46803	−13.2574
October 1991	1.481815	6.297559	10.6166	−4.70273	−61.5313
November 1991	−1.02602	−1.37405	−2.54786	−2.03036	−0.99
December 1991	−0.11832	−0.45457	0.142288	0.305906	−2.45165
January 1992	−3.45089	−6.53369	−5.46773	−4.85685	9.205542
February 1992	−4.4743	−7.66525	−2.54942	−1.20613	−3.75667
March 1992	−0.4027	0.067297	−0.20764	−2.0124	−8.1588
April 1992	0.18037	−7.97601	4.575535	−10.5292	−27.6842
May 1992	−1.47412	−1.22358	3.726013	−2.93782	3.724438
June 1992	−1.30489	4.6448	−3.83281	−3.51661	−3.37207
July 1992	−5.71789	−4.54015	−0.49471	14.30017	56.74889
August 1992	−3.00473	−5.27878	−4.09909	−0.54375	−9.90093
September 1992	−6.18748	3.30988	0.457789	−11.6907	−25.8013
October 1992	−4.16623	−7.5034	−0.57798	−5.5369	−3.83045
November 1992	0.936415	5.472804	−6.95797	−6.49773	20.11622
December 1992	−19.8389	14.52683	−23.3963	11.56755	−25.7411

Table 4. Descriptive Statistics from Table 3

	Argentina	*Brazil*	*Chile*	*Greece*	*Jordan*
Median	–1.20436	1.572404	–0.00164	–0.12173	–1.13931
Maximum	292.0298	3663.395	41.93493	40.75505	92.16606
Minimum	–883.938	–50.0296	–16.6914	–172.233	–745.767
Mean	–6.26038	81.05131	1.552424	–3.54726	–11.6609
Variance	20548.19	279645	110.6412	786.068	12310.54
Skewness	–4.79174	6.907922	1.82447	–4.7416	–6.39325

	Malaysia	*Mexico*	*Philippines*	*Thailand*	*Venezuela*	*All Countries*
Median	–0.00531	–0.89499	–0.53635	–1.10634	–2.07559	–0.55603434
Maximum	333.0511	205.3542	49.02951	325.6475	1418.128	3663.39471
Minimum	–19.8389	–7.97601	–91.5306	–19.1305	–1026.2	–1026.20086
Mean	6.575061	5.575897	–1.2642	6.598564	17.90065	9.47075681
Variance	2333.256	1041.38	291.0701	2261.783	67546.36	38562.7158
Skewness	6.856099	5.591542	–2.55068	6.702508	2.05448	13.6872877

coefficient in July 1990. Venezuela has its second most extreme in this month and Greece has its fourth most extreme. For each market, there is a pronounced spike in the coefficients. Those for June and for August are much smaller in magnitude. As occurred before, the low index return motivates the extreme results in this month. The market portfolio has an extremely low price of risk in this month. When comparing a small price of risk against the large, in terms of magnitude, prices in the emerging markets, the resulting segmentation coefficient must be extreme.

At the other extreme, there is no consistency when the least extreme coefficient occurs. The latest occurrence of the least extreme coefficient is August 1992 with Jordan; Brazil has its least extreme in April 1992. Malaysia and Venezuela both experience this value in 1989. Three countries have their least extreme results in both 1990 and 1991. The only demonstration of consistency in the last year is the existence of extreme coefficients in December. All the countries have results that fall in the upper tercile of their estimated coefficients. Overall, there seems to be less consistency in these coefficients than in the coefficients relative to the IFC index.

Applying the Page Test, though, gives an estimated statistic of 293,580. This leads to a normalized statistic of 1.2850 which is significant at the 9.9404% level. This is weak support for an increase in the level of integration between developed and emerging capital markets. Given the structure of the tests, however, the exact degree of integration cannot be discerned. Looking at the descriptive statistics and the observed coefficients, it would appear that they are still somewhat segmented from each other. The test does indicate though that the markets have moved closer than what is found by Errunza and Losq (1985).

Table 5. Annual Variance of Scaled Segmentation Coefficient with the Different Bases

Year	IFC Index	World Market Portfolio
1989	22,117.8422	2,234.7328
1990	733.8342	151,375.2236
1991	15,971.0267	829.9604
1992	5148.4592	233.5581

Excluding June 1990 from the results significantly influences the results. If we replace the estimated scaled segmentation coefficients with the average of the estimated coefficients for May 1990 and July 1990, the observed Page Statistic is reduced to 291,998.[4] This translates into a normalized statistic of 0.9126 which carries a p-value of 18.07%. This is not significant at conventional measures of significance. It appears that the observed coefficients for June 1990 have a major influence on the statistical tests. The consistency in that month across all countries drives the value for the Page statistic. These markets are seeing common events influencing their returns, but country specific events still have the greater influence on the return structure in these markets.

An examination of the variance in the segmentation coefficients on an annual basis verifies this assertion. Table 5 details the variance on a year-by-year basis. The coefficients relative to the world market tend to be a declining function of time. The second year, 1990, is the only year that does not fit into the pattern. The coefficients relative to the world market portfolio provide the most volatile results while the coefficients relative to the IFC index are the least volatile. However, 1990 is also the year where most countries experience their most extreme segmentation costs relative to the world market portfolio. The higher volatility reflects the extremeness of the coefficients in that year. The most dramatic decline in coefficient volatility against both benchmarks occurs in the final year. This provides a preliminary indication that the inflow of capital to those markets is having a stabilizing effect on their rates of return.

SUMMARY

Within the last few years, investors in developed countries have sought opportunities to take positions in emerging markets. This has strengthened the linkage between these markets and developed markets. In turn, this should increase the level of integration between markets. The increased level of integration changes the influence of monetary and fiscal policies in these countries. The inflow of capital into these economies provides another source of growth for the countries. However, the policies that induce capital inflows from other countries also promote the stability for the economies. Alford (1993b) indicates that this stability will lead to further growth in the economy as an important source of risk is being controlled. This, in turn, will adjust the price of risk to allow for an increased importance of global systematic risk. The end result would be a greater integration of emerging capital markets with the developed capital markets. However, this paper presents an argument that these emerging markets have not quite reached this point in their emergence.

The tests indicate that there is no change in the pricing of assets emerging markets with respect to each other, but, together, they have possibly moved closer to the pricing of assets in developed markets. The emerging markets are not collapsing toward a common core grouping. The results indicate that the price of risk is different among these countries. However, the tests do not indicate that the emerging markets have the same price of risk as do the developed markets. They only indicate that the differences between the two classes of markets may have narrowed over time. Emerging markets have a larger responsiveness to international events, but that responsiveness is dwarfed by their reaction to local events. This is consistent with Lessard's finding; there appears to be no common factor that determines the price of risk across markets. Still, there is preliminary evidence that global events can influence the price of risk in these markets. The observed segmentation coefficients of July 1990 demonstrate that. This may indicate the initial movements toward greater capital market integration for emerging markets.

This is consistent with the recent activities in the international capital markets. Changes in the structure of the emerging markets have altered investor access to the markets and, more importantly, investor perceptions of opportunities in these markets. Alford (1993b) indicates that the changes in the regulatory and economic environments have played an important part in the emergence of these markets. These economies are opening to increased trade and to increased investment, both portfolio and direct.

These changes are having positive influences on the emerging markets. They have a led to greater supply of capital to the markets which leads to a decrease in volatility. As a result, companies are finding an easier, more stable access to capital. The increased stability also reduces risk for investors. The downside for investors is that this increased international activity in these emerging countries will eventually reduce the available segmentation gains. The current arbitrage profits must subside as these markets emerge further.

ACKNOWLEDGMENT

An earlier version of this paper was presented at the Academy of International Business meeting in Maui, Hawaii, October 1993. The authors would like to thank Arvind Mahajan for his comments on earlier versions of this paper.

NOTES

1. In this model, R_i refers to the return on asset *i*; R_m is the return on the market portfolio, and R_f is the risk free rate of return. The variable σ_m^2 is the variance on the market return; σ_{im} denotes the covariance of asset *i* with the market portfolio. The variables λ_i and λ refer to the shadow costs of segmentation for asset *i* and the market portfolio, respectively, arising from the segmentational barriers.
2. These countries are: Argentina, Brazil, Chile, Greece, Jordan, Malaysia, Mexico, Philippine, Thailand, and Venezuela. Data for the other countries in the database are not complete and, for this reason, are not included in the analysis.
3. The absolute values for the coefficients of segmentation are ranked from least to greatest. These ranks are then multiplied by the hypothesized rank for that month. The most extreme coefficient of segmentation is posited to be the first month of the sample, January 1989; the least extreme would be the last month of the study, December 1992.
4. We would like to thank Arvind Mahajan for suggesting this approach.

REFERENCES

Alford, A. 1993a. "Assessing the Level of Capital Market Integration: A Review of the Literature." *Handbook of International Financial Market Integration*, edited by S. Stansell. London: Basil Blackwell.

———. 1993b. *Risk and Developing Capital Markets, Presentation: Financial Systems in Transition*. Mexico City.

Alford, A., and W.R. Folks, Jr. 1996. "A Test for Increased Capital Market Integration." *Financial Review* 31: 1–23.

Errunza, V. 1977. "Gains from Portfolio Diversification into Less Developed Countries' Securities." *Journal of International Business Studies*: 83–99.

Errunza, V., and E. Losq. 1985. "International Asset Pricing under Mild Segmentation: Theory and Test." *Journal of Finance* 40: 105–124.

Jorion, P., and E. Schwartz. 1986. "Integration vs. Segmentation in the Canadian Stock Market." *Journal of Finance* 41: 603–616.

Lessard, D.R. 1973. "International Portfolio Diversification: A Multivariate Analysis for a Group of Latin American Countries." *Journal of Finance* 28: 619–633.

Maldonado, R., and A. Saunders. 1981. "International Portfolio Diversification and the Inter-Temporal Stability of International Stock Market Relationships, 1957–78." *Financial Management*: 54–63.

Mullin, J. 1993. "Emerging Equity Markets in the Global Economy." *Federal Reserve Bank of New York Quarterly Review* (Summer): 54–83.

PRICE EFFECTS OF STOCK OWNERSHIP RESTRICTIONS FOR FOREIGNERS IN EMERGING MARKETS

C. Sherman Cheung, Clarence C. Y. Kwan, and Hugh A. Thomas

ABSTRACT

This paper investigates the design of restrictions to foreign portfolio equity investment in an international asset pricing framework. Our model explains the empirically observed discount of China's B shares and suggests policy implications concerning the design of restrictions for other Asia Pacific countries. We also show why closed-end, single-country, equity funds which invest in countries restricting foreign shareholding do not always trade at premiums. Whether the premium exists or not depends on the design of the restriction.

One of the ironies of political economy is that countries with the need for capital usually restrict the inflow of foreign capital by limiting foreigners' ability to invest. The phenomenon is evident among virtually all of the developing countries of the Asia Pacific region. Where the supply of shares available to foreign investors is restricted, one expects that foreigners would have to pay a premium for shares

Research in International Business and Finance, Supplement 1, pages 257–265.

ISBN: 0-7623-0110-4

relative to the price that local investors pay. In fact, evidence on markets with restrictions indicates that premia are the norm.[1] The significant discount for B shares in China is an empirical puzzle that calls for further investigation.[2]

The objectives of this study are twofold. First, drawing on the literature on pricing international assets subject to restrictions, we offer a theoretical explanation for the empirical discount puzzle for China's B shares and, building on that explanation, we consider how the design of ownership restrictions affect share pricing in other countries across the Asia Pacific region. Secondly, we clarify some common misconceptions concerning the discount/premium on closed-end, single-country, equity funds which invest in countries restricting foreign shareholding.

BARRIERS TO ENTRY

Table 1 lists the types of barriers to investment by non-nationals in domestic shares and gives examples of countries implementing the barriers. We distinguish two general types of barriers: (1) the rigid type whereby a fixed amount of the shares is made available to only foreign investors and (2) the flexible type whereby foreign investors can hold *up to* a certain fraction of a firm's shares outstanding. In addition, some countries such as Taiwan and Korea impose a further restriction that only approved financial institutions can invest.

China enforces a rigid restriction whereby a special class of shares, B shares, are made available exclusively to foreign investors. Domestic investors can only hold A shares. B shares are voting stock ranking equally with A shares. Purchases of B shares can only be made with foreign currency, with Shanghai B shares being U.S. dollar denominated and Shenzhen B shares being Hong Kong dollar denominated. The central bank converts the foreign currency to domestic currency at the official spot rate and stands ready to convert local currency distributions to foreign currency at the future prevailing official spot rate. As of the end of 1993, China had 32 companies with B shares.[3]

Table 1. Types of Barriers

	Discount/Premium Allowed	*Discount/Premium Not Allowed*
flexible restrictions: foreign investors holdings not to exceed certain fraction of shares outstanding	Thailand Certain companies in Singapore Philippines	Taiwan Korea
rigid restrictions: a constant amount of shares is made available to only foreign investors	China	none

Thailand enforces a flexible barrier that restricts foreign investors to holding no more than 45% of most domestic firms' shares and 25% of banking and finance company shares.

Excess foreign demand/supply is treated in different ways by different countries. One way is to allow the price mechanism to ration the restricted amount among the foreign investors. Under a flexible barrier, only excess foreign demand can occur. In the event that foreign buyers collectively wish to purchase less than their maximum percentage of shares of a company, the constraint is not binding and the price prevailing is the domestic price. In the event that the constraint is binding, some countries allow the price mechanism to ration the restricted amount of foreign shares among foreign investors, thus resulting in a premium. Thailand and certain companies such as Singapore Airlines in Singapore follow this approach. For example, Thailand and Indonesia have a separate foreign board on which foreign investors can trade stocks at premiums to the prices that local investors pay. Other countries disallow price rationing altogether. Taiwan and, to a certain extent, Korea follow non-price rationing.[4]

FORMAL MODEL OF ASSET PRICING WITH RIGID BARRIERS

The above discussion has pointed to one basic reason for the empirical puzzle of China's B share discount: the rigid restrictions allow the emergence of either excess demand or excess supply relative to A share pricing. In this section, we formalize and expand this analysis.

Our model is an extension of that of Eun and Janakiramanan (1986) who strive to model all types of barriers to investment within a one single period CAPM model[5] in a two country world. We enrich the model by introducing exchange rates and the division of the outstanding stock into A and B shares.

Each investor k, whether that investor be resident in the unrestricted global market ($k \in G$) or in the restricted domestic market ($k \in D$), maximizes the certainty equivalent (CEQ^k) of his or her end-of-period wealth $\widetilde{W}^k$.[6] He or she does so by investing in $\mathbf{n}$ shares, where $\mathbf{n}$ is a vector of the number of shares of each security purchased by the investor. Each investor k from the global market G invests in $\mathbf{n}_G^k$ shares in market G. Because the domestic government of country D restricts holdings of A shares to its own residents while restricting the holdings of B shares to residents of G, each $k \in G$ invests in $\mathbf{n}_B^k$ B shares of market D, while each $k \in D$ in $\mathbf{n}_A^k$ A shares of market D.

For investors $k \in G$,

$$CEQ^k = \overline{W} - \frac{\rho^k}{2} var(\widetilde{W}^k), \tag{1}$$

where the stochastic end-of-period wealth is

$$\tilde{W}^k = \mathbf{n}_G^{k'}\tilde{\mathbf{P}}_G + \mathbf{n}_B^{k'}\tilde{X}\tilde{\mathbf{P}}_B + r[w^k - \mathbf{n}_G^{k'}\mathbf{P}_G - \mathbf{n}_B^{k'}X\mathbf{P}_B]. \quad (2)$$

Investors have expected end-of-period wealth of

$$\overline{W}^k = \mathbf{n}_G^{k'}[\overline{\mathbf{P}}_G - \mathbf{P}_G r] + \mathbf{n}_B^{k'}[\overline{X\mathbf{P}}_B - X\mathbf{P}_B r] + W^k r. \quad (3)$$

In the above and subsequent equations,

$W^k, \tilde{W}^k$ and $\overline{W}^k$ = the beginning-of-period, stochastic end period, and expected end-of-period wealth of the kth investor, respectively,
ρ^k = the Arrow-Pratt measure of absolute risk aversion of the kth investor,
r = 1 + the risk free rate of interest in G currency,
$\mathbf{P}, \tilde{\mathbf{P}}$ and $\overline{\mathbf{P}}$ = the beginning-of-period, stochastic end-of-period, and expected end-of-period vector of share prices in local currency, respectively, and
$X, \tilde{X}$ and $\overline{X}$ = the beginning-of-period, stochastic end-of-period, and expected end-of-period direct quote exchange rate for the cost in G currency of one unit of country D currency, respectively.

Before we consider the solution of the model, we digress to explain the institutional structure of exchange rates. Note that the values X, $\tilde{X}$, and $\overline{X}$ are functions of changing official exchange rate policies. Like most developing countries, China has considered and implemented various currency exchange restrictions at various times. During most of the period when B shares have traded, foreigners (i.e., investors from the global economy in our model) have been restricted to use of perfectly convertible foreign exchange certificates (FECs) at official exchange rates whereas domestic investors use nonconvertible renminbi. The renminbi has always been convertible to foreign exchange in illegal black markets. Over the past three years, certain authorized local residents and designated foreign direct (i.e., not portfolio) investors have been able to swap foreign exchange legally for renminbi in regional swap centers. By late 1993 inter-swap center arbitrage by authorized domestic entities had cause regional swap rates to converge so that swap rates differed little from region to region.[7] At year end 1993, while the swap rate stood at 8.7 renminbi to the dollar, the official rate stood at 5.8 renminbi to the dollar. Effective January 1, 1994 the Chinese government committed to maintaining a "unitary and controlled floating exchange rate based on market supply and demand" but informed observers believe that the float implemented will continue to involve government restrictions and intervention which will cause the official rate of exchange to differ from the true market equilibrium.[8]

On one hand, an investor who bought B shares prior to January 1994 would have been effectively forced to pay the artificially high official price for the renminbi. On the other hand, the government undertaking to convert renminbi at the future official spot rate has an unknown value that would be considerable if the official rate remains above the true market equilibrium rate. In the model, the value of X reflects the initial high price and the volatility of $\tilde{X}$ reflects potential variance in the future value of the official exchange rate as a result of market and political forces. Returning to our model, if one assumes that there is no covariance between stock and exchange rate prices[9] the variance of the kth investor's end portfolio is

$$Var(\tilde{W}^k) = \mathbf{n}_G^{k'}\,\mathbf{\Gamma}_{GG}\,\mathbf{n}_G^k + \mathbf{n}_G^{k'}\overline{X}\mathbf{\Gamma}_{GB}\,\mathbf{n}_B^k + \mathbf{n}_B^{k'}\overline{X}\mathbf{\Gamma}_{BG}\,\mathbf{n}_G^k + \mathbf{n}_B^{k'}\,[\,(S^2+\overline{X}^2)\,\mathbf{\Gamma}_{BB} + S^2\overline{\mathbf{P}}_B\overline{\mathbf{P}}'_B\,]\,\mathbf{n}_B^k \tag{4}$$

where

$S =$ the standard deviation of the exchange rate $\tilde{X}$ and

$\mathbf{\Gamma}_{ij} =$ the covariance matrix of the share prices in the ith and jth share markets.

Maximizing equation (1) with regard to portfolio composition yields the result that each investor adjusts his or her portfolio so that the expected excess returns on each security expressed in G currency is a product of the risk aversion of the investor ρ^k and a function of the weighted covariance of the security in the portfolio with all other securities in the portfolio, both global G shares and domestic B shares, adjusted upwards (in the case of B shares) to reflect exchange rate risk. Excess returns of global shares are

$$\overline{\mathbf{P}}_G - \mathbf{P}_G r = \rho^k\,(\mathbf{\Gamma}_{GG}\mathbf{n}_G^k + \overline{X}\mathbf{\Gamma}_{GB}\mathbf{n}_B^k) \tag{5}$$

while excess returns of B shares are

$$\overline{X\mathbf{P}}_B - X\mathbf{P}_B r = \rho^k\,[\overline{X}\mathbf{\Gamma}_{BG}\mathbf{n}_G^k + (S^2+\overline{X}^2)\,(\mathbf{\Gamma}_{BB} + S^2\overline{\mathbf{P}}_B\overline{\mathbf{P}}'_B)\,\mathbf{n}_B^k]. \tag{6}$$

Assuming that all investors share the same expectations, one can aggregate across investors to derive the pricing relationships for global assets and B shares[10] as follows:

$$\mathbf{P}_G = \frac{1}{r}\,[\overline{\mathbf{P}}_G - \rho^G(\mathbf{\Gamma}_{GG}\mathbf{n}_G + \overline{X}\mathbf{\Gamma}_{GB}\alpha\mathbf{n}_D)\,] \tag{7}$$

$$\mathbf{P}_B = \frac{1}{Xr}\,\{\overline{X\mathbf{P}}_B - \rho^G[\overline{X}\mathbf{\Gamma}_{BG}\mathbf{n}_G + (\,(S^2+\overline{X}^2)\,\mathbf{\Gamma}_{BB} + S^2\overline{\mathbf{P}}_B\overline{\mathbf{P}}'_B)\,\alpha\mathbf{n}_D]\,\} \tag{8}$$

where

$\rho^G =$ the aggregated risk aversion of the global economy,

$\mathbf{n}_G = \Sigma_{k\in G}\mathbf{n}_G^k$,

$\alpha =$ the proportion of shares of companies in the restricted domestic economy D which are issued as B shares,

$\mathbf{n}_D =$ the vector giving the total number of shares of each of the companies in economy D, and

$\mathbf{n}_B = \Sigma_{k\in G}\mathbf{n}_B^k = \alpha\mathbf{n}_D$

It is noteworthy that by isolating entirely the purchasers of B shares from the demand of domestic investors $k \in D$, the demand of domestic investors does not enter into the pricing relationship of B shares at all. As we have not allowed investors in country D to invest abroad in the global economy G, solving for the equilibrium pricing relationship for A shares in currency of country D gives

$$\mathbf{P}_A = \frac{1}{r_D} [\overline{\mathbf{P}}_A - \rho^D \mathbf{\Gamma}_{AA} (1 - \alpha)\, \mathbf{n}_D] \tag{9}$$

where

$r_D =$ the risk free rate in the restricted domestic economy.

To explain the existence of a discount for B shares, one can easily see from equation (8) that

$$\frac{\partial \mathbf{P}_B}{\partial X} < 0. \tag{10}$$

In other words, if foreign investors are forced to pay a high artificial value for Chinese currency to begin with, they will compensate by paying a lower price for the B shares. Using equation (8), one can further demonstrate that

$$\frac{\partial \mathbf{P}_B}{\partial \rho^G} < 0 \text{ and } \frac{\partial \mathbf{P}_B}{\partial S^2} < 0. \tag{11}$$

Whenever the demand for B shares decreases due to shifts in, for example, global risk aversion or global investors' perception of domestic currency exchange risk or, for that matter, any other reason, the price of B shares will drop relative to A shares. In no case the local investors can step in to pick up the surplus. In the case of Thailand, on the other hand, the decrease in demand by foreign investors can be offset by domestic investors.

Finally, it can be shown from equation (8) that

$$\frac{\partial \mathbf{P}_A}{\partial r_D} < 0. \tag{12}$$

China's banking sector has not been deregulated, resulting in deposit rates being uncompetitive. Our model indicates that a low domestic deposit rate would cause local investors to allocate their funds in favor of A share, resulting in a premium of A shares relative to B shares.

FLEXIBLE BARRIERS

Countries like Taiwan[11] impose flexible barriers with the relatively restrictive level of 10%. Hence, one would expect that the constraint from the point of view of global investors is likely to be binding. The domestic investors are in effect left to determine the official stock exchange price for both the global and the domestic investors with a net supply of 90% of the outstanding stocks. In other words, one can determine equilibrium prices in a manner similar to equation (9) where $\alpha = 0.1$. Since the global investors are price takers, the P_A in this case would also be the price nominally available to them on the exchange. Note that the premium/discount does not exist, but that the shares would tend to be rationed by lack of availability on the exchange.

IMPLICATIONS FOR SINGLE COUNTRY CLOSED-END FUNDS

The above results have some interesting implications for the pricing of closed-end country funds. The common perception as expressed by Bosner-Neal, Brauer, Neal, and Wheatley (1990) is that "[t]he foreign government places limits on the fraction of shares that are unrestricted, and, when these limits are binding, the unrestricted shares sell at a premium relative to the restricted shares. . . . The underlying assets of closed-end country funds resemble restricted shares while the funds shares resemble unrestricted shares. Thus . . . binding quantitative restrictions a country imposes will increase the price-net asset value ratio of the fund investing in that country" (p. 526). The above perception ignores the design of the restrictions analyzed in this paper. In countries where the price mechanism is allowed to ration supply among foreign investors, the price premium on shares purchased in the local market and held by foreigners already reflects the restrictions in place. There is no more reason to expect an additional premium on such a country fund than there would be to expect a premium on a domestic American closed-end fund. In other words, the premium in the share prices of the stocks available to foreign investors from a country with flexible restrictions is already impounded into the net asset values and no further adjustment should be needed in the price of the closed-end fund. Of course, changes in the premium on the foreign board relative to the domestic board would be expected to diminish with the announcement of barrier-relaxing policy changes. And, in countries like Taiwan and Korea, where only one price prevails on the exchanges, the Bosner-Neal (1990) analysis applies fully and one would expect a premium to exist.[12]

CONCLUDING REMARKS

Our examination of the design of restrictions of foreign investment in domestic stocks has shown how the restrictions can result in a discount on share prices available only to foreign investors. In the case of China, the irrationally rigid design of A share and B share segmentation plus the controlled nature of exchange rates lead to a discount on the price of B shares. This means that a domestic firm contemplating going public may rationally wish to issue only domestic A shares in order to obtain better pricing and a consequent lower cost of capital. We also clarify a misunderstanding in the closed-end country fund literature. Specifically, a binding restriction imposed by a country on foreign investors does not always lead to a premium on the net asset value of the fund invested in the country. Whether the premium exists or not will depend on the design of the restriction.

ACKNOWLEDGMENT

Financial support for this study provided by the Social Sciences and Humanities Research Council of Canada is gratefully acknowledged.

NOTES

1. See, for example, Bailey and Jagtiani (1993) and Hietala (1989). Bosner-Neal, Brauer, Neal, and Wheatley (1990), extending this reasoning to explain the changing premia on closed-end funds investing in countries that restrict foreign investment in domestic shares, show that policy initiatives to increase/decrease restrictions of foreign shareholding of domestic shares tend to increase/decrease the price-net asset ratio of funds investing in that country.
2. Bailey (1993) reports discounts for B shares ranging from 40% to 70%.
3. See Steiner and McGough (1993).
4. Foreign investors in Korea can trade among themselves away from the exchange, thereby allowing an over-the-counter premium. Taiwan, however, prohibits this practice, making it impossible to trade at a premium. See Mark (1994) for a discussion.
5. The model generalizes easily to a multifactor model. As the conclusions drawn from the model are the same, we have used the traditional one factor approach.
6. We assume that all investors maximize their negative exponential utility functions (i.e., that they exhibit constant absolute risk aversion) and that security returns are multivariate normally distributed.
7. For a discussion of problems created by the swap centers, see Kentley (1993).
8. See *Wall Street Journal* Staff Reporter (1993) for a report on the announcement and year end exchange rates. Note that, although the FEC is now abolished, full convertibility is still not permitted. Control of access to swap centers is expected to be a key means to control the renminbi's new floating exchange rate. See Chen (1994) for a discussion.
9. This is admittedly a strong assumption, but although correlation risk exists (see Eun and Resnick 1988) it lacks a convincing theory for both its sign and magnitude. Practitioners hedging such risk tend to use numerical methods relying on historical observations rather than theoretical foundations (see Parsley 1993).
10. Note that we do not allow for participants in the domestic market to invest in the global market. This is consistent with capital controls in place in developing countries preventing the exporting of capital and with the little impact which the developing country would have on the global market in the event that those capital controls were ineffective.
11. See Mark (1994) for a discussion.
12. The actual premium/discount can be affected by other additional factors such as investor sentiment, as documented by Lee, Schleifer, and Thaler (1991).

REFERENCES

Bailey, W. forthcoming. "Risk and Return on China's New Stockmarkets: Some Preliminary Evidence." *Pacific Basin Finance Journal*.

Bailey, W., and J. Jagtiani. 1993. "Foreign Ownership Restrictions and Premiums for International Investment: Some Evidence from the Thai Capital Market." Working Paper, Cornell University, August.

Bosner-Neal, C., G. Brauer, R. Neal, and S. Wheatley. 1990. "Closed-End Country Fund Prices and International Investment Restrictions." *Journal of Finance* (June): 523–548.

Chen, K. 1994. "Beijing Unifies Dual Currency Exchange-Rate System." *Asian Wall Street Journal Weekly* (January 3): 2.

Eun, C., and B. Resnick. 1988. "Exchange Rate Uncertainty, Forward Contracts, and International Portfolio Selection." *Journal of Finance* (March): 197–215.

Eun, C., and S. Janakiramanan. 1989. "A Model of International Asset Pricing with a Constraint on the Foreign Equity Ownership." *Journal of Finance* (July): 897–914.

Hietala, P. 1989. "Asset Pricing in Partially Segmented Markets: Evidence from the Finnish Market." *Journal of Finance* (July): 697–718.

Kentley, R. 1993. "China's Currency 'Swap Centers' Draw U.S. Complaints of Trade Restraint." *Wall Street Journal* (July 9): p. 46.

Lee, C., A. Schleifer, and R. Thaler. 1991. "Investor Sentiment and the Closed-End Puzzle." *Journal of Finance* (March): 75–109.

Mark, J. 1994. "Foreign Investors Annoyed by Limits on Taiwan Stocks." *Asian Wall Street Journal Weekly* (January 17): 17, 20.

Parsley, M. 1993. "The Last Piece of the Jigsaw." *Euromoney* (November): 29–32.

Steiner, R., and R. McGough. 1993. "Mutual Interest." *Wall Street Journal* (December 10): 17.

Wall Street Journal Staff Reporter. 1993. "China Takes Steps to Make Its Currency Convertible." *Wall Street Journal* (December 30): p. A6.

NON-NORMALITY OF RETURNS IN EMERGING MARKETS:
A COMPARISON OF MEAN-VARIANCE VERSUS MEAN-LOWER PARTIAL MOMENT ASSET PRICING MODELS

Babak Eftekhari and Stephen E. Satchell

ABSTRACT

Emerging market returns typically exhibit non-normal returns. Theory suggests that when non-normal returns exist, the mean-variance (MV) beta should be statistically different from mean-lower partial (LPM) beta, unless investors have quadratic utility. We investigate this question, firstly by obtaining Bera-Jarque statistics for 17 emerging equity markets for the period 1985–1994 to test for normality. We note that none of the markets have normal returns. We then use regression analysis to test for the difference between the MV and LPM betas of the 17 countries. We find that in only four cases our expectations are satisfied—that is, non-normality leads to statistically different betas. This implies that even though theory suggests different betas when returns are non-normal, in practice traditional betas are not statistically different from an alternative beta robust to non-normality.

Research in International Business and Finance, Supplement 1, pages 267–277.

ISBN: 0-7623-0110-4

INTRODUCTION

The most common measure of risk used in finance by academics and practitioners is the variance. Markowitz (1952) showed that if risk is measured by variance and returns by the mean of the returns distribution, uncertain prospects can be ordered by their ranking in the mean-variance (MV) space. The MV model relies upon the assumption that the distribution of the returns is normal or the investor's utility function is quadratic. If at least one of these conditions holds, it can be shown that choosing among risky assets on the basis of the mean and variance only is consistent with the expected utility principle (Tobin 1958).[1] The asset pricing model resulting from the MV approach is the traditional Capital Asset Pricing Model (MV-CAPM) of Sharpe (1963, 1964), Mossin (1966), and Lintner (1969). However, it has been pointed out by Fama (1965), Hanoch and Levy (1969), and Pratt (1964) that the assumptions that the investor's utility function is quadratic or the distribution of returns is normal may lead to unsatisfactory conclusions. Fama has shown that the distribution of returns is not normal but conforms quite well to the four-parameter Paretian distribution. Even if in the case of many markets, (for monthly or higher length periods) the normal distribution is a true description of the data, this is not necessarily true for high frequency and emerging markets data. When returns are non-normal, traditional asset pricing models rely on quadratic utility. Hanoch and Levy have pointed out that a quadratic utility function implies that more wealth is preferred to less wealth in a bounded range and beyond this range investors prefer less wealth to more wealth. In particular, Pratt pointed out that the quadratic utility function, even in the acceptable range, implies increasing rather than decreasing absolute risk aversion, with the implication that a risky portfolio is an inferior good. In general MV analysis is inconsistent with second-order stochastic dominance.

Apart from the criticisms placed on the assumptions underpinning the MV-CAPM, it has been argued that the variance is not a good measure of risk. In response, Markowitz offered the semi-variance (SV) as an alternative. The SV measures the downside variability from the mean. Markowitz (1959) and Mao (1970) contend that investors frequently associate risk with the failure to achieve target return. Fishburn (1977) states that if the above argument is correct, then any measure of dispersion taken with respect to a parameter (e.g., mean) which changes from distribution to distribution is questionable. Partly in response to this criticism Bawa (1975) and Bawa and Lindenberg (1977) offered the lower partial moment (LPM) as an extension. The LPM is a measure of portfolio risk that focuses on returns below some target or reference point. This measurement leads to the LPM capital asset pricing model (LPM-CAPM).

It is known that these models reduce to the same relationship given normal returns, that is MV-CAPM is a special case of LPM-CAPM. However, the literature has failed to answer the question, whether the models imply the same measures of market risk (betas) given real financial data. If the betas are statistically identical, then the assumptions of the MV-CAPM are, either satisfied, or inconsequential, and the traditional CAPM is as good as the other models, that is, the use of variance is warranted. If the betas are statistically significantly different, as the theory would suggest, then this information is important in terms of assessing the impact on the investment of a change in the market portfolio. Such a finding would have implications in asset pricing, portfolio selection, and performance measurement. The contribution of this paper is to construct a method that tests for the difference between the betas resulting from the MV-CAPM and the LPM-CAPM, and apply this method to equity returns of a group of emerging markets. Emerging market data normally exhibit non-normality and are expected to violate the normality assumption of the MV-CAPM. We shall use the phrase normality to include a broader class of distributions for which the MV-CAPM is valid, the so-called elliptical class (see Ingersoll 1987, pp. 104–113 for details).

The plan of the paper is as follows. In the second section the LPM measure of risk and LPM-CAPM are reviewed. The third section presents the testing procedures, the fourth section discusses the data used in the empirical testing, results of which are given in the fifth section. The last section presents the conclusions.

LOWER PARTIAL MOMENT AND LPM-CAPM

Lower partial moment is a measure of portfolio risk that depends on only those portfolio returns that fall below some target level of returns. It is defined and measured as

$$\mathrm{LPM}_h(R_p) = \int_{-\infty}^{h} (R - h)^2 f_p(R)dR \tag{1}$$

where h is the target level and $f_p(R)$ represents the probability density function of returns for portfolio p. SV of returns is defined and measured in exactly this same way. In this sense, SV and LPM are interchangeable terms, except that for SV, h is the mean of R. However the literature does distinguish between the two terms because of their theoretical origins.

For expected utility maximizing investors, Bawa (1975) has provided a theoretical rationale for using LPM as the measure of portfolio risk. Stochastic Dominance (SD) rules can be used to derive the admissible set of portfolios for expected utility maximizing investors under far less restrictive assumptions regarding utility functions and probability distributions of returns than those required to rationalize the use of the mean-variance portfolio selection rule. Bawa related the mean-LPM portfolio selection rule to the SD rules and concluded that, at least on theoretical grounds, the mean-LPM rule is preferable to the popular MV selection rule. The basis for this preference is that while the mean-LPM rule can be derived from the

SD selection rules under very general assumptions regarding distributions of returns and utility functions, the MV rule can be derived only under very restrictive assumptions, as mentioned previously.

Hogan and Warren (1974) and Bawa and Lindenberg (1977) independently developed a LPM-CAPM.[2] The equilibrium pricing relationship of this model is stated as

$$E(R_i) - R_f = [E(R_m) - R_f] \frac{\text{CLPM}_{R_f}(R_m, R_i)}{\text{LPM}_{R_f}(R_m)} \tag{2}$$

where $E(R_i)$ is the equilibrium expected rate of return on asset i; $E(R_m)$ is the equilibrium expected rate of return on the market portfolio; $\text{LPM}_{R_f}(R_m)$ is the LPM of returns below R_f on the market portfolio; and $\text{CLPM}_{R_f}(R_m, R_i)$ is the co-LPM below R_f of the returns on the market portfolio with returns on security i, that is

$$\text{CLPM}_{R_f}(R_m, R_i) = \int_{-\infty}^{+\infty} \int_{-\infty}^{R_f} (R_m - R_f)(R_i - R_f) f(R_i, R_m)\, dR_m\, dR_i \tag{3}$$

where $f(R_i, R_m)$ is the joint probability density function of returns on asset i and returns on the market portfolio. In deriving equation (2), the target rate in all cases was set equal to the risk-free rate. The target rate can be set to any other rate.

In the LPM-CAPM, CLPM/LPM replaces COV/V from the MV-CAPM as the measure of systematic risk, where

$$\left(\frac{\text{COV}}{\text{V}}\right) = \frac{\sum_{t=1}^{k} (R_{it} - \overline{R}_i)(R_{mt} - \overline{R}_m)}{\sum_{t=1}^{k} \left(R_{mt} - \overline{R}_m\right)^2} \tag{4}$$

where $\overline{R}_i$ is the mean returns on security i for the k months, and $\overline{R}_m$ is the mean returns on the market index; and

$$\left(\frac{\text{CLPM}}{\text{LPM}}\right) = \frac{\sum_{t=1}^{k} (R_{it} - R_{ft})\,[\min(0, R_{mt} - R_{it})]}{\sum_{t=1}^{k} [\min(0, R_{mt} - R_{it})]^2} \tag{5}$$

where R_{ft} is the risk-free rate for period t. CLPM/LPM is a more general measure of systematic risk than is COV/V.

ECONOMETRIC TESTING PROCEDURE

Given a data set, our objective is to compare the beta from MV-CAPM (COV/V) and the beta from the LPM-CAPM (CLPM/LPM) from a statistical perspective. The betas can be calculated by using their definitions, so that the MV beta is calculated from (4) and the LPM beta from (5). However, if we estimate the betas this way, we would not be able to compare them accurately using known statistical techniques. Therefore, we will calculate the LPM beta using a regression model, which we shall call the "unrestricted model." By placing linear restrictions on this model we shall obtain the "restrictive model," which measures the MV beta. The validity of the restrictions and hence the statistical difference between the two betas, can then be tested via a simple F-test.

Our regression model of LPM-CAPM must separate the market distribution above and below the target rate of return so as to capture the downside response of asset returns. The model presented here is a variation of the Harlow and Rao (1989) model which itself is a modification of the asymmetric response model of Bawa et al. (1981) proposed for testing the Bawa-Lindenberg model. The *unrestricted* model is

$$R_{it} = \beta_{1i} R^{-}_{mt} + \beta_{2i} R^{+}_{mt} + \phi(\beta_{1i} - \beta_{2i})\delta_t + \varepsilon_{it} \qquad (6)$$
$$i = 1, \dots, N$$
$$t = 1, \dots, T$$

where $R^{-}_{mt} = R_{mt} - R_{ft}$ if $R_{mt} < R_{ft}$ and 0 otherwise; $R^{+}_{mt} = R_{mt} - R_{ft}$ if $R_{mt} > R_{ft}$ and 0 otherwise[3]; $\delta_t = 1$ if $R_{mt} > R_{ft}$ and 0 otherwise; and $\Phi \equiv E(R_{mt} \mid R_{mt} > R_{ft}) \equiv E(R^{+}_{mt})/P(R_{mt} > R_f)$.

The β_{1i} term in (6) is the LPM beta of asset i.[4] To see this, if $R_{mt} < R_{ft}$, then (6) becomes

$$R_{it} = \beta_{1i} R_{mt} + \varepsilon_{it} \qquad (7)$$

(7) is equivalent to (2), remembering that we are using excess returns. Furthermore, if we take expectations on both sides of (6), we get

$$E(R_i) = \beta_{1i} E(R^{-}_{mt}) + \beta_{2i} E(R^{+}_{mt}) + \phi(\beta_{1i} - \beta_{2i}) P(R_{mt} > R_{ft}) \qquad (8)$$

substituting for ϕ by using its definition results in

$$E(R_i) = \beta_{1i} E(R_{mt}) \qquad (9)$$

since $R^{+}_{mt} + R^{-}_{mt} = R_m$. Equations (6) and (8) assume that LPM-CAPM holds. Furthermore, β_{2i} represents the asymmetric response of the return on asset i to the return on the market portfolio. ϕ represents the expectation of the market return given that it falls above the target rate.

Consistent with equation (11) of Harlow and Rao (1989), we will estimate the reduced form of equation (6), where $\phi(\beta_{1i} - \beta_{2i}) = \pi_i$, and we get

$$R_{it} = \beta_{1i} R^-_{mt} + \beta_{2i} R^+_{mt} + \pi_i \delta_t + \varepsilon_{it} \tag{10}$$

To obtain the MV-CAPM all we have to do is to place the linear restrictions $\beta_{1i} = \beta_{2i}$ and $\pi = 0$ on the equation (10). The *restricted* model then is

$$R_{it} = \beta_{1i} R_{mt} + \varepsilon_{it} \tag{11}$$

This model is valid for *any* R_{mt} not for specific R_{mt}'s as is the case in (7). Given that we are using excess returns the slope in equation (11) is the MV-CAPM. This linear restriction can be tested via an F-test. Note that the restriction $\beta_{1i} = \beta_{2i}$ on (6) would have been enough to lead to (11), but we are estimating (10), which avoids the rather restrictive assumption about the interpretation of π_i. In our extended model (10)

$$E(R_{it}) = \beta_{1i} E(R^-_{mt}) + \beta_{2i} E(R^+_{mt}) + \pi_i P(R^+_{mt} > R_{ft}) \tag{12}$$

Our model (10) is broader in the sense that it still holds even if the LPM-CAPM fails to hold (i.e., $\phi(\beta_{1i} - \beta_{2i}) \neq \pi_i$).

The reasons for not using the restriction that $\phi = E(R_{mt} \mid R_{mt} > R_{ft})$ are compelling. Firstly, Harlow and Rao (1989) have ignored the impact on estimation of this restriction and so the OLS method they utilize will be inefficient. Secondly, if we made assumptions about the marginal distribution of R_{mt} and calculated an estimate of ϕ, $\hat{\phi}$, we could in principle substitute $\hat{\phi}$ into equation (6), rearrange and estimate by OLS. This would lead to errors in variable and possible inconsistent estimation. The correct solution is to write the joint likelihood of R_{it} and R_{mt} given (6) and the marginal distribution of R_{mt}. This would lead to optimal estimation of ϕ and any other parameters, but our results would be contingent on correct specification. For these reasons we have worked with the more general framework.

DATA DESCRIPTION

Emerging market data often exhibit non-normalities. To test the effect of this non-normality we use the International Finance Corporation's (IFC) Global Emerging Markets Index denominated in dollars for 17 countries as our asset returns. The market portfolio is taken as the monthly capital return on the S&P 500 index and the risk free rate of return is the U.S. Treasury rate. This also serves as our target rate of return. The justification for using S&P 500 is that we are looking at the risks of investment in emerging markets from the point of view of a U.S. investor. The data set spans 119 months, starting from January 1985 and ending November 1994. The countries used are: Argentina, Brazil, Chile, Colombia, Greece, India, Jordan, Korea, Malaysia, Mexico, Nigeria, Pakistan, Philippines, Taiwan, Thailand, Venezuela, and Zimbabwe. This is part of a larger data set analyzed extensively by Harvey (1995).

IFC began producing its own standardized stock indexes for developing countries in mid-1981 in response to the need for better means to evaluate the performance of these stock markets than local stock price indexes, which are each calculated in their own way and based on stocks selected by different criteria. The original IFC indexes were calculated only once a year, used month-end prices, were based on the 10 to 20 most active stocks in each of the 10 emerging markets, and were equally weighted and available on a "price only" and total return basis. Gradually, calculation periods increased to once a quarter using month-end prices. In late 1984, in response to growing interest in emerging markets among international fund managers, IFC decided to reorganize the methodology it used from equal to capitalization weighting, improve the timeliness of calculating its month-end indexes from a quarterly lag to a monthly lag, expand the number of stocks covered, and increase the number of markets covered from 10 to 17. Our sample period starts from this revision. These new indexes have proved very popular with money managers. Recently IFC has added more countries and stocks to its indexes, as well as a new set of indices named the IFC Investable indexes. The reason that these broader indexes and the new countries were not included in this study was due to the small sample periods that would have resulted.

Table 1 presents the summary statistics for the returns data used in this study. It can be seen that with the exception of Nigeria, all other markets exhibit positive mean return. The majority of the emerging markets also have higher average monthly return and variance than the United States, represented by the S&P 500. The most interesting aspect of the statistics is the non-normal nature of the data. The return distribution is normal if skewness and kurtosis are both near zero.[5]

As a preliminary check we obtain Bera-Jarque statistics for normality for all the countries used. The results of these tests are also presented in Table 1. If the data is normal we expect that the MV beta is not statistically different from the LPM beta. On the other hand if the returns for a country are non-normal we expect the LPM beta to be statistically significantly different from the MV beta.

The Bera-Jarque statistic is a popular test proposed by Jarque and Bera (1980) and measures departures from normality in terms of the third and fourth moments, that is, skewness and kurtosis, of the data. Letting μ_3 and μ_4 be the third and fourth (central) moments of a time series x_t, and defining $m_3 = (\mu_3 \setminus \sigma^3)$ and $m_4 = (\mu_4 \setminus \sigma^4)$ to be the moment measures of skewness and kurtosis, respectively, estimators of these measures are given by

$$\hat{m}_i = \left[\left(\frac{1}{T} \Sigma x_t^i \right) \Big/ \left(\frac{1}{T} \Sigma x_t^2 \right)^{i/2} \right], \qquad i = 3, 4 \tag{13}$$

Since these estimators are asymptotically independent, the squares of their standardized forms can be added to obtain

Table 1. Summary Statistics for 17 Emerging Markets and the S&P 500
119 Monthly Return Observations: 1.1985 to 11.1994

Country	*MIN*	*MAX*	*MEAN*	*VAR*	*SKEW*	*KURT*	*B.J.*
Argentina	−1.04849	1.021948	0.022094	0.058598	0.336518	6.754254	212.59*
Brazil	−0.84526	0.450684	0.010375	0.041363	−0.56042	1.990973	18.08*
Chile	−0.21746	0.195711	0.029736	0.006342	−0.21643	−0.01013	12.94*
Colombia	−0.19301	0.31594	0.024192	0.007036	1.178897	2.668001	118.93*
Greece	−0.36827	0.442639	0.010265	0.013582	0.795129	2.789404	61.86*
India	−0.27966	0.301743	0.012706	0.009362	0.126966	0.565918	6.60*
Jordan	−0.13788	0.149677	0.002839	0.002378	0.197381	1.234628	9.49*
Korea	−0.21872	0.235739	0.01549	0.00672	0.279991	−0.07627	12.99*
Malaysia	−0.36608	0.189096	0.009247	0.006475	−0.98899	3.333764	41.67*
Mexico	−0.90076	0.332953	0.026854	0.020081	−2.77300	16.67084	907.17*
Nigeria	−0.82218	0.689105	−0.00298	0.019946	−0.98000	15.81867	1163.65*
Pakistan	−0.17224	0.301036	0.011513	0.004068	1.496277	6.216449	286.07*
Philippines	−0.34813	0.352089	0.030315	0.010772	−0.01184	2.423282	30.31*
Taiwan	−0.43889	0.427493	0.018516	0.021155	−0.19407	1.452471	7.90*
Thailand	−0.41282	0.284458	0.019698	0.008224	−0.90315	4.287464	45.10*
Venezuela	−0.69493	0.388916	0.008285	0.019011	−1.02612	5.538779	136.44*
Zimbabwe	−0.262	0.371423	0.014833	0.008432	0.229336	2.138225	30.00*
Market - S&P500	−0.24543	0.12378	0.008911	0.002028	−1.53315	7.99872	189.13*

Notes: Summary statistics for 17 emerging markets and the S&P 500, representing the market index. MIN and MAX are the minimum and maximum return. MEAN and VAR are the mean and variance of the returns. SKEW is the skewness, and KURT is the kurtosis of the returns. B.J. is the Bera-Jarque statistic for normality. * Denotes a significant Bera-Jarque statistic at 5% significance level, implying non-normality.

$$\left[\frac{T}{6}\hat{m}_3^2 + \frac{T}{24}(\hat{m}_4 - 3)^2\right] \sim \chi_2^2 \tag{14}$$

where ~ means asymptotically (large T) distributed as. This is the Bera-Jarque statistic given in Table 1, and has a χ^2 distribution with 2 degrees of freedom, so that large values of this statistic would flag significant departures from normality.

From Table 1 we can see that all returns, including the returns on the market portfolio, are non-normal (with 5% significance level). Theory implies that the LPM beta should be statistically different from the MV beta in all 17 cases, unless investors have quadratic utility, or returns belong to the elliptical class. In the next section we present the test results.

We also obtained autocorrelation coefficients with lags of up to 12, for the 18 countries.[6] Only Zimbabwe appears to be highly autocorrelated. Considering the rest of the 204 autocorrelation coefficients, because of type I error set at 5%, we would expect 10 significant autocorrelations. 11 significant autocorrelation coefficients are obtained. Therefore, what autocorrelation we get is probably spurious.

Of the 11 significant autocorrelations, 5 are in the first period, 2 in the third, 2 in the fourth, 1 in the fifth, and 1 in the sixth. This is not random. Therefore there is a suggestion of a small one-month autocorrelation, but probably not enough to invalidate our modeling procedure.

EMPIRICAL RESULTS AND IMPLICATIONS

For each country two regressions were performed, corresponding to the unrestricted and restricted models (6) and (11). The betas obtained as well as the F-statistic for the restriction are reported in Table 2.

In only 4 cases out of 17 tested, our previous expectations are confirmed, that is, non-normal returns lead to different betas. In two of these cases the F-statistic is significant only at 25% significance value. For Chile and Colombia the F-statistic is significant at the 5% level. In both cases the LPM beta is less than the MV beta, and in the case of Colombia the LPM beta is negative whereas the MV beta is positive. Thailand and Venezuela have betas that are different at 25% significance level. An interesting aspect of the results is that in a number of cases the betas are

Table 2. MV and LPM betas for 17 Emerging Markets
119 Monthly Return Observations: 1.1985 to 11.1994

Country	*(1) MV beta*	*(2) LPM beta*	*F-stat for difference between (1) & (2)*
Argentina	0.4133	–0.1895	0.98
Brazil	0.3450	0.2615	0.04
Chile #	0.4300	0.1832	4.47*
Colombia #	0.1232	–0.2542	3.06*
Greece	0.4361	0.4614	0.23
India	0.0570	0.0279	0.52
Jordan	0.0129	0.0758	0.54
Korea	0.1703	–0.0601	1.20
Malaysia	–0.0260	–0.0157	0.08
Mexico	1.1399	1.5906	0.62
Nigeria	0.2058	0.5759	1.07
Pakistan	–0.1138	–0.1596	0.71
Philippines	0.3074	0.0299	1.27
Taiwan	0.4850	0.2407	0.66
Thailand #	0.2397	0.0394	1.70**
Venezuela #	–0.2886	–0.5888	1.64**
Zimbabwe	–0.0981	–0.2226	0.28

Notes: * Denotes a significant F-statistic at 5% and ** at 25% significance level. # Denotes a confirmed expectation for that country, that is, significantly different betas when returns are non-normal.

"visually" quite different, but statistically not so. For example the LPM beta for Argentina is 146% smaller than its MV beta, that being 0.6, even though this difference is statistically not significant. However, the LPM beta for Chile is only 0.24 smaller than its MV beta (57% smaller), but this difference is significant at 5% level.

CONCLUSIONS

Our results, that MV betas are statistically not different from LPM betas, may seem like good news for investors, if they use any of the standard risk analysis packages (such as APT, BARRA, and QUANTEC) all of which use (implicitly/explicitly) mean-variance analysis, and all of which are based on the decomposition of risk (variance) into sub-factors. However, our analysis is inconclusive as is often the case with nonlinear modeling. Our results are predicated on the maintained hypothesis that the data generating process (DGP) is that given by equation (10). Under (10) the equivalence of MV and LPM, taken together with non-normality, imply quadratic utility and/or elliptical distributions. However, if (10) were not to hold, that is, some other process generated the conditional distribution of emerging market returns given the U.S. returns, then our search would need to begin anew and our results could be different.

Also, an interesting result of this study is the observation that "visual" difference between betas does not necessarily imply statistical difference, and hence there exists a need for devising statistical methods like the ones in this paper to test the validity of the different models.

Finally, a precise description of what distributions validate the CAPM is discussed in Ingersoll (1987). Essentially the requirement, bar common factors, is that the idiosyncratic components of the asset returns are elliptical. Devising a test for ellipticity is complicated. Our simple procedure can be seen as a method to test that the returns distributions satisfy the ellipticity requirement. Our conclusions suggest, even with the above *caveats*, that the CAPM is a robust model and applicable to emerging markets.

NOTES

1. MV-CAPM still holds for return distributions that are members of the elliptical distribution family (see Ingersoll, 1987, p. 104–113). This condition may still be too restrictive.
2. Throughout this paper we have restricted our analysis to what Bawa and Lindenberg refer to as second order LPM. Given this, their pricing model and Hogan and Warren's pricing model are equivalent.
3. The target here is the risk free rate. Also note that we are using excess returns and that as a result, the regression model does not have an intercept term.
4. The betas obtained from (6) were compared to the ones that were obtained from (5). They were found to be the same.
5. The formula used for skewness is

$$\frac{n}{(n-1)(n-2)} \sum \left(\frac{x_i - \bar{x}}{s} \right)^3$$

and the formula used for kurtosis is

$$\left[\frac{n(n+1)}{(n-1)(n-2)(n-3)} \sum \left(\frac{x_i - \bar{x}}{s} \right)^4 \right] - \frac{3(n-1)^2}{(n-2)(n-3)}$$

6. The results are available from the authors on request.

REFERENCES

Bawa, V.S. 1975. "Optimal Rules for Ordering Uncertain Prospects." *Journal of Financial Economics* 2: 95–121.

Bawa, V.S., S. Brown, and R. Klein. 1981. "Asymmetric Response Asset Pricing Models: Testable Alternatives to Mean-Variance." Mimeo.

Bawa, V.S., and E.B. Lindenberg. 1977. "Capital Market Equilibrium in a Mean-Lower Partial Moment Framework." *Journal of Financial Economics* 5: 189–200.

Fama, E. 1965. "Portfolio Analysis in Stable Paretian Markets." *Management Science* 11: 404–419.

Fishburn, P.C. 1977. "Mean-Risk Analysis with Risk Associated with Below-Target Returns." *American Economic Review* 67: 116–126.

Hanoch, G., and H. Levy. 1969. "The Efficiency Analysis of Choices Involving Risk." *Review of Economic Studies* 36: 335–346.

Harlow, W.V., and R.K.S. Rao. 1989. "Asset Pricing in a Generalized Mean-Lower Partial Moment Framework: Theory and Evidence." *Journal of Financial & Quantitative Analysis* 24: 285–311.

Harvey, C.R. 1995. "Predictable Risk and Returns in Emerging Markets." *Review of Financial Studies* 8: 773–816.

Hogan, W., and J. Warren. 1974. "Toward the Development of an Equilibrium Capital Market Model Based on Semivariance." *Journal of Financial & Quantitative Analysis* 9: 1–12.

Ingersoll, J. 1987. *Theory of Financial Decision Making*. Totowa, NJ: Rowman and Littlefield.

Jarque, C.M., and A.K. Bera. 1980. "Efficient Tests for Normality, Homoskedasticity and Serial Dependence of Regression Residuals." *Economic Letters* 6: 255–259.

Lintner, J. 1969. "The Aggregation of Investor's Diverse Judgments and Preferences in Purely Competitive Security Markets." *Journal of Financial & Quantitative Analysis* 3: 347–400.

Mao, J. 1970. "Methods of Capital Budgeting: E-V vs. E-S." *Journal of Financial & Quantitative Analysis* 4: 657–675.

Markowitz, H. 1952. "Portfolio Selection." *Journal of Finance* 7: 77–91.

———. 1959. *Portfolio Selection*. New York: John Wiley and Sons Inc.

Mossin, J. 1966. "Equilibrium in a Capital Asset Market." *Econometrica* 34: 768–783.

Pratt, J.W. 1964. "Risk Aversion in the Small and in the Large." *Econometrica* 32: 122–136.

Sharpe, W.F. 1963. "A Simplified Model for Portfolio Analysis." *Management Science*: 277–293.

———. 1964. "Capital Asset Prices: A Theory of Market Equilibrium under Conditions of Risk." *Journal of Finance* 29: 425–442.

Tobin, J. 1958. "Liquidity Preference as a Behaviour Toward Risk." *Review of Economic Studies* 25: 65–86.

RISK AVERSION AND THE EFFICIENT MARKETS MODEL FOR STOCK PRICES: EVIDENCE FROM THE ATHENS STOCK EXCHANGE

Dimitris G. Kirikos

ABSTRACT

The statistical and economic importance of the efficient markets model with varying discount factors is tested on monthly data from the Athens Stock Exchange over the period 1981–1993. The time-series properties of the relevant information variables are determined by means of formal statistical tests and the relationship between stock price volatility and risk aversion is studied for admissible values of the Arrow-Pratt measure of relative risk aversion. In sharp contrast with existing evidence from well-organized markets, the results show a remarkably accurate fit of the model.

INTRODUCTION

The present value model for stock prices is among those simple stochastic dynamic models that have several important features. It is well-grounded on economic theory, it assumes that investors act in a rational manner, and it can be tested by means of alternative econometric techniques. However, there is considerable

Research in International Business and Finance, Supplement 1, pages 279–295.

ISBN: 0-7623-0110-4

evidence against the empirical relevance of the present value formula for stock prices, also known as the efficient markets model.

Early empirical rejections of the model, based on variance bounds tests, were attributed to fads that alter market psychology (Shiller 1981) and to inadequate testing procedures (LeRoy and Porter 1981).[1] Furthermore, several studies have identified the underlying assumption of risk neutrality as the main reason for the inability of the efficient markets model to explain the behavior of stock prices. For example, Lucas (1978) and LeRoy and LaCivita (1981) have shown that the variability of stock prices is an increasing function of the degree of risk aversion, while Salyer (1988) has demonstrated that stock price volatility depends on the autocorrelation properties of the dividend growth rate as well. Following this line, Grossman and Shiller (1981) showed that, indeed, under preferences that exhibit a coefficient of relative risk aversion of four, a series of perfect foresight prices reproduced the movements of actual stock prices fairly well over a 90-year period.

More recently, Campbell and Shiller (1987, 1988) suggested a testing procedure that accounts for the time-series properties of real asset prices and dividends. Specifically, they showed that the presence of common stochastic trends in stock prices and dividends is an implication of the present value model when each of these series has a unit root, and, therefore, the theory must be tested by using an error-correction model for dividends to generate expectations. This approach is useful not only for testing the model statistically,[2] but also for evaluating its *economic* significance on the basis of deviations from observed behavior measured by an appropriate metric. In this context, Campbell and Shiller (1987) provided evidence against the efficient markets model for stock prices, using annual data from the New York Stock Exchange (NYSE) covering the period 1871–1986, while Kirikos (1994) tested the model with varying discount factors on NYSE monthly data over the period 1974–1990 and found a poor fit for those values of the Arrow-Pratt measure of relative risk aversion for which the time-series implications of the theory are satisfied.

Nevertheless, the evidence against the present value model for stock prices with constant or varying discount factors may be misleading mainly because the description of the information variables by a vector autoregression (VAR) process may not be appropriate for a particular data set.[3] Therefore, before a conclusion is reached with regard to the statistical and economic relevance of the present value theory for the stock market, it would be very useful to reexamine its significance using a different data set.[4]

In this paper the efficient markets model with discount factors that vary over time (i.e., investors are risk averse) is tested on monthly data from an emerging market, namely the Athens Stock Exchange, over the period May 1981 to December 1993. The time series properties of the relevant information variables are determined by means of formal statistical tests and the relationship between stock price volatility and risk aversion is studied for admissible values of the Arrow-Pratt measure of relative risk aversion. The theory is presented in the second section and the empirical methodology is discussed in the third section. The empirical results reported in the fourth section reveal a remarkably accurate fit of the model, in sharp contrast with existing evidence from other markets. The last section contains final remarks.

RISK AVERSION AND STOCK PRICES[5]

Consider the following Euler equation resulting from the dynamic program of an infinitely-lived representative agent who maximizes discounted expected utility by allocating a finite endowment between consumption and share holdings in each period (see Lucas 1978; Mehra and Prescott 1985; Salyer 1988):

$$p_t\, u'(c_t) = \beta\, E_t u'(c_{t+1}) \cdot (p_{t+1} + d_{t+1}), \tag{1}$$

where p is the price in terms of consumption of an equity share, c denotes consumption, β $(0 < \beta < 1)$ is the subjective discount factor (the inverse of one plus the rate of time preference), d is real dividend, $u'(.)$ is the marginal utility of consumption, and $E_t = E(. \mid I_t)$ denotes expectations based on the full information set I_t which is available at time t. Given the recursive structure of the agent's problem, the interpretation of equation (1) is that, in equilibrium the utility foregone due to the purchase of an equity share in any given period should be equal to the discounted utility derived from expected consumption next period.

Forward iteration of equation (1) gives:

$$p_t\, u'(c_t) = \sum_{i=1}^{\infty} \beta^i\, E_t u'(c_{t+i}) \cdot d_{t+i}\,. \tag{2}$$

If we set $\theta = \beta/(1-\beta)$, that is, θ is the inverse of the rate of time preference, then equation (2) can be rewritten as:

$$p_t\, u'(c_t) = \theta(1-\beta) \sum_{i=0}^{\infty} \beta^i\, E_t u'(c_{t+1+i}) \cdot d_{t+1+i}\,, \tag{3}$$

and upon subtraction of $\theta u'(c_t) d_t$ from both sides of equation (3), we obtain:

$$(p_t - \theta d_t) \cdot u'(c_t) = \theta \sum_{i=0}^{\infty} \beta^i\, E_t\, \Delta u'(c_{t+1+i}) \cdot d_{t+1+i}\,, \tag{4}$$

where Δ is the difference operator $(\Delta x_t = x_t - x_{t-1})$.

Furthermore, let us assume that the utility function is of the constant relative risk aversion form:

$$u(c) = \frac{c^{1-\gamma}}{1-\gamma}, \gamma \neq 1$$

$$\ln c, \gamma = 1 \tag{5}$$

where γ is the coefficient of relative risk aversion. Thus, equations (4) and (5) give:

$$(p_t - \theta d_t) \cdot c_t^{-\gamma} = \theta \sum_{i=0}^{\infty} \beta^i E_t \Delta c_{t+1+i}^{-\gamma} \cdot d_{t+1+i}, \tag{6}$$

or, by defining $S_t = (p_t - \theta d_t)c_t^{-\gamma}$ and $y_t = d_t c_t^{-\gamma}$,[6]

$$S_t = \theta \sum_{i=0}^{\infty} \beta^i E_t \Delta y_{t+1+i}. \tag{7}$$

As it happens, equation (7) is more general than Campbell and Shiller's (1987) case of risk neutrality, which obtains here for $\gamma = 0$. Nevertheless, if $p_t c_t^{-\gamma}$ and $d_t c_t^{-\gamma}$ are difference stationary, then the series S_t, the analogue of what is referred to as the spread by Campbell and Shiller, must be stationary as equation (7) shows. That is, consumption-weighted asset prices and dividends must be cointegrated with cointegrating vector $[1 - \theta]$.

EMPIRICAL METHODOLOGY

Equation (7) has little empirical content because it includes expectations of future changes in y_t based on an unavailable information set. For this reason, these conditional expectations will be replaced here by linear projections on observed information, that is, a subset $\mathbf{\Phi}_t$ of the full information set I_t. In particular, it is assumed that available information is summarized by current and past values of the vector $\mathbf{x}_t = [\Delta y_t \; S_t]'$. This is a rather large information set because it includes current and past stock prices, that is, in effect it includes all information used by investors.

Now let the vector time series $\mathbf{x}_t$ have the following VAR representation:

$$\begin{bmatrix} \Delta y_t \\ S_t \end{bmatrix} = \begin{bmatrix} \pi(L) & \rho(L) \\ \psi(L) & \omega(L) \end{bmatrix} \begin{bmatrix} \Delta y_{t-1} \\ S_{t-1} \end{bmatrix} + \begin{bmatrix} u_{1t} \\ u_{2t} \end{bmatrix} \tag{8}$$

where $\pi(L)$, $\rho(L)$, $\psi(L)$, and $\omega(L)$ are polynomials in the lag or backshift operator L, all of order k. The VAR process (8) can be equivalently written in the companion form:

$$\begin{bmatrix} \Delta y_t \\ \cdot \\ \Delta y_{t-k+1} \\ S_t \\ \cdot \\ S_{t-k+1} \end{bmatrix} = \begin{bmatrix} \pi_1 & \cdot & \cdot & \pi_k & \rho_1 & \cdot & \cdot & \rho_k \\ 1 & 0 & \cdot & 0 & 0 & \cdot & \cdot & 0 \\ \cdot & \cdot & \cdot & \cdot & \cdot & \cdot & \cdot & \cdot \\ 0 & \cdot & 1 & 0 & 0 & \cdot & \cdot & 0 \\ \psi_1 & \cdot & \cdot & \psi_k & \omega_1 & \cdot & \cdot & \omega_k \\ 0 & \cdot & \cdot & 0 & 1 & 0 & \cdot & 0 \\ \cdot & \cdot & \cdot & \cdot & \cdot & \cdot & \cdot & \cdot \\ 0 & \cdot & \cdot & 0 & 0 & \cdot & 1 & 0 \end{bmatrix} \begin{bmatrix} \Delta y_{t-1} \\ \cdot \\ \Delta y_{t-k} \\ S_{t-1} \\ \cdot \\ S_{t-k} \end{bmatrix} + \begin{bmatrix} u_{1t} \\ 0 \\ \cdot \\ 0 \\ u_{2t} \\ 0 \\ \cdot \\ 0 \end{bmatrix} \tag{9}$$

or

$$\mathbf{z}_t = \mathbf{A}\mathbf{z}_{t-1} + \mathbf{v}_t, \tag{10}$$

where $\mathbf{z}_t$, $\mathbf{v}_t$, and the matrix of coefficients $\mathbf{A}$ are defined implicitly in (9) and (10).

The first-order companion form (10) is very convenient for taking conditional expectations since $E(\mathbf{z}_{t+i} \mid \mathbf{\Phi}_t) = \mathbf{A}^i\mathbf{z}_t$, $i > 0$, where $\mathbf{\Phi}_t$ is the econometrician's information set which contains the history through time t of the information variables included in the vector $\mathbf{z}_t$. Thus, equation (7) can be usefully written as:

$$\mathbf{e}_2' \mathbf{z}_t = \theta \sum_{i=0}^{\infty} \beta^i \mathbf{e}_1' \mathbf{A}^{i+1} \mathbf{z}_t = \theta \mathbf{e}_1' \mathbf{A}[\mathrm{I} - \beta\mathbf{A}]^{-1} \mathbf{z}_t, \tag{11}$$

where $\mathbf{e}_1$ and $\mathbf{e}_2$ are $2k \times 1$ vectors (k being the VAR lag length) with zeroes everywhere except for rows 1 and k+1, respectively, and unity there. Note that the infinite sum in equation (11) must converge because the information variables are stationary.

The reason for the choice of an error correction model for y_t, instead of a VAR in the first differences of $p_t c_t^{-\gamma}$ and $d_t c_t^{-\gamma}$, should now be clear. If the differences of two cointegrated variables were included in the information vector, that would impose a large number of unit roots on the system and a finite VAR representation would not exist, or, more formally, the Wold representation would not be invertible.

The implications of the present value model with varying discount factors for the parameters of our error-correction model can be easily derived from equation (11). If the asset pricing theory is correct, equation (11) must hold for any vector time series $\mathbf{z}_t$, and, therefore, it must be true that:

$$\mathbf{e}_2' = \theta \mathbf{e}_1' \mathbf{A}[\mathrm{I} - \beta\mathbf{A}]^{-1}. \tag{12}$$

Equation (12) represents a set of $2k$ cross-equation restrictions on the parameters of the error-correction model for y_t. These can be tested by means of the Wald test statistic which has an asymptotic χ^2 distribution with degrees of freedom equal to the number of restrictions in equation (12) (see Amemiya 1985, pp. 141–146). More precisely, letting $\lambda' = \mathbf{e}_2' - \theta\mathbf{e}_1'\mathbf{A}(\mathbf{I} - \beta\mathbf{A})^{-1}$ denote deviations from equation (12) and $\mathbf{b}$ the vector of parameters in the VAR with variance-covariance matrix Var($\mathbf{b}$), we have:

$$W = \lambda' \left[\frac{\partial \lambda}{\partial \mathbf{b}'} \mathrm{Var}(\mathbf{b}) \frac{\partial \lambda}{\partial \mathbf{b}} \right]^{-1} \lambda \rightarrow \chi^2 (2k), \tag{13}$$

where W is the Wald statistic. The partial derivatives in (13) involve highly non-linear expressions in $\mathbf{b}$, but they can be calculated numerically.

Nevertheless, a statistical rejection of the null hypothesis leaves us with no alternative theory as the model is tested against an unrestricted VAR model which presumably describes the dynamics of the information variables. In addition, a statistical rejection of the cross-equation restrictions is not very informative with regard to the economic importance of the underlying theory, that is, it does not reveal whether it is due to transitory deviations from the model or not.

Fortunately, the VAR approach provides measures of the economic significance of the model, which can be used to test against the alternative that asset prices are too choppy.[7] As suggested by Campbell and Shiller (1987), such measures are the correlation and the variance ratio of the actual spread S_t and the theoretical spread S_t' given by the right-hand side of equation (11). If these are not significantly different from one, then S_t' must trace the movements of the actual series S_t reasonably well in spite of a possible statistical rejection of the underlying restrictions.[8]

EMPIRICAL RESULTS

The statistical and economic importance of the efficient markets model with varying discount factors is tested here on monthly data from the Athens Stock Exchange covering the period May 1981 to December 1993 (152 observations). The composite stock price index of the Athens Stock Exchange, divided by the general wholesale price index, is used as the series of real stock prices. A dividend index is not available, and, therefore, one is constructed by following Standard & Poor's methodology (see Standard & Poor's *Dividend Record*). First, a dividend-yield series is computed by dividing the latest known annual aggregate cash dividends by the monthly aggregate market value of the stocks included in the composite price index.[9,10] The resulting series is then multiplied by the composite stock price index to obtain a nominal dividend series. The latter, divided by the general wholesale price index, is taken to be the series of real dividends. Consumption is proxied by the de-seasonalized index of industrial production because monthly data on the former are not available. This is justified by the requirement that a stationary equilibrium in intertemporal asset pricing models be characterized by market clearing, that is, the endowment is consumed. A detailed description of the data and their sources is given in the Appendix.

To obtain empirical results, we need specific values for the coefficient of relative risk aversion γ and the subjective discount factor β. Following Mehra and Prescott (1985), γ is allowed to vary within the reasonable range from zero to ten, but admissible values are those for which the series $p_t c_t^{-\gamma}$ and $d_t c_t^{-\gamma}$ are cointegrated as predicted by the theory. Then, estimates of $\beta = \theta/(1+\theta)$ are obtained from estimates of the cointegrating parameter θ.

A necessary preliminary step is to test for unit roots in the series $p_t c_t^{-\gamma}$ and $d_t c_t^{-\gamma}$ as our empirical results are valid only when they are difference stationary. The Phillips-Perron test (Phillips and Perron 1988) was conducted for all integer values of γ in the range [0 10] and the results are reported in Table 1. The null hypothesis

Table 1. Phillips-Perron Test for Unit Roots

		With Trend		*Without Trend*	
γ	*Truncation Lag*	4	13	4	13
0		−2.543	−2.452	−3.181	−2.440
		−2.792	−2.711	−2.189	−2.198
1		−2.563	−2.463	−1.536	−1.535
		−2.772	−2.697	−2.169	−2.155
2		−2.600	−2.493	−1.498	−1.586
		−2.788	−2.707	−2.267	−2.268
3		−2.655	−2.545	−1.659	−1.763
		−2.838	−2.742	−2.399	−2.426
4		−2.727	−2.623	−1.877	−1.983
		−2.918	−2.805	−2.548	−2.612
5		−2.817	−2.731	−2.133	−2.228
		−3.024	−2.896	−2.711	−2.810
6		−2.926	−2.872	−2.424	−2.488
		−3.154	−3.016	−2.884	−3.015
7		−3.054	−3.048	−2.743	−2.755
		−3.306	−3.164	−3.068	−3.222
8		−3.205	−3.262	−3.085	−3.020
		−3.478	−3.341	−3.262	−3.429
9		−3.380	−3.514	−3.441	−3.279
		−3.670	−3.544	−3.467	−3.633
10		−3.581	−3.805	−3.803	−3.529
		−3.882	−3.773	−3.683	−3.833

Notes: For each γ the first row contains the test statistic for the series $p_t c_t^{-\gamma}$ and the second row for the series $d_t c_t^{-\gamma}$. The truncation lag gives the maximum order of non-zero autocorrelations of the differenced series and is selected according to Schwert (1989) as maximum = int{12(T/100)$^{1/4}$} and minimum = int{4(T/100)$^{1/4}$}, where T is the sample size. Asymptotic critical values for testing the null hypothesis of a unit root are as follows (Fuller 1976, p. 373). With Trend: −3.96, −3.41, −3.12; Without Trend: −3.43, −2.86, −2.57 at the 1%, 5%, and 10% significance levels, respectively.

of a unit root is rejected when γ is 7 or higher, and, thus, only integer values of γ in the range [0 6] will be considered below.[11]

It is also important to test for common stochastic trends in consumption-weighted prices and dividends, because cointegration of these series is an implication of the asset pricing theory. Johansen's likelihood ratio test (Johansen 1988, 1991) for the full sample period is reported in Table 2, panel A, and it can be used to test the null hypothesis that there are at most r linearly independent cointegrating vectors in a VAR system with independent Gaussian errors. Unlike other tests for cointegration the Johansen test is robust, considers all cointegrating vectors, and provides maximum likelihood estimates (MLE) of these vectors as a byproduct of the testing procedure.[12]

Table 2. Johansen's Test for Cointegration of $p_t c_t^{-\gamma}$ and $d_t c_t^{-\gamma}$

A. Full sample 5/81–12/93

	Without Trend		*With Trend*			
γ	*r = 0* *(19.96)*	*r = 1* *(9.24)*	*r = 0* *(15.41)*	*r = 1* *(3.76)*	*Estimated* θ	β
0	18.787*	1.343	18.552	1.137	—	—
1	20.532	1.405*	20.284	1.240	45.437	0.978
2	23.583	1.709*	23.320	1.601	46.907	0.979
3	27.088	2.232*	26.811	2.173	48.232	0.979
4	30.729	2.866*	30.427	2.839	49.379	0.980
5	34.471	3.570*	34.126	3.561	50.271	0.980
6	38.329	4.372*	37.923	4.370	50.820	0.981

B. Full sample excluding observations 12/88–4/90

	Without Trend		*With Trend*	
γ	*r = 0* *(19.96)*	*r = 1* *(9.24)*	*r = 0* *(15.41)*	*r = 1* *(3.76)*
0	18.332*	1.731	18.096	1.532
1	20.250	1.692*	20.008	1.519
2	23.207	1.706*	22.935	1.555
3	26.717	1.781*	26.405	1.656
4	30.212	1.923*	29.865	1.829
5	33.362	2.122*	32.983	2.060
6	36.112	2.366*	35.697	2.331

Notes: Computations are based on an error-correction model with 17 lags. The null hypothesis is that there are at most r linearly independent cointegrating vectors and critical values at the 5% significance level (see Osterwald-Lenum 1992) are given below r. θ is obtained from the MLE of the cointegrating vector and β is the corresponding value for the subjective discount factor. An * indicates that the hypothesis is not rejected and there one should stop when reading from left to right (see note 14).

Results are reported for the null that there is a linear trend in the data and for sub-hypothesis that there is not, and they are based on an error-correction model with 17 lags.[13] As suggested by Johansen (1992), for each r one should read from left to right and stop when the null hypothesis is not rejected.[14] Thus, the results of Table 2, panel A, provide evidence of one cointegrating vector and no linear trend when the coefficient of relative risk aversion γ is in the range [1 6]. For the case of risk neutrality ($\gamma = 0$) the hypothesis of zero cointegrating vectors is not rejected.[15] Thus, if there is any truth in the efficient markets model, investors should be risk averse because the implication of the model, that consumption-weighted stock prices and dividends are cointegrated, is satisfied only for $\gamma > 0$.[16] The degree of risk aversion is determined by additional tests below.

Following the methodological approach of Arshanapalli and Doukas (1993), who use cointegration tests and error-correction modeling to study the relevance of linkages and dynamic interactions among major stock markets, Johansen's test for cointegration is also conducted for the full sample period but excluding observations from December 1988 to April 1990. The latter period included exceptional political events in Greece (see note 19) which might have affected our cointegration tests. However, the statistics reported in panel B of Table 2 reproduce the results obtained without excluding the politically turbulent period (panel A).[17]

Given the admissible range of the Arrow-Pratt measure of relative risk aversion suggested by the cointegration tests of Table 2, further tests of the present value model with varying discount factors are reported in Table 3. Those are based on

Table 3. Tests of Model Restrictions and Price Volatility Full Sample 5/81–12/93

γ	*VAR Lag*	*Wald Test*	$Cor(S_t, S'_t)$	$Var(S_t)/Var(S'_t)$
1	9	83.687 (0.0000)	0.988 (0.0067)	1.459 (0.4501)
	12	90.601 (0.0000)	0.988 (0.0078)	1.560 (0.4674)
2	9	95.686 (0.0000)	0.986 (0.0075)	1.341 (0.3501)
	12	89.414 (0.0000)	0.987 (0.0074)	1.397 (0.4003)
3	9	103.780 (0.0000)	0.984 (0.0079)	1.261 (0.2828)
	12	87.617 (0.0000)	0.986 (0.0077)	1.255 (0.3442)
4	9	104.461 (0.0000)	0.983 (0.0079)	1.200 (0.2383)
	12	88.122 (0.0000)	0.984 (0.0081)	1.142 (0.2961)
5	9	99.704 (0.0000)	0.982 (0.0079)	1.152 (0.2083)
	12	93.116 (0.0000)	0.982 (0.0083)	1.060 (0.2547)
6	9	95.607 (0.0000)	0.982 (0.0078)	1.114 (0.1876)
	12	103.547 (0.0000)	0.981 (0.0081)	1.004 (0.2195)

Notes: Numbers in parentheses next to the Wald test statistics are marginal significance levels (p-values) whereas those next to the correlations and the variance ratios are standard errors. In each case the Wald test statistic has an asymptotic χ^2 distribution with 2×(VAR Lag) degrees of freedom. Wald tests and standard errors are computed numerically by varying each parameter by 10^{-5}.

estimates of a VAR process[18] for the demeaned series Δy_t ($y_t = d_t c_t^{-\gamma}$) and $S_t = (p_t - \theta d_t)c_t^{-\gamma}$, where the spread S_t is derived using the MLEs of θ from Table 2, panel A.

The Wald test, reported in the third column of Table 3, rejects the cross-equation restrictions (12) in all cases. However, volatility tests based on the correlation and the variance ratio of actual and theoretical spreads, S_t and S'_t, suggest that the statistical rejections of the cross-equation restrictions are most likely due to transitory deviations from the model. Indeed, the correlation and the variance ratio

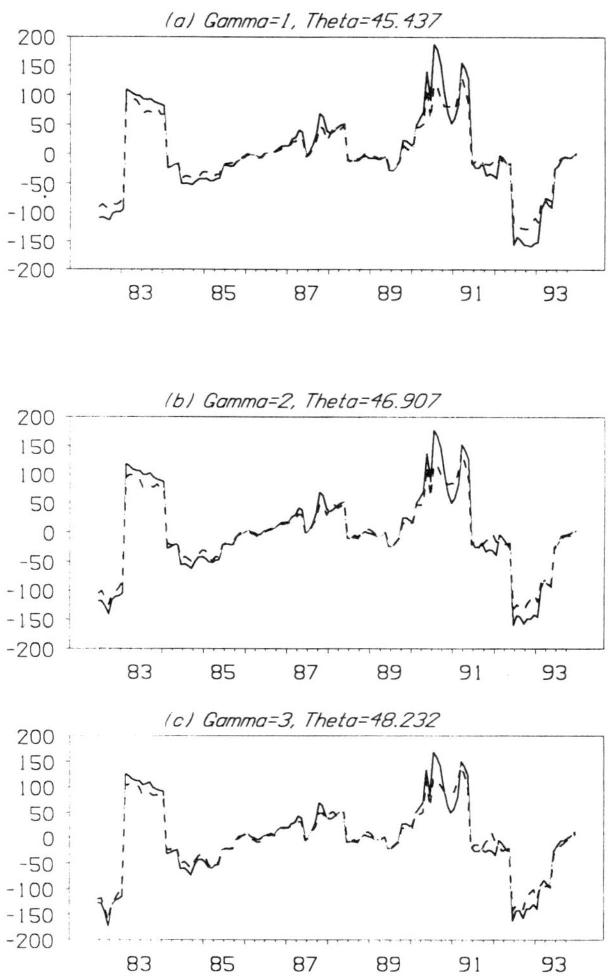

Figure 1. Spread (solid) & Theoretical Spread (dashed), Lags = 12

of S_t and S'_t, reported in the fourth and fifth columns of Table 3, are not significantly different from one. That is, differences between S_t and S'_t must be due to sampling error. Furthermore, the values of the variance ratio of actual and theoretical spreads show a monotonic relationship between risk aversion and stock price volatility and suggest that investors are strongly risk averse since the variance ratio is close to one when γ is 5 or 6.

The above results are verified by Figures 1 and 2 which depict the actual spread S_t (solid line) and the theoretical spread S'_t, that is, the unrestricted VAR forecast

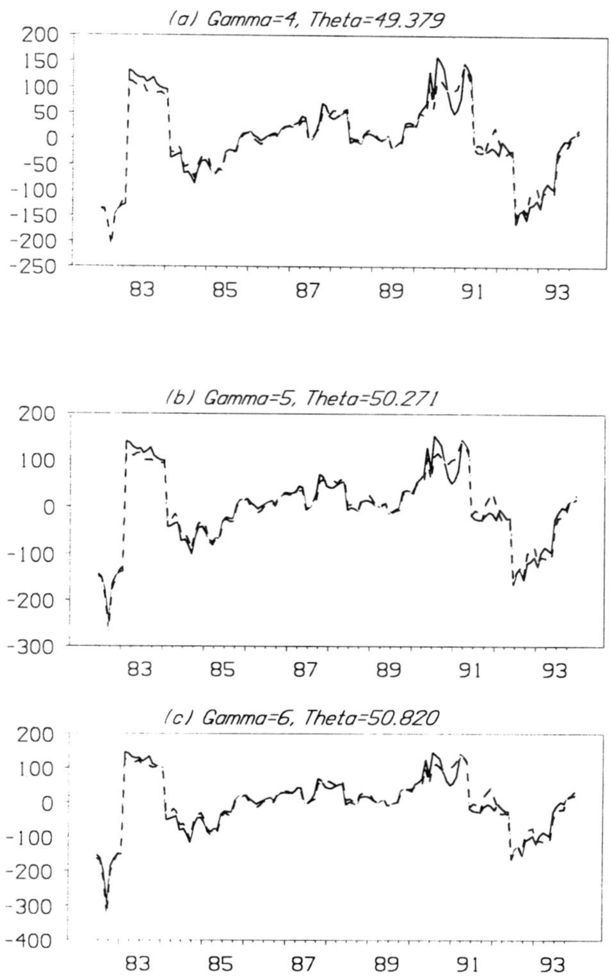

Figure 2. Spread (solid) & Theoretical Spread (dashed), Lags = 12

Table 4. Tests of Model Restrictions and Price Volatility Subsample 5/81–11/88

γ	*VAR Lag*	*Wald Test*	$Cor(S_t, S'_t)$	$Var(S_t)/Var(S'_t)$
1	9	18.573 (0.4185)	0.991 (0.0102)	1.016 (0.2142)
	12	17.809 (0.8121)	0.990 (0.0138)	1.022 (0.2175)
2	9	17.678 (0.4770)	0.993 (0.0086)	1.045 (0.2136)
	12	18.984 (0.7528)	0.993 (0.0103)	1.036 (0.2143)
3	9	17.210 (0.5087)	0.995 (0.0064)	1.073 (0.2114)
	12	22.357 (0.5579)	0.994 (0.0087)	1.034 (0.2040)
4	9	17.099 (0.5163)	0.996 (0.0044)	1.091 (0.2072)
	12	28.591 (0.2358)	0.993 (0.0082)	1.019 (0.1880)
5	9	17.659 (0.4783)	0.996 (0.0036)	1.100 (0.2019)
	12	39.326 (0.0252)	0.991 (0.0076)	1.001 (0.1707)
6	9	19.091 (0.3862)	0.997 (0.0040)	1.099 (0.1969)
	12	55.792 (0.0002)	0.990 (0.0071)	0.984 (0.1558)

Notes: See notes in Table 3.

of the present value of all future changes in consumption-weighted dividends (dashed line). These series are displayed for the admissible values of γ and the corresponding estimated cointegrating parameter θ. Except for a short period in 1989–1990, observed differences between S_t and S'_t are small and they can be conveniently attributed to sampling error. Thus, future excess stock returns are not likely to be predictable (see note 8) and the efficient markets model seems to be economically important when investors' risk averse behavior is taken into account.

Figures 1 and 2 suggest that the statistical rejections of the cross-equation restrictions implied by the asset pricing theory may be due to transitory deviations which occurred in the later period of our sample.[19] For this reason, tests were also conducted for two equal overlapping subperiods and the results are reported in Tables 4 and 5. Specifically, the tests reported in Table 4 are based on data that cover the period May 1981 to November 1988 while those in Table 5 are based on data from June 1986 to December 1993. Both subsamples are of the same size (91 observations).

Apparently, the model performs very well in the earlier subperiod where, as the Wald test shows, the cross-equation restrictions are not rejected at high levels of confidence in all but two cases. By contrast, when observations after 1988 are included the same restrictions are strongly rejected for all values of the coefficient of relative risk aversion γ. In addition, the correlation and the variance ratio of S_t and S'_t are not statistically different from unity and that verifies the superior performance of the model in the first subperiod. Finally, as in the case of the full

Table 5. Tests of Model Restrictions and Price Volatility Subsample 6/86–12/93

γ	*VAR Lag*	*Wald Test*	$Cor(S_t, S'_t)$	$Var(S_t)/Var(S'_t)$
1	9	111.310 (0.0000)	0.969 (0.0249)	2.406 (1.2506)
	12	129.114 (0.0000)	0.964 (0.0290)	2.396 (1.0772)
2	9	123.799 (0.0000)	0.964 (0.0259)	2.142 (0.9932)
	12	125.395 (0.0000)	0.963 (0.0283)	2.154 (0.9788)
3	9	140.987 (0.0000)	0.953 (0.0292)	1.986 (0.8059)
	12	122.045 (0.0000)	0.959 (0.0294)	1.945 (0.8806)
4	9	154.978 (0.0000)	0.942 (0.0327)	1.857 (0.6781)
	12	121.464 (0.0000)	0.954 (0.0314)	1.752 (0.7859)
5	9	164.099 (0.0000)	0.931 (0.0361)	1.731 (0.5885)
	12	125.683 (0.0000)	0.948 (0.0347)	1.592 (0.6977)
6	9	170.121 (0.0000)	0.922 (0.0396)	1.612 (0.5228)
	12	135.261 (0.0000)	0.942 (0.0393)	1.468 (0.6188)

Notes: See notes in Table 3.

sample, the results for the two overlapping subperiods point to a value of 5 or 6 for γ.

CONCLUDING REMARKS

The results obtained in this study are in sharp contrast with the received evidence on the present value theory of stock prices in well-organized markets. When investors are risk averse, the model with varying discount factors seems to explain the movements of stock prices in the Athens Stock Exchange with remarkable accuracy over the period 1981–1993. Moreover, the evidence suggests that observed deviations from the asset pricing theory around 1989–1990, a period of political instability in Greece, can be conveniently characterized as transitory. Thus, under risk averse behavior, the efficient markets model is economically significant for an emerging market.

Unlike previous studies (Shiller 1981; LeRoy and Porter 1981; Campbell and Shiller 1987), here investors are assumed to be risk averse and this implies that discount factors vary over time. Nevertheless, risk averse behavior of market participants does not make the validity of the model universal since it fails to explain the volatility of stock prices in a developed market (Kirikos 1994). Even though it would be misleading to conclude that risk aversion does not affect the movements of stock prices, one can safely assume that risk aversion is not the major cause of price volatility in well-organized and developed markets.

Emerging markets seem to operate somewhat differently.[20] The results reported in this paper suggest that risk is a major concern for investment decisions in a less organized market where the time-series implications of the theory are satisfied for relatively high degrees of risk aversion. Possible explanations for this include a deficient institutional setting and lack of instruments for hedging financial risks. In particular, a securities depository was instituted in the Athens Stock Exchange in 1990 while the system of electronic transactions did not operate before 1992. Such operating developments, which have long characterized well-organized markets, are necessary for fast and secure clearance of trades and eliminate risks associated with slow and inefficient transaction processing. In addition, new operating rules, which reduce government control over the Securities and Exchange Commission, were introduced only recently with a view to enhancing the efficiency and trustworthiness of the commission.

The development of a secondary market for government bonds and the introduction of forward transactions, market making, and derivatives should also help increase the scope for efficient risk management and thus smooth stock price movements.[21] The lack of such instruments until now seems to increase substantially the effects of risk averse behavior on stock price volatility, as our empirical results suggest.

By and large, emerging capital markets are characterized by small numbers of traded stocks and investors and by a low volume of transactions, which make them vulnerable to exogenous shocks. The effects of such shocks appear to be magnified by the behavior of investors who place little confidence in the organization of the market and who do not have access to alternative instruments to cover their positions.

Finally, it should be noted that the empirical results of this paper are dependent on the specification of preferences and on the VAR representation of the dynamics of the information variables. However, more complicated specifications should only be expected to improve the performance of the model.

APPENDIX

Description of Data

The composite stock price index, aggregate cash dividends, and the market value of the stocks included in the price index are all taken from various issues of the *Monthly Statistical Bulletin* and the *Annual Statistical Bulletin* of the Athens Stock Exchange. A dividend index was constructed using these data as described in the fourth section. Stock prices and dividends are deflated by the general wholesale price index (base year 1980) which is compiled by the National Statistical Service of Greece and is reported in the *Monthly Statistical Bulletin* of the Bank of Greece.

Consumption is proxied by the general index of industrial production (base year 1980) which is also taken from various issues of the *Monthly Statistical Bulletin* of the Bank of Greece. The index of industrial production was de-seasonalized using a Holt-Winter linear trend model with multiplicative seasonality.

ACKNOWLEDGMENT

The author is indebted to the editor, John Doukas, for his insightful comments and suggestions on an earlier draft. Of course, the author alone is responsible for any remaining errors.

NOTES

1. In general, variance bounds tests have been criticized by LeRoy (1984) and Kleidon (1986) on the grounds that they are based on wrong variance measures. Econometric problems, such as issues of stationarity, small sample bias, and statistical power have also been noted.

2. Single-equation statistical tests are equivalent to tests of cross-equation restrictions in a multivariate context (see Abel and Mishkin 1983).

3. Cecchetti, Lam, and Mark (1990, 1993) have reported evidence in favor of a Markov switching regimes model (the Hamilton model) for consumption and dividend growth rates, using the same data as Campbell and Shiller (1987).

4. It is worth quoting from LeRoy (1984): "It is remarkable how little evidence it takes to convince many economists, even some otherwise sympathetic to magical explanations of economic phenomena, that the stock market is exempt from the same economic theory that explains the price of rutabagas" (pp. 183–184).

5. This section follows the second section in Kirikos (1994).

6. The notation of Campbell and Shiller (1987) is used in order to facilitate comparisons.

7. For the advantages of the VAR approach over equivalent single-equation statistical tests, see Baillie (1989) and Mishkin (1989).

8. The difference $S_t - S_t'$ depends on the present value of all future excess returns on stock (see Campbell and Shiller 1987).

9. The aggregate cash dividends of a given year are divided by the end-of-month aggregate market value of the relevant stocks for the 12-month period beginning in May of the next year, because dividends are announced until May. For example, for the period May 1981 to April 1982 the aggregate cash dividends of 1980 are used to obtain monthly dividend yields. This ensures that stock prices and dividends are observed together and, thus, there is no need to lag dividends by one period as in Campbell and Shiller's (1987) tests with annual data.

10. Even though ex post dividend yields for each company are published by the Athens Stock Exchange, these series do not satisfy the requirement that stock prices and dividends be concurrently observed.

11. The Phillips-Perron test was also conducted for the first differences of the series $p_t c_t^{-\gamma}$ and $d_t c_t^{-\gamma}$ and the null hypothesis of a unit root was rejected for all values of γ. These results are available from the author.

12. The MLE of the cointegrating vector is the eigenvector that corresponds to the maximum eigenvalue of the residual moment matrix whose eigenvalues are used in computing the trace statistic for cointegration.

13. The Akaike information criterion suggests 8, 9, and 17 lags for the various values of γ. The greatest lag length is selected in order to ensure white noise errors.

14. Let H_r^* denote the hypothesis of at most r cointegrating vectors and no linear trend and H_r the corresponding hypothesis when a linear trend is relevant. Then, if $\subset$ denotes the relation between hypotheses (i.e., the hypothesis to the left of $\subset$ is a sub-hypothesis of that to the right) we have the following: $H_r^* \subset H_{r+1}^*$, $H_r \subset H_{r+1}$, and $H_r^* \subset H_r$. Thus, H_1 can only be rejected if H_0^*, H_0, and H_1^* are also rejected. Similarly, H_1^* can only be rejected if H_0^* and H_0 are also rejected (see table 1 in Johansen 1992, p. 391).

15. It is worth pointing out that even with annual data from NYSE which spanned a 116-year period, over which cointegration should be prominent (see Hakkio and Rush 1991), Campbell and Shiller (1987) reported borderline evidence of cointegration for $\gamma = 0$.

16. Note that in our analytical framework risk neutrality ($\gamma = 0$) is a prerequisite for weak form efficiency, that is, for the random walk property of stock prices (Sargent 1987, p. 94). However, in accord with our results there is compelling evidence against weak form efficiency of the Greek stock market (e.g., Theodossiou, Koutmos, and Negakis 1993; Moschos and Xanthakis 1995).

17. The results do not change when Johansen's test is conducted for the subperiods May 1981–November 1988 and May 1990–December 1993, the only exception being a borderline rejection of the hypothesis of zero cointegrating vectors and no linear trend for $\gamma = 0$ over the period May 1981 to November 1988 (test statistic = 20.462, critical value = 19.96 at the 5% significance level). These results are available from the author.

18. The VAR lag length is selected by the Akaike information criterion that suggests 9 or 12 lags for the various values of γ.

19. The period 1989–1990 was characterized by political instability in Greece (three general elections in a 10-month period) whose repercussions for stock prices are apparently not captured by the asset pricing theory.

20. Pertinent empirical results are reported in Moschos and Xanthakis (1995) who find evidence of little correlation between stock price movements in the Athens Stock Exchange and in the developed markets of London and New York.

21. A detailed description of recent developments in the Athens Stock Exchange is given in Niarchos (1995).

REFERENCES

Abel, A.B., and F.S. Mishkin. 1983. "An Integrated View of Tests of Rationality, Market Efficiency and the Short-run Neutrality of Monetary Policy." *Journal of Monetary Economics* 11: 3–24.

Amemiya, T. 1985. *Advanced Econometrics*. Cambridge, MA: Harvard University Press.

Arshanapalli, B., and J. Doukas. 1993. "International Stock Market Linkages: Evidence from the Pre- and Post-October 1987 Period." *Journal of Banking and Finance* 17: 193–208.

Baillie, R.T. 1989. "Econometric Tests of Rationality and Market Efficiency." *Econometric Reviews* 8: 151–86.

Campbell, J.Y., and R.J. Shiller. 1987. "Cointegration and Tests of Present Value Models." *Journal of Political Economy* 95: 1062–88.

———. 1988. "The Dividend-Price Ratio and Expectations of Future Dividends and Discount Factors." *Review of Financial Studies* 1: 195–228.

Cecchetti, S.G., P.-S. Lam, and N.C. Mark. 1990. "Mean Reversion in Equilibrium Asset Prices." *American Economic Review* 80: 398–418.

———. 1993. "The Equity Premium and the Risk-free Rate." *Journal of Monetary Economics* 31: 21–45.

Fuller, W.A. 1976. *Introduction to Statistical Time Series*. New York: Wiley.

Grossman, S.J., and R.J. Shiller. 1981. "The Determinants of the Variability of Stock Market Prices." *American Economic Review Papers and Proceedings* 71: 222–27.

Hakkio, C.S., and M. Rush. 1991. "Cointegration: How Short is the Long-run." *Journal of International Money and Finance* 10: 571–81.

Johansen, S. 1988. "Statistical Analysis of Cointegration Vectors." *Journal of Economic Dynamics and Control* 12: 231–54.

———. 1991. "Estimation and Hypothesis Testing of Cointegration Vectors in Gaussian Vector Autoregressive Models." *Econometrica* 59: 1551–80.

———. 1992. "Determination of Cointegration Rank in the Presence of a Linear Trend." *Oxford Bulletin of Economics and Statistics* 54: 383–97.

Kirikos, D.G. 1994. "Cointegration, Risk Aversion and Real Asset Prices." *Applied Economics Letters* 1: 236–40.

Kleidon, A.W. 1986. "Variance Bounds Tests and Stock Price Valuation Models." *Journal of Political Economy* 94: 953–1001.

LeRoy, S.F. 1984. "Efficiency and the Variability of Asset Prices." *American Economic Review Papers and Proceedings* 74: 183–87.

LeRoy, S.F., and R.D. Porter. 1981. "The Present Value Relation: Tests Based on Implied Variance Bounds." *Econometrica* 49: 555–74.

LeRoy, S.F., and C.J. LaCivita. 1981. "Risk-aversion and the Dispersion of Asset Prices." *Journal of Business* 54: 535–47.

Lucas, R.E., Jr. 1978. "Asset Prices in an Exchange Economy." *Econometrica* 46: 1429–45.

Mehra, R., and E.C. Prescott. 1985. "The Equity Premium: A Puzzle." *Journal of Monetary Economics* 15: 145–61.

Mishkin, F.S. 1989. "Econometric Tests of Rationality and Market Efficiency: A Comment." *Econometric Reviews* 8: 197–200.

Moschos, D., and M. Xanthakis. 1995. "The Domestic Capital Market and the Degree of its Comovement with Developed Markets." In *The Greek Financial System*, edited by G. Provopoulos. Athens: Institute of Economic and Industrial Research.

Niarchos, N.A. 1995. "The Greek Stock Market: Current Developments and Prospects." In *The Greek Financial System*, edited by G. Provopoulos. Athens: Institute of Economic and Industrial Research.

Osterwald-Lenum, M. 1992. "A Note with Quantiles of the Asymptotic Distribution of the Maximum Likelihood Cointegration Rank Test Statistics." *Oxford Bulletin of Economics and Statistics* 54: 461–72.

Phillips, P.C.B., and P. Perron. 1988. "Testing for a Unit Root in Time Series Regression." *Biometrika* 75: 335–46.

Salyer, K.D. 1988. "Risk Aversion and Stock Price Volatility when Dividends are Difference Stationary." *Economics Letters* 28: 255–58.

Sargent, T.J. 1987. *Dynamic Macroeconomic Theory*. Cambridge, MA: Harvard University Press.

Schwert, G.W. 1989. "Tests for Unit Roots: A Monte Carlo Investigation." *Journal of Business and Economic Statistics* 7: 147–59.

Shiller, R.J. 1981. "Do Stock Prices Move Too Much to be Justified by Subsequent Changes in Dividends?" *American Economic Review* 71: 421–36.

Theodossiou, P., G. Koutmos, and C. Negakis. 1993. "The Intertemporal Relation Between the U.S. and Greek Stock Markets: A Conditional Variance Tale Analysis." *International Journal of Finance* 5: 493–504.

LIQUIDITY, STOCK RETURNS, AND OWNERSHIP STRUCTURE: AN EMPIRICAL STUDY OF THE BOMBAY STOCK EXCHANGE

Venkat R. Eleswarapu and
Chandrasekhar Krishnamurthi

ABSTRACT

We study the problem of illiquidity that afflicts the stocks listed on the Bombay Stock Exchange (BSE). Trading on a regular basis is concentrated in only a few of the more than 6,000 stocks listed on the BSE. We examine this issue by empirically looking at the characteristics of firms leading to differential levels of trading frequency and also, the resultant effect on average returns. Based on the study of a random sample of 250 firms over the five-year period—1989 to 1993, we find evidence in favor of a liquidity premium for stocks on the BSE. Also, we find trading frequency is positively related to number of shareholders and shares outstanding. In addition, the ownership structure seems to matter, with concentration in the hands of insiders and government bodies having a deleterious effect on liquidity.

Research in International Business and Finance, Supplement 1, pages 297–311.

ISBN: 0-7623-0110-4

INTRODUCTION

In recent years globalization of capital flows has led to the growing relevance of "Emerging Capital Markets." In particular, India is one of the countries with an expanding stock market that is attracting foreign funds. The Indian capital market has grown phenomenally due to the recently initiated liberalization process. For instance, between 1985 and 1992 the number of listed companies on the Bombay Stock Exchange (BSE) increased from 4,344 to 6,480. In the same period, the market value of the listed companies increased from Rs.253 billion to Rs.3,541 billion (approximately US$110 billion in 1992). As a percentage of GNP, the market capitalization of the listed companies increased from 9.7% in 1985–1986 to 57% in 1991–1992. However, the stock markets in India are plagued by severe illiquidity with trading being very infrequent and concentrated in only a few stocks.

About 85% of the trading volume on the BSE is in 90 companies that are classified as "Group A." In fact, 32% of the volume is due to only the 10 most active issues. In terms of trading frequency, Joseph (1990) estimates that only 20% of the firms trade every day. In contrast, about 25% of the listed companies do not trade even once a year. In this paper, we examine this issue empirically by looking at the characteristics of the firms leading to the differential levels of trading frequency, and the resultant effect on average returns for the stocks on the BSE.

Illiquidity as measured by the absence of continuous trading implies that there is an extreme mismatch between the available buyers and sellers at a given point in time. As early as 1968, Demsetz noted the possibility that the available pool of liquidity-motivated traders (who demand immediacy) may not arrive at the same time. The consequent order imbalance can be cleared only if there exist traders who are willing to absorb the excess demand or supply at a price concession, of course. In other words, the traders who want to buy immediately can do so at a higher price and, similarly traders desiring immediate sale have to accept a lower price. On the BSE the liquidity traders do not have this facility at this time, since there are neither any predesignated dealers for the stocks nor a mechanism for aggregating limit orders.[1] Therefore, at a given point in time, if there are no liquidity-motivated traders on one side of the transaction, then one would expect no trade to occur.

On the New York Stock Exchange, Demsetz (1968) has shown that the probability of the arrival of a trader—the transaction rate—depends on the number of shareholders. Since then, other authors such as Benston and Hagerman (1974) and Glosten and Harris (1988) have used it as a proxy for the extent of liquidity traders for a particular stock. Recently, Bhide (1993) argues that liquidity of the stock can be enhanced by having a more diffused ownership but only at the cost of good internal monitoring. Also, Holmstrom and Tirole (1993) make a distinction between long-term investors and short-term liquidity traders. The idea is that the ownership structure affects the level of liquidity of the stock. While authors such as Glosten and Harris (1988) have used variables like insider concentration as a proxy for the adverse-selection component of the bid-ask spreads, the effect of ownership structure on the level of liquidity has not been tested directly.

In this paper, we attempt to shed light on the factors causing differential levels of trading frequency on the BSE by specifically focusing on ownership structure variables. Also, we investigate the effect of the lack of liquidity on the expected returns of the stocks that is predicted by Amihud and Mendelson (1986). We believe that our paper contributes to a better understanding of a hitherto relatively unresearched emerging market. Given the growing attention on India and its stock markets, the findings of this paper should be of interest to an international audience as well.

We conduct this study using a sample of 250 companies over a five-year period—1989 to 1993. We find evidence in favor of a liquidity premium in the Indian market with stocks with a lower trading frequency having a higher average returns. Also, we find that diffused stock ownership has a beneficial impact on the secondary market liquidity with trading frequency being positively related to the number of shareholders and shares outstanding. Also, liquidity is adversely affected by larger insider holdings or by government and financial institutions. The rest of the paper is organized as follows. In the second section, we provide an overview of the Bombay Stock Exchange. In the third section, we discuss the implications of differential liquidity across stocks. The data and empirical results are presented in the fourth section. We offer our concluding comments in the final section.

AN OVERVIEW OF THE BOMBAY STOCK EXCHANGE

The Bombay Stock Exchange (BSE) is the largest, and most active stock market in India. It accounts for 65 to 70% of all transactions in value terms and about 80% of market capitalization. As of 1991, 6,400 companies were listed on this exchange. The total number of shareholders in India is estimated to be about 15 million.

Classification: Listed securities are classified into Group A and Group B categories. Group A securities, also known as specified securities, can be traded with or without effecting deliveries. This facility, called the *Badla*-system, is equivalent to being able to short-sell or to buy with borrowed capital. There are about 90 stocks in this category which contains the larger and more liquid stocks. The BSE selects the firms to the Group A category based on the volume of transactions, market capitalization, public shareholding pattern, and dividend payment record. Transactions in Group B, also called the cash shares, are settled with delivery of shares in return for cash on the settlement day which occurs once every two weeks.

Role of Members: Even though the stock exchange does not prescribe any functional distinction between members, the BSE has a fairly well-established specialization covering the following types: (1) commission brokers; (2) floor brokers; (3) odd lot dealers; (4) *taravaniwalas* (jobbers or specialists); (5) *budliwalas* or financiers; and (6) dealers in non-cleared securities.

Commission brokers are members who buy and sell orders on the floor of exchange on behalf of their clients. The brokerage is currently 2.5% of the value of the contract. Floor brokers are the authorized assistants or sub-brokers and they execute orders for any member of the exchange. They receive a share in the brokerage fees paid by the client to the commission brokers.

Taravaniwalas specialize in one or more of the listed securities and operate mainly on their own account. They help to maintain a continuous market by standing ready to transact and charge a spread to compensate them for their services. However, they are under no obligation to give two-way quotes or act as a dealer continuously for any particular stock. Hence, dealers are not available for many stocks. A survey conducted by Gupta (1992) shows that spreads ranged from 0.2 to 4.5% for Group A shares and from 0.3 to 30% for Group B shares.

Budliwalas, acting as financiers, lend securities to those who have sold short or lend money to those who need funds to take delivery of securities that they have purchased. Thus, they act as the third party (inbetween the buyer and the seller) in certain transactions involving Group A stocks. Dealers in non-cleared securities perform a role similar to *taravaniwalas* but operate on Group B securities.

Trading System: Trading on the BSE is conducted on the exchange floor that is confined to members or their representatives. The brokers execute trades on behalf of their clients during the official trading session—11:30 a.m. to 2:30 p.m. on weekdays. The trading floor contains several trading posts for the different securities. Potential buyers and sellers gather at the trading post where a particular security is traded[2] and bargain bilaterally with an open out-cry system. The traders record the details of their consummated trades in "*sauda*" books. The "*sauda*" books are exchange-provided notepads and the entries in them are used as evidence in settling disputes.[3]

Settlement Procedures: For Group B shares, payment of money and physical delivery of shares takes place at the end of each account period which occurs once in two weeks. On the other hand, for Group A shares, settlement is done by either: (a) delivering shares against payment, or (b) an offsetting trade, that is, a purchase for a sale made earlier or vice versa within the account period of two weeks, or (c) carrying over the transaction to the next period. The following example illustrates the carry-over procedure. Suppose an investor buys 1,000 shares of XYZ Corporation at Rs.55 per share. On the settlement date, suppose XYZ sells for Rs.50 and the investor wishes to carry forward the transaction to the next settlement. The stock exchange rules stipulate that all transactions conducted during an account period (two weeks) must be settled on the settlement date. So, the investor must find a financier to help her. Typically her broker will help her to find a *budliwala*. The investor has to put up a 15% margin and the *budliwala* finances an amount equal to the number of shares multiplied by the make-up price. (The make-up price is determined by the stock exchange authorities and is fairly close to the price on settlement day.) Assuming a make-up price Rs.50, the investor takes delivery of 1,000 shares by paying Rs.55,000. She has to come up with Rs.12,500, which is equal to Rs. 5,000 (the loss incurred during the account period) plus Rs. 7,500 (the margin money of 15% of Rs. 50,000). The *budliwala* provides the remaining Rs.42,500. Now the investor sells the shares to the *badla* financier at the make-up price of Rs.50 and executes a resale contract for the subsequent settlement at a rate of Rs.50 plus the *badla* financing charge. The *badla* charges are normally 2% to 3% for each two-week period.

IMPLICATIONS OF DIFFERENTIAL LIQUIDITY ACROSS STOCKS

Prior literature has focused on several definitions of liquidity. For instance, Lippman and McCall (1986) have defined liquidity in terms of the time that it takes to transact. Hasbrouck and Schwartz (1988) characterize a liquid market by its depth, breadth, and resiliency. Depth refers to the existence of buy and sell orders near the current market price, breadth is the existence of orders in substantial volume, and resiliency is the responsiveness of new orders to price changes caused by short-term order flow imbalances. Other authors such as Amihud and Mendelson (1986) define liquidity as the observable bid-ask spread. Bernstein (1987) reviews the various measures of liquidity and points out the pitfalls of using any single measure of liquidity.

Liquidity and Asset Pricing

Trading frictions have an impact on the price behavior of a security. Other factors being equal, thinly traded stocks are found to have wider bid-ask spreads and greater short-period price volatility. Also, market model beta coefficients are biased downwards (see Schwartz 1988 for a summary of these issues). The issue of whether liquidity differences between assets have an effect on asset prices is an important one. Amihud and Mendelson (1986) model the impact of liquidity on asset pricing. They measure liquidity by the posted bid-ask spread[4] which is the cost of immediate execution. Their theoretical model posits, and their empirical results corroborate, that assets with wider percentage spreads yield higher returns on average and that investors with longer holding periods should select assets with wider spreads.[5] Amihud and Mendelson (1988) point out the benefits of increasing liquidity. They argue that by increasing liquidity firms reduce their cost of capital and increase their value. They analyze the role of a number of financial management policies and institutional mechanisms in enhancing the secondary market liquidity of firms. The implication of these findings is that we need to move from the two-dimensional risk/return framework to a three-dimensional risk/return/liquidity framework.

There are several reasons why it is useful to study the relation between liquidity and asset pricing in the context of an emerging market such as India. First, prior studies have largely focused on the more advanced Western capital markets. The association of liquidity with stock returns has not been tested in emerging capital markets. There are very important differences between the trading practices of the Bombay Stock Exchange and an advanced stock market such as the New York Stock Exchange. NYSE is a continuous market (except at the beginning of each day) with specialists providing liquidity. Trades are consummated at the quoted prices of the specialist with negligible time delay. In BSE there are no mandatory market-makers. Investors seeking liquidity are subjected to uncertainty regarding the transaction price as well as the time of completion of trade. Furthermore, the differences in liquidity across stocks are exacerbated by the BSE practice of categorizing stocks into two groups. It is therefore interesting to study whether, in spite of the differences in the market microstructure, there exists a liquidity premium in the Indian stock market.

Second, the study of liquidity in the Indian stock market, which is plagued by severe illiquidity problems, is likely to be useful to investors in making their investment decisions. Since 1993, Foreign Institutional Investors (FII) have been allowed to invest directly in the Indian stock market. FIIs find it useful to invest in Indian stocks on account of expectation of higher returns coupled with potential diversification benefits.[6] FIIs as of now only include the most liquid stocks in their portfolios. Empirical evidence on the liquidity premium in the Indian stock market is likely to be informative for FIIs who would like to know the potential compensation for investing in the illiquid stocks.

Ownership Structure and Liquidity

Demsetz (1968) states that one of the important determinants of secondary market liquidity is the number of shareholders. As the number of persons holding a particular share increases, the number of market participants interested in trading the asset increases in direct proportion. Therefore, the number of transactions per unit of time also increases. The number of transactions and the volume traded are observed to be highly correlated in Demsetz's study. Another consequence of an increase in the number of shareholders is the reduction in bid-ask spreads.

Benston and Hagerman (1974) observe a direct relation between a proxy for the extent of insider holding and bid-ask spread. Insiders possess shares for the purpose of controlling the firm and have privileged access to price-sensitive information not available to the public. Market-makers in order to reduce their potential losses on account of trading with insiders and/or other informed traders widen their bid-ask spreads (Bagehot 1971).

Holmstrom and Tirole (1993) in their study of the role of the stock market as a monitor of managerial performance, make a distinction between long-term investors and short-term speculators. In their model, the information content of stock prices improves with the liquidity of the secondary market. They show that in a liquid market, speculators will devote more resources on monitoring as they will realize more of the potential gains. Concentrated ownership reduces liquidity and consequently there is reduced monitoring by speculators. Thus, stock market liquidity is shown to have both a private and social value. On the other hand, Bhide (1993) argues that increased stock market liquidity due to diffused stock holding in the U.S. markets has been achieved at the cost of good internal monitoring by block-holders. Currently, block-holders owning 10% or more of a firm's stock are considered to be insiders, and section 16(b) of the Securities Exchange Act in the United States places restrictions on their short-term trading. Corporate and pension fund managers do not wish to compromise on the fiduciary responsibilities to their constituents and, thus protect the liquidity of their investments. Therefore, they may restrict their holdings to less than 10% to avoid triggering the provisions of Section 16(b). With smaller holdings, block-holders have less incentive to provide internal monitoring. Bhide (1993) considers this loss of internal monitoring as the cost of providing liquidity. The basic premise of both the papers is that the ownership structure affects the level of liquidity of the stock.

Governmental regulatory agencies in India have historically favored policies that attracted small investors. New issues of capital have been made on a nondiscretionary basis and investors who apply for a smaller number of shares have been favored. Also, listed companies paid taxes at lower rates than non-listed companies. This may be one main reason for many stocks to list on the BSE even though they have very few shares owned by outsiders. Consequently, there is little information put out by these companies nor any actual trading in the secondary markets. Joseph (1990) finds that in his sample, for about 50% of the stocks which did not trade even once a year, there is no publicly available earnings or dividend information!

However, ownership in stocks has also been concentrated in the hands of insiders, government, and financial institutions. Typically, about 40% of shares were held by insiders and about 15%–20% by financial institutions and government. At the extreme, public sector companies were wholly owned by the government of India and were absolutely illiquid. Even in larger private sector companies, it was not unusual to find governmental nominees sitting on the board of directors. The effect of ownership concentration on stock market liquidity in the Indian context has not been empirically studied.

Recently, the regulatory agency, Securities Exchange Board of India (SEBI), has started permitting private placement of stocks; increased the minimum amount of investment in public issues; and allowed companies to raise capital from Euro-Issues. These measures undermine the secondary market liquidity of stocks. An ostensible reason for these measures is to allow companies to raise capital at lower issue costs. But adequate attention has not been given to the potential adverse impact of these measures on the liquidity of stocks. Hence evidence on the effect of stock ownership patterns on liquidity should be potentially useful from a policy perspective as well.

DATA AND EMPIRICAL RESULTS

Data on stock prices were obtained from the database of Dateline and Research Technologies Limited (DART). The DART database covers nearly 2,000 companies out of a total of more than 6,000 listed companies on the Bombay Stock Exchange. The price data are available in computer-readable form and cover the period July 1988–June 1993. The data on shareholding pattern were obtained from DART and the Bombay Stock Exchange directory. The shareholding data contain the following variables: percentage of the total shares held by insiders, public, and governmental financial institutions; total number of shares outstanding; and number of shareholders.

Sample

We selected 250 companies randomly from the 2,000 companies in the DART database. The price data were collected from the DART database while the ownership information was hand-collected from the BSE directory as of the end of each year in our sample. Companies belonging to both Group A and Group B were selected to make our sample representative of the population as much as possible. Companies not in the DART database are likely to be infrequently traded stocks especially of small companies. Therefore, our sample systematically excludes the most illiquid stocks. Unfortunately, all the currently available Indian databases (in computer-readable form) will quite likely suffer from the same bias.

In our sample, we do not require that the firm has to survive for the entire five-year period. That is, firms are allowed to "die-out" in the middle of the year to avoid survivorship bias. Also, some firms enter our sample in the middle of the five-year period. Thus the actual number of stocks in a particular year will in general be less than 250. For each company that exists at the beginning of a given year over the period 1989 to 1993, we compute the average monthly return which is a geometric

Table 1. Descriptive Statistics of the Randomly Selected Sample of 250 Firms over the Period July 1988 to June 1993

Variable	*Mean*
Trading Frequency	0.814
Number of Shareholders	61,882
Shares Outstanding (in millions)	11.838
Percent held by Insiders	43.23
Percent held by Govt./F.I.	16.54
Percent held by Public	40.27

Notes: All the variables are observed at the end of each year. We compute a cross-sectional mean each year and then calculate a mean across the years.

mean computed every year. That is, for each company we have one annual observation for monthly return. This is done to minimize the likely impact of severe non-trading on return measurement. We measure the liquidity of a stock by its trading frequency, defined as the ratio of the number of days the particular stock traded to the total number of days on which the stock exchange operated during each year. Liquidity measures such as bid-ask spread and trading volume are not available for stocks on the BSE.[7] Table 1 gives a summary description of the sample.

Empirical Results

Initially, we study the impact of trading frequency on the average returns of the firms—a measure of the liquidity premium. This was estimated using a pooled time series and cross-section regression using the annual observations of trading frequency and average monthly returns to estimate the impact of trading frequency on stock returns. That is, we regress the average monthly returns of a particular stock on its trading frequency during the previous year.

The results of this regression (reported in Table 2) indicate the existence of a liquidity premium. The negative coefficient for the trading frequency variable (Tra_Frq) is statistically significant at conventional levels ($t = -2.55$). Of course, we could not control for beta risk on account of the severity of the thin-trading problem. For the more illiquid stocks we do not have enough data points, with trading not occurring for more than half the days. Furthermore, the evidence of

Table 2. Estimates of Coefficients (*t*-statistics) of the Pooled Cross-section and Time-series Regression of the Average Returns of Firms over the Period 1989–1993

	Regression		
Variable	*(I)*	*(II)*	*(III)*
Trading Frequency	−2.49	−3.06	−2.94
	(−255)	(−3.30)	(−2.90)
Shares Outstanding		7.84×10^{-9}	
		(1.11)	
No. of Shareholders			4.39×10^{-7}
			(0.53)
N	869	653	563
Adj. *R*-Square	0.163	0.204	0.195

Notes: (I): $R_{it} = a_0 + a_1$ Tra_Freq.$_{it-1} + \Sigma_t d_t DY_t + e_{it}$

(II): $R_{it} = b_0 + b_1$ Tra_Freq.$_{it-1} + b_2$ Shares_Out$_{it-1} + \Sigma_t d_t DY_t + e_{it}$

(III): $R_{it} = c_0 + c_1$ Tra_Freq.$_{it-1} + c_2$ Shareholders$_{it-1} + \Sigma_t d_t DY_t + e_{it}$

R_{it} is the annual observation of average monthly returns for each stock. Trading Frequency, Shares Outstanding and the number of shareholders for each stock are annual observations that are measured during the preceding year. Trading Frequency is the percentage of the days over which a particular stock traded in a year. DY_t is a dummy variable which indicates each of the years.

Fama and French (1992) indicates that control for size is more important than that of beta risk. They find a strong relation between returns and size, but they are unable to find a reliable relation between returns and beta. However, due to infrequent trading, we are unable to obtain year-end prices for most stocks. Therefore, we use the number of shares outstanding as the proxy for size. By regressing average monthly returns on the trading frequency and number of shares outstanding (regression II), we find that the trading frequency variable remains significant but the number of shares outstanding is not.

We next regress average monthly returns on the trading frequency and the number of shareholders. The number of shareholders is a proxy for the transaction rate according to Demsetz (1968). According to him, there exists an approximate linear relation between the number of transactions and the number of shareholders. We wish to test the relative importance of the liquidity proxies viz., trading frequency and number of shareholders. Also, the number of shareholders is a proxy for the extent of "investor awareness" in a equilibrium model with limited information such as Merton (1987). He predicts that in a world where investors have information on only a subset of securities and restrict their holdings to them, firms with lower investor base will have higher average returns. The results (regression III) indicate significance for the trading frequency variable but the number of shareholders variable is not statistically significant.

Next, to gauge the overall characteristics of the firms leading to differences in their trading frequency, we initially form portfolios based on the trading frequency and see how they differ in terms of the various shareholding variables. The portfolios are formed on the basis of the average trading frequency for each year and are rebalanced annually. LQ1 contains the lowest quintile of stocks based on trading frequency whereas LQ5 contains the most liquid stocks. Average values of the variables are shown for each of the liquidity portfolios—LQ1 through LQ5.

We can observe from Table 3 that the average trading frequency of the least liquid stocks is only 0.41. This implies that these stocks do not trade for approximately 60% of the days. The average trading frequency increases to 0.79 for the second most illiquid portfolio (LQ2). The average trading frequencies of LQ3, LQ4, and LQ5 are 0.90, 0.97, and 1.00, respectively. The average number of shares outstanding increases from 4.119 million to 24.023 million from LQ1 to LQ5. The increase is not strictly monotonic. The average number of shareholders shows an increasing pattern from 11,007 to 149,594 from LQ1 through LQ5. Once again, the increase is not strictly monotonic.

The descriptive statistics give us some idea of the effect of ownership structure on the observed liquidity. Liquid firms are characterized by a large number of shares outstanding and are owned by a large number of shareholders. That is, diffused ownership appears to be associated with higher trading frequency.[8] The shareholding pattern is as follows: approximately 40% is held by the public, 15–20% by government and financial institutions, and the rest is held by corporate insiders.[9] We group governmental holdings with financial institutions such as Unit Trust of

Table 3. Average Shareholding and Ownership Characteristics for Five Portfolios formed on the Basis of the Trading Frequency over the Period 1988–1993

Portfolio Number	*Average Trading Frequency*	*Number of Shares Outstanding (in millions)*	*Number of Shareholders*	*Percentage of Shares Held by Insiders*	*Percentage of Shares Held by Govt./FI*	*Percentage of Shares Held by Public*
LQ1	0.41	4.119	11,007	43.13	15.94	40.92
LQ2	0.79	10.480	51,598	43.76	15.12	41.07
LQ3	0.90	7.720	33,335	42.98	15.92	41.16
LQ4	0.97	12.850	63,875	43.44	15.40	41.37
LQ5	1.00	24.023	149,594	42.85	20.30	36.82

Notes: Each year firms are ranked and assigned to one of five portfolios based on the trading frequency during that year. Then the average of the shareholding and ownership structure variables is computed for each portfolio annually. The time-series average for each portfolio is reported in the above table.

India, Life Insurance Corp., and so on, since there were no privately owned mutual funds during the time period studied. The government, either directly through shareholdings or indirectly through directives, exercises a large degree of control on these financial institutions. The government nominees serve on the board of directors of these financial institutions. Anecdotal evidence suggests that these quasi-government bodies typically subscribed to large block of shares in the primary market but rarely sold them in the secondary markets.

We next use regression techniques to analyze the impact of shareholding pattern on trading frequency. The regressions (in Table 4) again use firm-level pooled cross-section and time-series data. The regression of trading frequency on the number of shares outstanding shows that it has a positive effect on the trading frequency and the relation is statistically significant. That is, we find that increasing the number of shares outstanding has a beneficial impact on the trading frequency. Potentially, policies such as stock-splits, as suggested by many, are likely to enhance liquidity. We next examine the impact of the number of shareholders on the trading frequency (regression II). A strong statistically significant positive relation exists between trading frequency and the number of shareholders. Our results conform with similar findings in the United States (for example, Demsetz 1968). Therefore, liquidity seems to improve with a more diffused ownership of the stock.

Next, we explore the impact of specific ownership structure variables on the trading frequency. That is, after controlling for the number of shares outstanding, we would like to know the effect of ownership of stocks (by different categories of investors) on the trading frequency. First, we examine impact of the extent of shareholding by the insiders. The rationale being that these shares are held for control purposes and hence will be traded less frequently than those held by outsiders. Thus, we expect an inverse relation (after controlling for the total shares

Table 4. Estimates of Coefficients (*t*-statistics) of the Pooled Cross-section and Time-series Regression of the Trading Frequency on Shareholding Variables of Firms over the Period 1988–1993

	Regression	
Variable	*(I)*	*(II)*
Shares Outstanding	1.30×10^{-9}	
	(4.92)	
No. of Shareholders		1.09×10^{-7}
		(3.40)
N	827	715
Adj. *R*-Square	0.071	0.054

Notes: (I): $\text{Tra\_Freq.}_{it} = a_0 + a_1 \text{ Shares\_Outstanding}_{it} + \Sigma_t\, d_t\, DY_t + e_{it}$

(II): $\text{Tra\_Freq.}_{it} = b_0 + b_1 \text{ Shareholders}_{it} + \Sigma_t\, d_t\, DY_t + e_{it}$

Trading Frequency, Shares Outstanding and the Number of shareholders for each stock are annual observations. Trading Frequency is the percentage of days during which a particular stock is traded in a year. Shares Outstanding and the Number of shareholders are as of March each year. DY_t is a dummy variable which indicates each of the years.

Table 5. Estimates of Coefficients (*t*-statistics) of the Pooled Cross-section and Time-series Regression of the Trading Frequency on Ownership Structure Variables of Firms over the Period 1988–1993

	Regression	
Variable	*(I)*	*(II)*
Shares Outstanding	4.16×10^{-9}	2.53×10^{-9}
	(5.77)	(3.55)
Insiders' Shares	-1.74×10^{-14}	
	(–4.35)	
Govt. & F.I.'s Shares		-3.63×10^{-9}
		(–1.86)
N	827	827
Adj. *R*-Square	0.079	0.074

Notes: (I): $\text{Tra\_Freq.}_{it} = a_0 + a_1 \text{ Shares\_Out.}_{it} + a_2 \text{ Inside\_Shares}_{it} + \Sigma_t\, d_t\, DY_t + e_{it}$

(II): $\text{Tra\_Freq.}_{it} = b_0 + b_1 \text{ Shares\_Out.}_{it} + b_2 \text{ G\&F.I.\_Shares}_{it} + \Sigma_t\, d_t\, DY_t + e_{it}$

Trading Frequency, Shares Outstanding and the shares held by different categories of investors are annual observations for each stock. Trading Frequency is the percentage of days during which a particular stock is traded in a year. Shares held by Insiders includes that by parent company in the case of subsidiaries. Shares held by the Government and Financial Institutions (such as U.T.I., L.I.C., etc.) are considered as "long-term" non-insiders. DY_t is a dummy variable which indicates each of the years.

outstanding) between the holdings of insiders and liquidity as measured by trading frequency in the secondary market.

Results in Table 5 confirm that insiders' holdings have a deleterious effect on trading frequency after controlling for the total number of shares outstanding. In some sense, this can be viewed as the price paid by the outsiders for the better monitoring by the insiders. Next, we examine the effect of shareholdings by government and financial institutions on the trading frequency. As per our earlier discussion, these are blocks of shares that are rarely traded in the secondary markets and hence should lower the trading frequency of the stocks. The reason being that their shareholding effectively reduces the potential number of "floating" stock. Our results confirm this conjecture. The number of shares held by the government or financial institutions variable has a negative and statistically significant effect on trading frequency, after controlling for the number of shares outstanding.

CONCLUDING REMARKS

Our results indicate that there exists a liquidity premium for stocks traded in the Bombay Stock Exchange with expected stock returns being inversely related to the trading frequency. Size and diffused ownership appear to have a positive effect on the liquidity measure. Specifically, trading frequency increases with the number of shareholders and number of shares outstanding. Also, liquidity is adversely affected by an increase in the holdings of insiders, government, and financial institutions that are quasi-government organizations.

Our study has several implications for the companies listed on the BSE. First, liquid firms face a lower cost of capital and, therefore have a higher market value. Liquidity enhancing measures are valuable in themselves. Increasing the number of shareholders and the number of shares by such actions as stock splits are some such measures. Diffused ownership has a beneficial impact on liquidity but comes with additional costs. The process of making public issues targeted at a very large number of investors is both time-consuming and expensive. These costs must be weighed with the benefits that accrue from better liquidity. The dynamics of costs and benefits of liquidity-enhancing measures is a fertile area for further research.

This study also pinpoints the effects of "long-term" investors, namely, insider holdings, and holdings of government and financial institutions. There is savings in terms of flotation costs when shares are held by insiders, and government and financial institutions, but at the cost of reduced liquidity. The ostensible argument for increasing the insider-ownership is better monitoring. However, anecdotal evidence suggests that board members representing the government or quasi-government bodies (such as the Unit Trust of India, Life Insurance Corporation of India, etc.) do not play any constructive nor active role in the companies in which they have significant holdings. Measurement of the benefit of improved monitoring versus the cost of reduced liquidity is another fruitful area for further research.

APPENDIX

Since September 1994, there is a new electronic stock exchange (National Stock Exchange) operating in India. It was originally started for trading Treasury bonds. A month later trading began on also equities. As of March 1995, the daily trading volume in equities is about Rs. 700 million. This compares to about Rs. 3,000 million on the BSE. The main features of the NSE are as follows:

1. Members are provided with computers connected to the central computer at the NSE headquarters. The order-driven system flashes the best buy-sell limit orders on the monitor.
2. Members can submit orders through their terminal which are immediately executed by the system.
3. There are no preassigned market makers and dealers can submit quotes only one side.
4. On the eighth day, each member is given a statement specifying his or her net position in each stock, indicating the cash to be transferred or securities to be delivered to the clearinghouse.
5. Delivery of securities and cash are to be completed by the thirteenth and fourteenth day, respectively. The fifteenth day is the last day for payouts.

ACKNOWLEDGMENTS

We would like to thank Henk Berkman, Jerry Bowman, J.B. Chay, and Usha Natarajan for their useful comments and suggestions. Also, we wish to acknowledge the assistance provided by Basvaraj and Crossley in data collection. This research project was partially funded by a grant from the Indian Institute of Management, Bangalore, India.

NOTES

1. Of course, since October 1994 the newly created National Stock Exchange (NSE) has an electronic trading mechanism. This is elaborated in the Appendix.

2. However, for most securities there are no designated trading posts. Especially, for the smaller illiquid stocks, a trader has to encounter, by chance, another person that is interested in taking the opposite side.

3. The transactions are not time-stamped and a trade may be reported to the exchange much later in the day. Thus, it will be almost impossible to determine whether the investor got the best possible price.

4. Studies such as Lee (1993), Blume and Goldstein (1992), and Petersen and Fialkowski (1994) suggest that the posted spreads may be poor proxy for the effective spreads.

5. Eleswarapu and Reinganum (1993) raise some doubts regarding the robustness of the model using evidence with NYSE data.

6. The returns in the Indian stock market have had a correlation of –0.17 with the U.S. market (S&P 500). Investing in the Indian market provides Western investors with a classic opportunity for risk reduction.

7. Volume data are available for Group A stocks but not for Group B stocks. Our sample is mainly composed of Group B stocks. The Indian stock markets at present do not have mandatory market-makers. Therefore, bid-ask spreads are not available.

8. An extreme example is the case of DSP Financial consultants which has less than 100 shareholders. The last trade recorded for the company in our sample period was in January 1992.

9. We classify the holdings by other companies and/or the parent company as insiders.

REFERENCES

Amihud, Y., and H. Mendelson. 1986. "Asset Pricing and the Bid-ask Spread." *Journal of Financial Economics* 17: 223–249.

———. 1988. "Liquidity and Asset Prices: Financial Management Implications." *Financial Management* 17: 5–15.

Bagehot, W. 1971. "The Only Game in Town." *Financial Analysts Journal* 8: 31–53.

Benston, G.J., and R.L. Hagerman. 1974. "Determinations of Bid-ask Spreads in the Over-the-Counter Market." *Journal of Financial Economics* 1: 353–364.

Bernstein, P.L. 1987. "Liquidity, Stock Markets, and Market Makers." *Financial Management* 16: 54–62.

Bhide, A. 1993. "The Hidden Costs of Stock Market Liquidity." *Journal of Financial Economics* 34: 31–51.

Blume, M.E., and M.A. Goldstein. 1992. "Displayed and Effective Spreads by Market." Working Paper no. 27-92, White Center for Financial Research, University of Pennsylvania, Philadelphia, PA.

Demsetz, H. 1968. "The Cost of Transacting." *Quarterly Journal of Economics* 82: 33–53.

Eleswarapu, V., and M. Reinganum. 1993. "The Seasonal Behavior of Liquidity Premium in Asset Pricing." *Journal of Financial Economics* 34: 373–386.

Fama, E.F., and K.R. French. 1992. "The Cross-section of Expected Stock Returns." *Journal of Finance* 47: 427–465.

Glosten, L.R., and L.E. Harris. 1988. "Estimating the Components of the Bid-ask Spread." *Journal of Financial Economics* 21: 123–142.

Gupta, L.C. 1992. *Stock Exchange Trading in India: Agenda for Reform*. Delhi, India: Society for Capital Market Research and Development.

Hasbrouck, J., and R.A. Schwartz. 1988. "Liquidity and Execution Costs Inequity Markets." *Journal of Portfolio Management* 14: 10–17.

Holmstrom, B., and J. Tirole. 1993. "Market Liquidity and Performance Monitoring." *Journal of Political Economy* 101: 678–709.

Joseph, P. 1990. "An Investigation into the Causes for Thinly Traded Shares in the Stock Exchanges in India and Alternative Sources of Capital for Companies." Unpublished MBA thesis, University of Hull, U.K.

Lee, C. 1993. "Market Integration and Price Execution for NYSE-listed Securities." *Journal of Finance* 48: 1009–1038.

Lippman, S., and J. McCall. 1986. "An Operational Measure of Liquidity." *American Economic Review* 76: 43–55.

Merton, R.C. 1987. "A Simple Model of Capital Market Equilibrium with Incomplete Information." *Journal of Finance* 42: 483–510.

Petersen, M.A., and D. Fialkowski. 1994. "Posted versus Effective Spreads: Good Prices or Bad Quotes?" *Journal of Financial Economics* 35: 269–292.

Schwartz, R. 1988. *Equity Markets: Structure, Trading and Performance*. New York: Harper and Row.

DO WE EXPECT MORE LATENT VARIABLES IN A STRUCTURALLY DIFFERENT MARKET: THE CASE OF HONG KONG

Wai Lee, Hung-Gay Fung, and Wai-Chung Lo

ABSTRACT

Using the Generalized Method of Moments (GMM) allowing for conditional heteroscedasticity, this study examines the time-varying expected returns of a sample of Hong Kong common stocks and industry groups for the period of 1986–1995. To our surprise, we find only one latent variable in a mean-variance pricing framework for the stock returns. Although we are able to find portfolios that can span the mean-variance space of stock returns within our sample for a relatively short period, little evidence is found to support the spanning hypothesis for a longer horizon.

INTRODUCTION

The latent variable model has been used extensively to examine the behavior of the time-varying expected stock returns in the United States (Ferson, Foerster, and Keim 1993; Ferson 1992; Campbell 1987, among others). In addition to analyzing

Research in International Business and Finance, Supplement 1, pages 313–328.

ISBN: 0-7623-0110-4

stock returns, many studies have extended such models to study financial assets such as bonds, foreign exchange, and other assets (Ferson 1992; Hansen and Hodrick 1983). However, little evidence on the time-varying asset return behaviors in other countries is available (see the literature review section for details).

Ferson, Foerster, and Keim (1993) find only two to three latent variables for the U.S. stock returns. That is, only a small number of latent variables can be used to explain the asset returns in the U.S. market. It would be interesting to examine whether this result holds for other markets, especially the emerging market. The Hong Kong stock market is structurally different from the U.S. market, and its price movements are quite volatile. Thus, this study examining the time-varying asset returns of the Hong Kong stock market, which is expected to have more latent variables, should be of interest for the following reasons.

First, the Hong Kong stock market represents an important emerging market in the Pacific Basin. The emerging markets are in a different stage of development as compared to the more matured and developed ones such as the U.S. market. Little evidence is available in the literature regarding the time-varying behavior of the expected returns for these markets. Because of few government interventions, the Hong Kong stock market serves a good case in analyzing the price behavior as compared to other Asian countries whereby government restrictions/interventions in the stock markets are typical.

Second, Hong Kong is an international financial center where its stock market has placed an important role in channelling and raising foreign funds. The stock market has a large trading volume and a relatively low price-earning ratio as compared to the other Asian countries, implying an active market with a good potential for large price increases (Lo, Fung, Chen, and Lai 1992). Furthermore, in recent years many new financial derivatives such as the stock index futures and stock index options have developed. These instruments tend to enhance the activity of the cash market.

Third, the Hong Kong stock market is well-known to be affected by political news. During the past several years, many companies in China have listed their shares in the Hong Kong stock market. After 1997 Hong Kong will become a part of Mainland China and thus will no longer be under British rule. It would be interesting to examine whether its stock market behavior would be comparable to the U.S. experience given the strong influence of its political climate.

Fourth, the behavior of the Hong Kong stock market is unique compared to other international stock markets. In a study of 17 stock markets by Harvey (1991), Hong Kong is shown to have the highest average return (i.e., about 2.3 times of that of the United States) and the highest variance (about 8 times of that of the United States). Interestingly, none of the stock markets can dominate Hong Kong in a mean-variance framework. In addition, Hong Kong has the second lowest correlation with the world portfolio, and it also has the lowest correlation with other stock markets in Harvey's sample. On the other hand, Hong Kong has the highest conditional covariance with the world portfolio and the second lowest excess return during the 1987 global stock crash. This evidence suggests that the Hong Kong stock market's behavior is "extreme and yet unique."

Finally, since 1983 the exchange rate of Hong Kong is closely tied to the U.S. dollar as maintained by the Hong Kong Monetary Authority. Given the exchange rate linkage between the Hong Kong and the U.S. markets, Malliaris and Urrutia (1992) find that the Hong Kong stock prices are moving closely with the U.S. prices. Thus, it is interesting to investigate whether the U.S. experience in the time-varying return behavior is also applicable to the Hong Kong stock market.

From the above discussions, we know that Hong Kong has been subject to many financial developments, large price movements, and impacts of various political forces in recent years. As a result, we do expect that there are more latent variables for the Hong Kong stock returns than that of the U.S. market.

Using an iterated Generalized Method of Moments (GMM), we study the time-varying behavior of a representative sample of the Hong Kong stock and industry group returns. Specifically, we investigate the number of latent variables in a mean-variance framework that can explain the behavior of these asset returns. We also attempt to identify the spanning portfolios that can generate the mean-variance space of all asset returns in our sample.

To our surprise, we only find one latent variable for the Hong Kong stock returns. That is, we have fewer latent variables found in the Hong Kong stock market than that of the U.S. market. We do not find the two portfolios that can span the stock returns for the whole period. This result, however, is quite similar to the U.S. experience.

The rest of the paper is organized as follows. The second section gives a brief review of the literature. The third section presents the latent variable approach and different hypotheses tested. The fourth section contains the empirical results. The last section is the conclusion.

LITERATURE REVIEW

In the finance literature, a number of studies have shown that asset returns are at least partially predictable. In a cross-sectional setting, early studies such as Black, Jensen, and Scholes (1972), Blume and Friend (1973), and Fama and MacBeth (1973) empirically confirm that on the average, assets with higher beta, or systematic risk, have higher excess returns. Since violations of the capital asset pricing model (CAPM) of Sharpe (1964), Lintner (1965), and Mossin (1966) have been commonly reported, subsequent studies thus focus on other anomalies, such as the size effect and earnings/price effect.

International evidence also indicates that, on the average, firms of smaller size and lower earnings/price ratio have higher returns. Hawawini and Keim (1994) provide an excellent survey on the cross-sectional predictability of stock returns, covering studies on 16 international stock markets. In addition, calendar anomalies of these markets have also been documented.[1]

While examination of the cross-sectional, unconditional moments in asset returns sheds light on the average relationship between returns and risks, recent studies focus on the time-varying asset returns and risks behavior. A time-series study is more appropriate and interesting to describe the dynamic relationship between returns and risks. One of the first group of early studies of this sort examines whether expected excess stock returns over Treasury bills are constant through time.

Fama and Schwert (1977) find that when monthly stock returns are regressed on the one-month bill rate, which is used as a proxy of expected inflation, the coefficient is significantly negative and thus the constant expected excess return hypothesis is strongly rejected. Fama (1981), and later elaborated by Geske and Roll (1983), attributes the predictability of stock returns to the proxy hypothesis that reflects the positive relationship between stock returns and expected real activities. Subsequently, we observe a growing body of research on using short-term interest rates to predict stock returns. Such negative relationship is also confirmed in many other stock markets by Gultekin (1983) and Solnik (1983).[2] In addition, Breen, Glosten, and Jagannathan (1989) find that the predictability of stock returns by the short-term interest rates are both statistically and economically significant. Ferson (1989) explains their relationship by a standard asset pricing theory which shows that the expected excess return is equal to the product of the expected covariance of the negative of a pricing kernal with the assets return and the gross return of the risk-free asset. Ferson concludes that changes in conditional betas are associated with risk-free rates.

Another group of research investigates the hypothesis whether expected excess returns on long-term Treasury bonds over the short-term bill rate are constant. Early studies such as Shiller (1979), Shiller, Campbell, and Schoenholtz (1983), and Fama (1984) find that the hypothesis is strongly rejected and confirm that excess bond returns can be predicted by yield spreads and short-term interest rates. Built on these previous evidence of stock and bond returns predictability, subsequent studies further extend the scope to cover many other asset classes. For example, Froot (1990) finds strong evidence that short-term interest rates can predict returns on stocks, bonds, foreign currencies, and commodities. Along a similar line of research, Cutler, Poterba, and Summers (1991) also find that excess returns on numerous international stock and bond markets, foreign currencies, real estate, collectibles, and precious metals are negatively correlated with short-term interest rates.

While the findings relating to the predictability of asset returns are well documented, a fundamental problem in finance is to characterize these time-varying expected returns with an asset pricing model. Previous research has reported that many implications of the CAPM are violated. As a result, numerous studies empirically examine the performance of some multifactor asset pricing models along the line of the Arbitrage Pricing Theory (APT) of Ross (1976), and the intertemporal CAPM (ICAPM) of Merton (1973). These models introduce additional factor risk premiums usually in the form of excess returns of some traded portfolios and factor mimicking portfolios, and propose that the time-varying expected excess return is a linear function of these factor risk premiums.

Motivated by the predictability of returns and these multifactor models, recent research efforts focus on using instrumental variables to proxy for the expected risk premiums. Some instrumental variables commonly used are, for example, lagged excess return of the asset, dividend yield of stock, short-term interest rate, term structure variables, default risk premium, dummy variable for January, among others. Two noticeable examples of these studies are Keim and Stambaugh (1986) and Campbell (1987) which report that both stock returns and bond returns are predictable.

Extension to international portfolios in analyzing the time- varying asset returns include Harvey (1991), Ferson and Harvey (1993), Solnik (1993), and Lee and Chiang (1995), among others. In particular, Ferson and Harvey (1993) not only proxy the expected risk premiums by the instrumental variables, but also construct the time-varying betas with those variables. They report that their model captures much of the predictability for many countries. On the other hand, the study by Giovannini and Jorion (1989) reports that estimated conditional variances cannot explain the observed time variation of risk premia but have significant positive predictive ability for second moments of asset returns in the U.S. stock market and in the foreign exchange market.

One particular class of studies of multifactor asset pricing models is the latent variable approach, which proposes that time-varying expected excess return is a linear function of a few unobservable factor risk premiums called latent variables. These models allow expected returns and risk premiums to vary over time, while holding the betas fixed. The latent variable model has been used extensively to investigate the asset returns and risk premiums in the U.S. market (Ferson and Foerster 1994; Ferson, Foerster, and Keim 1993; Ferson 1992; Campbell 1987). This study thus corroborates with these studies that employ the latent variable model and examines the time-varying return behavior for the Hong Kong stock market.

RESEARCH METHODOLOGY

In this section, we will discuss briefly two methods that examine the latent variable asset pricing models. The first one relates to testing different null hypotheses for the latent variable models while the second one examines the issue of mean-variance spanning.

Latent Variable Model

In the standard asset pricing framework such as Cox, Ingersoll, and Ross (1985), Merton (1973), and Sharpe (1964), the expected asset returns can be expressed as a linear combination of expected risk premiums as

$$E(R_{it} \mid Z_{t-1}) = (1 - \Sigma b_{ij})E(\lambda_{0t} \mid Z_{t-1}) + \Sigma b_{ij} E(\lambda_{jt} \mid Z_{t-1}) \tag{1}$$

where $\lambda_{jt}, j = 1,2, \ldots K$, are the unobserved risk premiums (state variables, hedge portfolios, or factors); b_{ij} are the betas of the asset i for the j risk factor conditional on the information Z_{t-1}; and λ_{0t} is the zero-beta security.

When the expected returns and risks of assets at time t are conditioned on the known information set, their betas and expected risk premiums are also time varying. The latent variable asset pricing model is an approach that relates the time varying expected returns to a small number of unobservable risk premiums, or latent variables, while assuming constant ratios of the beta coefficients. Empirical tests of the latent variable models are based on the assumption that expected returns are time varying but are correlated with observable instruments, Z_{t-1}, which are known at time t.

In examining the joint hypothesis (H_1) of linear expectations for expected returns and K latent variables, Ferson, Foerster, and Keim (1993) formulate the latent variable approach for the equation (1) as:

$$R_1 = Z\delta_1 + U_1 \tag{2a}$$

$$R_2 = Z\delta_1 C + U_2 \tag{2b}$$

$$l'C = l \tag{2c}$$

where $R = (R_1, R_2)$ is a $T \times N$ matrix of all asset returns, partitioned by columns with $K + l$ in R_1 and $N - K - l$ in R_2 where T is the number of observations. Because R contains the entire asset returns and there are fewer latent variables than the number of assets, there must be some restrictions on some asset returns in R. Thus, R can be partitioned into two types of asset returns, R_1 and R_2. R_1 contains the reference assets while R_2 contains the rest of the asset returns. The reference assets are chosen in such a way that their beta matrix and a unit vector are nonsingular. In addition, the reference assets must span the K risk factors and they cannot have identical betas on any combination of risk factors. In this way, R_2 can be thought of some linear combinations of R_1.[3] Z is a $T \times L$ matrix of predetermined instrumental variables; l is a vector of one. δ_1 and C are $L \times (K + l)$ and $(K + l) \times (N - K - l)$ matrices of parameters, respectively.

Examination of H_1 can be accomplished using the generalized method of moments (GMM) which allows autocorrelation and conditional heteroscedasticity in the disturbance term. The parameters are estimated to minimize the quadratic function of $Tg'Wg$ where g is the vector of the orthogonality conditions and W is the inverse of the covariance matrix of the orthogonality conditions. Under H_1, the orthogonality condition tested is $E(U'Z) = 0$, where $U = (U_1, U_2)$. Under the null hypothesis, the minimized value of the quadratic form is asymptotically distributed as a chi square statistic with degrees of freedom equal to the number of orthogonality conditions less the number of parameters. Following Ferson, Foerster, and Keim (1993), we label this chi-square statistic as the GMM1 test statistic.

On the other hand, we can also examine another null hypothesis (H_2) of K latent variables without imposing the linear expectations restriction in H_1 above as follows:

$$U = R_2 - R_1 C \tag{3a}$$

$$l'C = l \tag{3b}$$

Similarly, H_2 can be examined using the GMM test with the orthogonality condition as $E(U'Z) = 0$. GMM2 is the minimized chi-square value of the quadratic form imposed in equations (3a–3b).

Mean-Variance Spanning

Mean-variance spanning refers to the condition that only a subset of all asset returns (R_s) (also called the mimicking/spanning asset returns/portfolios) is required to generate the mean-variance boundary of all other assets (Huberman and Kandel 1987). Thus, it seems clear that mean-variance spanning is associated closely with equations (3a–3b) if R_1 is defined as the mimicking asset returns (portfolios) that can generate the time-varying behavior of the risk factors. The mean-variance spanning hypothesis can be examined with the following formulation:

$$V = R_2 - R_s C \tag{4a}$$

$$l'C = l \tag{4b}$$

where $R = (R_s, R_2)$ is a $T \times N$ matrix of asset returns. R_s is $T \times (K + l)$ spanning assets where K is number of latent variables in the asset-pricing model.[4] R_2 contains $N - K - l$ test asset returns to be spanned.

The test statistic examining the unconditional spanning is the minimized value of the GMM criterion function for the equations (4a–4b) with $E(V) = E(V'R_s) = 0$ as the orthogonality condition. Similarly, we can examine the conditional mean-variance spanning for the orthogonality condition $E(V'[R_s, Z]) = 0$ used in the quadratic function of the GMM test.

EMPIRICAL RESULTS

Weekly data sampled on Wednesday were collected from the Data Stream for the period June 1986 to March 1995. We select Wednesday data to avoid day of the week effects. Only individual stocks that are consistently part of the Hang Seng Index with continuous prices during this sampled period were selected. Thus, we ended up with 14 stocks and four industry groups (banking, commercial and industrial, utilities, and properties) in the data. To examine the subsample results, we break down the whole period into three subsample periods with about 150 observations in each.

Asset Returns with Instrumental Variables

To examine the predictability of returns by the predetermined instrumental variables, we use six instruments which are all lagged by one period in our weekly tests. These include a constant, the weekly return of the Hang Seng Index (RHSI), dividend yield of the Hang Seng Index (DHSI), and a January dummy variable (JAN) that is used to capture the seasonality changes in risk. In the literature, measures of the short- and long-term structure variables are used (for example, Solnik 1993; Harvey 1991; Campbell 1987, among others). However, the term structure variable in Hong Kong is not available. Since the Hong Kong exchange rate has been kept a close tie with U.S. dollars during our study period, the U.S. term structure variables would be a good proxy for the Hong Kong counterparts. As a result, for our analysis we use the U.S. short-term interest rate risk premium variable (STERM) that is the difference between the U.S. 3-month and U.S. 1-month interest rate. A long-term interest rate risk premium variable (LTERM) is computed using the U.S. 30-year government bond rate less the U.S. 1-month rate.

We conduct our tests for two different sets of assets. In the first set (set A), we include the 14 individual stocks and the four industry groups (i.e., $N = 18$). In the second set (set B), we include the four industry groups (i.e., $N = 4$). We run the following regression for the reference assets (R_1) as:

$$R_i = \alpha_0 + \alpha_1 RHSI_{t-1} + \alpha_2 DHSI_{t-1} + \alpha_3 STERM_{t-1} + \alpha_4 LTERM_{t-1} + \alpha_5 JAN + u_t \tag{5}$$

In testing H_1 and H_2, we need to select the referenced assets for the following latent variable models. We have experimented with different referenced assets; their results are similar (not reported here). We only report the results using the Bank of East Asia and Wheellock in the first set of assets, and using the commercial and industrial and utilities industry groups in the second set of assets in Table 1. Two interesting results are noteworthy.

First, the magnitude of the coefficients of the instrumental variables varies substantially depending on the subperiods. In addition, their significance level also changes. These results suggest that the linear projection of referenced asset returns on the predetermined instrumental variables may not be stable over time.

Second, the adjusted R^2 is surprisingly high for all subperiods. While the adjusted R^2 for each subperiod differs from each other substantially, it is higher for the subperiods than for the whole period, a result suggesting that instrumental variables may not have a consistent explanatory power across subperiods and they have relatively low explanatory power for the whole period.

Table 1. Regression Results for the Weekly Reference Asset Returns

$R_i = \alpha_0 + \alpha_1 RHSI_{t-1} + \alpha_2 DHSI_{t-1} + \alpha_3 STERM_{t-1} + \alpha_4 LTERM_{t-1} + \alpha_5 JAN + u_t$

	First Set		*Second Set*	
Model	*EAsia*	*Wheellock*	*C&I*	*Utilities*
Whole period: 1986/6–1995/3				
Constant	–0.215	–0.13	–0.017	–0.011
	(–4.62)	(–4.50)	(–1.33)	(–1.12)
RHSI	–0.008	0.062	0.122	0.063
	(–0.04)	(0.51)	(2.34)	(1.50)
DHSI	62.685	38.429	5.406	4.088
	(4.84)	(4.73)	(1.55)	(1.46)
STERM	–7.415	–28.360	–31.707	–28.786
	(–0.16)	(–0.95)	(–2.49)	(–2.80)
LTERM	19.085	12.929	2.807	2.288
	(2.72)	(2.94)	(1.48)	(1.51)
JAN	–0.010	–0.009	0.001	–0.003
	(–0.38)	(–5.2)	(0.18)	(–0.49)
adj R^2	0.042	0.047	0.029	0.024
First Subperiod: 1986/6–1989/5				
Constant	–0.026	–0.064	–0.046	–0.021
	(–0.88)	(–1.81)	(–1.79)	(–2.01)
RHSI	0.344	0.276	0.277	0.181
	(3.41)	(2.28)	(3.14)	(2.55)
DHSI	10.425	25.203	18.017	8.057
	(1.12)	(2.26)	(2.22)	(1.23)
STERM	–44.289	–72.543	–49.003	–47.442
	(–1.94)	(–2.59)	(–2.45)	(–2.90)
LTERM	2.2755	4.059	3.020	3.440
	(0.36)	(0.54)	(0.55)	(0.78)
JAN	–0.001	–0.021	–0.002	0.0005
	(–0.07)	(–1.06)	(–0.14)	(0.04)
adj R^2	0.108	0.109	0.139	0.105

(*continued*)

Table 1. Continued

	First Set		Second Set	
Model	*EAsia*	*Wheellock*	*C&I*	*Utilities*
Second Subperiod: 1989/5–1992/3				
Constant	–0.179	–0.300	–0.204	–0.131
	(–3.94)	(–5.16)	(–4.44)	(–3.68)
RHSI	–0.090	0.068	–0.034	0.013
	(–0.96)	(0.56)	(–0.37)	(0.17)
DHSI	45.771	76.600	51.178	33.966
	(3.99)	(5.14)	(4.42)	(3.77)
STERM	–1.061	–2.842	–4.253	–6.002
	(–0.05)	(–0.09)	(–0.19)	(–0.34)
LTERM	12.826	17.295	12.151	8.218
	(3.81)	(3.99)	(3.58)	(3.09)
JAN	0.002	0.001	0.008	–0.004
	(0.23)	(0.06)	(0.77)	(–0.47)
adj R^2	0.091	0.156	0.107	0.074
Third Subperiod: 1992/4–1995/3				
Constant	–0.715	–0.364	0.019	0.011
	(–4.62)	(–4.09)	(0.72)	(0.48)
RHSI	–0.461	–0.378	–0.114	–0.136
	(–0.91)	(–1.30)	(–1.31)	(–1.88)
DHSI	281.39	153.07	3.032	3.418
	(6.34)	(5.99)	(0.40)	(0.54)
STERM	42.783	–43.439	–72.269	–39.775
	(0.26)	(–0.45)	(–2.52)	(–1.65)
LTERM	–4.992	–8.011	–5.370	–4.007
	(–0.15)	(–0.41)	(–0.93)	(–0.61)
JAN	–0.041	–0.010	–0.008	–0.006
	(–0.56)	(–0.25)	(–0.67)	(–0.61)
adj R^2	0.190	0.178	0.022	0.010

Notes: *T*-values are in parentheses. EAsia is Bank of East Asia and C&I denotes Commercial and Industrial group.

Results on the Latent Variable Model

In estimating the models, we use the iterated GMM in which an identity matrix is used for W in the first stage, which obtains estimates of the error terms, and a new weighting matrix is then calculated after each iteration until convergence. Ferson and Foerster (1994) find that this iterative approach has superior finite sample properties.

Table 2 summaries the tests of the latent variable models using weekly data for the individual stocks and the industry groups. We examine H_1 and H_2 for three different subperiods and the whole period using GMM1 and GMM2.

At the standard significance level, we are not able to reject K=1 using GMM1 and GMM2 for (a) 14 individual stocks and the four industry groups, and (b) the four industry groups alone. The lowest p-value among all tests is 0.114 of the third subsample in the first set A. The results appear to be robust across different

Table 2. Tests of Asset-Pricing Models with $K = 1$ Latent Variable Model:

$$R_1 = Z\delta_1 + U_1$$

$$R_2 = Z\delta_1 C + U_2$$

$$l'C = l$$

where $R = (R_1, R_2)$ is a $T \times N$ matrix of all returns, partitioned by columns with $K + 1$ in R_1 and N-K-1 in R_2 where T is the number of observations. l is a vector of one. Z contains the instrumental variables. δ_1 is $L \times (K+1)$ and C is $L \times (N\text{-}K\text{-}1)$. GMM1 is the chi square value for the above model with $E(U'Z) = 0$ as the orthogonality condition. GMM2 statistic is computed for the reformulated model:

$$U = R_2 - R_1 C$$

$$l'C = l$$

Period	*Assets*	*GMM1 (p-value)*	*GMM2 (p-value)*
1986/6–1989/5	14 stocks & 4 IGPs	0.321	0.999
1989/5–1992/3		0.711	0.682
1992/4–1995/3		0.114	0.884
1986/6–1995/3		0.994	0.916
1986/6–1989/5	4 IGPs	0.844	0.843
1989/5–1992/3		0.726	0.694
1992/4–1995/3		0.740	0.650
1986/6–1995/3		0.947	0.900

Notes: IGPs denote industry groups. In the 14 stocks and 4 industry groups analysis, we use the stock returns of Bank of East Asia and Wheellock as the referenced assets. For the second analysis (i.e., 4 IGPs), we use returns of the commercial and industrial along with utilities industry groups as the referenced assets.

subperiods, implying that one latent variable (or two spanning portfolios) would be able to explain the expected asset returns in the mean-variance framework. This finding is striking because of the small number of latent variables found, and it is quite different from the results of Ferson, Foerster, and Keim (1993) who find two latent variables for the Dow Jones 30 common stocks but three latent variables for the New York Stock Exchange common stocks.[5]

Results on Mean-Variance Spanning

Mean-variance spanning is richer in economic implications than that of the latent variable model. If we cannot reject K latent variables, we should then be able to find $K+1$ spanning portfolios that can span the mean-variance space of all other asset returns.

Table 3 reports the results of our tests for unconditional and conditional mean-variance spanning. Because we cannot reject the hypothesis of $K=1$, we use two spanning portfolios to conduct the spanning tests. In our experiment, we use the industry returns of banking and properties groups as the two spanning portfolios.

Table 3. Tests of Unconditional and Conditional Mean-Variance Spanning for $K=1$ (one latent variable)

Model:

$$V = R_2 - R_s C$$

$$l'C = l.$$

where $R = (R_s, R_2)$ is a $T \times N$ matrix of asset returns. R_s is $T \times (K+1)$ spanning assets where K is number of latent variables in the asset-pricing model. $K=1$ (two spanning portfolios) is used here. R_2 contains $N-K-1$ test asset returns. The test statistic that examines the unconditional spanning is the minimized value of the GMM criterion function with $E(V'R_s) = 0$ as the orthogonality condition. Similarly, the conditional mean-variance spanning is tested for the orthogonality condition $E(V'[R_s, Z]) = 0$.

Period	*Test Assets*	*Unconditional Spanning (p-values)*	*Conditional Spanning (p-values)*
1986/6–1989/5	14 stocks & 4 IGPs	0.008	0.337
1989/5–1992/3		0.001	0.231
1992/4–1995/3		0.010	0.449
1986/6–1995/3		0.000	0.002
1986/6–1989/5	4 IGPs	0.001	0.015
1989/5–1992/3		0.029	0.406
1992/4–1995/3		0.001	0.006
1986/6–1995/3		0.000	0.000

Notes: IGPs denote industry groups. Returns of banking and properties industries are used as the spanning portfolios.

In the first analysis that includes 14 stocks and two other industry groups as the spanned assets, we consistently reject unconditional spanning for all three subperiods and the whole period. However, we find little evidence against conditional spanning for all three subperiods but reject conditional spanning for the whole period. For the second analysis including only four industry groups, similar results emerge as in the first analysis. We are able to reject the unconditional spanning across all subperiods, and it is less likely to reject conditional spanning according to the relatively higher p-values. However, we reject conditional spanning for first, third, and the whole period at the 5% level, a result consistent with the first analysis. Some interesting findings should be noted.

First, the difference in results in the unconditional and conditional spanning for the three subperiods probably reflects the importance of prior information in pricing assets. If investors at time t use prior information at t–1, they are able to span more effectively all other asset's return space for the three subperiods.

Second, the results of the conditional spanning are different for the 14 stocks/4 industry groups versus four industry groups for the three subperiods. The results indicate that the p-values for the four industry groups are generally lower than those of the 14 Stocks/4 industry groups, implying that it is relatively easier to span those individual stock returns space for the subperiods.

Finally, the difference in results for the three subperiods and the whole period for the two analyses (i.e., 14 stocks/4 industry groups versus four industry groups) is puzzling and is probably due to the fact that we have more observations in the whole period and thus have a higher power to reject the null hypothesis. This reasoning may further be supported from the results in Table 1. The instrumental variables appear to have time-varying effects on the reference assets. The adjusted R^2 is lowest in the whole period as compared to the subperiod, a result implying that the explanatory power for the instrumental variables differs across time. Thus, the spanning portfolios may not be able to span the mean-variance space of all assets for the whole period given the nature of the time-varying behavior in the expected returns. Indeed, the rejection of mean-variance spanning for the whole period remains a challenge for future research.

CONCLUSIONS

This study examines the time-varying behavior of expected returns of a representative sample of Hong Kong common stocks which are part of the Hang Seng Index for 1986–1995. Using Ferson, Foerster, and Keim's (1993) latent variable approach that allows for conditional heteroscedasticity, we find little evidence against the joint hypothesis of linear expectations for expected returns and one latent variable. When relaxing the linear expectations restriction, we also find that the hypothesis of one latent variable cannot be rejected. The small number of latent variable found for the Hong Kong stock returns is in sharp contrast to the U.S. experience that two or three latent variables are required in the asset pricing model.

Further analysis of the expected return behaviors using mean-variance spanning indicates that two spanning portfolios to some extent are able to span the mean-variance space for a relatively short subperiod when conditional information is used. However, over a longer time horizon, little evidence is found to support the spanning hypothesis. Although this result is consistent with the U.S. experience, it presents a challenge for future research to identify the proper spanning portfolios. Possible candidates include size-based portfolios, or other industry portfolios. It is equally possible that different spanning portfolios are found in different subperiods, when the underlying risk factors are better mimicked.

While identifying the spanning portfolios is left as further empirical exercise, our results on the number of latent variables provide insights for future research. Our finding of one latent variable is consistent and robust across different time periods as well as different sets of assets, implying that to a possibly large extent, the asset returns in our sample move together (Campbell 1987). It also suggests that the assets have constant ratios of betas on only two risk factors, or mimicking portfolios.

It is even more interesting to interpret our findings together with Harvey's (1991) results. It seems that the "unique" behavior of the Hong Kong stock market is driven by a very few common driving forces. It is quite plausible that the political force and the fundamental economic factor dominate the other factors so that we can only find one latent variable. Whether these driving forces are related to the unique economic and political environment in Hong Kong remain great challenges for future research.

ACKNOWLEDGMENT

The authors would like to thank Jim Bennett (referee), Joseph Cheng, Larry Lang (editor), and Yangru Wu (referee) for many helpful comments and suggestions.

NOTES

1. See also the citations therein.
2. A recent study of a market-timing strategy with short-term interest rate by Lee (1995) finds that the negative relationship between stock returns and the bill rate in the United States has gradually disappeared over time since 1954. Instead, the bill rate is found to be increasingly important in affecting stock return volatilities. The information content of the bill rate seems to have shifted from the first moment to the second moment of stock returns.
3. We thank the reviewer for clarifying this point.
4. The system of equations 4a–4b is overidentified (see note 10 in Ferson, Foerster, and Keim 1993).
5. The difference in the results may be most likely due to the assets examined, and not the time periods used, as rightfully pointed out by the reviewer. In addition, it would be more desirable to add debt instruments in the empirical tests as in the case of Ferson, Foerster, and Keim (1993). However, the debt market in Hong Kong is primitive and not well-developed. Return data for debt instruments are simply not available. Thus, we exclude them in the present study.

REFERENCES

Black, F., M. Jensen, and M. Scholes. 1972. "The Capital Asset Pricing Model: Some Empirical Tests." In *Studies in the Theory of Capital Markets,* edited by M. Jensen. New York: Praeger.

Blume, M.E., and I. Friend. 1973. "A New Look at the Capital Asset Pricing Model." *Journal of Finance* 28: 19–33.

Breen, W.L., L. Glosten, and R. Jagannathan. 1989. "Economic Significance of Predictable Variations in Stock Index Returns." *Journal of Finance* 44: 1177–1189.

Campbell, J.Y. 1987. "Stock Returns and the Term Structure." *Journal of Financial Economics* 18: 373–399.

Cox, J.C., J.E. Ingersoll, and S.A. Ross. 1985. "A Theory of the Term Structure of Interest Rates." *Econometrica* 53: 385–407.

Cutler, D.M., J.M. Poterba, and L.H. Summers. 1991. "Speculative Dynamics." *Review of Economic Studies* 58: 529–546.

Fama, E. 1981. "Stock Returns, Real Activity, Inflation and Money." *American Economic Review* 71: 545–565.

———. 1984. "The Information in the Term Structure." *Journal of Financial Economics* 13: 509–528.

Fama, E., and J. MacBeth. 1973. "Risk, Return and Equilibrium: Empirical Tests." *Journal of Political Economy* 71: 607–636.

Fama, E., and W. Schwert. 1977. "Asset Returns and Inflation." *Journal of Financial Economics* 5: 115–146.

Ferson, W.E. 1989. "Changes in Expected Security Returns, Risk, and the Level of Interest Rates." *Journal of Finance* 44: 1191–1217.

———. 1992. "Theory and Empirical Testing of Asset Pricing Models." In *Finance Handbook*, edited by R.A. Jarrow, W.T. Ziemba, and V. Maksimovich. Amsterdam: North Holland Publishers.

Ferson, W.E., and C.R. Harvey. 1993. "The Risk and Predictability of International Equity Returns." *Review of Financial Studies* 6: 527–566.

Ferson, W.E., and S.R. Foerster. 1994. "Finite Sample Properties of the Generalized Method of Moments in Tests of Conditional Asset Pricing Models." *Journal of Financial Economics* (August): 29–55.

Ferson, W.E., S.R. Foerster, and D.B. Keim. 1993. "General Tests of Latent Variable Models and Mean-Variance Spanning." *Journal of Finance* (March): 131–156.

Froot, K.A. 1990. "Short Rates and Expected Asset Returns." Working Paper, NBER.

Geske, R., and R. Roll. 1983. "The Fiscal and Monetary Linkage Between Stock Returns and Inflation." *Journal of Finance* 38: 1–33.

Giovannini, A., and P. Jorion. 1989. "The Time Variation of Risk and Return in the Foreign Exchange Market and Stock Markets." *Journal of Finance* (June): 307–325.

Gultekin, N.B. 1983. "Stock Market Returns and Inflation: Evidence from Other Countries." *Journal of Finance* 38: 49–65.

Hansen, L.P., and R.J. Hodrick. 1983. "Risk Adverse Speculation in the Forward Foreign Exchange Market: An Econometric Analysis of Linear Models." In *Exchange Rate and International Macroeconomics* Chicago: University of Chicago Press.

Hansen, L.P., and K. Singleton. 1982. "Generalized Instrumental Variables Estimation of Non-linear Rational Expectation Models." *Econometrica* 50: 1269–1285.

Harvey, C.R. 1991. "The World Price of Covariance Risk." *Journal of Finance* 46: 111–158.

Hawawini, G., and D.B. Keim. 1994. "On the Predictability of Common Stock Returns: World-wide Evidence." Working Paper, Rodney L. White Center for Financial Research, Wharton School.

Huberman, G., and S. Kandel. 1987. "Mean-Variance Spanning." *Journal of Finance* (September): 873–888.

Keim, D.B., and R.F. Stambaugh. 1986. "Predicting Returns in the Stock and Bond Markets." *Journal of Financial Economics* 17: 357–390.

Lee, W. 1995. "Market Timing and Short term Interest Rate." Unpublished manuscript, Harvard Business School.

Lee, W., and T.C. Chiang. 1995. "Covariance Risk, Coskewness Risk, and International Asset Pricing." Unpublished manuscript, Harvard Business School and Drexel University.

Lintner, J. 1965. "The Valuation of Risk Assets and the Selection of Risky Investment in Stock Portfolios and Capital Budgets." *Review of Economics and Statistics* 47: 13–37.

Lo, W.C., H.G. Fung, S.K. Chen, and G. Lai. 1992. "Dependency in Pacific Basin Stock Returns." *International Review of Financial Analysis* 2: 199–210.

Malliaris, A.G., and J.L. Urrutia. 1992. "The International Crash of October 1987: Causality Tests." *Journal of Financial and Quantitative Analysis* (September): 353–364.

Merton, R.C. 1973. "An Intertemporal Capital Asset Pricing Model." *Econometrica* 41: 876–887.

Mossin, J. 1966. "Equilibrium in a Capital Asset Market." *Econometrica* 34: 768–783.

Ross, S. 1976. "The Arbitrage Theory of Capital Asset Pricing." *Journal of Economic Theory* 13: 341–360.

Sharpe, W. 1964. "Capital Asset Prices: A Theory of Market Equilibrium under Conditions of Risk." *Journal of Finance* 19: 425–442.

Shiller, R.J. 1979. "The Volatility of Long-term Interest Rates and Expectations Models of the Term Structure." *Journal of Political Economy* 87: 1190–1219.

Shiller, R.J., J.Y. Campbell, and K.L. Schoenholtz. 1983. "Forward Rates and Future Policy: Interpreting the Term Structure of Interest Rates." *Brookings Paper on Economic Activity* 1: 173–217.

Solnik, B. 1983. "The Relation between Stock Prices and Inflationary Expectations." *Journal of Finance* 38: 35–48.

———. 1993. "The Performance of International Asset Allocation Strategies Using Conditioning Information." *Journal of Empirical Finance* (June): 33–56.

THE PHILIPPINES CALL MARKET FOR INTEREST RATE FUTURES:
MEAN REVERSION AND VOLATILITY STRUCTURE

Moon Hoe Lee and Osman Luis C. Ranit

ABSTRACT

In keeping with the recent interest in the literature on testing for mean reversion in asset prices, we analyzed the settlement yields of interest rate futures contracts from October 1992 when the instrument started trading on the Manila International Futures Exchange in Philippines. We report statistically significant evidence of mean reversion in the settlement yields. We also investigated the volatility structure of settlement yields of the Philippines interest rate futures contracts. We found that the volatility of the most nearby contract is about two and a half times the volatility of the next nearby contract, which is predicted by Samuelson's (1965) hypothesis. However, we did not find any evidence of monotonicity in the relation between volatility and maturity.

INTRODUCTION

The Philippines capital market for years has been limited to commercial banking and a secondary stock market in Manila. A major development in the emerging capital market for this country, which is located in the Asia Pacific basin, took place

Research in International Business and Finance, Supplement 1, pages 329–334.

ISBN: 0-7623-0110-4

in the 1980s. In October 1984 the Manila International Futures Exchange Inc. (MIFEI) and the Manila Futures Clearing House Inc. (MFCHI) were established. MIFEI opened for trading in October 1986. Agricultural commodity futures, currency futures, and interest rate futures contracts are traded on MIFEI and cleared through MFCHI. These non-equity transactions are closely monitored by the Philippines government's Securities and Exchange Commission (SEC). Representatives from the Brokers and Exchange Department (BED) in the SEC monitor daily trading. Price quotations for counters traded are picked up immediately by Reuter's and Telerate and beamed worldwide from their video screens.

The Manila International Futures Exchange is a unique market. Unlike most markets in North America, the futures market in Manila is a call market. Futures contracts are transacted by a sessional method of trading. Two trading sessions are conducted daily for agricultural, currency, and interest rate futures contracts with one morning session and one afternoon session from Monday to Friday, except holidays. The trading of currency and interest rate futures contracts follow after the trading of agricultural commodity futures contracts.

The international futures market in Manila is a relatively new market. But it is a fast growing market trading in futures products which are important to the Southeast Asian commercial center such as agricultural commodity futures contracts (sugar, copra, coffee, and soybean), local currency futures contracts, and local interest rate futures contracts. The Philippines interest rate futures contract was first traded in October 1992 and several maturities are actively traded. We selected this financial product for analysis for several reasons. Quotes for the interest rate futures contract take the form of yields for one-month, two-month, three-month, and four-month contracts. The design features of the Philippines interest rate futures contract are very different from those of the interest rate futures products seen in North America. A second reason is that, although Bessembinder et al. (1995) in a recent article reported statistically significant evidence of mean reversion in the futures prices for agricultural commodities, crude oil, and metals, they did not find statistically significant evidence for the futures price of a U.S. interest rate product. This result seems to be at odds with the well-known articles on models of the determination of interest rates. For instance, the well-known Vasicek (1977) and Cox, Ingersoll, and Ross (1985) models specify mean reversion as an attractive property of interest rate models. The recent literature has also focused on mean reversion in other asset prices. Poterba and Summers (1988), and Fama and French (1988) reported mean reversion in stock prices.

We further examined the volatility structure of the yield quotes of the Philippines futures interest rate product. Samuelson (1965) postulated that the volatility of nearby futures contracts in general could be expected to be higher than the volatility of more distant futures contracts. We reported evidence in partial support of Samuelson's hypothesis for settlement yields from the Manila futures market.

METHOD OF ESTIMATION

Let $r(t, \tau)$ be the settlement yield at time t of a futures contract which delivers a financial instrument at time $t + \tau$, where τ is the fixed maturity of the futures contract. Settlement yields are observed over the time interval, $t = 1, 2, ..N$, where N is the sample size. Suppose the settlement yields follow a first-order autoregressive process of the form:

$$r(t,\tau) - \bar{r} = y(t) \tag{1}$$

and

$$dy(t) = -\kappa y(t) + \nu dz(t) \tag{2}$$

where $\bar{r}$ is the mean settlement yield, $y(t)$ is the deviation from the mean settlement yield, κ is the speed of reversion toward the mean settlement yield, ν is the volatility of the change in the deviation from the mean settlement yield, and $dz(t)$ is the increment to a standard Wiener process.

The above specification of a first-order autoregressive process has the advantage that a measure of the coefficient of mean reversion is directly specified. In addition, we have a model where the coefficient of mean reversion and the volatility are jointly specified. This permits joint estimation of the parameter of mean reversion and the volatility of settlement yields.

Samuelson (1965, 1976) has suggested the use of a first-order autoregressive process to model equilibrium futures asset prices. He applied the first-order autoregressive process to demonstrate that nearby commodity futures contracts would show more price variability than distant commodity futures contracts. This has become known as Samuelson's hypothesis. Prices in a first-order autoregressive process would self-correct if external forces were to displace the price of the asset at any point in time from its equilibrium zone. The price system, therefore, has a stable equilibrium.

The set of parameters $\{\kappa, \nu, \bar{r}\}$ of the equation system (1) and (2) can be jointly estimated by maximum likelihood.

Evidence of mean reversion in financial futures settlement yields is provided by the significance of t-statistics for the coefficients of mean reversion, κ.

To extend the test of Samuelson's hypothesis to financial futures contracts, let ν_m be the volatility for the shorter maturity futures contract and ν_n be the volatility for the longer maturity futures contract, where m and n are the maturities of the financial futures contracts measured in months. The null hypothesis can be stated as follows:

$$\nu_m^2 \leq \nu_n^2 \tag{3}$$

This null hypothesis can be tested against the alternative hypothesis

$$\nu_m^2 > \nu_n^2 \tag{4}$$

The statistic for testing the null hypothesis is

$$F_{(N_m - 3),(N_n - 3)} = \frac{\nu_m^2}{\nu_n^2} \tag{5}$$

where $(N_m - 3)$ and $(N_n - 3)$ are the degrees of freedom for the terms in the numerator and in the denominator respectively. The sample sizes for the shorter and longer maturity contracts are N_m and N_n number of observations respectively. If the value for the F-statistic calculated from equation (5) is greater than the critical value of the F-statistic for an upper-tailed test, then the null hypothesis is rejected in favor of the alternative hypothesis of $\nu_m^2 > \nu_n^2$.

DATA AND RESULTS

Interest rate futures contracts commenced trading on the Manila International Futures Exchange in Philippines in October 1992. Interest rate futures contracts of one-month, two-month, three-month, and four-month maturity are traded on that exchange and cleared by the Manila Futures Clearing House. Contracts of one-month, two-month, and three-month maturity are traded daily. The four-month maturity contract is traded less frequently. The quotes are expressed in annualized percent yield.

The data for this study consist of daily settlement yields of the Philippines interest rate futures contracts with maturities of one month, two months, and three months for the period from October 1992 to February 1994. The settlement yields were collected from the files of futures brokers in Manila.

The estimates for the average speed of mean reversion, κ, the average volatility, ν, of the settlement yields of interest rate futures contracts, the mean, $\bar{r}$, of settlement yields, their standard errors and the F-test for the null hypotheses $\nu_1^2 \leq \nu_2^2$ and $\nu_2^2 \leq \nu_3^2$ are shown in Table 1. Subscripts for ν label the maturity of the futures contracts in months.

One objective of this study is to examine whether or not the settlement yields of the Philippines interest rate futures contracts are mean-reverting. Column 4 of Table 1 shows the estimated coefficients of mean reversion for the settlement yields. The coefficient of mean reversion has an average value of 0.052 for the one-month contract, 0.013 for the two-month contract, and 0.021 for the three-month contract. The t-values for these coefficients are 2.78, 1.83, and 2.27, respectively. All of these coefficients of mean reversion are significant at the 5% level of significance.

Column 5 gives the estimated values of the volatility parameter. The average volatility of the settlement yields for the one-month contract is 0.0045 with a t-value of 24. The average volatility for the two-month and three-month contracts is of the order of 0.0016 with a t-value of 24. All the volatility estimates are significant at

Table 1. Mean Reversion and Volatility Structure of Philippines Interest Rate Futures

Period	*Maturity (months)*	*N*	κ	v	$\bar{r}$	*F-value*
10/1/92–2/25/94	1	313	0.052188 (0.018756)	0.004518 (0.000185)	0.1440 (0.0049)	
10/1/92–2/25/94	2	320	0.013130 (0.007157)	0.001659 (0.000065)	0.1449 (0.0074)	7.41
10/1/92–2/25/94	3	320	0.021439 (0.009437)	0.001621 (0.000064)	0.1484 (0.0045)	1.04

Notes: N = number of observations
κ = rate of mean reversion
v = volatility
$\bar{r}$ = mean settlement yield of interest rate futures contracts
F value = value of F-test for the null hypotheses
$v_1^2 \le v_2^2$ and $v_2^2 \le v_3^2$ where subscripts denote maturity in months.
Standard errors are given within parentheses.

the 5% level. An F-test shows that the volatility of the settlement yield for the one-month contract is higher than that for the two-month contract. The computed F-value is 7.41. However, no monotonicity in the volatility structure is detected.

The estimated mean settlement yields are shown in column 6 of Table 1. The mean settlement yields are 14.40%, 14.49%, and 14.84% per annum, respectively, for the one-month, two-month, and three-month contracts. These mean settlement yields are all significant at the 5% level.

CONCLUSION

The financial futures contract is a new product traded in Philippines, one of the emerging capital markets in the Asia Pacific region. The Manila International Futures Exchange introduced the financial futures contract in October 1992. Since the start of trading, three maturities (one-month, two-months, and three-months) have been actively traded on that exchange.

There has been a fair deal of recent interest in the literature on the equilibrium conditions affecting asset prices. One of these conditions is the mean-reverting property of asset prices in equilibrium capital markets. One of the objectives of the present study is to investigate the property of mean reversion for interest rate futures contracts traded in an emerging capital market. We have chosen the financial futures contract recently introduced in an Asia Pacific country. The Philippines capital market is not generally known as a well-developed market in Southeast Asia. In recent years Philippines has introduced innovations to its secondary capital market. One of these innovations is the Manila International Futures Exchange. We find strong evidence of mean reversion in Philippines interest rate futures for all actively traded maturities. This evidence is present in the yield data from a new futures market. It shows that the Philippines financial futures market operates like a well-functioning capital market.

We examined the volatility structure of the Philippines interest rate futures. We found partial support of Samuelson's hypothesis in the Philippines financial futures market. The volatility of settlement yields for one-month contract is unmistakably greater than the volatility for the two-month contract. But we did not find any evidence of monotonicity in the volatility structure.

REFERENCES

Bessembinder, H. et al. 1995. "Mean Reversion in Equilibrium Asset Prices: Evidence from the Futures Term Structure." *Journal of Finance* 50: 361–375.

Cox, J.C., J.E. Ingersoll, and S.A. Ross. 1985. "A Theory of the Term Structure of Interest Rates." *Econometrica* 53: 385–407.

Fama, E.F., and K.R. French. 1988. "Permanent and Temporary Components of Stock Prices." *Journal of Political Economy* 96: 246–273.

Poterba, J.M., and L.H. Summers. 1988. "Mean Reversion in Stock Prices: Evidence and Implications." *Journal of Financial Economics* 22: 27–59.

Samuelson, P.A. 1965. "Proof that Properly Anticipated Prices Fluctuate Randomly." *Industrial Management Review* 6: 41–49.

———. 1976. "Is Real-world Price a Tale Told by the Idiot of Chance?" *Review of Economics and Statistics* 58: 120–123.

Vasicek, O. 1977. "An Equilibrium Characterization of the Term Structure." *Journal of Financial Economics* 5: 177–188.

THE EFFECTS OF ENVIRONMENTAL REGULATION ON STOCK PRICES ON THE MEXICAN STOCK EXCHANGE

Dan W. French, Martin J. Herrera, and Janet M. Tanski

ABSTRACT

This paper examines the impact of the announcement of environmental regulation on returns on stocks traded on the Bolsa Mexicana de Valores. Returns around 13 different announcements from 1987 to 1991 indicate that the market reacts negatively to new environmental regulation. The negative reaction appears to persist for at least several days following the announcement; 10 of 12 average daily returns following the point at which the information becomes known are negative. In addition, the event with the largest negative impact is the most significant environmental event, the passage of the National Program of Environmental Protection.

INTRODUCTION

The impact of events on common stock returns has been the subject of numerous articles in the finance literature. Most studies show that capital markets in developed countries are highly efficient in the sense that prices quickly adjust to publicly

Research in International Business and Finance, Supplement 1, pages 335–341.

ISBN: 0-7623-0110-4

available information as investors act to receive a return commensurate with the level of perceived risk. Hill and Schneeweis (1983) show an immediate impact of the Three Mile Island nuclear accident on equity prices for nuclear as well as non-nuclear public utility firms. Kalra, Henderson, and Raines (1993) show that the Chernobyl Nuclear Accident had a negative impact on utility share prices in the United States and attribute this impact to a change in market expectations for the future of the nuclear power industry.

The cost to firms of noncompliance with environmental regulation is increasing in both the United States (Hicks 1992; Burnett-Hall 1994) and Mexico (Ranger 1993). As information regarding new environmental regulation becomes public, increased costs of complying should become reflected in the stock prices of those companies affected. In this paper, we briefly review Mexico's recent changes in environmental policy and examine the effect of specific environmental regulation on rates of return of securities traded on the Bolsa Mexicana de Valores (BMV), the Mexican Stock Exchange. Depending on the expected level of enforcement of these regulations, we would expect rates of return to decline because of increased costs of complying with the new regulations. Our objective in the paper is to see if this is indeed the result as well as to see how rapidly prices on the BMV respond to public information regarding environmental regulation.

ENVIRONMENTAL POLICY IN MEXICO

As a result of many factors, including the rapid industrialization strategy followed since the 1940s, Mexico has faced increasing environmental problems. Air and water pollution, hazardous waste, soil erosion, salinization, the use of sewage water for irrigation, pesticides, solid waste dumps, industrial and toxic waste dumps, the international flow of toxic waste from the United States into Mexico, deforestation, loss of biodiversity: all are creating very serious problems.

Mexico's environmental policy began with the 1971 Federal Law for the Prevention and Control of Environmental Contamination which basically established an administrative regulatory power under the direction of the federal government. The Subsecretariat of Environmental Improvement was under the Secretariat of Health and for years was a very poorly funded agency with few qualified technical personnel that maintained solely symbolic and educational functions. In 1982 the de la Madrid administration created the Secretariat of Urban Development and Ecology (SEDUE), elevating the environment's importance in policy. However, SEDUE's poor performance and scandalous management, along with the fact that the economy was collapsing meant that environmental regulation and pollution cleanup languished (Mumme 1991). In March 1988 a new environmental law took effect called the General Law for Ecological Equilibrium and Environmental Protection. The law is specific in defining the terms of environmental regulation, and it is continuously being amended by new executive decrees which are published in the *Diario Oficial*, the official publication of record for the federal government in Mexico. Carlos Salinas de Gortari brought environmental issues to the fore in his campaign and throughout his administration.

Since Salinas de Gortari took office, SEDUE has been reorganized, and now environmental regulation and enforcement are under the umbrella of SEDESOL (the Ministry of Social Development). In the area of ecology, SEDESOL exercises its authority through two of its agencies, the *Instituto Nacional de Ecologia* (National Institute of Ecology), also known as INE, and the *Procuraduría Federal de Proteccíon al Ambiente* (Office of the Attorney General for Environmental Protection, or, PROFEPA). Generally speaking INE acts as the regulatory branch (creating policy, setting standards, issuing permits) and PROFEPA serves as an enforcement agency. However, the President, the Head of the Federal District Department, and the Congress also have constitutional authority to issue environmental regulations.

ENVIRONMENTAL EVENT DATA

To identify the effect, if any, of the passage of environmental legislation on Mexican stock returns, we use standard event study methods. The "events" in this study are

Table 1. Mexican Environmental Legislation and Regulations Used in the Study

Date	*Brief Description*
1 Jan 19, 1987	Import and export of hazardous materials that can cause damage to the environment or that are a risk to the public health
2 Aug 4, 1988	Maximum permissible limits for discharges of residual water into bodies of water by the sugar producing industry
3 Oct 19, 1988	Procedure for determining the concentration of carbon monoxide in the air
4 Dec 14, 1988	Establishes guidelines for formulating, issuing, and changing technical ecological standards
5 Dec 13, 1989	Requirements for operating a controlled confinement area for hazardous materials
6 Mar 1, 1990	Limits the use of gasoline and diesel powered vehicles on one day of the week in Mexico City
7 Jul 10, 1990	The National Program of Environmental Protection
8 Jan 16, 1991	Maximum permissible levels of the opaqueness of exhaust smoke from diesel powered vehicles
9 Feb 20, 1991	Maximum limits of contaminants in water discharges from the coffee industry
10 Sep 20, 1991	Maximum levels of emissions of solid particulates from the manufacture, distribution, or storage of cement
11 Oct 1, 1991	Establishes the method for measuring the concentration of solid particulate matter suspended in the air
12 Oct 29, 1991	Minimum contaminant gas conversion efficiency of catalytic converters
13 Aug 9, 1991	Control of cross-border movement and disposal of hazardous waste

the passage of laws or the issuance of decrees, accords, or regulations under Mexican environmental legislation. Each event date is the date on which the event was published in the *Diario Oficial*. During the 1987 to 1991 period, we identify as potentially important and record a total of 13 environmental events. Table 1 lists these events.

The source of stock prices is the BMV's comprehensive daily price report which contains detailed prices and dividend information for all securities traded on the BMV. For each event, we compute daily returns of all stocks traded on the BMV for 10 days prior to the event and for 10 days after the event. We then compute an average market return which is the arithmetic mean of all stocks traded for each day. The number of stocks included in the calculation depends on the number trading during the event time period and varies from 32 to 140.

RESULTS

To examine the impact of environmental regulation in general on stock prices, we average all returns over all 13 events. Each event day is defined as day 0, days prior to the event are –1 to –10, and days after the event are +1 to +10. For example, day 0 then has the average return on the event publication date for all 13 environmental events. Figure 1 presents the average returns for all events accumulated from day –10 (cumulative average returns). The figure shows that, in general, stock prices tended to rise prior to the environmental events and fall afterward.

For a more detailed view of the results, Table 2 presents daily mean returns, *t*-statistics for the daily mean returns (testing for a difference from zero), and the

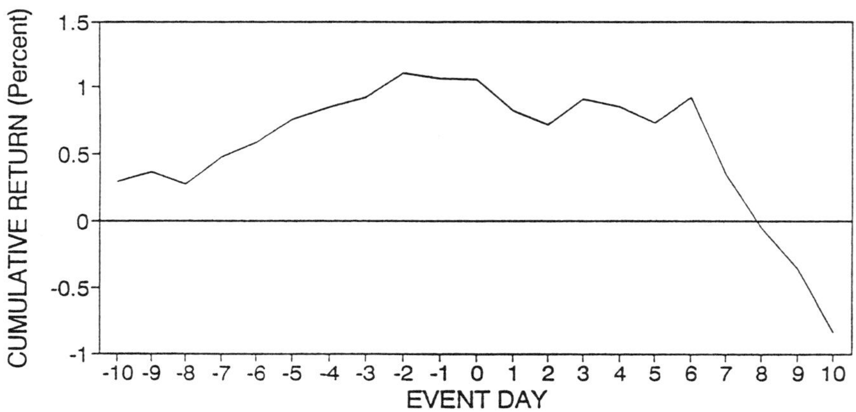

Figure 1. Cumulative Average Returns for All Companies with All Events Combined

Table 2. Returns for All Companies with All Events Combined

Event Day	*Average Return (percent)*	*Average Return t-statistic*	*Cumulative Return (percent)*
–10	.30	2.55*	.30
–9	.07	.63	.37
–8	–.09	–.79	.28
–7	.20	1.74	.48
–6	.10	.90	.58
–5	.18	1.58	.77
–4	.09	.77	.86
–3	.07	.61	.93
–2	.18	1.57	1.11
–1	–.05	–.40	1.06
0	–.01	–.05	1.06
+1	–.23	–1.96*	.83
+2	–.11	–.92	.72
+3	.19	1.61	.91
+4	–.05	–.47	.85
+5	–.12	–1.02	.74
+6	.19	1.61	.92
+7	–.58	–4.96*	.35
+8	–.39	–3.40*	–.05
+9	–.30	–2.62*	–.35
+10	–.48	–4.16*	–.83

Note: * Significant at the $\alpha = .05$ level.

numerical cumulative average returns used to construct Figure 1. Although the event day is day 0, we would likely expect to see a market reaction beginning on day –1 because day 0 is the day of publication, and the material to be published becomes known on the day prior to publication. With the exception of day –8, the first day to exhibit negative returns is day –1. This is consistent with a negative reaction to environmental events, and it is consistent with the notion that a market reaction would begin on day –1.

Within the time period –10 to –2, 8 of the 9 returns are positive. This is not surprising because positive returns occurred much more often than negative returns during the period under study. Of the 12 returns between –1 and +10, only 2 are positive and 10 are negative. The probability of finding 10 of 12 returns negative using the binomial distribution, if there is a 50% chance of negative returns, is only .019. This result gives statistical support to a negative market reaction following the knowledge of new environmental regulation.

Table 3. Cumulative Average Returns for Each Event on Days –2, –1, 0, +1, and +10

	Event Day				
Event Number	*–2*	*–1*	*0*	*+1*	*+10*
1	1.0	0.0	0.5	1.7	8.6
2	1.6	1.7	1.5	1.9	1.3
3	4.9	3.1	1.5	2.3	0.5
4	0.7	1.6	2.4	4.0	9.9
5	–3.7	–4.1	–3.7	–3.4	–3.9
6	1.2	1.8	2.1	1.6	1.7
7	0.1	–0.3	–1.5	–3.3	–6.9
8	8.1	7.1	7.3	2.1	1.2
9	–3.5	–2.9	–1.9	–1.6	–7.5
10	0.9	–0.1	–0.4	0.7	1.3
11	0.5	1.5	1.8	2.1	–4.0
12	0.7	1.4	1.4	1.1	–3.5
13	3.8	3.9	3.9	4.3	–.4

To examine possible effects of specific types of environmental regulation on stock returns, Table 3 provides cumulative average returns for selected event days (–2, –1, 0, +1, +10) for each of the 13 events. Based on negative returns (declining cumulative average returns) around the event day 0 and negative cumulative average returns on day +10, the following events appear to generate the greatest market reactions:

Event 5 - the requirements for operating a controlled confinement area for hazardous materials,
Event 7 - the passage of the National Program of Environmental Protection, and
Event 8 - the maximum permissible levels of exhaust smoke from diesel powered vehicles.

Of these events, the passage of the National Program of Environmental Protection had the most negative cumulative average return on day +10 and had more negative reactions around day 0. This is logical since the passage of the national program is more likely to affect a broader range of companies than regulation aimed at specific segments.

Note that events 9, 11, and 12 also exhibit large negative cumulate average returns by day +10. However, their returns are not consistently negative around day 0, so we cannot attribute the strong negative reaction to the event alone.

CONCLUSION

The evidence presented in this paper strongly indicates that there is a negative reaction on the Bolsa Mexicana de Valores to the announcement of environmental regulation. The market reaction begins on the day that the information becomes known, the day prior to publication in the *Diario Oficial*. The negative returns associated with the announcement appear to continue at least for several days, indicating that the market does not fully absorb new information immediately.

Negative returns also persist throughout the 10-day period following the announcement of environmental regulation. However, we cannot say with confidence the negative returns later in the period (days +4 to +10) are necessarily tied to the environmental regulation announcement. It is quite possible that other events unidentified in this study have negatively influenced security returns during those days. Possibly a larger sample over a longer time period, once such data become available, will provide for stronger conclusions on the subject.

REFERENCES

Burnett-Hall, R. 1994. "Asset Values and Environmental Legislation." *Accountancy* (January):126.

Hicks, R.C. 1992. "Environmental Legislation and the Costs of Compliance." *Government Finance Review* (April): 7–10.

Hill, J., and T. Schneeweis. 1983. "The Effect of Three Mile Island on Electric Utility Stock Prices: A Note." *The Journal of Finance* XXXVIII (4): 1285–1292.

Kalra, R.G.V. Henderson, Jr., and G.A. Raines. 1993. "Effects of the Chernobyl Nuclear Accident on Utility Share Prices." *Quarterly Journal of Business and Economics* 32(2): 52–77.

Mumme, S.P. 1991. "Clearing the Air: Environmental Reform in Mexico." *Environment* 33 (10): 7–30.

Ranger, E.M., Jr. 1993. "The High Cost of Noncompliance." *Business Mexico* (July): 44, 49.

THE ROBUSTNESS OF THE DAY-OF-THE-WEEK EFFECT: EVIDENCE FROM THE TAIWAN STOCK EXCHANGE

Che-Peng Lin and M. Mark Walker

ABSTRACT

This study examines the existence of the day-of-the-week effect in an emerging international market, Taiwan, during the period from January 6, 1986 to September 30, 1994. Test methodologies include the Ordinary Least Squares (OLS) approach and robustness tests. Using the OLS approach we find that the average returns for Saturday are abnormally high in Taiwan. However, after we correct for (1) the large sample size problem and (2) violations in the conventional assumptions regarding the OLS error terms, the abnormal "Saturday effect" becomes insignificant. This result, which is consistent with Connolly's (1989, 1991) evidence for U.S. stocks, supports the efficient market hypothesis.

INTRODUCTION

Financial theory indicates that stock prices should follow a random walk (see Fama 1965, 1970). According to the random walk hypothesis, an invariant relationship should exist between stock market returns and time flows. There has been substan-

Research in International Business and Finance, Supplement 1, pages 343–359.

ISBN: 0-7623-0110-4

tial empirical research, however, which reports that calendar anomalies do exist. One such anomaly is the day-of-the-week effect.

Studies using daily stock returns usually assume that the distribution of stock returns is identical for each day of the week. This assumption has been shown to be inappropriate by numerous studies which find that U.S. stocks tend to earn lower returns on Monday, while foreign stocks, such as those traded in Japan and Australia, tend to earn lower returns on Tuesday. Because the day-of-the week effect exists in various countries, it is difficult for researchers to determine whether the effect is generated independently within each country or whether the effect is generated by the behavior of security holders who actively trade in international markets. That is, international holders could "export" calendar anomalies from one country to another (Pettengill 1986). To avoid this problem, we test whether stocks listed on the Taiwan Stock Exchange (TSE) exhibit a day-of-the-week effect.

Taiwan currently has the world's second largest foreign exchange reserves (Japan is ranked first).[1] However, Taiwan did not open its stock market to foreign investors until December 28, 1990, when the government of Taiwan passed a law that allowed foreign institutions to invest directly in the Taiwan stock market.[2] Because this locality feature reduces the international market integration problem (also known as the exporting calendar anomalies problem), the Taiwan Stock Exchange is an interesting market to reexamine the day-of-the-week effect. While several prior studies have tested for the presence of the day-of-the-week effect in the Taiwan stock market, the results are mixed (see Ho 1990; Jeng 1991; Tong 1992).[3]

The present study uses several methodologies to examine the day-of-the-week effect in Taiwan. First, we employ ordinary least squares (OLS) linear regression models with strong statistical assumptions. Both traditional and modified regression models are examined. The traditional OLS model has been widely adopted in previous studies that examine weekly patterns in daily stock returns. The modified OLS model, on the other hand, incorporates the return on a risk-free asset as an independent variable in order to incorporate the impact of local interest rate changes on stock prices. Second, this study investigates the robustness of the day-of-the-week effect in the Taiwan stock market. Previous studies that have examined calendar anomalies in the Taiwan stock market have not conducted robustness tests.

The paper is organized as follows. The first section reviews prior studies that have examined the day-of-the-week effect. The following sections describe the data, methodology, and results. The final section presents the conclusions.

BACKGROUND

The day-of-the-week effect was first documented in the U.S. stock markets by Cross (1973) and French (1980). In general, they found that stock returns on Mondays were significantly negative, while stock returns on Fridays were significantly higher. Gibbons and Hess (1981) proposed the settlement hypothesis as one explanation of the day-of-the-week effect. The settlement hypothesis suggests that different settlement dates cause the day-of-the-week effect. In the U.S. stock market, trades are settled several business days after the transaction date. Because business days (rather than calendar days) determine the settlement date, the length of the settlement period does vary. Before February 10, 1968, for example, settlement was to occur in four business days. Thus, one could argue that a transaction price on Monday should represent a four-day forward price equal to the transaction price on Monday plus four days interest (at the risk-free rate). A transaction price on Tuesday, on the other hand, should reflect a six-day forward price (four business days plus two non-trading days). As a result, Gibbons and Hess (1981) argued that stock prices on Tuesdays, Wednesdays, Thursdays, and Fridays should be grossed up by the riskless rate of interest for six days. While Gibbons and Hess (1981) hypothesized that different settlement periods may have caused the significant negative returns on Mondays, their empirical findings did not support the settlement hypothesis.

In addition to the settlement hypothesis, there have been two other attempts to explain the abnormal negative returns observed on Mondays in the U.S. market. However, neither the measurement error hypothesis (see, e.g., Gibbons and Hess 1981; Keim and Stambaugh 1984) nor the specialist-related biases hypothesis (see, e.g., Keim and Stambaugh 1984) are able to fully explain the day-of-the-week effect.

A second line of inquiry has investigated whether international stock markets exhibit a day-of-the-week effect. While Theobald and Price (1984) reported a similar effect in U.K. equity markets, Pettway and Tapley (1984) studied the weekly pattern in the Japanese stock market. Using three market indexes over the period 1979 through 1982, they found that Tuesday returns were the lowest and Wednesday returns were the highest. Jaffe and Westerfield (1985a) examined stock market returns in the United States, U.K., Japan, Canada, and Australia and also found evidence of a significant day-of-the-week effect. Japanese and Australian stock markets, for example, experienced lower returns on Tuesdays. Jaffe and Westerfield (1985b) proposed the time zone hypothesis: the significant negative return on Tuesday for Japan and Australia was affected by the Monday effect in the United States. Tokyo, Japan, is 14 hours ahead of New York and Sydney, Australia, is 15 hours ahead. The time zone hypothesis explains some of the Australian results, but it does not explain the Japanese results. Moreover, while the authors also tested the settlement and measurement error hypotheses, they found no evidence to support these potential explanations.

Solnik and Bousquet (1990) found evidence of the day-of-the-week effect in the Paris Bourse. Similar to the cases in Japan and Australia, the Paris Bourse exhibits a strong and consistent negative return on Tuesdays. When compared to other stock markets, however, the Paris Bourse has a peculiar market structure. All major companies listed on the Paris exchange are traded on a forward basis. This forward market has no marking-to-market and provides a one-time monthly settlement of all transactions at the end of the month. Solnik and Bousquet (1990) tested whether this unique settlement procedure caused the negative returns on Tuesday, but they concluded that the settlement hypothesis did not explain the negative Tuesday returns.

Barone (1990) analyzed the Italian stock market based on the Milan Stock Exchange's "MIB storico" stock index over the period January 2, 1975 to August 22, 1989. He reported negative returns for both Monday and Tuesday, and positive returns for Friday.

Kato (1990) reexamined the weekly patterns in Japanese stock returns over the period from April 1978 through June 1987 by using the Value Weighted Index of the Tokyo Stock Exchange. In Japan the Tokyo Stock Exchange was open from Monday through Saturday until 1972. After 1972 the Tokyo stock market sometimes closed on either the second or third Saturday of each month. During the period between July 1986 and January 1989, the market closed on both the second and third Saturday of each month. There has been no Saturday trading since February 1989. Kato (1990) indicated that after October 7, 1972 there has been no cash settlement on Saturday even when the market was open. This peculiar trading structure provides an interesting opportunity to reexamine the settlement effect hypothesis. In Japan transactions are settled three business days after the transaction date. Thus, if the settlement hypothesis fully explains the day-of-the-week effect, "the Thursday returns in the week closed by Friday trading should be higher than Thursday returns in the week closed by Saturday trading" (Kato 1990, p. 1037). The results did not support this hypothesis. Instead, Kato (1990) found low returns on Mondays and Tuesdays, and high returns on Saturdays.

Ho (1990) examined the daily returns of the U.K., United States, and 10 other stock markets in the Asia Pacific area and reported the existence of a strong day-of-the-week effect for most markets. Using daily stock returns on the Taiwan Weighted Stock Index for the period January 1975 to November 1987, Ho (1990) found significant results for Tuesday, Wednesday, and Saturday. Jeng (1991), on the other hand, examined returns from January 1987 to September 1990, and found that a day-of-the-week effect existed only for one index. Finally, Tong (1992) examined daily returns from 1980–1988 and found evidence that Saturday returns are abnormally high in the Taiwan stock market.

More recently, Connolly (1989, 1991) analyzed the day-of-the-week effect in the U.S. markets. In contrast to prior research, however, Connolly (1989, 1991) examined alternative testing procedures. Because previous empirical tests of the day-of-the-week effect are often based on foundations of models with strong statistical assumptions, Connolly (1989, 1991) argued that previous results may be biased if these foundations are not evaluated systematically. For example, there is a problem of interpreting classical test statistics when researchers use very large samples. Connolly (1989) noted that "Standard F-statistics, . . . , will distort sample evidence if the significance level is not adjusted as the sample size increases." In addition, Connolly (1989) examined the robustness of the day-of-the-week effect after correcting for violations in the conventional assumptions about the ordinary least squares (OLS) error terms. After appropriately adjusting for the large sample size problem, as well as heteroskedasticity and autocorrelation in the daily stock returns, Connolly (1989, 1991) found that the day-of-the-week effect in the U. S. market no longer existed by the mid-1970s.

Following Connolly (1989, 1991), Chang, Pinegar, and Ravichandran (1993) analyzed the robustness of the day-of-the-week effect in international markets. They found that the day-of-the-week effect remains in several international markets even when robustness tests are included. This finding "further complicates the international day-of-the-week effect puzzle" (see Chang, Pinegar, and Ravichandran 1993, p. 497).

DATA AND METHODOLOGY

Data

This study examines daily stock market returns calculated using the Weighted Stock Index provided by the Taiwan Stock Exchange for the period January 6, 1986 to September 30, 1994. The calendar dates in this study are indicated by year/month/day. For example, the main study period begins 86/01/06 and ends 94/09/30.

A sub-period from January 6, 1986 to June 30, 1992 is also examined. The sub-period ends on June 30, 1992 to further control for the international market integration problem. On December 28, 1990, the amended *Security Investment*

Table 1. Direct Investment in Taiwan Stock Market from Foreign Investment Institutions

	Number of Applications		*Applied Amount*	*Approved Amount*	*Total Remittance*	*Stockholding in % of*
	Applied	*Approved*	*($mil - U.S.)*		*($mil - U.S.)*	*Remittance*
1988	–	–	–	–	–	–
1989	–	–	–	–	–	–
1990	–	–	–	–	–	–
1991	25	19	$ 1244.80	$ 522.40	–	–
1992	27	23	1189.40	569.10	$ 846.40	–
1993	74	58	4709.50	2788.10	2599.00	85.57
1994*	38	22	4457.70	2005.00	4073.80	75.95

Notes: 1. The Taiwan Stock Exchange committee granted foreign investment in the Taiwan stock market on Dec. 28, 1990.

2. By July 1994 the TSEC had permitted 71 foreign investment institutions to invest directly in Taiwan's security market.

*Accumulated up to June 1994.

Source: Taiwan Stock Exchange Committee (TSEC).

Regulations and Exchange Settlement Rules for Overseas Chinese and Foreigners was enacted. This law allowed foreign institutions to invest directly in the Taiwan stock market. According to the statistical record, foreign institutions started to remit money into Taiwan in 1992 and officially hold shares of Taiwanese companies in 1993 (see Table 1). Thus, the locality feature of the Taiwan stock market is strongest for the sub-period ending on June 30, 1992.

The maximum allowance for direct investment by foreign institutions is currently 7.5 billion U.S. dollars. As a result, direct investment by foreign institutions is limited to about 4% of the total market value in Taiwan (*Central Daily News—International Edition* 1994b). Since the impact of direct foreign investments is still very limited in Taiwan, the locality feature of this market should be strong throughout the January 6, 1986 to September 30, 1994 study period.

We also recognize the effect of the worldwide October crash in 1987. In Taiwan the fluctuation limits on daily price movements in the TSE caused the effects of the October crash to be spread throughout the week of October 19 to October 24, 1987. To avoid any potential bias caused by the crash, six observations (87/10/19–87/10/24, Monday–Saturday) are excluded from the main data set. The main data set is divided into two periods. The complete data set contains 2,496 daily returns over the period 86/01/06–94/09/30, while the sub-period contains 1,851 daily returns from 86/01/06–92/06/30. We call this Data Set I.

In order to test whether the potential day-of-the-week effect is a non-trading weekend effect or a non-trading holiday effect, returns following holidays (or holiday returns) are deleted. Holidays are defined as days when "trading would normally have occurred but did not" (Lakonishok and Smidt 1988, p. 411). We delete the holiday returns from the main data set and refer to this modified data set as Data Set II. Data Set II contains 2,363 and 1,755 daily returns for the period 86/01/06–94/09/30 and the sub-period 86/01/06–92/06/30, respectively.

Daily stock returns, *Rt*, are calculated as follows.

$$Rt = \ln\left(Index_t / Index_{t-1} \right), \tag{1}$$

where *Index* = the value of the TSE Weighted Index.

Methodology

Traditional OLS Model

The following regression model is used to examine the day-of-the-week effect in Taiwan:

$$R_t = \gamma_1 D_{1t} + \gamma_2 D_{2t} + \gamma_3 D_{3t} + \gamma_4 D_{4t} + \gamma_5 D_{5t} + \gamma_6 D_{6t} + e_t \tag{2}$$

where R_t is the daily return of the TSE Weighted Index on date *t*. D_{1t} is a dummy variable that is equal to 1 if *t* is a Monday and zero otherwise. D_{2t} is a dummy variable for Tuesday and so on. The disturbance term is e_t. The coefficients γ_1

through γ_6 represent the mean returns for Monday through Saturday. The F-statistic for this non-intercept regression model tests the null hypothesis that $\gamma_1 = \gamma_2 = \ldots. = \gamma_6$ and examines if any coefficient deviates significantly from zero.

Modified OLS Model

Financial theory indicates that stock returns are a function of the return on a risk-free asset. As a result, we test whether the interest accumulation on a risk-free asset during non-trading weekends or holidays, as well as local interest rate changes, affect daily stock price patterns in the Taiwan stock market. We modify the traditional OLS model by adding the daily return on a risk-free asset as an independent variable. The annualized three-month time-deposit rates offered by the First Commercial Bank (one of three commercial banks which are backed by the government in Taiwan) are used as the short-term risk-free rate. The Appendix explains the procedure for calculating the daily interest returns. After incorporating the return on the risk-free asset, the modified equation is as follows.

$$R_t = \gamma_0 INT + \sum_{j=1}^{6} \gamma_j D_{jt} + e_t, \tag{3}$$

where INT = the daily return on the risk-free asset.

Robustness Tests

Robustness tests are conducted using the following model specification.

$$R_t = \gamma_0 + \sum_{i=1}^{n} \gamma_i DAY_{it} + \varepsilon_t, \tag{4}$$

where n equals the number of days which show a significant abnormal return (n = 1, 2, . . 6), γ_0 is the intercept term, and γ_i equals the coefficient on dummy variable DAY_{it}. The dummy variables, DAY_{it}, take a value of one if the return is observed on a particular day which exhibits an abnormal average return (e.g., Monday), and assume a value of zero on days that do not exhibit an abnormal return.

This study incorporates two robustness tests: the large sample size problem and error term adjustments. The large sample size problem was recognized by Lindley (1957), who analyzed how a hypothesis testing procedure can be influenced by varying the sample size. Lindley (1957) pointed out that for a given significance level, a larger sample will cause the null hypothesis to be rejected more easily even when the posterior odds favor the null. If the null hypothesis is meant to be favored (i.e., a type I error is considered more serious than a type II error), then the significance level should be decreased as the sample size increases (Leamer 1978). Leamer (1978) advocated the Bayesian approach to adjust for the large sample size distortion. Chang, Pinegar, and Ravichandran (1993) claimed that given "diffuse priors about expected values and variances of regression coefficients and even prior odds about the null and alternative hypotheses," the adjusted Bayesian-t critical value should be calculated as follows.

$$t - \text{crit} = [(T - k) \cdot (T^{1/T} - 1)]^{0.5}, \tag{5}$$

where T is the number of observations, k is the number of parameters to be estimated, and $T - k$ is the number of degrees of freedom (Chang et al. 1993, p. 502).

In addition to the sample size adjustment, we also test for violations in the conventional assumptions about the regression error terms. Chang, Pinegar, and Ravichandran (1993) noted that heteroskedasticity and autocorrelation problems can bias inferences based on the results of ordinary least squares. We evaluate the homoskedasticity assumption using the Breusch-Pagan-Godfrey test, and adjust for heteroskedasticity using the approach advocated by White (1980). We test for autocorrelation using coefficients of lag 1, and adjust the OLS error terms using the Yule-Walker (YW) estimation procedure. The latter technique is referred to as a two-step full transform method in the SAS program. For a first-order auto-regressive process, the estimates generated by the default method with SAS are the same as the Prais-Winsten estimates (Prais and Winsten 1954).

Finally, we evaluate two critical aspects of normality: skewness and kurtosis. If the normality assumption of the OLS error terms is violated, then a trimmed least squares (TRLS) regression will be applied. Prior research indicates that the disturbance terms obtained from regression equations involving stock returns are generally not normally distributed (see Mandelbrot 1963; Fama 1963, 1965; Blattberg and Gonedes 1974). As noted by Connolly (1989), failure to adjust for non-normality can lead to incorrect inferences because outliers often distort the results.

Both Connolly (1989) and Chang, Pinegar, and Ravichandran (1993) use TRLS to solve the non-normality problem. We use a symmetric trimming proportion α by dropping the highest $T\alpha$ and lowest Tα observations from the data set. "T" represents the number of observations in a specific data set, and "highest" and "lowest" refer to the highest and lowest returns. The remaining observations are then used to obtain the TRLS estimates. Based on Connolly's (1989) assertion that "a trim of 0.05 is almost certainly necessary [and a] trim of 0.20 is almost certainly as large as the data require," we use trimming proportions of 0.05 and 0.20 in the TRLS regressions.

EMPIRICAL RESULTS AND ANALYSIS

Results Using the Traditional OLS Approach

The results using the traditional OLS model are shown in Table 2. Panel A reports the results for Data Set I (the main data set), and Panel B reports the results for Data

Table 2. Tests for the Day-of-the-Week Effect (Traditional OLS Model)$^{+}$

Model: $R_t = \gamma_1 D_{1t} + \gamma_2 D_{2t} + \gamma_3 D_{3t} + \gamma_4 D_{4t} + \gamma_5 D_{5t} + \gamma_6 D_{6t} + e_t$

	Panel A (Data Set I)$^{++}$		*Panel B (Data Set II)*$^{++}$	
YYMMDD and DAY	*860106 to 940930*	*860106 to 920630*	*860106 to 940930*	*860106 to 920630*
MON	.000902 (0.850)	.001608 (1.219)	.001464 (1.330)	.002004 (1.464)
TUE	.000323 (0.312)	.001054 (0.816)	–.000349 (–0.331)	.000431 (0.326)
WED	.000343 (0.331)	–.000193 (–0.148)	–.000029 (–0.028)	–.000658 (–0.506)
THU	.000086 (0.082)	–.000291 (–0.223)	.000509 (0.489)	.000250 (0.190)
FRI	.001344 (1.290)	.001241 (0.952)	.001400 (1.342)	.001235 (0.940)
SAT	.002749 (2.555)**	.002814 (2.102)**	.002717 (2.561)**	.002805 (2.112)**
F-statistic	1.521	1.258	1.746	1.314
Obs. (n)	2496	1851	2363	1755

Notes: $^{+}$ *t*-statistics in parentheses.
$^{++}$ Data Set I = main data set, Data Set II = main data set excluding returns following holidays.
* Significant at 10% level.
** Significant at 5% level.
*** Significant at 1% level.

Set II (the main data set excluding "holiday returns"). The results for both data sets suggest that while no negative Monday or Tuesday effect exists in the Taiwan stock market, a potential Saturday effect does exist (the *t*-statistics are shown in parentheses).

Results using the Modified OLS Approach

The results using the modified OLS model, which are similar to the results using the traditional OLS model, are shown in Table 3. The null hypotheses that the average returns for either Monday or Tuesday are equal to zero cannot be rejected, but the null hypothesis that the average return for Saturday is equal to zero can be rejected at the 5% level. These results suggest that a potential Saturday effect does exist in the Taiwan stock market. No abnormal returns are found for the remaining days of the week.

Table 3. Tests for the Day-of-the-Week Effect (Modified OLS Model)+

Model: $R_t = \gamma_0 INT + \Sigma\, \gamma_j\, D_{jt} + e_t$

YYMMDD and INT, DAY	*860106 to 940930*	*860106 to 920630*
INT	−.742376	.074956
	(−0.357)	(0.032)
MON	.001172	.001581
	(0.899)	(1.014)
TUE	.000468	.001040
	(0.420)	(0.762)
WED	.000482	−.000206
	(0.435)	(−0.151)
THU	.000211	−.000303
	(0.192)	(−0.223)
FRi	.001481	.001227
	(1.333)	(0.893)
SAT	.002873	.002802
	(2.540)**	(2.012)**
F-statistic	1.322	1.078
Obs. (n)	2496	1851

Notes: + *t*-statistics in parentheses.

++ Daily interest returns are derived by assuming that interest rate changes are unexpected.

The results are similar for Data Set II.

* Significant at 10% level.

** Significant at 5% level.

*** Significant at 1% level.

Specification and Robustness Tests

Because Saturday returns are potentially higher than the other days of the week, we use the following model specification.

$$R_t = \gamma_0 + \gamma_1 SAT + \varepsilon_t, \tag{6}$$

where *SAT* is a dummy variable that is equal to one for a Saturday return and zero otherwise.

The results of the specification tests, which are shown in Table 4, indicate that the normality assumption is violated. The returns for both study periods exhibit skewness and excess kurtosis (the absolute values of the coefficients for skewness

Table 4. Specification Tests for the Day-of-the-Week Effect[+]

Model: $R_t = \gamma_0 + \gamma_1 SAT + e_t$

YYMMDD & Specification test Results	*860106 to 940930*	*860106 to 920630*	*Approximate Critical Values for Specification Tests at the 5% Significance Level*
Observation	2496	1851	
Coefficient of Skewness	–0.3006	–0.3251	0.08 ~ 0.095
Coefficient of Excess Kurtosis	1.3177	0.9162	0.16 ~ 0.20
Breusch-Pagan/Godfrey Tests for Heteroskedasticity	7.3236	4.9027	3.84
Coefficient of Lag One Autocorrelation	0.133	0.150	0.05

Notes: [+] Critical values for the coefficients of skewness and excess kurtosis are based on sample size between 1800 and 2500. The Breusch-Pagan-Godfrey test for heteroskedasticity yields a χ^2-statistic with one degree of freedom.

and excess kurtosis exceed the range of approximate critical values at the 5% level). The critical values are based on sample sizes between 1,800 and 2,500 observations. We show a range of critical values in order to reflect the different sample sizes observed in this diagnostic procedure.

The assumption of homoskedasticity is examined using the Breusch-Pagan/Godfrey test. The diagnostics of the Breusch-Pagan/Godfrey test, which yield a χ^2-statistic with one degree of freedom, indicate that the assumption that the OLS error terms are homoskedastic is rejected at the 5% significance level. The assumption of non-autocorrelation is examined using coefficients of lag 1 autocorrelation. All lag 1 autocorrelation coefficients exceed the critical value at the 5% level. This finding indicates that the regression error terms are autocorrelated.

Table 5 reports the results of robustness tests that correct for the violations in the conventional assumptions about the OLS error terms. Part A in Table 5 presents the sample size and OLS estimates for γ_0 and γ_1. Part B reports corrected t-values for γ_0 and γ_1 as well as Bayesian-t critical values.

The values presented in the row labeled "None" are t-statistics for γ_1 under conventional OLS error term assumptions without any adjustment. The values listed in "White" are ts calculated after using White's (1980) adjustment for heteroskedasticity. The next set of t-statistics, labeled "Y-W", are corrected t-values using the Yule-Walker estimation for adjusting autocorrelation among the OLS error terms. The t-statistics listed in rows labeled "Trim(0.05)" and "Trim(0.20)" are adjusted ts using trimmed least squares regressions to adjust for the non-normality problem. The Bayesian-t statistics are reported in the last row of Table 5.

Table 5. Robustness Tests for the Day-of-the-Week Effect[+]

Model: $R_t = \gamma_0 + \gamma_1 SAT + e_t$

Part A Number of Observations (*n*) and *OLS estimates* for γ_0 and γ_1		
YYMMDD and Estimates	*860106 to 940930*	*8360106 to 920630*
Obs. (n)	2496	1851
γ_0	.000596	.000680
γ_1	.002153	.002134
Part B The t–statistics for γ_1 *with Robustness Adjustments*[+]		
YYMMDD and Test Results	*860106 to 940930*	*860106 to 920630*
None	1.837*	1.462
White	1.986**	1.573
Y-W	1.617	1.208
Trim(0.05)	0.633	1.054
Trim(0.20)	0.957	0.246
Bayesian-*t* Crit.	2.7979	2.7442

Notes: [+] The *t*-statistics in the various rows are reported by applying: OLS(None); White's (1980) 'consistent standard error' heteroskedasticity adjustment (White); Yule-Walker estimation for adjusting lag 1 autocorrelation (Y-W); and trimmed least squares regressions with trims of 0.05 and 0.20 respectively. The *t*-values are marked with one, two or three asterisks if the *t*s are greater than 1.645, 1.96 and 2.567, respectively (significant at 10%, 5%, and 1% under an OLS approach) and are underlined if these *t*s exceed the Bayesian-*t* critical values.

In Part B of Table 5, one, two, or three asterisks are assigned to the adjusted *t*-values to reflect significance at the 10%, 5%, and 1% levels, respectively. The associated critical values are 1.645, 1.96, and 2.576, respectively. It is important to note, however, that none of the *t*-statistics exceed the Bayesian-*t* critical values. As a result, sample size adjustments under a Bayesian approach render the day-of-the-week effect in the Taiwan stock market insignificant. For example, the *t*-statistic for the row marked "None" is insignificant when the *t*-value of 1.837 (for the 86/01/06 to 94/09/30 period) is compared to the Bayesian-*t* statistic of 2.7979.

The robustness of the day-of-the-week effect is also evaluated after adjusting for heteroskedasticity, autocorrelation and non-normality. Before the simultaneous imposition of the Bayesian approach and regression error adjustments, γ_1 retains its significance even when the heteroskedasticity adjustment is made. However, this variable loses its significance when both autocorrelation and nonnormality adjustments are applied. When both the Bayesian approach (i.e., the sample size adjustment) and error term adjustments are imposed simultaneously, no significant day-of-the-week effect is found.

CONCLUSION

The day-of-the-week effect is one of the most interesting empirical anomalies in finance. In the U.S. stock market the average return on common stocks is negative on Monday. In the Japanese stock market the lowest average return is observed on Tuesday. This study extends this research by examining the day-of-the-week effect in Taiwan, an emerging international market.

Because the Taiwan stock market has a distinct locality feature, the stock return patterns in Taiwan should not be affected by international trading activities. As a result, any day-of-the-week effect observed in Taiwan should be unique in reflecting the locality characteristic of this market. Stated differently, a Monday or Tuesday effect observed in the Taiwan market should not be related to either the Monday effect in the United States or the Tuesday effect in Japan.

The results of this study indicate that while the Taiwan stock market does not exhibit a significant Monday or Tuesday effect, average returns for Saturday are significantly positive and are the largest across the days of the week. Further testing, however, reveals that the observed Saturday effect becomes insignificant when robustness tests are applied.

The results of this study indicate that the day-of-the-week effect in the Taiwan stock market disappears when adjustments are made to reflect the large sample size problem and correct for violations in the conventional assumptions regarding the OLS error terms. As a result, we conclude that the evidence for the Taiwan stock market is consistent with the efficient market hypothesis.

APPENDIX

Daily Interest Return Calculation

To examine the impact of interest rate changes on the day-of-the-week effect, we modify the traditional OLS regression model by including the return on a risk-free asset as an independent variable. The annualized three-month time deposit rates offered by First Commercial Bank are used to derive the daily interest return. First Commercial Bank is one of three commercial banks backed by the Taiwanese government. Over the period 86/01/06–94/09/30, the annualized interest rate on three-month time deposits was changed 23 times (see Table A1). We assume that all of the interest rate changes were unanticipated. The following discussion illustrates the calculation of the daily interest returns from 86/01/10 to 86/01/30.

Date	*Day*	*Daily Int. Ret. (unexpected)*
860110	Friday	0.000142144
860111	Saturday	0.000142144
860113	Monday	0.000284288

Date	Day	Daily Int. Ret. (unexpected)
860114	Tuesday	0.000142144
860115	Wednesday	0.000142144
860116	Thursday	0.000142144
860117	Friday	0.000142144
860118	Saturday	0.000142144
860120	Monday	0.000865978
860121	Tuesday	0.000135537
860122	Wednesday	0.000135537
860123	Thursday	0.000135537
860124	Friday	0.000135537
860125	Saturday	0.000135537
860127	Monday	0.000271074
860128	Tuesday	0.000135537
860129	Wednesday	0.000135537
860130	Thursday	0.000135537

Calculation for Days when Interest Rates Are Not Changed

As shown in Table A1, the annualized interest rate for the three-month time deposits was changed from 5.25% to 5.00% on January 20, 1986 (86/01/20). Thus, the daily interest returns for dates before and after 86/01/20 were 0.000142144 and 0.000135537, respectively. These daily returns are estimated as follows.

$$(1 + r_1)^{360} - 1 = 0.0525 \Rightarrow r_1 = 0.000142144$$

and,

$$(1 + r_2)^{360} - 1 = 0.05 \Rightarrow r_2 = 0.000135537$$

where, r_1 and r_2 indicate the daily interest returns.

These daily returns are used for those trading days in which interest rates were (1) not changed and (2) were not preceded by a non-trading day. When a trading day is preceded by one or more non-trading day(s), the daily interest returns are accumulated. For example, on January 13, 1986 (Monday) the offered interest rate for a three-month time deposit was 5.25%. The daily interest return for this date is 0.000284288, which is equal to 0.000142144 times 2. January 13, 1986 was preceded by a non-trading day (Sunday). On January 27, 1986 (Monday) when the offered interest rate for three-month time deposits was 5.00%, the daily interest return was 0.000271074 (0.000135537 times 2).

Calculation for Days When Interest Rates Are Changed

The annualized interest rate for three-month time deposits was changed from 5.25% to 5.00% on 86/01/20. Thus, if we assume that investors did not anticipate

Table A1. Annualized Interest Rates for 3-month Time Deposits

Reported Rates are Offered by First Commercial Bank in Taiwan

YYMMDD and Interest Rates	*Offered Interest Rate Changes*	
	From	*To*
860120	5.25%	5.00%
860221	5.00%	4.75%
860306	4.75%	4.50%
861020	4.50%	4.00%
880715	4.00%	4.50%
890404	4.50%	5.25%
890422	5.25%	6.25%
890511	6.25%	9.25%
890625	9.25%	9.00%
890824	9.00%	8.75%
891127	8.75%	8.25%
900205	8.25%	8.80%
900301	8.80%	9.00%
900504	9.00%	8.75%
900921	8.75%	8.40%
901005	8.40%	7.75%
910912	7.75%	7.45%
910925	7.45%	7.15%
911120	7.15%	6.775%
920111	6.775%	6.50%
930914	6.50%	6.35%
940414	6.35%	6.10%
540604	6.10%	5.95%

Source: First Commercial Bank Offered Interest Rates.

this interest rate change, then the daily interest return for 86/01/20 is 0.00086597849. This result is calculated using the following procedure.

1. On Saturday, January 18, 1986, the present value (PV) of a three-month time deposit which will pay \$1 after 90 days is 0.987289419 (i.e, $i = 0.0142144\%$, $FV = 1$, $n = 90$, and $PMT = 0$).
2. Two days later (on Monday, January 20, 1986) the interest rate was changed from 5.25% to 5.00%. The PV of this time deposit is 0.98814439 (i.e, $i = 0.0135537\%$, $FV = 1$, $n = 88$, and $PMT = 0$).
3. On January 20, 1986 the one-period interest return associated with the interest rate change is 0.0865978% (i.e., $FV = 0.98814439$, $PV = 0.987289419$, $n = 1$, and $PMT = 0$).

ACKNOWLEDGMENT

The authors wish to thank Professors Keith Womer, Steven Graham, and Morris Stocks for their helpful comments and suggestions. The usual disclaimer applies.

NOTES

1. The accumulated foreign exchange reserves in Taiwan were equal to about $90,986,000,000 at the end of August 1994 (*Central Daily News—International Edition* 1994a).

2. On December 28, 1990 the amended "Security Investment Regulations and Exchange Settlement Rules for Overseas Chinese and Foreigners" was enacted (the title was translated from the *Taiwan Stock Exchange: A Thirty-Year Perspective*, p. 190).

3. Chou (1989) also examines calendar anamolies in the Taiwan stock market, but he does not examine the day-of-the-week effect.

REFERENCES

Barone, E. 1990. "The Italian Stock Market: Efficiency and Calendar Anomalies." *Journal of Banking and Finance* 14: 483–510.

Blattberg, R.C., and N.J. Gonedes. 1974. "A Comparison of the Stable and Student Distributions as Statistical Models for Stock Prices." *Journal of Business* 47: 244–280.

Central Daily News-International Edition. October 17, 1994a.

Central Daily News-International Edition. November 7, 1994b.

Chang, E.C., J.M. Pinegar, and R. Ravichandran. 1993. "International Evidence on the Robustness of the Day-of-the-Week Effect." *Journal of Financial and Quantitative Analysis* 28: 497–513.

Chou, S.-R. 1989. "An Empirical Analysis of Stock Market Anomalies: Evidence from the Republic of China in Taiwan." Unpublished doctoral dissertation, The University of Kentucky.

Connolly, R.A. 1989. "An Examination of the Robustness of the Weekend Effect." *Journal of Financial and Quantitative Analysis* 24: 133–169.

———. 1991. "A Posterior Odds Analysis of the Weekend Effect." *Journal of Econometrics* 49: 51–104.

Cross, F. 1973. "The Behavior of Stock Prices on Fridays and Mondays." *Financial Analysts Journal* (November-December): 67–69.

Fama, E.F. 1963. "Mandlebrot and the Stable Paretain Hypothesis." *Journal of Business* 36: 420–429.

———. 1965. "The Behavior of Stock Market Prices." *Journal of Business* 38: 34–105.

———. 1970. "Efficient Capital Markets: A Review of Theory and Empirical Work." *Journal of Finance* 25: 383–417.

French, K. 1980. "Stock Returns and The Weekend Effect." *Journal of Financial Economics* 8: 55–69.

Gibbons, M., and P. Hess. 1981. "Day of the Week Effects and Asset Returns." *Journal of Business* 54: 579–596.

Ho, Y.K. 1990. "Stock Return Seasonalities in Asia Pacific Markets." *Journal of International Financial Management and Accounting* 2: 47–77.

Jaffe, J., and R. Westerfield. 1985a. "The Week-End Effect in Common Stock Returns: The International Evidence." *Journal of Finance* 40: 433–454.

———. 1985b. "Patterns in Japanese Common Stock Returns: Day of The Week and Turn of the Year Effects." *Journal of Financial and Quantitative Analysis* 20: 261–272.

Jeng, Y. 1991. "Two Essays on the Closed-end Country Funds." Unpublished doctoral thesis, The University of Iowa.

Kato, K. 1990. "Weekly Patterns in Japanese Stock Returns." *Management Science* 36: 1031–1043.

Keim, D., and R. Stambaugh. 1984. "A Further Investigation of the Weekend Effect in Stock Returns." *Journal of Finance* 39: 819–834.

Lakonishok, J., and S. Smidt. 1988. "Are Seasonal Anomalies Real? A Ninety-Year Perspective." *Review of Financial Studies* 1: 403–425.

Leamer, E.E. 1978. *Specification Searches: Ad-Hoc Inference with Non-Experimental Data*. New York: John Wiley and Sons.

Lindley, D.V. 1957. "A Statistical Paradox." *Biometrika* 44: 187–192.

Mandelbrot, B.B. 1963. "The Variation of Certain Speculative Prices." *Journal of Business* 36: 394–419.

Pettengill, G. 1986. "A Non-Tax Cause for the January Effect? Evidence from Early Data." *Quarterly Journal of Business and Economics* 25: 15–34.

Pettway, R., and T. Tapley. 1984. "The Tokyo Stock Exchange: An Analysis of Stock Market Prices." *Keio Business Review*: 75–93.

Prais, S., and C. Winsten. 1954. "Trend Estimation and Serial Correlation." Cowles Commission Discussion Paper Number 282, Chicago.

Solnik, B., and L. Bousquet. 1990. "Day-of-the-Week Effect on the Paris Bourse." *Journal of Banking and Finance* 14: 461–468.

Taiwan Stock Exchange: A Thirty-Year Perspective. Taiwan: TSE Publication.

Theobald, M., and V. Price. 1984. "Seasonality Estimation in Thin Markets." *Journal of Finance* 39: 377–392.

Tong, W.H.S. 1992. "The Analysis of Stock Return Anomalies in the Asian Markets (Taiwan and South Korea) and an Examination of Dynamic Hedging." Unpublished doctoral dissertation, Arizona State University.

White, H. 1980. "A Heteroscedasticity-Consistent Covariance Matrix Estimator and a Direct Test for Heteroscedasticity." *Econometrica* 48: 817–838.

CAPITAL STRUCTURES IN MIDDLE-INCOME COUNTRIES:
A STUDY OF INDONESIA AND MALAYSIA

Qaizar Hussain

ABSTRACT

This paper analyzes the determinants of average cost of capital and debt-equity ratios in Indonesia and Malaysia following banking deregulation during the early 1980s. Indonesia experienced high debt-equity ratios and an infant stock market, whereas Malaysia enjoyed lower debt-equity ratios along with a well-functioning equity market. This study extends the existing empirical work on capital structure by introducing shareholder concentration and examines its impact on the cost of capital and debt-equity ratios in these countries. It was found that shareholder concentration has an adverse impact on these financial variables in Indonesia and a neutral or even a beneficial effect in the case of Malaysia. Finally, by taking advantage of a model explaining the various stages of financial development, we found that the role and size of the largest shareholders (who are effective monitors) declined in Malaysia over the 1980s.

Research in International Business and Finance, Supplement 1, pages 361–400.

ISBN: 0-7623-0110-4

INTRODUCTION

In recent years a number of studies have dealt with capital structures in developing countries. These studies have primarily focused on a combination of highly developed equity markets and repressed banking sectors (see Dailami 1986; Sundararajan 1985; Cho 1986). This paper takes an alternative route by examining an economy with a developed banking sector and an underdeveloped equity market, and compares it with an economy enjoying a relatively well-developed financial system.[1] For this purpose two countries, Indonesia and Malaysia, have been selected for analyses. Both these countries underwent banking deregulation during the early 1980s. At that time, Indonesia had a highly developed banking sector but a relatively "thin" equity market. However, Malaysia had well-developed banking (and bond) and equity sectors.

Our primary objective is to explore the implications of the presence of market power or buyer concentration in the market for equity. In this respect, we shall relax the Miller-Modigliani assumptions by introducing shareholder market power (monopsonistic competition) in the equity sector, sometimes coined as "non-dilution of control" in the literature.[2] The main questions examined include: to what extent do large shareholders distort the financial system in the "middle-income" country (Indonesia) versus that in the "newly-developed" country (Malaysia)?[3] In particular, what is the impact of shareholder concentration on the *cost of capital* and *debt-equity ratios*? Finally, can we expect shareholder concentration to decline over time? These questions are important because if significant distortions, such as high shareholder concentration, are present in the financial sector, the cost of capital[4] may be adversely affected, resulting in lower investment in the economy and a loss of advantage in international trade. Further, firms will continue to rely on intermediaries for their financing needs, despite high lending rates (as in Indonesia following banking deregulation), which may prevent the direct sources of finance from being developed for an extended period.[5]

It may be noted that Zeckhauser and Pound (1990) find a positive role of large shareholders as a consequence of monitoring effort in the United States.[6] The main conclusions in their study are that these large shareholders, through their effective monitoring, contribute to lower earnings/price ratios, there is no significant effect on dividend payouts, and also there is no close connection between leverage and the presence of sizable shareholders. The Zeckhauser and Pound story may be correct for significantly developed financial markets such as the United States or Malaysia, but not for underdeveloped markets such as Indonesia.

The paper is organized as follows: the second section presents a model, the third section provides some motivation and facts about Indonesia and Malaysia, the fourth section lists some hypotheses and data, the fifth and sixth sections report empirical evidence on Indonesia and Malaysia, and the final section concludes the paper.

THE MODEL

The model (based on Zeckhauser and Pound 1990; Diamond 1991) provides a simple framework for predicting high levels of equilibrium debt to equity ratios and it is a convenient vehicle for explaining the transition from "middle-income" to "newly-developed" countries, resulting in declining debt-equity ratios. The story is divided into three related paradigms.

(A) The financial sector of a "middle-income" country consists of banks and an equity market. The firms in this country depend heavily on bank debt for their financing needs. The equity market is "thin"[7] with an overwhelming presence of large shareholders and a few small shareholders. The small shareholders are highly risk-averse and rely on large shareholders who have the resources to monitor the firms. Thus, small shareholders care about the reputation of firms. In the presence of asymmetric information in both the banking and the equity sector, the primary function of banks and large shareholders is to monitor borrowers (firms).

Large shareholders behave as monopsonistic competitors in the shares market. These monopsonists have little interest in diluting their shares to the public. Like monopsonists in any other market, they force the prices of shares to remain low and the returns (mainly dividends) high. Low share prices further discourage the firms from issuing new shares. This phenomenon causes the equilibrium value of shares to be small and the equilibrium size of bank-debt to be large resulting in significantly high debt-equity ratios. Finally, the return on equity is greater than the return on debt in these "middle-income" countries, even more than in industrialized countries.[8]

Figures 2 and 3 describe the debt and equity markets in a "middle-income" country and also explain the transition to a "newly-developed" country.[9] The demand and supply schedules are as follows.

Assume equity and bank debt are substitutes, the *demand* functions are:

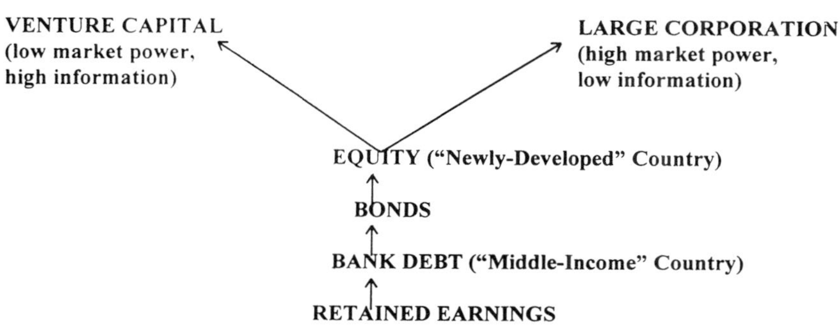

Figure 1. Stages of Financial Development

Note: These are typically observed stages of financial develpment in most economies.

$$D_{\text{debt funding}} = f(\overset{-}{r}_D, \overset{+}{r}_E)$$

$$D_{\text{equity funding}} = f(\overset{-}{r}_E, \overset{+}{r}_D)$$

where r_D and r_E refer to the rates of return on debt and equity.

The *supply* function in the debt market is as follows:

$$S_{\text{debt funding}} = f(\overset{+}{r}_D, M_D)$$

where M_D is the degree of monitoring by banks. The *supply* functions in the equity market are:

$$S_{LS} = f(r_E, M_E)$$

$$S_{SS} = g(r_E, \Omega)$$

LS and *SS* denote large and small shareholders respectively, M_E is the degree of monitoring performed only by *LS*, and Ω is an index of the degree of reputation developed by firms in the banking sector. The initial equilibriums in both the bank and equity markets are given by points *E* in Figure 2.

The reason why firms do not obtain all their financing from banks is that monitoring is expensive. Following Diamond (1991), after a certain period when firms have earned a good reputation and a valuable track record, it is suboptimal for such firms to be consistently monitored. Diamond divides the firms into *G* (good or less risky), *BG* (sometimes safe and at other times risky), and *B* (bad or most risky) firms. In our model, when the *BG* type firms become well-known following consistent monitoring by banks, even small, risk-averse agents are willing to buy equities. As a result, the supply curve for small savers (*S*) in Figure 3 shifts to the

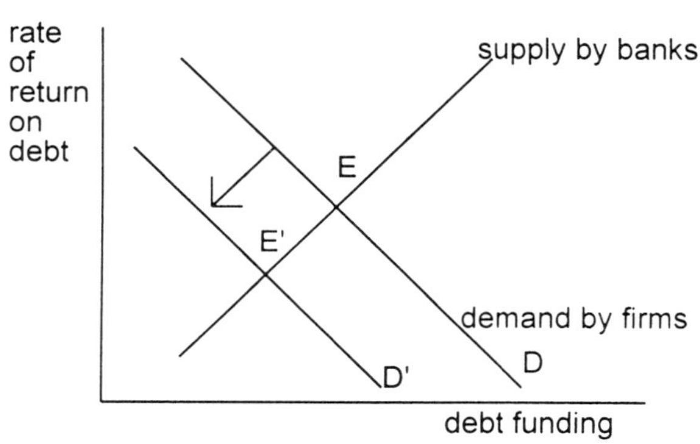

Figure 2.

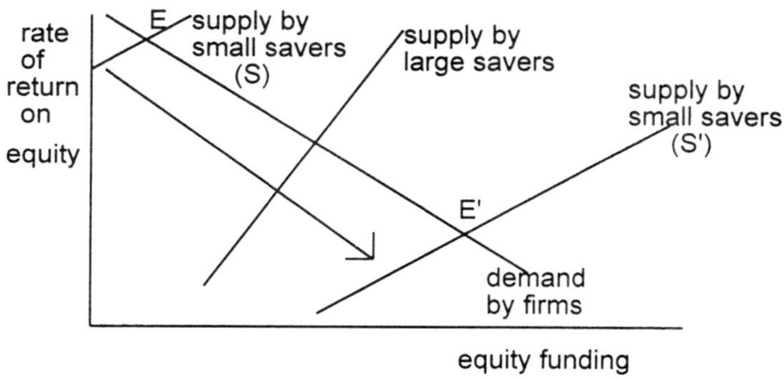

Figure 3.

right to S'. The supply curve for small savers is a function of the degree of reputation (Ω) of the firm. At S' the rate of return on equity has fallen and the size of equity funds has grown. When the return on equity falls, some firms in the debt market reduce their demand for debt funding, since debt and equity are assumed to be substitutes. This causes the demand curve (D) for debt in Figure 2 to shift to the left (D') resulting in a lower level of equilibrium debt funding by banks. The interesting feature in these "newly-developed" countries is that the supply curve for the large shareholder is less relevant once firms have earned a favorable reputation. Overall, these stages of financial development from indirect to direct finance explain the decline in the economy's debt to equity ratio and the cost of capital (defined as the weighted average of the returns on equity and debt). In addition, the narrowing of the differentials between the returns on equity and debt is partly explained by this model.

(B) An economy consists of two types of firms: Firm A and Firm B. The objective of Firm A is to maximize its profits. In order to finance its investments, it can rely on retained earnings, borrow from banks, or issue equity. In case the firm runs out of retained earnings, it either uses bank debt or issues shares to build the factory.

Let us assume if Firm A decides to rely on equity, its shares turn out to be predominantly owned by a large shareholder B[10] who behaves as a monopsonistic competitor in the shares market.[11] The main objective of Firm B is to conduct effective monitoring of Firm A on behalf of all shareholders who own shares of Firm A. Shareholder B faces an upward-sloping shares supply curve.[12] As indicated above, assume no bankruptcy costs, no taxes, and no uncertainty. Note that in the following model monitoring is conducted both by banks and the large shareholder B. The principal-agent problem in this model is reduced through effective monitoring by shareholders and the moral hazard and adverse selection problems of banks are solved through monitoring and reputation effects maintained by frequent borrowings.[13] The large shareholder (LS) B's maximization problem is:

$$\text{Max } nV(n) - \int_0^n P(x)dx \qquad w.r.t.\ n \tag{1a}$$

where the first term denotes the total benefit from acquiring all shares, and the second term represents their total cost respectively. n is the number of shares held by LS, V is the value of shares, and $P(n)$ is the cost of a marginal share. As indicated earlier, in this model the main benefit that the LS derives is through monitoring of the owner.

$$FOC \quad nV'(n) + V(n) - P(n) = 0 \tag{1b}$$

$$\text{or} \qquad nV'(n) = P(n) - V(n)$$

One important factor contributing to the upward-sloping supply curve for shares in the monopsonistic competitor case above is the existence of large buyer of shares whose monitoring is believed to be beneficial for future performance of Firm A. Like the monopsonist in the labor market who succeeds in forcing the equilibrium wage to be low, the monopsonist here pushes the equilibrium price of shares low.

However, in a limiting case of *perfect competition* in the buyers market for shares we would expect a large number of shareholders $s_1 \ldots s_m$ who do not conduct effective monitoring. Under that scenario, the representative small shareholder (SS) has the following objective function:

$$\text{Max } (nV - Pn) \qquad w.r.t.\ n \tag{2a}$$

$$FOC \qquad V - P = 0 \tag{2b}$$

or $V = P$ is the Pareto efficient solution for the purchase of shares. The price of shares in this situation would be higher than in the monopsonist case.

(C) The dynamics of shareholder concentration are illustrated in Figure 4 where we introduce the marginal cost (MC) and marginal benefit (MB) of monitoring.

Monitoring cost = $k^*(s_i/s)$ where k is a constant, s is total shares of the firm, and s_i is shares owned by the largest shareholder.

Monitoring benefit = $f(s_i/s)$ where $f < 0$, $f' < 0$.

Marginal cost of monitoring is assumed to be constant (k)[14] and marginal benefit schedule eventually falls with the size of the shareholders, because after a certain size of the largest shareholder, the additional benefits derived from monitoring (such as raising value of the firm in terms of higher expected profits) diminish.

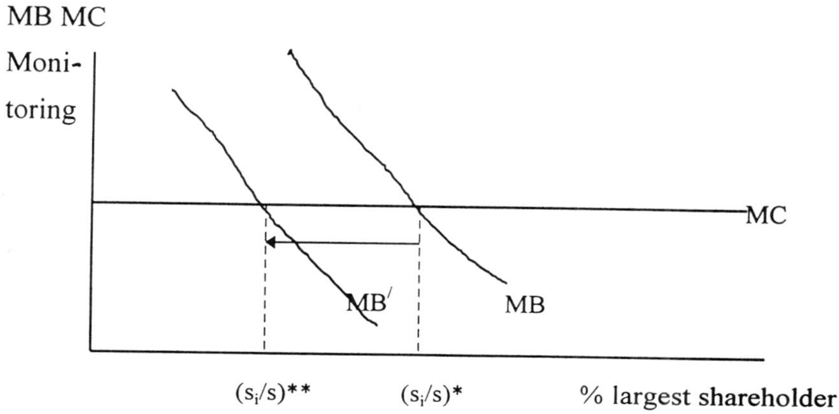

Figure 4. Dynamics of Concentration

With an improvement in technology and greater information available on firms, the marginal benefit of monitoring in the equity market shifts down. As a result, the optimal size of the largest shareholder $(s_i/s)^*$, declines to a lower level $(s_i/s)^{**}$. This is beneficial because an increased number of shareholders, each controlling a smaller proportion of firm's shares, will emerge in the economy and equity markets will play a greater role. In sum, the monitoring role, as measured by the equilibrium size of the large shareholders, should decline over time.

MOTIVATION AND FACTS—INDONESIA AND MALAYSIA

In this section we describe some important financial characteristics of the two countries in our sample in order to motivate the model and empirical research.

Taking market capitalization/GDP as a measure of the size of the stock market, Table 1 shows that the Jakarta Stock Exchange occupies the twelfth position in Asia whereas the Kuala Lumpur Stock Exchange ranks sixth (Ariff and Johnson 1990, tables 1, 2). Other measures of performance such as mean and volatility of annual returns indicate that Jakarta has the highest, and Kuala Lumpur one of the lowest means and standard deviations (Ariff and Johnson 1990, table 4). Interestingly, the total daily trading activity lasted only about fifteen minutes on the Jakarta Stock Exchange during the 1980s.

A measure of debt to equity ratios in Indonesia and Malaysia for the period 1983–1989 is constructed by taking the ratio of claims of the banking system on the private sector (as a proxy for bank debt) to market capitalization (as a proxy for equity). Throughout the 1980s the ratio averaged about 130 for Indonesia and only 0.96 in the case of Malaysia suggesting a marked contrast between the two countries.[15]

Table 1. Stock Markets in Asia: 1988

Stock Exchange	*Listing of Co.'s*	*Market Capitalization (US$ Bn)*	*GDP*	*Cap/GDP*	*Rank (Cap/GDP)*	*Mean Return (80–89)*	*Standard Deviation of Return (80–89)*
Bahrain/Kuwait	65	11.84	19.50	0.610	7	50	100
Bangkok	141	8.81	52.45	0.170	8	17.11	24.47
Bombay	2238	23.85	274.88	0.090	10	28.96	32.17
Hong Kong	284	74.37	46.25	1.620	2	7.47	40.44
Jakarta	**24**	**0.25**	**72.00**	**0.004**	**12**	**52.61**	**109.69**
Karachi	404	2.46	36.98	0.067	11	12.04	18.65
Kuala Lumpur	**238**	**23.32**	**33.73**	**0.691**	**6**	**13.24**	**31.90**
Manila	141	4.28	39.40	0.109	9	38.92	73.09
Seoul	502	94.24	131.99	0.714	5	33.43	35.47
Singapore	325	62.56	22.50	2.91	1	15.30	27.86
Taipei	163	120.02	101.46	1.18	3	43.06	52.42
Tokyo	1649	2,725.00	3,819.91	1.100	4	11.61	30.18

Source: Ariff and Johnson (1990).

Dailami and Atkin (1990) compare developing countries and find that the ex post real return on stocks far exceeded the real interest rate[16] in almost all of them during the 1980s. In Indonesia the real return on stocks was 36.7% whereas on bank deposits it was only 4.4%. Malaysia, however, enjoyed a relatively small differential (7.3%). According to the authors, the large differences are due to high risk premiums in equity markets combined with other factors such as differential levels of taxation.[17] I contend that there is more to these large differentials than merely the risk premium argument. The supply constraints are playing an important role. Two factors on the supply side could be responsible for such a large differential. First, the continued presence of interest rate ceilings in several countries. Governments and financial institutions in these developing countries contributed to a favorable bias toward debt finance by providing heavy subsidies on bank loans when interest rate ceilings were in place. Second, the focus of this study, the existence of shareholder market power, have forced the return on stocks to remain phenomenally high.[18] The fact that the existing finance literature dealing with debt-equity choice pertains more to developed markets, may have resulted in emphasizing the role of taxation and bankruptcy costs more than other factors, such as interest rate policies and market power in the financial markets.

The final feature of the two markets is far higher average economy-wide dividend rates and significantly lower prices (and price-earnings) of shares in Indonesia relative to Malaysia. Table 2 provides contrasting figures for dividend yield and price-earning ratios for Indonesia and Malaysia. The country with an infant stock market (Indonesia) enjoys remarkably higher dividends but lower price-earnings

Table 2.

Year	Market Dividend Yield: Indonesia	Price-Earnings Ratio: Indonesia	Market Dividend Yield: Malaysia	Price-Earnings Ratio: Malaysia
1980	12.07	1.10	4.50	22.10
1981	13.08	0.89	4.60	23.30
1982	12.10	6.48	4.60	23.80
1983	17.39	4.98	3.00	29.80
1984	16.07	3.85	5.10	23.40
1985	15.26	3.50	5.45	18.10
1986	17.66	3.58	4.69	27.90
1987	13.90	3.46	2.45	30.74

Source: International Finance Corporation (1993).

ratios in contrast to Malaysia with a relatively more advanced stock market. Indonesia and Malaysia have strikingly different financial characteristics despite numerous cultural and economic similarities, such as minority Chinese ownership of businesses, high economic growth, low inflation, and sound macroeconomic policies. We examine the proposition that the degree of market power on the part of shareholders may be partly responsible for such marked differences in financial characteristics.

HYPOTHESES AND DATA

We compare and contrast Indonesian and Malaysian financial markets by examining the following hypotheses:

- Market power exerted by significant shareholders plays a stronger role in influencing debt to equity ratios[19] in Indonesia during the 1980s than in Malaysia. The influence in Malaysia tends to decrease over time (1984–1987).[20]
- The cost of capital is affected by market power and the degree of influence falls over time (1984–1987) with less need for monitoring as market develops.[21]
- Shareholder concentration lowers the price-earnings ratio and raises the return on equity. Producer concentration has a relatively more beneficial impact on these variables.

Data—Indonesia

The data set for Indonesia appears in the form of balance sheets, income statements, and financial ratios for individual companies listed on the Jakarta Stock

Table 3. Indonesia

PUBLIC					
PMDN		*PMA*		*ALL*	
Mean	*Range*	*Mean*	*Range*	*Mean*	*Range*
24.8	10.0–52.2	25.2	2.3–59.2	24.9	2.3–59.2
LS					
PMDN		*PMA*		*ALL*	
Mean	*Range*	*Mean*	*Range*	*Mean*	*Range*
62.2	16.1–89.3	65.6	19.2–85	63.4	16.1–89.3

Note: *PMDN* refers to domestic firms and *PMA* to foreign joint-ventures

Exchange.[22] Balance sheet and income statement figures are expressed in millions of rupiah for the years 1988, 1989, and 1990.

In order to understand how the financing decisions of domestic firms differ from those of foreign firms, we have separated them into two groups. The first category consists of firms that are wholly nationally-owned (PMDN), and those classified as foreign joint-ventures (PMA) occupy the second category.[23] The sample consists of 33 PMDN firms and 19 PMA firms for a total of 52 firms.

There are two important variables obtained from the Indonesian Capital Market Directory pertaining to the degree of concentration among shareholders. First is *PUBLIC*, which is the proportion of shares owned by the public (sometimes called float), and second is *LS*, the proportion of shares owned by all the large shareholders (each controlling shares in excess of 15%) in a company.[24] The means and ranges of these variables are given in Table 3.

Data—Malaysia

The data set for Malaysia was only available for the top 98 manufacturing companies listed on the Kuala Lumpur Stock Exchange (even though the total number of companies listed were three times this number). The time period spans the 1980s decade depending on the availability of data. The cross-sectional regression analyses are performed for 1984 and 1987. The data sources are in the form of balance sheets and income statements included in the *Annual Companies Handbook* (various years) published by the Exchange, which were organized and analyzed in the World Bank study conducted by Singh and Hamid (1992).[25] Balance sheets and income statements are expressed in thousands of ringgits.

Two caveats are in order. First, the series reflect information on only the largest manufacturing firms in Malaysia and thus they are by no means representative of

Table 4. Number of Listed Companies and Market Value, 1987–1991

Year	*Domestic*	*Foreign*	*Total*	*Value M$ Million*
1987	232	59	291	73,791
1988	238	57	295	99,106
1989	250	55	305	155,984
1990	282	3	285	130,235
1991	321	3	324	159,855

Source: The G-T Guide to World Equity Markets (1991).

the whole economy. Second, in contrast to Indonesia, domestic firms are not easily distinguishable from foreign firms. This makes comparisons between the two countries difficult. Nevertheless, the cross-sectional analyses provide valuable insights into the financing decisions of firms in Malaysia.

Two variables are constructed to estimate the degree of shareholder market power in Malaysia. First, for each firm listed on the Exchange the sum of the three largest shareholders (*SUMLS*) measures the *Concentration Ratio*. Second, we also constructed the *Herfindahl Index* (*H*) for the three largest shareholders in each of the largest 98 companies.[26] Both of these indices are available for 1981, 1984, 1987, and 1988. Other important financial variables will be defined in the sections pertaining to the respective countries.

EMPIRICAL EVIDENCE—INDONESIA

The financial ratios are presented for three years: 1988, 1989, and 1990. The average debt-equity ratios for the sample of firms are summarized in Table 6.

Table 5. Malaysia
Basic Statistics Regarding the Concentration Ratio and Herfindahl Index

	Mean	*Standard Deviation*	*Minimum*	*Maximum*
SUMLS81	0.557	0.174	0.217	0.998
SUMLS84	0.541	0.157	0.192	0.871
SUMLS87	0.526	0.168	0.176	0.885
SUMLS88	0.514	0.169	0.188	0.922
H81	0.206	0.149	0.017	0.570
H84	0.192	0.145	0.012	0.598
H87	0.173	0.138	0.010	0.598
H88	0.167	0.141	0.012	0.562

Table 6. Indonesia
Average Debt-Equity Ratios

	1988	*1989*	*1990*
PMDN	6.13	1.09	1.12
PMA	1.59	0.89	1.04
ALL	3.92	0.99	1.08

Note: PMDN refers to domestic firms and PMA to foreign joint-ventures.

Table 6 indicates that the average debt-equity ratios are significantly higher for domestic firms than for foreign firms and the ratios decline over the time period. Further, the correlation between debt-equity ratios of firms and float (calculated separately) is significantly negative for the three years (–.32, –.31, and –.34) for PMDN firms, and less significant for the PMA firms (+.03, –.22, and –.05). Our model predicts a significantly low value since the companies with high debt to equity ratios would likely be dominated by big shareholders behaving as monopsonists rather than by the public. The variables used in the regressions for Indonesia are as follows:

ROE: Return on equity or the profit after taxes divided by equity
LROE: Log of ROE
DE: Debt-equity ratio[27]
LDE: Log of *DE*
PUBLIC: Proportion of firm's shares owned by the public
LPUBLIC: Log of *PUBLIC*
LS: Proportion of shares owned by the largest shareholders (shares greater than or equal to 15%)
LLS: Log of *LS*
LSSH: Ratio of number of large shareholders (>15%) to total number of shareholders
LCON: Shareholder concentration proxy—*LPUBLIC* or *LLS*
PE: Price-earnings ratio
LOIS: Log of (profit after taxes/net sales)
DIVP: Dividend payout or the dividend per share/earnings per share
LNSALES: Log of net sales
LTAXES: Log of corporate taxes (taken as the difference between profit before taxes and profit after taxes)

The regressions for Indonesia below are be divided into two parts. First, the effect of concentration and other relevant variables on the cost of capital (return on equity) is examined. Second, the important determinants of firms' debt-equity financing decisions are studied.

Regression Equations

1) $LROE = \alpha + \theta_1 LDE + \theta_2 LTAXES + \theta_3 LNSALES + \theta_4 LCON + \varepsilon$

H_A: $\theta_1 > 0$; $\theta_2 > 0$; $\theta_3 > 0$; $\theta_4 > 0$ if *LLS* and < 0 if *LPUBLIC*

2) $LDE = \alpha + \beta_1 PE + \beta_2 LOIS + \beta_3 LTAXES + \beta_4 LNSALES + \beta_5 LCON + \varepsilon$

H_A: $\beta_1 < 0$; $\beta_2 > 0$; $\beta_3 > 0$; $\beta_4 > 0$; $\beta_5 > 0$ if *LLS* and < 0 if *LPUBLIC.*

Determinants of Return on Equity

Tables (A1–A4) in this section are presented in Appendix A for Indonesia. Table A1 summarizes the results for the return on equity in levels (*ROE*). The results in logs for this dependent variable (*LROE*) are reported in Tables A2, A3, and A4.

The results in Table A1 give support to the hypothesis that the higher the debt to equity ratio (*DE*), the higher is the return on equity.[28] Note that this table examines only domestic (*PMDN*) firms generating a relatively small sample size. The reason is that we are primarily interested in studying the role of domestic firms, whenever possible. In addition, large shareholders help raise the rate of return (t = 1.83 in equation 1). Finally, an important result is the effect of *DE* and *LSSH* on *PE*. Both are significantly[29] negative, indicating that the presence of higher debt-equity ratios and large shareholders contributes to lower price-earnings ratios. This result contrasts with the findings of Zeckhauser and Pound (1990) who find a positive role of large shareholders in improving price-earnings ratios for the case of U.S. firms, and hence boosting future corporate performance. Apparently, the effect of shareholder market power is a function of the stage of development an economy is passing through.

In Tables A2, A3, and A4 we have transformed the variables into logarithms. Except for Table A1 in levels, all the other tables show results in log form. There are several reasons why we tried the regressions in logs. Logs provide superior results and interpretations (elasticities) of the coefficient estimates. For example, *PUBLIC* produced insignificant results in levels which changed markedly in logs. Finally, one reason why we are including Table A1 is to treat *PE* as a dependent variable in levels, that would not have been possible in logs. Table A2 summarizes results for ALL firms, Table A3 for domestic (PMDN) firms, and Table A4 for foreign-joint venture (PMA) firms.

As indicated above, information on return on debt was unavailable, therefore return on equity is used as a proxy for the cost of capital. The main difference between the equations in each of the tables is that the first three equations include

LPUBLIC (log of *PUBLIC*), and the last three include *LLS* (log of proportion of large shareholders) as measures of concentration.

First, *LDE* (log of debt-equity ratio) has an ambiguous effect on the cost of capital. Ideally, *LDE* should be treated as an endogenous variable (see Frankel 1992) in a two-stage least squares regression, but there are too few observations in the data set. Second, *LNSALES* which estimates the impact of market power on the sellers' side, has coefficients which are generally negative, and particularly significant for the PMA firms and for the later years. This indicates an increased favorable influence of large firms on the cost of capital, especially in the case of foreign companies. Thus, market power in the output sector seems to exert a downward pressure on the return on equity. Third, as expected, the coefficient estimates of *LTAXES* appear to be positive and significant in all cases showing an adverse impact of taxes on *LROE*.

Finally, *LLS* and *LPUBLIC* are used as proxies for market power (or lack of) or concentration (or lack of) of shareholders. In our hypothesis we expect a positive sign for *LLS* and a negative sign for *LPUBLIC*. As expected, *LLS* performs well with (t = 1.84 and 2.22) for *ALL* firms in 1988 and 1990 respectively. When *ALL* firms are disaggregated into domestic and foreign firms, even then the coefficient estimates for *LLS* are significantly positive. However, *LPUBLIC* is not so significant, though it is negative, suggesting that the ownership by small shareholders has a favorable impact on the cost of capital.[30]

Determinants of Debt-Equity Ratios

Tables A5, A6, and A7 (see Appendix A) for Indonesia summarize the results for the determinants of debt-equity ratios, where the log of the debt-equity ratio (*LDE*) is taken as the dependent variable. Before we discuss the results, several points should be mentioned. First, often we are constrained by the number of observations especially when we divide our sample into domestic firms and foreign joint-ventures. This is why econometric techniques, such as two-stage least squares are not applied here, even though some simultaneity may exist among the variables. Moreover, given a small-sized sample in this study firms have not been classified into industries as is done in Zeckhauser and Pound (1990). Second, logs provide superior results and interpretations than levels and thus there is no a priori reason why we ought not to use logs. In case of price-earnings ratio, for example, we did not take logs because earnings can sometimes be negative.[31] In the foregoing analysis several issues pertaining to the determinants of debt-equity ratios are discussed.

Shareholder Concentration

The log of *PUBLIC* (*LPUBLIC*) is a proxy for the degree of concentration in the equity market. As indicated earlier, the central thesis is that firms predominantly owned by large shareholders primarily rely on debt and those owned by small shareholders tend to equity financing. In this case we would expect a negative relationship between *LPUBLIC* and *LDE*.

Table A5 presents the regressions in the absence of taxes. The coefficient estimates (elasticities) for *LPUBLIC* are negative and significant with *t*-statistics of (–1.97), (–2.13), and (–1.45) for *ALL*, *PMDN*, and *PMA* firms respectively. When the log of taxes is included as an explanatory variable (Table A6), the coefficients of *LPUBLIC* become less significant with *t*-statistics of (–1.14) and (–0.87) for *ALL* and *PMDN* firms, but remain more significant for *PMA* firms (–1.88). The results indicate that if float is high, firms prefer to conduct their additional financing through the issuance of equity, or rely on retained earnings, rather than debt. It holds even more true for foreign-owned firms than domestic firms. The presence and frequent trading of small shareholders in the secondary market helps in giving firms an incentive to benefit from higher stock prices. Since *LPUBLIC* is inversely related to *LLS*, the familiar "non-dilution of control" argument is valid here which suggests that large shareholders buy up large chunks of the company's shares and keep prices low, thereby dissuading the company from issuing additional equity for investment. They force the secondary market for shares to remain "thin" further increasing the firms' reliance on bank-debt. This argument is confirmed for both foreign-incorporated (PMA) and domestic-incorporated (PMDN) firms.

Firm Size

The log of net sales of firms (*LNSALES*) acts as proxy for firm size for all the firms listed on the Jakarta Stock Exchange. Theory suggests that large firms tend to be highly leveraged (Titman and Wessels 1988). The main argument is that large firms enjoy a low probability of bankruptcy since they are often significantly diversified. On the other hand, small firms suffer higher costs of issuing equity and may resort to bank borrowing. This cost-benefit argument would support a positive correlation between firm size and debt-equity ratio.

The results are inconclusive for *LNSALES*. In Table A5 for the category of *ALL* firms, the elasticity of net sales is positive in 1988, but turns negative in 1989 and 1990. In fact, the positive correlation between firm size and debt-equity reverses in the later years for all firms in the sample. Large firms eventually begin to rely on equity, and not on debt as the theory would indicate. In summary, the adverse effects on debt-equity ratios of monopsonistic competition are unambiguous, and do not necessarily hold for market power on the output side.

Current Profitability

LOIS measures the log of profits after taxes as a proportion of firm's net sales. Traditional theories such as the "static trade-off"[32] or the "pecking order" theory (Donaldson 1961) have been used as arguments for profitable firms choosing debt over equity. For example, according to the pecking order theory of financial development, firms prefer financing investment first through retained earnings, then debt, and finally through issuing equity. This theory proposes that it is cheaper to borrow from banks than sell shares. Thus we would expect a positive correlation between profitability and debt/equity.[33]

In contrast to the positive relationship implied by the pecking order theory, Tables A5, A6, and A7 show significantly negative elasticities for all the categories of firms and for all the three years. In our sample profitable firms rely on external equity financing.[34] Our results bear striking similarities to a recent study[35] indicating that profitable firms resort to equity mode of financing in the United States. Apparently, equity financing is not as expensive as is commonly believed; the traditional pecking order theory does not hold for many companies. We accept the hypothesis that profitability leads to high debt-equity ratios in Indonesia.

Taxation

The log of corporate taxes (*LTAXES*) is included as a measure of taxation. Since the seminal Miller and Modigliani (1958) work, a plethora of papers have successfully attempted to invalidate the neutrality propositions. One manner is through the introduction of taxation. Due to the presence of double taxation on equity, both firms and savers show a preference for bank funds. It should be noted that we could not obtain data on taxes on dividends. Nevertheless, we hypothesize that corporate taxes reduce profits after taxes, and thereby retained earnings, which are a part of shareholders' equity. Therefore, in our regressions we expect a positive relationship between *LTAXES* and *LDE*.

The regression results indicate that the tax elasticity of debt is clearly positive and partly significant in both 1989 and 1990 ($t = 1.69$ and 1.47) for ALL firms. It is also positive for the sub-categories of PMDN and PMA in 1989. However, the coefficient estimates for 1988 portray a different picture. There appears to be a tax advantage to equity and not debt in that year. The elasticities are negative and statistically significant for *ALL* and PMA firms with ($t = -1.50$ and -2.19) in 1988. Therefore, the tax bias toward debt is not completely unambiguous in all of our cross-sectional regressions.

Expected Future Profitability

The variable that best serves as a proxy here is the price-earnings ratio (*PE*). Expected future profitability should directly influence the choices firms make in financing their additions to capital. Several studies point out that companies that have high price-earnings ratios are more likely to issue equity (see, e.g., Martin and Scott 1974). Thus we would expect a negative relationship between *PE* and *LDE*. Because the price-earnings ratio can be negative, it is used in level form as an explanatory variable.[36]

The coefficient estimates (semi-log elasticity) for ALL firms remain negative, but not so significant, for all the three years in the regressions without taxes (Table A5). Even when taxes are included, either the results are still negative or insignificantly positive for each of the subcategories of firms (Table A6 and A7). The results suggest that, in general, higher expected future profitability has a negative effect on debt-equity ratios. In other words, firms which expect promising results in the future prefer to rely on equity or retained earnings than debt, even in an economy such as Indonesia which faced a less-developed equity market during the sample period. The null hypothesis signifying no relationship between PE and LDE is rejected in favor of the alternative suggesting a negative relationship. In conclusion, the presence of high price-earnings ratios may be a necessary condition for firms in reducing their reliance on the banking sector.

EMPIRICAL EVIDENCE—MALAYSIA

As in Indonesia, the regressions for Malaysia are divided into two parts. First, the variables affecting the cost of capital are analyzed, then the important determinants of firms' debt-equity financing decisions are studied.

The variables used in the regressions for Malaysia are as follows:

WACC: (dividends+interest on debt)/(total liabilities + total equity)
LWACC: Log of *WACC*
LSUMLS: Log of sum of the three largest shareholders
LH: Log of Herfindahl Index for the three largest shareholders
LCON: Shareholder concentration proxy—*LSUMLS* or *LH*
LLTDEQ: Log of long-term debt/total equity
LSTDEQ: Log of short-term debt/total equity
LLOANEQ: Log of long-term loans/total equity
PE: Price-earnings ratio
OIS: Earnings after taxes and extraordinary expenses/net sales
INTSOEQ: Internal sources/total equity
LTASS: Log of total assets
LTAXES: Log of corporate income taxes
LINVESTEQ: Log of investment/total equity
LINTANGEQ: Log of intangibles/total equity

Table 7. Malaysia
Average Debt-Equity Ratios

	1984	*1987*
Short-term Debt/Eq	0.30	0.79
Long-term Debt/Eq	0.17	0.41
Long-term Loans/Eq	0.14	0.51
Internal Sources/Eq	0.03	–0.05

Regression Equations

1) $$LWACC = \alpha + \theta_1 LLTDEQ + \theta_2 LTAXES + \theta_3 LTASS + \theta_4 LCON + \theta_5 INTSOEQ + \varepsilon$$

$$H_A\colon \theta_1 \neq 0; \theta_2 > 0; \theta_3 > 0; \theta_4 \neq 0 \text{ if } LSUMLS \text{ or } H; \theta_5 < 0$$

2) $$LDE = \alpha + \beta_1 PE + \beta_2 OIS + \beta_3 LTAXES + \beta_4 LTASS + \beta_5 LCON + \beta_6 INTSOEQ + \beta_7 LINTANGEQ + \beta_8 LINVESTEQ + \varepsilon$$

LDE* is either *LLTDEQ*, *LSTDEQ*, or *LLOANEQ

$$H_A\colon \beta_1 < 0; \beta_2 > 0; \beta_3 > 0; \beta_4 > 0;$$

$$\beta_5 \neq 0 \text{ if } LSUMLS \text{ or } LH; \beta_6 < 0; \beta_7 < 0; \beta_8 > 0$$

Determinants of Cost of Capital

We attempt to identify the variables affecting the weighted average cost of capital.[37] The analysis follows in the spirit of Miller and Modigliani (1958) in testing for the neutrality of financing for Malaysia. As mentioned earlier, the weighted average cost of capital is defined as the weighted average of the returns on equity and debt. One shortcoming of the proxy used here (*WACC*) is that it excludes ex post capital gains as part of the return on assets.

Table B1 in Appendix B summarizes the cross-sectional analyses for the log of the cost of capital (*WACC*) performed separately for 1984 and 1987.[38] The first two equations in Table B1 take advantage of ordinary least squares and the last two of two-stage least squares.

First, long-term debt to equity in logs (*LLTDEQ*) is insignificant in all the four equations. According to Frankel (1992) and others, high levels of debt-equity ratios taken as weights in the formula for the cost of capital, may endogenously increase the returns on debt and equity. In the case of Malaysia we find no evidence of such a phenomenon. Second, the role of internal funds (*INTSOEQ*) is negative and very significant.[39] The more that the firms have internal funds left over at the end of the year, the lower is the average cost of capital for that year.[40] Third, large firms (*LTASS*) have a favorable (negative) and a statistically significant effect on the cost of capital. Fourth, taxes (*LTAXES*) for both 1984 and 1987 are positively correlated with the cost of capital. This result may have a fiscal policy implication. An expansionary fiscal policy through reduction in the corporate taxes may help lower the cost of capital and boost investment in the economy.

Finally, the proxies for shareholder market power—*LSUMLS* and *LH* both show a negative, but not so significant, relationship with *LWACC*, with the *t*-statistic for *SUMLS* falling from 1984 to 1987. This possibly suggests a small and a declining

Table 8. Malaysia
Correlations between Price-Earnings (*PE*) and Concentration Ratio(*SUMLS*), and between Price-Earnings and Total Assets (*TASS*) for 98 Manufacturing Firms

	PE(1984)	*PE(1987)*
SUMLS	–0.167	0.020
TASS	–0.094	0.029

role of the large shareholders in the equity sector which had reached an intermediate stage of financial development, in contrast to an influential role of large shareholders in Indonesia whose equity market was at an infant stage (see Tables B1–B4 for Indonesia).

In Table 8, we examine the impact of shareholder size and firm size on price-earnings ratios. The simple correlation coefficient between *SUMLS* and *PE* rises from 1984 to 1987, but there is a relatively smaller increase for the correlation between *TASS* and *PE* over the same period. Table 8 provides support to the argument that the adverse monopsonistic impact on prices in 1984 is larger than the adverse monopolistic impact. The table also indicates that the negative influence of both large shareholders and large firms declines by 1987. The results are in contrast to Zeckhauser and Pound (1990), who obtain a positive relationship between the degree of concentration and price-earnings in the United States.

Determinants of Debt-Equity Ratios

In this section we explore the determinants of debt-equity ratios in our cross-sectional sample of 98 firms for 1984 and 1987. The analysis follows Titmann and Wessels (1988) and Taggart (1985). Along with other important variables, we will include the proxies for market power—Concentration Ratio and Herfindahl Index. In addition, fortunately due to the availability of far richer data for Malaysia than Indonesia, we can conduct separate analyses for long-term debt to equity, long-term loan to equity, and short-term debt to equity. We are able to distinguish between the key determinants of long-term and short-term financing decision of firms.

Tables (B2–B7) in Appendix B provide cross-sectional regression results for 1984 and 1987. The three dependent variables are logs of long-term debt to equity, (*LLTDEQ*), short-term debt to equity (*LSTDEQ*), and finally long-term loans to equity (*LLOANEQ*).[41] Tables B2 and B3 present results for the determinants of *LLTDEQ*, Tables B4 and B5 for *LSTDEQ*, and Tables B6 and B7 for *LLOANEQ*.[42] The independent variables have been defined above and are expressed in logs except for *OIS*, *PE*, and *INTSOEQ* which are in level form. The following discussion of the tables will be conducted according to independent variables and not dependent variables.

Shareholder Concentration

The variables included as proxies for concentration are concentration ratio (*LSUMLS*) and Herfindahl Index (*LH*), both expressed in log form. The regressions for either of the two measures are similar; so in most cases we have presented only those with *LSUMLS*. Our model predicts that the distortionary role of shareholders declines over time.

As expected, in contrast to Indonesia, shareholder concentration in Malaysia has a positive but insignificant effect on *LLTDEQ*, *LLOANEQ*, and *LSTDEQ* in 1984. More importantly, the effect subsides in 1987, and even turns negative in some regressions signifying a relatively minor impact of shareholder concentration on debt-equity ratios. Thus sizable shareowners may be contributing to an increased reliance on shareholders' equity as compared to debt. In sum, for countries which have attained an "intermediate" stage of financial development, such as Malaysia, buyer concentration does not produce higher debt-equity ratios. An obvious criticism of this conclusion may be that the power of the test may be low (we may be falsely accepting the null when the alternative hypothesis may be true).

Firm Size

LTASS measures the size of firms in terms of assets. As discussed for the case of Indonesia, theories suggest that firm size is correlated with leverage (Titman and Wessels 1988).

The regression results indicate that large firms rely more on long-term debt and loans than short-term debt. In case of long-term debt the positive coefficient estimates observed in 1984 (Table B2) become highly significant in 1987 (with a *t*-statistic of 3.12 in equation 6). We can conclude for Malaysia, whose financial sector is quite advanced, that market power from the production side has a greater impact on raising debt/equity than market power from the stockholder side.

Current Profitability

As in Indonesia, profit/sales (*OIS*) is used as a proxy for current profitability. As discussed for Indonesia, various theories such as the "pecking order" approach to financial development argue that profitable firms would prefer to raise funds through debt than issue equity.

The last equation in each table (Tables B2–B7) highlights the influence of current profitability on debt to equity. In all cases, contrary to what is expected from the "pecking order" approach to corporate finance, the coefficient estimates of OIS are negative and significant, suggesting that profitable firms rely more on shareholders' equity for their financing decisions than any form of debt. For details on more recent work on this issue, please refer to the corresponding discussion of current profitability in Indonesia. As in Indonesia, we can reject the hypothesis that profitable firms rely on debt rather than equity for additional financing.

Taxation

LTAXES represents the log of corporate income taxes. Despite the fact that information on dividend tax was not available, we still expect a positive coefficient because income taxes reduce retained earnings which form a part of shareholders' equity.

The influence of corporate income taxes on debt-equity ratios is positive and insignificant in 1984, but negative and not so significant in 1987, suggesting the fact that overall they play a minor role. In addition, though not statistically significant, the negative sign may be indicating a puzzling result that taxes encourage firms to rely on equity financing rather than on long-term debt or loans for their investment.

Expected Future Profitability

As in Indonesia, *PE* represents the price-earnings ratio taken in level form. Studies, for example, Martin and Scott (1974) find that firms enjoying high price-earnings prefer to issue equity. We expect this to be the case for Malaysia as well.

The effect of *PE* on *LLTDEQ* and *LLOANEQ* is highly significant and positive for 1984, and insignificant on *LSTDEQ*. Firms, apparently, prefer long-term debt and long-term bank loans over short-term debt if they are optimistic about their future profitability. In 1987, however, the semi-log elasticity for *LLTDEQ* and especially for *LSTDEQ* turns significantly negative. In the later years firms show a greater reliance on equity if they expect future profitability to be high. Overall, our results are comparable to Martin and Scott (1974) for 1987 but are reversed for 1984.

Internal Sources

We have computed *INTSOEQ* which represents the fraction of internal sources of finance in total equity of a company. The variable highlights a standard contemporaneous choice between retained earnings and debt.

In the case of short-term debt and long-term loans, the semi-log elasticity for *INTSOEQ* is negative and highly significant as compared to that of long-term debt, pointing out that the choice may be more relevant for short-term instruments than long-term instruments. It may be noted that retained earnings from the last period are more relevant for investment in the current period, but since we are analyzing cross-sectional regressions we have only used current-period retained earnings.

Moral Hazard

The presence of asymmetric information affects the choice between debt and equity. Following Shnure (1992) and Zeckhauser and Pound (1990), we approximate moral hazard with the log of the proportion of intangibles in firm's equity (LINTANGEQ). These studies point out that firms that spend a lot on intangibles engage in risky and opportunistic behavior, hence contributing to greater moral hazard. Therefore, firms that possess a greater share of intangibles will have less leverage since it will be difficult for them to obtain loans or short-term debt. In contrast to these above-mentioned studies, it is quite possible that firms that enjoy a higher share of intangibles, such as goodwill and research and development, may have a *lower* risk of moral hazard and thus will have greater access to leverage. In case of bankruptcy these intangibles are not easily valued and traded as tangible assets. It is, therefore, difficult to regain the goodwill developed by firms in the past. This is why firms may be discouraged from engaging in risky activities. We extracted information on intangibles from the asset side of the firms' balance sheets.

As expected, intangibles has a positive effect on long-term and short-term debt which increases in importance in 1987. On the other hand, the coefficients on bank loans are insignificant. We can deduce that since generally banks require physical collateral as a security for granting loans, intangibles will have little effect on loans. However, other types of leverage, such as bonds, may be easily demanded by savers based on both tangible and intangible asset values of the firm.

Collateral

The proxy for collateral as in Shnure (1992) is the log of firm's capital expenditures or investment as a fraction of equity—*LINVESTEQ*. We expect a positive relationship between collateral and debt/equity, especially bank loans/equity.

Except in case of regressions for loans where the coefficient is positive and partly significant for 1987, overall *LINVESTEQ* has hardly any effect on leverage.

Dynamics of Concentration

The third hypothesis emerging from our model is that the share of large stockholders in a firm (s_i/s) is expected to decline over time[43] (see Table 5). Monitoring eventually becomes less useful as improvement in the principal-agent problem causes the marginal cost curve for monitoring to shift down. The equilibrium size of the largest shareholders falls.

We take the case of Malaysia[44] and observe the trend of the sum of the shares of three largest shareholder (*SUMLS*) and the sum of squares of the three largest shareholders (*H*), and analyze the changes over the 1980s (1981, 1984, 1987, 1988). The main thesis put foreword in our model is that large shareholders are able provide an effective monitoring function in order to reduce the agency costs, and the need for monitoring falls as the financial markets grow. For the case of Malaysia, which

Table 9. Malaysia
Changes in the Concentration Ratio

	CH8481	*CH8784*	*CH8887*	*CH8881*
No. of observations	29	67	96	38
No. of observation < 0	22	60	81	21
% of observations < 0	76	90	84	55

can be classified as a "newly-developed" market, we expect the measure of concentration to display a declining trend following financial liberalization in the early 1980s. The proposition is derived in the form of stages of financial development from the Diamond (1991) model which suggests that the firms' need for monitoring declines as they gain reputation over time. Small shareholders progressively own greater shares of the companies that are able to take advantage of cheaper sources of finance, with prices of shares determined in the secondary market.[45]

Concentration Ratio

The frequency distributions for the changes in the shares indicated by *SUMLS* (CH8481, CH8784, CH8887, and CH8881) are presented in Table 9. Though the time gap is relatively small, the negative signs dominate the positive signs suggesting that the size of the largest shareholders is declining during the 1980s. The correlation coefficient between the *SUMLS* for 1988 and 1981 (calculated separately) is only 0.51 signifying a marked change in the concentration ratio across firms over the time period.

Herfindahl Index

Following are the changes in the shares measured by the Herfindahl Index (*H*) which adjusts for outliers in the data. Again Table 10 shows the preliminary statistics for CH8481, CH8784, CH8887, and CH8881. The correlation coefficient between the series for 1988 and 1981 (again calculated separately) is only 0.71 which sheds light on the fact that the market share gap widens to an extent with time even though the time gap is only seven years.

Table 10. Malaysia
Changes in the Herfindahl Index

	CH8481	*CH8784*	*CH8887*	*CH8881*
No. of observations	29	67	96	38
No. of observation < 0	21	63	94	18
% of observations < 0	72	94	98	47

Table 11. Malaysia
Basic Statistics Regarding the Weighted Average Cost of Capital

Mean	*Standard*	*Deviation*	*Minimum*	*Maximum*
WACC(81)	0.046	0.031	0.0018	0.234
WACC(84)	0.050	0.043	0.0009	0.328
WACC(87)	0.044	0.039	0.0119	0.303
WACC(88)	0.038	0.018	0.0016	0.103

Finally, Table 11 reports a declining trend in the cost of capital (*WACC*) for Malaysia over the period 1981–1988. Not only do the mean and the standard deviation fall over seven years, but the minimum and maximum values of *WACC* are smaller in 1988 than in 1981. The figures show that the largest Malaysian manufacturing firms experienced a fall in their required rates of return in the later stages of the financial reforms period.

SUMMARY AND CONCLUSIONS

We have conducted a cross-sectional empirical study of the financial sectors in Indonesia and Malaysia for the 1980s. Indonesia's financial sector was at an "early" stage of financial development in contrast to that of Malaysia which had reached an "intermediate" stage following financial liberalization during the early 1980s. We found that, in contrast to other empirical work, shareholder concentration (in the form of large minority holdings) is an important source of financial distortions and is a determinant of the cost of capital and debt-equity ratios. The primary findings are that concentration influences the dependent variables differently in Indonesia and Malaysia. It raises the debt-equity ratios and the cost of capital in Indonesia, but has an insignificant or even a beneficial effect on these variables in Malaysia. Concentration also lowers price-earnings of domestic firms in Indonesia. As mentioned in the text, the conclusions of this study differ from Zeckhauser and Pound (1990) for Indonesia but are quite similar for Malaysia, since the authors also find a positive role of large shareholders in influencing corporate performance for U.S. firms.[46] A highly concentrated shareholder sector, such as Indonesia, imposes a supply constraint in the sense that it discourages firms from issuing new shares to finance their investment, further strengthening their reliance on banks. In addition to concentration, we examined several other variables such as firm size, current and future profitability, taxes, retained earnings, moral hazard, and collateral, and analyzed their role in the regressions for both the cost of capital and debt-equity ratios.

In addition to concentration, other factors are worth noting. The impact of producer concentration is more severe in Malaysia than in Indonesia. Profitable firms in both countries rely on equity more than debt. Firms that expect higher future profitability are also likely to raise funds through equity than debt. If they chose debt, they prefer long-term debt and long-term loans over short-term debt. The choice between retained earnings and debt is more relevant for short-term instruments than long-term instruments. The effect of taxation on debt-equity ratios is mixed in both countries. Finally, intangibles as a proxy for (lack of) moral hazard, increase firms' ability to raise total debt but have little effect on their ability to borrow from banks. Banks often require tangible assets as collateral. In sum, low shareholder concentration combined with high current and expected profitability have a favorable impact on the financial sectors in the two countries.

Distortions present in the financial sector also have an impact on the real sector. They contribute to high levels of cost of capital, which results in lower domestic investment, and a comparative disadvantage in international trade.

The importance of developing equity markets cannot be over-emphasized. They provide risk-diversification of assets, serve as channels for coordination and information, provide alternative and cheaper sources of finance, reduce credit-rationing and monopolistic powers of banks, and finally, they lower debt-equity ratios, equity premiums, and the cost of capital as was found for Malaysia.

The authorities can speed up the "stages of financial development" by introducing certain reforms. These reforms should include: (1) providing tax incentives to issuing companies especially those with large public ownership, (2) requirements for greater disclosure by shareholders and firms, (3) restriction of bank loans to undercapitalized firms, (4) imposition of taxes on bank deposits in order to reduce the differential between the returns to equity and bank deposits, and (5) removal of restrictions on international capital flows.

ACKNOWLEDGMENTS

This paper is an adapted version of Chapter 3 of the doctoral dissertation at the University of California, Berkeley. The author is grateful to Professors Jeffrey Frankel, Maurice Obstfeld, Dwight Jaffee, Roger Craine, and especially to his Thesis Advisor, Professor James Pierce, for valuable comments and suggestions.

APPENDIX A

Indonesia[47]

The variables used in the regressions for Indonesia are as follows:

ROE: Return on equity or the profit after taxes divided by equity
LROE: Log of *ROE*
DE: Debt-equity ratio
LDE: Log of *DE*
PUBLIC: Proportion of firm's shares owned by the public

LPUBLIC: Log of *PUBLIC*
LS: Proportion of shares owned by the largest shareholders (shares greater than or equal to 15%)
LLS: Log of *LS*
LSSH: Ratio of number of large shareholders (>15%) to total number of shareholders
PE: Price-earnings ratio
LOIS: Log of (profit after taxes/net sales)
DIVP: Dividend payout or the dividend per share/earnings per share
LNSALES: Log of net sales
LTAXES: Log of corporate taxes (taken as the difference between profit before taxes and profit after taxes)

Table A1. Regression Results for Return on Equity and Price-Earnings Ratios for Domestic Firms in Levels

Country: Indonesia					
Equation	*1*	*2*	*3*	*4*	*5*
Dependent Variable	*ROE* (1989)	*ROE* (1989)	*PE* (1989)	*ROE* (1990)	*ROE* (1990)
Estimation Method	OLS	OLS	OLS	OLS	OLS
Number of Observations	20	20	14	20	20
FIRMS	*PMDN*	*PMDN*	*PMDN*	*PMDN*	*PMDN*
C	–2.58	7.61	7.32	0.64	15.3
	(–0.44)	(2.10)	(4.33)	(0.10)	(3.77)
DE	2.98	1.99	–3.18	2.08	0.90
	(3.07)	(2.17)	(–1.14)	(2.18)	(0.98)
DIVP			0.06		
			(0.47)		
PUBLIC		0.009			–0.11
		(0.08)			(–0.89)
LSSH	0.11		–0.45	0.12	
	(1.83)		(–2.62)	(1.81)	
R^2	0.36	0.23	0.42	0.24	0.13

Table A2. Regression Results for the Log of Return on Equity for a Sample of ALL Firms

Country: Indonesia						
Equation	*1*	*2*	*3*	*4*	*5*	*6*
Dependent Variable	*LROE* (1988)	*LROE* (1989)	*LROE* (1990)	*LROE* (1988)	*LROE* (1989)	*LROE* (1989)
Estimation Method	OLS	OLS	OLS	OLS	OLS	OLS
Number of Observations	18	29	30	29	29	30
FIRMS	*ALL*	*ALL*	*ALL*	*ALL*	*ALL*	*ALL*
C	2.51	–1.67	3.62	–2.97	–1.61	1.12
	(1.44)	(–0.72)	(3.88)	(–1.16)	(–0.34)	(0.99)
LDE	–0.02	0.31	0.21	–0.07	–0.20	0.18
	(–0.10)	(1.01)	(1.65)	(–0.34)	(–0.52)	(1.53)
LNSALES	0.05	–0.28	–0.31	0.08	–0.32	–0.34
	(0.22)	(–1.06)	(–2.50)	(0.36)	(–0.99)	(–2.89)
LTAXES	0.12	0.57	0.39	0.14	0.65	0.44
	(0.64)	(2.65)	(3.32)	(0.77)	(2.53)	(3.88)
LPUBLIC	–0.38	0.98	–0.16			
	(–1.70)	(3.30)	(–1.21)			
LLS				0.92	0.63	0.48
				(1.84)	(0.78)	(2.22)
R^2	0.23	0.47	0.40	0.24	0.25	0.47

Table A3. Regression Results for the Log of Return on Equity for a Sample of Domestic Firms

Country: Indonesia						
Equation	*1*	*2*	*3*	*4*	*5*	*6*
Dependent Variable	*LROE* (1988)	*LROE* (1989)	*LROE* (1990)	*LROE* (1988)	*LROE* (1989)	*LROE* (1989)
Estimation Method	OLS	OLS	OLS	OLS	OLS	OLS
Number of Observations	13	14	15	13	14	15
FIRMS	*PMDN*	*PMDN*	*PMDN*	*PMDN*	*PMDN*	*PMDN*
C	3.25	2.47	3.39	–11.92	–3.16	1.59
	(0.66)	(1.32)	(2.18)	(1.63)	(–0.97)	(0.98)
LDE	–0.09	0.21	0.33	–0.32	0.18	0.33
	(–0.21)	(1.02)	(1.85)	(–0.08)	(0.91)	(1.93)
LNSALES	0.26	–0.12	–0.18	0.41	0.005	–0.18
	(0.70)	(–0.73)	(–1.33)	(1.13)	(0.03)	(–1.37)
LTAXES	0.07	0.35	0.25	0.03	0.26	0.26
	(0.23)	(2.80)	(1.92)	(0.11)	(2.28)	(2.02)
LPUBLIC	–1.15	–0.35	–0.21			
	(–1.09)	(–0.99)	(–0.65)			
LLS				2.39	0.90	0.25
				(1.54)	(1.54)	(0.87)
R^2	0.33	0.66	0.52	0.41	0.70	0.53

Table A4. Regression Results for the Log of Return on Equity for a Sample of Foreign Firms

Country: Indonesia Equation	1	2	3	4	5	6
Dependent Variable	LROE (1988)	LROE (1989)	LROE (1990)	LROE (1988)	LROE (1989)	LROE (1989)
Estimation Method	OLS	OLS	OLS	OLS	OLS	OLS
Number of Observations	16	15	15	16	15	15
FIRMS	PMA	PMA	PMA	PMA	PMA	PMA
C	5.30 (3.10)	–0.69 (–0.17)	4.62 (3.57)	0.41 (0.17)	–2.82 (–0.46)	2.12 (1.50)
LDE	–0.03 (–0.11)	0.55 (1.03)	0.22 (1.13)	–0.10 (–0.32)	–0.46 (–0.69)	0.12 (0.75)
LNSALES	–0.26 (–1.08)	–1.01 (–1.69)	–0.67 (–2.15)	–0.30 (–1.30)	–1.55 (–2.57)	–0.69 (–2.72)
LTAXES	0.16 (0.71)	1.48 (2.45)	0.73 (2.21)	0.27 (1.26)	1.98 (3.14)	0.74 (2.77)
LPUBLIC	–0.34 (–1.86)	1.01 (2.19)	–0.04 (–0.26)			
LLS				0.85 (1.94)	1.64 (1.43)	0.60 (2.28)
R^2	0.34	0.65	0.35	0.36	0.57	0.57

Table A5. Regression Results for the Log of Debt-Equity Ratios in the Absence of Taxes

Country: Indonesia Equation	1	2	3	4	5
Dependent Variable	LDE(1988)	LDE(1989)	LDE(1990)	LDE(1989)	LDE(1989)
Estimation Method	OLS	OLS	OLS	OLS	OLS
Number of Observations	18	37	37	20	17
FIRMS	ALL	ALL	ALL	PMDN	PMA
C	–3.70 (–2.61)	1.63 (0.92)	2.00 (1.13)	0.71 (0.29)	2.20 (0.80)
PE	–0.006 (–0.56)	–0.002 (–1.50)	–0.003 (–0.72)	–0.006 (–2.69)	–0.001 (–1.11)
LOIS	–0.86 (–4.46)	–0.27 (–1.28)	–0.33 (–1.62)	0.25 (0.82)	–0.22 (–1.09)
LNSALES	0.16 (1.32)	–0.09 (–0.66)	–0.18 (–1.42)	0.32 (1.57)	–0.22 (–1.09)
LPUBLIC	–0.18 (–1.41)	–0.52 (–1.97)	–0.32 (–1.28)	–1.05 (–2.13)	–0.45 (–1.45)
R^2	0.69	0.15	0.12	0.37	0.35

Table A6. Regression Results for the Log of Debt-Equity Ratios for ALL and Domestic Firms in the Presence of Taxes

Country: Indonesia				
Equation	*1*	*2*	*3*	*4*
Dependent Variable	*LDE*(1988)	*LDE* (1989)	*LDE*(1990)	*LDE*(1989)
Estimation Method	OLS	OLS	OLS	OLS
Number of Observations	18	28	30	14
FIRMS	*ALL*	*ALL*	*ALL*	*PMDN*
C	−3.82	−3.27	−1.43	−3.77
	(−2.82)	(−2.22)	(−0.93)	(−1.40)
PE	−0.008	−0.0009	0.001	0.009
	(−0.83)	(−1.10)	(0.33)	(0.69)
LOIS	−0.69	−0.81	−0.73	−0.57
	(−3.18)	(−2.97)	(−2.19)	(−1.11)
LNSALES	0.37	−0.09	−0.34	0.05
	(2.04)	(−0.41)	(−1.09)	(0.13)
LTAXES	−0.23	0.33	0.44	0.37
	(−1.50)	(1.69)	(1.47)	(1.01)
LPUBLIC	−0.15	−0.22	−0.12	−0.51
	(−1.25)	(−1.14)	(−0.58)	(−0.87)
R^2	0.74	0.56	0.29	0.63

Table A7. Regression Results for the Log of Debt-Equity Ratios for Foreign Firms in the Presence of Taxes

Country: Indonesia			
Equation	*1*	*2*	*3*
Dependent Variable	*LDE*(1988)	*LDE*(1989)	*LDE*(1990)
Estimation Method	OLS	OLS	OLS
Number of Observations	15	14	15
FIRMS	*PMA*	*PMA*	*PMA*
C	−2.82	−0.96	−1.08
	(−2.98)	(−0.47)	(−0.50)
PE	0.002	−0.002	−0.002
	(0.25)	(−1.74)	(−0.40)
LOIS	−0.63	−1.37	−0.51
	(−4.06)	(−3.13)	(−1.39)
LNSALES	0.31	−0.89	0.45
	(2.48)	(−1.83)	(0.83)
LTAXES	−0.23	1.04	−0.55
	(−2.19)	(1.94)	(−0.99)
LPUBLIC	−0.30	−0.40	−0.27
	(−3.23)	(−1.88)	(−1.11)
R^2	0.90	0.72	0.51

APPENDIX B

Malaysia[48]

The variables used in the regressions for Malaysia are defined as follows:

WACC: (dividends + interest on debt)/(total liabilities + total equity)
LWACC: Log of *WACC*
LSUMLS: Log of sum of the three largest shareholders
LH: Log of Herfindahl Index for the three largest shareholders
LLTDEQ: Log of long-term debt/total equity
LSTDEQ: Log of short-term debt/total equity
LLOANEQ: Log of long-term loans/total equity
PE: Price-earnings ratio
OIS: Earnings after taxes and extraordinary expenses/net sales
INTSOEQ: Internal sources/total equity
LTASS: Log of total assets
LTAXES: Log of corporate income taxes
LINVESTEQ: Log of investment/total equity
LINTANGEQ: Log of intangibles/total equity

Table B1. Regression Results for the Log of Weighted Average Cost of Capital

Country: Malaysia				
Equation	*1*	*2*	*3*	*4*
Dependent Variable	LWACC(1984)	LWACC(1987)	LWACC(1987)	LWACC(1987)
Estimation Method	OLS	OLS	2SLS	2SLS
Number of Observations	44	64	30	30
C	–1.77	–1.20	1.14	0.02
	(–1.48)	(–1.15)	(0.60)	(0.01)
LLTDEQ	–0.002	0.009	0.09	0.08
	(–0.04)	(0.17)	(0.38)	(0.36)
LINVESTEQ			0.02	0.02
			(0.59)	(0.55)
INTSOEQ	–5.65	–2.29	–2.77	–2.67
	(–5.97)	(–3.50)	(–3.66)	(–3.47)
LTASS	–0.17	–0.15	–0.25	–0.25
	(–1.86)	(–2.21)	(–2.43)	(–2.39)
LTAXES	0.18	0.07		
	(2.56)	(1.74)		
LSUMLS	–0.16	–0.18	–0.24	
	(–0.85)	(–1.17)	(–0.99)	
LH				(–0.06)
				(–0.71)
R^2	0.51	0.23	0.41	0.40

Notes: *LLTDEQ* is endogenous in *2SLS*.
Adjusted R^2 for 1984 in equation 3 and 4 for both *LSUMLS* and *LH* were negative so the results are not presented here.

Table B2. Regression Results for the Log of Long Term Debt-Equity Ratios for 1984

Country: Malaysia Year: 1984						
Equation	*1*	*2*	*3*	*4*	*5*	*6*
Dependent Variable	*LLTDEQ*	*LLTDEQ*	*LLTDEQ*	*LLTDEQ*	*LLTDEQ*	*LLTDEQ*
Estimation Method	2SLS	2SLS	OLS	OLS	OLS	OLS
Number of Observations	20	20	20	20	18	52
C	–8.80 (–3.04)	–5.15 (–2.07)	–7.85 (–2.66)	–5.55 (–2.50)	–6.63 (–1.98)	–9.72 (–2.73)
PE	0.003 (1.64)	0.003 (1.61)	0.002 (1.75)	0.002 (1.97)	0.002 (1.74)	0.001 (1.14)
OIS						–3.76 (–2.57)
LINVESTEQ	–0.06 (–0.64)	–0.07 (–0.68)		–0.02 (–0.18)	–0.05 (–0.40)	
LINTANGEQ			0.04 (0.39)	0.009 (0.10)	0.008 (0.09)	
INTSOEQ	–4.61 (–1.09)	–5.03 (–1.11)	–3.98 (–2.10)	–4.55 (–1.27)	–5.46 (–1.15)	0.76 (0.32)
LTASS	0.28 (1.64)	0.28 (1.63)			0.08 (0.15)	0.35 (1.33)
LTAXES					0.05 (0.13)	0.005 (0.03)
LSUMLS	0.81 (1.27)		0.69 (1.23)	0.89 (1.50)	0.80 (1.07)	0.80 (1.35)
LH		0.28 (1.09)				
R^2	0.43	0.41	0.32	0.33	0.47	0.22

Note: *PE* is endogenous in *2SLS*.

Table B3. Regression Results for the Log of Long Term Debt-Equity Ratios for 1987

Country: Malaysia Year 1987						
Equation	*1*	*2*	*3*	*4*	*5*	*6*
Dependent Variable	*LLTDEQ*	*LLTDEQ*	*LLTDEQ*	*LLTDEQ*	*LLTDEQ*	*LLTDEQ*
Estimation Method	2SLS	2SLS	OLS	OLS	OLS	OLS
Number of Observations	38	38	46	46	35	80
C	–12.9	–10.89	–9.18	–8.14	–8.53	–8.68
	(–3.04)	(–3.03)	(–2.91)	(–3.23)	(–2.65)	(–3.54)
PE	–0.006	–0.006	–0.0007	–0.0007	0.0003	–0.002
	(–1.71)	(–1.71)	(–0.59)	(–0.54)	(0.10)	(–0.27)
OIS						–1.99
						(–1.70)
LINVESTEQ	0.04	0.04			0.13	
	(0.35)	(0.37)			(1.51)	
LINTANGEQ			0.23	0.24	0.29	
			(2.21)	(2.26)	(2.45)	
INTSOEQ	0.73	0.74	–0.25	–0.32	0.24	1.98
	(0.60)	(0.60)	(–0.31)	(–0.40)	(0.26)	(1.26)
LTASS	0.77	0.78	0.57	0.57	0.70	0.52
	(2.72)	(2.73)	(2.88)	(2.88)	(2.80)	(3.12)
LTAXES					–0.26	–0.12
					(–2.02)	(–1.44)
LSUMLS	0.45		0.26		0.37	0.26
	(0.66)		(0.52)		(0.70)	(0.65)
LH		0.17		0.01		
		(0.62)		(0.08)		
R_r^2	0.43	0.17	0.30	0.29	0.43	0.16

Note: *PE* is endogenous in *2SLS*.

Table B4. Regression Results for the Log of Short Term Debt-Equity Ratios for 1984

Country: Malaysia Year: 1984					
Equation	*1*	*2*	*3*	*4*	*5*
Dependent Variable	*LSTDEQ*	*LSTDEQ*	*LSTDEQ*	*LSTDEQ*	*LSTDEQ*
Estimation Method	2SLS	2SLS	OLS	OLS	OLS
Number of Observations	18	18	18	17	45
C	–3.30 (–0.73)	1.06 (0.40)	–0.37 (–0.11)	4.62 (1.25)	–3.74 (–0.82)
PE	0.005 (0.70)	0.005 (0.68)	–0.0007 (–0.24)	–0.002 (–0.69)	0.0006 (0.16)
OIS					–4.91 (–2.69)
LINVESTEQ	0.04 (0.33)	0.02 (0.19)		0.20 (1.53)	
LINTANGEQ			0.02 (0.17)	0.12 (0.96)	
INTSOEQ	–13.37 (–3.47)	–13.60 (–3.52)	–4.35 (–2.15)	–15.72 (–4.21)	0.11 (0.04)
LTASS	–0.12 (–0.59)	–0.12 (–0.53)	–0.09 (–0.54)	–0.80 (–1.83)	0.13 (0.40)
LTAXES				0.33 (1.15)	–0.16 (–0.82)
LSUMLS	0.99 (1.08)		0.11 (0.18)	0.68 (0.98)	0.47 (0.62)
LH		0.34 (1.08)			
R^2	0.45	0.46	0.24	0.73	0.20

Note: *PE* is endogenous in *2SLS*.

Table B5. Regression Results for the Log of Short Term Debt-Equity Ratios for 1987

Country: Malaysia Year: 1987						
Equation	*1*	*2*	*3*	*4*	*5*	*6*
Dependent Variable	*LSTDEQ*	*LSTDEQ*	*LSTDEQ*	*LSTDEQ*	*LSTDEQ*	*LSTDEQ*
Estimation Method	2SLS	2SLS	OLS	OLS	OLS	OLS
Number of Observations	38	38	46	62	35	70
C	–0.02	1.60	3.93	0.85	4.59	4.21
	(–0.004)	(0.36)	(0.98)	(0.31)	(1.05)	(1.01)
PE	–0.012	–0.01	–0.006	–0.006	–0.004	–0.004
	(–2.79)	(–2.75)	(–3.64)	(–3.14)	(–2.95)	(–2.88)
OIS						-3.49
						(–1.78)
LINVESTEQ	0.07	0.07		0.06	0.17	
	(0.52)	(0.51)		(0.44)	(1.45)	
LINTANGEQ			0.25		0.30	
			(1.85)		(1.88)	
INTSOEQ	–1.07	–1.09	–1.93	–3.52	–1.34	1.54
	(–0.70)	(–0.72)	(–1.87)	(–3.12)	(–1.06)	(0.59)
LTASS	–0.19	–0.19	–0.31		–0.30	–0.16
	(–0.55)	(–0.53)	(–1.24)		(–0.88)	(–0.56)
LTAXES					–0.18	–0.19
					(–1.05)	(–1.41)
LSUMLS	0.38		–0.23	–0.78	0.16	–0.80
	(0.44)		(–0.36)	(–1.09)	(0.23)	(–1.20)
LH		0.11				
		(0.33)				
R^2	0.45	0.45	0.46	0.30	0.54	0.27

Note: *PE* is endogenous in *2SLS*.

Table B6. Regression Results for the Log of Long Term Bank Loan-Equity Ratios for 1984

Country: Malaysia Year: 1984						
Equation	*1*	*2*	*3*	*4*	*5*	*6*
Dependent Variable	*LLOANEQ*	*LLOANEQ*	*LLOANEQ*	*LLOANEQ*	*LLOANEQ*	*LLOANEQ*
Estimation Method	2SLS	2SLS	OLS	OLS	OLS	OLS
Number of Observations	18	18	18	18	17	33
C	–11.36	–5.50	–8.39	–1.25	–13.05	–9.55
	(–1.39)	(–1.74)	(–3.55)	(–1.54)	(–3.93)	(–2.70)
PE	0.006	0.008	0.006	0.005	0.006	–0.0003
	(0.45)	(0.48)	(2.14)	(1.81)	(1.85)	(–0.09)
OIS						1.22
						(0.65)
LINVESTEQ	–0.03	–0.04	0.03	0.009	–0.10	
	(–0.26)	(–0.35)	(0.29)	(0.09)	(–0.83)	
LINTANGEQ			–0.02	–0.01	0.006	
			(–0.28)	(–0.11)	(0.06)	
INTSOEQ	–7.26	–7.61	–8.90	–9.24	–4.46	0.07
	(–2.28)	(–2.18)	(–2.60)	(–2.55)	(–1.01)	(0.03)
LTASS	0.29	0.33			0.78	0.67
	(1.21)	(1.13)			(1.55)	(2.00)
LTAXES					–0.38	–0.23
					(–1.07)	(–1.13)
LSUMLS	1.37		1.56		0.99	0.16
	(0.92)		(2.52)		(1.30)	(0.27)
LH		0.52		0.50		
		(0.84)		(2.11)		
R^2	0.63	0.58	0.54	0.49	0.68	0.18

Note: *PE* is endogenous in *2SLS*.

Table B7. Regression Results for the Log of Long Term Bank Loan-Equity Ratios for 1987

Country: Malaysia Year: 1987					
Equation	*1*	*2*	*3*	*4*	*5*
Dependent Variable	*LLOANEQ*	*LLOANEQ*	*LLOANEQ*	*LLOANEQ*	*LLOANEQ*
Estimation Method	2SLS	OLS	OLS	OLS	OLS
Number of Observations	27	42	33	25	45
C	–4.54 (–1.22)	4.29 (–2.06)	–7.67 (–2.50)	–6.74 (–2.01)	–6.84 (–2.69)
PE	0.002 (0.26)	–0.008 (–0.20)		–0.004 (–0.72)	0.001 (0.78)
OIS					–5.76 (–2.54)
LINVESTEQ	0.12 (1.06)	0.13 (1.38)		0.04 (0.38)	
LINTANGEQ			0.09 (0.82)	0.12 (0.68)	
INTSOEQ	0.03 (0.01)	–3.31 (–3.80)	–1.48 (–1.20)	–1.28 (–0.40)	2.37 (1.03)
LTASS	0.27 (1.06)		0.33 (1.62)	0.34 (1.07)	0.29 (1.50)
LTAXES				–0.08 (–0.56)	–0.11 (–1.29)
LSUMLS		0.60 (1.09)	0.45 (0.82)	0.45 (0.66)	0.49 (1.06)
LH	0.28 (1.01)				
R^2	0.20	0.35	0.21	0.25	0.31

Note: *PE* is endogenous in *2SLS*.

NOTES

1. In this paper we will build on the studies by Taggart (1985), Marsh (1982), Singh and Hamid (1992), Zeckhauser and Pound (1990), and Titman and Wessels (1988).

2. This argument goes back to Wai and Patrick (1973) and Drake (1977), who suggest that family-controlled entities, for fear of losing control and secrecy, buy up huge chunks of company shares. These large shareholders are presumed to be effective monitors aimed at reducing the principal-agent problem.

3. The terms "middle-income" and "newly-developed" refer to middle-income countries. These terms are used to make the distinction between countries at early and medium stages of financial development. Also note that the Jakarta Stock Exchange was founded in 1977 and the Kuala Lumpur Stock Exchange in 1973.

4. The cost of capital, or the minimum acceptable rate of return on capital, is defined as the weighted average of the cost of debt and the cost of equity, where the weights represent shares of debt and equity in total funding. Assuming the costs are dependent on leverage, then the cost of equity would rise with higher leverage due to an increase in the riskiness of equity streams in the portfolio of investors, and the cost of debt may also increase due to the fall in credit rating of additional debt since riskier borrowers will obtain loans at higher lending rates (see Frankel 1992).

5. The benefits of an equity market have been widely discussed in the literature. Some benefits include risk diversification of assets, channels for coordination and information, and enhancement of allocative efficiency through the reduction in the monopolistic powers of the existing intermediaries.

6. They analyzed a cross-sectional sample of 286 firms in 22 industries during 1988.

7. A market characterized by low levels of liquidity is termed a "thin" market.

8. See Dailami and Atkin (1990) for empirical confirmation of high equity premiums in several middle-income countries.

9. Note that the horizontal axes in Figure 2 and 3 denote funding for debt and equity and the vertical axes their respective rates of return. The framework is analogous to the loanable funds model.

10. This model has been partly borrowed from Zeckhauser and Pound (1990). The authors define a large shareholder as a single entity holding more than 15% of outstanding voting stock.

11. Deviation from perfectly elastic demand and supply curves for debt and equity mainly due to the presence of asymmetric information is sufficient to invalidate the Miller-Modigliani propositions making the financial structure of firms determinate.

12. The supply curve is upward-sloping because in order to buy more shares the large shareholder must offer a higher price for additional shares. The main reason is that new purchases increase the value of his previous holdings of shares.

13. Despite the presence of asymmetric information problems in this model, we have not explicitly included the theoretical framework involved in our simple model.

14. Note that the basic insight of this analysis would not change if *MC* were upward-sloping.

15. Obtained from *Emerging Stock Markets Factbook* (1991) and *International Financial Statistics* (1992).

16. In general the interest rate refers to the rate on short-term time deposits (under 6 months).

17. The differences between the two seem to be huge for most countries in the sample as compared to developed countries.

18. For details refer to the preceding model.

19. Note that total equity used in the computation of debt-equity ratios for both Indonesia and Malaysia is analogous to shareholders' equity or net worth of companies obtained from the balance sheet of companies.

20. Shareholder data for Indonesia were unavailable for the 1980s which made the dynamic analysis impossible for Indonesia. However, data for the 1990s are available and is analyzed in our subsequent paper.

21. The hypothesis that the degree of influence falls is tested only for Malaysia, since time series data are unavailable for Indonesia.

22. The data were obtained from the 1991 issue of the *Indonesian Capital Market Directory* and manually entered into a spreadsheet.

23. The acronyms originate from the Indonesian language. PMDN stands for Penanaman Modal Dalam Negari (a company established the under domestic investment law). PMA stands for Penanaman Modal Asing (a company established under the foreign investment law).

24. The information on the largest shareholders and public ownership is as of 1990–1991. Clearly, earlier information would be valuable but is not available. Moreover, taking 1990–1991 seems to be conservative since market power would be an even bigger issue in the 1980s. Finally, the 15% figure is consistent with the cutoff adopted by Zeckhauser and Pound (1990).

25. The original data set was obtained in diskette form from the International Finance Corporation, and information on shareholders was derived from the *Annual Companies Handbook* according to respective company and year, and manually entered into a spreadsheet.

26. Herfindahl Index is defined as Σs_i^2 where s_i denotes the percentage shares owned by the three largest shareholders. One key advantage of such index is that it is less sensitive to extreme values.

27. Information on bonds issued by firms is unavailable for Indonesia which makes it difficult to distinguish components of debt. However, since the bond market was almost nonexistent, we can regard debt as primarily bank loans.

28. In contrast to Malaysia, cost of capital has not been computed since data on return on debt is unavailable. Therefore, only return on equity (*ROE*) is examined here. Note that the positive relationship between increases in the debt-equity ratio and the return on equity is formally presented in Copeland and Weston (1983).

29. In the regression results reported in this paper, whenever we refer to the coefficient estimate as being significant, the *t*-statistic is close to or greater than an absolute value of 2. When a variable is insignificant, the *t*-statistic is between 0 and 1 in absolute terms.

30. Unfortunately, we are constrained by the number of observations particularly when we separate *ALL* firms into *PMDN* and *PMA* firms. Moreover, *LDE* may be insignificant in part due to the simultaneity problem.

31. However, taking a log of (profit after taxes/net sales) will not create a problem, since profit after taxes have only one negative observation in each year.

32. This approach suggests that firms choose a level of debt by estimating the benefits and costs of incurring additional debt (see, for example, Jensen and Meckling 1976).

33. Of course, ideally past profitability would be a superior measure than current profitability but we are limited by our data set since it is only available for three years.

34. Or rely on retained earnings since they are included in shareholders' equity.

35. The study was conducted by Jean Helwege and Nellie Liang of the Federal Reserve Board who focus on 367 American firms that went public in 1983. This study is cited in the October 8, 1994 issue of *The Economist*, p. 88.

36. Two-stage least squares regressions were tried separately with *PE* as an endogenous variable; the results changed very little.

37. Though theoretical work deals with the relationship between the marginal cost of capital and investment, the marginal cost of capital is difficult to quantify in empirical analysis. Therefore, we will restrict ourselves to the average cost of capital.

38. Of course it would have been ideal if the gap was larger between the two time periods but we are limited by data availability.

39. The coefficient estimate here measures semi-log elasticity. We did not take logs of *INTSOEQ* because some values were zero.

40. See Bernanke and Gertler (1987) for a model relating high balance sheet positions and lower costs of obtaining external funds.

41. In this particular case logarithm proves to be a superior functional form than linear estimations. There is no a priori reason for not taking logarithms where the coefficients represent elasticities. In a few cases where the explanatory variables had non-positive values such as *INTSOEQ*, *OIS* and *PE*, we kept the original level form in the regressions.

42. It should be noted that, though each of the dependent variables has been treated separately, we could alternatively have created a vector of these four variables (three shares and the fourth as a residual) and run joint regressions but this method would have complicated our analyses. Moreover, the determinants of these dependent variables may not be the same in all cases.

43. Figure 4 of the model describes a dynamic framework indicating how equilibrium size of big stockholders declines over time.

44. Though Indonesia would be more relevant here when discussing concentration, time series data on concentration were not available.

45. See Figures 2 and 3 of the model above pertaining to a "newly-developed" country.

46. Two main limitations of our study are data unavailability and low power of the tests for shareholder concentration in Malaysia.

47. Note that *t*-statistics are presented in parenthesis in all the tables.

48. Note that *t*-statistics are presented in parenthesis in all the tables.

REFERENCES

Ariff, M., and L.W. Johnson. 1990. *Securities Markets & Stock Pricing: Evidence From A Developing Capital Market In Asia*. Longman Singapore Publishers (Pte) Ltd.

Bernanke, B., and G. Gertler. 1987. "Financial Fragility and Economic Performance." *NBER Working Paper* No. 2318, July.

Cho, Y.J. 1986. "Inefficiencies from Financial Liberalization in the Absence of Well-Functioning Equity Markets." *Journal of Money, Credit, and Banking* 18 (2): 191–99.

Copeland, T.E., and J.F. Weston. 1983. *Financial Theory and Corporate Policy*. New York: Addison-Wesley Publishing Company.

Dailami, M. 1986. "Optimal Corporate Debt Financing and Real Investment Decisions Under Controlled Banking Systems." Development Research Department, The World Bank. November.

Dailami, M., and M. Atkin. 1990. "Stock Markets in Developing Countries: Key Issues and a Research Agenda." *World Bank Working Paper Series* No. 515, October.

Diamond, D.W. 1991. "Monitoring and Reputation: The Choice between Bank Loans and Directly Placed Debt." *Journal of Political Economy* 99 (4): 689–721.

Donaldson, G. 1961. *Corporate Debt Capacity*. Graduate School of Business Research, Harvard University, Boston.

Drake, P.J. 1977. "Securities Markets in Less-Developed Countries." *Journal of Development Studies* 13, January.

The Economist. 1994. October 8, 333 (7884).

Frankel, J.A. 1992. "The Evolving Japanese Financial System, and the Cost of Capital." Mimeo, University of California, Berkeley.

Indonesian Capital Market Directory. various issues. Jakarta: Institute for Economic and Financial Research.

International Finance Corporation. 1991. *Emerging Stock Markets Factbook*.

International Finance Corporation. 1993. *Emerging Markets Data Base*.

International Monetary Fund. 1992. *International Financial Statistics*.

Jensen, M.C., and W.J. Meckling. 1976. "Theory of the Firm: Managerial Behavior, Agency Costs and Ownership Structure." *Journal of Financial Economics* 3: 305–360.

Kuala Lumpur Stock Exchange. various issues. *Annual Companies Handbook* XVI.

Marsh, P. 1982. "The Choice Between Debt and Equity: An Empirical Study." *The Journal of Finance* XXXVII (1): 121–144.

Martin, J.D., and D.F. Scott. 1974. "A Discriminant Analysis of the Corporate Debt-Equity Decision." *Financial Management* (Winter): 71–79.

Modigliani, F., and M. Miller. 1958. "The Cost of Capital, Corporation Finance and the Theory of Investment." *American Economic Review* 48 (June): 261–97.

Shleifer, A., and R.W. Vishny. 1986. "Large Shareholders and Corporate Control." *Journal of Political Economy* 94 (3): 461–468.

Shnure, C.D. 1992. "Asymmetric Information, Financial Intermediaries and Debt." Ph.D. Dissertation, University of California at Berkeley.

Singh, A., and J. Hamid. 1992. "Corporate Financial Structures in Developing Countries." *International Finance Corporation Technical Paper* 1, World Bank.

Sundararajan, V. 1985. "Debt-Equity Ratios of Firms and Interest Rate Policy." *International Monetary Fund Staff Papers*, No. 3, September: 430–434.

Taggart, R.J. 1985. "Secular Patterns in the Financing of US Corporations." In *Corporate Capital Structures in the United States*, edited by B.M. Friedman. NBER Report. Chicago: University of Chicago Press.

Titman, S., and R. Wessels. 1988. "The Determinants of Capital Structure Choice." *The Journal of Finance* XI (1): 1–19.

Wai, U.T., and H.T. Patrick. 1973. "Stock and Bond Issues and Capital Markets in Less Developed Countries." *International Monetary Fund Staff Papers*, July: 253–317.

Zeckhauser, R.J., and J. Pound. 1990. "Are Large Shareholders Effective Monitors? An Investigation of Share Ownership and Corporate Performance." In *Asymmetric Information, Corporate Finance, and Investment*, edited by R. Glenn Hubbard. Washington, DC: National Bureau of Economic Research.

Advances in Pacific Basin Business, Economics and Finance

Edited by **Cheng-Few Lee**,
Department of Finance, School of Business

Volume 1, 1995, 370 pp. $73.25
ISBN 1-55938-737-8

CONTENTS: PART A: MACROECONOMICS. Outlook for Japan-EC-United States Political-Economic Relations, *Richard J. Sweeney.* New Economic Policies for the U.S., *John Clark Francis.* Japan and the Threat of Laura Tyson, *Jeremiah J. Sullivan.* An Overview of Recent Economic Development in China, *Wuu-Long Lin and Thomas P. Chen.* Linkage Effects of Foreign Enterprises on Chinese Economy: Problems and Prospects in the 1990s, *Peter C. Y. Chow.* Linkage Effects of Foreign Enterprises in China: Problems and Prospects - Comment, *Chao-Nan Liu.* Financial System in China, *Frank C. Jen.* Trade Policy of Taiwan, *Rong-I Wu.* A Re-Evaluation of Taiwan Domestic Economic Policy: A Political-Economy Approach, *Pai-Hsien Pang and Shih-Ming Chen.* China's Foreign Exchange Rate Policy, *Jizu Wang.* Trade and Investment Across the Taiwan Straits: Maintaining Competitive Advantage, Pursuing Complementarity, *Koong-lian Kao.* Privatization and Productivity Growth in China: 1979-1990, *Chi-Chu Chou.* Japan's ODA and Its Role in China's Economic Reform, *David C. Cheng.* A Comparative Study of Economic Development: The Case of Shanghai, *Hong Kong and Taiwan, Chang-Hsien Chang and Peter Koveos.* Economic Relationships between Taiwan and China, *M. Jan Dutta.* Globalization of the Taiwanese Economy and U.S. - Taiwan Trade Relations, *Frank S. T. Hsiao.* The Pattern of U.S. - Asian Pacific Rim Trade, 1965-1987, *Ira N. Gang, Catherine Y. Co.* PART B: BUSINESS, FINANCE AND ACCOUNTING. An International Comparison of the Accuracy of Analysts' Forecasts of Earnings, *Jang Youn Cho and Andrew Pitcher.* Earnings Forecasting in Efficient Japanese Portfolios, *John B. Guerard Jr., Suzuki Makoto and Unmesh Bhide.* A Comparative Study of the Weekend Effects in the United States, British and the Pacific Rim Stock Markets: An Application of the ARCH Model, *Bwo-Nung Huang, Yu-Jane Liu and Chin W. Yang.* Corporate Ownership Structure and Corporate Governance Mechanism: With Experience of Korean Firms, *Ungki Lim.* On the Pricing of the Deposit Insurance Liabilities of the CDIC of Taiwan, *Jin-Chuan Duan, Mao-Wei Hung and Thomas Liaw.* The US, Japan and the Emerging Stock Markets of the Pacific Basin: A Test of Regional and Intertemporal Stability, *Richard Ajayi, Jongmoo Jay Choi and Seyed M. Mehdian.* Excess Returns of Unseasoned New Issues in Taiwan: An Institutional Perspective, *Gili Yen, E.C. Yen and S. Chen.* An Analysis of Mergers Between Mutual Banks and Credit Cooperatives in Japan, *Yasuo Hoshino.*